The life and

Edward Gibbon

With his History of the crusades.

Verbatim reprint, with copious index

Edward Gibbon

Alpha Editions

This edition published in 2019

ISBN : 9789353957407

Design and Setting By
Alpha Editions
email - alphaedis@gmail.com

THE "CHANDOS CLASSICS."

THE

LIFE AND LETTERS

OF

EDWARD GIBBON:

WITH HIS

HISTORY OF THE CRUSADES.

VERBATIM REPRINT,

WITH COPIOUS INDEX BY

W. J. DAY.

LONDON AND NEW YORK
FREDERICK WARNE AND CO.
1889

MEMOIRS OF MY LIFE AND WRITINGS.

In the fifty-second year of my age, after the completion of an arduous and successful work, I now propose to employ some moments of my leisure in reviewing the simple transactions of a private and literary life. Truth, naked unblushing truth, the first virtue of more serious history, must be the sole recommendation of this personal narrative. The style shall be simple and familiar; but style is the image of character; and the habits of correct writing may produce, without labour or design, the appearance of art and study. My own amusement is my motive, and will be my reward: and if these sheets are communicated to some discreet and indulgent friends, they will be secreted from the public eye till the author shall be removed beyond the reach of criticism or ridicule.*

A lively desire of knowing and of recording our ancestors so generally prevails, that it must depend on the influence of some common principle in the minds of men. We seem to have lived in the persons of our forefathers; it is the labour and reward of vanity to extend the term of this ideal longevity. Our imagination is always active to enlarge the narrow circle in which Nature has confined us. Fifty or an hundred years may be allotted to an individual, but we step forward beyond death with such hopes as religion and philosophy will suggest; and we fill up the silent vacancy that precedes our birth, by associating ourselves to the authors of our existence. Our calmer judgment will rather tend to moderate, than to suppress, the pride of an ancient and worthy race. The satirist may laugh, the philosopher may preach; but Reason herself will respect the prejudices and habits, which have been consecrated by the experience of mankind.

Wherever the distinction of birth is allowed to form a superior order in the state, education and example should always, and will often, produce among them a dignity of sentiment and propriety of conduct, which is guarded from dishonour by their own and the public esteem. If we read of some illustrious line so ancient that it has no beginning, so worthy that it ought to have no end, we sympathize in its various

* This passage is found in one only of the six sketches, and in that which seems to have been the first written, and which was laid aside among loose papers. Mr. Gibbon, in his communications with me on the subject of his Memoirs, a subject which he had never mentioned to any other person, expressed a determination of publishing them in his lifetime ; and never appears to have departed from that resolution, excepting in one of his letters annexed, in which he intimates a doubt, though rather carelessly, whether in his time, or at any time, they would meet the eye of the public. In a conversation, however, not long before his death, it was suggested to him, that, if he should make them a full image of his mind, he would not have nerves to publish them in his lifetime, and that they should be posthumous ;—He answered, rather eagerly, that he was determined to publish them *in his lifetime*. **S.**

fortunes; nor can we blame the generous enthusiasm, or even the harmless vanity, of those who are allied to the honours of its name. For my own part, could I draw my pedigree from a general, a states-man, or a celebrated author, I should study their lives with the diligence of filial love.   In the investigation of past events, our curiosity is stimulated by the immediate or indirect reference to ourselves; but in the estimate of honour we should learn to value the gifts of Nature above those of Fortune; to esteem in our ancestors the qualities that best promote the interests of society; and to pronounce the descendant of a king less truly noble than the offspring of a man of genius, whose writings will instruct or delight the latest posterity.   The family of Confucius is, in my opinion, the most illustrious in the world.   After a painful ascent of eight or ten centuries, our barons and princes of Europe are lost in the darkness of the middle ages; but, in the vast equality of the empire of China, the posterity of Confucius have main-tained, above two thousand two hundred years, their peaceful honours and perpetual succession.   The chief of the family is still revered, by the sovereign and the people, as the lively image of the wisest of man-kind.   The nobility of the Spencers has been illustrated and enriched by the trophies of Marlborough; but I exhort them to consider the "Fairy Queen" as the most precious jewel of their coronet.   I have exposed my private feelings, as I shall always do, without scruple or reserve.   That these sentiments are just, or at least natural, I am inclined to believe, since I do not feel myself interested in the cause; for I can derive from my ancestors neither glory nor shame.

Yet a sincere and simple narrative of my own life may amuse some of my leisure hours; but it will subject me, and perhaps with justice, to the imputation of vanity.   I may judge, however, from the experience both of past and of the present times, that the public are always curious to know the men, who have left behind them any image of their minds: the most scanty accounts of such men are compiled with diligence, and perused with eagerness; and the student of every class may derive a lesson, or an example, from the lives most similar to his own.   My name may hereafter be placed among the thousand articles of a Biographia Britannica; and I must be conscious, that no one is so well qualified, as myself, to describe the series of my thoughts and actions.   The authority of my masters, of the grave Thuanus, and the philosophic Hume, might be sufficient to justify my design; but it would not be difficult to produce a long list of ancients and moderns, who, in various forms, have exhibited their own portraits.   Such por-traits are often the most interesting, and sometimes the only interesting parts of their writings; and if they be sincere, we seldom complain of the minuteness or prolixity of these personal memorials.   The lives of the younger Pliny, of Petrarch, and of Erasmus, are expressed in the epistles, which they themselves have given to the world.   The essays of Montaigne and Sir William Temple bring us home to the houses and bosoms of the authors: we smile without contempt at the head-strong passions of Benevenuto Cellini, and the gay follies of Colley Cibber.   The confessions of St. Austin and Rousseau disclose the secrets of the human heart; the commentaries of the learned Huet have survived his evangelical demonstration; and the memoirs of Goldoni are more truly dramatic than his Italian comedies. The heretic and the churchman are strongly marked in the characters and fortunes of Whiston and Bishop Newton; and even the dullness of Michael de Marolles and Anthony Wood acquires some value from the faithful representation of men and manners. That I am equal or superior to some of these, the effects of modesty or affectation cannot force me to dissemble.

MY family is originally derived from the county of Kent. The southern district, which borders on Sussex and the sea, was formerly overspread with the great forest Anderida, and even now retains the denomination of the Weald or Woodland. In this district, and in the hundred and parish of Rolvenden, the Gibbons were possessed of lands in the year one thousand three hundred and twenty-six; and the elder branch of the family, without much increase or diminution of property, still adheres to its native soil. Fourteen years after the first appearance of his name, John Gibbon is recorded as the Marmorarius or architect of King Edward the Third: the strong and stately castle of Queensborough, which guarded the entrance of the Medway, was a monument of his skill; and the grant of an hereditary toll on the passage from Sandwich to Stonar, in the Isle of Thanet, is the reward of no vulgar artist. In the visitations of the heralds, the Gibbons are frequently mentioned; they held the rank of esquire in an age, when that title was less promiscuously assumed: one of them, under the reign of Queen Elizabeth, was captain of the militia of Kent; and a free school, in the neighbouring town of Benenden, proclaims the charity and opulence of its founder. But time, or their own obscurity, has cast a veil of oblivion over the virtues and vices of my Kentish ancestors; their character or station confined them to the labours and pleasures of a rural life: nor is it in my power to follow the advice of the poet, in an inquiry after a name,—

> " Go ! search it there, where to be born, and die,
> Of rich and poor makes all the history."

So recent is the institution of our parish registers. In the beginning of the seventeenth century, a younger branch of the Gibbons of Rolvenden migrated from the country to the city; and from this branch I do not blush to descend. The law requires some abilities; the church imposes some restraints; and before our army and navy, our civil establishments, and India empire, had opened so many paths of fortune, the mercantile profession was more frequently chosen by youths of a liberal race and education, who aspired to create their own independence. Our most respectable families have not disdained the counting-house, or even the shop; their names are enrolled in the Livery and Companies of London; and in England, as well as in the Italian commonwealths, heralds have been compelled to declare that gentility is not degraded by the exercise of trade.

The armorial ensigns which, in the times of chivalry, adorned the crest and shield of the soldier, are now become an empty decoration, which every man, who has money to build a carriage, may paint according to his fancy on the panels. My family arms are the same, which were borne by the Gibbons of Kent in an age, when the College of Heralds religiously guarded the distinctions of blood and name: a lion rampant gardant, between three schallop-shells argent, on a field azure.* I should not however have been tempted to blazon my coat of arms, were it not connected with a whimsical anecdote.—About the reign of James the First, the three harmless schallop-shells were changed by Edmund Gibbon esq. into three ogresses, or female cannibals, with a design of stigmatizing three ladies, his kinswomen, who had provoked him by an unjust law-suit. But this singular mode of revenge, for which he obtained the sanction of Sir William Seagar, king at arms, soon expired with its author; and, on his own monument in the Temple church, the monsters vanish, and the three schallop-shells resume their proper and hereditary place.

Our alliances by marriage it is not disgraceful to mention. The chief honour of my ancestry is James Fiens, Baron Say and Seale, and Lord High Treasurer of England, in the reign of Henry the Sixth; from whom by the Phelips, the Whetnalls, and the Cromers, I am lineally descended in the eleventh degree. His dismission and imprisonment in the Tower were insufficient to appease the popular clamour; and the Treasurer, with his son-in-law Cromer, was beheaded (1450), after a mock trial by the Kentish insurgents. The black list of his offences, as it is exhibited in Shakespeare, displays the ignorance and envy of a plebeian tyrant. Besides the vague reproaches of selling Maine and Normandy to the Dauphin, the Treasurer is specially accused of luxury, for riding on a foot-cloth; and of treason, for speaking French, the language of our enemies: "Thou hast most traitorously corrupted the youth of the realm," says Jack Cade to the unfortunate Lord, "in erecting a grammar-school; and whereas before our forefathers had no other books than the score and the tally, thou hast caused printing to be used; and, contrary to the king, his crown, and dignity, thou hast built a paper-mill. It will be proved to thy face, that thou hast men about thee, who usually talk of a noun and a verb, and such abominable words, as no christian ear can endure to hear." Our dramatic poet is generally more attentive to character than to history; and I much fear that the art of printing was not introduced into England, till several years after Lord Say's death; but of some of these meritorious crimes I should hope to find my ancestor guilty; and a man of letters may be proud of his descent from a patron and martyr of learning.

In the beginning of the last century Robert Gibbon esq. of Rolvenden in Kent (who died in 1618), had a son of the same name of Robert, who settled in London, and became a member of the Clothworkers' Company. His wife was a daughter of the Edgars, who flourished about four hundred years in the county of Suffolk, and produced an eminent and wealthy serjeant-at-law, Sir Gregory Edgar, in the reign of Henry the Seventh. Of the sons of Robert Gibbon, (who died in 1643,) Matthew did not aspire above the station of a linen-draper in Leadenhall-street; but John has given to the public some

---

* The father of Lord Chancellor Hardwicke married an heiress of this family of Gibbon. The Chancellor's escutcheon in the Temple Hall quarters the arms of Gibbon, as does also that, in Lincoln's Inn Hall, of Charles York, Chancellor in 1770. S.

curious memorials of his existence, his character, and his family. He was born on Nov. 3d, 1629; his education was liberal, at a grammar-school, and afterwards in Jesus College at Cambridge; and he celebrates the retired content which he enjoyed at Allesborough, in Worcestershire, in the house of Thomas Lord Coventry, where John Gibbon was employed as a domestic tutor, the same office which Mr. Hobbes exercised in the Devonshire family. But the spirit of my kinsman soon immerged into more active life: he visited foreign countries as a soldier and a traveller, acquired the knowledge of the French and Spanish languages, passed some time in the Isle of Jersey, crossed the Atlantic, and resided upwards of a twelvemonth (1659) in the rising colony of Virginia. In this remote province his taste, or rather passion, for heraldry found a singular gratification at a war-dance of the native Indians. As they moved in measured steps, brandishing their tomahawks, his curious eye contemplated their little shields of bark, and their naked bodies, which were painted with the colours and symbols of his favourite science. "At which I exceedingly wondered;" and concluded that heraldry was ingrafted *naturally* into the sense of human race. If so, it deserves a greater esteem than now-a-days is put upon it." His return to England after the Restoration was soon followed by his marriage—his settlement in a house in St. Catherine's Cloister, near the Tower, which devolved to my grandfather—and his introduction into the Heralds' College (in 1671) by the style and title of Blue-mantle Pursuivant at Arms. In this office he enjoyed near fifty years the rare felicity of uniting, in the same pursuit, his duty and inclination: his name is remembered in the College, and many of his letters are still preserved. Several of the most respectable characters of the age, Sir William Dugdale, Mr. Ashmole, Dr. John Betts, and Dr. Nehemiah Grew, were his friends; and in the society of such men, John Gibbon may be recorded without disgrace as the member of an astrological club. The study of hereditary honours is favourable to the Royal prerogative; and my kinsman, like most of his family, was a high Tory both in church and state. In the latter end of the reign of Charles the Second, his pen was exercised in the cause of the Duke of York: the Republican faction he most cordially detested; and as each animal is conscious of its proper arms, the heralds' revenge was emblazoned on a most diabolical escutcheon. But the triumph of the Whig government checked the preferment of Blue-mantle; and he was even suspended from his office, till his tongue could learn to pronounce the oath of abjuration. His life was prolonged to the age of ninety: and, in the expectation of the inevitable though uncertain hour, he wishes to preserve the blessings of health, competence, and virtue. In the year 1682 he published in London his *Introductio ad Latinam Blasoniam*, an original attempt, which Camden had desiderated, to define, in a Roman idiom, the terms and attributes of a Gothic institution. It is not two years since I acquired, in a foreign land, some domestic intelligence of my own family; and this intelligence was conveyed to Switzerland from the heart of Germany. I had formed an acquaintance with Mr. *Langer*, a lively and ingenious scholar, while he resided at Lausanne as preceptor to the Hereditary Prince of *Brunswick*. On his return to his proper station of Librarian to the Ducal Library of

Wolfenbuttel, he accidentally found among some literary rubbish a small old English volume of heraldry, inscribed with the name of *John Gibbon.* From the title only *Mr. Langer* judged that it might be an acceptable present to his friend ; and he judged rightly. His manner is quaint and affected; his order is confused : but he displays some wit, more reading, and still more enthusiasm: and if an enthusiast be often absurd, he is never languid. An English text is perpetually interspersed with Latin sentences in prose and verse ; but in his own poetry he claims an exemption from the laws of prosody. Amidst a profusion of genealogical knowledge, my kinsman could not be forgetful of his own name ; and to him I am indebted for almost the whole of my information concerning the Gibbon family. From this small work the author expected immortal fame.

Such are the hopes of authors ! In the failure of those hopes John Gibbon has not been the first of his profession, and very possibly may not be the last of his name. His brother Matthew Gibbon, the draper, had one daughter and two sons—my grandfather Edward, who was born in the year 1666, and Thomas, afterwards Dean of Carlisle. According to the mercantile creed, that the best book is a profitable ledger, the writings of John the herald would be much less precious than those of his nephew Edward : but an author professes at least to write for the public benefit ; and the slow balance of trade can be pleasing to those persons only, to whom it is advantageous. The successful industry of my grandfather raised him above the level of his immediate ancestors ; he appears to have launched into various and extensive dealings : even his opinions were subordinate to his interest ; and I find him in Flanders clothing King William's troops, while he would have contracted with more pleasure, though not perhaps at a cheaper rate, for the service of King James. During his residence abroad, his concerns at home were managed by his mother Hester, an active and notable woman. Her second husband was a widower of the name of Acton : they united the children of their first nuptials. After his marriage with the daughter of Richard Acton, goldsmith in Leadenhall-street, he gave his own sister to Sir Whitmore Acton, of Aldenham ; and I am thus connected, by a triple alliance, with that ancient and loyal family of Shropshire baronets. It consisted about that time of seven brothers, all of gigantic stature ; one of whom, a pigmy of six feet two inches, confessed himself the last and least of the seven ; adding, in the true spirit of party, that such men were not born since the Revolution. Under the Tory administration of the four last years of Queen Anne (1710—1714) Mr. Edward Gibbon was appointed one of the Commissioners of the Customs ; he sat at that Board with Prior ; but the merchant was better qualified for his station than the poet ; since Lord Bolingbroke has been heard to declare, that he had never conversed with a man, who more clearly understood the commerce and finances of England. In the year 1716 he was elected one of the Directors of the South Sea Company ; and his books exhibited the proof that, before his acceptance of this fatal office, he had acquired an independent fortune of sixty thousand pounds.

But his fortune was overwhelmed in the shipwreck of the year twenty, and the labours of thirty years were blasted in a single day. Of the use or abuse of the South Sea scheme, of the guilt or innocence of my grandfather and his brother Directors, I am neither a competent nor a disinterested judge. Yet the equity of modern times must condemn the violent and arbitrary proceedings, which would have disgraced the cause of justice, and would render injustice still more odious. No sooner had the nation awakened from its golden dream, than a popular and even a parliamentary clamour demanded their victims : but it was acknowledged on all sides that the South Sea Directors, however guilty, could not be touched by any known laws of the land. The speech of Lord Molesworth, the author of the State of Denmark, may shew the temper, or rather the intemperance, of the House of Commons. "Extraordinary crimes (exclaimed that ardent Whig) call aloud for extraordinary remedies. The Roman lawgivers had not foreseen the possible existence of a parricide ; but as soon as the first monster appeared, he was sewn in a sack, and cast headlong into the river ; and I shall be content to inflict the same treatment on the authors of our present ruin." His motion was not literally adopted ; but a bill of pains and penalties was introduced, a retroactive statute, to punish the offences, which did not exist at the time they were committed. Such a pernicious violation of liberty and law can be excused only by the most imperious necessity ; nor could it be defended on this occasion by the plea of impending danger or useful example. The legislature restrained the persons of the Directors, imposed an exorbitant security for their appearance, and marked their characters with a previous note of ignominy : they were compelled to deliver, upon oath, the strict value of their estates ; and were disabled from making any transfer or alienation of any part of their property. Against a bill of pains and penalties it is the common right of every subject to be heard by his counsel at the bar : they prayed to be heard ; their prayer was refused ; and their oppressors, who required no evidence, would listen to no defence. It had been at first proposed that one-eighth of their respective estates should be allowed for the future support of the Directors ; but it was speciously urged, that in the various shades of opulence and guilt such an unequal proportion would be too light for many, and for some might possibly be too heavy. The character and conduct of each man were separately weighed ; but, instead of the calm solemnity of a judicial inquiry, the fortune and honour of three and thirty Englishmen were made the topic of hasty conversation, the sport of a lawless majority ; and the basest member of the committee, by a malicious word or a silent vote, might indulge his general spleen or personal animosity. Injury was aggravated by insult, and insult was embittered by pleasantry. Allowances of twenty pounds, or one shilling, were facetiously moved. A vague report that a Director had formerly been concerned in *another* project, by which some unknown persons had lost their money, was admitted as a proof of his actual guilt. One man was ruined because he had dropped a foolish speech, that his horses should feed upon gold ; another because he was grown so proud, that, one day at the Treasury, he had refused a civil answer to persons much above him. All were condemned, absent and unheard, in arbitrary fines and forfeitures, which swept away the greatest part of their substance. Such bold oppression can scarcely be shielded by the omnipotence of parliament ; and yet it may be seriously questioned, whether the Judges of the South Sea Directors were the true and legal representatives of their country. The first parliament of George the First had been chosen (1715) for three years : the term had elapsed, their trust was expired ; and the four additional years (1718—1722), during which they continued to sit, were derived not from the people, but from themselves ; from the strong measure of the septennial bill, which can only be paralleled by *il serar di consiglio* of the Venetian history. Yet candour will own that to the same parliament every Englishman is deeply indebted : the septennial act, so vicious in its origin, has been sanctioned by time, experience, and the national consent. Its first operation secured the House of Hanover on the throne, and its permanent influence maintains the peace and stability of government. As often as a repeal has been moved in the House of Commons, I have given in its defence a clear and conscientious vote.

My grandfather could not expect to be treated with more lenity than his companions. His Tory principles and connections rendered him obnoxious to the ruling powers : his name is reported in a suspicious secret ; and his well-known abilities could not plead the excuse of ignorance or error. In the first proceedings against the South Sea Directors, Mr. Gibbon is one of the few who were taken into custody ; and, in the final sentence, the measure of his fine proclaims him eminently guilty. The total estimate which he delivered on oath to the House of Commons amounted to £106,543 5s. 6d., exclusive of antecedent settlements. Two different allowances of £15,000 and of £10,000 were moved for Mr. Gibbon ; but, on the question being put, it was carried without a division for the smaller sum. On these ruins, with the skill and credit, of which parliament had not been able to despoil him, my grandfather at a mature age erected the edifice of a new fortune : the labours of sixteen years were amply rewarded ; and I have reason to believe that the second structure was not much inferior to the first. He had realized a very considerable property in Sussex, Hampshire, Buckinghamshire, and the New River Company ; and had acquired a spacious house,* with gardens and lands, at Putney, in Surrey, where he resided in decent hospitality. He died in December 1736, at the age of seventy; and by his last will, at the expense of Edward, his only son, (with whose marriage he was not perfectly reconciled,) enriched his two daughters, Catherine and Hester. The former became the wife of Mr. Edward Elliston, an East India captain : their daughter and heiress Catherine was married in the year 1756 to Edward Eliot, Esq. (now lord Eliot), of Port Eliot, in the county of Cornwall ; and their three sons are my nearest male relations on the father's side. A life of devotion and celibacy was the choice of my aunt, Mrs. Hester Gibbon, who, at the age of eighty-five, still resides in a hermitage at Cliffe, in Northamptonshire; having long survived her spiritual guide and faithful companion Mr. William Law, who, at an advanced age, about the year 1761, died in her house. In our family he had left the reputation of a worthy and pious man, who believed all that he professed, and practised all that he enjoined. The character of a non-juror, which he maintained to the last, is a sufficient evidence of his principles in church and state ; and the

* Since inhabited by Mr. Wood, Sir John Shelley, the Duke of Norfolk, &c.—S.

sacrifice of interest to conscience will be always respectable. His theo-logical writings, which our domestic connection has tempted me to peruse, preserve an imperfect sort of life, and I can pronounce with more confidence and knowledge on the merits of the author. His last compositions are darkly tinctured by the incomprehensible visions of Jacob Behmen ; and his discourse on the absolute unlawfulness of stage entertainments is sometimes quoted for a ridiculous intemperance of sentiment and language.—" The actors and spectators must all be damned : the playhouse is the porch of Hell, the place of the Devil's abode, where he holds his filthy court of evil spirits : a play is the Devil's triumph, a sacrifice performed to his glory, as much as in the heathen temples of Bacchus or Venus, &c., &c." But these sallies of religious frenzy must not extinguish the praise, which is due to Mr. William Law as a wit and a scholar. His argument on topics of less absurdity is specious and acute, his manner is lively, his style forcible and clear ; and, had not his vigorous mind been clouded by enthusiasm, he might be ranked with the most agreeable and ingenious writers of the times. While the Bangorian controversy was a fashionable theme, he entered the lists on the subject of Christ's kingdom, and the authority of the priesthood : against the plain account of the sacra-ment of the Lord's Supper he resumed the combat with Bishop Hoad-ley, the object of Whig idolatry, and Tory abhorrence ; and at every weapon of attack and defence the non-juror, on the ground which is common to both, approves himself at least equal to the prelate. On the appearance of the Fable of the Bees, he drew his pen against the licentious doctrine that private vices are public benefits, and morality as well as religion must join in his applause. Mr. Law's master-work, the *Serious Call*, is still read as a popular and powerful book of devotion. His precepts are rigid, but they are founded on the gospel ; his satire is sharp, but it is drawn from the knowledge of human life ; and many of his portraits are not unworthy of the pen of La Bruyère. If he finds a spark of piety in his reader's mind, he will soon kindle it to a flame ; and a philosopher must allow that he exposes, with equal severity and truth, the strange contradiction between the faith and prac-tice of the Christian world. Under the names of Flavia and Miranda he has admirably described my two aunts—the heathen and the Chris-tian sister.

My father, Edward Gibbon, was born in October, 1707 : at the age of thirteen he could scarcely feel that he was disinherited by act of par-liament ; and, as he advanced towards manhood, new prospects of fortune opened to his view. A parent is most attentive to supply in his children the deficiencies, of which he is conscious in himself :· my grandfather's knowledge was derived from a strong understanding, and the experience of the ways of men ; but my father enjoyed the benefits of a liberal education as a scholar and a gentleman. At Westminster School, and afterwards at Emanuel College in Cambridge, he passed through a regular course of academical discipline ; and the care of his learning and morals was intrusted to his private tutor, the same Mr. William Law. But the mind of a saint is above or below the present world ; and while the pupil proceeded on his travels, the tutor remained at Putney, the much-honoured friend and spiritual director of the whole family. My father resided some time at Paris to acquire the fashionable exercises; and as his temper was warm and social, he indulged in those pleasures, for which the strictness of his former education had given him a keener relish. He afterwards visited several provinces of France; but his excursions were neither long nor remote; and the slender knowledge, which he had gained of the French language, was gradually obliterated. His passage through Besançon is marked by a singular consequence in the chain of human events. In a dangerous illness Mr. Gibbon was attended, at his own request, by one of his kinsmen of the name of Acton, the younger brother of a younger brother, who had applied himself to the study of physic. During the slow recovery of his patient, the physician himself was attacked by the malady of love: he married his mistress, renounced his country and religion, settled at Besançon, and became the father of three sons; the eldest of whom, General Acton, is conspicuous in Europe as the principal Minister of the king of the Two Sicilies. By an uncle whom another stroke of fortune had transplanted to Leghorn, he was educated in the naval service of the Emperor; and his valour and conduct in the command of the Tuscan frigates protected the retreat of the Spaniards from Algiers. On my father's return to England he was chosen, in the general election of 1734, to serve in parliament for the borough of Petersfield; a burgage tenure, of which my grandfather possessed a weighty share, till he alienated (1 know not why) such important property. In the opposition to Sir Robert Walpole and the Pelhams, prejudice and society connected his son with the Tories,—shall 1 say Jacobites? or, as they were pleased to style themselves, the country gentlemen? with them he gave many a vote; with them he drank many a bottle. Without acquiring the fame of an orator or a statesman, he eagerly joined in the great opposition, which, after a seven years' chase, hunted down Sir Robert Walpole: and in the pursuit of an unpopular minister, he gratified a private revenge against the oppressor of his family in the South Sea persecution.

I was born at Putney, in the county of Surrey, April 27th, O. S., in the year one thousand seven hundred and thirty-seven; the first child of the marriage of Edward Gibbon, esq., and of Judith Porten.* My lot might have been that of a slave, a savage, or a peasant; nor can I reflect without pleasure on the bounty of Nature, which cast my birth in a free and civilized country, in an age of science and philosophy, in a family of honourable rank, and decently endowed with the gifts of fortune. From my birth I have enjoyed the right of primogeniture; but I was succeeded by five brothers and one sister, all of whom were snatched away in their infancy. My five brothers, whose names may be found in the parish register of Putney, I shall not pretend to lament: but from my childhood to the present hour I have deeply and sincerely regretted my sister, whose life was somewhat prolonged, and whom I remember to have been an amiable infant. The relation of a brother

* The union to which I owe my birth was a marriage of inclination and esteem. Mr. James Porten, a merchant of London, resided with his family at Putney, in a house adjoining to the bridge and churchyard, where I have passed many happy hours of my childhood. He left one son (the late Sir Stanier Porten) and three daughters; Catherine, who preserved her maiden name, and of whom I shall hereafter speak; another daughter married Mr. Darrel of Richmond, and left two sons, Edward and Robert: the youngest of the three sisters was Judith, my mother.

and a sister, especially if they do not marry, appears to me of a very singular nature. It is a familiar and tender friendship with a female, much about our own age ; an affection perhaps softened by the secret influence of sex, and the sole species of Platonic love that can be indulged with truth, and without danger.

At the general election of 1741, Mr. Gibbon and Mr. Delmé stood an expensive and successful contest at Southampton, against Mr. Dummer and Mr. Henly, afterwards Lord Chancellor and Earl of Northington. The Whig candidates had a majority of the resident voters ; but the corporation was firm in the Tory interest : a sudden creation of one hundred and seventy new freemen turned the scale ; and a supply was readily obtained of respectable volunteers, who flocked from all parts of England to support the cause of their political friends. The new parliament opened with the victory of an opposition, which was fortified by strong clamour and strange coalitions. From the event of the first divisions, Sir Robert Walpole perceived that he could no longer lead a majority in the House of Commons, and prudently resigned (after a dominion of one-and-twenty years) the guidance of the state (1742). But the fall of an unpopular minister was not succeeded, according to general expectation, by a millennium of happiness and virtue : some courtiers lost their places, some patriots lost their characters, Lord Orford's offences vanished with his power ; and after a short vibration, the Pelham government was fixed on the old basis of the Whig aristocracy. In the year 1745, the throne and the constitution were attacked by a rebellion, which does not reflect much honour on the national spirit ; since the English friends of the Pretender wanted courage to join his standard, and his enemies (the bulk of the people) allowed him to advance into the heart of the kingdom. Without daring, perhaps without desiring, to aid the rebels, my father invariably adhered to the Tory opposition. In the most critical season he accepted, for the service of the party, the office of alderman in the city of London : but the duties were so repugnant to his inclination and habits, that he resigned his gown at the end of a few months. The second parliament in which he sat was prematurely dissolved (1747) : and as he was unable or unwilling to maintain a second contest for Southampton, the life of the senator expired in that dissolution.

The death of a new-born child before that of its parents may seem an unnatural, but it is strictly a probable, event : since of any given number the greater part are extinguished before their ninth year, before they possess the faculties of the mind or body. Without accusing the profuse waste or imperfect workmanship of Nature, I shall only observe, that this unfavourable chance was multiplied against my infant existence. So feeble was my constitution, so precarious my life, that, in the baptism of each of my brothers, my father's prudence successively repeated my Christian name of Edward, that, in case of the departure of the eldest son, this patronymic appellation might be still perpetuated in the family.

—————— Uno avulso non deficit alter.

To preserve and to rear so frail a being, the most tender assiduity was scarcely sufficient, and my mother's attention was somewhat diverted by an exclusive passion for her husband, and by the dissipation of the world, in which his taste and authority obliged her to mingle. But the maternal office was supplied by my aunt, Mrs. Catherine Porten; at whose name I feel a tear of gratitude trickling down my cheek. A life of celibacy transferred her vacant affection to her sister's first child: my weakness excited her pity; her attachment was fortified by labour and success: and if there be any, as I trust there are some, who rejoice that I live, to that dear and excellent woman they must hold themselves indebted. Many anxious and solitary days did she consume in the patient trial of every mode of relief and amusement. Many wakeful nights did she sit by my bedside in trembling expectation that each hour would be my last. Of the various and frequent disorders of my childhood my own recollection is dark. Suffice it to say, that while every practitioner, from Sloane and Ward to the Chevalier Taylor, was successively summoned to torture or relieve me, the care of my mind was too frequently neglected for that of my health: compassion always suggested an excuse for the indulgence of the master, or the idleness of the pupil; and the chain of my education was broken, as often as I was recalled from the school of learning to the bed of sickness.

As soon as the use of speech had prepared my infant reason for the admission of knowledge, I was taught the arts of reading, writing, and arithmetic. So remote is the date, so vague is the memory of their origin in myself, that, were not the error corrected by analogy, I should be tempted to conceive them as innate. In my childhood I was praised for the readiness with which I could multiply and divide, by memory alone, two sums of several figures; such praise encouraged my growing talent; and had I persevered in this line of application, I might have acquired some fame in mathematical studies.

After this previous institution at home, or at a day school at Putney, I was delivered at the age of seven into the hands of Mr. John Kirkby, who exercised about eighteen months the office of my domestic tutor. His learning and virtue introduced him to my father; and at Putney he might have found at least a temporary shelter, had not an act of indiscretion driven him into the world. One day reading prayers in the parish church, he most unluckily forgot the name of King George: his patron, a loyal subject, dismissed him with some reluctance, and a decent reward; and *how* the poor man ended his days I have never been able to learn. Mr. John Kirkby is the author of two small volumes; he Life of Automathes (London, 1745), and an English and Latin Grammar (London, 1746); which, as a testimony of gratitude, he dedicated (Nov. 5th, 1745) to my father. The books are before me: from them the pupil may judge the preceptor; and, upon the whole, his judgment will not be unfavourable. The grammar is executed with accuracy and skill, and I know not whether any better existed at the time in our language: but the Life of Automathes aspires to the honours of a philosophical fiction. It is the story of a youth, the son of a shipwrecked exile, who lives alone on a desert island from infancy to the age of manhood. A hind is his nurse; he inherits a cottage, with many useful and curious instruments; some ideas remain of the education of his two first years; some arts are borrowed from the beavers of a neighbouring lake; some truths are revealed in supernatural visions. With these helps, and his own industry, Automathes becomes a self-taught though speechless philosopher, who had investigated with success his own mind, the natural world, the abstract sciences, and the great principles of morality and religion. The author is not entitled to the merit of invention, since he has blended the English story of Robinson Crusoe with the Arabian romance of Hai Ebn Yokhdan, which he might have read in the Latin version of Pocock. In the Automathes I cannot praise either the depth of thought or elegance of style ; but the book is not devoid of entertainment or instruction ; and among several interesting passages, I would select the discovery of fire, which produces by accidental mischief the discovery of conscience. A man who had thought so much on the subjects of language and education was surely no ordinary preceptor: my childish years, and his hasty departure, prevented me from enjoying the full benefit of his lessons ; but they enlarged my knowledge of arithmetic, and left me a clear impression of the English and Latin rudiments.

In my ninth year (Jan., 1746), in a lucid interval of comparative health, my father adopted the convenient and customary mode of English education ; and I was sent to Kingston-upon-Thames, to a school of about seventy boys, which was kept by Dr. Wooddeson and his assistants. Every time I have since passed over Putney Common, I have always noticed the spot where my mother, as we drove along in the coach, admonished me that I was now going into the world, and must learn to think and act for myself. The expression may appear ludicrous ;. yet there is not, in the course of life, a more remarkable change than the removal of a child from the luxury and freedom of a wealthy house, to the frugal diet and strict subordination of a school ; from the tenderness of parents, and the obsequiousness of servants, to the rude familiarity of his equals, the insolent tyranny of his seniors, and the rod, perhaps, of a cruel and capricious pedagogue. Such hardships may steel the mind and body against the injuries of fortune ; but my timid reserve was astonished by the crowd and tumult of the school ; the want of strength and activity disqualified me for the sports of the play-field ; nor have I forgotten how often in the year forty-six I was reviled and buffeted for the sins of my Tory ancestors. By the common methods of discipline, at the expence of many tears and some blood, I purchased the knowledge of the Latin syntax : and not long since I was possessed of the dirty volumes of Phædrus and Cornelius Nepos, which I painfully construed and darkly understood. The choice of these authors is not injudicious. The *lives* of Cornelius Nepos, the friend of Atticus and Cicero, are composed in the style of the purest age : his simplicity is elegant, his brevity copious ; he exhibits a series of men and manners ; and with such illustrations, as every pedant is not indeed qualified to give, this classic biographer may initiate a young student in the history of Greece and Rome. The use of fables or apologues has been approved in every age from ancient India to modern Europe. They convey in familiar images the truths of morality and prudence ; and the most childish understanding (I advert to the scruples of Rousseau) will not suppose either that beasts *do* speak, or that men *may* lie. A fable represents the genuine characters of animals ; and a skilful master might extract from Pliny and Buffon some pleasing lessons of natural history, a science well adapted to the taste and capacity of children.   The Latinity of Phædrus is not exempt from an alloy of the silver age ; but his manner is concise, terse, and sententious : the Thracian slave discreetly breathes the spirit of a freeman ; and when the text is found, the style is perspicuous.   But his fables, after a long oblivion, were first published by Peter Pithou, from a corrupt manuscript.   The labours of fifty editors confess the defects of the copy, as well as the value of the original ; and the school-boy may have been whipped for misapprehending a passage, which Bentley could not restore, and which Burman could not explain.

My studies were too frequently interrupted by sickness ; and after a real or nominal residence at Kingston School of near two years, I was finally recalled (Dec., 1747) by my mother's death, in her thirty-eighth year.   I was too young to feel the importance of my loss ; and the image of her person and conversation is faintly imprinted in my memory.   The affectionate heart of my aunt, Catherine Porten, bewailed a sister and a friend ; but my poor father was inconsolable, and the transport of grief seemed to threaten his life or his reason.   I can never forget the scene of our first interview, some weeks after the fatal event ; the awful silence, the room hung with black, the mid-day tapers, his sighs and tears ; his praises of my mother, a saint in heaven ; his solemn adjuration that I would cherish her memory and imitate her virtues ; and the fervor with which he kissed and blessed me as the sole surviving pledge of their loves.   The storm of passion insensibly subsided into calmer melancholy.   At a convivial meeting of his friends, Mr. Gibbon might affect or enjoy a gleam of cheerfulness ; but his plan of happiness was for ever destroyed : and after the loss of his companion he was left alone in a world, of which the business and pleasures were to him irksome or insipid.   After some unsuccessful trials he renounced the tumult of London and the hospitality of Putney, and buried himself in the rural or rather rustic solitude of Beriton ; from which, during several years, he seldom emerged.

As far back as I can remember, the house, near Putney-bridge and churchyard, of my maternal grandfather appears in the light of my proper and native home.   It was there that I was allowed to spend the greatest part of my time, in sickness or in health, during my school vacations and my parents' residence in London, and finally after my mother's death.   Three months after that event, in the spring of 1748, the commercial ruin of her father, Mr. James Porten, was accomplished and declared.   He suddenly absconded : but as his effects were not sold, nor the house evacuated, till the Christmas following, I enjoyed during the whole year the society of my aunt, without much consciousness of her impending fate.   I feel a melancholy pleasure in repeating my obligations to that excellent woman, Mrs. Catherine Porten, the true mother of my mind as well as of my health.   Her natural good sense was improved by the perusal of the best books in the English language ; and if her reason was sometimes clouded by prejudice, her sentiments were never disguised by hypocrisy or affectation.   Her indulgent tenderness, the frankness of her temper, and my innate rising curiosity, soon removed all distance between us : like friends of an equal age, we freely conversed on every topic, familiar or abstruse ; and it was her delight and reward to observe the first shoots of my young ideas. Pain and languor were often soothed by the voice of instruction and amusement ; and to her kind lessons I ascribe my early and invincible love of reading, which I would not exchange for the treasures of India. I should perhaps be astonished, were it possible to ascertain the date, at which a favourite tale was engraved, by frequent repetition, in my memory : the Cavern of the Winds ; the Palace of Felicity ; and the fatal moment, at the end of three months or centuries, when Prince Adolphus is overtaken by Time, who had worn out so many pair of wings in the pursuit. Before I left Kingston school I was well acquainted with Pope's Homer and the Arabian Nights Entertainments, two books which will always please by the moving picture of human manners and specious miracles : nor was I then capable of discerning that Pope's translation is a portrait endowed with every merit, excepting that of likeness to the original. The verses of Pope accustomed my ear to the sound of poetic harmony : in the death of Hector, and the shipwreck of Ulysses, I tasted the new emotions of terror and pity ; and seriously disputed with my aunt on the vices and virtues of the heroes of the Trojan war. From Pope's Homer to Dryden's Virgil was an easy transition ; but I know not how, from some fault in the author, the translator, or the reader, the pious Æneas did not so forcibly seize on my imagination ; and I derived more pleasure from Ovid's Metamorphoses, especially in the fall of Phæton, and the speeches of Ajax and Ulysses. My grandfather's flight unlocked the door of a tolerable library ; and I turned over many English pages of poetry and romance, of history and travels. Where a title attracted my eye, without fear or awe I snatched the volume from the shelf ; and Mrs. Porten, who indulged herself in moral and religious speculations, was more prone to encourage than to check a curiosity above the strength of a boy. This year (1748), the twelfth of my age, I shall note as the most propitious to the growth of my intellectual stature.

The relics of my grandfather's fortune afforded a bare annuity for his own maintenance ; and his daughter, my worthy aunt, who had already passed her fortieth year, was left destitute. Her noble spirit scorned a life of obligation and dependence ; and after revolving several schemes, she preferred the humble industry of keeping a boarding-house for Westminster-school,* where she laboriously earned a competence for her old age. This singular opportunity of blending the advantages of private and public education decided my father. After the Christmas holidays in January, 1749, I accompanied Mrs. Porten to her new house in College-street ; and was immediately entered in the school, of which Dr. John Nicoll was at that time head-master. At first I was alone : but my aunt's resolution was praised ; her character was esteemed ; her friends were numerous and active : in the course of some years she became the mother of forty or fifty boys, for the most part of family and fortune ; and as her primitive habitation was too narrow, she built and occupied a spacious mansion in

---

* It is said in the family, that she was principally induced to this undertaking by her affection for her nephew, whose weak constitution required her constant and unremitted attention.—S.

Dean's Yard. I shall always be ready to join in the common opinion, that our public schools, which have produced so many eminent characters, are the best adapted to the genius and constitution of the English people. A boy of spirit may acquire a previous and practical experience of the world ; and his playfellows may be the future friends of his heart or his interest. In a free intercourse with his equals, the habits of truth, fortitude, and prudence will insensibly be matured. Birth and riches are measured by the standard of personal merit ; and the mimic scene of a rebellion has displayed, in their true colours, the ministers and patriots of the rising generation. Our seminaries of learning do not exactly correspond with the precept of a Spartan king, "that the child should be instructed in the arts, which will be useful to the man ;" since a finished scholar may emerge from the head of Westminster or Eton, in total ignorance of the business and conversation of English gentlemen in the latter end of the eighteenth century. But these schools may assume the merit of teaching all that they pretend to teach, the Latin and Greek languages : they deposit in the hands of a disciple the keys of two valuable chests ; nor can he complain, if they are afterwards lost or neglected by his own fault. The necessity of leading in equal ranks so many unequal powers of capacity and application, will prolong to eight or ten years the juvenile studies, which might be despatched in half that time by the skilful master of a single pupil. Yet even the repetition of exercise and discipline contributes to fix in a vacant mind the verbal science of grammar and prosody : and the private or voluntary student, who possesses the sense and spirit of the classics, may offend, by a false quantity, the scrupulous ear of a well-flogged critic. For myself, I must be content with a very small share of the civil and literary fruits of a public school. In the space of two years (1749, 1750), interrupted by danger and debility, I painfully climbed into the third form ; and my riper age was left to acquire the beauties of the Latin, and the rudiments of the Greek tongue. Instead of audaciously mingling in the sports, the quarrels, and the connections of our little world, I was still cherished at home under the maternal wing of my aunt ; and my removal from Westminster long preceded the approach of manhood.

The violence and variety of my complaint, which had excused my frequent absence from Westminster School, at length engaged Mrs. Porten, with the advice of physicians, to conduct me to Bath : at the end of the Michaelmas vacation (1750) she quitted me with reluctance, and I remained several months under the care of a trusty maid-servant. A strange nervous affection, which alternately contracted my legs, and produced, without any visible symptoms, the most excruciating pain, was ineffectually opposed by the various methods of bathing and pumping. From Bath I was transported to Winchester, to the house of a physician ; and after the failure of his medical skill, we had again recourse to the virtues of the Bath waters. During the intervals of these fits, I moved with my father to Beriton and Putney ; and a short unsuccessful trial was attempted to renew my attendance at Westminster School. But my infirmities could not be reconciled with the hours and discipline of a public seminary ; and instead of a domestic tutor, who might have watched the favourable moments, and gently advanced the progress of my learning, my father was too easily content with such occasional teachers as the different places of my residence could supply. I was never forced, and seldom was I persuaded, to admit these lessons: yet 1 read with a clergyman at Bath some odes of Horace, and several episodes of Virgil, which gave me an imperfect and transient enjoyment of the Latin poets. It might now be apprehended that I should continue for life an illiterate cripple; but, as I approached my sixteenth year, Nature displayed in my favour her mysterious energies: my constitution was fortified and fixed; and my disorders, instead of growing with my growth and strengthening with my strength, most wonderfully vanished. 1 have never possessed or abused the insolence of health: but since that time few persons have been more exempt from real or imaginary ills; and, till I am admonished by the gout, the reader will no more be troubled with the history of my bodily complaints. My unexpected recovery again encouraged the hope of my education; and I was placed at Esher, in Surrey, in the house of the Reverend Mr. Philip Francis, in a pleasant spot, which promised to unite the various benefits of air, exercise, and study (Jan., 1752). The translator of Horace might have taught me to relish the Latin poets, had not my friends discovered in a few weeks, that he preferred the pleasures of London, to the instruction of his pupils. My father's perplexity at this time, rather than his prudence, was urged to embrace a singular and desperate measure. Without preparation or delay he carried me to Oxford; and I was matriculated in the university as a gentleman commoner of Magdalen college, before I had accomplished the fifteenth year of my age (April 3, 1752).

The curiosity, which had been implanted in my infant mind, was still alive and active; but my reason was not sufficiently informed to understand the value, or to lament the loss, of three precious years from my entrance at Westminster to my admission at Oxford. Instead of repining at my long and frequent confinement to the chamber or the couch, I secretly rejoiced in those infirmities, which delivered me from the exercises of the school, and the society of my equals. As often as I was tolerably exempt from danger and pain, reading, free desultory reading, was the employment and comfort of my solitary hours. At Westminster, my aunt sought only to amuse and indulge me; in my stations at Bath and Winchester, at Beriton and Putney, a false compassion respected my sufferings; and 1 was allowed, without controul or advice, to gratify the wanderings of an unripe taste. My indiscriminate appetite subsided by degrees in the *historic* line: and since philosophy has exploded all innate ideas and natural propensities, I must ascribe this choice to the assiduous perusal of the Universal History, as the octavo volumes successively appeared. This unequal work, and a treatise of Hearne, the *Ductor historicus*, referred and introduced me to the Greek and Roman historians, to as many at least as were accessible to an English reader. All that I could find were greedily devoured, from Littlebury's lame Herodotus, and Spelman's valuable Xenophon, to the pompous folios of Gordon's Tacitus, and a ragged Procopius of the beginning of the last century. The cheap acquisition of so much knowledge confirmed my dislike to the study of languages; and I argued with Mrs. Porten, that, were I master of Greek and Latin, I must interpret to myself in English the thoughts of the original, and that such extemporary versions must be inferior to the elaborate translations of professed scholars ; a silly sophism, which could not easily be confuted by a person ignorant of any other language than her own. From the ancient I leaped to the modern world : many crude lumps of Speed, Rapin, Mezeray, Davila, Machiavel, Father Paul, Bower, &c., I devoured like so many novels ; and I swallowed with the same voracious appetite the descriptions of India and China, of Mexico and Peru.

My first introduction to the historic scenes, which have since engaged so many years of my life, must be ascribed to an accident. In the summer of 1751, I accompanied my father on a visit to Mr. Hoare's, in Wiltshire ; but I was less delighted with the beauties of Stourhead, than with discovering in the library a common book, the Continuation of Echard's Roman History, which is indeed executed with more skill and taste than the previous work. To me the reigns of the successors of Constantine were absolutely new ; and I was immersed in the passage of the Goths over the Danube, when the summons of the dinner-bell reluctantly dragged me from my intellectual feast. This transient glance served rather to irritate than to appease my curiosity ; and as soon as I returned to Bath I procured the second and third volumes of Howel's History of the World, which exhibit the Byzantine period on a larger scale. Mahomet and his Saracens soon fixed my attention ; and some instinct of criticism directed me to the genuine sources. Simon Ockley, an original in every sense, first opened my eyes ; and I was led from one book to another, till I had ranged round the circle of Oriental history. Before I was sixteen, I had exhausted all that could be learned in English of the Arabs and Persians, the Tartars and Turks ; and the same ardour urged me to guess at the French of D'Herbelot, and to construe the barbarous Latin of Pocock's Abulfaragius. Such vague and multifarious reading could not teach me to think, to write, or to act ; and the only principle that darted a ray of light into the indigested chaos, was an early and rational application to the order of time and place. The maps of Cellarius and Wells imprinted in my mind the picture of ancient geography : from Stranchius I imbibed the elements of chronology : the Tables of Helvicus and Anderson, the Annals of Usher and Prideaux, distinguished the connection of events, and engraved the multitude of names and dates in a clear and indelible series. But in the discussion of the first ages I overleaped the bounds of modesty and use. In my childish balance I presumed to weigh the systems of Scaliger and Petavius, of Marsham and Newton, which I could seldom study in the originals ; and my sleep has been disturbed by the difficulty of reconciling the Septuagint with the Hebrew computation. I arrived at Oxford with a stock of erudition, that might have puzzled a doctor, and a degree of ignorance, of which a school-boy would have been ashamed.

At the conclusion of this first period of my life, I am tempted to enter a protest against the trite and lavish praise of the happiness of our boyish years, which is echoed with so much affectation in the world. That happiness I have never known, that time I have never regretted ; and were my poor aunt still alive, she would bear testimony to the early and constant uniformity of my sentiments. It will indeed be replied, that *I* am not a competent judge; that pleasure is incompatible with pain; that joy is excluded from sickness; and that the felicity of a schoolboy consists in the perpetual motion of thoughtless and playful agility, in which I was never qualified to excel. My name, it is most true, could never be enrolled among the sprightly race, the idle progeny of Eton or Westminster,

"Who foremost may delight to | With pliant arm, the glassy wave,
    cleave, | Or urge the flying ball."

The poet may gaily describe the short hours of recreation; but he forgets the daily tedious labours of the school, which is approached each morning with anxious and reluctant steps.

A traveller, who visits Oxford or Cambridge, is surprised and edified by the apparent order and tranquillity that prevail in the seats of the English muses. In the most celebrated universities of Holland, Germany, and Italy, the students, who swarm from different countries, are loosely dispersed in private lodgings at the houses of the burghers: they dress according to their fancy and fortune; and in the intemperate quarrels of youth and wine, their *swords*, though less frequently than of old, are sometimes stained with each other's blood. The use of arms is banished from our English universities; the uniform habit of the academics, the square cap, and black gown, is adapted to the civil and even clerical profession; and from the doctor in divinity to the under-graduate, the degrees of learning and age are externally distinguished. Instead of being scattered in a town, the students of Oxford and Cambridge are united in colleges; their maintenance is provided at their own expense, or that of the founders; and the stated hours of the hall and chapel represent the discipline of a regular, and, as it were, a religious community. The eyes of the traveller are attracted by the size or beauty of the public edifices; and the principal colleges appear to be so many palaces, which a liberal nation has erected and endowed for the habitation of science. My own introduction to the university of Oxford forms a new æra in my life; and at the distance of forty years I still remember my first emotions of surprise and satisfaction. In my fifteenth year I felt myself suddenly raised from a boy to a man: the persons, whom I respected as my superiors in age and academical rank, entertained me with every mark of attention and civility; and my vanity was flattered by the velvet cap and silk gown, which distinguish a gentleman commoner from a plebeian student. A decent allowance, more money than a schoolboy had ever seen, was at my own disposal; and I might command, among the tradesmen of Oxford, an indefinite and dangerous latitude of credit. A key was delivered into my hands, which gave me the free use of a numerous and learned library; my apartment consisted of three elegant and well-furnished rooms in the new building, a stately pile, of Magdalen College; and the adjacent walks, had they been frequented by Plato's disciples, might have been compared to the Attic shade on the banks of the Ilissus. Such was the fair prospect of my entrance (April 3, 1752) into the university of Oxford.

A venerable prelate, whose taste and erudition must reflect honour on the society in which they were formed, has drawn a very interesting picture of his academical life.—" I was educated (says Bishop Lowth) in the UNIVERSITY OF OXFORD. I enjoyed all the advantages, both public and private, which that famous seat of learning so largely affords. I spent many years in that illustrious society, in a well-regulated course of useful discipline and studies, and in the agreeable and improving commerce of gentlemen and of scholars ; in a society where emulation without envy, ambition without jealousy, contention without animosity, incited industry, and awakened genius ; where a liberal pursuit of knowledge, and a genuine freedom of thought, were raised, encouraged, and pushed forward by example, by commendation, and by authority. I breathed the same atmosphere that the HOOKERS, the CHILLING-WORTHS, and the LOCKES had breathed before ; whose benevolence and humanity were as extensive as their vast genius and comprehensive knowledge ; who always treated their adversaries with civility and respect ; who made candour, moderation, and liberal judgment as much the rule and law as the subject of their discourse. And do you reproach me with my education in this place, and with my relation to this most respectable body, which I shall always esteem my greatest advantage and my highest honour?" I transcribe with pleasure this eloquent passage, without examining what benefits or what rewards were derived by Hooker, or Chillingworth, or Locke, from their academical institution ; without inquiring, whether in this angry controversy the spirit of Lowth himself is purified from the intolerant zeal, which Warburton had ascribed to the genius of the place. It may indeed be observed, that the atmosphere of Oxford did not agree with Mr. Locke's constitution ; and that the philosopher justly despised the academical bigots, who expelled his person and condemned his principles. The expression of gratitude is a virtue and a pleasure : a liberal mind will delight to cherish and celebrate the memory of its parents ; and the teachers of science are the parents of the mind. I applaud the filial piety, which it is impossible for me to imitate ; since I must not confess an imaginary debt, to assume the merit of a just or generous retribution. To the university of Oxford *I* acknowledge no obligation ; and she will as cheerfully renounce me for a son, as I am willing to disclaim her for a mother. I spent fourteen months at Magdalen College ; they proved the fourteen months the most idle and unprofitable of my whole life : the reader will pronounce between the school and the scholar ; but I cannot affect to believe that Nature had disqualified me for all literary pursuits. The specious and ready excuse of my tender age, imperfect preparation, and hasty departure, may doubtless be alleged ; nor do I wish to defraud such excuses of their proper weight. Yet in my sixteenth year I was not devoid of capacity or application ; even my childish reading had displayed an early though blind propensity for books ; and the shallow flood might have been taught to flow in a deep channel and a clear stream. In the discipline of a well-constituted academy, under the guidance of skilful and vigilant professors, I should gradually have risen from translations to originals, from the Latin to the Greek classics, from dead languages to living science : my hours would have been occupied by useful and agreeable studies, the wanderings of fancy would have been restrained, and I should have escaped the temptations of idleness, which finally precipitated my departure from Oxford.

Perhaps in a separate annotation I may coolly examine the fabulous and real antiquities of our sister universities, a question which has kindled such fierce and foolish disputes among their fanatic sons. In the meanwhile it will be acknowledged that these venerable bodies are sufficiently old to partake of all the prejudices and infirmities of age. The schools of Oxford and Cambridge were founded in a dark age of false and barbarous science; and they are still tainted with the vices of their origin. Their primitive discipline was adapted to the education of priests and monks; and the government still remains in the hands of the clergy, an order of men whose manners are remote from the present world, and whose eyes are dazzled by the light of philosophy. The legal incorporation of these societies by the charters of popes and kings had given them a monopoly of the public instruction; and the spirit of monopolists is narrow, lazy, and oppressive; their work is more costly and less productive than that of independent artists; and the new improvements so eagerly grasped by the competition of freedom, are admitted with slow and sullen reluctance in those proud corporations, above the fear of a rival, and below the confession of an error. We may scarcely hope that any reformation will be a voluntary act; and so deeply are they rooted in law and prejudice, that even the omnipotence of parliament would shrink from an inquiry into the state and abuses of the two universities.

The use of academical degrees, as old as the thirteenth century, is visibly borrowed from the mechanic corporations; in which an apprentice, after serving his time, obtains a testimonial of his skill, and a licence to practise his trade and mystery. It is not my design to depreciate those honours, which could never gratify or disappoint my ambition; and I should applaud the institution, if the degrees of bachelor or licentiate were bestowed as the reward of manly and successful study: if the name and rank of doctor or master were strictly reserved for the professors of science, who have approved their title to the public esteem.

In all the universities of Europe, excepting our own, the languages and sciences are distributed among a numerous list of effective professors: the students, according to their taste, their calling, and their diligence, apply themselves to the proper masters; and in the annual repetition of public and private lectures, these masters are assiduously employed. Our curiosity may inquire what number of professors has been instituted at Oxford? (for I shall now confine myself to my own university;) by whom are they appointed, and what may be the probable chances of merit or incapacity; how many are stationed to the three faculties, and how many are left for the liberal arts? what is the form, and what the substance, of their lessons? But all these questions are silenced by one short and singular answer, "That in the university of Oxford, the greater part of the public professors have for these many years given up altogether even the pretence of teaching." Incredible as the fact may appear, I must rest my belief on the positive and impartial evidence of a master of moral and political wisdom, who had himself resided at Oxford. Dr. Adam Smith assigns as the cause of their indolence, that, instead of being paid by voluntary contributions, which would urge them to increase the number, and to deserve the gratitude of their pupils, the Oxford professors are secure in the enjoyment of a fixed stipend, without the necessity of labour, or the apprehension of controul. It has indeed been observed, nor is the observation absurd, that excepting in experimental sciences, which demand a costly apparatus and a dexterous hand, the many valuable treatises, that have been published on every subject of learning, may now supersede the ancient mode of oral instruction. Were this principle true in its utmost latitude, I should only infer that the offices and salaries, which are become useless, ought without delay to be abolished. But there still remains a material difference between a book and a professor; the hour of the lecture enforces attendance; attention is fixed by the presence, the voice, and the occasional questions of the teacher; the most idle will carry something away; and the more diligent will compare the instructions, which they have heard in the school, with the volumes, which they peruse in their chamber. The advice of a skilful professor will adapt a course of reading to every mind and every situation; his authority will discover, admonish, and at last chastise the negligence of his disciples; and his vigilant inquiries will ascertain the steps of their literary progress. Whatever science he professes he may illustrate in a series of discourses, composed in the leisure of his closet, pronounced on public occasions, and finally delivered to the press. I observe with pleasure, that in the university of Oxford Dr. Lowth, with equal eloquence and erudition, has executed this task in his incomparable *Prælections* on the Poetry of the Hebrews.

The college of St. Mary Magdalen was founded in the fifteenth century by Wainfleet, bishop of Winchester; and now consists of a president, forty fellows, and a number of inferior students. It is esteemed one of the largest and most wealthy of our academical corporations, which may be compared to the Benedictine abbeys of Catholic countries; and I have loosely heard that the estates belonging to Magdalen College, which are leased by those indulgent landlords at small quit-rents and occasional fines, might be raised, in the hands of private avarice, to an annual revenue of nearly thirty thousand pounds. Our colleges are supposed to be schools of science, as well as of education; nor is it unreasonable to expect that a body of literary men, devoted to a life of celibacy, exempt from the care of their own subsistence, and amply provided with books, should devote their leisure to the prosecution of study, and that some effects of their studies should be manifested to the world. The shelves of their library groan under the weight of the Benedictine folios, of the editions of the fathers, and the collections of the middle ages, which have issued from the single abbey of St. Germain de Préz at Paris. A composition of genius must be the offspring of one mind; but such works of industry, as may be divided among many hands, and must be continued during many years, are the peculiar province of a laborious community. If I inquire into the manufactures of the monks of Magdalen, if I extend the inquiry to the other colleges of Oxford and Cambridge, a silent blush, or a scornful frown, will be the only reply. The fellows or monks of my time were decent easy men, who supinely enjoyed the gifts of the founder; their days were filled by a series of uniform employments; the chapel and the hall, the coffee-house and the common room, till they retired, weary and well satisfied, to a long slumber. From the toil of reading, or thinking, or writing, they had absolved their conscience; and the first shoots of learning and ingenuity withered on the ground, without yielding any fruits to the owners or the public. As a gentleman commoner, I was admitted to the society of the fellows, and fondly expected that some questions of literature would be the amusing and instructive topics of their discourse. Their conversation stagnated in a round of college business, Tory politics, personal anecdotes, and private scandal: their dull and deep potations excused the brisk intemperance of youth; and their constitutional toasts were not expressive of the most lively loyalty for the house of Hanover. A general election was now approaching: the great Oxfordshire contest already blazed with all the malevolence of party-zeal. Magdalen College was devoutly attached to the old interest! and the names of Wenman and Dashwood were more frequently pronounced, than those of Cicero and Chrysostom. The example of the senior fellows could not inspire the under-graduates with a liberal spirit or studious emulation; and I cannot describe, as I never knew, the discipline of college. Some duties may possibly have been imposed on the poor scholars, whose ambition aspired to the peaceful honours of a fellowship (*ascribi quietis ordinibus - - - - Deorum*); but no independent members were admitted below the rank of a gentleman commoner, and our velvet cap was the cap of liberty. A tradition prevailed that some of our predecessors had spoken Latin declamations in the hall; but of this ancient custom no vestige remained: the obvious methods of public exercises and examinations were totally unknown; and I have never heard that either the president or the society interfered in the private economy of the tutors and their pupils.

The silence of the Oxford professors, which deprives the youth of public instruction, is imperfectly supplied by the tutors, as they are styled, of the several colleges. Instead of confining themselves to a single science, which had satisfied the ambition of Burman or Bernoulli, they teach, or promise to teach, either history or mathematics, or ancient literature, or moral philosophy; and as it is possible that they may be defective in all, it is highly probable that of some they will be ignorant. They are paid, indeed, by voluntary contributions; but their appointment depends on the head of the house: their diligence is voluntary, and will consequently be languid, while the pupils themselves, or their parents, are not indulged in the liberty of choice or change. The first tutor into whose hands I was resigned appears to have been one of the best of the tribe: Dr. Waldegrave was a learned and pious man, of a mild disposition, strict morals, and abstemious life, who seldom mingled in the politics or the jollity of the college. But his knowledge of the world was confined to the university; his learning was of the last, rather than the present age; his temper was indolent; his faculties, which were not of the first rate, had been relaxed by the climate, and he was satisfied, like his fellows, with the slight and superficial discharge of an important trust. As soon as my tutor had sounded the insufficiency of his pupil in school-learning, he proposed that we should read every morning from ten to eleven the comedies of Terence. The sum of my improvement in the university of Oxford is confined to three or four Latin plays; and even the study of an elegant classic, which might have been illustrated by a comparison of ancient and modern theatres, was reduced to a dry and literal interpretation of the author's text. During the first weeks I constantly attended these lessons in my tutor's room; but as they appeared equally devoid of profit and pleasure I was once tempted to try the experiment of a formal apology. The apology was accepted with a smile. I repeated the offence with less ceremony; the excuse was admitted with the same indulgence: the slightest motive of laziness or indisposition, the most trifling avocation at home or abroad, was allowed as a worthy impediment; nor did my tutor appear conscious of my absence or neglect. Had the hour of lecture been constantly filled, a single hour was a small portion of my academic leisure. No plan of study was recommended for my use; no exercises were prescribed for his inspection; and, at the most precious season of youth, whole days and weeks were suffered to elapse without labour or amusement, without advice or account. I should have listened to the voice of reason and of my tutor; his mild behaviour had gained my confidence. I preferred his society to that of the younger students; and in our evening walks to the top of Heddington-hill, we freely conversed on a variety of subjects. Since the days of Pocock and Hyde, Oriental learning has always been the pride of Oxford, and I once expressed an inclination to study Arabic. His prudence discouraged this childish fancy; but he neglected the fair occasion of directing the ardour of a curious mind. During my absence in the summer vacation, Dr. Waldegrave accepted a college living at Washington in Sussex, and on my return I no longer found him at Oxford. From that time I have lost sight of my first tutor; but at the end of thirty years (1781) he was still alive; and the practice of exercise and temperance had entitled him to a healthy old age.

The long recess between the Trinity and Michaelmas terms empties the colleges of Oxford, as well as the courts of Westminster. I spent, at my father's house at Beriton in Hampshire, the two months of August and September. It is whimsical enough, that as soon as I left Magdalen College, my taste for books began to revive; but it was the same blind and boyish taste for the pursuit of exotic history. Unprovided with original learning, unformed in the habits of thinking, unskilled in the arts of composition, I resolved—to write a book. The title of this first Essay, *The Age of Sesostris*, was perhaps suggested by Voltaire's Age of Lewis XIV. which was new and popular; but my sole object was to investigate the probable date of the life and reign of the conqueror of Asia. I was then enamoured of Sir John Marsham's Canon Chronicus; an elaborate work, of whose merits and defects I was not yet qualified to judge. According to his specious, though narrow plan, I settled my hero about the time of Solomon, in the tenth century before the Christian era. It was therefore incumbent on me, unless I would adopt Sir Isaac Newton's shorter chronology, to remove a formidable objection; and my solution, for a youth of fifteen, is not devoid of ingenuity. In his version of the Sacred Books, Manetho the high priest has identified Sethosis, or Sesostris, with the elder brother of Danaus, who landed in Greece, according to the Parian Marble, fifteen hundred and ten years before Christ. But in my supposition the high priest is guilty of a voluntary error; flattery is the prolific parent of falsehood. Manetho's History of Egypt is dedicated to Ptolemy Philadelphus, who derived a fabulous or illegitimate pedigree from the Macedonian kings of the race of Hercules. Danaus is the ancestor of Hercules; and after the failure of the elder branch, his descendants, the Ptolemies, are the sole representatives of the royal family, and may claim by inheritance the kingdom which they hold by conquest. Such were my juvenile discoveries; at a riper age I no longer presume to connect the Greek, the Jewish, and the Egyptian antiquities, which are lost in a distant cloud. Nor is this the only instance, in which the belief and knowledge of the child are superseded by the more rational ignorance of the man. During my stay at Beriton, my infant-labour was diligently prosecuted, without much interruption from company or country diversions; and I already heard the music of public applause. The discovery of my own weakness was the first symptom of taste. On my return to Oxford, the Age of Sesostris was wisely relinquished; but the imperfect sheets remained twenty years at the bottom of a drawer, till, in a general clearance of papers (Nov., 1772,) they were committed to the flames.

After the departure of Dr. Waldgrave, I was transferred, with his other pupils, to his academical heir, whose literary character did not command the respect of the college. Dr. —— well remembered that he had a salary to receive, and only forgot that he had a duty to perform. Instead of guiding the studies, and watching over the behaviour of his disciple, I was never summoned to attend even the ceremony of a lecture; and, excepting one voluntary visit to his rooms, during the eight months of his titular office, the tutor and pupil lived in the same college as strangers to each other. The want of experience, of advice, and of occupation, soon betrayed me into some improprieties of conduct, ill-chosen company, late hours, and inconsiderate expense. My growing debts might be secret; but my frequent absence was visible and scandalous: and a tour to Bath, a visit into Buckinghamshire, and four excursions to London in the same winter, were costly and dangerous frolics. They were, indeed, without a meaning, as without an excuse. The irksomeness of a cloistered life repeatedly tempted me to wander; but my chief pleasure was that of travelling; and I was too young and bashful to enjoy, like a Manly Oxonian in Town, the pleasures of London. In all these excursions I eloped from Oxford; I returned to college; in a few days I eloped again, as if I had been an independent stranger in a hired lodging, without once hearing the voice of admonition, without once feeling the hand of control. Yet my time was lost, my expenses were multiplied, my behaviour abroad was unknown; folly as well as vice should have awakened the attention of my superiors, and my tender years would have justified a more than ordinary degree of restraint and discipline.

It might at least be expected, that an ecclesiastical school should inculcate the orthodox principles of religion. But our venerable mother had contrived to unite the opposite extremes of bigotry and indifference : an heretic, or unbeliever, was a monster in her eyes ; but she was always, or often, or sometimes, remiss in the spiritual education of her own children. According to the statutes of the university, every student, before he is matriculated, must subscribe his assent to the thirty-nine articles of the church of England, which are signed by more than read, and read by more than believe them. My insufficient age excused me, however, from the immediate performance of this legal ceremony ; and the vice-chancellor directed me to return, as soon as I should have accomplished my fifteenth year ; recommending me, in the mean while, to the instruction of my college. My college forgot to instruct : I forgot to return, and was myself forgotten by the first magistrate of the university. Without a single lecture, either public or private, either christian or protestant, without any academical subscription, without any episcopal confirmation, I was left by the dim light of my catechism to grope my way to the chapel and communion-table, where I was admitted, without a question, how far, or by what means, I might be qualified to receive the sacrament. Such almost incredible neglect was productive of the worst mischiefs. From my childhood I had been fond of religious disputation : my poor aunt has been often puzzled by the mysteries which she strove to believe ; nor had the elastic spring been totally broken by the weight of the atmosphere of Oxford. The blind activity of idleness urged me to advance without armour into the dangerous mazes of controversy ; and at the age of sixteen, I bewildered myself in the errors of the church of Rome.

The progress of my conversion may tend to illustrate, at least, the history of my own mind. It was not long since Dr. Middleton's free inquiry had founded an alarm in the theological world : much ink and much gall had been spilt in the defence of the primitive miracles ; and the two dullest of their champions were crowned with academic honours by the university of Oxford. The name of Middleton was unpopular ; and his proscription very naturally led me to peruse his writings, and those of his antagonists. His bold criticism, which approaches the precipice of infidelity, produced on my mind a singular effect ; and had I persevered in the communion of Rome, I should now apply to my own fortune the prediction of the Sibyl,

———Via prima salutis,
Quod minimè reris, Graiâ, pandetur ab urbe.

The elegance of style and freedom of argument were repelled by a shield of prejudice. I still revered the character, or rather the names, of the saints and fathers whom Dr. Middleton exposes ; nor could he destroy my implicit belief, that the gift of miraculous powers was continued in the church, during the first four or five centuries of Christianity. But I was unable to resist the weight of historical evidence, that within the same period most of the leading doctrines of popery were already introduced in theory and practice : nor was my conclusion absurd, that miracles are the test of truth, and that the church must be orthodox and pure, which was so often approved by the visible interposition of the Deity. The marvellous tales which are so boldly attested by the Basils and Chrysostoms, the Austins and Jeroms, compelled me to embrace the superior merits of celibacy, the institution of the monastic life, the use of the sign of the cross, of holy oil, and even of images, the invocation of saints, the worship of relics, the rudiments of purgatory in prayers for the dead, and the tremendous mystery of the sacrifice of the body and blood of Christ, which insensibly swelled into the prodigy of transubstantiation. In these dispositions, and already more than half a convert, I formed an unlucky intimacy with a young gentleman of our college, whose name I shall spare. With a character less resolute, Mr. —— had imbibed the same religious opinions; and some Popish books, I know not through what channel, were conveyed into his possession. I read, I applauded, I believed: the English translations of two famous works of Bossuet, Bishop of Meaux, the Exposition of the Catholic Doctrine, and the History of the Protestant Variations, achieved my conversion, and I surely fell by a noble hand.* I have since examined the originals with a more discerning eye, and shall not hesitate to pronounce, that Bossuet is indeed a master of all the weapons of controversy. In the Exposition, a specious apology, the orator assumes, with consummate art, the tone of candour and simplicity; and the ten-horned monster is transformed, at his magic touch, into the milk-white hind, who must be loved as soon as she is seen. In the History, a bold and well-aimed attack, he displays, with a happy mixture of narrative and argument, the faults and follies, the changes and contradictions of our first reformers; whose variations (as he dexterously contends) are the mark of historical error, while the perpetual unity of the catholic church is the sign and test of infallible truth. To my present feelings it seems incredible that I should ever believe that I believed in transubstantiation. But my conqueror oppressed me with the sacramental words, " Hoc est corpus meum," and dashed against each other the figurative half-meanings of the protestant sects: every objection was resolved into omnipotence; and after repeating at St. Mary's the Athanasian creed, I humbly acquiesced in the mystery of the real presence.

" To take up half on trust, and half to try,
Name it not faith, but bungling bigotry,
Both knave and fool, the merchant we may call,
To pay great sums, and to compound the small,
For who would break with Heaven, and would not break for all ? "

No sooner had I settled my new religion than I resolved to profess myself a catholic. Youth is sincere and impetuous; and a momentary glow of enthusiasm had raised me above all temporal considerations.†

By the keen protestants, who would gladly retaliate the example of persecution, a clamour is raised of the increase of popery: and they are always loud to declaim against the toleration of priests and jesuits, who pervert so many of his majesty's subjects from their religion and allegiance. On the present occasion, the fall of one or more of her sons directed this clamour against the university: and it was con-

* Mr. Gibbon never talked with me on the subject of his conversion to popery but once: and then he imputed his change to the works of Parsons the jesuit, who lived in the reign of Elizabeth, and who, he said, had urged all the best arguments in favour of the Roman catholic religion. S.
† He described the letter to his father, announcing his conversion, as written with all the pomp, the dignity, and self-satisfaction of a martyr. S.

fidently affirmed that popish missionaries were suffered, under various disguises, to introduce themselves into the colleges of Oxford. But justice obliges me to declare, that, as far as relates to myself, this assertion is false; and that I never conversed with a priest, or even with a papist, till my resolution from books was absolutely fixed. In my last excursion to London, I addressed myself to Mr. Lewis, a Roman catholic bookseller in Russell-street, Covent Garden, who recommended me to a priest, of whose name and order I am at present ignorant. In our first interview he soon discovered that persuasion was needless. After sounding the motives and merits of my conversion, he consented to admit me into the pale of the church; and at his feet, on the eighth of June 1753, I solemnly, though privately, abjured the errors of heresy. The seduction of an English youth of family and fortune was an act of as much danger as glory; but he bravely over-looked the danger, of which I was not then sufficiently informed. "Where a person is reconciled to the see of Rome, or procures others to be reconciled, the offence (says Blackstone) amounts to high treason." And if the humanity of the age would prevent the execution of this sanguinary statute, there were other laws of a less odious cast, which condemned the priest to perpetual imprisonment, and trans-ferred the proselyte's estate to his nearest relation. An elaborate con-troversial epistle, approved by my director, and addressed to my father, announced and justified the step which I had taken. My father was neither a bigot nor a philosopher; but his affection deplored the loss of an only son; and his good sense was astonished at my strange departure from the religion of my country. In the first sally of passion he divulged a secret which prudence might have suppressed, and the gates of Magdalen College were for ever shut against my return. Many years afterwards, when the name of Gibbon was become as notorious as that of Middleton, it was industriously whispered at Oxford, that the historian had formerly "turned papist;" my character stood exposed to the reproach of inconstancy; and this invidious topic would have been handled without mercy by my opponents, could they have separated my cause from that of the university. For my own part, I am proud of an honest sacrifice of interest to conscience. I can never blush, if my tender mind was entangled in the sophistry that seduced the acute and manly understandings of CHILLINGWORTH and BAYLE, who afterwards emerged from superstition to scepticism.

While Charles the First governed England, and was himself governed by a catholic queen, it cannot be denied that the missionaries of Rome laboured with impunity and success in the court, the country, and even the universities. One of the sheep,

> ——Whom the grim wolf with privy paw
> Daily devours apace, and nothing said,

is Mr. William Chillingworth, Master of Arts, and Fellow of Trinity College, Oxford; who, at the ripe age of twenty-eight years, was per-suaded to elope from Oxford, to the English seminary at Douay in Flanders. Some disputes with Fisher, a subtle jesuit, might first awaken him from the prejudices of education; but he yielded to his own victorious argument, "that there must be somewhere an infallible judge; and that the church of Rome is the only christian society which either does or can pretend to that character." After a short trial of a few months, Mr. Chillingworth was again tormented by religious scruples : he returned home, resumed his studies, unravelled his mistakes, and delivered his mind from the yoke of authority and superstition. His new creed was built on the principle, that the Bible is our sole judge, and private reason our sole interpreter : and he ably maintains this principle in the Religion of a Protestant, a book which, after startling the doctors of Oxford, is still esteemed the most solid defence of the Reformation. The learning, the virtue, the recent merits of the author, entitled him to fair preferment : but the slave had now broken his fetters ; and the more he weighed, the less was he disposed to subscribe to the thirty-nine articles of the church of England. In a private letter he declares, with all the energy of language, that he could not subscribe to them without subscribing to his own damnation ; and that if ever he should depart from this immoveable resolution, he would allow his friends to think him a madman, or an atheist. As the letter is without a date, we cannot ascertain the number of weeks or months that elapsed between this passionate abhorrence and the Salisbury Register, which is still extant. " Ego Gulielmus Chillingworth, ... omnibus hisce articulis, ... et singulis in iisdem contentis volens, et ex animo subscribo, et consensum meum iisdem præbeo. 20 die Julii 1638." But, alas! the chancellor and prebendary of Sarum soon deviated from his own subscription : as he more deeply scrutinized the article of the Trinity, neither scripture nor the primitive fathers could long uphold his orthodox belief; and he could not but confess, "that the doctrine of Arius is either the truth, or at least no damnable heresy." From this middle region of the air, the descent of his reason would naturally rest on the firmer ground of the Socinians : and if we may credit a doubtful story, and the popular opinion, his anxious inquiries at last subsided in philosophic indifference. So conspicuous, however, were the candour of his nature and the innocence of his heart, that this apparent levity did not affect the reputation of Chillingworth. His frequent changes proceeded from too nice an inquisition into truth. His doubts grew out of himself; he assisted them with all the strength of his reason : he was then too hard for himself; but finding as little quiet and repose in those victories, he quickly recovered, by a new appeal to his own judgment : so that in all his sallies and retreats, he was in fact his own convert.

Bayle was the son of a Calvinist minister in a remote province of France, at the foot of the Pyrenees. For the benefit of education, the protestants were tempted to risk their children in the catholic universities ; and in the twenty-second year of his age, young Bayle was seduced by the arts and arguments of the jesuits of Toulouse. He remained about seventeen months (Mar. 19 1669—Aug. 19 1670) in their hands, a voluntary captive : and a letter to his parents, which the new convert composed or subscribed (April 15 1670), is darkly tinged with the spirit of popery. But Nature had designed him to think as he pleased, and to speak as he thought : his piety was offended by the excessive worship of creatures ; and the study of physics convinced him of the impossibility of transubstantiation, which is abundantly refuted by the testimony of our senses. His return to the communion of a falling sect was a bold and disinterested step, that exposed him to the rigour of the laws ; and a speedy flight to Geneva protected him from the resentment of his spiritual tyrants, unconscious as they were of the full value of the prize, which they had lost. Had Bayle adhered to the catholic church, had he embraced the ecclesiastical profession, the genius and favour of such a proselyte might have aspired to wealth and honours in his native country : but the hypocrite would have found less happiness in the comforts of a benefice, or the dignity of a mitre, than he enjoyed at Rotterdam in a private state of exile, indigence, and freedom. Without a country, or a patron, or a prejudice, he claimed the liberty and subsisted by the labours of his pen : the inequality of his voluminous works is explained and excused by his alternately writing for himself, for the booksellers, and for posterity ; and if a severe critic would reduce him to a single folio, that relic, like the books of the Sibyl, would become still more valuable. A calm and lofty spectator of the religious tempest, the philosopher of Rotterdam condemned with equal firmness the persecution of Lewis the Fourteenth, and the republican maxims of the Calvinists ; their vain prophecies, and the intolerant bigotry which sometimes vexed his solitary retreat. In reviewing the controversies of the times, he turned against each other the arguments of the disputants ; successively wielding the arms of the catholics and protestants, he proves that neither the way of authority, nor the way of examination can afford the multitude any test of religious truth ; and dexterously concludes that custom and education must be the sole grounds of popular belief. The ancient paradox of Plutarch, that atheism is less pernicious than superstition, acquires a tenfold vigor, when it is adorned with the colours of his wit, and pointed with the acuteness of his logic. His critical dictionary is a vast repository of facts and opinions ; and he balances the *false* religions in his sceptical scales, till the opposite quantities (if I may use the language of algebra) annihilate each other. The wonderful power which he so boldly exercised, of assembling doubts and objections, had tempted him jocosely to assume the title of the νεφεληγερετα Ζευς, the cloud-compelling Jove ; and in a conversation with the ingenious Abbé (afterwards Cardinal) de Polignac, he freely disclosed his universal Pyrrhonism. " I am most truly (said Bayle) a protestant ; for I protest indifferently against all systems and all sects."

The academical resentment, which I may possibly have provoked, will prudently spare this plain narrative of my studies, or rather of my idleness ; and of the unfortunate event which shortened the term of my residence at Oxford. But it may be suggested, that my father was unlucky in the choice of a society, and the chance of a tutor. It will perhaps be asserted, that in the lapse of forty years many improvements have taken place in the college and in the university. I am not unwilling to believe, that some tutors might have been found more active than Dr. Waldgrave, and less contemptible than Dr. ****. About the same time, and in the same walk, a Bentham was still treading in the footsteps of a Burton, whose maxims he had adopted, and whose life he had published. The biographer indeed preferred the school-logic to the new philosophy, Burgursdicius to Locke ; and the hero appears, in his own writings, a stiff and conceited pedant. Yet even these men, according to the measure of their capacity, might be diligent and useful ; and it is recorded of Burton, that he taught his pupils what he knew ; some Latin, some Greek, some ethics and metaphysics ; referring them to proper masters for the languages and sciences of which he was ignorant. At a more recent period, many students have been attracted by the merit and reputation of Sir William Scott, then a tutor in University College, and now conspicuous in the profession of the civil law : my personal acquaintance with that gentleman has inspired me with a just esteem for his abilities and knowledge ; and I am assured that his lectures on history would compose, were they given to the public, a most valuable treatise. Under the auspices of the present Archbishop of York, Dr. Markham, himself an eminent scholar, a more regular discipline has been introduced, as I am told, at Christ Church ;* a course of classical and philosophical studies is proposed, and even pursued, in that numerous seminary : learning has been made a duty, a pleasure, and even a fashion ; and several young gentlemen do honour to the college in which they have been educated. According to the will of the donor, the profit of the second part of Lord Clarendon's History has been applied to the establishment of a riding-school, that the polite exercises might be taught, I know not with what success, in the university. The Vinerian professorship is of far more serious importance ; the laws of his country are the first science of an Englishman of rank and fortune, who is called to be a magistrate, and may hope to be a legislator. This judicious institution was coldly entertained by the graver doctors, who complained (I have heard the complaint) that it would take the young people from their books : but Mr. Viner's benefaction is not unprofitable, since it has at least produced the excellent commentaries of Sir William Blackstone.

After carrying me to Putney, to the house of his friend Mr. Mallet,†

* This was written on the information Mr. Gibbon had received, and the observation he had made, previous to his late residence at Lausanne. During his last visit to England, he had an opportunity of seeing at Sheffield-place some young men of the college above alluded to ; he had great satisfaction in conversing with them, made many inquiries respecting their course of study, applauded the discipline of Christ Church, and the liberal attention shown by the Dean, to those whose only recommendation was their merit. Had Mr. Gibbon lived to revise this work, I am sure he would have mentioned the name of Dr. Jackson with the highest commendation. There are other colleges at Oxford, with whose discipline my friend was unacquainted, to which, without doubt, he would willingly have allowed their due praise, particularly Brazen Nose and Oriel Colleges ; the former under the care of Dr. Cleaver, bishop of Chester, the latter under that of Dr. Eveleigh. It is still greatly to be wished that the general expence, or rather extravagance, of young men at our English universities may be more effectually restrained. The expence, in which they are permitted to indulge, is inconsistent not only with a necessary degree of study, but with those habits of morality which should be promoted, by all means possible, at an early period of life. An academical education in England is at present an object of alarm and terror to every thinking parent of moderate fortune. It is the apprehension of the expence, of the dissipation, and other evil consequences, which arise from the want of proper restraint at our own universities, that forces a number of our English youths to those of Scotland, and utterly excludes many from any sort of academical instruction. If a charge be true, which I have heard insisted on, that the heads of our colleges in Oxford and Cambridge are vain of having under their care chiefly men of opulence, who may be supposed exempt from the necessity of œconomical controul, they are indeed highly censurable ; since the mischief of allowing early habits of expence and dissipation is great, in various respects, even to those possessed of large property ; and the most serious evil from this indulgence must happen to youths of humbler fortune, who certainly form the majority of students both at Oxford and Cambridge.—S.

† The author of a life of Bacon, which has been rated above its value ; of some forgotten poems and plays ; and of the pathetic ballad of William and Margaret.

by whose philosophy I was rather scandalized than reclaimed, it was necessary for my father to form a new plan of education, and to devise some method which, if possible, might effect the cure of my spiritual malady. After much debate it was determined, from the advice and personal experience of Mr. Eliot (now Lord Eliot) to fix me, during some years, at Lausanne in Switzerland. Mr. Frey, a Swiss gentleman of Basil, undertook the conduct of the journey : we left London the 19th of June, crossed the sea from Dover to Calais, travelled post through several provinces of France, by the direct road of St. Quentin, Rheims, Langres, and Besançon, and arrived the 30th of June at Lausanne, where I was immediately settled under the roof and tuition of Mr. Pavilliard, a Calvinist minister.

The first marks of my father's displeasure rather astonished than afflicted me : when he threatened to banish, and disown, and disinherit a rebellious son, I cherished a secret hope that he would not be able or willing to effect his menaces ; and the pride of conscience encouraged me to sustain the honourable and important part which I was now acting. My spirits were raised and kept alive by the rapid motion of my journey, the new and various scenes of the Continent, and the civility of Mr. Frey, a man of sense, who was not ignorant of books or the world. But after he had resigned me into Pavilliard's hands, and I was fixed in my new habitation, I had leisure to contemplate the strange and melancholy prospect before me. My first complaint arose from my ignorance of the language. In my childhood I had once studied the French grammar, and I could imperfectly understand the easy prose of a familiar subject. But when I was thus suddenly cast on a foreign land, I found myself deprived of the use of speech and of hearing ; and, during some weeks, incapable not only of enjoying the pleasures of conversation, but even of asking or answering a question in the common intercourse of life. To a home-bred Englishman every object, every custom was offensive; but the native of any country might have been disgusted with the general aspect of his lodging and entertainment. I had now exchanged my elegant apartment in Magdalen College, for a narrow, gloomy street, the most unfrequented of an unhandsome town, for an old inconvenient house, and for a small chamber ill-contrived and ill-furnished, which, on the approach of Winter, instead of a companionable fire, must be warmed by the dull invisible heat of a stove. From a man I was again degraded to the dependence of a schoolboy. Mr. Pavilliard managed my expences, which had been reduced to a diminutive state : I received a small monthly allowance for my pocket-money ; and helpless and awkward as I have ever been, I no longer enjoyed the indispensable comfort of a servant. My condition seemed as destitute of hope, as it was devoid of pleasure : I was separated for an indefinite, which appeared an infinite term from my native country; and I had lost all connexion with my catholic friends. I have since reflected with surprise, that as the Romish clergy of every part of Europe maintain a close correspondence with each other, they never attempted, by letters or messages, to rescue me from the hands of the heretics, or at least to confirm my zeal and constancy in the profession of the faith. Such was my first introduction to Lausanne ; a place where I spent nearly five years with pleasure and profit, which I afterwards revisited without compulsion, and which I have finally selected as the most grateful retreat for the decline of my life.

But it is the peculiar felicity of youth that the most unpleasing objects and events seldom make a deep or lasting impression ; it forgets the past, enjoys the present, and anticipates the future. At the flexible age of sixteen I soon learned to endure, and gradually to adopt, the new forms of arbitrary manners: the real hardships of my situation were alienated by time. Had I been sent abroad in a more splendid style, such as the fortune and bounty of my father might have supplied, I might have returned home with the same stock of language and science, which our countrymen usually import from the Continent. An exile and a prisoner as I was, their example betrayed me into some irregularities of wine, of play, and of idle excursions: but I soon felt the impossibility of associating with them on equal terms ; and after the departure of my first acquaintance, I held a cold and civil correspondence with their successors. This seclusion from English society was attended with the most solid benefits. In the *Pays de Vaud*, the French language is used with less imperfection than in most of the distant provinces of France : in Pavilliard's family, necessity compelled me to listen and to speak ; and if I was at first disheartened by the apparent slowness, in a few months I was astonished by the rapidity of my progress. My pronunciation was formed by the constant repetition of the same sounds ; the variety of words and idioms, the rules of grammar, and distinctions of genders, were impressed in my memory : ease and freedom were obtained by practice ; correctness and elegance by labour ; and before I was recalled home, French, in which I spontaneously thought, was more familiar than English to my ear, my tongue, and my pen. The first effect of this opening knowledge was the revival of my love of reading, which had been chilled at Oxford ; and I soon turned over, without much choice, almost all the French books in my tutor's library. Even these amusements were productive of real advantage : my taste and judgment were now somewhat riper. I was introduced to a new mode of style and literature : by the comparison of manners and opinions, my views were enlarged, my prejudices were corrected, and a copious voluntary abstract of the *Histoire de l'Eglise et de l'Empire;* by le Sueur, may be placed in a middle line between my childish and my manly studies. As soon as I was able to converse with the natives, I began to feel some satisfaction in their company : my awkward timidity was polished and emboldened; and I frequented, for the first time, assemblies of men and women. The acquaintance of the Pavilliards prepared me by degrees for more elegant society. I was received with kindness and indulgence in the best families of Lausanne ; and it was in one of these that I formed an intimate and lasting connection with Mr. Deyverdun, a young man of an amiable temper and excellent understanding. In the arts of fencing and dancing, small indeed was my proficiency; and some months were idly wasted in the riding-school. My unfitness to bodily exercise reconciled me to a sedentary life, and the horse, the favourite of my countrymen, never contributed to the pleasures of my youth.

My obligations to the lessons of Mr. Pavilliard, gratitude will not suffer me to forget : he was endowed with a clear head and a warm heart; his innate benevolence had assuaged the spirit of the church; he was rational, because he was moderate : in the course of his studies he had acquired a just though superficial knowledge of most branches of literature ; by long practice, he was skilled in the arts of teaching; and he laboured with assiduous patience to know the character, gain the affection, and open the mind of his English pupil.* As soon as we began to understand each other, he gently led me, from a blind and undistinguishing love of reading, into the path of instruction. I consented with pleasure that a portion of the morning hours should be consecrated to a plan of modern history and geography, and to the critical perusal of the French and Latin classics ; and at each step I felt myself invigorated by the habits of application and method. His prudence repressed and dissembled some youthful sallies; and as soon as I was confirmed in the habits of industry and temperance, he gave the reins into my own hands. His favourable report of my behaviour and progress gradually obtained some latitude of action and expence ; and he wished to alleviate the hardships of my lodging and entertainment. The principles of philosophy were associated with the examples of taste ; and by a singular chance, the book, as well as the man, which contributed the most effectually to my education, has a stronger claim on my gratitude than on my admiration. Mr. De Crousaz, the adversary of Bayle and Pope, is not distinguished by lively fancy or profound reflection ; and even in his own country, at the end of a few years, his name and writings are almost obliterated. But his philosophy had been formed in the school of Locke, his divinity in that of Limborch and Le Clerc ; in a long and laborious life, several genera‑ tions of pupils were taught to think, and even to write ; his lessons rescued the academy of Lausanne from Calvinistic prejudice ; and he had the rare merit of diffusing a more liberal spirit among the clergy and people of the Pays de Vaud. His system of logic, which in the last editions has swelled to six tedious and prolix volumes, may be praised as a clear and methodical abridgment of the art of reasoning, from our simple ideas to the most complex operations of the human understanding. This system I studied, and meditated, and abstracted, till I have obtained the free command of an universal instrument,

* *Extract of a letter from* M. PAVILLIARD *to* EDWARD GIBBON esq.

A Lausanne, ce 25 Juillet, 1753.

Monsieur de Gibbon se porte très bien par la Grace de Dieu, et il me paroit qu'il ne se trouve pas mal de nôtre Maison ; j'ai même lieu de penser qu'il prend de l'attachement pour moi, ce dont je suis charmé et que je travaillerai a augmenter, parce qu'il aura plus de confiance en moi, dans ce que je me propose de lui dire.

Je n'ai point encore enterpris de lui parler sur les matieres de religion, parce que je n'entens pas assez la langue Angloise pour soutenir une longue conversation en cette langue, quoique je lise les auteurs Anglois avec assez de facilité ; et Monsieur de Gibbon n'entend pas assez de François, mais il y fait beaucoup de progrès.

Je suis fort content de la politesse et de la douceur de caractere de Monsieur votre Fils, et je me flatte que je pourrai toujours vous parler de lui avec eloge; il s applique beaucoup à la lecture.

From the Same to the Same.　　　　A Lausanne, ce 13 Aout, 1753.

Monsieur de Gibbon se porte bien par la grace de Dieu ; je l'aime, et je me suis extrêmement attaché à lui parce qu'il est doux et tranquille. Pour ce que regard ses sentimens, quoique je ne lui aie encore rien dit la dessus, j'ai lui d'esperer qu'il ouvrira les yeux à la verité. Je le pense ainsi, parce qu'étant dans mon cabinet il a choisi deux livres de controverse qu'il a pris dans sa chambre et qu'il les lit. Il m'a chargé de vous offrir ses très humble respects, et de vous demander la permission de le laisser monter au manege : cet exercice pourroit contri‑ buer à donner de la force à son corps, c'est l'idée qu'il en a.

which I soon presumed to exercise on my catholic opinions. Pavilliard was not unmindful that his first task, his most important duty, was to reclaim me from the errors of popery. The intermixture of sects has rendered the Swiss clergy acute and learned on the topics of controversy; and I have some of his letters in which he celebrates the dexterity of his attack, and my gradual concessions after a firm and well-managed defence.* I was willing, and I am now willing, to allow him a handsome share of the honour of my conversion: yet I must observe, that it was principally effected by my private reflections; and I still remember my solitary transport at the discovery of a philosophical argument against the doctrine of transubstantiation: *that* the text of scripture, which seems to inculcate the real presence, is attested only by a single sense—our sight; while the real presence itself is disproved by three of our senses—the sight, the touch, and the taste. The various articles of the Romish creed disappeared like a dream; and after a full conviction, on Christmas-day, 1754, I received the sacrament in the church of Lausanne. It was here that I suspended my religious inquiries, acquiescing with implicit belief in the tenets and mysteries, which are adopted by the general consent of catholics and protestants.†

* M. Pavilliard has described to me the astonishment with which he gazed on Mr. Gibbon standing before him: a thin little figure, with a large head, disputing and urging, with the greatest ability, all the best arguments that had ever heen used in favour of popery. Mr. Gibbon many years ago became very fat and corpulent, but he had uncommonly small bones, and was very slight made. S.

† *Letter from* MR. PAVILLIARD *to* EDWARD GIBBON esq.

Monsieur, June 26th, 1754.

J'espère que vous pardonnerez mon long silence en faveur des nouvelles que j'ai à vous apprendre. Si j'ai tant tardé, ce n'a été ni par oubli, ni par negligence, mais je croyois de semaine en semaine pouvoir vous annoncer que Monsieur votre fils avoit entierement renoncé aux fausse idées qu'il avoit embrassées; mais il a fallu disputer le terrein pié à pié, et je n'ai pas trouvé en lui un homme leger, et qui passe rapidement d'un sentiment à un autre. Souvent après avoir detruit toutes ses idées sur un article de maniere qu'il n'avoit rien à repliquer, ce qu'il avouoit sans detour, il me disoit qu'il ne croioit pas, qu'il n'y eut rien à me repondre. La dessus je n'ai pas jugé qu'il fallut le pousser à bout, et extorquer de lui un aveu que son cœur desavoueroit; je lui donnois alors du tems pour réfléchir; tous mes livres etoient à sa disposition; je revenois à la charge quand il m'avouoit qu'il avoit etudié la matiere aussi bien qu'il l'avoit pu, et enfin j'etablissoit une verité.

Je me persuadois, que quand j'aurois detruit les principales erreurs de l'eglise Romaine, je n'aurois qu'à faire voir que les autres sont des consequences des premières, et qu'elles ne peuvent subsister quand les fundamentales sont renversées; mais, comme je l'ai dit, je me suis trompé, il a fallu traitter chaque article dans son entier. Par la grace de Dieu, je n'ai pas perdu mon tems, et aujourdhui, si meme il conserve quelques restes de ces pernicieuses erreurs, j'ose dire qu'il n'est plus membre de l'eglise Romaine; voici dans où nous en sommes.

J'ai renversé l'infallibilité de l'eglise; j'ai prouvé que jamais St. Pierre n'a été chef des apôtres: que quand il l'auroit été, le pape n'est point son successeur; qu'il est douteuse que St. Pierre a jamais été à Rome, mais, supposé qu'il y ait été, il n'a pas été evêque de cette ville: que la transubstantiation est un invention humaine, et peu ancien ne dans l'eglise; que l'adoration de l'Eucharistie et le retranchement de la coupe sont contraires à la parole de Dieu: qu'il y a des saints, mais que nous ne savons pas que ils sont, et par consequent qu'on ne peut pas le prier; que le respect et le culte qu'on rend aux reliques est condamnable; qu'il n'y a point de purgatoire, et que la doctrine des indulgences est fausse; que la Careme et les jeunes du Vendredi et du Samedi sont ridicules aujourdhui, et de la maniere que l'eglise Romaine les prescrit; que les imputations que l'eglise de Rome nous fait de varier dans notre doctrine, et d'avoir pour reformateurs des personnes dont la conduite et les mœurs ont été en scandale, sont entierement fausses.

Vous comprenez bien, Monsieur, que ces articles sont d'un longue discussion, qu'il a fallu du tems à Monsieur votre fils pour mediter mes raisons et pour y chercher des reponses. Je lui ai demandé plusieurs fois, si mes preuves et mes raisons lui paroissoient convainquantes; il m'a toujours assuré qu'oui, de façon que j'ose assurer, aussi comme je le lui a dit à lui meme, il y a peu de tems qu'il n'étoit plus catholique Romain. Je me flatte, qu'après avoir obtenu la victoire sur ces articles, je l'aurai sur le reste avec le secours de Dieu. Tellement que je compte de vous marquer dans peu que cette ouvrage est fini, je dois vous dire encore, que quoique j'ai trouvé Mr. votre fils très ferme dans ses idées, je l'ai trouvé raisonnable, qu'il s'est rendu à la lumière, et qu'il n'est pas, ce qu'on appelle, chicaneur. Par raport à l'article du

Such, from my arrival at Lausanne, during the first eighteen or twenty months (July 1753—March 1755), were my useful studies, the foundation of all my future improvements. But every man who rises above the common level has received two educations : the first from his teachers ; the second, more personal and important, from himself. He will not, like the fanatics of the last age, define the moment of grace ; but he cannot forget the æra of his life, in which his mind has expanded to its proper form and dimensions. My worthy tutor had the good sense and modesty to discern how far he could be useful : as soon as he felt that I advanced beyond his speed and measure, he wisely left me to my genius ; and the hours of lesson were soon lost in the voluntary labour of the whole morning, and sometimes of the whole day. The desire of prolonging my time, gradually confirmed the salutary habit of early rising, to which I have always adhered, with some regard to seasons and situations ; but it is happy for my eyes and my health, that my temperate ardour has never been seduced to trespass on the hours of the night. During the last three years of my residence at Lausanne, I may assume the merit of serious and solid application ; but I am tempted to distinguish the last eight months of the year 1755, as the period of the most extraordinary diligence and rapid progress.* In my French and Latin translations I adopted an excellent method, which, from my own success, I would recommend to the imitation of students. I chose some classic writer, such as Cicero and Vertot, the most approved for purity and elegance of style. I translated, for instance, an epistle of Cicero into French ; and after throwing it aside, till the words and phrases were obliterated from my memory, I re-translated my French into such Latin as I could find ; and then compared each sentence of my imperfect version, with the

---

jeune le Vendredi et Samedi, long tems apres que je vous eus ecrit qu'il n'avoit jamais marqué qu'il voulut l'observer, environ le commencement du mois de Mars je m'aperçus un Vendredi qu'il ne mangeoit point de viande ; je lui parlai en particulier pour en savoir la raison, craignant que ce ne fut par indisposition : il me repondit qu'il l'avoit fait à dessein, et qu'il avoit cru être obligé de se conformer à la pratique d'un eglise dont il etoit membre : nous parlames quelques tems sur ce sujet ; il m'assura qu'il n'invisageoit cela que comme une pratique bonne à la verité, et qu'il devoit suivre, quoiqu'il ne la crus pas sainte en elle meme, ni d'institution divine. Je ne crus pas devoir insister pour lors, ni le forcer à agir contre ses lumières : j'ai traitté cette article qu'est certainement un des moins importans des moins fondés ; et cepeondant il m'a fallu un tems considerable pour le detromper, et pour lui faire comprendre qu'il avoit tort de s'assujettir à la pratique d'un Eglise qu'il ne reconnoissoit plus pour infaillible ; que si meme cette pratique avoit en quelque utilité dans son institution, cependant elle n'en avoit aucune en elle meme, puis qu'elle ne contribuoit en rien à la pureté des mœurs ; qu'ainsi il n'y avoit aucune raison, ni dans l'institution de cette pratique, ni dans la pratique en elle même, que l'autorisât à s'y soumettre : qu'aujourdhui ce n'etoit qu'une affaire d'interet, puis qu'avec de l'argent on obtennoit des dispenses pour manger gras, &c. de manier que je l'ai ramené à la liberté Chretienne avec beaucoup de peine et seulement depuis quelques se maines. Je l'ai engagé a vous ecrire, pour vous manifester les sentimens où il est, et l'etat de sa santé, et je crois qu'il l'a fait.

* JOURNAL, December 1755.]—In finishing this year, I must remark how favourable it was to my studies. In the space of eight months, from the beginning of April, I learnt the principles of drawing ; made myself complete master of the French and Latin languages, with which I was very superficially acquainted before, and wrote and translated a great deal in both ; read Cicero's Epistles ad Familiares, his Brutus, all his Orations, his Dialogues de Amicitiâ, and De Senectute ; Terence, twice ; and Pliny's Epistles. In French, Giannone's History of Naples, and l'Abbé Bannier's Mythology, and M. de Boehat's Memoirs sur la Suisse, and wrote a very ample relation of my tour. I likewise began to study Greek, and went through the Grammar. I begun to make very large collections of what I read. But what I esteem most of all, from the perusal and meditation of De Crousaz's Logic, I not only understood the principles of that science, but formed my mind to a habit of thinking and reasoning I had no idea of before.

ease, the grace, the propriety of the Roman orator. A similar experiment was made on several pages of the Revolutions of Vertot ; I turned them into Latin, returned them after a sufficient interval into my own French, and again scrutinized the resemblance or dissimilitude of the copy and the original. By degrees I was less ashamed, by degrees I was more satisfied with myself ; and I persevered in the practice of these double translations, which filled several books, till I had acquired the knowledge of both idioms, and the command at least of a correct style. This useful exercise of writing was accompanied and succeeded by the more pleasing occupation of reading the best authors. The perusal of the Roman classics was at once my exercise and reward. Dr. Middleton's History, which I then appreciated above its true value, naturally directed me to the writings of Cicero. The most perfect editions, that of Olivet, which may adorn the shelves of the rich, that of Ernesti, which should lie on the table of the learned, were not in my power. For the familiar epistles I used the text and English commentary of Bishop Ross : but my general edition was that of Verburgius, published at Amsterdam in two large volumes in folio, with an indifferent choice of various notes. I read, with application and pleasure, *all* the epistles, *all* the orations, and the most important treatises of rhetoric and philosophy ; and as I read, I applauded the observation of Quintilian, that every student may judge of his own proficiency, by the satisfaction which he receives from the Roman orator. I tasted the beauties of language, I breathed the spirit of freedom, and I imbibed from his precepts and examples the public and private sense of a man. Cicero in Latin, and Xenophon in Greek, are indeed the two ancients whom I would first propose to a liberal scholar; not only for the merit of their style and sentiments, but for the admirable lessons, which may be applied almost to every situation of public and private life. Cicero's Epistles may in particular afford the models of every form of correspondence, from the careless effusions of tenderness and friendship, to the well-guarded declaration of discreet and dignified resentment. After finishing this great author, a library of eloquence and reason, I formed a more extensive plan of reviewing the Latin classics,* under the four divisions of, 1. historians, 2. poets, 3. orators, and 4. philosophers, in a chronological series, from the days of Plautus and Sallust, to the decline of the language and empire of Rome : and this plan, in the last twenty-seven months of my residence at Lausanne (Jan. 1756—April 1758), I *nearly* accomplished. Nor was this review, however rapid, either hasty or superficial. I indulged myself in a second and even a third perusal of Terence, Virgil, Horace, Tacitus, &c., and studied to imbibe the sense and spirit most congenial to my own. I never suffered a difficult or corrupt passage to escape, till I had viewed it in every light of which it was susceptible : though often disappointed, I always consulted the most learned or ingenious commentators, Torrentius and Dacier on Horace, Catrou and Servius on Virgil, Lipsius on Tacitus, Meziriac on Ovid, &c.; and in the ardour of my inquiries, I embraced a large circle of historical and

* JOURNAL, Jan. 1756.]—I determined to read over the Latin authors in order ; and read this year, Virgil, Sallust, Livy, Velleius Paterculus, Valerius Maximus, Tacitus, Suetonius, Quintus Curtius, Justin, Florus, Plautus, Terence, and Lucretius. I also read and meditated Locke upon the Understanding.

critical erudition. My abstracts of each book were made in the French language: my observations often branched into particular essays; and I can still read, without contempt, a dissertation of eight folio pages on eight lines (287—294) of the fourth Georgic of Virgil. Mr. Deyverdun, my friend, whose name will be frequently repeated, had joined with equal zeal, though not with equal perseverance, in the same undertaking. To him every thought, every composition, was instantly communicated; with him I enjoyed the benefits of a free conversation on the topics of our common studies.

But it is scarcely possible for a mind endowed with any active curiosity to be long conversant with the Latin classics, without aspiring to know the Greek originals, whom they celebrate as their masters, and of whom they so warmly recommend the study and imitation;

> ——Vos exemplaria Græca
> Nocturnâ versate manu, versate diurnâ.

It was now that I regretted the early years which had been wasted in sickness or idleness, or mere idle reading; that I condemned the perverse method of our schoolmasters, who, by first teaching the mother-language, might descend with so much ease and perspicuity to the origin and etymology of a derivative idiom. In the nineteenth year of my age I determined to supply this defect; and the lessons of Pavilliard again contributed to smooth the entrance of the way, the Greek alphabet, the grammar, and the pronunciation according to the French accent. At my earnest request we presumed to open the Iliad; and I had the pleasure of beholding, though darkly and through a glass, the true image of Homer, whom I had long since admired in an English dress. After my tutor had left me to myself, I worked my way through about half the Iliad, and afterwards interpreted alone a large portion of Xenophon and Herodotus. But my ardour, destitute of aid and emulation, was gradually cooled, and, from the barren task of searching words in a lexicon, I withdrew to the free and familiar conversation of Virgil and Tacitus. Yet in my residence at Lausanne I had laid a solid foundation, which enabled me, in a more propitious season, to prosecute the study of Grecian literature.

From a blind idea of the usefulness of such abstract science, my father had been desirous, and even pressing, that I should devote some time to the mathematics;* nor could I refuse to comply with so reasonable a wish. During two winters I attended the private lectures of Monsieur de Traytorrens, who explained the elements of algebra and geometry, as far as the conic sections of the Marquis de l'Hôpital,

---

* *Extract of a Letter from* M. Pavilliard *to* Edward Gibbon esq.

Monsieur,   January 12th, 1757.

Vous avez souhaitté que Monsieur votre fils s'appliquâlt à l'algebre; le gout qu'il a pour les belles lettres lui faisoit apprendre que l'algebre ne nuissit à ses études favorites: je lui ai persuadé qu'il ne se faisoit pas une juste idée de cette partie des mathematiques; l'obeissance qu il vous dois, jointe à mes raisons, l'ont determiné à en faire un cours. Je ne croiois pas qu'avec cette repugnance il y fit de grand progrés: je me suis trompé: il fait bien tout ce qu'il fait; il est exact à ses leçons, il s'applique à lire avant sa leçon, et il repasse avec soin, de maniere qu'il avance beaucoup, et plus que je ne me serois attendu: il est charmé d'avoir commencé, et je pense qu'il fera un petit cours de geometrie, ce que en tout ne lui prendra que sept à huit mois. Pendant qu'il fait ses leçons, il ne s'est point relaché sur ses autres études: il avance beaucoup dans le Grec, et il a presque lu la moieté de l'Iliade d'Homere; je lui fais regulierement des leçons sur cet auteur: il a aussi fini les Historiens Latins; il en est à present aux Poetes; et il a lu entierement Plaute et Terence, et bientôt il aura fini Lucrece. Au reste,

and appeared satisfied with my diligence and improvement.* But as my childish propensity for numbers and calculations was totally extinct, I was content to receive the passive impression of my Professor's lectures, without any active exercise of my own powers. As soon as I understood the principles, I relinquished for ever the pursuit of the mathematics ; nor can I lament that I desisted, before my mind was hardened by the habit of rigid demonstration, so destructive of the finer feelings of moral evidence, which must, however, determine the actions and opinions of our lives. I listened with more pleasure to the proposal of studying the law of nature and nations, which was taught in the academy of Lausanne by Mr. Vicat, a professor of some learning and reputation. But instead of attending his public or private course, I preferred in my closet the lessons of his masters, and my own reason. Without being disgusted by Grotius or Puffendorf, I studied in their writings the duties of a man, the rights of a citizen, the theory of justice (it is, alas ! a theory), and the laws of peace and war, which have had some influence on the practice of modern Europe. My fatigues were alleviated by the good sense of their commentator Barbeyrac. Locke's Treatise of Government instructed me in the knowledge of Whig principles, which are rather founded in reason than experience ; but my delight was in the frequent perusal of Montesquieu, whose energy of style, and boldness of hypothesis, were powerful to awaken and stimulate the genius of the age. The logic of De Crousaz had prepared me to engage with his master Locke and his antagonist Bayle ; of whom the former may be used as a bridle, and the latter applied as a spur, to the curiosity of a young philosopher. According to the nature of their respective works, the schools of argument and objection, I carefully went through the Essay on Human Understanding, and occasionally consulted the most interesting articles of the Philosophic Dictionary. In the infancy of my reason I

---

il ne lît pas ces auteurs à la legere, il veut s'eclaircir sur tout ; de façon, qu'avec le genie qu'il a, l'excellente memoire et l'application, il ira loin dans les sciences.

J'ai eu l'honneur de vous dire ci-devant, que malgré ses études il voioit compagnie ; je puis vous le dire encore aujourdhui.

From the Same to the Same.

Monsieur,   Jan. 14th, 1758.

J'ai eu l'honneur de vous ecrire le 27 Juillet et le 26 8bre passés, et je vous ai rendu compte de la santé, des études, et de la conduite de Monsieur votre fils. Je n'ai rien à ajouter à tout ce que je vous en ai dit : il se porte parfaitement bien par la grace de Dieu : il continue à etudier avec application, et je puis vous assurer qu'il fait de progrés considerable dans les études, et il se fait extrémement estimer par tous ceux qui les connoissent, et j'espere que quand il vous montrera en detail ce qu'il fait, vous en serez très content. Les Belles Lettres que sont son étude favorite ne l'occupent pas entierement ; il continue les mathematiques, et son professeur m'assure qu'il n'a jamais vu personne avancer autant que lui, ni avoir plus d'ardeur et d'application qu'il en a. Son genie heureux et penetrant est secondé par un memoire de plus henreuse, tellement qu'iln'oublie presque rien de ce qu'il apprend. Je n'ai pas moins lieu d'être content de sa conduite ; quoiqu'il étude beaucoup, il voit cependant compagnie, mais il ne voit que des personnes dont le commerce peut lui être utile.

* JOURNAL, January 1757.]—I began to study algebra under M. de Traytorrens, went through the elements of algebra and geometry, and the three first books of the Marquis de l'Hôpital's Conic Sections. I also read Tibullus, Catullus, Propertius, Horace, (with Dacier's and Torrentius's Notes,) Virgil, Ovid's Epistles, with Meziriac's Commentary, the Ars Amandi, and the Elegics ; likewise the Augustus and Tiberius of Suetonius, and a Latin translation of Dion Cassius, from the death of Julius Cæsar to the death of Augustus. I also continued my correspondence begun last year with M. Allemand of Bex, and the Professor Breitinger of Zurich ; and opened a new one with the Professor Gesner of Gottingen.

N.B. Last year and this, I read St. John's Gospel, with part of Xenophon's Cyropœdia ; the Iliad, and Herodotus ; but upon the whole, I rather neglected my Greek.

turned over, as an idle amusement, the most serious and important treatise : in its maturity, the most trifling performance could exercise my taste or judgment, and more than once I have been led by a novel into a deep and instructive train of thinking. But I cannot forbear to mention three particular books, since they may have remotely contributed to form the historian of the Roman empire. 1. From the Provincial Letters of Pascal, which almost every year I have perused with new pleasure, I learned to manage the weapon of grave and temperate irony, even on subjects of ecclesiastical solemnity. 2. The Life of Julian, by the Abbé de la Bleterie, first introduced me to the man and the times ; and I should be glad to recover my first essay on the truth of the miracle which stopped the rebuilding of the Temple of Jerusalem. 3. In Giannone's Civil History of Naples I observed with a critical eye the progress and abuse of sacerdotal power, and the revolutions of Italy in the darker ages. This various reading, which I now conducted with discretion, was digested, according to the precept and model of Mr. Locke, into a large common-place book ; a practice, however, which I do not strenuously recommend. The action of the pen will doubtless imprint an idea on the mind as well as on the paper : but I much question whether the benefits of this laborious method are adequate to the waste of time ; and I must agree with Dr. Johnson, (Idler, No. 74.) "that what is twice read, is commonly better remembered, than what is transcribed."

During two years, if I forget some boyish excursions of a day or a week, I was fixed at Lausanne ; but at the end of the third summer, my father consented that I should make the tour of Switzerland with Pavilliard : and our short absence of one month (Sept. 21st—Oct. 20th, 1755) was a reward and relaxation of my assiduous studies.* The fashion of climbing the mountains and reviewing the *Glaciers*, had not yet been introduced by foreign travellers, who seek the sublime beauties of nature. But the political face of the country is not less diversified

---

* *From* EDWARD GIBBON *to* MRS. PORTEN. * * * * * Now for myself. As my father has given me leave to make a journey round Switzerland, we set out to-morrow. Buy a map of Switzerland, it will cost you but a shilling, and follow me. I go by Iverdun, Neufchatel, Bienne or Biel, Soleurre or Solothurn, Bale or Basil, Bade, Zurich, Lucerne, and Berne. The voyage will be of about four weeks ; so that *I hope to find a letter from you waiting for me.* As my father had given me leave to learn what I had a mind, I have learned to ride, and learn actually to dance and draw. Besides that, I often give ten or twelve hours a day to my studies. I find a great many agreeable people here ; see them sometimes, and can say upon the whole, without vanity, that though I am the Englishman here who spends the least money, I am he who is the most generally liked. I told you that my father had promised to send me into France and Italy. I have thanked him for it ; but if he would follow my plan, he won't do it yet a while. I never liked young travellers : they go too raw to make any great remarks, and they lose a time which is (in my opinion) the most precious part of a man's life. My scheme would be, to spend this winter at Lausanne : for though it is a very good place to acquire the air of good company and the French tongue, we have no good professors. To spend (I say) the winter at Lausanne ; go into England to see my friends a couple of months, and after that, finish my studies, either at Cambridge (for after what has passed one cannot think of Oxford), or at an university in Holland. If you liked the scheme, *could you not propose it to my father by Metcalf, or somebody* who has *a certain credit over him?* I forgot to ask you whether, in case my father writes to tell me of his marriage, would you advise me to compliment my mother-in-law? I think so. My health is so very regular, that I have nothing to say about it.

I have been the whole day writing you this letter ; the preparations for our voyage gave me a thousand interruptions. Besides that, I was obliged to write in English. This last reason will seem a paradox, but I assure you the French is much more familiar to me. I am, &c.

LAUSANNE, Sept. 20, 1755.   E. GIBBON,

by the forms and spirit of so many various republics, from the jealous government of the *few* to the licentious freedom of the *many*. I contemplated with pleasure the new prospects of men and manners; though my conversation with the natives would have been more free and instructive, had I possessed the German, as well as the French language. We passed through most of the principal towns of Switzerland ; Neufchâtel, Bienne, Soleurre, Arau, Baden, Zurich, Basil, and Berne. In every place we visited the churches, arsenals, libraries, and all the most eminent persons ; and after my return, I digested my notes in fourteen or fifteen sheets of a French journal, which I dispatched to my father, as a proof that my time and his money had not been mis-spent. Had I found this journal among his papers, I might be tempted to select some passages ; but I will not transcribe the printed accounts, and it may be sufficient to notice a remarkable spot, which left a deep and lasting impression on my memory. From Zurich we proceeded to the Benedictine Abbey of Einfidlen, more commonly styled Our Lady of the Hermits. I was astonished by the profuse ostentation of riches in the poorest corner of Europe ; amidst a savage scene of woods and mountains, a palace appears to have been erected by magic ; and it was erected by the potent magic of religion. A crowd of palmers and votaries was prostrate before the altar. The title and worship of the Mother of God provoked my indignation ; and the lively naked image of superstition suggested to me, as in the same place it had done to Zuinglius, the most pressing argument for the reformation of the church. About two years after this tour, I passed at Geneva a useful and agreeable month ; but this excursion, and short visits in the Pays de Vaud, did not materially interrupt my studious and sedentary life at Lausanne.

My thirst of improvement, and the languid state of science at Lausanne, soon prompted me to solicit a literary correspondence with several men of learning, whom I had not an opportunity of personally consulting. 1. In the perusal of Livy, (xxx. 44,) I had been stopped by a sentence in a speech of Hannibal, which cannot be reconciled by any torture with his character or argument. The commentators dissemble, or confess their perplexity. It occurred to me, that the change of a single letter, by substituting *otio* instead of *odio*, might restore a clear and consistent sense ; but I wished to weigh my emendation in scales less partial than my own. I addressed myself to M. Crevier, the successor of Rollin, and a professor in the university of Paris, who had published a large and valuable edition of Livy. His answer was speedy and polite ; he praised my ingenuity, and adopted my conjecture. 2. I maintained a Latin correspondence, at first anonymous, and afterwards in my own name, with Professor Breitinger of Zurich, the learned editor of a Septuagint Bible. In our frequent letters we discussed many questions of antiquity, many passages of the Latin classics. I proposed my interpretations and amendments. His censures, for he did not spare my boldness of conjecture, were sharp and strong ; and I was encouraged by the consciousness of my strength, when I could stand in free debate against a critic of such eminence and erudition. 3. I corresponded on similar topics with the celebrated Professor Matthew Gesner, of the university of Gottingen ; and he accepted, as courteously as the two former, the invitation of an unknown youth.

But his abilities might possibly be decayed ; his elaborate letters were feeble and prolix ; and when I asked his proper direction, the vain old man covered half a sheet of paper with the foolish enumeration of his titles and offices. 4. These Professors of Paris, Zurich, and Gottingen, were strangers, whom I presumed to address on the credit of their name ; but Mr. Allamand, Minister at Bex, was my personal friend, with whom I maintained a more free and interesting correspondence. He was a master of language, of science, and, above all, of dispute ; and his acute and flexible logic could support, with equal address, and perhaps with equal indifference, the adverse sides of every possible question. His spirit was active, but his pen had been indolent. Mr. Allamand had exposed himself to much scandal and reproach, by an anonymous letter (1745) to the Protestants of France ; in which he labours to persuade them that *public* worship is the exclusive right and duty of the state, and that their numerous assemblies of dissenters and rebels were not authorized by the law or the gospel. His style is animated, his arguments specious ; and if the papist may seem to lurk under the mask of a protestant, the philosopher is concealed under the disguise of a papist. After some trials in France and Holland, which were defeated by his fortune or his character, a genius that might have enlightened or deluded the world, was buried in a country living, unknown to fame, and discontented with mankind. *Est sacrificulus in pago, et rusticos decipit.* As often as private or ecclesiastical business called him to Lausanne, I enjoyed the pleasure and benefit of his conversation, and we were mutually flattered by our attention to each other. Our correspondence, in his absence, chiefly turned on Locke's metaphysics, which he attacked, and I defended ; the origin of ideas, the principles of evidence, and the doctrine of liberty ;

And found no end, in wandering mazes lost.

By fencing with so skilful a master, I acquired some dexterity in the use of my philosophic weapons ; but I was still the slave of education and prejudice. He had some measures to keep ; and I much suspect that he never showed me the true colours of his secret scepticism.

Before I was recalled from Switzerland, I had the satisfaction of seeing the most extraordinary man of the age ; a poet, an historian, a philosopher, who has filled thirty quartos, of prose and verse, with his various productions, often excellent, and always entertaining. Need I add the name of Voltaire ? After forfeiting, by his own misconduct, the friendship of the first of kings, he retired, at the age of sixty, with a plentiful fortune, to a free and beautiful country, and resided two winters (1757 and 1758) in the town or neighbourhood of Lausanne. My desire of beholding Voltaire, whom I then rated above his real magnitude, was easily gratified. He received me with civility as an English youth ; but I cannot boast of any peculiar notice or distinction, *Virgilium vidi tantum.*

The ode which he composed on his first arrival on the banks of the Leman Lake, *O Maison d'Aristippe ! O Jardin d'Epicure, &c.* had been imparted as a secret to the gentleman by whom I was introduced. He allowed me to read it twice ; I knew it by heart ; and as my discretion was not equal to my memory, the author was soon displeased by the circulation of a copy. In writing this trivial anecdote, I wished to observe whether my memory was impaired, and I have the comfort of finding that every line of the poem is still engraved in fresh and indelible characters. The highest gratification which I derived from Voltaire's residence at Lausanne, was the uncommon circumstance of hearing a great poet declaim his own productions on the stage. He had formed a company of gentlemen and ladies, some of whom were not destitute of talents. A decent theatre was framed at Monrepos, a country-house at the end of a suburb; dresses and scenes were provided at the expense of the actors; and the author directed the rehearsals with the zeal and attention of paternal love. In two successive winters his tragedies of Zayre, Alzire, Zulime, and his sentimental comedy of the Enfant Prodigue, were played at the theatre of Monrepos. Voltaire represented the characters best adapted to his years, Lusignan, Alvaréz, Benassar, Euphemon. His declamation was fashioned to the pomp and cadence of the old stage; and he expressed the enthusiasm of poetry, rather than the feelings of nature. My ardour, which soon became conspicuous, seldom failed of procuring me a ticket. The habits of pleasure fortified my taste for the French theatre, and that taste has perhaps abated my idolatry for the gigantic genius of Shakespeare, which is inculcated from our infancy as the first duty of an Englishman. The wit and philosophy of Voltaire, his table and theatre, refined, in a visible degree, the manners of Lausanne; and, however addicted to study, I enjoyed my share of the amusements of society. After the representation of Monrepos I sometimes supped with the actors. I was now familiar in some, and acquainted in many houses; and my evenings were generally devoted to cards and conversation, either in private parties or numerous assemblies.

I hesitate, from the apprehension of ridicule, when I approach the delicate subject of my early love. By this word I do not mean the polite attention, the gallantry, without hope or design, which has originated in the spirit of chivalry, and is interwoven with the texture of French manners. I understand by this passion the union of desire, friendship, and tenderness, which is inflamed by a single female, which prefers her to the rest of her sex, and which seeks her possession as the supreme or the sole happiness of our being. I need not blush at recollecting the object of my choice; and though my love was disappointed of success, I am rather proud that I was once capable of feeling such a pure and exalted sentiment. The personal attractions of Mademoiselle Susan Curchod were embellished by the virtues and talents of the mind. Her fortune was humble, but her family was respectable. Her mother, a native of France, had preferred her religion to her country. The profession of her father did not extinguish the moderation and philosophy of his temper, and he lived content with a small salary and laborious duty, in the obscure lot of minister of Crassy, in the mountains that separate the Pays de Vaud from the county of Burgundy.* In the solitude of a sequestered village he

* *Extracts from the Journal.*—March 1757.—I wrote some critical observations upon Plautus. March 8.—I wrote a long dissertation on some lines of Virgil. June.—I saw Mademoiselle Curchod—*Omnia vincit amor, et nos cedamus amori.* August.—I went to Crassy, and staid two days. Sept. 15.—I went to Geneva. Oct. 15.—I came back to

bestowed a liberal, and even learned, education on his only daughter. She surpassed his hopes by her proficiency in the sciences and languages; and in her short visits to some relations at Lausanne, the wit, the beauty, and erudition of Mademoiselle Curchod were the theme of universal applause. The report of such a prodigy awakened my curiosity; I saw and loved. I found her learned without pedantry, lively in conversation, pure in sentiment, and elegant in manners; and the first sudden emotion was fortified by the habits and knowledge of a more familiar acquaintance. She permitted me to make her two or three visits at her father's house. I passed some happy days there, in the mountains of Burgundy, and her parents honourably encouraged the connection. In a calm retirement the gay vanity of youth no longer fluttered in her bosom; she listened to the voice of truth and passion, and I might presume to hope that I had made some impression on a virtuous heart. At Crassy and Lausanne I indulged my dream of felicity: but on my return to England, I soon discovered that my father would not hear of this strange alliance, and that without his consent I was myself destitute and helpless. After a painful struggle I yielded to my fate : I sighed as a lover, I obeyed as a son*; my wound was insensibly healed by time, absence, and the habits of a new life. My cure was accelerated by a faithful report of the tranquillity and cheerfulness of the lady herself, and my love subsided in friendship and esteem. The minister of Crassy soon afterwards died ; his stipend died with him: his daughter retired to Geneva, where, by teaching young ladies, she earned a hard subsistence for herself and her mother ; but in her lowest distress she maintained a spotless reputation, and a dignified behaviour. A rich banker of Paris, a citizen of Geneva, had the good fortune and good sense to discover and possess this inestimable treasure ; and in the capital of taste and luxury she resisted the temptations of wealth, as she had sustained the hardships of indigence. The genius of her husband has exalted him to the most conspicuous station in Europe. In every change of prosperity and disgrace he has reclined on the bosom of a faithful friend ; and Mademoiselle Curchod is now the wife of M. Necker, the minister, and perhaps the legislator, of the French monarchy.

Whatsoever have been the fruits of my education, they must be ascribed to the fortunate banishment which placed me at Lausanne. I have sometimes applied to my own fate the verses of Pindar, which remind an Olympic champion that his victory was the consequence of his exile ; and that at home, like a domestic fowl, his days might have rolled away inactive or inglorious.

Lausanne, having passed through Crassy. Nov. 1.—I went to visit M. de Watteville at Loin, and saw Mademoiselle Curchod in my way through Rolle. Nov. 17.—I went to Crassy, and staid there six days. Jan. 1758.—In the three first months of this year I read Ovid's Metamorphoses, finished the conic sections with M. de Traytorrens, and went as far as the infinite series ; I likewise read Sir Isaac Newton's Chronology, and wrote my critical observations upon it. Jan. 23.—I saw Alzire acted by the society at Monrepos. Voltaire acted Alvares ; D'Hermanches, Zamore ; de St. Cierge, Cusman ; M. de Gentil, Monteze ; and Madame Denys, Alzire.

* See Oeuvres de Rousseau, tom. xxxiii. p. 88, 89. octavo edition. As an author I shall not appeal from the judgment, or taste, or caprice of *Jean Jaques:* but that extraordinary man, whom I admire and pity, should have been less precipitate in condemning the moral character and conduct of a stranger.

. . . . ἤτοι καὶ τεά κεν,
᾽Ενδομάχας ἅτ᾽ ἀλέκτωρ,
Συγγόνω παρ᾽ ἑστίᾳ
᾽Ακλεὴς τιμὰ κατεφυλλορόησε ποδῶν·
Εἰ μὴ στᾶσις ἀντιάνειρα
Κνωσίας ἄμερσε πάτρας. *

     Olymp. xii.

* Thus, like the crested bird of Mars, at home
 Engag'd in foul domestic jars,
 And wasted with intestine wars,
Inglorious hadst thou spent thy vig'rous bloom;
 Had not sedition's civil broils
 Expell'd thee from thy native *Crete*,
 And driv'n thee with more glorious toils
Th' *Olympic* crown in *Pisa's* plain to meet.
       West's Pindar.

If my childish revolt against the religion of my country had not stripped me in time of my academic gown, the five important years, so liberally improved in the studies and conversation of Lausanne, would have been steeped in port and prejudice among the monks of Oxford. Had the fatigue of idleness compelled me to read, the path of learning would not have been enlightened by a ray of philosophic freedom. I should have grown to manhood ignorant cf the life and language of Europe, and my knowledge of the world would have been confined to an English cloister. But my religious error fixed me at Lausanne, in a state of banishment and disgrace. The rigid course of discipline and abstinence, to which I was condemned, invigorated the constitution of my mind and body; poverty and pride estranged me from my countrymen. One mischief, however, and in their eyes a serious and irreparable mischief, was derived from the success of my Swiss education; I had ceased to be an Englishman. At the flexible period of youth, from the age of sixteen to twenty-one, my opinions, habits, and sentiments were cast in a foreign mould; the faint and distant remembrance of England was almost obliterated; my native language was grown less familiar; and I should have cheerfully accepted the offer of a moderate independence on the terms of perpetual exile. By the good sense and temper of Pavilliard my yoke was insensibly lightened: he left me master of my time and actions; but he could neither change my situation, nor increase my allowance, and with the progress of my years and reason I impatiently sighed for the moment of my deliverance. At length, in the spring of the year 1758, my father signified his permission and his pleasure that I should immediately return home. We were then in the midst of a war: the resentment of the French at our taking their ships without a declaration, had rendered that polite nation somewhat peevish and difficult. They denied a passage to English travellers, and the road through Germany was circuitous, toilsome, and perhaps in the neighbourhood of the armies, exposed to some danger. In this perplexity, two Swiss officers of my acquaintance in the Dutch service, who were returning to their garrisons, offered to conduct me through France as one of their companions; nor did we sufficiently reflect that my borrowed name and regimentals might have been considered, in case of a discovery, in a very serious light. I took my leave of Lausanne on April 11 1758, with a mixture of joy and regret, in the firm resolution of revisiting, as a man, the persons and places which had been so dear to my youth. We travelled slowly, but pleasantly, in a hired coach, over the hills of Franche-compté and the fertile province of Lorraine, and passed, without accident or inquiry, through several fortified towns of the French frontier: from thence we entered the wild Ardennes of the Austrian dutchy of Luxemburg; and after crossing the Meuse at Liege, we traversed the heaths of Brabant, and reached, on April 26, our Dutch garrison of Bois le Duc. In our passage through Nancy, my eye was gratified by the aspect of a regular and beautiful city, the work of Stanislaus, who, after the storms of Polish royalty, reposed in the love and gratitude of his new sub. jects of Lorraine. In our halt at Maestricht I visited Mr. de Beaufort, a learned critic, who was known to me by his specious arguments against the five first centuries of the Roman History. After dropping my regimental companions, I stepped aside to visit Rotterdam and the Hague. I wished to have observed a country, the monument of freedom and industry; but my days were num- bered, and a longer delay would have been ungraceful. I hastened to embark at the Brill, landed the next day at Harwich, and pro- ceeded to London, where my father awaited my arrival. The whole term of my first absence from England was four years ten months and fifteen days.

In the prayers of the church our personal concerns are judiciously reduced to the threefold distinction of *mind, body,* and *estate.* The sentiments of the mind excite and exercise our social sympathy. The review of my moral and literary character is the most interesting to myself and to the public; and I may expatiate, without reproach, on my private studies; since they have produced the public writings, which can alone entitle me to the esteem and friendship of my readers. The experience of the world inculcates a discreet reserve on the subject of our person and estate, and we soon learn that a free disclosure of our riches or poverty would provoke the malice of envy, or encourage the insolence of contempt.

The only person in England whom I was impatient to see was my aunt Porten, the affectionate guardian of my tender years. I hastened to her house in College-street, Westminster; and the evening was spent in the effusions of joy and confidence. It was not without some awe and apprehension that I approached the presence of my father. My infancy, to speak the truth, had been neglected at home; the severity of his look and language at our last parting still dwelt on my memory; nor could I form any notion of his character, or my probable reception. They were both more agreeable than I could expect. The domestic discipline of our ancestors has been relaxed by the philosophy and softness of the age; and if my father remembered that he had trembled before a stern parent, it was only to adopt with his own son an opposite mode of behaviour. He received me as a man and a friend; all constraint was banished at our first interview, and we ever afterwards continued on the same terms of easy and equal politeness. He applauded the success of my education; every word and action was expressive of the most cordial affection; and our lives would have passed without a cloud, if his œconomy had been equal to his fortune, or if his fortune had been equal to his desires. During my absence he had married his second wife, Miss Dorothea Patton, who was intro- duced to me with the most unfavourable prejudice. I considered his second marriage as an act of displeasure, and I was disposed to hate the rival of my mother. But the injustice was in my own fancy, and the imaginary monster was an amiable and deserving woman. I could ιot be mistaken in the first view of her understanding, her knowledge, ιnd the elegant spirit of her conversation : her polite welcome, and her ιssiduous care to study and gratify my wishes, announced at least that he surface would be smooth; and my suspicions of art and falsehood vere gradually dispelled by the full discovery of her warm and exquisite ιensibility. After some reserve on my side, our minds associated in ;onfidence and friendship ; and as Mrs. Gibbon had neither children ιor the hopes of children, we more easily adopted the tender names ιnd genuine characters of mother and of son. By the indulgence of :hese parents, I was left at liberty to consult my taste or reason in the :hoice of place, of company, and of amusements; and my excursions were bounded only by the limits of the island, and the measure of my ιncome. Some faint efforts were made to procure me the employment οf secretary to a foreign embassy; and I listened to a scheme which would again have transported me to the continent. Mrs. Gibbon, with ιeeming wisdom, exhorted me to take chambers in the Temple, and devote my leisure to the study of the law. I cannot repent of having neglected her advice. Few men, without the spur of necessity, have resolution to force their way, through the thorns and thickets of that gloomy labyrinth. Nature had not endowed me with the bold and ready eloquence which makes itself heard amidst the tumult of the bar; and I should probably have been diverted from the labours of literature, without acquiring the fame or fortune of a successful pleader. I had no need to call to my aid the regular duties of a profession; every day, every hour, was agreeably filled; nor have I known, like so many of my countrymen, the tediousness of an idle life.

Of the two years (May 1758—May 1760,) between my return to England and the embodying of the Hampshire militia, I passed about nine months in London, and the remainder in the country. The metropolis affords many amusements, which are open to all. It is itself an astonishing and perpetual spectacle to the curious eye; and each taste, each sense may be gratified by the variety of objects which will occur in the long circuit of a morning walk. I assiduously frequented the theatres at a very propitious æra of the stage, when a constellation of excellent actors, both in tragedy and comedy, was eclipsed by the meridian brightness of Garrick in the maturity of his judgment, and vigour of his performance. The pleasures of a town-life are within the reach of every man who is regardless of his health, his money, and his company. By the contagion of example I was sometimes seduced; but the better habits, which I had formed at Lausanne, induced me to seek a more elegant and rational society; and if my search was less easy and successful than I might have hoped, I shall at present impute the failure to the disadvantages of my situation and character. Had the rank and fortune of my parents given them an annual establishment in London, their own house would have introduced me to a numerous and polite circle of acquaintance. But my father's taste had always preferred the highest and the lowest company, for which he was equally qualified ; and after a twelve years' retirement, he was no longer in the memory of the great with whom he had associated. I found myself a stranger in the midst of a vast and unknown city; and at my entrance into life I was reduced to some dull family parties, and some scattered connections, which were not such as I should have chosen for myself. The most useful friends of my father were the Mallets: they received me with civility and kindness at first on his account, and afterwards on my own; and (if I may use Lord Chesterfield's words) I was soon *domesticated* in their house. Mr. Mallet, a name among the English poets, is praised by an unforgiving enemy, for the ease and elegance of his conversation, and his wife was not destitute of wit or learning. By his assistance I was introduced to Lady Hervey, the mother of the present earl of Bristol. Her age and infirmities confined her at home; her dinners were select; in the evening her house was open to the best company of both sexes and all nations; nor was I displeased at her preference and affectation of the manners, the language, and the literature of France. But my progress in the English world was in general left to my own efforts, and those efforts were languid and slow. I had not been endowed by art or nature with those happy gifts of confidence and address, which unlock every door and every bosom; nor would it be reasonable to complain of the just consequences of my sickly childhood, foreign education, and reserved temper. While coaches were rattling through Bond-street, I have passed many a solitary evening in my lodging with my books. My studies were sometimes interrupted by a sigh, which I breathed towards Lausanne; and on the approach of Spring, I withdrew without reluctance from the noisy and extensive scene of crowds without company, and dissipation without pleasure. In each of the twenty-five years of my acquaintance with London (1758—1783) the prospect gradually brightened; and this unfavourable picture most properly belongs to the first period after my return from Switzerland.

My father's residence in Hampshire, where I have passed many light, and some heavy hours, was at Beriton, near Petersfield, one mile from the Portsmouth road, and at the easy distance of fifty-eight miles from London.* An old mansion, in a state of decay, had been converted into the fashion and convenience of a modern house: and if strangers had nothing to see, the inhabitants had little to desire. The spot was not happily chosen, at the end of the village and the bottom of the hill: but the aspect of the adjacent grounds was various and cheerful; the downs commanded a noble prospect, and the long hanging woods in sight of the house could not perhaps have been improved by art or expence. My father kept in his own hands the whole of the estate, and even rented some additional land; and whatsoever might be the balance of profit and loss, the farm supplied him with amusement and plenty. The produce maintained a number of men and horses, which were multiplied by the intermixture of domestic and rural servants; and in the intervals of labour the favourite team, a handsome set of bays or greys, was harnessed to the coach. The œconomy of the house was regulated by the taste and prudence of Mrs. Gibbon. She prided herself in the elegance of her occasional dinners; and from the uncleanly avarice of Madame Pavilliard, I was suddenly transported to the daily neatness and luxury of an English

* The estate and manor of Beriton, otherwise Buriton, were considerable, and were sold a few years ago to Lord Stawell.—S.

table. Our immediate neighbourhood was rare and rustic ; but from the verge of our hills, as far as Chichester and Goodwood, the western district of Sussex was interspersed with noble seats and hospitable families, with whom we cultivated a friendly, and might have enjoyed a very frequent, intercourse. As my stay at Buriton was always voluntary, I was received and dismissed with smiles; but the comforts of my retirement did not depend on the ordinary pleasures of the country. My father could never inspire me with his love and knowledge of farming. I never handled a gun, I seldom mounted an horse; and my philosophic walks were soon terminated by a shady bench, where I was long detained by the sedentary amusement of reading or meditation. At home I occupied a pleasant and spacious apartment; the library on the same floor was soon considered as my peculiar domain; and I might say with truth, that I was never less alone than when by myself. My sole complaint, which I piously suppressed, arose from the kind restraint imposed on the freedom of my time. By the habit of early rising I always secured a sacred portion of the day, and many scattered moments were stolen and employed by my studious industry. But the family hours of breakfast, of dinner, of tea, and of supper, were regular and long: after breakfast Mrs. Gibbon expected my company in her dressing-room; after tea my father claimed my conversation and the perusal of the newspapers ; and in the midst of an interesting work I was often called down to receive the visit of some idle neighbours. Their dinners and visits required, in due season, a similar return ; and I dreaded the period of the full moon, which was usually reserved for our more distant excursions. I could not refuse attending my father, in the summer of 1759, to the races at Stockbridge, Reading, and Odiam, where he had entered a horse for the hunter's plate; and I was not displeased with the sight of our Olympic games, the beauty of the spot, the fleetness of the horses, and the gay tumult of the numerous spectators. As soon as the militia business was agitated, many days were tediously consumed in meetings of deputy-lieutenants at Petersfield, Alton, and Winchester. In the close of the same year, 1759, Sir Simeon (then Mr.) Stewart attempted an unsuccessful contest for the county of Southampton, against Mr. Legge, Chancellor of the Exchequer : a well-known contest, in which Lord Bute's influence was first exerted and censured. Our canvas at Portsmouth and Gosport lasted several days; but the interruption of my studies was compensated in some degree by the spectacle of English manners, and the acquisition of some practical knowledge.

If in a more domestic or more dissipated scene my application was somewhat relaxed, the love of knowledge was inflamed and gratified by the command of books ; and I compared the poverty of Lausanne with the plenty of London. My father's study at Buriton was stuffed with much trash of the last age, with much high church divinity and politics, which have long since gone to their proper place : yet it contained some valuable editions of the classics and the fathers, the choice, as it should seem, of Mr. Law ; and many English publications of the times had been occasionally added. From this slender beginning I have gradually formed a numerous and select library, the foundation of my works, and the best comfort of my life, both at home

E

and abroad. On the receipt of the first quarter, a large share of my allowance was appropriated to my literary wants. I cannot forget the joy with which I exchanged a bank-note of twenty pounds for the twenty volumes of the Memoirs of the Academy of Inscriptions; nor would it have been easy, by any other expenditure of the same sum, to have procured so large and lasting a fund of rational amusement. At a time when I most assiduously frequented this school of ancient literature, I thus expressed my opinion of a learned and various collection, which since the year 1759 has been doubled in magnitude, though not in merit—" Une de ces societés, qui ont mieux immortalisé Louis XIV. qu'un ambition souvent pernicieuse aux hommes, commençoit deja ces recherches qui réunissent la justesse de l'esprit, l'ameneté & l'erudition : où l'on voit tant des decouvertes, et quelquefois, ce qui ne cede qu'à peine aux decouvertes, une *ignorance* modeste et *savante.*" The review of my library must be reserved for the period of its maturity ; but in this place I may allow myself to observe, that I am not conscious of having ever bought a book from a motive of ostentation, that every volume, before it was deposited on the shelf, was either read or sufficiently examined, and that I soon adopted the tolerating maxim of the elder Pliny, " nullum esse librum tam malum ut non ex aliquâ parte prodesset." I could not yet find leisure or courage to renew the pursuit of the Greek language, excepting by reading the lessons of the Old and New Testament every Sunday, when I attended the family to church. The series of my Latin authors was less strenuously completed ; but the acquisition, by inheritance or purchase, of the best editions of Cicero, Quintilian, Livy, Tacitus, Ovid, &c. afforded a fair prospect, which I seldom neglected. I persevered in the useful method of abstracts and observations ; and a single example may suffice, of a note which had almost swelled into a work. The solution of a passage of Livy (xxxviii. 38,) involved me in the dry and dark treatises of Greaves, Arbuthnot, Hooper, Bernard, Eisenschmidt, Gronovius, La Barré, Freret, &c. ; and in my French essay (chap. 20,) I ridiculously send the reader to my own *manuscript* remarks on the weights, coins, and measures of the ancients, which were abruptly terminated by the militia drum.

As I am now entering on a more ample field of society and study, I can only hope to avoid a vain and prolix garrulity, by overlooking the vulgar crowd of my acquaintance, and confining myself to such intimate friends among books and men, as are best entitled to my notice by their own merit and reputation, or by the deep impression which they have left on my mind. Yet I will embrace this occasion of recommending to the young student a practice, which about this time I myself adopted. After glancing my eye over the design and order of a new book, I suspended the perusal till I had finished the task of self-examination, till I had revolved, in a solitary walk, all that I knew or believed, or had thought on the subject of the whole work, or of some particular chapter: I was then qualified to discern how much the author added to my original stock ; and I was sometimes satisfied by the agreement, I was sometimes armed by the opposition of our ideas. The favourite companions of my leisure were our English writers since the Revolution ; they breathe the spirit of reason and liberty; and they most seasonably contributed to restore the purity of my own language, which had been corrupted by the long use of a foreign idiom. By the judicious advice of Mr. Mallet, I was directed to the writings of Swift and Addison; wit and simplicity are their common attributes: but the style of Swift is supported by manly original vigour; that of Addison is adorned by the female graces of elegance and mildness. The old reproach, that no British altars had been raised to the muse of history, was recently disproved by the first performances of Robertson and Hume, the histories of Scotland and of the Stuarts. I will assume the presumption of saying, that I was not unworthy to read them: nor will I disguise my different feelings in the repeated perusals. The perfect composition, the nervous language, the well-turned periods of Dr. Robertson, inflamed me to the ambitious hope that I might one day tread in his footsteps: the calm philosophy, the careless, inimitable beauties of his friend and rival, often forced me to close the volume with a mixed sensation of delight and despair.

The design of my first work, the Essay on the Study of Literature, was suggested by a refinement of vanity, the desire of justifying and praising the object of a favourite pursuit. In France, to which my ideas were confined, the learning and language of Greece and Rome were neglected by a philosophic age. The guardian of those studies, the Academy of Inscriptions, was degraded to the lowest rank among the three royal societies of Paris: the new appellation of Erudits was contemptuously applied to the successors of Lipsius and Casàubon; and I was provoked to hear (see M. d'Alembert Discours preliminaire à l'Encyclopedie) that the exercise of the memory, their sole merit, had been superseded by the nobler faculties of the imagination and the judgment. I was ambitious of proving by my own example, as well as by my precepts, that all the faculties of the mind may be exercised and displayed by the study of ancient literature: 1 began to select and adorn the various proofs and illustrations which had offered themselves in reading the classics; and the first pages or chapters of my essay were composed before my departure from Lausanne. The hurry of the journey, and of the first weeks of my English life, suspended all thoughts of serious application: but my object was ever before my eyes; and no more than ten days, from the first to the eleventh of July, were suffered to elapse after my summer establishment at Buriton. My essay was finished in about six weeks; and as soon as a fair copy had been transcribed by one of the French prisoners at Petersfield, I looked round for a critic and judge of my first performance. A writer can seldom be content with the doubtful recompence of solitary approbation; but a youth ignorant of the world, and of himself, must desire to weigh his talents in some scales less partial than his own: my conduct was natural, my motive laudable, my choice of Dr. Maty judicious and fortunate. By descent and education Dr. Maty, though born in Holland, might be considered as a Frenchman; but he was fixed in London by the practice of physic, and an office in the British Museum. His reputation was justly founded on the eighteen volumes of the *Journal Britannique*, which he had supported, almost alone, with perseverance and success. This humble though useful labour, which had once been dignified by the genius of Bayle and the learning of Le Clerc, was not disgraced by the taste, the knowledge, and the judgment of Maty : he exhibits a candid and pleasing view of the state of litera-ture in England during a period of six years (January 1750—December 1755); and, far different from his angry son, he handles the rod of criticism with the tenderness and reluctance of a parent. The author of the *Journal Britannique* sometimes aspires to the character of a poet and philosopher : his style is pure and elegant ; and in his virtues, or even in his defects, he may be ranked as one of the last disciples of the school of Fontenelle. His answer to my first letter was prompt and polite : after a careful examination he returned my manuscript, with some animadversion and much applause ; and when I visited London in the ensuing winter, we discussed the design and execution in several free and familiar conversations. In a short excur-sion to Buriton I reviewed my essay, according to his friendly advice ; and after suppressing a third, adding a third, and altering a third, I consummated my first labour by a short preface, which is dated Feb. 3, 1759. Yet I still shrunk from the press with the terrors of virgin modesty : the manuscript was safely deposited in my desk ; and as my attention was engaged by new objects, the delay might have been pro-longed till I had fulfilled the precept of Horace, "nonumque prematur in annum." Father Sirmond, a learned jesuit, was still more rigid, since he advised a young friend to expect the mature age of fifty, before he gave himself or his writings to the public (Olivet Hist. de l'Acad. Françoise, tom. ii. p. 143). The counsel was singular ; but it is still more singular that it should have been approved by the example of the author. Sirmond was himself fifty-five years of age when he published (in 1614) his first work, an edition of Sidonius Apollinaris, with many valuable annotations : (see his life, before the great edition of his works in five volumes folio, Paris, 1696, é Typographiâ Regiâ).

Two years elapsed in silence : but in the spring of 1761 I yielded to the authority of a parent, and complied, like a pious son, with the wish of my own heart.* My private resolves were influenced by the state of Europe. About this time the belligerent powers had made and ac-cepted overtures of peace; our English plenipotentiaries were named to assist at the Congress of Augsburg, which never met : I wished to attend them as a gentleman or a secretary ; and my father fondly

* JOURNAL, March 8, 1758.]—I began my Essai sur l'Etude de la Litterature, and wrote the 23 first chapters (excepting the following ones, 11, 12, 13, 18, 19, 20, 21, 22.) before I left Switzerland.

July 11.—I again took in hand my Essay : and in about six weeks finished it, from C. 23—55. (excepting 27, 28, 29, 30, 31, 32, 33. and note to C. 38.) besides a number of chapters from C. 55. to the end, which are now struck out.

Feb. 11, 1759.—I wrote the chapters of my Essay, 27, 28, 29, 30, 31. the note to C. 38. and the first part of the preface.

April 23, 1761.—Being at length, by my father's advice, determined to publish my Essay, I revised it with great care, made many alterations, struck out a considerable part, and wrote the chapters from 57—78, which I was obliged myself to copy out fair.

June 10, 1761.—Finding the printing of my book proceeded but slowly, I went up to town, where I found the whole was finished. I gave Becket orders for the presents : 20 for Lausanne ; copies for the Duke of Richmond, Marquis of Carnarvon, Lords Waldegrave, Litchfield, Bath, Granville, Bute, Shelbourn, Chesterfield, Hardwicke, Lady Hervey, Sir Joseph Yorke, Sir Matthew Featherstone, M. M. Mallet, Maty, Scott, Wray, Lord Egremont, M. de Bussy, Mademoiselle la Duchesse d'Aguillon, and M. le Comte de Caylus : great part of these were only my father's or Mallet's acquaintance,

believed that the proof of some literary talents might introduce me to public notice, and second the recommendations of my friends. After a last revisal I consulted with Mr. Mallet and Dr. Maty, who approved the design and promoted the execution. Mr. Mallet, after hearing me read my manuscript, received it from my hands, and delivered it into those of Becket, with whom he made an agreement in my name ; an easy agreement : I required only a certain number of copies ; and, without transferring my property, I devolved on the bookseller the charges and profits of the edition. Dr. Maty undertook, in my absence, to correct the sheets : he inserted, without my knowledge, an elegant and flattering epistle to the author ; which is composed, however, with so much art, that, in case of a defeat, his favourable report might have been ascribed to the indulgence of a friend for the rash attempt of a *young English* gentleman. The work was printed and published, under the title of Essai sur l'Etude de la Litterature, à Londres, chez T. Becket et P. A. de Hondt, 1761, in a small volume in duodecimo : my dedication to my father, a proper and pious address, was composed the twenty-eighth of May : Dr. Maty's letter is dated June 16 ; and I received the first copy (June 23) at Alresford, two days before I marched with the Hampshire militia. Some weeks afterwards, on the same ground, I presented my book to the late Duke of York, who breakfasted in Colonel Pitt's tent. By my father's direction, and Mallet's advice, many literary gifts were distributed to several eminent characters in England and France ; two books were sent to the Count de Caylus, and the Duchesse d'Aiguillon, at Paris : I had reserved twenty copies for my friends at Lausanne, as the first fruits of my education, and a grateful token of my remembrance : and on all these persons I levied an unavoidable tax of civility and compliment. It is not surprising that a work, of which the style and sentiments were so totally foreign, should have been more successful abroad than at home. I was delighted by the copious extracts, the warm commendations, and the flattering predictions of the Journals of France and Holland : and the next year (1762) a new edition (I believe at Geneva) extended the fame, or at least the circulation, of the work. In England it was received with cold indifference, little read, and speedily forgotten : a small impression was slowly dispersed ; the bookseller murmured, and the author (had his feelings been more exquisite) might have wept over the blunders and baldness of the English translation. The publication of my History fifteen years afterwards revived the memory of my first performance, and the Essay was eagerly sought in the shops. But I refused the permission which Becket solicited of reprinting it : the public curiosity was imperfectly satisfied by a pirated copy of the booksellers of Dublin ; and when a copy of the original edition has been discovered in a sale, the primitive value of half-a-crown has risen to the fanciful price of a guinea or thirty shillings.

I have expatiated on the petty circumstances and period of my first publication, a memorable æra in the life of a student, when he ventures to reveal the measure of his mind : his hopes and fears are multiplied by the idea of self-importance, and he believes for a while that the eyes of mankind are fixed on his person and performance. Whatever may be my present reputation, it no longer rests on the merit of this first essay ; and at the end of twenty-eight years I may appreciate my juvenile work with the impartiality, and almost with the indifference, of a stranger.   In his answer to Lady Hervey, the Count de Caylus admires, or affects to admire, " les livres sans nombre que Mr. Gibbon a lus et tres bien lus."   But, alas ! my stock of erudition at that time was scanty and superficial ; and if I allow myself the liberty of naming the Greek masters, my genuine and personal acquaintance was confined to the Latin classics.   The most serious defect of my Essay is a kind of obscurity and abruptness which always fatigues, and may often elude, the attention of the reader.   Instead of a precise and proper definition of the title itself, the sense of the word *Litterature* is loosely and variously applied : a number of remarks and examples, historical, critical, philosophical, are heaped on each other without method or connection ; and if we except some introductory pages, all the remaining chapters might indifferently be reversed or transposed.   The obscure passages is often affected, *brevis esse laboro, obscurus fio;* the desire of expressing perhaps a common idea with sententious and oracular brevity : alas ! how fatal has been the imitation of Montesquieu !   But this obscurity sometimes proceeds from a mixture of light and darkness in the author's mind ; from a partial ray which strikes upon an angle, instead of spreading itself over the surface of an object. After this fair confession I shall presume to say, that the Essay does credit to a young writer of two and twenty years of age, who had read with taste, who thinks with freedom, and who writes in a foreign language with spirit and elegance.   The defence of the early History of Rome and the new Chronology of Sir Isaac Newton form a specious argument.   The patriotic and political design of the Georgics is happily conceived ; and any probable conjecture, which tends to raise the dignity of the poet and the poem, deserves to be adopted, without a rigid scrutiny.   Some dawnings of a philosophic spirit enlighten the general remarks on the study of history and of man.   I am not displeased with the inquiry into the origin and nature of the gods of polytheism, which might deserve the illustration of a riper judgment.   Upon the whole, I may apply to the first labour of my pen the speech of a far superior artist, when he surveyed the first productions of his pencil. After viewing some portraits which he had painted in his youth, my friend Sir Joshua Reynolds acknowledged to me, that he was rather humbled than flattered by the comparison with his present works ; and that after so much time and study, he had conceived his improvement to be much greater than he found it to have been.

At Lausanne I composed the first chapters of my Essay in French, the familiar language of my conversation and studies, in which it was easier for me to write than in my mother tongue.   After my return to England I continued the same practice, without any affectation, or design of repudiating (as Dr. Bentley would say) my vernacular idiom. But I should have escaped some Anti-gallican clamour, had I been content with the more natural character of an English author.   I should have been more consistent had I rejected Mallet's advice, of prefixing an English dedication to a French book ; a confusion of tongues that seemed to accuse the ignorance of my patron.   The use of a foreign dialect might be excused by the hope of being employed as a negociator, by the desire of being generally understood on the continent ; but my true motive was doubtless the ambition of new and singular fame, an Englishman claiming a place among the writers of France. The latin tongue had been consecrated by the service of the church, it was refined by the imitation of the ancients ; and in the fifteenth and sixteenth centuries the scholars of Europe enjoyed the advantage, which they have gradually resigned, of conversing and writing in a common and learned idiom. As that idiom was no longer in any country the vulgar speech, they all stood on a level with each other ; yet a citizen of old Rome might have smiled at the best Latinity of the Germans and Britons ; and we may learn from the *Ciceronianus* of Erasmus, how difficult it was found to steer a middle course between pedantry and barbarism. The Romans themselves had sometimes attempted a more perilous task, of writing in a living language, and appealing to the taste and judgment of the natives. The vanity of Tully was doubly interested in the Greek memoirs of his own consulship ; and if he modestly supposes that some Latinisms might be detected in his style, he is confident of his own skill in the art of Isocrates and Aristotle ; and he requests his friend Atticus to disperse the copies of his work at Athens, and in the other cities of Greece, (*Ad Atticum*, i. 19. ii. 1.) But it must not be forgotten, that from infancy to manhood Cicero and his contemporaries had read and declaimed, and composed with equal diligence in both languages ; and that he was not allowed to frequent a Latin school till he had imbibed the lessons of the Greek grammarians and rhetoricians. In modern times, the language of France has been diffused by the merit of her writers, the social manners of the natives, the influence of the monarchy, and the exile of the protestants. Several foreigners have seized the opportunity of speaking to Europe in this common dialect, and Germany may plead the authority of Leibnitz and Frederick, of the first of her philosophers, and the greatest of her kings. The just pride and laudable prejudice of England has restrained this communication of idioms ; and of all the nations on this side of the Alps, my countrymen are the least practised, and least perfect in the exercise of the French tongue. By Sir William Temple and Lord Chesterfield it was only used on occasions of civility and business, and their printed letters will not be quoted as models of composition. Lord Bolingbroke may have published in French a sketch of his Reflections on Exile : but his reputation now reposes on the address of Voltaire, " Docte sermones utriusque linguæ ; " and by his English dedication to Queen Caroline, and his Essay on Epic Poetry, it should seem that Voltaire himself wished to deserve a return of the same compliment. The exception of Count Hamilton cannot fairly be urged ; though an Irishman by birth, he was educated in France from his childhood. Yet I am surprised that a long residence in England, and the habits of domestic conversation, did not affect the ease and purity of his inimitable style ; and I regret the omission of his English verses, which might have afforded an amusing object of comparison. I might therefore assume the *primus ego in patriam, &c.;* but with what success I have explored this untrodden path must be left to the decision of my French readers. Dr. Maty, who might himself be questioned as a foreigner, has secured his retreat at my expense. " Je ne crois pas que vous vous piquiez d'être moins facile à reconnoitre pour un Anglois que Lucullus pour un Romain." My friends at Paris have been more indulgent, they received me as a countryman, or at least as a provincial ; but they were friends and Parisians.* The defects which Maty insinuates, " Ces traits saillans, ces figures hardies, ce sacrifice de la régle àu sentiment, et de la cadence à la force," are the faults of the youth, rather than of the stranger : and after the long and laborious exercise of my own language, I am conscious that my French style has been ripened and improved.

I have already hinted, that the publication of my essay was delayed till I had embraced the military profession. I shall now amuse myself with the recollection of an active scene, which bears no affinity to any other period of my studious and social life.

In the outset of a glorious war, the English people had been defended by the aid of German mercenaries. A national militia has been the cry of every patriot since the Revolution ; and this measure, both in parliament and in the field, was supported by the country gentlemen or Tories, who insensibly transferred their loyalty to the house of Hanover : in the language of Mr. Burke, they have changed the idol, but they have preserved the idolatry. In the act of offering our names and receiving our commissions, as major and captain in the Hampshire regiment, (June 12, 1759,) we had not supposed that we should be dragged away, during two years and a half, (May 10, 1760— December 23, 1762,) to a wandering life of military servitude. But a weekly or monthly exercise of thirty thousand provincials would have left them useless and ridiculous ; and after the pretence of an invasion had vanished, the popularity of Mr. Pitt gave a sanction to the illegal step of keeping them till the end of the war under arms, in constant pay and duty, and at a distance from their respective homes. When the King's order for our embodying came down, it was too late to retreat, and too soon to repent. The South battalion of the Hampshire militia was a small independent corps of four hundred and seventy-six, officers and men, commanded by lieutenant-colonel Sir Thomas Worsley, who, after a prolix and passionate contest, delivered us from the tyranny of the lord lieutenant, the Duke of Bolton. My proper station, as first captain, was at the head of my own, and afterwards of the grenadier, company ; but in the absence, or even in the presence, of the two field officers, I was entrusted by my friend and my father with the effective labour of dictating the orders, and exercising the battalion. With the help of an original journal, I could write the history of my bloodless and inglorious campaigns ; but as these events have lost much of their importance in my own eyes, they shall be dispatched in a few words. From Winchester, the first place of assembly, (June 4, 1760,) we were removed, at our own request, for the benefit of a foreign education. By the arbitrary, and often capricious, orders of the War-office, the battalion successively marched to

---

* The copious extracts which were given in the *Journal Etranger* by Mr. Suard, a judicious critic, must satisfy both the author and the public. I may here observe, that I have never seen in any literary review a tolerable account of my History. The manufacture of journals, at least on the continent, is miserably debased.

the pleasant and hospitable Blandford (June 17); to Hilsea barracks, a seat of disease and discord (Sept. 1); to Cranbrook in the weald of Kent (Dec. 11); to the sea-coast of Dover (Dec. 27); to Winchester camp (June 25, 1761); to the populous and disorderly town of Devizes (Oct. 23); to Salisbury (Feb. 28, 1762); to our beloved Blandford a second time (March 9); and finally, to the fashionable resort of Southampton (June 2); where the colours were fixed till our final dissolution (Dec. 23). On the beach at Dover we had exercised in sight of the Gallic shores. But the most splendid and useful scene of our life was a four months' encampment on Winchester Down, under the command of the Earl of Effingham. Our army consisted of the thirty-fourth regiment of foot and six militia corps. The consciousness of our defects was stimulated by friendly emulation. We improved our time and opportunities in morning and evening field-days; and in the general reviews the South Hampshire were rather a credit than a disgrace to the line. In our subsequent quarters of the Devizes and Blandford, we advanced with a quick step in our military studies; the ballot of the ensuing summer renewed our vigour and youth; and had the militia subsisted another year, we might have contested the prize with the most perfect of our brethren.

The loss of so many busy and idle hours was not compensated by any elegant pleasure; and my temper was insensibly soured by the society of our rustic officers. In every state there exists, however, a balance of good and evil. The habits of a sedentary life were usefully broken by the duties of an active profession: in the healthful exercise of the field I hunted with a battalion, instead of a pack; and at that time I was ready, at any hour of the day or night, to fly from quarters to London, from London to quarters, on the slightest call of private or regimental business. But my principal obligation to the militia, was the making me an Englishman, and a soldier. After my foreign education, with my reserved temper, I should long have continued a stranger in my native country, had I not been shaken in this various scene of new faces and new friends: had not experience forced me to feel the characters of our leading men, the state of parties, the forms of office, and the operation of our civil and military system. In this peaceful service I imbibed the rudiments of the language, and science of tactics, which opened a new field of study and observation. 1 diligently read, and meditated, the *Memoires Militaires* of Quintus Icilius, (Mr. Guichardt,) the only writer who has united the merits of a professor and a veteran. The discipline and evolutions of a modern battalion gave me a clearer notion of the phalanx and the legion; and the captain of the Hampshire grenadiers (the reader may smile) has not been useless to the historian of the Roman empire.

A youth of any spirit is fired even by the play of arms, and in the first sallies of my enthusiasm I had seriously attempted to embrace the regular profession of a soldier. But this military fever was cooled by the enjoyment of our mimic Bellona, who soon unveiled to my eyes her naked deformity. How often did I sigh for my proper station in society and letters. How often (a proud comparison) did I repeat the complaint of Cicero in the command of a provincial army: "Clitellæ bovi sunt impositæ. Est incredibile quam me negotii tædeat. Non habet satis magnum campum ille tibi non ignotus cursus animi; et industriæ meæ præclara opera cessat. Lucem, *libros*, urbem domum, vos desidero. Sed feram, ut potero ; sit modo annuum. Si prorogatur, actum est."—Epist. ad Atticum, lib. v. 15. From a service without danger I might indeed have retired without disgrace ; but as often as I hinted a wish of resigning, my fetters were riveted by the friendly intreaties of the colonel, the parental authority of the·major, and my own regard for the honour and welfare of the battalion. When I felt that my personal escape was impracticable, I bowed my neck to the yoke : my servitude was protracted far beyond the annual patience of Cicero ; and it was not till after the preliminaries of peace that I received my discharge, from the act of government which disembodied the militia.*

When I complain of the loss of time, justice to myself and to the militia must throw the greatest part of that reproach on the first seven or eight months, while I was obliged to learn as well as to teach: The dissipation of Blandford, and the disputes of Portsmouth, consumed the hours which were not employed in the field ; and amid the perpetual hurry of an inn, a barrack, or a guard-room, all literary ideas were banished from my mind. After this long fast, the longest which I have ever known, I once more tasted at Dover the pleasures of

* JOURNAL, 1761, Jan. 11.]—In these seven or eight months of a most disagreeably active life, I have had no studies to set down ; indeed, I hardly took a book in my hand the whole time. The first two months at Blandford, I might have done something ; but the novelty of the thing, of which for some time I was so fond as to think of going into the army, our field-days, our dinners abroad, and the drinking and late hours we got into, prevented any serious reflections. From the day we marched from Blandford I had hardly a moment I could call my own, almost continually in motion ; if I was fixed for a day, it was in the guard-room, a barrack, or an inn. Our disputes consumed the little time I had left. Every letter, every memorial relative to them fell to my share ; and our evening conferences were used to bear all the morning hours strike. At last I got to Dover, and Sir Thomas left us for two months. The charm was over, I was sick of so hateful a service ; I was settled in a comparatively quiet situation. Once more I began to taste the pleasure of thinking.

Recollecting some thoughts I had formerly had in relation to the system of Paganism, which I intended to make use of in my Essay, I resolved to read Tully de Natura Deorum, and finished it in about a month. I lost some time before I could recover my habit of application.

Oct. 23.]—Our first design was to march through Marlborough ; but finding on inquiry that it was a bad road, and a great way about, we resolved to push for Devizes in one day, though nearly thirty miles. We accordingly arrived there about three o'clock in the afternoon.

Nov. 2.]—I have very little to say for this and the following month. Nothing could be more uniform than the life I led there. The little civility of the neighbouring gentlemen gave us no opportunity of dining out ; the time of year did not tempt us to any excursions round the coutry ; and at first my indolence, and afterwards a violent cold, prevented my going over to Bath. I believe in the two monthsI never dined or lay from quarters. I can therefore only set down what I did in the literary way. Designing to recover my Greek, which I had somewhat neglected, I set myself to read Homer, and finished the four first books of the Iliad, with Pope's translation and notes : at the same time, to understand the geography of the Iliad, and particularly the catalogue, I read books 8, 9, 10, 12, 13, and 14 of Strabo, in Casaubon's Latin translation : I likewise read Hume's History of England to the Reign of Henry the Seventh; just published, *ingenious but superficial; * and the *Journals des Sçavans * for Aug., Sept., and Oct. 1761, with the *Bibliotheque des Sciences,* &c. from July to Oct. Both these Journals speak very handsomely of my book.

December 25, 1761.]—When, upon finishing the year, I take a review of what I have done, I am not dissatisfied with what I did in it, upon making proper allowances. On the one hand, I could begin nothing before the middle of January. The Deal duty lost me part of February; although I was at home part of March, and all April, yet electioneering is no friend to the Muses. May, indeed, though dissipated by our sea parties, was pretty quiet ; but June was absolutely lost, upon the march, at Alton, and settling ourselves in camp. The four succeeding months in camp allowed me little leisure and less quiet. November and December were indeed as much my own as any time can be whilst I remain in the militia ; but still it is, reading and thinking; and the hungry appetite with which I opened a volume of Tully's philosophical works is still present to my memory. The last review of my Essay before its publication, had prompted me to investigate the *nature of the gods;* my inquiries led me to the Historie Critique du Manichèisme of Beausobre, who discusses many

---

at best, not a life for a man of letters. However, in this tumultuous year, (besides smaller things which I have set down,) I read four books of Homer in Greek, six of Strabo in Latin, Cicero de Naturâ Deorum, and the great philosophical and theological work of M. de Beausobre: I wrote in the same time a long dissertation on the succession of Naples; reviewed, fitted for the press, and augmented above a fourth, my Essai sur l'Etude de la Litterature.

In the six weeks I passed at Beriton, as I never stirred from it, every day was like the former. I had neither visits, hunting, or walking. My only resources were myself, my books, and family conversations. – But to me these were great resources.

April 24, 1762.]—I waited upon Colonel Harvey in the morning, to get him to apply for me to be brigade major to Lord Effiogham, as a post I should be very fond of, and for which I am not unfit. Harvey received me with great good-nature and candour, told me he was both willing and able to serve me: that indeed he had already applied to Lord Effingham for * * * *, one of his own officers, and though there would be more than one brigade major, he did not think he could properly recommend two; but that if I could get some other person to break the ice, he would second it, and believed he should succeed: should that fail, as * * * * was in bad circumstances, he believed he could make a compromise with him (this was my desire) to let me do the duty without pay. I went from him to the Mallets, who promised to get Sir Charles Howard to speak to Lord Effingham.

August 22.]—I went with Ballard to the French church, where I heard a most indifferent sermon preached by M. * * * * *. A very bad style, a worse pronunciation and action, and a very great vacuity of ideas, composed this excellent performance. Upon the whole, which is preferable, the philosophic method of the English, or the rhetoric of the French preachers? The first (though less glorious) is certainly safer for the preacher. It is difficult for a man to make himself ridiculous, who proposes only to deliver plain sense on a subject he has thoroughly studied. But the instant he discovers the least pretentions towards the sublime, or the pathetic, there is no medium; we must either admire or laugh: and there are so many various talents requisite to form the character of an orator, that it is more than probable we shall laugh. As to the advantage of the hearer, which ought to be the great consideration, the dilemma is much greater. Excepting in some particular cases, where we are blinded by popular prejudices, we are in general so well acquainted with our duty, that it is almost superfluous to convince us of it. It is the heart, and not the head, that holds out; and it is certainly possible, by a moving eloquence, to rouse the sleeping sentiments of that heart, and incite it to acts of virtue. Unluckily it is not so much acts, as habits of virtue, we should have in view; and the preacher who is inculcating, with the eloquence of a Bourdaloue, the necessity of a virtuous life, will dismiss his assembly full of emotions, which a variety of other objects, the coldness of our northern constitutions, and no immediate opportunity of exerting their good resolutions, will dissipate in a few moments.

Aug. 24.]—The same reason that carried so many people to the assembly to-night, was what kept me away; I mean the dancing.

28.]—To-day Sir Thomas came to us to dinner. The Spa has done him a great deal of good, for he looks another man. Pleased to see him, we kept bumperizing till after roll-calling; Sir Thomas assuring us, every fresh bottle, how infinitely soberer he was grown.

29.]—I felt the usual consequences of Sir Thomas's company, and lost a morning, because I had lost the day before. However, having finished Voltaire, I returned to Le Clerc (I mean for the amusement of my leisure hours); and laid aside for some time his *Bibliotheque Universelle,* to look into the *Bibliotheque Choisie,* which is by far the better work.

Sept. 23.]—Colonel Wilkes, of the Buckinghamshire militia, dined with us, and renewed the acquaintance Sir Thomas and myself had begun with him at Reading. I scarcely ever met with a better companion; he has inexhaustible spirits, infinite wit and humour, and a great deal of knowledge. He told us himself, that in this time of public dissension he was resolved to make his fortune. Upon this principle he has connected himself closely with Lord Temple and Mr. Pitt, commenced a public adversary to Lord Bute, whom he abuses weekly in the North Briton, and other political papers in which he is concerned. This proved a very debauched day: we drank a good deal both after dinner and supper; and when at last Wilkes had retired, Sir Thomas and some others (of whom I was not one) broke into his room, and made him drink a bottle of claret in bed.

Oct. 5.]—The review, which lasted about three hours, concluded, as usual, with marching by Lord Effingham, by grand divisions. Upon the whole, considering the camp had done both the Winchester and the Gosport duties all the summer, they behaved very well, and made a fine appearance. As they marched by, I had my usual curiosity to count their files. The following is my field return: I think it a curiosity; I am sure it is more exact than is commonly made to a reviewing general.

deep questions of Pagan and Christian theology: and from this rich treasury of facts and opinions, I deduced my own consequences, beyond the holy circle of the author. After this recovery I never relapsed into indolence ; and my example might prove, that in the life most averse to study, some hours may be stolen, some minutes may be

			Number of Files.		Number of Men.		Establishment.
Berkshire,	{	Grenadiers, 19 Battalion, 72	} 91	—	273	—	560
W. Essex,	{	Grenadiers, 15 Battalion, 80	} 95	—	285	—	480
S. Glôster,	{	Grenadiers, 20 Battalion, 84	} 104	—	312	—	600
N. Glôster,	{	Grenadiers, 13 Battalion, 52	} 65	—	195	—	360
Lancashire,	{	Grenadiers, 20 Battalion, 88	} 108	—	324	—	800
Wiltshire,	{	Grenadiers, 24 Battalion, 120	} 144	—	432	—	800
		Total,	607		1821		3600

N.B. The Gosport detachment from the Lancashire consisted of two hundred and fifty men. The Buckinghamshire took the Winchester duty that day.

So that this camp in England, supposed complete, with only one detachment, had under arms, on the day of the grand review, little more than half their establishment. This amazing deficiency (though exemplified in every regiment I have seen) is an extraordinary military phœnomenon : what must it be upon foreign service ? I doubt whether a nominal army of an hundred thousand men often brings fifty into the field.

Upon our return to Southampton in the evening, we found Sir Thomas Worsley.

October 21.]—One of those impulses, which it is neither very easy nor very necessary to withstand, drew me from Longinus to a very different subject, the Greek Calendar. Last night, when in bed, I was thinking of a dissertation of M. de la Nauze upon the Roman calendar, which I read last year. This led me to consider what was the Greek, and finding myself very ignorant of it, I determined to read a short, but very excellent abstract of Mr. Dodwell's book de Cyclis, by the famous Dr. Halley. It is only twenty-five pages ; but as I meditated it thoroughly, and verified all the calculations, it was a very good morning's work.

Oct. 28.]—I looked over a new Greek Lexicon which I have just received from London. It is that of Robert Constantine, Lugdon. 1637. It is a very large volume in folio, in two parts, comprising in the whole 1785 pages. After the great Thesaurus, this is esteemed the best Greek Lexicon. It seems to be so. Of a variety of words for which I looked, I always found an exact definition ; the various senses well distinguished, and properly supported, by the best authorities. However, I still prefer the radical method of Scapula to this alphabetical one.

Dec. 11.]—I have already given an idea of the Gosport duty; I shall only add a trait which characterizes admirably our unthinking sailors. At a time when they knew that they should infallibly be discharged in a few weeks, numbers, who had considerable wages due to them, were continually jumping over the walls, and risquing the losing of it for a few hours' amusement at Portsmouth.

17.]—We found old Captain Meard at Alresford, with the second division of the fourteenth. He and all his officers supped with us, and made the evening rather a drunken one.

18.]—About the same hour our two corps paraded to march off. They, an old corps of regulars, who had been two years quiet in Dover castle. We, part of a young body of militia, two-thirds of our men recruits, of four months' standing, two of which they had passed upon very disagreeable duty. Every advantage was on their side, and yet our superiority, both as to appearance and discipline, was so striking, that the most prejudiced regular could not have hesitated a moment. At the end of the town our two companies separated ; my father's struck off for Petersfield, whilst I continued my rout to Alton : into which place I marched my company about noon ; two years six months and fifteen days after my first leaving it. I gave the men some beer at roll-calling, which they received with great cheerfulness and decency. I dined and lay at Harrison's, where I was received with that old-fashioned breeding, which is at once so honourable and so troublesome.

23.]—Our two companies were disembodied ; mine at Alton, and my father's at Buriton. Smith marched them over from Petersfield : they fired three vollies, lodged the major's colours, delivered up their arms, received their money, partook of a dinner at the major's expence, and then separated with great cheerfulness and regularity. Thus ended the militia : I may say ended, since our annual assemblies in May are so very precarious, and can be of so little use. However, our serjeants and drums are still kept up, and quartered at the rendezvous of their company, and the adjutant remains at Southampton in full pay.

snatched. Amidst the tumult of Winchester camp I sometimes thought and read in my tent; in the more settled quarters of the Devizes, Blandford, and Southampton, I always secured a separate lodging, and the necessary books; and in the summer of 1762, while the new militia was raising, I enjoyed at Buriton two or three months of literary repose *. In forming a new plan of study, I hesitated between the mathematics and the Greek language; both of which I had neglected since my return from Lausanne. I consulted a learned and friendly mathematician, Mr. George Scott, a pupil of de Moivre; and his map of a country which I have never explored, may perhaps be more serviceable to others. As soon as I had given the preference to Greek, the example of Scaliger and my own reason determined me on the choice of Homer, the father of poetry, and the Bible of the ancients: but Scaliger ran through the Iliad in one and twenty days; and I was not dissatisfied with my own diligence for performing the same labour in an equal number of weeks. After the first difficulties were surmounted, the language of nature and harmony soon became easy and familiar, and each day I sailed upon the ocean with a brisker gale and a more steady course.

As this was an extraordinary scene of life, in which I was engaged above three years and a half from the date of my commission, and above two years and a half from the time of our embodying, I cannot take my leave of it without some few reflections. When I engaged in it, I was totally ignorant of its nature and consequences. I offered, because my father did, without ever imagining that we should be called out, till it was too late to retreat with honour. Indeed, I believe it happens throughout, that our most important actions have been often determined by chance, caprice, or some very inadequate motive. After our embodying, many things contributed to make me support it with great impatience. Our continual disputes with the duke of Bolton; our unsettled way of life, which hardly allowed me books or leisure for study; and more than all, the disagreeable society in which I was forced to live.

After mentioning my sufferings, I must say something of what I found agreeable. Now it is over, I can make the separation much better than I could at the time. 1. The unsettled way of life itself had its advantages. The exercise and change of air and of objects amused me, at the same time that it fortified my health. 2. A new field of knowledge and amusement opened itself to me; that of military affairs, which, both in my studies and travels, will give me eyes for a new world of things, which before would have passed unheeded. Indeed, in that respect I can hardly help wishing our battalion had continued another year. We had got a fine set of new men, all our difficulties were over; we were perfectly well clothed and appointed; and, from the progress our recruits had already made, we could promise ourselves that we should be one of the best militia corps by next summer; a circumstance that would have been the more agreeable to me, as I am now established the real acting major of the battalion. But what I value most, is the knowledge it has given me of mankind in general, and of my own country in particular. The general system of our government, the methods of our several offices, the departments and powers of their respective officers, our provincial and municipal administration, the views of our several parties, the characters, connections, and influence of our principal people, have been impressed on my mind, not by vain theory, but by the indelible lessons of action and experience. I have made a number of valuable acquaintance, and am myself much better known, than (with my reserved character) I should have been in ten years, passing regularly my summers at Buriton, and my winters in London. So that the sum of all is, that I am glad the militia has been, and glad that it is no more.

* Journal, May 8, 1762.]—This was my birth-day, on which I entered into the twenty-sixth year of my age. This gave me occasion to look a little into myself, and consider impartially my good and bad qualities. It appeared to me, upon this inquiry, that my character was virtuous, incapable of a base action, and formed for generous ones; but that it was proud, violent, and disagreeable in society. These qualities I must endeavour to cultivate, extirpate, or restrain, according to their different tendency. Wit I have none. My imagination is rather strong than pleasing. My memory both capacious and retentive. The shining qualities of my understanding are extensiveness and penetration; but I want both quickness and exactness. As to my situation in life, though I may sometimes repine at it, it perhaps is the best adapted to my character. I can command all the conveniences of life, and I can command too that independence, (that first earthly blessing,) which is hardly to be met with in a higher or lower fortune. When I talk of my situation, I must exclude that temporary one, of being in the militia. Though I go through it with spirit and application, it is both unfit for, and unworthy of me.

'Εν δ' ἄνεμος πρῆσεν μέσον ἱστίον, ἀμφὶ, δε κῦμα
Στείρη πορφήρεον μεγάλ' ἴαχε, νηός ἰούσης·
'Η δ' ἔθεεν κατα κῦμα διαπρήσσουσα κέλευθα.*   *Ilias*, A. 481.

In the study of a poet who has since become the most intimate of my friends, I successively applied many passages and fragments of Greek writers; and among these I shall notice a life of Homer, in the Oposcula Mythologica of Gale, several books of the geography of Strabo, and the entire treatise of Longinus, which, from the title and the style, is equally worthy of the epithet of *sublime.* My grammatical skill was improved, my vocabulary was enlarged ; and in the militia I acquired a just and indelible knowledge of the first of languages. On every march, in every journey, Horace was always in my pocket, and often in my hand: but I should not mention his two critical epistles, the amusement of a morning, had they not been accompanied by the elaborate commentary of Dr. Hurd, now Bishop of Worcester. On the interesting subjects of composition and imitation of epic and dramatic poetry, I presumed to think for myself ; and thirty close-written pages in folio could scarcely comprise my full and free discussion of the sense of the master and the pedantry of the servant.

After his oracle Dr. Johnson, my friend Sir Joshua Reynolds denies all original genius, any natural propensity of the mind to one art or science rather than another. Without engaging in a metaphysical or rather verbal dispute, I *know*, by experience, that from my early youth I aspired to the character of an historian. While I served in the militia, before and after the publication of my essay, this idea ripened in my mind ; nor can I paint in more lively colours the feelings of the moment, than by transcribing some passages, under their respective dates, from a journal which I kept at that time.

Beriton, April 14, 1761. (In a short excursion from Dover.)— "Having thought of several subjects for an historical composition, I chose the expedition of Charles VIII. of France into Italy. I read two memoirs of Mr. de Foncemagne in the Academy of Inscriptions (tom. xvii. p. 539—607.), and abstracted them. I likewise finished this day a dissertation, in which I examine the right of Charles VIII. to the crown of Naples, and the rival claims of the House of Anjou and Arragon: it consists of ten folio pages, besides large notes."

Beriton, August 4, 1761. (In a week's excursion from Winchester camp.)—"After having long revolved subjects for my intended historical essay, I renounced my first thought of the expedition of Charles VIII. as too remote from us, and rather an introduction to great events, than great and important in itself. I successively chose and rejected the crusade of Richard the First, the barons' wars against John and Henry the Third, the History of Edward the Black Prince, the lives and comparisons of Henry V. and the Emperor Titus, the life of Sir Philip Sidney, and that of the Marquis of Montrose. At length I have fixed on Sir Walter Raleigh for my hero. His eventful story is varied by the characters of the soldier and sailor, the courtier and historian ; and

* —— Fair wind, and blowing fresh,
Apollo sent them : quick they rear'd the mast,
Then spread th'unsullied canvas to the gale,

And the wind fill'd it.   Roar'd the sable flood
Around the bark, that ever as she went
Dash'd wide the brine, and scudded swift away,
COWPER'S *Homer*,

it may afford such a fund of materials as I desire, which have not yet been properly manufactured. At present I cannot attempt the execution of this work. Free leisure, and the opportunity of consulting many books, both printed and manuscript, are as necessary as they are impossible to be attained in my present way of life. However, to acquire a general insight into my subject and resources, I read the life of Sir Walter Raleigh by Dr. Birch, his copious article in the General Dictionary by the same hand, and the reigns of Queen Elizabeth and James the First in Hume's History of England."

Beriton, January 1762. (In a month's absence from the Devizes.)—"During this interval of repose, I again turned my thoughts to Sir Walter Raleigh, and looked more closely into my materials. I read the two volumes in quarto of the Bacon Papers, published by Dr. Birch ; the Fragmenta Regalia of Sir Robert Naunton, Mallet's Life of Lord Bacon, and the political treatises of that great man in the first volume of his works, with many of his letters in the second ; Sir William Monson's Naval Tracts, and the elaborate life of Sir Walter Raleigh, which Mr. Oldys has prefixed to the best edition of his History of the World. My subject opens upon me, and in general improves upon a nearer prospect."

Beriton, July 26, 1762. (During my summer residence.)—"I am afraid of being reduced to drop my hero ; but my time has not, however, been lost in the research of his story, and of a memorable æra of our English annals. The life of Sir Walter Raleigh, by Oldys, is a very poor performance ; a servile panegyric, or flat apology, tediously minute, and composed in a dull and affected style. Yet the author was a man of diligence and learning, who had read everything relative to his subject, and whose ample collections are arranged with perspicuity and method. Excepting some anecdotes lately revealed in the Sidney and Bacon Papers, I know not what I should be able to add. My ambition (exclusive of the uncertain merit of style and sentiment) must be confined to the hope of giving a good abridgment of Oldys. I have even the disappointment of finding some parts of this copious work very dry and barren ; and these parts are unluckily some of the most characteristic : Raleigh's colony of Virginia, his quarrels with Essex, the true secret of his conspiracy, and, above all, the detail of his private life, the most essential and important to a biographer. My best resource would be in the circumjacent history of the times, and perhaps in some digressions artfully introduced, like the fortunes of the Peripatetic philosophy in the portrait of Lord Bacon. But the reigns of Elizabeth and James the First are the periods of English history, which have been the most variously illustrated : and what new lights could I reflect on a subject, which has exercised the accurate industry of *Birch,* the lively and curious acuteness of *Walpole,* the critical spirit of *Hurd,* the vigorous sense of *Mallet* and *Robertson,* and the impartial philosophy of *Hume ?* Could I even surmount these obstacles, I should shrink with terror from the modern history of England, where every character is a problem, and every reader a friend or an enemy ; where a writer is supposed to hoist a flag of party, and is devoted to damnation by the adverse faction. Such would be *my* reception at home : and abroad, the historian of Raleigh must encounter an indifference far more bitter than censure or reproach. The events of his life are interesting : but his character is ambiguous, his actions are obscure, his writings are English, and his fame is confined to the narrow limits of our language and our island. I must embrace a safer and more extensive theme.

There is one which I should prefer to all others, *The History of the Liberty of the Swiss,* of that independence which a brave people rescued from the House of Austria, defended against a Dauphin of France, and finally sealed with the blood of Charles of Burgundy. From such a theme, so full of public spirit, of military glory, of examples of virtue, of lessons of government, the dullest stranger would catch fire ; what might not *I* hope, whose talents, whatsoever they may be, would be inflamed with the zeal of patriotism. But the materials of this history are inaccessible to me, fast locked in the obscurity of an old barbarous German dialect, of which I am totally ignorant, and which I cannot resolve to learn for this sole and peculiar purpose.

I have another subject in view, which is the contrast of the former history : the one a poor, warlike, virtuous republic, which emerges into glory and freedom ; the other a commonwealth, soft, opulent, and corrupt ; which, by just degrees, is precipitated from the abuse to the loss of her liberty : both lessons are, perhaps, equally instructive. This second subject is, *The History of the Republic of Florence under the House of Medicis:* a period of one hundred and fifty years, which rises or descends from the dregs of the Florentine democracy, to the title and dominion of Cosmo de Medicis in the Grand Duchy of Tuscany. I might deduce a chain of revolutions not unworthy of the pen of Vertot ; singular men, and singular events ; the Medicis four times expelled, and as often recalled ; and the Genius of Freedom reluctantly yielding to the arms of Charles V. and the policy of Cosmo. The character and fate of Savanerola, and the revival of arts and letters in Italy, will be essentially connected with the elevation of the family and the fall of the republic. The Medicis (stirps quasi fataliter nata ad instauranda vel fovenda studia (Lipsius ad Germanos et Gallos, Epist. viii.) were illustrated by the patronage of learning ; and enthusiasm was the most formidable weapon of their adversaries. On this splendid subject I shall most probably fix ; but *when,* or *where,* or *how* will it be executed ? I behold in a dark and doubtful perspective."

Res altâ terrâ, et caligine mersas.*

* JOURNAL, July 27, 1762.]—The reflections which I was making yesterday I continued and digested to-day. I don't absolutely look on that time as lost, but that it might have been better employed than in revolving schemes, the execution of which is so far distant. I must learn to check these wanderings of my imagination.

Nov. 24.]—I dined at the Cocoa Tree with * * * * * ; who, under a great appearance of oddity, conceals more real honour, good sense, and even knowledge, than half those who laugh at him. We went thence to the play (the Spanish Friar) ; and when it was over, returned to the Cocoa Tree. That respectable body, of which I have the honour of being a member, affords every evening a sight truly English. Twenty or thirty perhaps, of the first men in the kingdom, in point of fashion and fortune, supping at little tables covered with a napkin, in the middle of a coffee-room, upon a bit of cold meat, or a Sandwich, and drinking a glass of punch. At present, we are full of king's counsellers and lords of the bedchamber ; who, having jumped into the ministry, make a very singular medley of their old principles and language, with their modern ones.

Nov. 26.]—I went with Mallet to breakfast with Garrick ; and thence to Drury-lane House, where I assisted at a very private rehearsal, in the Green-room, of a new tragedy of Mallet's

The youthful habits of the language and manners of France had left in my mind an ardent desire of revisiting the Continent on a larger and more liberal plan. According to the law of custom, and perhaps of reason, foreign travel completes the education of an English gentleman : my father had consented to my wish, but I was detained above four years by my rash engagement in the militia. I eagerly grasped the first moments of freedom : three or four weeks in Hampshire and London were employed in the preparations of my journey, and the farewell visits of friendship and civility : my last act in town was to applaud Mallet's new tragedy of Elvira ;* a post-chaise conveyed me

---

called Elvira. As I have since seen it acted, I shall defer my opinion of it till then ; but I cannot help mentioning here the surprising versatility of Mrs. Pritchard's talents, who rehearsed, almost at the same time, the part of a furious queen in the Green-room, and that of a coquette on the stage ; and passed several times from one to the other with the utmost ease and happiness.

Dec. 30.]—Before I close the year I must balance my accounts—not of money, but of time. I may divide my studies into four branches ; 1. Books that I have read for themselves, classic writers, or capital treatises on any science ; such books as ought to be perused with attention, and meditated with care. Of these I read *the twenty last books of the Iliad twice, the three first books of the Odyssey, the Life of Homer, and Longinus* περι Ύψους. 2. Books which I have read or consulted, to illustrate the former. Such as this year, *Blackwall's Inquiry into the Life and Writings of Homer, Burke's Sublime and Beautiful, Hurd's Horace, Guichard's Memoires Militaires,* a great variety of passages of the ancients occasionally useful : large extracts from *Mezeriac, Bayle,* and *Potter ;* and many memoirs and· abstracts from the *Academy of Belles Letsres :* among these I shall only mention here two long and curious suites of dissertations—*the one upon the Temple of Delphi, the Amphictyonic Council, and the Holy Wars, by M. M. Hardion and De Valois ; the other upon the games of the Grecians, by M. M. Burette, Gedoyne, and de la Barre.* 3. Books of amusement and instruction, perused at my leisure hours, without any reference to a regular plan of study. Of these, perhaps, I read too many, since I went through the Life of Erasmus, by Le Clerc and Burigny, many extracts from *Le Clerc's Bibliotheques, The Ciceronians,* and *Colloquies of Erasmus, Barclay's Argenis, Terasson's Sethos, Voltaire's Siecle de Louis XIV., Madame de Motteville's Memoirs,* and *Fontenelle's Works.* 4. Compositions of my own. I find hardly any, except *this Journal,* and the *Extract of Hwd's Horace,* which (like a chapter of Montaigne) contains many things very different from its title. To these four heads I must this year add a fifth. 5. Those treatises of English history which I read in January, with a view to my now abortive scheme of the *Life of Sir Walter Raleigh.* I ought indeed to have known my own mind better before I undertook them. Upon the whole, after making proper allowances, I am not dissatisfied with the year.

The three weeks which I passed at Beriton, at the end of this and the beginning of the ensuing year, are almost a blank. I seldom went out ; and as the scheme of my travelling was at last entirely settled, the hurry of impatience, the cares of preparations, and the tenderness of friends I was going to quit, allowed me hardly any moments for study.

* JOURNAL, Jan. 11, 1763.]—I called upon Dr. Matey in the morning. He told me that the Duke de Nivernois desired to be acquainted with me. It was indeed with that view that I had written to Matey from Beriton to present, in my name, a copy of my book to him. Thence I went to Becket, paid him his bill, (fifty-four pounds,) and gave him back his translation. It must be printed, though very indifferent. My comfort is, that my misfortune is not an uncommon one. We dined and supped at the Mallets.

12.—I went with Matey to visit the Duke in Albemarle Street. He is a little emaciated figure, but appears to possess a good understanding, taste, and knowledge. He offered me very politely letters for Paris. We dined at our lodgings. I went to Covent Garden to see Woodward in Bobadil, and supped with the Mallets at George Scott's.

JOURNAL, Jan. 19, 1763.]—I waited upon Lady Herbert and the Duke de Nivernois, and received my credentials. Lady Hervey's are for M. le Comte de Caylus, and Madame Geoffrin. The Duke received me very civilly, but (perhaps through Matey's fault) treated me more as a man of letters than as a man of fashion. His letters are entirely in that style ; for the Count de Caylus and M. M. de la Bleterie, de Ste. Palaye, Capcronier, du Clos, de Forcemagne, and d'Alembert. I then undressed for the play. My father and I went to the Rose, in the passage of the play-house, where we found Mallet, with about thirty friends. We dined together, and went thence into the pit, where we took our places in a body, ready to silence all opposition. However, we had no occasion to exert ourselves. Notwithstanding the malice of party, Mallet's nation, connections, and, indeed, imprudence, we heard nothing but applause. I think it was deserved· The plan was taken from de la Motte, but the details and language have great merit. A fine vein of dramatic poetry runs through the piece. The scenes between the father and son awaken almost every sensation of the human breast ; and

F

to Dover, the packet to Boulogne, and such was my diligence, that I reached Paris on Jan. 28, 1763, only thirty-six days after the disbanding of the militia. Two or three years were loosely defined for the term of my absence ; and I was left at liberty to spend that time in such places and in such a manner as was most agreeable to my taste and judgment.

In this first visit I passed three months and a half, (Jan. 28—May 9,) and a much longer space might have been agreeably filled, without any intercourse with the natives. At home we are content to move in the daily round of pleasure and business ; and a scene which is always present is supposed to be within our knowledge, or at least within our power. But in a foreign country, curiosity is our business and our pleasure ; and the traveller, conscious of his ignorance, and covetous of his time, is diligent in the search and the view of every object that can deserve his attention. I devoted many hours of the morning to the circuit of Paris and the neighbourhood, to the visit of churches and palaces conspicuous by their architecture, to the royal manufactures, collections of books and pictures, and all the various treasures of art, of learning, and of luxury. An Englishman may hear without reluctance, that in these curious and costly articles Paris is superior to London ; since the opulence of the French capital arises from the defects of its government and religion. In the absence of Louis XIV. and his successors, the Louvre has been left unfinished : but the millions which have been lavished on the sands of Versailles, and the morass of Marli, could not be supplied by the legal allowance of a British king. The splendour of the French nobles is confined to their town residence ; that of the English is more usefully distributed in their country seats ; and we should be astonished at our own riches, if the labours of architecture, the spoils of Italy and Greece, which are now scattered from Inverary to Wilton, were accumulated in a few streets between Marylebone and Westminster. All superfluous ornament is rejected by the cold frugality of the protestants ; but the catholic superstition, which is always the enemy of reason, is often the parent of the arts. The wealthy communities of priests and monks expend their revenues in stately edifices ; and the parish church of St. Sulpice, one of the noblest structures in Paris, was built and adorned by the private industry of a late curé. In this outset, and still more in the sequel of my tour, my eye was amused ; but the pleasing vision cannot be fixed by the pen ; the particular images are darkly seen through the medium

---

the counsel would have equally moved, but for the inconvenience unavoidable upon all theatres, that of entrusting fine speeches to indifferent actors. The perplexity of the catastrophe is much, and I believe justly, criticised. But another defect made a stronger impression upon me. When a poet ventures upon the dreadful situation of a father who condemns his son to death, there is no medium, the father must either be a monster or a hero. His obligations of justice, of the public good, must be as binding, as apparent, as perhaps those of the first Brutus. The cruel necessity consecrates his actions, and leaves no room for repentance. The thought is shocking, if not carried into action. In the execution of Brutus's sons I am sensible of that fatal necessity. Without such an example, the unsettled liberty of Rome would have perished the instant after its birth. But Alonzo might have pardoned his son for a rash attempt, the cause of which was a private injury, and whose consequences could never have disturbed an established government. He might have pardoned such a crime in any other subject ; and as the laws could exact only an equal rigour for a son, a vain appetite for glory, and a mad affectation of heroism, could alone have influenced him to exert an unequal and superior severity.

of five-and-twenty years, and the narrative of my life must not degenerate into a book of travels.*

But the principal end of my journey was to enjoy the society of a polished and amiable people, in whose favour I was strongly prejudiced, and to converse with some authors, whose conversation, as I fondly imagined, must be far more pleasing and instructive than their writings. The moment was happily chosen. At the close of a successful war the British name was respected on the continent.

Clarum et venerabile nomen
Gentibus.

Our opinions, our fashions, even our games, were adopted in France, a ray of national glory illuminated each individual, and every Englishman was supposed to be born a patriot and a philosopher. For myself, I carried a personal recommendation; my name and my Essay were already known; the compliment of having written in the French language entitled me to some returns of civility and gratitude. I was considered as a man of letters, who wrote for amusement. Before my departure I had obtained from the Duke de Nivernois, Lady Hervey, the Mallets, Mr. Walpole, &c. many letters of recommendation to their private or literary friends. Of these epistles the reception and success were determined by the character and situation of the persons by whom and to whom they were addressed : the seed was sometimes cast on a barren rock, and it sometimes multiplied an hundred fold in the production of new shoots, spreading branches, and exquisite fruit. But upon the whole, I had reason to praise the national urbanity, which from the court has diffused its gentle influence to the shop, the cottage, and the schools. Of the men of genius of the age, Montesquieu and Fontenelle were no more ; Voltaire resided on his own estate near Geneva ; Rousseau in the preceding year had been driven from his hermitage of Montmorency; and I blush at my having neglected to seek, in this journey, the acquaintance of Buffon. Among the men of letters whom I saw, D'Alembert and Diderot held the foremost rank in merit, or at least in fame. I shall content myself with enumerating the well-known names of the Count de Caylus, of the Abbé de la Bleterie, Barthelemy, Reynal, Arnaud, of Messieurs de la Condamine, du Clos, de Ste Palaye, de Bougainville, Caperonnier, de Guignes, Suard, &c. without attempting to discriminate the shades of their characters, or the degrees of our connection. Alone, in a morning visit, I commonly found the artists and authors of Paris less vain,

---

* JOURNAL, 21 Fevrier 1763.]—Aujourdhui j'ai commencé ma tournée, pour voir les endroits dignes d'attention dans la ville. D'Augny m'a accompagné. Nous sommes allés d'abord à la bibliotheque de l'Abbayé de St. Germain des Prez, où tout le monde étoit occupé à l'arrangement d'un cabinet de curiosités, et à l'hôpital des invalides, où le dôme étoit fermé à cause des reparations qu'on y faisoit. Il faut donc differer la visite et la description de ces deux endroits. De là nous sommes allés voir l'école militaire. Comme ce bâtiment s'éleve à coté des Invalides, bien des gens y verroient un moyen assez facile d'apprecier les ames differentes de leurs fondateurs. Dans l'un tout est grand et fastueux, dans l'autre tout est petit et mesquin. De petits corps de logis blancs et assez propres, qui, au lieu de 500 gentils-hommes, dont on a parlé, en contiennent 258, composent tout l'etablissement ; car le manége et les ecuries ne sont rien. Il est vrai qu'on dit que ces batimens ne sont qu'un échaffaudage, qu'on doit ôtre, pour élever le véritable ouvrage sur ces débris. Il faut bien en effet qu'on n'ait pas bâti pour l'éternité, puisque dans vingt ans la plûpart des poutres se sont pourries. Nous jettâmes ensuite un coup d'oeil sur l'église de St. Sulpice, dont la façade (le prétexte et le fruit de tant de lotteries) n'est point encore achevée.

and more reasonable, than in the circles of their equals, with whom they mingle in the houses of the rich. Four days in a week, I had a place, without invitation, at the hospitable tables of Mesdames Geoffrin and du Bocage, of the celebrated Helvetius, and of the Baron d'Olbach. In these symposia the pleasures of the table were improved by lively and liberal conversation; the company was select, though various and voluntary.*

The society of Madame du Bocage was more soft and moderate than that of her rivals, and the evening conversations of M. de Foncemagne were supported by the good sense and learning of the principal members of the Academy of Inscriptions. The opera and the Italians I occasionally visited; but the French theatre, both in tragedy and comedy, was my daily and favourite amusement. Two famous actresses then divided the public applause. For my own part, I preferred the consummate art of the Claron, to the intemperate sallies of the Dumesnil, which were extolled by her admirers, as the genuine voice of nature and passion. Fourteen weeks insensibly stole away; but had I been rich and independent, I should have prolonged, and perhaps have fixed, my residence at Paris.

Between the expensive style of Paris and of Italy it was prudent to interpose some months of tranquil simplicity; and at the thoughts of Lausanne I again lived in the pleasures and studies of my early youth. Shaping my course through Dijon and Besançon, in the last of which places I was kindly entertained by my cousin Acton, I arrived in the month of May 1763 on the banks of the Leman Lake. It had been my intention to pass the Alps in the autumn, but such are the simple attractions of the place, that the year had almost expired before my departure from Lausanne in the ensuing spring. An absence of five years had not made much alteration in manners, or even in persons. My old friends, of both sexes, hailed my voluntary return; the most

* JOURNAL, Fevrier 23, 1763.]—Je fis une visite à l'Abbé de la Bleterie, qui veut me mener chez la Duchesse d'Aiguillon; je me fis ecrire chez M. de Bougainville que j'ai grande envie de connoitre, et me rendis ensuite chez le Baron d'Olbach, ami de M. Helvetius. C'etoit ma première visite, et le premier pas dans une fort bonne maison. Le Baron a de l'esprit et des connoissances, et surtout il donne souvent et fort bien à diner.

Fevrier 24.]—L'Abbé Barthelemy est fort aimable et n'a de l'antiquaire qu'une très grande érudition. Je finis la soirée par une souper très agréable chez Madame Bontems avec M. le Marquis de Mirabeau. Cet homme est singulier; il a assez d'imagination pour dix autres, et pas assez de sens rassis pour lui seul. Je lui ai fait beaucoup de questions sur les titres de la noblesse Francoise; mais tout ce que j'en ai pu comprendre, c'est que personne n'a là dessus des idées bien nettes.

Mai 1763.]—Muni d'une double lettre de recommandation pour M. le Comte de Caylus, je m'etois imaginé que je trouverois reunis en lui l'homme de lettres et l'homme de qualité. Je le vis trois ou quatre fois, et je vis un homme simple, uni, bon, et qui me temoignoit une bonté extrême. Si je n'en ai point profité, je l'attribué moins à son caractére qu'à son genre de vie. Il se leve de grande matin, court les atteliers des artistes pendant tout le jour, et rentre chez lui à six heurs du soir pour se mettre en robe de chambre, et s'enfermer dans son cabinet. Le moyen de voir ses amis?

Si ces recommendations etoient steriles, il y en eut d'autres que devinrent aussi sécondes par leurs suites, qu'elles etoient agréables en elles mêmes. Dans une capitale comme Paris, il est necessaire, il est juste que des lettres de recommandation vous nyent distingué de la foule. Mais dèsque la glace est rompue, vos connoissances se multiplient, et vos nouveaux amis se font un plaisir de vous en procurer d'autres plus nouveaux encore. Heureux effet de ce caractere leger et aimable du François, qui a établi dans Paris une douceur et une liberté dans la société, inconnues à l'antiquité, et encore ignorées des autres nations. A Londres il faut faire son chemin dans les maisons que ne s'ouvrent qu'avec peine. Là on croit vous faire plaisir en vous recevant. Ici on croit s'en faire à soi-meme. Aussi je connois plus de maisons à Paris qu'à Londres: le fait n'est pas vraisemblable, mais il est vrai.

genuine proof of my attachment. They had been flattered by the present of my book, the produce of their soil ; and the good Pavilliard shed tears of joy as he embraced a pupil, whose literary merit he might fairly impute to his own labours. To my old list I added some new acquaintance, and among the strangers I shall distinguish Prince Lewis of Wirtemberg, the brother of the reigning Duke, at whose country-house, near Lausanne, I frequently dined : a wandering meteor, and at length a falling star, his light and ambitious spirit had successively dropped from the firmament of Prussia, of France, and of Austria ; and his faults, which he styled his misfortunes, had driven him into philosophic exile in the Pays de Vaud. He could now moralize on the vanity of the world, the equality of mankind, and the happiness of a private station. His address was affable and polite, and as he had shone in courts and armies, his memory could supply, and his eloquence could adorn, a copious fund of interesting anecdotes. His first enthusiasm was that of charity and agriculture ; but the sage gradually lapsed in the saint, and Prince Lewis of Wirtemberg is now buried in a hermitage near Mayence, in the last stage of mystic devotion. By some ecclesiastical quarrel, Voltaire had been provoked to withdraw himself from Lausanne, and retire to his castle at Ferney, where I again visited the poet and the actor, without seeking his more intimate acquaintance, to which I might now have pleaded a better title. But the theatre which he had founded, the actors whom he had formed, survived the loss of their master ; and, recent from Paris, I attended with pleasure at the representation of several tragedies and comedies. I shall not descend to specify particular names and characters ; but I cannot forget a private institution, which will display the innocent freedom of Swiss manners. My favourite society had assumed, from the age of its members, the proud denomination of the spring (*la société du printems*). It consisted of fifteen or twenty young unmarried ladies, of genteel, though not of the very first families ; the eldest perhaps about twenty, all agreeable, several handsome, and two or three of exquisite beauty. At each other's houses they assembled almost every day, without the controul, or even the presence, of a mother or an aunt ; they were trusted to their own prudence, among a crowd of young men of every nation in Europe. They laughed, they sung, they danced, they played at cards, they acted comedies ; but in the midst of this careless gaiety, they respected themselves, and were respected by the men ; the invisible line between liberty and licentiousness was never transgressed by a gesture, a word, or a look, and their virgin chastity was never sullied by the breath of scandal or suspicion. A singular institution, expressive of the innocent simplicity of Swiss manners. After having tasted the luxury of England and Paris, I could not have returned with satisfaction to the coarse and homely table of Madame Pavilliard ; nor was her husband offended that I now entered myself as a *pensionaire*, or boarder, in the elegant house of Mr. De Mesery, which may be entitled to a short remembrance, as it has stood above twenty years, perhaps, without a parallel in Europe. The house in which we lodged was spacious and convenient, in the best street, and commanding, from behind, a noble prospect over the country and the Lake. Our table was served with neatness and plenty ; the boarders were select ; we had the liberty of inviting any guests at a stated price ; and in the summer the scene was occasionally transferred to a pleasant villa, about a league from Lausanne. The characters of Master and Mistress were happily suited to each other, and to their situation. At the age of seventy-five, Madame de Mesery, who has survived her husband, is still a graceful, I had almost said, a handsome woman. She was alike qualified to preside in her kitchen and her drawing-room ; and such was the equal propriety of her conduct, that of two or three hundred foreigners, none ever failed in respect, none could complain of her neglect, and none could ever boast of her favour. Mesery himself, of the noble family of De Crousaz, was a man of the world, a jovial companion, whose easy manners and natural sallies maintained the cheerfulness of his house. His wit could laugh at his own ignorance : he disguised, by an air of profusion, a strict attention to his interest ; and in this situation he appeared like a nobleman who spent his fortune and entertained his friends. In this agreeable society I resided nearly eleven months (May 1763—April 1764) ; and in this second visit to Lausanne, among a crowd of my English companions, I knew and esteemed Mr. Holroyd (now Lord Sheffield) ; and our mutual attachment was renewed and fortified in the subsequent stages of our Italian journey. Our lives are in the power of chance, and a slight variation on either side, in time or place, might have deprived me of a friend, whose activity in the ardour of youth was always prompted by a benevolent heart, and directed by a strong understanding.*

* JOURNAL, Sept. 16, 1763.]—* * * * et * * * * nous ont quitté. Le premier est une mechante bête, grossier, ignorant, et sans usage du monde. Sa violence lui a fait vingt mauvaises affaires ici. On vouloit cependant lui faire entreprendre le voyage d'Italie, mais * * * * refusant de l'y accompagner, on a pris le partie de le rapeller en Angleterre en le faisant passer par Paris. * * * * est philosophe, et fort instruit, mais froid et nullement homme d'esprit. Il est las de courir le monde avec des jeunes foux. Apres avoir rendu celui-ci à sa famille, il compte venir chercher le repos et la retraite dans ce pays. Qu'il a raison !
Sept. 21me.]—J'ai essuyé une petite mortification au cercle. Le départ de Frey ayant fait vacquer l'emploi de directeur des etrangers, on m'avoit fait entrevoir qu'on me le destinoit, et ma franchise naturelle ne m'avoit pas permis de dissimuler que je le recevrois avec plaisir, et que je m'y attendois. Cependant la pluralité des voix l'a donné à M. Roel Hollandois. J'ai vu qu'on a saisi le premier moment que les loix permettoient de balloter, et que, si j'avois voulu rassembler mes amis, je l'aurois emporté ; mais je sais en même tems que je l'aurois eu il y a trois mois, sans y songer un moment. Ma reputation baisse ici avec quelque raison, et j'ai des ennemis.
Sept. 25me.]—J'ai passé l'après diner chez Madame de * * * * *. Je ne l'avois pas vue depuis le 14 de ce mois. Elle ne m'a point parlé, ni n'a paru s'etre apperçue de mon absence. Ce silence m'a fait de la peine. J'avois une très belle reputation ici pour les mœurs, mais je vois qu'on commence à me confondre avec mes compatriotes et à me regarder comme un homme qui aime le vin et le desordre.
Oct. 15me.]—J'ai passé l'après midi chez Madame de Mesery. Elle vouloit me faire rencontrer avec une Demoiselle Françoise qu'elle a prié à souper ; cette Demoiselle, qui s'apelle Le Franc, a six pieds de haut. Sa taille, sa figure, son ton, sa conversation, tout annonce le grenadier le plus déterminé, mais un grenadier, que a de l'esprit, des connoissances, et l'usage du monde. Aussi son sexe, son nom, son etat, tout est mystere. Elle se dit Parisienne, fille de condition, qui s'est retirée dans ce pays pour cause de religion. Ne seroit ce pas plûtot pour une affaire d'honneur ?
Lausanne, Dec. 16me, 1763.]—Je me suis levé tard, et une visite fort amicale de M. de Chandieu Villars,* m'a enlevé ce qui me restoit de la matinée. M. de Chandieu a servi en France avec distinction et s'est retiré avec le grade de maréchal de camp. C'est un homme

* The father of Madame de Severy, whose family were Mr. Gibbon's most intimate friends, after he had settled at Lausanne in the year 1783. S.

If my studies at Paris had been confined to the study of the world, three or four months would not have been unprofitably spent. My visits, however superficial, to the Academy of Medals and the public libraries, opened a new field of inquiry; and the view of so many manuscripts of different ages and characters induced me to consult the two great

d'une grande politesse, d'un esprit vif et facile; il feroit aujourdhui à soixante ans, l'agrément d'une société de jeunes filles. C'est presque le seul étranger qui ait pu acquérir l'aisance des maniéres Françoises, sans en prendre en même tems les airs bruyans et étourdis.

Lausanne, Dec. 18me, 1763.]—C'étoit un Dimanche de communion. Les cérémonies religieuses sont bein entendues dans ce pays. Elles sont rares, et par là même plus respectées; les Viellards se plaignent à la vérité du refroidissement de la dévotion; cependant un jour, comme celui-ci, offre encore un spectacle très édifiant. Point d'affaires, point d'assemblée; on s'interdit jusqu'au *whist* si nécessaire a l'existence d'un Lausannois.

Déc. 31me.]—Jettons un coup d'œil sur cette année 1763. Voyons comment j'ai employé cette portion de mon existence qui s'est écoulée et qui ne reviendra plus. Le mois de Janvier s'est passé dans le sein de ma famille à qui il falloit sacrifier tous mes momens, parcequ'ils étoient les derniers dans les soins d'un départ et dans l'embarras d'un voyage. Dans ce voyage cependant je trouvai moyen de lire les lettres de *Busbequius*, Ministre Imperial à la Porte. Elles sont aussi intéressantes qu'instructives. Je restai à Paris depuis le 28 JANVIER jusqu'au 9 MAI. Pendant tout ce tems je n'étudiai point. Les amusemens m'occupoient beaucoup, et l'habitude de la dissipation, qu'on prend si facilement dans les grandes villes, ne me permettoient pas de mettre à profit le tems qui me demeuroit. A la verité, si j'ai peu feuilleté les livres, l'observation de tous les objets curieux qui se presentent dans une grande capitale, et la conversation avec les plus grands hommes du siécle, m'ont instruit de beaucoup de choses que je n'aurois point trouvé dans les livres. Les sept ou huit derniers mois de cette année ont été plus tranquilles. Dès que je me suis vu etabli à Lausanne, j'ai entrepris une étude suivie sur la géographie ancienne de l'Italie. Mon ardeur s'est très bien soutenue pendant six semaines jusqu'à la fin du mois de Juin. Ce fut alors qu'un voyage de Geneve interrompit un peu mon assiduité, que le sejour de Mesery m'offrit mille distractions, et que la société de Saussure acheva de me faire perdre mon tems. Je repris mon travail avec ce Journal au milieu d'*Aout*, et depuis ce tems, jusqu'au commencement de *Novembre*, j'ai mis a profit tous mes instans; j'avoue que pendant les deux derniers mois mon ardeur s'est un peu rallantie. Irement, Dans cette étude suivie j'ai lu: 1, Près de deux livres de la géographie de *Strabon* sur l'Italie deux fois. 2. Une partie du deuxiéme livre de l'histoire naturelle de *Pline.* 3. Le quatriéme chapitre du deuxiéme livre de *Pomponius Mela.* 4. Les Itineraires d'Antonin, et de Jerusalem pour ce qui regarde l'Italie. Je les ai lus avec les Commentaires de Wesseling, &c. J'en ai tiré des tables de toutes les grandes routes de l'Italie, reduisant partout les milles Romains, en milles Anglois, et en lieues de France, selon les calculs de M. d'Anville. 5. L'Histoire des Grands Chemins de l'Empire Romain, par M. Bergier, deux volumes in 4to. 5. Quelques Extraits choisis de Ciceron, Tite Live, Velleius Paterculus, Tacite, et les deux Plines. La *Roma Vetus* de Nardini et plusieurs autres opuscules sur le même sujet qui composent presque tout le quatriéme tome du Tresor des Antiquités Romaines de Grævius. 7. L'*Italia Antiqua* de Cluvier, en deux volumes in folio. 8. L'*Iter* ou le Voyage de Cl. Rutillius Numatianus dans les Gaules. 9. Les Catalogues de Virgile. 10. Celui de Silius Italicus. 11. Le Voyage d'Horace a Brundusium. N.B. J'ai lu deux fois ces trois derniers morceaux. 12. Le Traité sur les Mesures Itineraires par M. d'Anville, et quelques Memoires de l'Academie des Belles Lettres. IIment, On me fit attendre Nardini de la Bibliotheque de Geneve. Je voulus remplir ce moment de vuide par la lecture de *Juvenal,* poëte qui je ne connoissois encore que de réputation. Je le lu deux fois avec plaisir et avec soin. IIIment, Pendant l'année j'ai lu quelques journaux, entre autres le Journal Etranger depuis son commencement, un tome des Nouvelles de Bayle, et les xxxv premiers volumes de la Bibliotheque raisonnée. IVment, J'ai beaucoup ecrit de mon Recueil Géographique de l'Italie qui est deja bien bein ample et assez curieux. Vment, Je ne dois point oublier ce journal même qui est devenu un ouvrage; 214 pages en quatre mois et demi et des pages des mieux fournies font un objet considerable. Aussi sans compter un grand nombre d'observations détachées, il s'y trouve des dissertations savantes et raisonées. Celle du passage d'Annibal contient dix pages, et celle sur le guerre sociale en a douze. Mais ces morceaux sont trop etendus, et le journal même a besoin d'une reforme qui lui retranche quantité de pieces qui sont assez étrangeres à son veritable plan. Après avoir un peu reflechi là dessus, voici quelques regles que je me suis faites sur les objets qui lui conviennent. Iment, Toute ma vie civile et privée, amusemens, mes liaisons, mes ecarts même, et toutes mes réfléxions qui ne roulent que sur des sujets qui me sont personels, je conviens que tout cela n'est interessant que pour moi, mais aussi ce n'est que pour moi que j'ecris mon journal. IIment, Tout ce que j'apprens par l'observation ou la conversation. A l'egard de celle-ci je ne rapporterai ce que que je tiens de personnes tout à la fois instruites et véridiques, lorsqu'il est question de faits, ou du petit nombre de ceux qui meritent le titre de grand homme, s'il s'agit de sentimens et d'opinions. IIIment, J'y mettrai soigneusement tout ce qu'on peut

Benedictine works, the *Diplomatica* of Mabillon, and the *Palæographia* of Montfaucon. I studied the theory without attaining the practice of the art : nor should I complain of the intricacy of Greek abbreviations and Gothic alphabets, since every day, in a familiar language, I am at a loss to decipher the hieroglyphics of a female note. In a tranquil scene, which revived the memory of my first studies, idleness would have been less pardonable : the public libraries of Lausanne and Geneva liberally supplied me with books ; and if many hours were lost in dissipation, many more were employed in literary labour. In the country, Horace and Virgil, Juvenal and Ovid, were my assiduous companions : but, in town, I formed and executed a plan of study for the use of my Transalpine expedition : the topography of old Rome, the ancient geography of Italy, and the science of medals. 1. I diligently read, almost always with my pen in my hand, the elaborate treatises of Nardini, Donatus, &c., which fill the fourth volume of the Roman Antiquities of Grævius. 2. I next undertook and finished the *Italia Antiqua* of Cluverius, a learned native of Prussia, who had measured, on foot, every spot, and has compiled and digested every passage of

appeller la partie materielle de mes études ; combein d'heures j'ai travaillé, combien de pages j'ai ecrit ou lu, avec une courte notice du sujet qu'elles contenoient. IVment, Je serois faché de lire sans réfléchir sur mes lectures, sans porter des jugemens raisonnés sur mes auteurs, et sans éplucher avec soin leurs idées et leurs expressions. Mais toute lecture ne fournit pas egalement. Il y a des livres qu'on parcourt, et il y en a qu'on lit ; il y en a eofin qu'on doit étudier. Mes observations sur ceux de la premiere classe ne peuvent qu'etre courtes et detachées. Elles conviennent au journal. Celles qui regardent la seconde classe n'y entreront qu'autant qu'elles auront le même caractère Vment, Mes réfléxions sur ce petit nombre d'auteurs classiques, qu'on medite avec soin, seront naturellement plus approfondies et plus suivies. C'est pour elles, er pour des pieces plus etendues et plus originales, aux quelles la lecture ou la meditation peut donner lieu, que je ferai .n recueil séparé. Je conserverai cependant sa liaison avec le journal par des renvois constans qui marqueront le numero de chaque piece avec le tems et l'occasion de sa composition. Moyennant ces précautions mon journal ne peut que m'être utile. Ce compte exact de mon tems m'en fera mieux sentir le prix ; il dissipera par son detail, l'illusion qu'on se fait d'envisager seulement les années et les mois et de mepriser les heures et les jours. Je ne dis rien de l'agrément. C'en est un bien grand cependant de pouvoir repasser chaque epoque de sa vie, et de se placer, dès qu'on le veut, au milieu de toutes les petites scenes qu'on a joué, ou qu'on a vu jouer.

6 Avril 1764.]—J'ai été eveillé par Pavilliard et H * * * * pour arrêter une facheuse affaire qui s'etoit passée au bal après notre départ. G * * * * qui faisoit sa cour a Mademoiselle * * * * * depuis long tems, voyoit avec peine que * * * * * * (* * * * *) menacoit de le supplanter. Il ne répondoit jamais aux politesses de son rival, que par des brusqueries ; et a la fin a l'occasion de la main de Mademoiselle * * * * * * il s'emporta contre lui le plus mal a propos du monde, et le traita devant tout le monde *d'impertinent*, &c. J'ai appris de Pavilliard que * * * * * * lui avoit envoyé un cartel ; et que la reponse de G * * * * ne l'ayant point contenté ils devoient se rencontrer à cinq heures du soir. Au désespoir de voir mon ami engagé dans une affaire qui ne pouvoit que lui faire du tort, j'ai couru chez M. de Crousaz où demeuroit * * * * * *. J'ai bientot vu qu'il ne lui falloit qu'une explication assez légere, jointe a quelque apologie de la part de G * * * * pour le désarmer, et je suis retourné chez lui avec H * * * * pour l'engager a la donner. Nous lui avons fait comprendre que l'aveu d'une veritable tort ne blessoit jamais l'honneur, et que son insulte envers les dames aussi bien qu'envers * * * * * étoit sans excuse. Je lui ai dicté un billet convenable, mais sans la moindre bassesse, que j'ai porté au Hollandois. Il a rendu les armes sur le champ, lui a fait la réponse la plus polie, et m'a remercié mille fois du rôle que j'avois fait. En vérité cet homme n'est pas difficile. Après diner j'ai vu nos dames à qui j'ai porté une lettre d'excuses. La mere n'en veut plus a G * * * *, mais Mademoiselle * * * * * * est desolée du tort que cette affaire peut lui faire dans le monde. Cette négociation m'a pris le jour entier ; mais peut on mieux employer un jour qu'à sauver la vie, peutêtre a deux personnes, et a conserver la réputation d'un ami ? Au reste j'ai vu au fond plus d'un caractére. G * * * * est brave, vrai, et sensé, mais d'une impétuosité qui n'est que plus dangereuse pour être supprimée a l'ordinaire. C * * * * est d'une étourderie d'enfant. De S * * * * d'une indifference qui vient bien plus d'un défaut de sensibilité, que d'un excès de raison. J'ai conçu une véritable amitié pour H * * * *. Il a beaucoup de raison et des sentimens d'honneur avec un cœur des mieux placé.

the ancient writers. These passages in Greek or Latin authors I perused in the text of Cluverius, in two folio volumes : but I separately read the descriptions of Italy by Strabo, Pliny, and Pomponius Mela, the Catalogues of the Epic poets, the Itineraries of Wesseling's Antoninus, and the coasting Voyage of Rutilius Numatianus ; and I studied two kindred subjects in the Measures Itineraires of d'Anville, and the copious work of Bergier, *Histoire des grands Chemins de l'Empire Romain.* From these materials I formed a table of roads and distances reduced to our English measure ; filled a folio common-place book with my collections and remarks on the geography of Italy ; and inserted in my journal many long and learned notes on the insulæ and populousness of Rome, the social war, the passage of the Alps by Hannibal, &c. 3. After glancing my eye over Addison's agreeable dialogues, I more seriously read the great work of Ezechiel Spanheim *de Præstantiâ et Usù Numismatum,* and applied with him the medals of the kings and emperors, the families and colonies, to the illustration of ancient history. And thus was I armed for my Italian journey.*

I shall advance with rapid brevity in the narrative of this tour, in which somewhat more than a year (April 1764—May 1765) was agreeably employed. Content with tracing my line of march, and slightly touching on my personal feelings, I shall waive the minute investigation of the scenes which have been viewed by thousands, and described by hundreds, of our modern travellers. ROME is the great object of our pilgrimage : and 1st, the journey ; 2d, the residence ; and 3d, the return ; will form the most proper and perspicuous division. 1. I climbed Mount Cenis, and descended into the plain of Piedmont, not on the back of an elephant, but on a light osier seat, in the hands of the dextrous and intrepid chairmen of the Alps. The architecture and government of Turin presented the same aspect of tame and tiresome uniformity :

* JOURNAL, Lausanne, Avril 17, 1764.]—Guise et moi, nous avons donné un diner excellent et beaucoup de vin à Dupleix, et à beaucoup d'autres. Après diner nous sommes échappés pour faire quelques visites aux * * *, aux * * *, et aux * * *. Je pars avec quelques regrets : cependant un peu de vin, et une gayeté dont je ne pouvois rendre raison, m'ont rendu d'une étourderie sans pareille, vis-a-vis de ces petites. Je leur ai dit cent folies, et nous nous sommes embrassés en riant. Mesery nous a donné un très beau souper avec une partie de la compagnie du matin, augmentée de Bourgeois et de Pavilliard. Ce souper, les adieux sur tout à Pavilliard, que j'aime véritablement, et les préparatifs du départ, m'ont occupé jusqu'a deux heures du matin.

Je quitte Lausanne avec moins de regret que la première fois. Je n'y laisse plus que des connoissances. C'etoit la maitresse et l'ami dont je pleurois la perte. D'ailleurs je voyois Lausanne avec les yeux encore novices d'un jeune homme, qui lui devoit la partie raisonable de son existence, et qui jugeoit sans objets de comparaison. Aujourdhui j'y vois une ville mal batie, au milien d'un pays delicieux, qui jouit de la paix et du repos, et qui les prend pour la liberté. Un peuple nombreux et bien élevé, qui aime la société, qui y est propre, et qui admet avec plaisir les étrangers dans ses cotteries, qui seroient bien plus agréables, si la conversation n'avoit pas cédé la place au jeu. Les femmes sont jolies, et malgré leur grande liberté, elles sont très sages. Tout au plus peuvent elles être un peu complaisantes, dans l'idée honnête, mais incertaine, de prendre un étranger dans leurs filets. L'affectation est le péché originel des Lausannois. Affectation de depense, affectation de noblesse, affectation d'esprit : les deux premiéres sont fort repandues, pendant que la troisiéme est fort rare. Comme ce vice se choque a tout instant avec celui des autres, Lausanne se trouve partagée dans un grand nombre d'etats, dont les principes et le langage varient a l'infini, et qui n'ont de commun que leur mepris reciproque les uns pour les autres. Leur gout pour la depense s'accorde mal avec celui de la noblesse. Ils périroient plutot que de renoncer a leurs grandeurs, ou d'embrasser la seule profession qui puisse les y soutenir. La maison de M. de Mesery est charmante : le caractére franc et genereux du Mari, les agrémens de la femme, une situation délicieuse, une chere excellente, la compagnie de ses compatriotes, et une liberté parfaite, font aimer ce séjour a tout Anglois. Que je voudrois en trouver un semblable a Londres ! J'y regrette encore Holroyd, mais il nous suit de près.

but the court was regulated with decent and splendid œconomy; and I was introduced to his Sardinian majesty Charles Emanuel, who, after the incomparable Frederic, held the second rank (proximus longo tamen intervallo) among the kings of Europe. The size and populousness of Milan could not surprise an inhabitant of London: but the fancy is amused by a visit to the Boromean Islands, an enchanted palace, a work of the fairies in the midst of a lake encompassed with mountains, and far removed from the haunts of men. I was less amused by the marble palaces of Genoa, than by the recent memorials of her deliverance (in December 1746) from the Austrian tyranny; and I took a military survey of every scene of action within the inclosure of her double walls. My steps were detained at Parma and Modena, by the precious relics of the Farnese and Este collections: but, alas! the far greater part had been already transported, by inheritance or purchase, to Naples and Dresden. By the road of Bologna and the Apennine I at last reached Florence, where I reposed from June to September, during the heat of the summer months. In the Gallery, and especially in the Tribune, I first acknowledged, at the feet of the Venus of Medicis, that the chisel may dispute the pre-eminence with the pencil, a truth in the fine arts which cannot on this side of the Alps be felt or understood. At home I had taken some lessons of Italian: on the spot I read, with a learned native, the classics of the Tuscan idiom: but the shortness of my time, and the use of the French language, prevented my acquiring any facility of speaking; and I was a silent spectator in the conversations of our envoy, Sir Horace Mann, whose most serious business was that of entertaining the English at his hospitable table.* After leaving Florence, I compared the solitude of Pisa with the industry of Lucca and Leghorn, and continued my journey through Sienna to Rome, where I arrived in the beginning of October. 2. My temper is not very susceptible of enthusiasm; and the enthusiasm which I do not feel, I have ever scorned to affect. But, at the distance of twenty-five years, I can neither forget nor express the strong emotions which agitated my mind as I first approached and entered the *eternal city*. After a sleepless night, I trod, with a lofty step, the ruins of the Forum; each memorable spot where Romulus *stood*, or Tully spoke, or Cæsar fell, was at once present to my eye; and several days of intoxication were lost or enjoyed before I could descend to a cool and minute investigation. My guide was Mr. Byers, a Scotch antiquary of experience and taste; but, in the daily labour of eighteen weeks, the powers of attention were sometimes fatigued, till I was myself qualified, in a last review, to select and study the capital works of ancient and modern art. Six weeks were borrowed for my tour of Naples, the most populous of cities, relative to its size, whose luxurious inhabitants seem to dwell on the confines of paradise and hell-fire. I was presented to the boy-

---

* JOURNAL, Florence, Aout 9me, 1764.]—Cocchi a diné avec nous. Nous avons beaucoup causé, mais je ne lui trouve pas le genre qu'on lui attribue, c'est peutetre, parceque les notres ne sont pas analogues. J'entrevois de l'extravagance dans ses idées, de l'affectation dans ses maniéres. Il se plaint a tout moment de sa pauvreté. Il connoit peu la veritable dignité d'un homme de lettres. S'il a beaucoup de science, elle est bornée a la physique. Il m'a demandé si Lord Spenser ne pouvoit pas faire des évêques, et m'a fait un conte de Lord Lyttelton (dont il le ne peut souffrir le fils) ou il étoit question des Parlemens de Campagne.

king by our new envoy, Sir William Hamilton ; who, wisely diverting his correspondence from the Secretary of State to the Royal Society and British Museum, has elucidated a country of such inestimable value to the naturalist and antiquarian. On my return, I fondly embraced, for the last time, the miracles of Rome ; but I departed without kissing the feet of Rezzonico (Clement XIII.), who neither possessed the wit of his predecessor Lambertini, nor the virtues of his successor Ganganelli. 3. In my pilgrimage from Rome to Loretto I again crossed the Apennine ; from the coast of the Adriatic I traversed a fruitful and populous country, which could alone disprove the paradox of Montesquieu, that modern Italy is a desert. Without adopting the exclusive prejudice of the natives, I sincerely admire the paintings of the Bologna school. I hastened to escape from the sad solitude of Ferrara, which in the age of Cæsar was still more desolate. The spectacle of Venice afforded some hours of astonishment ; the university of Padua is a dying taper : but Verona still boasts her amphitheatre, and his native Vicenza is adorned by the classic architecture of Palladio : the road of Lombardy and Piedmont (did Montesquieu find them without inhabitants ?) led me back to Milan, Turin, and the passage of Mount Cenis, where I again crossed the Alps in my way to Lyons.

The use of foreign travel has been often debated as a general question ; but the conclusion must be finally applied to the character and circumstances of each individual. With the education of boys, *where* or *how* they may pass over some juvenile years with the least mischief to themselves or others, I have no concern. But after supposing the previous and indispensable requisites of age, judgment, a competent knowledge of men and books, and a freedom from domestic prejudices, I will briefly describe the qualifications which I deem most essential to a traveller. He should be endowed with an active, indefatigable vigour of mind and body, which can seize every mode of conveyance, and support, with a careless smile, every hardship of the road, the weather, or the inn. The benefits of foreign travel will correspond with the degrees of these qualifications ; but, in this sketch, those to whom I am known will not accuse me of framing my own panegyric. It was at Rome, on the 15th of October 1764, as I sat musing amidst the ruins of the Capitol, while the bare-footed fryars were singing vespers in the temple of Jupiter,* that the idea of writing the decline and fall of the city first started to my mind. But my original plan was circumscribed to the decay of the city rather than of the empire : and though my reading and reflections began to point towards that object, some years elapsed, and several avocations intervened, before I was seriously engaged in the execution of that laborious work.

I had not totally renounced the southern provinces of France, but the letters which I found at Lyons were expressive of some impatience. Rome and Italy had satiated my curious appetite, and I was now ready to return to the peaceful retreat of my family and books. After a happy fortnight I reluctantly left Paris, embarked at Calais, again landed at Dover, after an interval of two years and five months, and hastily drove through the summer dust and solitude of London. On June 25 1765 I arrived at my father's house : and the five years and a half between

* Now the Church of the Zoccolants, or Franciscan Friars. S.

my travels and my father's death (1770) are the portion of my life which I passed with the least enjoyment, and which I remember with the least satisfaction. Every spring I attended the monthly meeting and exercise of the militia at Southampton; and by the resignation of my father, and the death of Sir Thomas Worsley, I was successively promoted to the rank of major and lieutenant-colonel commandant; but I was each year more disgusted with the inn, the wine, the company, and the tiresome repetition of annual attendance and daily exercise. At home, the œconomy of the family and farm still maintained the same creditable appearance. My connection with Mrs. Gibbon was mellowed into a warm and solid attachment : my growing years abolished the distance that might yet remain between a parent and a son, and my behaviour satisfied my father, who was proud of the success, however imperfect in his own life-time, of my literary talents. Our solitude was soon and often enlivened by the visit of the friend of my youth, Mr. Deyverdun, whose absence from Lausanne I had sincerely lamented. About three years after my first departure, he had emigrated from his native lake to the banks of the Oder in Germany. The *res angusta domi*, the waste of a decent patrimony, by an improvident father, obliged him, like many of his countrymen, to confide in his own industry ; and he was entrusted with the education of a young prince, the grandson of the Margrave of Schavedt, of the Royal Family of Prussia. Our friendship was never cooled, our correspondence was sometimes interrupted ; but I rather wished than hoped to obtain Mr. Deyverdun for the companion of my Italian tour. An unhappy, though honourable passion, drove him from his German court ; and the attractions of hope and curiosity were fortified by the expectation of my speedy return to England. During four successive summers he passed several weeks or months at Beriton, and our free conversations, on every topic that could interest the heart or understanding, would have reconciled me to a desert or a prison. In the winter months of London my sphere of knowledge and action was somewhat enlarged, by the many new acquaintance which I had contracted in the militia and abroad ; and 1 must regret, as more than an acquaintance, Mr. Godfrey Clarke of Derbyshire, an amiable and worthy young man, who was snatched away by an untimely death. A weekly convivial meeting was established by myself and travellers, under the name of the Roman Club*.

The renewal, or perhaps the improvement, of my English life was embittered by the alteration of my own feelings. At the age of twenty-one 1 was, in my proper station of a youth, delivered from the yoke of education, and delighted with the comparative state of liberty and affluence. My filial obedience was natural and easy ; and in the gay prospect of futurity, my ambition did not extend beyond the enjoyment of my books, my leisure, and my patrimonial estate, undisturbed by the cares of a family and the duties of a profession. But in the militia I was armed with power ; in my travels, I was exempt from

----

* The members were Lord Mountstuart (now Earl of Bute), Col. Edmonstone, Weddal, Palgrave, Lord Berkley, Godfrey Clarke, Holroyd (Lord Sheffield), Major Ridley, Sir William Guize, Sir John Aubrey, Lord Abingdon, Hon. Peregrine Bertie, Cleaver, Hon. John Damer, Hon. George Damer (Lord Milton), Sir Thomas Goscoygne, Sir John Hort, E. Gibbon.

controul; and as I approached, as I gradually passed my thirtieth year, I began to feel the desire of being master in my own house. The most gentle authority will sometimes frown without reason, the most cheerful submission will sometimes murmur without cause; and such is the law of our imperfect nature, that we must either command or obey; that our personal liberty is supported by the obsequiousness of our own dependants. While so many of my acquaintance were married or in parliament, or advancing with a rapid step in the various roads of honour and fortune, I stood alone, immoveable and insignificant; for after the monthly meeting of 1770, I had even withdrawn myself from the militia, by the resignation of an empty and barren commission. My temper is not susceptible of envy, and the view of successful merit has always excited my warmest applause. The miseries of a vacant life were never known to a man whose hours were insufficient for the inexhaustible pleasures of study. But I lamented that at the proper age I had not embraced the lucrative pursuits of the law or of trade, the chances of civil office or India adventure, of even the fat slumbers of the church; and my repentance became more lively as the loss of time was more irretrievable. Experience shewed me the use of grafting my private consequence on the importance of a great professional body; the benefits of those firm connections which are cemented by hope and interest, by gratitude and emulation, by the mutual exchange of services and favours. From the emoluments of a profession I might have derived an ample fortune, or a competent income, instead of being stinted to the same narrow allowance, to be increased only by an event which I sincerely deprecated. The progress and the knowledge of our domestic disorders aggravated my anxiety, and I began to apprehend that I might be left in my old age without the fruits either of industry or inheritance.

In the first summer after my return, whilst I enjoyed at Beriton the society of my friend Deyverdun, our daily conversations expatiated over the field of ancient and modern literature; and we freely discussed my studies, my first Essay, and my future projects. The Decline and Fall of Rome I still contemplated at an awful distance: but the two historical designs which had balanced my choice were submitted to his taste: and in the parallel between the Revolutions of Florence and Switzerland, our common partiality for a country which was *his* by birth, and *mine* by adoption, inclined the scale in favour of the latter. According to the plan, which was soon conceived and digested, I embraced a period of two hundred years, from the association of the three peasants of the Alps to the plenitude and prosperity of the Helvetic body in the sixteenth century. I should have described the deliverance and victory of the Swiss, who have never shed the blood of their tyrants but in a field of battle; the laws and manners of the confederate states; the splendid trophies of the Austrian, Burgundian, and Italian wars; and the wisdom of a nation, which, after some sallies of martial adventure, has been content to guard the blessings of peace with the sword of freedom.

—— Manus hæc inimica tyrannis
Ense petit placidam sub libertate quietem.

My judgment, as well as my enthusiasm, was satisfied with the gorious] theme ; and the assistance of Deyverdun seemed to remove an insu- perable obstacle. The French or Latin memorials, of which I was not ignorant, are inconsiderable in number and weight ; but in the perfect acquaintance of my friend with the German language, I found the key of a more valuable collection. The most necessary books were pro- cured ; he translated, for my use, the folio volume of Schilling, a copious and contemporary relation of the war of Burgundy; we read and marked the most interesting parts of the great chronicle of Tschudi ; and by his labour, or that of an inferior assistant, large extracts were made from the History of Lauffer and the Dictionary of Lew : yet such was the distance and delay, that two years elapsed in these preparatory steps ; and it was late in the third summer (1767) before I entered, with these slender materials, on the more agreeable task of composi- tion. A specimen of my History, the first book, was read the following winter in a literary society of foreigners in London ; and as the author was unknown, I listened, without observation, to the free strictures, and unfavourable sentence, of my judges.* The momentary sensation was painful ; but their condemnation was ratified by my cooler thoughts. I delivered my imperfect sheets to the flames,† and for ever renounced a design in which some expence, much labour, and more time had been so vainly consumed. I cannot regret the loss of a slight and superficial essay, for such the work must have been in the hands of a stranger, uninformed by the scholars and statesmen, and remote from the libraries and archives of the Swiss republics. My ancient habits, and the presence of Deyverdun, encouraged me to write in French for the continent of Europe ; but I was conscious myself that my style, above prose and below poetry, degenerated into a verbose and turgid declamation. Perhaps I may impute the failure to the injudicious choice of a foreign language. Perhaps I may suspect

* Mr. Hume seems to have had a different opinion of this work.

From Mr. HUME *to* Mr. GIBBON.

SIR,

It is but a few days since M. Deyverdun put your manuscript into my hands, and I have perused it with great pleasure and satisfaction. I have only one objection, derived from the language in which it is written. Why do you compose in French, and carry faggots into the wood, as Horace says with regard to the Romans who wrote in Greek ? I grant that you have a like motive to those Romans, and I adopt a language much more generally diffused than your native tongue : but have you not remarked the fate of those two ancient languages in following ages ? The Latin, though then less celebrated, and confined to more narrow limits, has in some measure outlived the Greek, and is now more generally understood by men of letters. Let the French, therefore, triumph in the present diffusion of their tongue. Our solid and increasing establishments in America, where we need less dread the inundation of Barbarians, promise a superior stability and duration to the English language.

Your use of the French tongue has also led you into a style more poetical and figurative, and more highly coloured, than our language seems to admit of in historical productions ; for such is the practice of French writers, particularly the more recent ones, who illuminate their pic- tures more than custom will permit us. On the whole, your History, in my opinion, is written with spirit and judgment; and I exhort you very earnestly to continue it. The objections that occurred to me on reading it, were so frivolous, that I shall not trouble you with them, and should, I believe, have a difficulty to recollect them. I am, with great esteem,

SIR, &c.

DAVID HUME.

LONDON,
24th of Oct. 1767.

† He neglected to burn them. He left at Sheffield-Place the introduction, or first book, in forty-three pages folio, written in a very small hand, besides a considerable number of notes. If Mr. Gibbon had not declared his judgment, perhaps Mr. Hume's opinion, expressed in the letter in the last note, might have justified the publication of it. S.

that the language itself is ill adapted to sustain the vigour and dignity of an important narrative. But if France, so rich in literary merit, had produced a great original historian, his genius would have formed and fixed the idiom to the proper tone, the peculiar model of historical eloquence.

It was in search of some liberal and lucrative employment that my friend Deyverdun had visited England. His remittances from home were scanty and precarious. My purse was always open, but it was often empty; and I bitterly felt the want of riches and power, which might have enabled me to correct the errors of his fortune. His wishes and qualifications solicited the station of the travelling governor of some wealthy pupil; but every vacancy provoked so many eager candidates, that for a long time I struggled without success; nor was it till after much application that I could even place him as a clerk in the office of the secretary of state. In a residence of several years he never acquired the just pronunciation and familiar use of the English tongue, but he read our most difficult authors with ease and taste : his, critical knowledge of our language and poetry was such as few foreigners have possessed; and few of our countrymen could enjoy the theatre of Shakspeare and Garrick with more exquisite feeling and discernment. The consciousness of his own strength, and the assurance of my aid, emboldened him to imitate the example of Dr. Maty, whose *Journal Britannique* was esteemed and regretted; and to improve his model, by uniting with the transactions of literature a philosophic view of the arts and manners of the British nation. Our Journal for the year 1767, under the title of *Memoires Literaires de la Grand Bretagne*, was soon finished, and sent to the press. For the first article, Lord Lyttelton's History of Henry II. I must own myself responsible; but the public has ratified my judgment of that voluminous work, in which sense and learning are not illuminated by a ray of genius. The next specimen was the choice of my friend, *the Bath Guide*, a light and whimsical performance, of local, and even verbal, pleasantry. I started at the attempt : he smiled at my fears : his courage was justified by success; and a master of both languages will applaud the curious felicity with which he has transfused into French prose the spirit, and even the humour, of the English verse. It is not my wish to deny how deeply I was interested in these Memoirs, of which I need not surely be ashamed; but at the distance of more than twenty years, it would be impossible for me to ascertain the respective shares of the two associates. A long and intimate communication of ideas had cast our sentiments and style in the same mould. In our social labours we composed and corrected by turns; and the praise which I might honestly bestow, would fall perhaps on some article or passage most properly my own. A second volume (for the year 1768) was published of these Memoirs. I will presume to say, that their merit was superior to their reputation; but it is not less true, that they were productive of more reputation than emolument. They introduced my friend to the protection, and myself to the acquaintance, of the Earl of Chesterfield, whose age and infirmities secluded him from the world; and of Mr. David Hume, who was under-secretary to the office in which Deyverdun was more humbly employed. The former accepted a dedication,

(April 12, 1769,) and reserved the author for the future education of his successor : the latter enriched the Journal with a reply to Mr. Walpole's Historical Doubts, which he afterwards shaped into the form of a note. The materials of the third volume were almost completed, when I recommended Deyverdun as governor to Sir Richard Worsley, a youth, the son of my old Lieutenant-colonel, who was lately deceased. They set forwards on their travels ; nor did they return to England till some time after my father's death.

My next publication was an accidental sally of love and resentment; of my reverence for modest genius, and my aversion for insolent pedantry. The sixth book of the Æneid is the most pleasing and perfect composition of Latin poetry. The descent of Æneas and the Sibyl to the infernal regions, to the world of spirits, expands an awful and boundless prospect, from the nocturnal gloom of the Cumæan grot,

> Ibant obscuri solâ sub nocte per umbram,

to the meridian brightness of the Elysian fields ;

> Largior hic campos æther et lumine vestit
> Purpureo———

from the dreams of simple Nature, to the dreams, alas ! of Egyptian theology, and the philosophy of the Greeks. But the final dismission of the hero through the ivory gate, whence

> Falsa ad cœlum mittunt insomnia manes,

seems to dissolve the whole enchantment, and leaves the reader in a state of cold and anxious scepticism. This most lame and impotent conclusion has been variously imputed to the taste or irreligion of Virgil ; but, according to the more elaborate interpretation of Bishop Warburton, the descent to hell is not a false, but a mimic scene; which represents the initiation of Æneas, in the character of a lawgiver, to the Eleusinian mysteries. This hypothsis, a singular chapter in the Divine Legation of Moses, had been admitted by many as true; it was praised by all as ingenious ; nor had it been exposed, in a space of thirty years, to a fair and critical discussion. The learning and the abilities of the author had raised him to a just eminence ; but he reigned the dictator and tyrant of the world of literature. The real merit of Warburton was degraded by the pride and presumption with which he pronounced his infallible decrees ; in his polemic writings he lashed his antagonists without mercy or moderation ; and his servile flatterers, (see the base and malignant Essay on the *Delicacy of Friendship,*) exalting the master critic far above Aristotle and Longinus, assaulted every modest dissenter who refused to consult the oracle, and to adore the idol. In a land of liberty, such despotism must provoke a general opposition, and the zeal of opposition is seldom candid or impartial. A late professor of Oxford, (Dr. Lowth,) in a pointed and polished epistle, (Aug. 31, 1765,) defended himself, and attacked the Bishop ; and, whatsoever might be the merits of an insignificant controversy, his victory was clearly established by the silent confusion of

Warburton and his slaves. *I* too, without any private offence, was ambitious of breaking a lance against the giant's shield ; and in the beginning of the year 1770, my Critical Observations on the Sixth Book of the Æneid were sent, without my name, to the press. In this short Essay, my first English publication, 1 aimed my strokes against the person and the hypothesis of Bishop Warburton. I proved, at least to my own satisfaction, *that* the ancient lawgivers did not invent the mysteries, and *that* Æneas was never invested with the office of lawgiver : *that* there is not any argument, any circumstance, which can melt a fable into allegory, or remove the scene from the Lake Avernus to the Temple of Ceres: *that* such a wild supposition is equally injurious to the poet and the man : *that* if Virgil was not initiated he could not, if he were, he would not, reveal the secrets of the initiation : *that* the anathema of Horace (*vetabo qui Cereris sacrum vulgarit, &c.*) at once attests his own ignorance and the innocence of his friend. As the Bishop of Gloucester and his party maintained a discreet silence, my critical disquisition was soon lost among the pamphlets of the day ; but the public coldness was overbalanced to my feelings by the weighty approbation of the last and best editor of Virgil, Professor Heyne of Gottingen, who acquiesces in my confutation, and styles the unknown author, *doctus -   et elegantissimus Britannus.* But I cannot resist the temptation of transcribing the favourable judgment of Mr. Hayley, himself a poet and a scholar : "An intricate hypothesis, twisted into a long and laboured chain of quotation and argument, the Dissertation on the Sixth Book of Virgil, remained some time unrefuted. - - - At length, a superior, but anonymous, critic arose, who, in one of the most judicious and spirited essays that our nation has produced, on a point of classical literature, completely overturned this ill-founded edifice, and exposed the arrogance and futility of its assuming architect." He even condescends to justify an acrimony of style, which had been gently blamed by the more unbiassed German ; "*Paullo acrius quam velis   · perstrinxit.*"* But I cannot forgive myself the contemptuous treatment of a man who, with all his faults, was entitled to my esteem ;† and I can less forgive, in a personal attack, the cowardly concealment of my name and character.

In the fifteen years between my Essay on the Study of Literature and the first volume of the Decline and Fall, (1761—1776,) this criticism on Warburton, and some articles in the Journal, were my sole publications. It is more especially incumbent on me to mark the employment, or to confess the waste of time, from my travels to my father's death, an interval in which I was not diverted by any professional duties from the labours and pleasures of a studious life. 1. As soon as I was released from the fruitless task of the Swiss revolutions, (1768,) I began

---

* The editor of the Warburtonian tracks, Dr. Parr, (p. 192,) considers the allegorical interpretation "as completely refuted in a most clear, elegant, and decisive work of criticism ; which could not, indeed, derive authority from the greatest name ; but to which the greatest name might with propriety have been affixed."

† The Divine Legation of Moses is a monument, already crumbling in the dust, of the rigour and weakness of the human mind. If Warburton's new argument proved anything, it would be a demonstration against the legislator, who left his people without the knowledge of a future state. But some episodes of the work, on the Greek philosophy, the hieroglyphics of Egypt, &c. are entitled to the praise of learning, imagination, and discernment.

gradually to advance from the wish to the hope, from the hope to the design, from the design to the execution, of my historical work, of whose limits and extent I had yet a very inadequate notion. The Classics, as low as Tacitus, the younger Pliny, and Juvenal, were my old and familiar companions. I insensibly plunged into the ocean of the Augustan history; and in the descending series I investigated, with my pen almost always in my hand, the original records, both Greek and Latin, from Dion Cassius to Ammianus Marcellinus, from the reign of Trajan to the last age of the Western Cæsars. The subsidiary rays of medals, and inscriptions of geography and chronology, were thrown on their proper objects; and I applied the collections of Tillemont, whose inimitable accuracy almost assumes the character of genius, to fix and arrange within my reach the loose and scattered atoms of historical information. Through the darkness of the middle ages I explored my way in the Annals and Antiquities of Italy of the learned Muratori; and diligently compared them with the parallel or transverse lines of Sigonius and Maffei, Baronius and Pagi, till I almost grasped the ruins of Rome in the fourteenth century, without suspecting that this final chapter must be attained by the labour of six quartos and twenty years. Among the books which I purchased, the Theodocian Code, with the commentary of James Godefroy, must be gratefully remembered. I used it (and much I used it) as a work of history, rather than of jurisprudence: but in every light it may be considered as a full and capacious repository of the political state of the empire in the fourth and fifth centuries. As I believed, and as I still believe, that the propagation of the Gospel, and the triumph of the church, are inseparably connected with the decline of the Roman monarchy, I weighed the causes and effects of the revolution, and contrasted the narratives and apologies of the Christians themselves, with the glances of candour or enmity which the Pagans have cast on the rising sects. The Jewish and Heathen testimonies, as they are collected and illustrated by Dr. Lardner, directed, without superseding, my search of the originals; and in an ample dissertation on the miraculous darkness of the passion, I privately withdrew my conclusions from the silence of an unbelieving age. I have assembled the preparatory studies, directly or indirectly relative to my history; but, in strict equity, they must be spread beyond this period of my life, over the two summers (1771 and 1772) that elapsed between my father's death and my settlement in London. 2. In a free conversation with books and men, it would be endless to enumerate the names and characters of all who are introduced to our acquaintance; but in this general acquaintance we may select the degrees of friendship and esteem, according to the wise maxim, *Multum legere potius quam multa.* I reviewed, again and again, the immortal works of the French and English, the Latin and Italian classics. My Greek studies (though less assiduous than I designed) maintained and extended my knowledge of that incomparable idiom. Homer and Xenophon were still my favourite authors; and I had almost prepared for the press an Essay on the Cyropœdia, which, in my own judgment, is not unhappily laboured. After a certain age, the new publications of merit are the sole food of the many; and the most austere student will be often tempted to break the line, for the sake of indulging his own curiosity, and of providing the topics of fashionable currency. A more respectable motive may be assigned for the third perusal of Blackstone's Commentaries, and a copious and critical abstract of that English work was my first serious production in my native language. 3. My literary leisure was much less complete and independent than it might appear to the eye of a stranger. In the hurry of London I was destitute of books ; in the solitude of Hampshire I was not master of my time. My quiet was gradually disturbed by our domestic anxiety, and I should be ashamed of my unfeeling philosophy, had I found much time or taste for study in the last fatal summer (1770) of my father's decay and dissolution.

The disembodying of the militia at the close of the war (1763) had restored the Major (a new Cincinnatus) to a life of agriculture. His labours were useful, his pleasures innocent, his wishes moderate ; and my father *seemed* to enjoy the state of happiness which is celebrated by poets and philosophers, as the most agreeable to nature, and the least accessible to fortune.

Beatus ille, qui procul negotiis (Ut prisca gens mortalium) Paterna rura bubus exercet suis, Solutus omni fœnore. <div align=right>Hor. *Epod.* ii.</div>	Like the first mortals, blest is he, From debts, and usury, and business free, With his own team who ploughs the soil, Which grateful once confessed his father's toil. <div align=right>Francis.</div>

But the last indispensable condition, the freedom from debt, was wanting to my father's felicity ; and the vanities of his youth were severely punished by the solicitude and sorrow of his declining age. The first mortgage, on my return from Lausanne, (1758,) had afforded him a partial and transient relief. The annual demand of interest and allowance was a heavy deduction from his income ; the militia was a source of expence, the farm in his hands was not a profitable adventure, he was loaded with the costs and damages of an obsolete law-suit ; and each year multiplied the number, and exhausted the patience, of his creditors. Under these painful circumstances, I consented to an additional mortgage, to the sale of Putney, and to every sacrifice that could alleviate his distress. But he was no longer capable of a rational effort, and his reluctant delays postponed not the evils themselves, but the remedies of those evils (*remedia malorum potius quam mala differebat*). The pangs of shame, tenderness, and self-reproach, incessantly preyed on his vitals ; his constitution was broken ; he lost his strength and his sight ; the rapid progress of a dropsy admonished him of his end, and he sunk into the grave on Nov. 10, 1770, in the sixty-fourth year of his age. A family tradition insinuates that Mr. William Law had drawn his pupil in the light and inconstant character of *Flatus*, who is ever confident, and ever disappointed in the chace of happiness. But these constitutional failings were happily compensated by the virtues of the head and heart, by the warmest sentiments of honour and humanity. His graceful person, polite address, gentle manners, and unaffected cheerfulness, recommended him to the favour of every company ; and in the change of times and opinions, his liberal spirit had long since delivered him from the zeal and prejudice of a Tory education. I submitted to the order of Nature ; and my grief was soothed by the conscious satisfaction that I had discharged all the duties of filial piety.

As soon as I had paid the last solemn duties to my father, and obtained, from time and reason, a tolerable composure of mind, I began to form the plan of an independent life, most adapted to my circumstances and inclination. Yet so intricate was the net, my efforts were so awkward and feeble, that nearly two years (Nov. 1770—Oct. 1772) were suffered to elapse before I could disentangle myself from the management of the farm, and transfer my residence from Beriton to a house in London. During this interval I continued to divide my year between town and the country ; but my new situation was brightened by hope ; my stay in London was prolonged into the summer ; and the uniformity of the summer was occasionally broken by visits and excursions at a distance from home. The gratification of my desires (they were not immoderate) has been seldom disappointed by the want of money or credit ; my pride was never insulted by the visit of an importunate tradesman ; and my transient anxiety for the past or future has been dispelled by the studious or social occupation of the present hour. My conscience does not accuse me of any act of extravagance or injustice, and the remnant of my estate affords an ample and honourable provision for my declining age. I shall not expatiate on my œconomical affairs, which cannot be instructive or amusing to the reader. It is a rule of prudence, as well as of politeness, to reserve such confidence for the ear of a private friend, without exposing our situation to the envy or pity of strangers ; for envy is productive of hatred, and pity borders too nearly on contempt. Yet I may believe, and even assert, that in circumstances more indigent or more wealthy, I should never have accomplished the task, or acquired the fame, of an historian ; that my spirit would have been broken by poverty and contempt, and that my industry might have been relaxed in the labour and luxury of a superfluous fortune.

I had now attained the first of earthly blessings, independence: I was the absolute master of my hours and actions : nor was I deceived in the hope that the establishment of my library in town would allow me to divide the day between study and society. Each year the circle of my acquaintance, the number of my dead and living companions, was enlarged. To a lover of books, the shops and sales of London present irresistible temptations ; and the manufacture of my history required a various and growing stock of materials. The militia, my travels, the House of Commons, the fame of an author, contributed to multiply my connections : I was chosen a member of the fashionable clubs ; and, before I left England in 1783, there were few persons of any eminence in the literary or political world to whom I was a stranger.* It would most assuredly be in my power to amuse the

* From the mixed, though polite, company of Boodle's, White's, and Brooks's, I must honourably distinguish a weekly society, which was instituted in the year 1764, and which still continues to flourish, under the title of the Literary Club. (Hawkins's Life of Johnson, p. 415. Boswell's Tour to the Hebrides, p. 97.) The names of Dr. Johnson, Mr. Burke, Mr. Topham Beauclerc, Mr. Garrick, Dr. Goldsmith, Sir Joshua Reynolds, Mr. Colman, Sir

reader with a gallery of portraits and a collection of anecdotes. But I have always condemned the practice of transforming a private memorial into a vehicle of satire or praise. By my own choice I passed in town the greatest part of the year; but whenever I was desirous of breathing the air of the country, I possessed an hospitable retreat at Sheffield-place in Sussex, in the family of my valuable friend Mr. Holroyd, whose character, under the name of Lord Sheffield, has since been more conspicuous to the public.

No sooner was I settled in my house and library, than I undertook the composition of the first volume of my History. At the outset all was dark and doubtful; even the title of the work, the true æra of the Decline and Fall of the Empire, the limits of the introduction, the division of the chapters, and the order of the narrative; and I was often tempted to cast away the labour of seven years. The style of an author should be the image of his mind, but the choice and command of language is the fruit of exercise. Many experiments were made before I could hit the middle tone between a dull chronicle and a rhetorical declamation: three times did I compose the first chapter, and twice the second and third, before I was tolerably satisfied with their effect. In the remainder of the way I advanced with a more equal and easy pace; but the fifteenth and sixteenth chapters have been reduced by three successive revisals, from a large volume to their present size; and they might still be compressed, without any loss of facts or sentiments. An opposite fault may be imputed to the concise and superficial narrative of the first reigns from Commodus to Alexander; a fault of which I have never heard, except from Mr. Hume in his last journey to London. Such an oracle might have been consulted and obeyed with rational devotion; but I was soon disgusted with the modest practice of reading the manuscript to my friends. Of such friends some will praise from politeness, and some will criticise from vanity. The author himself is the best judge of his own performance; no one has so deeply meditated on the subject; no one is so sincerely interested in the event.

By the friendship of Mr. (now Lord) Eliot, who had married my first cousin, I was returned at the general election for the borough of Liskeard. I took my seat at the beginning of the memorable contest between Great Britain and America, and supported, with many a sincere and silent vote, the rights, though not, perhaps, the interest, of the mother country. After a fleeting illusive hope, prudence condemned me to acquiesce in the humble station of a mute. I was not armed by Nature and education with the intrepid energy of mind and voice.

Vincentem strepitus, et natum rebus agendis.

Timidity was fortified by pride, and even the success of my pen discouraged the trial of my voice[*]. But I assisted at the debates of a

---

William Jones, Dr. Percy, Mr. Fox, Mr. Sheridan, Mr. Adam Smith, Mr. Steevens, Mr. Dunning, Sir Joseph Banks, Dr. Warton, and his brother Mr. Thomas Warton, Dr. Burney, &c., form a large and luminous constellation of British stars.

[*] A French sketch of Mr. Gibbon's Life, written by himself, probably for the use of some foreign journalist or translator, contains no fact not mentioned in his English Life. He there describes himself with his usual candour. Depuis huit ans il a assisté aux deliberations les

free assembly; I listened to the attack and defence of eloquence and reason; I had a near prospect of the characters, views, and passions of the first men of the age. The cause of government was ably vindicated by *Lord North*, a statesman of spotless integrity, a consummate master of debate, who could wield, with equal dexterity, the arms of reason and of ridicule. He was seated on the Treasury-bench between his Attorney and Solicitor General, the two pillars of the law and state, *magis pares quam similes;* and the minister might indulge in a short slumber, whilst he was upholden on either hand by the majestic sense of *Thurlow*, and the skilful eloquence of *Wedderburne.* From the adverse side of the house an ardent and powerful opposition was supported, by the lively declamation of *Barré*, the legal acuteness of *Dunning*, the profuse and philosophic fancy of *Burke*, and the argumentative vehemence of *Fox*, who in the conduct of a party approved himself equal to the conduct of an empire. By such men every operation of peace and war, every principle of justice or policy, every question of authority and freedom, was attacked and defended; and the subject of the momentous contest was the union or separation of Great Britain and America. The eight sessions that I sat in parliament were a school of civil prudence, the first and most essential virtue of an historian.

The volume of my History, which had been somewhat delayed by the novelty and tumult of a first session, was now ready for the press. After the perilous adventure had been declined by my friend Mr. Elmsly, I agreed, upon easy terms, with Mr. Thomas Cadell, a respectable bookseller, and Mr. William Strahan, an eminent printer; and they undertook the care and risk of the publication, which derived more credit from the name of the shop than from that of the author. The last revisal of the proofs was submitted to my vigilance; and many blemishes of style, which had been invisible in the manuscript, were discovered and corrected in the printed sheet. So moderate were our hopes, that the original impression had been stinted to five hundred, till the number was doubled by the prophetic taste of Mr. Strahan. During this awful interval I was neither elated by the ambition of fame, nor depressed by the apprehension of contempt. My diligence and accuracy were attested by my own conscience. History is the most popular species of writing, since it can adapt itself to the highest or the lowest capacity. I had chosen an illustrious subject. Rome is familiar to the school-boy and the statesman; and my narrative was deduced from the last period of classical reading. I had likewise flattered myself, that an age of light and liberty would receive, without scandal, an inquiry into the human *causes* of the progress and establishment of Christianity.

I am at a loss how to describe the success of the work, without betraying the vanity of the writer. The first impression was exhausted in a few days; a second and third edition were scarcely adequate to

---

plus importantes, mais il ne s'est jamais trouvé *le courage*, ni *le talent*, de parler dans une assemblée publique. This sketch was written before the publication of his three last volumes, as in closing it he says of his History: Cette entreprise lui demande encore plusieurs années d'une application soutenue; mais quelqu'en soit le succès, il trouve dans cette application même un plaisir toujours varié et toujours renaissant.——S.

the demand; and the bookseller's property was twice invaded by the pirates of Dublin. My book was on every table, and almost on every toilette; the historian was crowned by the taste or fashion of the day; nor was the general voice disturbed by the barking of any *profane* critic. The favour of mankind is most freely bestowed on a new acquaintance of any original merit; and the mutual surprise of the public and their favourite is productive of those warm sensibilities, which at a second meeting can no longer be rekindled. If I listened to the music of praise, I was more seriously satisfied with the approbation of my judges. The candour of Dr. Robertson embraced his disciple. A letter from Mr. Hume overpaid the labour of ten years. but I have never presumed to accept a place in the triumvirate of British historians.

That curious and original letter will amuse the reader, and his gratitude should shield my free communication from the reproach of vanity.

"DEAR SIR,   EDINBURGH, 18th March 1776.

"As I ran through your volume of history with great avidity and impatience, I cannot forbear discovering somewhat of the same impatience in returning you thanks for your agreeable present, and expressing the satisfaction which the performance has given me. Whether I consider the dignity of your style, the depth of your matter, or the extensiveness of your learning, I must regard the work as equally the object of esteem; and I own that if I had not previously had the happiness of your personal acquaintance, such a performance from an Englishman in our age would have given me some surprise. You may smile at this sentiment; but as it seems to me that your countrymen, for almost a whole generation, have given themselves up to barbarous and absurd faction, and have totally neglected all polite letters, I no longer expected any valuable production ever to come from them. I know it will give you pleasure (as it did me) to find that all the men of letters in this place concur in the admiration of your work, and in their anxious desire of your continuing it.

"When I heard of your undertaking, (which was some time ago,) I own I was a little curious to see how you would extricate yourself from the subject of your two last chapters. I think you have observed a very prudent temperament; but it was impossible to treat the subject so as not to give grounds of suspicion against you, and you may expect that a clamour will arise. This, if anything, will retard your success with the public; for in every other respect your work is calculated to be popular. But among many other marks of decline, the prevalence of superstition in England prognosticates the fall of philosophy and decay of taste; and though nobody be more capable than you to revive them, you will probably find a struggle in your first advances.

"I see you entertain a great doubt with regard to the authenticity of the poems of Ossian. You are certainly right in so doing. It is indeed strange that any men of sense could have imagined it possible, that above twenty thousand verses, along with numberless historical facts, could have been preserved by oral tradition during fifty generations, by the rudest, perhaps, of all the European nations, the most necessitous, the most turbulent, and the most unsettled. Where a supposition is so contrary to common sense, any positive evidence of it ought never to be regarded. Men run with great avidity to give their evidence in favour of what flatters their passions and their national prejudices. You are therefore over and above indulgent to us in speaking of the matter with hesitation.

"I must inform you that we all are very anxious to hear that you have fully collected the materials for your second volume, and that you are even considerably advanced in the composition of it. I speak this more in the name of my friends than in my own ; as I cannot expect to live so long as to see the publication of it. Your ensuing volume will be more delicate than the preceding, but I trust in your prudence for extricating you from the difficulties ; and, in all events, you have courage to despise the clamour of bigots.

I am, with great regard,
Dear Sir, &c.   DAVID HUME."

Some weeks afterwards I had the melancholy pleasure of seeing Mr. Hume in his passage through London ; his body feeble, his mind firm. On Aug. 25 of the same year (1776) he died, at Edinburgh, the death of a philosopher.

My second excursion to Paris was determined by the pressing invitation of M. and Madame Necker, who had visited England in the preceding summer. On my arrival I found M. Necker Director-general of the finances, in the first bloom of power and popularity. His private fortune enabled him to support a liberal establishment, and his wife, whose talents and virtues I had long admired, was admirably qualified to preside in the conversation of her table and drawing-room. As their friend, I was introduced to the best company of both sexes ; to the foreign ministers of all nations, and to the first names and characters of France ; who distinguished me by such marks of civility and kindness, as gratitude will not suffer me to forget, and modesty will not allow me to enumerate. The fashionable suppers often broke into the morning hours ; yet I occasionally consulted the Royal Library, and that of the Abbey of St. Germain, and in the free use of their books at home I had always reason to praise the liberality of those institutions. The society of men of letters I neither courted nor declined ; but I was happy in the acquaintance of M. de Buffon, who united with a sublime genius the most amiable simplicity of mind and manners. At the table of my old friend, M. de Foncemagne, I was involved in a dispute with the Abbé de Mably ; and his jealous irascible spirit revenged itself on a work which he was incapable of reading in the original.

As I might be partial in my own cause, I shall transcribe the words of an unknown critic, observing only, that this dispute had been preceded by another on the English constitution, at the house of the Countess de Froulay, an old Jansenist lady.

" Vous étiez chez M. de Foncemagne, mon cher Theodon, le jour que M. l'Abbé de Mably et M. Gibbon y dinerent en grande compagnie. La conversation roula presque entièrement sur l'histoire. L'Abbé etant un profond politique, la tourna sur l'administration, quand on fut au desert : et comme par caractère, par humeur, par l'habitude d'admirer Tite Live, il ne prise que le système republicain, il se mit à vanter l'excellence des republiques : bien persuadé que le savant Anglois l'approuveroit en tout, et admireroit la profondeur de génie qui avoit fait deviner tous ces avantages à un François. Mais M. Gibbon, instruit par l'experience des inconveniens d'un gouvernement populaire, ne fut point du tout de son avis, et il prit généreusement la défense du gouvernement monarchique. L'Abbé voulut le convaincre par Tite Live, et par quelques argumens tirés de Plutarque en faveur des Spartiates. M. Gibbon, doué de la memoire la plus heureuse, et ayant tous les faits presens à la pensée, domina bien-tot la conversation ; l'Abbé se facha, il s'emporta, il dit des choses dures ; l'Anglois, conservant le phlegme de son pays, prenoit ses avantages, et pressoit l'Abbé avec d'autant plus de succès que la colere le troubloit de plus en plus. La conversation s'echauffoit, et M. de Foncemagne la rompit en se levant de table, et en passant dans le salon, où personne ne fut tenté de la renouer."—*Supplement de la Manière d'ecrire l'Histoire,* p. 125, &c.*

Nearly two years had elapsed between the publication of my first and the commencement of my second volume ; and the causes must be assigned of this long delay. 1. After a short holiday, I indulged my curiosity in some studies of a very different nature, a course of anatomy, which was demonstrated by Doctor Hunter ; and some lessons of chymistry, which were delivered by Mr. Higgins. The principles of these sciences, and a taste for books of natural history, contributed to multiply my ideas and images ; and the anatomist and chymist may sometimes track me in their own snow. 2. I dived, perhaps too deeply, into the mud of the Arian controversy ; and many days of reading, thinking, and writing were consumed in the pursuit of a phantom. 3. It is difficult to arrange, with order and perspicuity, the various transactions of the age of Constantine ; and so much was I displeased with the first essay, that I committed to the flames above fifty sheets. 4. The six months of Paris and pleasure must be deducted from the account. But when I resumed my task I felt my improvement ; I was now master of my style and subject, and while the measure of my daily performance was enlarged, I discovered less reason to cancel or correct. It has always been my practice to cast a long paragraph in a single mould, to try it by my ear, to deposit it in my memory, but to suspend the action of the pen till I had given the last polish to my work. Shall I add, that I never found my mind more vigorous, nor my composition more happy, than in the winter hurry of society and parliament ?

Had I believed that the majority of English readers were so fondly

---

* Of the voluminous writings of the Abbé de Mably, (see his Eloge by the Abbé Brizard,) the *Principes du droit public de l'Europe,* and the first part of the *Observ. sur l'Hist de France,* may be deservedly praised ; and even the *Maniere d'ecrire l'Hist.* contains several useful precepts and judicious remarks. Mably was a lover of virtue and freedom ; but his virtue was austere, and his freedom was impatient of an equal. Kings, magistrates, nobles, and successful writers were the objects of his contempt, or hatred, or envy ; but his illiberal abuse of Voltaire, Hume, Buffon, the Abbé Reynal, Dr. Robertson, and *tutti quanti* can be injurious only to himself.

"Est il rien de plus fastidieux (says the polite Censor) qu'un M. Gibbon ; qui dans son eternelle Histoire des Empereurs Romains, suspend à chaque instant son insipide et lente narration, pour vous expliquer la cause de faits que vous allez lire." (Manière d'ecrire l'Histoire, p. 184. See another passage, p. 280.) Yet I am indebted to the Abbé de Mably for two such advocates as the anonymous French Critic and my friend Mr Hayley. (Hayley's Works, 8vo Ed. Vol. ii. 261.)

attached even to the name and shadow of Christianity ; had I foreseen that the pious, the timid, and the prudent, would feel, or affect to feel, with such exquisite sensibility; I might, perhaps, have softened the two invidious chapters, which would create many enemies, and conciliate few friends. But the shaft was shot, and the alarm was sounded, and I could only rejoice, that if the voice of our priests was clamorous and bitter, their hands were disarmed from the powers of persecution. I adhered to the wise resolution of trusting myself and my writings to the candour of the public, till Mr. Davies of Oxford presumed to attack, not the faith, but the fidelity, of the historian. *My Vindication*, expressive of less anger than contempt, amused for a moment the busy and idle metropolis; and the most rational part of the laity, and even of the clergy, appear to have been satisfied of my innocence and accuracy. I would not print this Vindication in quarto, lest it should be bound and preserved with the history itself. At the distance of twelve years, I calmly affirm my judgment of Davies, Chelsum, &c. A victory over such antagonists was a sufficient humiliation. They, however, were rewarded in this world. Poor Chelsum was indeed neglected; and I dare not boast the making Dr. Watson a bishop ; he is a prelate of a large mind and liberal spirit : but I enjoyed the pleasure of giving a Royal pension to Mr. Davies, and of collating Dr. Apthorpe to an archiepiscopal living. Their success encouraged the zeal of Taylor the Arian,* and Milner the Methodist,† with many others, whom it would be difficult to remember, and tedious to rehearse. The list of my adversaries, however, was graced with the more respectable names of Dr. Priestley, Sir David Dalrymple, and Dr. White ; and every polemic, of either university, discharged his sermon or pamphlet against the impenetrable silence of the Roman historian. In his History of the Corruptions of Christianity, Dr. Priestley threw down his two gauntlets to Bishop Hurd and Mr. Gibbon. I declined the challenge in a letter, exhorting my opponent to enlighten the world by his philosophical discoveries, and to remember that the merit of his predecessor Servetus is now reduced to a single passage, which indicates the smaller circulation of the blood through the lungs, from and to the heart.‡ Instead of listening to this friendly advice, the dauntless philosopher of Birmingham continued to fire away his double battery against those who believed too little, and those who believed too much. *From my* replies he has nothing to hope or fear : but his Socinian shield has repeatedly been pierced by the spear of Horsley, and his trumpet of sedition may at length awaken the magistrates of a free country.

The profession and rank of Sir David Dalrymple (now a Lord of Session) has given a more decent colour to his style. But he scrutinized each separate passage of the two chapters with the dry minuteness of a special pleader ; and as he was always solicitous to make, he may

---

* The stupendous title, *Thoughts on the Causes of the grand Apostacy*, at first agitated my nerves, till I discovered that it was the apostacy of the whole church, since the Council of Nice, from Mr. Taylor's private religion. His book is a thorough mixture of *high* enthusiasm and *low* buffoonery, and the Millennium is a fundamental article of his creed.

† From his grammar-school at Kingston upon Hull, Mr. Joseph Milner pronounces an anathema against all rational religion. *His* faith is a divine taste, a spiritual inspiration : *his* church is a mystic and invisible body : the *natural* Christians, such as Mr. Locke, who believe and interpret the Scriptures, are, in his judgment, no better than profane infidels.

‡ Astruc de la Structure du Cœur, i. 77, 79.

have succeeded sometimes in finding, a flaw. In his Annals of Scotland, he has shewn himself a diligent collector and an accurate critic.

I have praised, and I still praise, the eloquent sermons which were preached in St. Mary's pulpit at Oxford by Dr. White. If he assaulted me with some degree of illiberal acrimony, in such a place, and before such an audience, he was obliged to speak the language of the country. I smiled at a passage in one of his private letters to Mr. Badcock; "The part where we encounter Gibbon must be brilliant and striking."

In a sermon preached before the university of Cambridge, Dr. Edwards complimented a work, "which can only perish with the language itself;" and esteems the author a formidable enemy. He is, indeed, astonished that more learning and ingenuity has not been shewn in the defence of Israel; that the prelates and dignitaries of the church (alas, good man!) did not vie with each other, whose stone should sink the deepest in the forehead of this Goliah.

"But the force of truth will oblige us to confess, that in the attacks which have been levelled against our sceptical historian, we can discover but slender traces of profound and exquisite erudition, of solid criticism and accurate investigation; but we are too frequently disgusted by vague and inconclusive reasoning; by unseasonable banter and senseless witticisms; by imbittered bigotry and enthusiastic jargon; by futile cavils and illiberal invectives. Proud and elated by the weakness of his antagonists, he condescends not to handle the sword of controversy."—Monthly Review, Oct. 1790.

Let me frankly own that I was startled at the first discharge of ecclesiastical ordnance; but as soon as I found that this empty noise was mischievous only in the intention, my fear was converted into indignation; and every feeling of indignation or curiosity has long since subsided in pure and placid indifference.

The prosecution of my history was soon afterwards checked by another controversy of a very different kind. At the request of the Lord Chancellor, and of Lord Weymouth, then Secretary of State, I vindicated, against the French manifesto, the justice of the British arms. The whole correspondence of Lord Stormont, our late ambassador at Paris, was submitted to my inspection, and the *Memoire Justificatif,* which I composed in French, was first approved by the Cabinet Ministers, and then delivered as a State paper to the courts of Europe. The style and manner are praised by Beaumarchais himself, who, in his private quarrel, attempted a reply; but he flatters me, by ascribing the memoir to Lord Stormont; and the grossness of his invective betrays the loss of temper and of wit; he acknowledged, Oeuv. de Beaumarchais, iii. 299, 355, that *le style ne seroit pas sans grace, ni la logique sans justesse,* &c. if the facts were true which he undertakes to disprove. For these facts my credit is not pledged; I spoke as a lawyer from my brief, but the veracity of Beaumarchais may be estimated from the assertion that France, by the treaty of Paris (1763) was limited to a certain number of ships of war. On the application of the Duke of Choiseul, he was obliged to retract this daring falsehood.

Among the honourable connections which I had formed, I may justly be proud of the friendship of Mr. Wedderburne, at that time Attorney-

General, who now illustrates the title of Lord Loughborough, and the office of Chief Justice of the Common Pleas. By his strong recommendation, and the favourable disposition of Lord North, I was appointed one of the Lords Commissioners of Trade and Plantations; and my private income was enlarged by a clear addition of between seven and eight hundred pounds a-year. The fancy of an hostile orator may paint, in the strong colours of ridicule, "the perpetual virtual adjournment, and the unbroken sitting vacation of the Board of Trade."* But it must be allowed that our duty was not intolerably severe, and that I enjoyed many days and weeks of repose, without being called away from my library to the office. My acceptance of a place provoked some of the leaders of opposition, with whom I had lived in habits of intimacy; and I was most unjustly accused of deserting a party, in which I had never enlisted.†

The aspect of the next session of parliament was stormy and perilous; county meetings, petitions, and committees of correspondence, announced the public discontent; and instead of voting with a triumphant majority, the friends of government were often exposed to a struggle, and sometimes to a defeat. The House of Commons adopted Mr. Dunning's motion, "That the influence of the Crown had increased, was increasing, and ought to be diminished :" and Mr. Burke's bill of reform was framed with skill, introduced with eloquence, and supported by numbers. Our late president, the American Secretary of State, very narrowly escaped the sentence of proscription; but the unfortunate Board of Trade was abolished in the committee by a small

---

* I can never forget the delight with which that diffusive and ingenious orator, Mr. Burke, was heard by all sides of the house, and even by those whose existence he proscribed. (Speech on the Bill of Reform, p. 72—80.) The Lords of Trade blushed at their insignificancy, and Mr. Eden's appeal to the 2,500 volumes of our Reports, served only to excite a general laugh. I take this opportunity of certifying the correctness of Mr. Burke's printed speeches, which I have heard and read.

† *From* EDWARD GIBBON, esq. *to* ―――― esq.

DEAR SIR,   2nd July 1779.
Yesterday I received a very interesting communication from my friend, whose kind and honourable behaviour towards me I must always remember with the highest gratitude. He informed me that, in consequence of an arrangement, a place at the Board of Trade was reserved for me, and that as soon as I signified my acceptance of it, he was satisfied no farther difficulties would arise. My answer to him was sincere and explicit. I told him that I was far from approving all the past measures of the administration, even some of those in which I myself had silently concurred ; that I saw, with the rest of the world, many capital defects in the characters of some of the present ministers, and was sorry that in so alarming a situation of public affairs, the country had not the assistance of several able and honest men who are now in opposition. But that I had not formed with any of those persons in opposition any engagements or connections which could in the least restrain or affect my parliamentary conduct : that I could not discover among them such superior advantages, either of measures or of abilities, as could make me consider it as a duty to attach myself to their cause ; and that I clearly understood, from the public and private language of ――――, one of their leaders, that in the actual state of the country, he himself was seriously of opinion that opposition could not tend to any good purpose, and might be productive of much mischief ; that, for those reasons, I saw no objections which could prevent me from accepting an office under the present government, and that I was ready to take a step which I found to be consistent both with my interest and my honour.

It must now be decided, whether I may continue to live in England, or whether I must soon withdraw myself into a kind of philosophical exile in Switzerland. My father left his affairs in a state of embarrassment, and even of distress. My attempts to dispose of a part of my landed property have hitherto been disappointed, and are not likely at present to be more successful ; and my plan of expence, though moderate in itself, deserves the name of extravagance, since it exceeds my real income. The addition of the salary which is now offered will make my situation perfectly easy ; but I hope you will do me the justice to believe that my mind could not be so, unless I were satisfied of the rectitude of my own conduct.

majority (207 to 199) of eight votes. The storm, however, blew over for a time ; a large defection of country gentlemen eluded the sanguine hopes of the patriots : the Lords of Trade were revived ; administration recovered their strength and spirit ; and the flames of London, which were kindled by a mischievous madman, admonished all thinking men of the danger of an appeal to the people. In the premature dissolution which followed this session of parliament I lost my seat. Mr. Elliot was now deeply engaged in the measures of opposition, and the electors of Leskeard* are commonly of the same opinion as Mr. Elliot.

In this interval of my senatorial life, I published the second and third volumes of the Decline and Fall. My eccesiastical history still breathed the same spirit of freedom ; but protestant zeal is more indifferent to the characters and controversies of the fourth and fifth centuries. My obstinate silence had damped the ardour of the polemics. Dr. Watson, the most candid of my adversaries, assured me that he had no thoughts of renewing the attack, and my impartial balance of the virtues and vices of Julian was generally praised. This truce was interrupted only by some animadversions of the Catholics of Italy, and by some angry letters from Mr. Travis, who made me personally responsible for condemning, with the best critics, the spurious text of the three heavenly witnesses.

The piety or prudence of my Italian translator has provided an antidote against the poison of his original. The 5th and 7th volumes are armed with five letters from an anonymous divine to his friends, Foothead and Kirk, two English students at Rome : and this meritorious service is commended by Monsignor Stonor, a prelate of the same nation, who discovers much venom in the *fluid* and nervous style of Gibbon. The critical essay at the end of the third volume was furnished by the Abbate Nicola Spedalieri, whose zeal has gradually swelled to a more solid confutation in two quarto volumes.—Shall I be excused for not having read them ?

The brutal insolence of Mr. Travis's challenge can only be excused by the absence of learning, judgment, and humanity ; and to that excuse he has the fairest or foulest pretension. Compared with Archdeacon Travis, Chelsum and Davies assume the title of respectable enemies.

The bigoted advocate of popes and monks may be turned over even to the bigots of Oxford ; and the wretched Travis still smarts under the lash of the merciless Porson. I consider Mr. Porson's answer to Archdeacon Travis as the most acute and accurate piece of criticism which has appeared since the days of Bentley. His strictures are founded in argument, enriched with learning, and enlivened with wit ; and his adversary neither deserves nor finds any quarter at his hands. The evidence of the three heavenly witnesses would now be rejected in any court of justice : but prejudice is blind, authority is deaf, and our vulgar bibles will ever be polluted by this spurious text, "*sedet œternumque sedebit.*" The more learned ecclesiastics will indeed have the secret satisfaction of reprobating in the closet what they read in the church.

* The borough which Mr. Gibbon had represented in Parliament.

I perceived, and without surprise, the coldness and even prejudice of the town ; nor could a whisper escape my ear, that, in the judgment of many readers, my continuation was much inferior to the original attempts.   An author who cannot ascend will always appear to sink : envy was now prepared for my reception, and the zeal of my religious, was fortified by the motive of my political, enemies.   Bishop Newton, in writing his own life, was at full liberty to declare how much he himself and two eminent brethren were disgusted by Mr. G.'s prolixity, tediousness, and affectation.   But the old man should not have indulged his zeal in a false and feeble charge against the historian,✻ who had faithfully and even cautiously rendered Dr. Burnet's meaning by the alternative of sleep or repose.   That philosophic divine supposes, that, in the period between death and the resurrection, human souls exist without a body, endowed with internal consciousness, but destitute of all active or passive connection with the external world. " Secundum communem dictionem sacræ scripturæ, mors dicitur somnus, et morientes dicuntur *abdormire*, quod innuere mihi videtur statum mortis esse statum quietis, silentii, et αεργασεας." (*De Statû Mortuorum*, ch. v. p. 98.)

✻ Extract from* Mr. GIBBON's *Common Place Book.
Thomas Newton, Bishop of Bristol and Dean of St. Paul's, was born at Litchfield on Dec. 21 1703, O. S. (1st Jan. 1704, N. S.), and died Feb. 14 1782, in the 79th year of his age. A few days before his death he finished the memoirs of his own life, which have been prefixed to an edition of his posthumous works, first published in quarto, and since (1787) re-published in six volumes octavo.

P. 173, 174.   Some books were published in 1781, which employed some of the Bishop's leisure hours, and during his illness.   Mr. Gibbon's *History of the Decline and Fall of the Roman Empire* he read throughout, but it by no means answered his expectation ; for he found it rather a prolix and tedious performance, his matter uninteresting, and his style affected ; his testimonies not to be depended upon, and his frequent scoffs at religion offensive to every sober mind.   He had before been convicted of making false quotations, which should have taught him more prudence and caution.   But, without examining his authorities, there is one which must necessarily strike every man who has read Dr. Burnet's Treatise *de Statû Mortuorum*.   In vol. iii. p. 99, Mr. G. has the following note :—" Burnet (*de S. M.* p. 56—84) collects the opinions of the Fathers, as far as they assert the sleep or repose of human souls till the day of judgment.   He afterwards exposes (p. 91) the inconveniences which must arise if they possessed a more active and sensible existence.   Who would not from hence infer that Dr. B. was an advocate for the sleep or insensible existence of the soul after death ? whereas his doctrine is directly the contrary.   He has employed some chapters in treating of the state of human souls in the interval between death and the resurrection ; and after various proofs from reason, from scripture, and the Fathers, his conclusions are, that human souls exist after their separation from the body, that they are in a good or evil state according to their good or ill behaviour, but that neither their happiness nor their misery will be complete or perfect before the day of judgment.   His argumentation is thus summed up at the end of the 4th chapter—*Ex quibus constat primo, animas superesse extincto corpore ; secundo, bonas bene, malas male se habituras ; tertio, nec illis summam felicitatem, nec bis summam miseriam, accessuram esse ante diem judicii.*"   (The Bishop's reading the whole was a greater compliment to the work than was paid to it by two of the most eminent of his brethren for their learning and station.   The one entered upon it, but was soon wearied, and laid it aside in disgust : the other returned it upon the bookseller's hands ; and it is said that Mr. G. himself happened unluckily to be in the shop at the same time.)
Does the Bishop comply with his own precept in the next page ? (p. 175.)   " Old age should lenify, should soften men's manners, and make them more mild and gentle ; but often has the contrary effect, hardens their hearts, and makes them more sour and crabbed."—He is speaking of Dr. Johnson.
Have I ever insinuated that preferment-hunting is the great occupation of an ecclesiastical life ? (Memoirs *passim*) ; that a minister's influence and a bishop's patronage are sometimes pledged eleven deep ? (p. 151 ;) that a prebendary considers the audit week as the better part of the year ? (p. 127 ;) or that the most eminent of priests, the pope himself, would change their religion, if any thing better could be offered them ? (p. 56).   Such things are more than insinuated in the Bishop's Life, which afforded some scandal to the church, and some diversion to the profane laity.

I was however encouraged by some domestic and foreign testimonies of applause; and the second and third volumes insensibly rose in sale and reputation to a level with the first. But the public is seldom wrong; and I am inclined to believe that, especially in the beginning, they are more prolix and less entertaining than the first: my efforts had not been relaxed by success, and I had rather deviated into the opposite fault of minute and superfluous diligence. On the Continent, my name and writings were slowly diffused; a French translation of the first volume had disappointed the booksellers of Paris; and a passage in the third was construed as a personal reflection on the reigning monarch.*

Before I could apply for a seat at the general election the list was already full; but Lord North's promise was sincere, his recommendation was effectual, and I was soon chosen on a vacancy for the borough of Lymington, in Hampshire. In the first session of the new parliament, administration stood their ground; their final overthrow was reserved for the second. The American war had once been the favourite of the country: the pride of England was irritated by the resistance of her colonies, and the executive power was driven by national clamour into the most vigorous and coercive measures. But the length of a fruitless contest, the loss of armies, the accumulation of debt and taxes, and the hostile confederacy of France, Spain, and Holland, indisposed the public to the American war, and the persons by whom it was conducted; the representatives of the people, followed, at a slow distance, the changes of their opinion; and the ministers who refused to bend, were broken by the tempest. As soon as Lord North had lost, or was about to lose, a majority in the House of Commons, he surrendered his office, and retired to a private station, with the tranquil assurance of a clear conscience and a cheerful temper: the old fabric was dissolved, and the posts of government were occupied by the victorious and veteran troops of opposition. The lords of trade were not immediately dismissed, but the board itself was abolished by Mr. Burke's bill, which decency had compelled the patriots to revive; and I was stripped of a convenient salary, after having enjoyed it about three years.

So flexible is the title of my History, that the final æra might be fixed at my own choice; and I long hesitated whether I should be content with the three volumes, the fall of the Western empire, which fulfilled my first engagement with the public. In this interval of suspense, nearly a twelvemonth, I returned by a natural impulse to the Greek authors of antiquity; I read with new pleasure the Iliad and the Odyssey, the Histories of Herodotus, Thucydides, and Xenophon, a large portion of the tragic and comic theatre of Athens, and many interesting dialogues of the Socratic school. Yet in the luxury of freedom I began to wish for the daily task, the active pursuit, which

---

* It may not be generally known that Louis XVI. is a great reader, and a reader of English books. On perusing a passage of my History which seems to compare him to Arcadius or Honorius, he expressed his resentment to the Prince of B * * *, from whom the intelligence was conveyed to me. I shall neither disclaim the allusion, nor examine the likeness; but the situation of the late King of France excludes all suspicion of flattery; and I am ready to declare that the concluding observations of my third volume were written before his accession to the throne.

gave a value to every book, and an object to every inquiry; the preface of a new edition announced my design, and I dropped without reluctance from the age of Plato to that of Justinian. The original texts of Procopius and Agathias supplied the events and even the characters of his reign: but a laborious winter was devoted to the Codes, the Pandects, and the modern interpreters, before I presumed to form an abstract of the civil law. My skill was improved by practice, my diligence perhaps was quickened by the loss of office; and, excepting the last chapter, I had finished the fourth volume before I sought a retreat on the banks of the Leman Lake.

It is not the purpose of this narrative to expatiate on the public or secret history of the times: the schism which followed the death of the Marquis of Rockingham, the appointment of the Earl of Shelburne, the resignation of Mr. Fox, and his famous coalition with Lord North. But I may assert, with some degree of assurance, that in their political conflict those great antagonists had never felt any personal animosity to each other, that their reconciliation was easy and sincere, and that their friendship has never been clouded by the shadow of suspicion or jealousy. The most violent or venal of their respective followers embraced this fair occasion of revolt, but their alliance still commanded a majority in the House of Commons; the peace was censured, Lord Shelburne resigned, and the two friends knelt on the same cushion to take the oath of secretary of state. From a principle of gratitude I adhered to the coalition: my vote was counted in the day of battle, but I was overlooked in the division of the spoil. There were many claimants more deserving and importunate than myself: the board of trade could not be restored; and, while the list of places was curtailed, the number of candidates was doubled. An easy dismission to a secure seat at the board of customs or excise was promised on the first vacancy: but the chance was distant and doubtful; nor could I solicit with much ardour an ignoble servitude, which would have robbed me of the most valuable of my studious hours: at the same time the tumult of London, and the attendance on parliament, were grown more irksome; and, without some additional income, I could not long or prudently maintain the style of expence to which I was accustomed.

From my early acquaintance with Lausanne I had always cherished a secret wish, that the school of my youth might become the retreat of my declining age. A moderate fortune would secure the blessings of ease, leisure, and independence: the country, the people, the manners, the language, were congenial to my taste; and I might indulge the hope of passing some years in the domestic society of a friend. After travelling with several English,[*] Mr. Deyverdun was now settled at home, in a pleasant habitation, the gift of his deceased aunt: we had long been separated, we had long been silent; yet in my first letter I exposed, with the most perfect confidence, my situation, my sentiments, and my designs. His immediate answer was a warm and joyful acceptance: the picture of our future life provoked my impatience; and the terms of arrangement were short and simple, as he possessed the property, and I undertook the expence of our common house.

[*] Sir Richard Worsley, Lord Chesterfield, Broderick Lord Midleton, and Mr. Hume, brother to Sir Abraham.

Before I could break my English chain, it was incumbent on me to struggle with the feelings of my heart, the indolence of my temper, and the opinion of the world, which unanimously condemned this voluntary banishment. In the disposal of my effects, the library, a sacred deposit, was alone excepted : as my post-chaise moved over Westminster-bridge I bid a long farewell to the "fumum et opes strepitumq ; Romæ." My journey by the direct road through France was not attended with any accident, and I arrived at Lausanne nearly twenty years after my second departure. Within less than three months the coalition struck on some hidden rocks : had I remained on board, I should have perished in the general shipwreck.

Since my establishment at Lausanne, more than seven years have elapsed; and if every day has not been equally soft and serene, not a day, not a moment, has occurred in which I have repented of my choice. During my absence, a long portion of human life, many changes had happened: my elder acquaintance had left the stage; virgins were ripened into matrons, and children were grown to the age of manhood. But the same manners were transmitted from one generation to another: my friend alone was an inestimable treasure ; my name was not totally forgotten, and all were ambitious to welcome the arrival of a stranger and the return of a fellow-citizen. The first winter was given to a general embrace, without any nice discrimination of persons and characters. After a more regular settlement, a more accurate survey, I discovered three solid and permanent benefits of my new situation. 1. My personal freedom had been somewhat impaired by the House of Commons and the Board of Trade; but I was now delivered from the chain of duty and dependence, from the hopes and fears of political adventure: my sober mind was no longer intoxicated by the fumes of party, and I rejoiced in my escape, as often as I read of the midnight debates which preceded the dissolution of parliament. 2. My English œconomy had been that of a solitary bachelor, who might afford some occasional dinners. In Switzerland I enjoyed at every meal, at every hour, the free and pleasant conversation of the friend of my youth; and my daily table was always provided for the reception of one or two extraordinary guests. Our importance in society is less a positive than a relative weight: in London I was lost in the crowd; I ranked with the first families of Lausanne, and my style of prudent expence enabled me to maintain a fair balance of reciprocal civilities. 3. Instead of a small house between a street and a stable-yard, I began to occupy a spacious and convenient mansion, connected on the north side with the city, and open on the south to a beautiful and boundless horizon. A garden of four acres had been laid out by the taste of Mr. Deyverdun: from the garden a rich scenery of meadows and vineyards descends to the Leman Lake, and the prospect far beyond the Lake is crowned by the stupendous mountains of Savoy. My books and my acquaintance had been first united in London; but this happy position of my library in town and country was finally reserved for Lausanne. Possessed of every comfort in this triple alliance, I could not be tempted to change my habitation with the changes of the seasons.

My friends had been kindly apprehensive that I should not be able

H

to exist in a Swiss town at the foot of the Alps, after having so long conversed with the first men of the first cities of the world. Such lofty connections may attract the curious, and gratify the vain; but I am too modest, or too proud, to rate my own value by that of my associates; and whatsoever may be the fame of learning or genius, experience has shown me that the cheaper qualifications of politeness and good sense are of more useful currency in the commerce of life. By many, conversation is esteemed as a theatre or a school: but, after the morning has been occupied by the labours of the library, I wish to unbend rather than to exercise my mind; and in the interval between tea and supper I am far from disdaining the innocent amusement of a game at cards. Lausanne is peopled by a numerous gentry, whose companionable idleness is seldom disturbed by the pursuits of avarice or ambition: the women, though confined to a domestic education, are endowed for the most part with more taste and knowledge than their husbands and brothers: but the decent freedom of both sexes is equally remote from the extremes of simplicity and refinement. I shall add as a misfortune rather than a merit, that the situation and beauty of the Pays de Vaud, the long habits of the English, the medical reputation of Dr. Tissot, and the fashion of viewing the mountains and *Glaciers*, have opened us on all sides to the incursions of foreigners. The visits of Mr. and Madame Necker, of Prince Henry of Prussia, and of Mr. Fox, may form some pleasing exceptions; but, in general, Lausanne has appeared most agreeable in my eyes, when we have been abandoned to our own society. I had frequently seen Mr. Necker, in the summer of 1784, at a country house near Lausanne, where he composed his Treatise on the Administration of the Finances. I have since, in October 1790, visited him in his present residence, the castle and barony of Copet, near Geneva. Of the merits and measures of that statesman various opinions may be entertained; but all impartial men must agree in their esteem of his integrity and patriotism.

In August 1784, Prince Henry of Prussia, in his way to Paris, passed three days at Lausanne. His military conduct has been praised by professional men; his character has been vilified by the wit and malice of a dæmon (Mem. Secret de la Cour de Berlin); but I was flattered ····
by his affability, and entertained by his conversation.

In his tour of Switzerland (Sept. 1788) Mr. Fox gave me two days of free and private society. He seemed to feel, and even to envy, the happiness of my situation; while I admired the powers of a superior man, as they are blended in his attractive character with the softness and simplicity of a child. Perhaps no human being was ever more perfectly exempt from the taint of malevolence, vanity, or falsehood

My transmigration from London to Lausanne could not be effected without interrupting the course of my historical labours. The hurry of my departure, the joy of my arrival, the delay of my tools, suspended their progress; and a full twelvemonth was lost before I could resume the thread of regular and daily industry. A number of books most requisite and least common had been previously selected; the academical library of Lausanne, which I could use as my own, con-

tained at least the fathers and councils ; and I have derived some
occasional succour from the public collections of Berne and Geneva.
The fourth volume was soon terminated, by an abstract of the controversies of the Incarnation, which the learned Dr. Prideaux was apprehensive of exposing to profane eyes. It had been the original design
of the learned Dean Prideaux to write the history of the ruin of the
Eastern Church. In this work it would have been necessary, not only
to unravel all those controversies which the Christians made about the
hypostatical union, but also to unfold all the niceties and subtle notions
which each sect entertained concerning it. The pious historian was
apprehensive of exposing that incomprehensible mystery to the cavils
and objections of unbelievers : and he durst not, " seeing the nature of
this book, venture it abroad in so wanton and lewd an age " (Preface
to the Life of Mahomet, p. 10).

In the fifth and sixth volumes the revolutions of the empire and the
world are most rapid, various, and instructive; and the Greek or Roman
historians are checked by the hostile narratives of the barbarians of
the East and the West.*

It was not till after many designs, and many trials, that I preferred,
as I still prefer, the method of grouping my picture by nations ; and
the seeming neglect of chronological order is surely compensated by
the superior merits of interest and perspicuity. The style of the first
volume is, in my opinion, somewhat crude and elaborate ; in the second
and third it is ripened into ease, correctness, and numbers ; but in the
three last I may have been seduced by the facility of my pen, and the
constant habit of speaking one language and writing another may have
infused some mixture of Gallic idioms. Happily for my eyes, I have
always closed my studies with the day, and commonly with the morning;
and a long, but temperate, labour has been accomplished, without
fatiguing either the mind or body; but when I computed the remainder
of my time and my task, it was apparent that, according to the season
of publication, the delay of a month would be productive of that of a
year. I was now straining for the goal, and in the last winter many
evenings were borrowed from the social pleasures of Lausanne. I
could now wish that a pause, an interval, had been allowed for a
serious revisal.

I have presumed to mark the moment of conception : I shall now
commemorate the hour of my final deliverance. It was on the day, or
rather night, of the 27th of June, 1787, between the hours of eleven
and twelve, that I wrote the last lines of the last page, in a summer-
house in my garden. After laying down my pen, I took several turns
in a *berceau*, or covered walk of acacias, which commands a prospect
of the country, the lake, and the mountains. The air was temperate,
the sky was serene, the silver orb of the moon was reflected from the
waters, and all nature was silent. I will not dissemble the first emotions of joy on the recovery of my freedom, and, perhaps, the establishment of my fame. But my pride was soon humbled, and a sober

* I have followed the judicious precept of the Abbé de Mably, (Manière d'ecrire l'Hist.,
p. 110,) who advises the historian not to dwell too minutely on the decay of the eastern empire;
but to consider the barbarian conquerors as a more worthy subject of his narrative. " Fas est
et ab hoste doceri."

melancholy was spread over my mind, by the idea that I had taken an everlasting leave of an old and agreeable companion, and that whatsoever might be the future date of my History, the life of the historian must be short and precarious. I will add two facts, which have seldom occurred in the composition of six, or at least of five quartos. 1. My first rough manuscript, without any intermediate copy, has been sent to the press. 2. Not a sheet has been seen by any human eyes, excepting those of the author and the printer : the faults and the merits are exclusively my own.*

I cannot help recollecting a much more extraordinary fact, which is affirmed of himself by Retif de la Bretorme, a voluminous and original writer of French novels. He laboured, and may still labour, in the humble office of corrector to a printing-house ; but this office enabled him to transport an entire volume from his mind to the press ; and his work was given to the public without ever having been written with a pen.

After a quiet residence of four years, during which I had never moved ten miles from Lausanne, it was not without some reluctance and terror, that I undertook, in a journey of two hundred leagues, to cross the mountains and the sea. Yet this formidable adventure was achieved without danger or fatigue ; and at the end of a fortnight I found myself in Lord Sheffield's house and library, safe, happy, and at home. The character of my friend (Mr. Holroyd) had recommended him to a seat in parliament for Coventry, the command of a regiment of light dragoons, and an Irish peerage. The sense and spirit of his political writings have decided the public opinion on the great questions of our commercial interest with America and Ireland.†

The sale of his Observations on the American States was diffusive, their effect beneficial ; the Navigation Act, the palladium of Britain, was defended, and perhaps saved, by his pen ; and he proves, by the weight of fact and argument, that the mother-country may survive and flourish after the loss of America. My friend has never cultivated the arts of composition ; but his materials are copious and correct, and he leaves on his paper the clear impression of an active and vigorous mind. His " Observations on the Trade, Manufactures, and present State of Ireland," were intended to guide the industry, to correct the prejudices, and to assuage the passions of a country which seemed to forget that she could be free and prosperous only by a friendly connection with Great Britain. The concluding observations are written with so much ease and spirit, that they may be read by those who are the least interested in the subject.

He fell (in 1784) with the unpopular coalition ; but his merit has been acknowledged at the last general election, 1790, by the honourable

---

* *Extract from* Mr. GIBBON's *Common-place Book.*
The IVth Volume of the History of the Decline and Fall of the Roman Empire, begun March 1st, 1782—ended June 1784.
The Vth Volume, begun July 1784—ended May 1st, 1786.
The VIth Volume, begun May 18th, 1786—ended June 27th, 1787.
These three volumes were sent to press August 15th, 1787, and the whole impression was concluded April following. [*The edition—six volumes quarto—is referred to.*]

† Observations on the Commerce of the American States, by John Lord Sheffield, 6th ed., Lond., 1784, in 8vo.

invitation and free choice of the city of Bristol. During the whole time of my residence in England I was entertained at Sheffield-Place and in Downing-Street by his hospitable kindness ; and the most pleasant period was that which I passed in the domestic society of the family. In the larger circle of the metropolis I observed the country and the inhabitants with the knowledge, and without the prejudices, of an Englishman ; but I rejoiced in the apparent increase of wealth and prosperity, which might be fairly divided between the spirit of the nation and the wisdom of the minister. All party-resentment was now lost in oblivion : since I was no man's rival, no man was my enemy. I felt the dignity of independence, and as I asked no more, I was satisfied with the general civilities of the world. The house in London which I frequented with most pleasure and assiduity was that of Lord North. After the loss of power and of sight, he was still happy in himself and his friends ; and my public tribute of gratitude and esteem could no longer be suspected of any interested motive. Before my departure from England, I was present at the august spectacle of Mr. Hastings's trial in Westminster Hall. It is not my province to absolve or condemn the Governor of India ; but Mr. Sheridan's eloquence demanded my applause ; nor could I hear without emotion the personal compliment which he paid me in the presence of the British nation.*

From this display of genius, which blazed four successive days, I shall stoop to a very mechanical circumstance. As I was waiting in the managers' box, I had the curiosity to inquire of the short-hand writer, how many words a ready and rapid orator might pronounce in an hour ? From 7000 to 7500 was his answer. The medium of 7200 will afford 120 words in a minute, and two words in each second. But this computation will only apply to the English language.

As the publication of my three last volumes was the principal object, so it was the first care of my English journey. The previous arrangements with the bookseller and the printer were settled in my passage through London, and the proofs, which I returned more correct, were transmitted every post from the press to Sheffield-Place. The length of the operation, and the leisure of the country, allowed some time to review my manuscript. Several rare and useful books, the Assises de Jerusalem, Ramusius de Bello C. P^{aro}, the Greek Acts of the Synod of Florence, the Statuta Urbis Romæ, &c. were procured, and introduced in their proper places the supplements which they afforded. The impression of the fourth volume had consumed three months Our common interest required that we should move with a quicker pace ; and Mr. Strahan fulfilled his engagement, which few printers could sustain, of delivering every week three thousand copies of nine sheets. The day of publication was, however, delayed, that it might coincide with the fifty-first anniversary of my own birthday ; the double festival was celebrated by a cheerful literary dinner at Mr. Cadell's house ; and I seemed to blush while they read an elegant com-

* He said the facts that made up the volume of narrative were unparalleled in atrociousness, and that nothing equal in criminality was to be traced, either in ancient or modern history, in the correct periods of Tacitus, or the luminous page of Gibbon.—*Morning Chronicle, June 14, 1788.*

pliment from Mr. Hayley,* whose poetical talents had more than once been employed in the praise of his friend. Before Mr. Hayley inscribed with my name his epistles on history, I was not acquainted with that amiable man and elegant poet. He afterwards thanked me in verse for my second and third volumes ;† and in the summer of 1781, the Roman Eagle ‡ (a proud title) accepted the invitation of the English

* OCCASIONAL STANZAS, *by* Mr. HAYLEY, *read after the Dinner at* Mr. CADELL'S, *May* 8, 1788 ; *being the Day of the Publication of the three last Volumes of* Mr. GIBBON'S *History, and his Birthday.*

GENII of ENGLAND and of ROME !
In mutual triumph here assume
    The honours each may claim !
This social scene with smiles survey !
And consecrate the festive day
    To Friendship and to Fame !

Enough, by Desolation's tide,
With anguish, and indignant pride,
    Has ROME bewail'd her fate ;
And mourn'd that Time, in Havoc's hour,
Defac'd each monument, of power
    To speak her truly great.

O'er maim'd POLYBIUS, just and sage,
O'er LIVY'S mutilated page,
    How deep was her regret !
Touch'd by this Queen, in ruin grand,
See ! Glory, by an English hand,
    Now pays a mighty debt :

Lo ! sacred to the ROMAN Name,
And rais'd, like ROME'S immortal Fame,
    By Genius and by Toil,

The splendid Work is crown'd to-day,
On which Oblivion ne'er shall prey,
    Nor Envy make her spoil !

ENGLAND, exult ! and view not now,
With jealous eye each nation's brow,
    Where Hist'ry's palm has spread !
In every path of liberal art,
Thy Sons to prime distinction start,
    And no superior dread.

Science for Thee a NEWTON rais'd ;
For thy renown a SHAKESPEARE blaz'd,
    Lord of the drama's sphere !
In different fields to equal praise
See History now thy GIBBON raise
    To shine without a peer !

Eager to honour living worth,
And bless to-day the double birth,
    That proudest joy may claim,
Let artless Truth this homage pay,
And consecrate the festive day
    To Friendship and to Fame !

† SONNET *to* EDWARD GIBBON, esq.
On the Publication of his Second and Third Volumes, 1781.

WITH proud delight th' imperial founder gaz'd
    On the new beauty of his second Rome,
When on his eager eye rich temples blaz'd,
    And his fair city rose in youthful bloom ;
A pride more noble may thy heart assume,
    O GIBBON ! gazing on thy growing work,
In which, constructed for a happier doom,
    No hasty marks of vain ambition lurk :
Thou may'st deride both Time's destructive sway,
    And baser Envy's beauty-mangling dirk ;
Thy gorgeous fabric, plann'd with wise delay,
    Shall baffle foes more savage than the Turk ;
As ages multiply, its fame shall rise,
And earth must perish ere its splendour dies.

HAYLEY'S *Works,* 8vo. ed. i. 162.

‡ A CARD *of* INVITATION *to* Mr. GIBBON, *at Brighthelmstone,* 1781.

AN English sparrow, pert and free,
Who chirps beneath his native tree,
Hearing the Roman eagle's near,
And feeling more respect than fear,
Thus, with united love and awe,
Invites him to his shed of straw.
    Tho' he is but a twittering sparrow,
The field he hops in rather narrow,
When nobler plumes attract his view,
He ever pays them homage due,
He looks with reverential wonder
On him whose talons bear the thunder ;
Nor could the Jackdaws e'er inveigle
His voice to vilify the eagle,
Tho' issuing from the holy tow'rs,
In which they build their warmest bow'rs,
Their sovereign's haunt they slyly search,

In hopes to catch him on his perch,
(For Pindar says, beside his God
The thunder-bearing bird will nod,)
Then, peeping round his still retreat,
They pick from underneath his feet
Some moulted feather he lets fall,
And swear he cannot fly at all.——
    Lord of the sky ! whose pounce can tear
These croakers, that infest the air,
Trust him ! the sparrow loves to sing
The praise of thy imperial wing !
He thinks thou'lt deem him, on his word,
An honest, though familiar bird :—
And hopes thou soon wilt condescend
To look upon thy little friend ;
That he may boast around his grove
A visit from the bird of Jove.

HAYLEY'S *Works,* i. 189.

Sparrow, who chirped in the groves of Eartham, near Chichester. As most of the former purchasers were naturally desirous of completing their sets, the sale of the quarto edition was quick and easy ; and an octavo size was printed, to satisfy at a cheaper rate the public demand. The conclusion of my work was generally read, and variously judged. The style has been exposed to much academical criticism ; a religious clamour was revived, and the reproach of indecency has been loudly echoed by the rigid censors of morals. I never could understand the clamour that has been raised against the indecency of my three last volumes. 1. An equal degree of freedom in the former part, especially in the first volume, had passed without reproach. 2. I am justified in painting the manners of the times ; the vices of Theodora form an essential feature in the reign and character of Justinian. 3. My English text is chaste, and all licentious passages are left in the obscurity of a learned language. *Le Latin dans ses mots brave l'hon-nêteté,* says the correct Boileau, in a country and idiom more scrupulous than our own. Yet, upon the whole, the History of the Decline and Fall seems to have struck root, both at home and abroad, and may, perhaps, a hundred years hence still continue to be abused. I am less flattered by Mr. Porson's high encomium on the style and spirit of my history, than I am satisfied with his honourable testimony to my attention, diligence, and accuracy ; those humble virtues, which religious zeal had most audaciously denied. The sweetness of his praise is tempered by a reasonable mixture of acid. As the book may not be common in England, I shall transcribe my own character from the Bibliotheca Historica of Meuselius, a learned and laborious German. " Summis ævi nostri historicis Gibbonus sine dubio adnumerandus est. Inter capitolii ruinas stans primum hujus operis scribendi concilium cepit. Florentissimos vitæ annos colligendo et laborando eidem impendit. Enatum inde monumentum ære perennius, licet passim appareant sinistrè dicta, minus perfecta, veritati non satis consentanea. Videmus quidem ubique fere studium scrutandi veritatemque scribendi maximum : tamen sine Tillemontio duce ubi scilicet hujus historia finitur sæpius noster titubat atque hallucinatur. Quod vel maxime fit ubi de rebus Ecclesiasticis vel de juris prudentiâ Romanâ (tom. iv.) tradit, et in aliis locis. Attamen nævi hujus generis haud impediunt quo minus operis summam et οικονομιαν præclare dispositam, delectum rerum sapientissimum, argutum quoque interdum, dictionemque seu stylum historico æque ac philosopho dignissimum, et vix a quoque alio Anglo, Humio ac Robertsono haud exceptis (*præreptum ?*) vehementer laudemus, atque sæculo nostro de hujusmodi historiâ gratulemur . . . . . Gibbonus adversarios cum in tum extra patriam nactus est, quia propagationem religionis Christianæ, non, ut vulgo, fieri solet, aut more Theologorum, sed ut Historicum et Philosophum decet, exposuerat."

The French, Italian, and German translations have been executed with various success ; but, instead of patronizing, I should willingly suppress such imperfect copies, which injure the character, while they propagate the name of the author. The first volume had been feebly, though faithfully, translated into French by M. Le Clerc de Septchenes, a young gentleman of a studious character and liberal fortune. After his decease the work was continued by two manufacturers of Paris, M. M. Desmuniers and Cantwell : but the former is now an active member in the national assembly, and the undertaking languishes in the hands of his associate. The superior merit of the interpreter, or his language, inclines me to prefer the Italian version : but I wish that it were in my power to read the German, which is praised by the best judges. The Irish pirates are at once my friends and my enemies, But I cannot be displeased with the too numerous and correct impressions which have been published for the use of the continent at Basil in Switzerland.* The conquests of our language and literature are not confined to Europe alone, and a writer who succeeds in London, is speedily read on the banks of the Delaware and the Ganges.

In the preface of the fourth volume, while I gloried in the name of an Englishman, I announced my approaching return to the neighbourhood of the Lake of Lausanne. This last trial confirmed my assurance that I had wisely chosen for my own happiness ; nor did I once, in a year's visit, entertain a wish of settling in my native country. Britain is the free and fortunate island ; but where is the spot in which I could unite the comforts and beauties of my establishment at Lausanne ? The tumult of London astonished my eyes and ears ; the amusements of public places were no longer adequate to the trouble ; the clubs and assemblies were filled with new faces and young men ; and our best society, our long and late dinners, would soon have been prejudicial to my health. Without any share in the political wheel, I must be idle and insignificant : yet the most splendid temptations would not have enticed me to engage a second time in the servitude of Parliament or office. At Tunbridge, some weeks after the publication of my History, I reluctantly quitted Lord and Lady Sheffield, and, with a young Swiss friend, M. Wilhelm. de Severy, whom I had introduced to the English world, I pursued the road of Dover and Lausanne. My habitation was embellished in my absence, and the last division of books, which followed my steps, increased my chosen library to the number of between six and seven thousand volumes. My seraglio was ample, my choice was free, my appetite was keen. After a full repast on Homer and Aristophanes, I involved myself in the philosophic maze of the writings of Plato, of which the dramatic is, perhaps, more interesting than the argumentative part : but I stepped aside into every path of inquiry which reading or reflection accidentally opened.

Alas ! the joy of my return, and my studious ardour, were soon damped by the melancholy state of my friend Mr. Deyverdun. His health and spirits had long suffered a gradual decline, a succession of apoplectic fits announced his dissolution ; and before he expired, those who loved him could not wish for the continuance of his life. The voice of reason might congratulate his deliverance, but the feelings of nature and friendship could be subdued only by time : his amiable character was still alive in my remembrance ; each room, each walk, was imprinted with our common footsteps ; and I should blush at my

---

* Of their 14 8vo. vols. the two last include the whole body of the notes. The public importunity had forced *me* to remove them from the end of the volume to the bottom of the page ; but I have often repented of my compliance.

own philosophy, if a long interval of study had not preceded and followed the death of my friend. By his last will he left to me the option of purchasing his house and garden, or of possessing them during my life, on the payment either of a stipulated price, or of an easy retribution to his kinsman and heir. I should probably have been tempted by the dæmon of property, if some legal difficulties had not been started against my title ; a contest would have been vexatious, doubtful, and invidious ; and the heir most gratefully subscribed an agreement, which rendered my life-possession more perfect, and his future condition more advantageous. Yet I had often revolved the judicious lines in which Pope answers the objections of his long-sighted friend :

> Pity to build without or child or wife ;
> Why, you'll enjoy it only all your life :
> Well, if the use be mine, does it concern one,
> Whether the name belong to Pope or Vernon?

The certainty of my tenure has allowed me to lay out a considerable sum in improvements and alterations : they have been executed with skill and taste ; and few men of letters, perhaps, in Europe, are so desirably lodged as myself. But I feel, and with the decline of years I shall more painfully feel, that I am alone in Paradise. Among the circle of my acquaintance at Lausanne, I have gradually acquired the solid and tender friendship of a respectable family, the family of de Severy : the four persons of whom it is composed are all endowed with the virtues best adapted to their age and situation ; and I am encouraged to love the parents as a brother, and the children as a father. Every day we seek and find the opportunities of meeting : yet even this valuable connection cannot supply the loss of domestic society.

Within the last two or three years our tranquillity has been clouded by the disorders of France : many families at Lausanne were alarmed and affected by the terrors of an impending bankruptcy; but the revolution, or rather the dissolution of the kingdom has been heard and felt in the adjacent lands.

I beg leave to subscribe my assent to Mr. Burke's creed on the revolution of France. I admire his eloquence, I approve his politics, I adore his chivalry, and I can almost excuse his reverence for church establishments. I have sometimes thought of writing a dialogue of the dead, in which Lucian, Erasmus, and Voltaire should mutually acknowledge the danger of exposing an old superstition to the contempt of the blind and fanatic multitude.

A swarm of emigrants of both sexes, who escaped from the public ruin, has been attracted by the vicinity, the manners, and the language of Lausanne ; and our narrow habitations in town and country are now occupied by the first names and titles of the departed monarchy. These noble fugitives are entitled to our pity; they may claim our esteem, but they cannot, in their present state of mind and fortune, much contribute to our amusement. Instead of looking down as calm and idle spectators on the theatre of Europe, our domestic harmony is somewhat embittered by the infusion of party spirit : our ladies and gentlemen assume the character of self-taught politicians; and the sober dictates of wisdom and experience are silenced by the clamour of the triumphant *democrates.* The fanatic missionaries of sedition have scattered the seeds of discontent in our cities and villages, which had flourished above two hundred and fifty years without fearing the approach of war, or feeling the weight of government. Many individuals, and some communities, appear to be infested with the Gallic phrenzy, the wild theories of equal and boundless freedom; but I trust that the body of the people will be faithful to their sovereign and to themselves; and I am satisfied that the failure or success of a revolt would equally terminate in the ruin of the country. While the aristocracy of Berne protects the happiness, it is superfluous to enquire whether it be founded in the rights of man : the œconomy of the state is liberally supplied without the aid of taxes; and the magistrates *must* reign with prudence and equity, since they are unarmed in the midst of an armed nation.

The revenue of Berne, excepting some small duties, is derived from church lands, tithes, feudal rights, and interest of money. The republic has nearly 500,000l. sterling in the English funds, and the amount of their treasure is unknown to the citizens themselves. For myself (may the omen be averted) I can only declare, that the first stroke of a rebel drum would be the signal of my immediate departure.

When I contemplate the common lot of mortality, I must acknowledge that I have drawn a high prize in the lottery of life. The far greater part of the globe is overspread with barbarism or slavery : in the civilized world, the most numerous class is condemned to ignorance and poverty ; and the double fortune of my birth in a free and enlightened country, in an honourable and wealthy family, is the lucky chance of an unit against millions. The general probability is about three to one, that a new-born infant will not live to complete his fiftieth year.* I have now passed that age, and may fairly estimate the present value of my existence in the three-fold division of mind, body, and estate.

1. The first and indispensable requisite of happiness is a clear conscience, unsullied by the reproach or remembrance of an unworthy action.

> —— Hic murus aheneus esto,
> Nil conscire sibi, nullâ pallescere culpâ.

I am endowed with a cheerful temper, a moderate sensibility, and a natural disposition to repose rather than to activity : some mischievous appetites and habits have perhaps been corrected by philosophy or time. The love of study, a passion which derives fresh vigour from enjoyment, supplies each day, each hour, with a perpetual source of independent and rational pleasure ; and I am not sensible of any decay of the mental faculties. The original soil has been highly improved by cultivation ; but it may be questioned, whether some flowers of fancy, some grateful errors, have not been eradicated with the weeds of prejudice. 2. Since I have escaped from the long perils

---

* Buffon, Supplement à l'Hist. naturelle, vii. p. 158—164, of a given number of new-born infants, one half, by the fault of nature or man, is extinguished before the age of puberty and reason,—a melancholy calculation !

of my childhood, the serious advice of a physician has seldom beer. requisite. "The madness of superfluous health" I have never known: but my tender constitution has been fortified by time, and the inestimable gift of the sound and peaceful slumbers of infancy may be imputed both to the mind and body. 3. I have already described the merits of my society and situation; but these enjoyments would be tasteless or bitter if their possession were not assured by an annual and adequate supply. According to the scale of Switzerland, I am a rich man; and I am indeed rich, since my income is superior to my expence, and my expence is equal to my wishes. My friend Lord Sheffield has kindly relieved me from the cares to which my taste and temper are most adverse: shall I add, that since the failure of my first wishes, I have never entertained any serious thoughts of a matrimonial connection?

I am disgusted with the affectation of men of letters, who complain that they have renounced a substance for a shadow; and that their fame (which sometimes is no insupportable weight) affords a poor compensation for envy, censure, and persecution.* My own experience, at least, has taught me a very different lesson: twenty happy years have been animated by the labour of my History; and its success has given me a name, a rank, a character, in the world, to which I should not otherwise have been entitled. The freedom of my writings has indeed provoked an implacable tribe; but, as I was safe from the stings, I was soon accustomed to the buzzing of the hornets: my nerves are not tremblingly alive, and my literary temper is so happily framed, that I am less sensible of pain than of pleasure. The rational pride of an author may be offended, rather than flattered, by vague indiscriminate praise; but he cannot, he should not, be indifferent to the fair testimonies of private and public esteem. Even his moral sympathy may be gratified by the idea, that now, in the present hour, he is imparting some degree of amusement or knowledge to his friends in a distant land: that one day his mind will be familiar to the grandchildren of those who are yet unborn.† I cannot boast of the friendship or favour of princes; the patronage of English literature has long since been devolved on our booksellers, and the measure of their liberality is the least ambiguous test of our common success. Perhaps the golden mediocrity of my fortune has contributed to fortify my application.

The present is a fleeting moment, the past is no more; and our prospect of futurity is dark and doubtful. This day may *possibly* be

---

* M. d'Alembert relates, that as he was walking in the gardens of Sans Souci with the King of Prussia, Frederic said to him, "Do you see that old woman, a poor weeder, asleep on that sunny bank? she is probably a more happy being than either of us." The king and the philosopher may speak for themselves; for my part I do not envy the old woman.

† In the first of ancient or modern romances (Tom Jones), this proud sentiment, this feast of fancy, is enjoyed by the genius of Fielding.—"Come, bright love of fame, &c. fill my ravished fancy with the hopes of charming ages yet to come. Foretel me that some tender maid, whose grandmother is yet unborn, hereafter, when, under the fictitious name of Sophia, she reads the real worth which once existed in my Charlotte, shall from her sympathetic breast send forth the heaving sigh. Do thou teach me not only to foresee but to enjoy, nay even to feed on future praise. Comfort me by the solemn assurance, that, when the little parlour in which I sit at this moment shall be reduced to a worse furnished box, I shall be read with honour by those who never knew nor saw me, and whom I shall neither know nor see." Book xiii. ch. 1.

my last ; but the laws of probability, so true in general, so fallacious in particular, still allow about fifteen years.* I shall soon enter into the period which, as the most agreeable of my long life, was selected by the judgment and experience of the sage Fontenelle. His choice is approved by the eloquent historian of nature, who fixes our moral happiness to the mature season in which our passions are supposed to be calmed, our duties fulfilled, our ambition satisfied, our fame and fortune established on a solid basis (see Buffon). In private conversation, that great and amiable man added the weight of his own experience; and this autumnal felicity might be exemplified in the lives of Voltaire, Hume, and many other men of letters. I am far more inclined to embrace than to dispute this comfortable doctrine. I will not suppose any premature decay of the mind or body; but I must reluctantly observe that two causes, the abbreviation of time, and the failure of hope, will always tinge with a browner shade the evening of life.

WHEN I first undertook to prepare Mr. Gibbon's Memoirs for the press, I supposed that it would be necessary to introduce some continuation of them, from the time when they cease, namely, soon after his return to Switzerland in the year 1788; but the examination of his correspondence with me suggested, that the best continuation would be the publication of his letters from that time to his death. I shall thus give more satisfaction, by employing the language of Mr. Gibbon, instead of my own; and the public will see him in a new and (I think) an admirable light, as a writer of letters. By the insertion of a few occasional sentences, I shall obviate the disadvantages that are apt to arise from an interrupted narration. A prejudiced or a fastidious critic may condemn, perhaps, some parts of the letters as trivial; but many readers, I flatter myself, will be gratified by discovering even in these my friend's affectionate feelings, and his character in familiar life. His letters in general bear a strong resemblance to the style and turn of his conversation; the characteristics of which were vivacity, elegance, and precision, with knowledge astonishingly extensive and correct. He never ceased to be instructive and entertaining; and in general there was a vein of pleasantry in his conversation which prevented its becoming languid, even during a residence of many months with a family in the country.

It has been supposed that he always arranged what he intended to say, before he spoke; his quickness in conversation contradicts this notion: but it is very true, that before he sat down to write a note or letter, he completely arranged in his mind what he meant to express. He pursued the same method in respect to other composition; and he occasionally would walk several times about his apartment before he

---

* Mr. Buffon, from our disregard of the possibility of death within the four and twenty hours, concludes that a chance, which falls below or rises above ten thousand to one, will never affect the hopes or fears of a reasonable man. The fact is true, but our courage is the effect of thoughtlessness, rather than of reflection. If a public lottery were drawn for, the choice of an immediate victim, and if our name were inscribed on one of the ten thousand tickets, should we be perfectly easy?

had rounded a period to his taste. He has pleasantly remarked to me, that it sometimes cost him many a turn before he could throw a sentiment into a form that gratified his own criticism. His systematic habit of arrangement in point of style, assisted, in his instance, by an excellent memory and correct judgment, is much to be recommended to those who aspire to any perfection in writing.

Although the Memoirs extend beyond the time of Mr. Gibbon's return to Lausanne, I shall insert a few Letters, written immediately after his arrival there, and combine them so far as to include even the last note which he wrote a few days previously to his death. Some of them contain few incidents; but they connect and carry on the account either of his opinions or of his employment.

LETTERS FROM EDWARD GIBBON, ESQ.,

TO THE

Right Hon. LORD SHEFFIELD.

LAUSANNE, July 30, 1788.—Wed., 3 p.m.

I HAVE but a moment to say, before the departure of the post, that after a very pleasant journey I arrived here about half an hour ago; that I am as well arranged, as if I had never stirred from this place; and that dinner on the table is just announced. Severy I dropt at his country-house about two leagues off. I just saluted the family, who dine with me the day after to-morrow, and return to town for some days, I hope weeks, on my account. The son is an amiable and grateful youth; and even this journey has taught me to know and to love him still better. My satisfaction would be complete, had I not found a sad and serious alteration in poor Deyverdun: but thus our joys are chequered! I embrace all; and at this moment feel the last pang of our parting at Tunbridge. Convey this letter or information, without delay, from Sheffield-Place to Bath. In a few days I shall write more amply to both places.

Oct. 1, 1788.

AFTER such an act of vigor as my first letter, composed, finished, and dispatched within half an hour after my landing, while the dinner was smoaking on the table, your knowledge of the animal must have taught you to expect a proportionable degree of relaxation; and you will be satisfied to hear, that, for many Wednesdays and Saturdays, I have consumed more time than would have sufficed for the epistle, in devising reasons for procrastinating it to the next post. At this very moment I begin so very late, as I am just going to dress, and dine in the country, that I can take only the benefit of the date, October the first, and must be content to seal and send my letter next Saturday.

Oct. the 4th.

SATURDAY is now arrived, and I much doubt whether I shall have time to finish. I rose, as usual, about seven; but as I knew I should have so much time, you know it would have been ridiculous to begin anything before breakfast. When I returned from my break-fast-room to the library, unluckily I found on the table some new and interesting books, which instantly caught my attention; and without injuring my correspondent, I could safely bestow a single hour to gratify my curiosity. Some things which I found in them insensibly led me to other books, and other enquiries; the morning has stolen away, and I shall be soon summoned to dress and dine with the two Severys, father and son, who are returned from the country on a disagreeable errand, an illness of Madame, from which she is however recovering. Such is the faithful picture of my mind and manners, and from a single day *disce omnes.* After having been so long chained to the oar, in a splendid galley indeed, I freely and fairly enjoy my liberty as I promised in my preface: range without control over the wide expanse of my library; converse, as my fancy prompts me, with poets and historians, philosophers and orators, of every age and language; and often indulge my meditations in the invention and arrangement of mighty works, which I shall probably never find time or application to execute. My garden, berceau, and pavilion often varied the scene of my studies; the beautiful weather which we have enjoyed exhilarated my spirits, and I again tasted the wisdom and happiness of my retirement, till that happiness was inter-rupted by a very serious calamity, which took from me for above a fortnight all thoughts of study, of amusement, and even of correspond-ence. I mentioned in my first letter the uneasiness I felt at poor Deyverdun's declining health, how much the pleasure of my life was embittered by the sight of a suffering and languid friend. The joy of our meeting appeared at first to revive him; and, though not satisfied, I began to think, at least to hope, that he was every day gaining ground; when, alas! one morning I was suddenly recalled from my berceau to the house, with the dreadful intelligence of an apoplectic stroke; I found him senseless: the best assistance was instantly collected: and he had the aid of the genius and experience of Mr. Tissot, and of the assiduous care of another physician, who for some time scarcely quitted his bedside either night or day. While I was in momentary dread of a relapse, with a confession from his physicians that such a relapse must be fatal, you will feel that I was much more to be pitied than my friend. At length, art or nature triumphed over the enemy of life. I was soon assured that all immediate danger was past; and now for many days I have had the satisfaction of seeing him recover, though by slow degrees, his health and strength, his sleep and appetite. He now walks about the garden, and receives his particular friends, but has not yet gone abroad. His future health will depend very much upon his own prudence: but, at all events, this has been a very serious warning; and the slightest indisposition will hereafter assume a very formidable aspect. But let us turn from this melancholy subject.—The Man of the People escaped from the tumult, the bloody tumult of the Westminster election, to the lakes and mountains of

Switzerland, and I was informed that he was arrived at the Lyon d'Or. I sent a compliment; he answered it in person, and settled at my house for the remainder of the day. I have eat and drank, and conversed and sat up all night with Fox in England; but it never has happened, perhaps it never can happen again, that I should enjoy him as I did that day, alone, from ten in the morning till ten at night. Poor Deyverdun, before his accident, wanted spirits to appear, and has regretted it since. Our conversation never flagged a moment; and he seemed thoroughly pleased with the place and with his company. We had little politics; though he gave me, in a few words, such a character of Pitt, as one great man should give of another his rival: much of books, from my own, on which he flattered me very pleasantly, to Homer and the Arabian Nights; much about the country, my garden (which he understands far better than I do), and, upon the whole, I think he envies me, and would do so were he minister. The next morning I gave him a guide to walk him about the town and country, and invited some company to meet him at dinner. The following day he continued his journey to Berne and Zurich, and I have heard of him by various means. The people gaze on him as a prodigy, but he shows little inclination to converse with them, &c. &c. &c. Our friend *Douglas* has been curious, attentive, agreeable; and in every place where he has resided some days, he has left acquaintance who esteem and regret him: I never knew so clear and general an impression.

After this long letter I have yet many things to say, though none of any pressing consequence. I hope you are not idle in the deliverance of Beriton, though the late events and edicts in France begin to reconcile me to the possession of dirty acres. What think you of Necker and the States Generales? Are not the public expectations too sanguine? Adieu. I will write soon to my lady separately, though I have not any particular subject for her ear. Ever yours.

LAUSANNE, Nov. 29, 1788.

As I have no correspondents but yourself, I should have been reduced to the stale and stupid communications of the newspapers, if you had not dispatched me an excellent sketch of the extraordinary state of things. In so new a case the *salus populi* must be the first law: and any extraordinary acts of the two remaining branches of the legislature must be excused by necessity, and ratified by general consent. * * Till things are settled, I expect a regular journal. From kingdoms I descend to farms. * * Adieu.

LAUSANNE, Dec. 13, 1788.

* * * OF public affairs I can only hear with curiosity and wonder: careless as you may think me, I feel myself deeply interested. You must now write often; make Miss Firth copy any curious fragments: and stir up any of my well-informed acquaintance, Batt, Douglas, Adam, perhaps Lord Loughborough, to correspond with me; I *will* answer them.

We are now cold and gay at Lausanne. The Severys came to town yesterday. I saw a good deal of Lords Malmsbury and Beauchamp, and their ladies ; Ellis, of the Rolliad, was with them ; I like him much : I gave them a dinner.

Adieu for the present. Deyverdun is not worse.

LAUSANNE, April 25, 1789.

BEFORE your letter, which I received yesterday, I was in the anxious situation of a king, who hourly expects a courier from his general, with the news of a decisive engagement. I had abstained from writing, for fear of dropping a word, or betraying a feeling, which might render you too cautious or too bold. On the famous 8th of April, between twelve and two, I reflected that the business was determined ; and each succeeding day I computed the speedy approach of your messenger, with favourable or melancholy tidings. When I broke the seal, I expected to read, "What a damned unlucky fellow you are ! Nothing tolerable was offered, and I indignantly withdrew the estate." I *did* remember the fate of poor Lenborough, and I was afraid of your magnanimity, &c. It is whimsical enough, but it is human nature, that I now begin to think of the deep-rooted founda-tions of land, and the airy fabric of the funds. I not only consent, but even wish, to have eight or ten thousand pounds on a good mortgage. The pipe of wine you sent to me was seized, and would have been confiscated, if the government of Berne had not treated me with the most flattering and distinguished civility : they not only released the wine, but they paid out of their own pocket the shares to which the bailiff and the informer were entitled by law. I should not forget that the bailiff refused to accept of his part. Poor Deyverdun's constitu-tion is quite broken ; he has had two or three attacks, not so violent as the first : every time the door is hastily opened, I expect to hear of some fatal accident : the best or worst hopes of the physicians are only that he may linger some time longer ; but if he lives till the summer, they propose sending him to some mineral waters at Aix, in Savoy. You will be glad to hear that I am now assured of pos-sessing, during my life, this delightful house and garden. The act has been lately executed in the best form, and the handsomest manner. I know not what to say of your miracles at home : we rejoice in the king's recovery, and its ministerial consequences ; and I cannot be insensible to the hope, at least the chance, of seeing in this country a first lord of trade, or secretary at war. In your answer, which I shall impatiently expect, you will give me a full and true account of your designs, which by this time must have dropt, or be determined at least, for the present year. If you come, it is high time that we should look out for a house—a task much less easy than you may possibly imagine. Among new books, I recommend to you the Count de Mirabeau's great work, "Sur la Monarchie Prussienne ;" it is in your own way, and gives a very just and complete idea of that wonderful machine. His "Correspondence Secrette" is diabolically good. Adieu. Ever yours.

LAUSANNE, June 13, 1789.

YOU are in truth a wise, active, indefatigable, and inestimable friend ; and as our virtues are often connected with our faults, if you were more tame and placid, you would be perhaps of less use and value. A very important and difficult transaction seems to be nearly terminated with success and mutual satisfaction : we seem to run before the wind with a prosperous gale ; and, unless we should strike on some secret rocks which I do not foresee, shall, on or before the 31st July, enter the harbour of Content ; though I cannot pursue the metaphor by adding we shall *land*, since our operation is of a very opposite tendency. I could not easily forgive myself for shutting you up in a dark room with parchments and attornies, did I not reflect that this probably is the last material trouble that you will ever have on my account ; and that after the labours and delays of twenty years, I shall at last attain what I have always sighed for, a clear and competent income, above my wants, and equal to my wishes. In this contemplation you will be sufficiently rewarded. I hope ***** will be content with our title-deeds, for I cannot furnish another shred of parchment. Mrs. Gibbon's jointure is secured on the Beriton estate, and her legal consent is requisite for the sale. Again and again I must repeat my hope that she is perfectly satisfied, and that the close of her life may not be embittered by suspicion, or fear, or discontent. What new security does she prefer,—the funds, the mortgage, or your land ? At all events she must be made easy. I wrote to her again some time ago, and begged that if she were too weak to write, she would desire Mrs. Gould or Mrs. Holroyd to give me a line concerning her state of health. To this no answer ; I am afraid she is displeased.

Now for the disposal of the money : I approve of the 8000 l. mortgage on Beriton ; and honour your prudence in not shewing, by the comparison of the rent and interest, how foolish it is to purchase land. * * * There is a chance of my drawing a considerable sum into this country, for an arrangement which you yourself must approve, but which I have not time to explain at present. For the sake of dispatching, by this evening's post, an answer to your letter which arrived this morning, I confine myself to the *needful*, but in the course of a few days I will send a more familiar epistle. Adieu. Ever yours.

LAUSANNE, July 14, 1789.

POOR Deyverdun is no more : he expired Saturday the 4th instant ; and in his unfortunate situation, death could only be viewed by himself, and by his friends, in the light of a consummation devoutly to be wished. Since September he has had a dozen apoplectic strokes, more or less violent : in the intervals between them his strength gradually decayed ; every principle of life was exhausted ; and had he continued to drag a miserable existence, he must probably have survived the loss of his faculties. Of all misfortunes this was what he himself most apprehended : but his reason was clear and calm to the last ; he beheld his approaching dissolution with the firmness of a philosopher. I fancied that time and reflection had prepared me for the event ; but the habits of three-and-thirty years friendship are not so easily broken. The first days, and more especially the first nights, were indeed painful. Last Wednesday and Saturday it would not have been in my power to write. I must now recollect myself, since it is necessary for me not only to impart the news, but to ask your opinion in a very serious and doubtful question, which must be decided without loss of

I

time. I shall state the facts, but as I am on the spot, and as new lights may occur, I do not promise implicit obedience.

Had my poor friend died without a will, a female *first* cousin settled somewhere in the north of Germany, and whom I believe he had never seen, would have been his heir at law. In the next degree he had several cousins ; and one of these, an old companion, by name Mr. de Montagny, he has chosen for his heir. As this house and garden was the best and clearest part of poor Deyverdun's fortune : as there is a heavy duty or fine (what they call *lods*) on every change of property out of the legal descent ; as Montagny has a small estate and a large family, it was necessary to make some provision in his favour. The will therefore leaves me the option of enjoying this place during my life, on paying the sum of 250 l. (I reckon in English money) at present, and an annual rent of 30 l.; or else, of purchasing the house and garden for a sum which, including the duty, will amount to 2500 l. If I value the rent of 30 l. at twelve years purchase, I may acquire my enjoyment for life at about the rate of 600 l.; and the remaining 1900 l. will be the difference between that tenure and absolute perpetual property. As you have never accused me of too much zeal for the interest of posterity, you will easily guess which scale at first preponderated. I deeply felt the advantage of acquiring, for the smaller sum, every possible enjoyment, as long as I myself should be capable of enjoying: I rejected, with scorn, the idea of giving 1900 l. for ideal posthumous property ; and I deemed it of little moment whose name, after my death, should be inscribed on my house and garden at Lausanne. How often did I repeat to myself the philosophical lines of Pope, which seem to determine the question.

In this state of self-satisfaction I was not much disturbed by all my real or nominal friends, who exhort me to prefer the right of purchase; among such friends, some are careless and some are ignorant ; and the judgment of those, who are able and willing to form an opinion, is often biassed by some selfish or social affection, by some visible or invisible interest. But my own reflections have gradually and forcibly driven me from my first propensity; and these reflections I will now proceed to enumerate :

1. I can make this purchase with ease and prudence. As I have had the pleasure of *not* hearing from you very lately, I flatter myself that you advance on a carpet road, and that almost by the receipt of this letter (July 31st) the acres of Beriton will be transmuted into sixteen thousand pounds : if the payment be not absolutely completed by that day, ***** will not scruple, I suppose, depositing the 2600 l. at Gosling's, to meet my draught. Should he hesitate, I can desire Darrell to sell *quantum sufficit* of my short annuities. As soon as the new settlement of my affairs is made, I shall be able, after deducting this sum, to square my expence to my income, &c.

2. On mature consideration, I am perhaps less selfish and less philosophical than I appear at first sight : indeed, were I not so, it would now be in my power to turn my fortune into life-annuities, and let the Devil take the hindmost. I feel, (perhaps it is foolish,) but I feel that this little paradise will please me still more when it is absolutely my own ; and that I shall be encouraged in every improvement of use or

beauty, by the prospect that, after my departure, it will be enjoyed by some person of my own choice. I sometimes reflect with pleasure that my writings will survive me ; and that idea is at least as vain and chimerical.

3. The heir, Mr. de Montagny, is an old acquaintance. My situation of a life-holder is rather new and singular in this country ; the laws have not provided for many nice cases which may arise between the landlord and tenant : some I can foresee, others have been suggested, many more I might feel when it would be too late. His right of property might plague and confine me ; he might forbid my lending to a friend, inspect my conduct, check my improvements, call for securities, repairs, &c. But if I purchase, I walk on my own terrace fierce and erect, the free master of one of the most delicious spots on the globe.

Should I ever migrate homewards, (you stare, but such an event is less improbable than I could have thought it two years ago,) this place would be disputed by strangers and natives.

Weigh these reasons, and send me without delay a rational explicit opinion, to which I shall pay such regard as the nature of circumstances will allow. But, alas! when all is determined, I shall possess this house, by whatsoever tenure, without friendship or domestic society. I did not imagine, six years ago, that a plan of life so congenial to my wishes, would so speedily vanish. I cannot write upon any other subject. Adieu, your's ever.

LAUSANNE, August 1789.

AFTER receiving and dispatching the power of attorney, last Wednesday, I opened, with some palpitation, the unexpected missive which arrived this morning. The perusal of the contents spoiled my breakfast. They are disagreeable in themselves, alarming in their consequences, and peculiarly unpleasant at the present moment, when I hoped to have formed and secured the arrangements of my future life. I do not perfectly understand what are these deeds which are so inflexibly required ; the wills and marriage-settlements I have sufficiently answered. But your arguments do not convince ****, and I have very little hope from the Lenborough search. What will be the event ? If his objections are only the result of legal scrupulosity, surely they might be removed, and every chink might be filled, by a general bond of indemnity, in which I boldly ask you to join, as it will be a substantial important act of friendship, without any possible risk to yourself or your successors. Should he still remain obdurate, I must believe what I already suspect, that **** repents of his purchase, and wishes to elude the conclusion. Our case would be then hopeless, *ibi omnis effusus labor*, and the estate would be returned on our hands with the taint of a bad title. The refusal of mortgage does not please me ; but surely our offer shews some confidence in the goodness of my title. If he will not take eight thousand pounds at *four per cent.* we must look out elsewhere ; new doubts and delays will arise, and I am persuaded that you will not place an implicit confidence in my attorney. I know not as yet your opinion about my Lausanne purchase. If you are against it, the present position of affairs gives you great advantage,

&c. &c. The Severys are all well; an uncommon circumstance for the four persons of the family at once. They are now at Mex, a country-house six miles from hence, which I visit to-morrow for two or three days. They often come to town, and we shall contrive to pass a part of the autumn together at Rolle. I want to change the scene; and beautiful as the garden and prospect must appear to every eye, I feel that the state of my own mind casts a gloom over them; every spot, every walk, every bench, recals the memory of those hours, of those conversations, which will return no more. But I tear myself from the subject. I could not help writing to-day, though I do not find I have said any thing very material. As you must be conscious that you have agitated me, you will not postpone any agreeable, or even *decisive* intelligence. I almost hesitate, whether I shall run over to England, to consult with you on the spot, and to fly from poor Deyverdun's shade, which meets me at every turn. I did not expect to have felt his loss so sharply. But six hundred miles! Why are we so far off?

Once more, What is the difficulty of the title? Will men of sense, in a sensible country, never get rid of the tyranny of lawyers? more oppressive and ridiculous than even the old yoke of the clergy. Is not a term of seventy or eighty years, nearly twenty in my own person, sufficient to prove our legal possession? Will not the records of fines and recoveries attest that *I* am free from any bar of entails and settlements? Consult some sage of the law, whether their present demand be necessary and legal. If your ground be firm, force them to execute the agreement or forfeit the deposit. But if, as I much fear, they have a right, and a wish, to elude the consummation, would it not be better to release them at once, than to be hung up for five years, as in the case of Lovegrove, which cost me in the end four or five thousand pounds? You are bold, you are wise; consult, resolve, act. In my penultimate letter I dropped a strange hint, that a migration homeward was not impossible. I know not what to say; my mind is all afloat; yet you will not reproach me with caprice or inconstancy. How many years did you damn my scheme of retiring to Lausanne! I executed that plan; I found as much happiness as is compatible with human nature, and during four years (1783—1787) I never breathed a sigh of repentance. On my return from England the scene was changed: I found only a faint semblance of Deyverdun, and that semblance was each day fading from my sight. I have passed an anxious year, but my anxiety is now at an end, and the prospect before me is a melancholy solitude. I am still deeply rooted in this country; the possession of this paradise, the friendship of the Severys, a mode of society suited to my taste, and the enormous trouble and *expence* of a migration. Yet in England (when the present clouds are dispelled) I could form a very comfortable establishment in London, or rather at Bath; and I have a very noble country-seat at about ten miles from East Grinstead in Sussex (*alluding to Sheffield-Place*). That spot is dearer to me than the rest of the three kingdoms; and I have sometimes wondered how two men, so opposite in their tempers and pursuits, should have imbibed so long and lively a propensity for each other. Sir Stanier Porten is just dead. He has left his widow with a moderate pension, and two children, my nearest relations: the eldest, Charlotte, is about

Louisa's age, and also a most amiable, sensible young creature. I have conceived a romantic idea of educating and adopting her; as we descend into the vale of years our infirmities require some domestic female society : Charlotte would be the comfort of my age, and I could reward her care and tenderness with a decent fortune. A thousand difficulties oppose the execution of the plan, which I have never opened but to you; yet it would be less impracticable in England than in Switzerland. Adieu. I am wounded; pour some oil into my wounds : yet I am less unhappy since I have thrown my mind upon paper.

Are you not amazed at the French revolution ? They have the power, will they have the moderation, to establish a good constitution ? Adieu, ever yours.

LAUSANNE, Sept. 9, 1789.

WITHIN an hour after the reception of your last, I drew my pen for the purpose of a reply, and my exordium ran in the following words : " I find by experience, that it is much more rational, as well as easy, to answer a letter of real business by the return of the post." This important truth is again verified by my own example. After writing three pages I was called away by a very rational motive, and the post departed before I could return to the conclusion. A second delay was coloured by some decent pretence. Three weeks have slipped away, and I now force myself on a task, which I should have dispatched without an effort on the first summons. My only excuse is, that I had little to write about English business, and that I could write nothing definitive about my Swiss affairs. And first, as Aristotle says of the first,

1. I was indeed in low spirits when I sent what you so justly stile my dismal letter ; but I do assure you, that my own feelings contributed much more to sink me, than any events or terrors relative to the sale of Beriton. But I again hope and trust, from your consolatory epistle, that, &c. &c.

2. My Swiss transaction has suffered a great alteration. I shall not become the proprietor of my house and garden at Lausanne, and I relinquish the phantom with more regret than you could easily imagine. But I have been determined by a difficulty, which at first appeared of little moment, but which has gradually swelled to an alarming magnitude. There is a law in this country, as well as in some provinces of France, which is styled *le droit de retrait, le retrait lignagere,* (Lord Loughborough must have heard of it,) by which the relations of the deceased are entitled to redeem a house or estate at the price for which it has been sold ; and as the sum fixed by poor Deyverdun is much below its known value, a crowd of competitors are beginning to start. The best opinions (for they are divided) are in my favour, that I am not subject to *le droit de retrait,* since I take not as a purchaser, but as a legatee. But the words of the will are somewhat ambiguous, the event of law is always uncertain, the administration of justice at Berne (the last appeal) depends too much on favour and intrigue : and it is very doubtful whether I could revert to the life-holding, after having chosen and lost the property. These considerations engaged me to open a negotiation with Mr. de Montagny, through the medium of my friend the judge : and as he most ardently wishes to keep the house,

he consented, though with some reluctance, to my proposals. Yesterday he signed a covenant in the most regular and binding form, by which he allows my power of transferring my interest, interprets in the most ample sense my right of making alterations, and expressly renounces all claim, as landlord, of visiting or inspecting the premises. I have promised to lend him twelve thousand livres, (between seven and eight hundred pounds,) secured on the house and land. The mortgage is four times its value; the interest of four pounds *per cent.* will be annually discharged by the rent of thirty guineas. So that I am now tranquil on that score for the remainder of my days. I hope that time will gradually reconcile me to the place which I have inhabited with my poor friend; for in spite of the *cream* of London, I am still persuaded that no other place is so well adapted to my taste and habits of studious and social life.

Far from delighting in the whirl of a metropolis, my only complaint against Lausanne is the great number of strangers, always of English, and now of French, by whom we are infested in summer. Yet we have escaped the *damned* great ones, the Count d'Artois, the Polignacs, &c., who slip by us to Turin. What a scene is France! While the assembly is voting abstract propositions, Paris is an independent republic; the provinces have neither authority nor freedom, and poor Necker declares that credit is no more, and that the people refuse to pay taxes. Yet I think you must be seduced by the abolition of tithes. If Eden goes to Paris you may have some curious information. Give me some account of Mr. and Mrs. Douglas. Do they live with Lord North? I hope they do. When will parliament be dissolved? Are you still Coventry-mad? I embrace my Lady, the sprightly Maria, and the smiling Louisa. Alas! alas! you will never come to Switzerland. Adieu, ever yours.

LAUSANNE, Sept. 25, 1789.

Alas! what perils do environ | The man who meddles with cold iron.

ALAS! what delays and difficulties do attend the man who meddles with legal and landed business! Yet if it be only to disappoint your expectation, I am not so very nervous at this new provoking obstacle. I had totally forgotten the deed in question, which was contrived in the last year of my father's life, to tie his hands and regulate the disorder of his affairs; and which might have been so easily cancelled by Sir Stannier, who had not the smallest interest in it, either for himself or his family. The amicable suit, which is now become necessary, must, I think, be short and unambiguous, yet I cannot help dreading the crotchets, that lurk under the chancellor's great wig; and, at all events, I foresee some additional delay and expence. The golden pill of the two thousand eight hundred pounds has soothed my discontent; and if it be safely lodged with the Goslings, I agree with you, in considering it as an unequivocal pledge of a fair and willing purchaser. It is indeed chiefly in that light I now rejoice in so large a deposit, which is no longer necessary in its full extent. You are apprised by my last letter that I have reduced myself to the life-enjoyment of the house and garden. And, in spite of my feelings, I am every day more convinced that I have chosen the safer side. I believe my cause to have been good, but it was doubtful. Law in this country is not so expensive as in England, but it is more troublesome; I must have gone to Berne, have solicited my judges in person; a vile custom! the event was uncertain; and during at least two years, I should have been in a state of suspense and anxiety; till the conclusion of which it would have been madness to have attempted any alteration or improvement. According to my present arrangement I shall want no more than eleven hundred pounds of the two thousand, and I suppose you will direct Gosling to lay out the remainder in India bonds, that it may not lie quite dead, while I am accountable to * * * * for the interest The elderly lady in a male habit, who informed me that Yorkshire is a register county, is a certain judge, one Sir William Blackstone, whose name you may possibly have heard. After stating the danger of purchasers and creditors, with regard to the title of estates on which they lay out or lend their money, he thus continues: "In Scotland every act and event regarding the transmission of property is regularly entered on record; and some of our own provincial divisions, particularly the extended county of York and the populous county of Middlesex, have prevailed with the legislature to erect such registers in their respective districts." (Blackstone's Comment., ii. 343, ed. 1774, qto.) If I am mistaken, it is in pretty good company; but I suspect that we are all right, and that the register is confined to one or two ridings. As we have, alas! two or three months before us, I should hope that your prudent sagacity will discover some sound land, in case you should not have time to arrange another mortgage. I now write in a hurry, as I am just setting out for Rolle, where I shall be settled with cook and servants in a pleasant apartment, till the middle of November. The Severys have a house there, where they pass the autumn. I am not sorry to vary the scene for a few weeks, and I wish to be absent while some alterations are making in my house at Lausanne. I wish the change of air may be of service to Severy the father, but we do not at all like his present state of health. How completely, alas, how completely! could I now lodge you: but your firm resolve of making me a visit seems to have vanished like a dream. Next summer you will not find five hundred pounds for a rational friendly expedition; and should parliament be dissolved, you will perhaps find five thousand for ———. I cannot think of it with patience. Pray take serious strenuous measures for sending me a pipe of excellent Madeira in cask, with some dozens of Malmsey Madeira. It should be consigned to Messrs. Romberg Voituriers at Ostend, and I must have timely notice of its march. We have so much to say about France, that I suppose we shall never say anything. That country is now in a state of dissolution. Adieu.

LAUSANNE, Dec. 15, 1789.
YOU have often reason to accuse my strange silence and neglect in the most important of *my own* affairs; for I will presume to assert, that in a business of yours of equal consequence, you should not find me cold or careless. But on the present occasion my silence is, perhaps, the highest compliment I ever paid you. You remember the answer of Philip of Macedon: Philip may sleep, while he knows that

Parmenio is awake." I expected, and to say the truth, I wished that my Parmenio would have decided and acted, without expecting my dilatory answer, and in his decision I should have acquiesced with implicit confidence. But since you will have my opinion, let us consider the present state of my affairs. In the course of my life I have often known, and sometimes felt, the difficulty of getting money, but I now find myself involved in a more singular distress, the difficulty of placing it, and if it continues much longer, I shall almost wish for my land again.

I perfectly agree with you that it is bad management to purchase in the funds when they do not yield four pounds *per cent.* * * * Some of this money I can place safely, by means of my banker here ; and I shall possess, what I have always desired, a command of cash, which I cannot abuse to my prejudice, since I have it in my power to supply with my pen any extraordinary or fanciful indulgence of expense. And so much, much indeed, for pecuniary matters. What would you have me say of the affairs of France? We are too near, and too remote, to form an accurate judgment of that wonderful scene. The abuses of the court and government called aloud for reformation ; and it has happened, as it will always happen, that an innocent well-disposed Prince has paid the forfeit of the sins of his predecessors ; of the ambition of Louis the Fourteenth, of the profusion of Louis the Fifteenth. The French nation had a glorious opportunity, but they have abused, and may lose their advantages. If they had been content with a liberal translation of our system, if they had respected the prerogatives of the crown, and the privileges of the nobles, they might have raised a solid fabric on the only true foundation, the natural aristocracy of a great country. How different is the prospect ! Their King brought a captive to Paris, after his palace had been stained with the blood of his guards ; the nobles in exile; the clergy plundered in a way which strikes at the root of all property ; the capital an independent republic ; the union of the provinces dissolved ; the flames of discord kindled by the worst of men ; (in that light I consider Mirabeau ;) and the honestest of the assembly a set of wild visionaries (like our Dr. Price,) who gravely debate, and dream about the establishment of a pure and perfect democracy of five-and-twenty millions, the virtues of the golden age, and the primitive rights and equality of mankind, which would lead, in fair reasoning, to an equal partition of lands and money. How many years must elapse before France can recover any vigour, or resume her station among the Powers of Europe? As yet there is no symptom of a great man, a Richlieu or a Cromwell, arising, either to restore the monarchy, or to lead the commonwealth. The weight of Paris, more deeply engaged in the funds than *all* the rest of the kingdom, will long delay a bankruptcy ; and if it should happen, it will be, both in the cause and the effect, a measure of weakness, rather than of strength. You send me to Chamberry, to see a Prince and an Archbishop. Alas ! we have exiles enough here, with the Marshal de Castries and the Duke de Guignes at their head ; and this inundation of strangers, which used to be confined to the summer, will now stagnate all the winter. The only ones whom I have seen with pleasure are Mr. Mounier, the late president of the national assembly, and the Count de Lally; they have both dined with me. Mounier, who is a serious dry politician, is returned to Dauphiné. Lally is an amiable man of the world, and a poet; he passes the winter here. You know how much I prefer a quiet select society to a crowd of names and titles, and that I always seek conversation with a view to amusement, rather than information. What happy countries are England and Switzerland, if they know and preserve their happiness.

I have a thousand things to say to my Lady, Maria, and Louisa, but I can add only a short postscript about the Madeira. Good Madeira is now become essential to my health and reputation. May your hogshead prove as good as the last; may it not be intercepted by the rebels or the Austrians. What a scene again in that country! Happy England! Happy Switzerland! I again repeat, adieu.

LAUSANNE, Jan. 27, 1790.

YOUR two last epistles, of the 7th and 11th instant, were somewhat delayed on the road; they arrived within two days of each other, the last this morning (27th); so that I answer by the first, or at least by the second post. Upon the whole, your French method, though sometimes more rapid, appears to me less sure and steady than the old German highway, &c. &c. * * * But enough of this. A new and brighter prospect seems to be breaking upon us, and few events of *that kind* have ever given me more pleasure than your successful negociation and * * * *'s satisfactory answer. The agreement is, indeed, equally convenient for both parties: no time or expence will be wasted in scrutinizing the title of the estate; the interest will be secured by the clause of five *per cent.* and I lament with you, that no larger sum than eight thousand pounds can be placed on Beriton, without asking (what might be somewhat impudent) a collateral security, &c. * * * But I wish you to choose and execute one or the other of these arrangements with sage discretion and absolute power. I shorten my letter, that I may dispatch it by this post. I see the time, and I shall rejoice to see it at the end of twenty years, when my cares will be at an end, and our friendly pages will be no longer sullied with the repetition of dirty land and vile money; when we may expatiate on the politics of the world and our personal sentiments. Without expecting your answer of business, I mean to write soon in a purer style, and I wish to lay open to my friend the state of my mind, which (exclusive of all worldly concerns) is not perfectly at ease. In the mean while, I must add two or three short articles. 1. I am astonished at Elmsley's silence, and the immobility of your picture, Mine should have departed long since, could I have found a sure opportunity, &c. Adieu, yours.

LAUSANNE, May 15, 1790.

SINCE the first origin (*ab ovo*) of our connection and correspondence, so long an interval of silence has not intervened, as far as I remember, between us, &c.

From my silence you conclude that the moral complaint, which I had insinuated in my last, is either insignificant or fanciful. The conclusion is rash. But the complaint in question is of the nature of a slow lingering disease, which is not attended with any immediate danger. As I have not leisure to expatiate, take the idea in three words : "Since the loss of poor Deyverdun, I am *alone;* and even in Paradise, solitude is painful to a social mind. When I was a dozen years younger, I *scarcely* felt the weight of a single existence amidst the crowds of London, of parliament, of clubs; but it will press more heavily upon me in this tranquil land, in the decline of life, and with the increase of infirmities. Some expedient, even the most desperate, must be embraced, to secure the domestic society of a male or female companion. But I am not in a hurry ; there is time for reflection and advice." During this winter such finer feelings have been suspended by the grosser evil of bodily pain. On the ninth of February I was seized by such a fit of the gout as I had never known, though I must be thankful that its dire effects have been confined to the feet and knees, without ascending to the more noble parts. With some vicis-situdes of better and worse, I have groaned between two and three months ; the debility has survived the pain, and though now easy, I am carried about in my chair, without any power, and with a very distant chance, of supporting myself, from the extreme weakness and contraction of the joints of my knees. Yet I am happy in a skilful physician, and kind assiduous friends : every evening, during more than three months, has been enlivened (excepting when I have been forced to refuse them) by some cheerful visits, and very often by a chosen party of both sexes. How different is such society from the solitary evenings which I have passed in the tumult of London ! It is not worth while fighting about a shadow, but should I ever return to England, Bath, not the metropolis, would be my last retreat.

Your portrait is at last arrived in perfect condition, and now occupies a conspicuous place over the chimney-glass in my library. It is the object of general admiration ; good judges (the few) applaud the work ; the name of Reynolds opens the eyes and mouths of the many ; and were not I afraid of making you vain, I would inform you that the original is not allowed to be more than five-and-thirty. In spite of private reluctance and public discontent, I have honourably dismissed *myself* (his portrait). I shall arrive at Sir Joshua's before the end of the month ; he will give me a look, and perhaps a touch ; and you will be indebted to the president one guinea for the carriage. Do not be nervous, I am not rolled up ; had I been so, you might have gazed on my charms four months ago. I want some account of yourself, of my Lady, (shall we never directly correspond ?) of Louisa, and of Maria. How has the latter since her launch supported a quiet winter in Sussex ? I so much rejoice in your divorce from that b—— Kitty Coventry, that I care not what marriage you contract. A great city would suit your dignity, and the duties which would kill me in the first session, would supply your activity with a constant fund of amusement. But tread softly and surely ; the ice is deceitful, the water is deep, and you may be soused over head and ears before you are aware. · Why did not you or Elmsley send me the African pamphlet* by the post ? it would not have cost much. You have such a knack of turning a nation, that I am afraid you will triumph (perhaps by the force of argument) over justice and humanity. But do you not expect to work at Belzebub's

* Observations on the Project for abolishing the Slave Trade, by Lord Sheffield.

sugar plantations in the infernal regions, under the tender government of a negro-driver? I should suppose both my Lady and Miss Firth very angry with you.

As to the bill for prints, which has been too long neglected, why will you not exercise the power, which I have never revoked, over all my cash at the Goslings? The Severy family has passed a very favourable winter; the young man is impatient to hear from a family which he places above all others: yet he will generously write next week, and send you a drawing of the alterations in the house. Do not raise your ideas; you know *I* am satisfied with convenience in architecture, and some elegance in furniture. I admire the coolness with which you ask me to epistolize Reynell and Elmsley, as if a letter were so easy and pleasant a task; it appears less so to me every day.

1790.

YOUR indignation will melt into pity, when you hear that for several weeks past I have been again confined to my chamber and my chair. Yet I must hasten, generously hasten, to exculpate the gout, my old enemy, from the curses which you already pour on his head. He is not the cause of this disorder, although the consequences have been somewhat similar. I am satisfied that this effort of nature has saved me from a very dangerous, perhaps a fatal crisis; and I listen to the flattering hope that it may tend to keep the gout at a more respectful distance, &c.

The whole sheet has been filled with dry selfish business; but I must and will reserve some lines of the cover for a little friendly conversation. I passed four days at the castle of Copet with Necker; and could have wished to have shown him, as a warning to any aspiring youth possessed with the dæmon of ambition. With all the means of private happiness in his power, he is the most miserable of human beings: the past, the present, and the future are equally odious to him. When I suggested some domestic amusements of books, building, &c. he answered, with a deep tone of despair, "Dans l'état ou je suis, je ne puis sentir que le coup de vent qui m'a abbatû." How different from the careless cheerfulness with which our poor friend Lord North supported his fall! Madame Necker maintains more external composure, *mais le Diable n'y perd rien.* It is true that Necker wished to be carried into the closet, like old Pitt, on the shoulders of the people; and that he has been ruined by the democracy which he had raised. I believe him to be an able financier, and know him to be an honest man; too honest, perhaps, for a minister. His rival Calonne has passed through Lausanne, in his way from Turin; and was soon followed by the Prince of Condé, with his son and grandson; but I was too much indisposed to see them. They have, or have had, some wild projects of a counter-revolution: horses have been bought, men levied: such foolish attempts must end in the ruin of the party. Burke's book is a most admirable medicine against the French disease, which has made too much progress even in this happy country. I admire his eloquence, I approve his politics, I adore his chivalry, and I can forgive even his superstition. The primitive church, which I have treated with some freedom, was itself at that time an innovation, and I was attached to the old Pagan establishment. The French spread so many lies about the sentiments of the English nation, that I wish the most considerable men of all parties and descriptions would join in some public act, declaring themselves satisfied and resolved to support our present constitution. Such a declaration would have a wonderful effect in Europe; and, were I thought worthy, I myself would be proud to subscribe it. I have a great mind to send you something of a sketch, such as all thinking men might adopt.

I have intelligence of the approach of my Madeira. I accept with equal pleasure the second pipe, now in the Torrid Zone. Send me some pleasant details of your domestic state, of Maria, &c. If my Lady thinks that my silence is a mark of indifference, my Lady is a goose. I *must* have you all at Lausanne next summer.

LAUSANNE, August 7, 1790.

I ANSWER at once your two letters; and I should probably have taken earlier notice of the first, had I not been in daily expectation of the second. I must begin on the subject of what really interests me the most, your glorious election for Bristol. Most sincerely do I congratulate your exchange of a cursed expensive jilt, who deserted you for a rich Jew, for an honourable connection with a chaste and virtuous matron, who will probably be as constant as she is disinterested. In the whole range of election from Caithness to St. Ives, I much doubt whether there be a single choice so truly honourable to the member and the constituents. The second commercial city invites, from a distant province, an independent gentleman, known only by his active spirit, and his writings on the subject of trade; and names him, without intrigue or expence, for her representative; even the voice of party is silenced, while factions strive which shall applaud the most. You are now sure, for seven years to come, of never wanting food; I mean business: what a crowd of suitors or complainants will besiege your door! what a load of letters and memorials will be heaped on your table! I much question whether even you will not sometimes exclaim, *Ohe! jam satis est!* but that is your affair. Of the excursion to Coventry I cannot decide, but I hear it is pretty generally blamed: but, however, I love gratitude to an old friend; and shall not be very angry if you damned them with a farewell to all eternity. But I cannot repress my indignation at the use of those foolish, obsolete, odious words, Whig and Tory. In the American war they might have some meaning; and then your Lordship was a Tory, although you supposed yourself a Whig: since the coalition, all general principles have been confounded; and if there ever was an opposition to men, not measures, it is the present. Luckily both the leaders are great men; and, whatever happens, the country must fall upon its legs. What a strange mist of peace and war seems to hang over the ocean! We can perceive nothing but secrecy and vigour; but those are excellent qualities to perceive in a minister. From yourself and politics I now return to my private concerns, which I shall methodically consider under the three great articles of mind, body, and estate.

1. I am not absolutely displeased at your firing so hastily at the hint, a tremendous hint, in my last letter. But the danger is not so serious or imminent as you seem to suspect ; and I give you my word, that, before I take the slightest step which can bind me either in law, conscience, or honour, I will faithfully communicate, and we will freely discuss, the whole state of the business. But at present there is not anything to communicate or discuss ; I do assure you that I have not any particular object in view : I am not in love with any of the hyænas of Lausanne, though there are some who keep their claws tolerably well pared. Sometimes, in a solitary mood, I have fancied myself married to one or another of those whose society and conversation are the most pleasing to me ; but when I have painted in my fancy all the probable consequences of such an union, I have started from my dream, rejoiced in my escape, and ejaculated a thanksgiving that I was still in possession of my natural freedom. Yet I feel, and shall continue to feel, that domestic solitude, however it may be alleviated by the world, by study, and even by friendship, is a comfortless state, which will grow more painful as I descend in the vale of years. At present my situation is very tolerable ; and if at dinner-time, or at my return home in the evening, I sometimes sigh for a companion, there are many hours, and many occasions, in which I enjoy the superior blessing of being sole master of my own house. But your plan, though less dangerous, is still more absurd than mine : such a couple as you describe could not be found ; and, if found, would not answer my purpose ; their rank and position would be awkward and ambiguous to myself and my acquaintance, and the agreement of three persons of three characters would be still more impracticable. My plan of Charlotte Porten is undoubtedly the most desirable ; and she might either remain a spinster (the case is not without example), or marry some Swiss of my choice, who would increase and enliven our society ; and both would have the strongest motives for kind and dutiful behaviour. But the mother has been indirectly sounded, and will not hear of such a proposal for some years. On my side, I would not take her, but as a piece of soft wax which I could model to the language and manners of the country : I must therefore be patient.

Young Severy's letter, which may be now in your hands, and which, for these three or four last posts, has furnished my indolence with a new pretence for delay, has already imformed you of the means and circumstances of my resurrection. Tedious indeed was my confinement, since I was not able to move from my house or chair, from the ninth of February to the first of July, very nearly five months. The first weeks were accompanied with more pain than I have ever known in the gout, with anxious days and sleepless nights ; and when that pain subsided, it left a weakness in my knees which seemed to have no end. My confinement was however softened by books, by the possession of every comfort and convenience, by a succession each evening of agreeable company, and by a flow of equal spirits and general good health. During the last weeks I descended to the ground floor, poor Deyverdun's apartment, and constructed a chair like Merlin's, in which I could wheel myself in the house and on the terrace. My patience has been universally admired; yet how many thousands have passed those five months less easily than myself. I remember making a remark perfectly simple, and perfectly true; "At present (I said to Madame de Severy,) I am not positively miserable, and I may reasonably hope a daily or weekly improvement, till sooner or later in the summer I shall recover new limbs, and new pleasures, which I do not now possess: have any of you such a prospect?" The prediction has been accomplished, and I have arrived to my present condition of strength, or rather of feebleness: I now can walk with tolerable ease in my garden and smooth places; but on the rough pavement of the town I use, and perhaps shall use, a sedan chair. The Pyrmont waters have performed wonders; and my physician (not Tissot, but a very sensible man) allows me to hope, that the term of the interval will be in proportion to that of the fit.

Have you read in the English papers, that the government of Berne is overturned, and that we are divided into three democratical leagues? true as what I have read in the French papers, that the English have cut off Pitt's head, and abolished the House of Lords. The people of this country are happy; and in spite of some miscreants, and more foreign emissaries, they are sensible of their happiness.

Finally—Inform my Lady, that I am indignant at a false and heretical assertion in her last letter to Severy, "that friends at a distance cannot love each other, if they do not write." I love her better than any woman in the world; indeed I do; and yet I do not write. And she herself—but I am calm. We have now nearly one hundred French exiles, some of them worth being acquainted with; particularly a Count de Schomberg, who is become almost my friend; he is a man of the world, of letters, and of sufficient age, since in 1753 he succeeded to Marshal Saxe's regiment of dragoons. As to the rest, I entertain them, and they flatter me: but I wish we were reduced to our Lausanne society. Poor France! the state is dissolved, the nation is mad! Adieu.

LAUSANNE, April 9, 1791.

FIRST, of my health: it is now tolerably restored, my legs are still weak, but the animal in general is in a sound and lively condition; and we have great hopes from the fine weather and the Pyrmont waters. I most sincerely wished for the presence of Maria, to embellish a ball which I gave the 29th of last month to all the best company, natives and foreigners, of Lausanne, with the aid of the Severys, especially of the mother and son, who directed the œconomy, and performed the honours of the *fête*. It opened about seven in the evening; the assembly of men and women was pleased and pleasing, the music good, the illumination splendid, the refreshments profuse: at twelve, one hundred and thirty persons sat down to a very good supper: at two, I stole away to bed, in a snug corner; and I was informed at breakfast, that the remains of the veteran and young troops, with Severy and his sister at their head, had concluded the last dance about a quarter before seven. This magnificent entertainment has gained me great credit; and the expence was more reasonable than you can easily imagine. This was an extraordinary event, but I give frequent dinners ; and in the summer I have an assembly every Sunday evening. What a wicked wretch ! says my Lady.

I cannot pity you for the accumulation of business, as you ought not to pity *me*, if I complained of the tranquillity of Lausanne ; we suffer or enjoy the effects of our own choice. Perhaps you will mutter something, of our not being born for ourselves, of public spirit (I have formerly read of such a thing), of private friendship, for which I give you full and ample credit, &c. But your parliamentary operations, at least, will probably expire in the month of June ; and I shall refuse to sign the Newhaven conveyance, unless I am satisfied that you will execute the Lausanne visit this summer. On the 15th of June, suppose Lord, Lady, Maria, and Maid, (poor Louisa !) in a post coach, with Elienne on horseback, set out from Downing-Street, or Sheffield-Place, across the channel from Brighton to Dieppe, visit the National Assembly, buy caps at Paris, examine the ruins of Versailles, and arrive at Lausanne, without danger or fatigue, the second week in July ; you will be lodged pleasantly and comfortably, and will not perhaps despise my situation. A couple of months will roll, alas ! too hastily away : you will all be amused by new scenes, new people ; and whenever Maria and you, with Severy, mount on horseback to visit the country, the glaciers, &c. my Lady and myself shall form a very quiet tête-à-tête at home. In September, if you are tired, you may return by a direct or indirect way ; but I only desire that you will not make the plan impracticable, by grasping at too much. In return, I promise you a visit of three or four months in the autumn of ninety-two : you and my booksellers are now my principal attractions in England. You had some right to growl at hearing of my supplement in the papers : but Cadell's indiscretion was founded on a hint which I had thrown out in a letter, and which in all probability will never be executed. Yet I am not totally idle. Adieu.

LAUSANNE, May 18, 1791.

I WRITE a short letter, on small paper, to inform you, that the various deeds, which arrived safe and in good condition, have this morning been sealed, signed, and delivered, in the presence of respectable and well-known English witnesses. To have read the aforesaid acts, would have been difficult ; to have understood them, impracticable. I therefore signed them with my eyes shut, and in that implicit confidence, which we freemen and Britons are humbly content to yield to our lawyers and ministers. I hope, however, most seriously hope, that every thing has been carefully examined, and that I am not totally ruined. It is not without much impatience that I expect an account of the payment and investment of the purchase-money. It was my intention to have added a new edition of my will ; but I have an unexpected call to go to Geneva to-morrow with the Severys, and must defer that business a few days till after my return. On my return I may possibly find a letter from you, and will write more fully in answer : my posthumous work, contained in a single sheet, will not ruin you in postage. In the mean while let me desire you either never to talk of Lausanne, or to execute the journey this summer ; after the dispatch of public and *private* business, there can be no real obstacle but in yourself. Pray do not go to war with Russia ; it is very foolish. I am quite angry with Pitt. Adieu.

LAUSANNE, May 31, 1791.

AT length I see a ray of sunshine breaking from a dark cloud. Your epistle of the 13th arrived this morning, the 25th instant, the day after my return from Geneva; it has been communicated to Severy. We now believe that you intend a visit to Lausanne this summer, and we hope that you will execute that intention. If you are a man of honour, you shall find me one; and, on the day of your arrival at Lausanne, I will ratify my engagement of visiting the British isle before the end of the year 1792, excepting only the fair and foul exception of the gout. You rejoice me, by proposing the addition of dear Louisa; it was not without a bitter pang that I threw her overboard, to lighten the vessel and secure the voyage: I was fearful of the governess, a second carriage, and a long train of difficulty and expence, which might have ended in blowing up the whole scheme. But if you can bodkin the sweet creature into the coach, she will find an easy welcome at Lausanne. The first arrangements which I must make before your arrival, may be altered by your own taste, on a survey of the premises, and you will all be commodiously and pleasantly lodged. You have heard a great deal of the beauty of my house, garden, and situation; but such are their intrinsic value, that, unless I am much deceived, they will bear the test even of exaggerated praise. From my knowledge of your Lordship, I have always entertained some doubt how you would get through the society of a Lausanne winter: but I am satisfied that, exclusive of friendship, your summer visits to the banks of the Leman Lake will long be remembered as one of the most agreeable periods of your life; and that you will scarcely regret the amusement of a Sussex Committee of Navigation in the dog days. You ask for details: what details? a map of France and a post-book are easy and infallible guides. If the ladies are not afraid of the ocean, you are not ignorant of the passage from Brighton to Dieppe: Paris will then be in your direct road; and even allowing you to look at the Pandæmonium, the ruins of Versailles, &c., a fortnight diligently employed will clear you from Sheffield Place to Gibbon Castle. What can I say more?

As little have I to say on the subject of my worldly matters, which seem now, Jupiter be praised, to be drawing towards a final conclusion; since when people part with their money, they are indeed serious. I do not perfectly understand the ratio of the precise sum which you have poured into Gosling's reservoir, but suppose it will be explained in a general account.

You have been very dutiful in sending me, what I have always desired, a cut Woodfall on a remarkable debate; a debate, indeed, most remarkable! Poor ***** is the most eloquent and rational madman that I ever knew. I love ***'s feelings, but I detest the political principles of the man, and of the party. Formerly, you detested them more strongly during the American war, than myself. I am half afraid that you are corrupted by your unfortunate connections. Should you admire the National Assembly, we shall have many an altercation, for I am as high an aristocrat as Burke himself: and he has truly observed, that it is impossible to debate with temper on the subject of that cursed revolution. In my last excursion to Geneva I frequently saw the

Neckers, who by this time are returned to their summer residence at Copet. He is much restored in health and spirits, especially since the publication of his last book, which has probably reached England. Both parties, who agree in abusing him, agree likewise that he is a man of virtue and genius ; but I much fear that the purest intentions have been productive of the most baneful consequences. Our military men, I mean the French, are leaving us every day for the camp of the Princes at Worms, and support what is called * * * representation. Their hopes are sanguine ; I will not answer for their being well grounded ; it is *certain*, however, that the emperor had an interview the 19th instant with the Count of Artois at Mantua ; and the aristocrats talk in mysterious language of Spain, Sardinia, the Empire, four or five armies, &c. They will doubtless strike a blow this summer : may it not recoil on their own heads ! Adieu. Embrace our female travellers. A short delay !

LAUSANNE, June 12, 1791.

I NOW begin to see you all in real motion, swimming from Brighton to Dieppe, according to my scheme, and afterwards treading the direct road, which you cannot well avoid, to the turbulent capital of the late kingdom of France. I know not what more to say, or what further instructions to send ; they would indeed be useless, as you are travelling through a country which has been sometimes visited by Englishmen : only this let me say, that in the midst of anarchy the roads were never more secure than at present. As you will wish to assist at the national assembly, you will act prudently in obtaining from the French in London a good recommendation to some leading member ; Cazales, for instance, or the Abbé Maury. I soon expect from Elmsley a cargo of books ; but you may bring me any new pamphlet of exquisite flavour, particularly the last works of John Lord Sheffield, which the dog has always neglected to send. You will have time to write once more, and you must endeavour, as nearly as possible, to mark the day of your arrival. You may come either by Lyons and Geneva, by Dijon and les Rousses, or by Dole and Pontarliere. The post will fail you on the edge of Switzerland, and must be supplied by hired horses. I wish you to make your last day's journey easy, so as to dine upon the road, and arrive by tea-time. The pulse of the counter-revolution beats high, but I cannot send you any certain facts. Adieu. I want to *hear* my Lady abusing me for never writing. *All* the Severys are very impatient.

Notwithstanding the high premium, I do not absolutely wish you drowned. Besides all other cares, I must marry and propagate, which would give me a great deal of trouble.

LAUSANNE, July 1st, 1791.

IN obedience to your orders I direct a flying shot to Paris, though I have not anything particular to add, excepting that our impatience is increased in the *inverse ratio* of time and space. Yet I almost doubt whether you have passed the sea. The news of the King of France's escape must have reached you before the 28th, the day of your departure, and the prospect of strange unknown disorder may well have

K

suspended your firmest resolves. The royal animal is again caught, and all may probably be quiet. I was just going to exhort you to pass through Brussels and the confines of Germany; a fair Irishism, since if you read this, you are already at Paris. The only reasonable advice which now remains, is to obtain, by means of Lord Gower, a sufficiency, or even superfluity, of forcible passports, such as leave no room for cavil on a jealous frontier. The frequent intercourse with Paris has proved that the best and shortest road, instead of Besançon, is by Dijon, Dole, Les Rousses, and Niyon. Adieu. I warmly embrace the Ladies. It would be idle now to talk of business.

IT has appeared from the foregoing Letters, that a visit from myself and my family, to Mr. Gibbon at Lausanne, had been for some time in agitation. This long-promised excursion took place in the month of June 1791, and occasioned a considerable cessation of our correspondence. I landed at Dieppe immediately after the flight from, and return to, Paris of the unfortunate Lewis XVI. During my stay in that capital, I had an opportunity of seeing the extraordinary ferment of men's minds, both in the national assembly, in private societies, and in my passage through France to Lausanne, where I recalled to my memory the interesting scenes I had witnessed, by frequent conversations with my deceased friend. I might have wished to record his opinions on the subject of the French revolution, if he had not expressed them so well in the annexed Letters. He seemed to suppose, as some of his Letters hint, that I had a tendency to the new French opinions. Never indeed, I can with truth aver, was suspicion more unfounded; nor could it have been admitted into Mr. Gibbon's mind, but that his extreme friendship for me, and his utter abhorrence of these notions, made him anxious and jealous, even to an excess, that I should not entertain them. He was, however, soon undeceived; he found that I was full as averse to them as himself. I had from the first expressed an opinion, that such a change as was aimed at in France, must derange all the regular governments in Europe, hazard the internal quiet and dearest interests of this country, and probably end in bringing on mankind a much greater portion of misery, than the most sanguine reformer had ever promised to himself or others to produce of benefit, by the visionary schemes of liberty and equality, with which the ignorant and vulgar were misled and abused.

Mr. Gibbon at first, like many others, seemed pleased with the prospect of the reform of inveterate abuses; but he very soon discovered the mischief which was intended, the imbecility with which concessions were made, and the ruin that must arise, from the want of resolution or conduct, in the administration of France. He lived to reprobate, in the strongest terms possible, the folly of the first reformers, and the something worse than extravagance and ferocity of their successors. He saw the wild and mischievous tendency of those pretended reformers, which, while they professed nothing but amendment, really meant destruction to all social order; and so strongly was his opinion fixed as to the danger of hasty innovation, that he became a warm and zealous advocate for every sort of old establishment, which he marked in various ways, sometimes rather ludicrously; and I recollect, in a circle where French affairs were the topic, and some Portuguese present, he, seemingly with seriousness, argued in favour of the inquisition at Lisbon, and said he would not, at the present moment, give up even that old establishment.

It may, perhaps, not be quite uninteresting to the readers of these Memoirs, to know, that I found Mr. Gibbon at Lausanne in possession of an excellent house; the view from which, and from the terrace, was so uncommonly beautiful, that even his own pen would with difficulty describe the scene which it commanded. This prospect comprehended everything grand and magnificent, which could be furnished by the finest mountains among the Alps, the most extensive view of the Lake of Geneva, with a beautifully varied and cultivated country, adorned by numerous villas, and picturesque buildings, inter-mixed with beautiful masses of stately trees. Here my friend received us with an hospitality and kindness which I can never forget. The best apartments of the house were appropriated to our use; the choicest society of the place was sought for, to enliven our visit, and render every day of it cheerful and agreeable. It was impossible for any man to be more esteemed and admired than Mr. Gibbon was at Lausanne. The preference he had given to that place, in adopting it for a residence, rather than his own country, was felt and acknowledged by all the inhabitants; and he may have been said almost to have given the law to a set of as willing subjects as any man ever presided over. In return for the deference shewn to him, he mixed, without any affectation, in all the society, I mean all the best society, that Lausanne afforded; he could indeed command it, and was, perhaps, for that reason the more partial to it; for he often declared that he liked society more as a relaxation from study, than as expecting to derive from it amusement or instruction; that to books he looked for improvement, not to living persons. But this I considered partly as an answer to my expressions of wonder, that a man who might choose the most various and most generally improved society in the world, namely, in England, that he should prefer the very limited circle of Lausanne, which he never deserted, but for an occasional visit to M. and Madame Necker. It must not, however, be understood, that in chusing Lausanne for his home, he was insensible to the merits of a residence in England: he was not in possession of an income which corresponded with his notions of ease and comfort in his own country. In Switzerland, his fortune was ample. To this consideration of fortune may be added another, which also had its weight; from early youth Mr. Gibbon had contracted a partiality for foreign taste and foreign habits of life, which made him less a stranger abroad than he was, in some respects, in his native country. This arose, perhaps, from having been out of England from his sixteenth to his twenty-first year; yet, when I came to Lausanne, I found him apparently without relish for French society. During the stay I made with him he renewed his intercourse with the principal French who were at Lausanne; **of whom** there happened to be a considerable number, distinguished for rank or talents; many indeed respectable for both.* During my stay in Switzerland I was not absent from my friend's house, except during a short excursion that we made together to Mr. Necker's at Copet, and a tour to Geneva, Chamouny, over the Col de Balme, to Martigny, St. Maurice, and round the Lake by Vevay to Lausanne. In the social and singularly pleasant months that I passed with Mr. Gibbon, he enjoyed his usual cheerfulness, with good health. Since he left England, in 1788, he had had a severe attack, mentioned in one of the foregoing letters, of an Erysipelas, which at last settled in one of his legs, and left something of a dropsical tendency; for at this time I first perceived a considerable degree of swelling about the ancle.

In the beginning of October I left this delightful residence; and some time after my return to England, our correspondence recommenced.

LETTERS FROM E. GIBBON, Esq.,

TO

LORD SHEFFIELD, and Others.

EDWARD GIBBON, *Esq., to the Hon. Miss* HOLROYD.

LAUSANNE, 9 Nov. 1791.

GULLIVER is made to say, in presenting his interpreter, " My tongue is in the mouth of my friend." Allow me to say, with proper expressions and excuses, " My pen is in the hand of my friend;" and the aforesaid friend begs leave thus to continue.†

I remember to have read somewhere in Rousseau, of a lover quitting very often his mistress, to have the pleasure of corresponding with her. Though not absolutely your lover, I am very much your admirer, and should be extremely tempted to follow the same example. The spirit and reason which prevail in your conversation, appear to great advantage in your letters. The three which I have received from Berne, Coblentz, and Brussels have given me much real pleasure; first, as a proof that you are often thinking of me; secondly, as an evidence that you are capable of keeping a resolution; and thirdly, from their intrinsic merit and entertainment. The style, without any allowance for haste or hurry, is perfectly correct; the manner is neither too light, nor too grave; the dimensions neither too long, nor too short: they are such, in a word, as I should like to receive from the daughter of my best friend. I attend your lively journal, through bad

---

* Marshal de Castries and several branches of his family, Duc de Guignes and daughters, Duc and Duchesse de Guiche, Madame de Grammont, Princesse d'Henin, Princesse de Bouillon, Duchesse de Biron, Prince de Salms, Comte de Schomberg, M. Lally Tolendal, M. de Mounier, Madame d'Aguesseau and family, M. de Malherbes, &c. &c.

† The remainder of the letter was dictated by Mr. Gibbon, and written by M. Wilh. de Severy. S.

roads, and worse inns. Your description of men and manners conveys very satisfactory information ; and I am particularly delighted with your remark concerning the irregular behaviour of the Rhine. But the Rhine, alas ! after some temporary wanderings, will be content to flow in his old channel, while man—man is the greatest fool of the whole creation.

I direct this letter to Sheffield-Place, where I suppose you arrived in health and safety. I congratulate my Lady on her quiet establishment by her fireside ; and hope you will be able, after all your excursions, to support the climate and manners of Old England. Before this epistle reaches you, I hope to have received the two promised letters from Dover and Sheffield-Place. If they should not meet with a proper return, you will pity and forgive me. I have not yet heard from Lord Sheffield, who seems to have devolved on his daughter, the task which she has so gloriously executed. 1 shall probably not write to him, till I have received his first letter of business from England ; but with regard to my Lady, 1 have most excellent intentions.

I never could understand how two persons of such superior merit, as Miss Holroyd and Miss Lausanne, could have so little relish for one another, as they appeared to have in the beginning ; and it was with great pleasure that I observed the degrees of their growing intimacy, and the mutual regret of their separation. Whatever you may imagine, your friends at Lausanne have been thinking as frequently of yourself and company, as you could possibly think of them ; and you will be very ungrateful, if you do not seriously resolve to make them a second visit, under such name and title as you may judge most agreeable. None of the Severy family, except perhaps my secretary, are inclined to forget you ; and 1 am continually asked for some account of your health, motions, and amusements. Since your departure, no great events have occurred. I have made a short excursion to Geneva and Copet, and found Mr. Necker in much better spirits than when you saw him. They pressed me to pass some weeks this winter in their house at Geneva ; and 1 may possibly comply, at least, in part, with their invitation. The aspect of Lausanne is peaceful and placid ; and you have no hopes of a revolution driving me out of this country. We hear nothing of the proceedings of the commission,* except by playing at cards every evening with Monsieur Fischer, who often speaks of Lord Sheffield with esteem and respect. There is no appearance of Rosset and La Motte being brought to a speedy trial, and they still remain in the castle of Chillon, which (according to the geography of the National Assembly) is washed by the sea. Our winter begins with great severity ; and we shall not probably have many balls, which, as you may imagine, I lament much. Angletine does not consider two French words as a letter. Montrond sighs and

* A commission, at the head of which was Monsieur Fischer, one of the principal members of the government of Berne, a very active and intelligent man, who would have distinguished himself in the administration of any country. This commission, which was accompanied by two or three thousand of the best of the German militia of the Canton of Berne, was sent for the examining into some attempts to introduce the French revolutionary principles into the Pays de Vaud. Several persons were seized ; the greater part were released ; the examination was secret, but Rosset and La Motte were confined in the castle of Chillon ; and being afterwards condemned for correspondence with the French, to a long imprisonment, were trar sferred to the castle of Arbourg. S.

blushes whenever Louisa's name is mentioned : Philippine wishes to converse with her on men and manners. The French ladies are settled in town for the winter, and they form, with Mrs. Trevor, a very agreeable addition to our society. It is now enlivened by a visit of the Chevalier de Boufflers, one of the most accomplished men in the *ci devant* kingdom of France.

As Mrs. Wood, Madame de Silva, who has miscarried, is about to leave us, I must either cure or die ; and, upon the whole, I believe the former will be most expedient. You may see her in London, with dear Corea, next winter. My rival magnificently presents me with an hogshead of Madeira : so that in honour I could not supplant him : yet I do assure you, from my heart, that another departure is much more painful to me. The apartment below* is shut up, and I know not when I shall again visit it with pleasure. Adieu. Believe me, one and all, most affectionately yours.

EDWARD GIBBON, *Esq., to the Right Hon. Lord* SHEFFIELD.

LAUSANNE, December 28, 1791.

ALAS ! alas ! the dæmon of procrastination has again possessed me. Three months have nearly rolled away since your departure; and seven letters, five from the most valuable Maria, and two from yourself, have extorted from me only a single epistle, which perhaps would never have been written, had I not used the permission of employing my own tongue and the hand of a secretary. Shall I tell you, that, for these last six weeks, the eve of every day has witnessed a *firm* resolution, and the day itself has furnished some ingenious delay? This morning, for instance, I determined to invade you as soon as the breakfast things should be removed : they were removed; but I had something to read, to write, to meditate, and there was time enough before me. Hour after hour has stolen away, and I finally begin my letter at two o'clock, evidently too late for the post, as I must dress, dine, go abroad, &c. A foundation, however, *shall be* laid, which will stare me in the face ; and next Saturday I shall probably be roused by the awful reflection that it is the last day in the year.

After realizing this summer an event which I had long considered as a dream of fancy, I know not whether I should rejoice or grieve at your visit to Lausanne. While I possessed the family, the sentiment of pleasure highly predominated ; when, just as we had subsided in a regular, easy, comfortable plan of life, the last trump sounded, and, without speaking of the pang of separation, you left me to one of the most gloomy, solitary months of October which I have ever passed. For yourself and daughters, however, you have contrived to snatch some of the most interesting scenes of this world. Paris, at such a moment, Switzerland and the Rhine, Strasburg, Coblentz, have suggested a train of lively images and useful ideas, which will not be speedily erased. The mind of the young damsel, more especially, will be enlarged and enlightened in every sense. In four months she has lived many years ; and she will much deceive and displease me, if she

* The apartment principally inhabited during the residence of my family at Lausanne. S.

does not review and methodize her journal, in such a manner as she is capable of performing, for the amusement of her particular friends. Another benefit which will redound from your recent view is, that every place, person, and object, about Lausanne, are now become familiar and interesting to you. In our future correspondence (do I dare pronounce the word correspondence ?) I can talk to you as freely of every circumstance as if it were actually before your eyes. And first, of my own improvements.—All those venerable piles of ancient verdure which you *admire* have been eradicated in one fatal day. Your faithful substitutes, William de Severy and Levade, have never ceased to persecute me, till I signed their death warrant. Their place is now supplied by a number of picturesque naked poles, the foster-fathers of as many twigs of Platanusses, which may afford a grateful but distant shade to the founder, or to his seris Nepotibus. In the mean while l must confess that the terrace appears broader, and that I discover a much larger quantity of snow than I should otherwise do. The workmen admire your ingenious plan for cutting out a new bed-chamber and book-room ; but, on mature consideration, we all unanimously prefer the old scheme of adding a third room on the terrace beyond the library, with two spacious windows, and a fire-place between. It will be larger (28 feet by 21), and pleasanter, and warmer : the difference of expence will be much less considerable than I imagined : the door of communication with the library will be artfully buried in the wainscot : and, unless it be opened by my own choice, may always remain a profound secret. Such is the design ; but, as it will not be executed before next summer, you have time and liberty to state your objections. I am much colder about the staircase, but it may be finished, according to your idea, for thirty pounds ; and I feel they will persuade me. Am I not a very rich man ? When these alterations are completed, few authors of six volumes in quarto will be more agreeably lodged than myself. Lausanne is now full and lively ; all our native families are returned from the country ; and, praised be the Lord ! we are infested with few foreigners, either French or English. Even our democrats are more reasonable or more discreet ; it is agreed, to wave the subject of politics, and all seem happy and cordial. I have a grand dinner this week, a supper of thirty or forty people on Twelfth-day, &c.; some concerts have taken place ; some balls are talked of ; and even Maria would allow (yet it is ungenerous to say even Maria) that the winter scene at Lausanne is tolerably gay and active. I say nothing of the Severys, as Angletine has epistolized Maria last post. She has probably hinted that her brother meditates a short excursion to Turin ; that worthy fellow Trevor has given him a pressing invitation to his own house. In the beginning of February I propose going to Geneva for three or four weeks. I shall lodge and eat with the Neckers ; my mornings will be my own, and l shall spend my evenings in the society of the place, where I have many acquaintance. This short absence will agitate my stagnant life, and restore me with fresh appetite to my house, my library, and my friends. Before that time (the end of February) what events may happen, or be ready to happen ! The National Assembly (compared to which the former was a senate of heroes and demi-gods) seem resolved to attack

Germany *avec quatre millions de bayonettes libres;* the army of the princes must soon either fight, or starve, or conquer. Will Sweden draw his sword? will Russia draw her purse? an empty purse! All is darkness and anarchy : neither party is strong enough to oppose a settlement ; and 1 cannot see a possibility of an amicable arrangement, where there are no heads (in any sense of the word) who can answer for the multitude. Send me your ideas and those of Lord Guildford, Lord Loughborough, Fox, &c.

Before I conclude, a word of my vexatious affairs.—Shall I never sail on the smooth stream of good security and half-yearly interest? will everybody refuse my money? I had already written to Darrel and Gosling to obey your commands, and was in hopes that you had already made large and salutary evacuations. During your absence I never expected much effect from the cold indifference of agents ; but you are now in England—you will be speedily in London : set all your setting-dogs to beat the field, hunt, inquire, why should you not advertise? Yet 1 am almost ashamed to complain of some stagnation of interest, when 1 am witness to the natural and acquired philosophy of so many French, who are reduced from riches, not to indigence, but to absolute want and beggary. A Count Argout has just left us, who possessed ten thousand a year in the island of St. Domingo ; he is utterly burnt and ruined ; and a brother, whom he tenderly loved, has been murdered by the negroes. These are real misfortunes. 1 have much revolved the plan of the Memoirs 1 once mentioned ; and, as you do not think it ridiculous, I believe I shall make an attempt : if I can please myself, 1 am confident of not displeasing ; but let this be a profound secret between us : people must not be prepared to laugh ; they must be taken by surprise. Have you looked over your, or rather my, letters? Surely, in the course of the year, you may find a safe and cheap occasion of sending me a parcel ; they may assist me. Adieu. I embrace my Lady : send me a favourable account of her health. I kiss the Marmaille. By an amazing push of remorse and diligence I have finished my letter (three pages and a half) this same day since dinner ; but I have not time to read it. Ever yours.

Half past Six.

LAUSANNE, Dec. 31, 1791.

To the same.   To-morrow a new year, *multos et felices!*

I NOW most sincerely repent of my late repentance, and do almost swear never to renounce the amiable and useful practice of procrastination. Had I delayed, as I was strongly tempted, another post, your missive of the 13th, which did not reach me till this morning (three mails were due), would have arrived in time, and I might have avoided this second Herculean labour. 1t will be, however, no more than an infant Hercules. The topics of conversation have been fully discussed, and I shall now confine myself to the needful of the new business. *Felix faustumque sit!* may no untoward accident disarrange your Yorkshire mortgage ; the conclusion of which will place me in a clear and easy state, such as I have never known since the first hour of property. * * *

The three per cents are so high, and the country is in such a damned state of prosperity under that fellow Pitt, that it goes against me to purchase at such low interest. In my visit to England next autumn, or in the spring following, (alas! you *must* acquiesce in the alternative,) I hope to be armed with sufficient materials to draw a sum, which may be employed as taste or fancy shall dictate, in the improvement of my library, a service of plate, &c. I am not very sanguine, but surely this is no uncomfortable prospect. This pecuniary detail, which has not indeed been so unpleasant as it used formerly to be, has carried me farther than I expected. Let us now drink and be merry. I flatter myself that your Madeira, improved by its travels, will set forwards for Messrs. Romberg, at Ostend, early in the spring; and I should be very well pleased if you could add a hogshead of excellent Claret, for which we should be entitled to the drawback : they must halt at Basle, and send notice to me for a safe-conduct. Have you had any intelligence from Lord Auckland about the wine which he was to order from Bourdeaux, by Marseilles and the Rhone? The one need not impede the other ; I wish to have a large stock. Corea has promised me a hogshead of his native Madeira, for which I am to give him an order on Cadell for a copy of the Decline and Fall : he vanished without notice, and is now at Paris. Could you not fish out his direction by Mrs. Wood, who by this time is in England? I rejoice in Lally's prosperity. Have you reconsidered my proposal of a declaration of constitutional principles from the heads of the party? I think a foolish address from a body of Whigs to the National Assembly renders it still more incumbent on you. Achieve my worldly concerns, *et eris mihi magnus Apollo.* Adieu, ever yours.

To the same.   LAUSANNE, April 4, 1792.

FOR fear you should abuse me, as usual, I will begin the attack, and scold at you for not having yet sent me the long-expected intelligence of the completion of my mortgage. You had positively assured me that the second of February would terminate my worldly cares, by a consummation so devoutly to be wished. The news, therefore, might reach me about the eighteenth : and I argued with the gentle logic of laziness, that it was perfectly idle to answer your letter, till I could chant a thanksgiving song of gratitude and praise. As every post disappointed my hopes, the same argument was repeated for the next ; and twenty empty-handed postillions have blown their insignificant horns, till I am provoked at last to write by sheer impatience and vexation. *Facit indignatio versum. Cospetto di Baccho ;* for I must ease myself by swearing a little. What is the cause, the meaning, the pretence, of this delay? Are the Yorkshire mortgagers inconstant in their wishes? Are the London lawyers constant in their procrastination? Is a letter on the road, to inform me that all is concluded, or to tell me that all is broken to pieces? Had the money been placed in the three per cents last May ; besides the annual interest, it would have gained by the rise of stock nearly twenty *per cent.* Your Lordship is a wise man, a successful writer, and an useful senator : you understand America and Ireland, corn and slaves, but your prejudice against the funds,* in which I am often tempted to join,

---

* It would be more correct if he had said, my preference for land. S.

makes you a little blind to their increasing value in the hands of our virtuous and excellent minister. But our regret is vain; one pull more and we reach the shore; and our future correspondence will be no longer tainted with business. Shall I then be more diligent and regular? I hope and believe so; for now that I have got over this article of worldly interest, my letter seems to be almost finished. *A propos* of letters, am I not a sad dog to forget my Lady and Maria? Alas! the dual number has been prejudicial to both. How happy could I be with either, were t'other dear charmer away. I am like the ass of famous memory; I cannot tell which way to turn first, and there I stand mute and immoveable. The baronial and maternal dignity of my Lady, supported by twenty years' friendship, may claim the preference. But the five incomparable letters of Maria!—Next week, however.—Am I not ashamed to talk of next week?

I have most successfully, and most agreeably, executed my plan of spending the month of March at Geneva, in the Necker-house, and every circumstance that I had arranged turned out beyond my expectation; the freedom of the morning, the society of the table and drawing-room, from half an hour past two till six or seven; an evening assembly and card party, in a round of the best company, and, excepting one day in the week, a private supper of free and friendly conversation. You would like Geneva better than Lausanne; there is much more information to be got among the men; but though I found some agreeable women, their manners and style of life are, upon the whole, less easy and pleasant than our own. I was much pleased with Necker's brother Mr. De Germain, a good-humoured, polite, sensible man, without the genius and fame of the statesman, but much more adapted for private and ordinary happiness. Madame de Stael is expected in a few weeks at Copet, where they receive her, and where "to dumb forgetfulness a prey," she will have leisure to regret "the pleasing anxious being," which she enjoyed amidst the storms of Paris. But what can the poor creature do? her husband is in Sweden, her lover is no longer secretary at war, and her father's house is the only place where she can reside with the least degree of prudence and decency. Of that father I have really a much higher idea than I ever had before; in our domestic intimacy he cast away his gloom and reserve; I saw a great deal of his mind, and all that I saw is fair and worthy. He was overwhelmed by the hurricane, he mistook his way in the fog, but in such a perilous situation, I much doubt whether any mortal could have seen or stood. In the meanwhile, he is abused by all parties, and none of the French in Geneva will set their foot in his house. He remembers Lord Sheffield with esteem; his health is good, and he would be tranquil in his private life, were not his spirits continually wounded by the arrival of every letter and every newspaper. His sympathy is deeply interested by the fatal consequences of a revolution, in which he had acted so leading a part; and he feels as a friend for the danger of M. de Lessart, who may be guilty in the eyes of the Jacobins, or even of his judges, by those very actions and dispatches which would be most approved by all the lovers of his country. What a momentous event is the Emperor's death! In the forms of a new reign, and of the Imperial election, the Democrats have at least gained time, if they knew how to use it. But the new monarch, though of a weak complexion, is of a martial temper; he loves the soldiers, and is beloved by them; and the slow fluctuating politics of his uncle may be succeeded by a direct line of march to the gates of Strasbourg and Paris. It is the opinion of the master movers in France, (I know it most certainly,) that their troops will not fight, that the people have lost all sense of patriotism, and that on the first discharge of an Austrian cannon the game is up. But what occasion for Austrians or Spaniards? the French are themselves their greatest enemies; four thousand Marseillois are marched against Arles and Avignon, the *troupes de ligne* are divided between the two parties, and the flame of civil war will soon extend over the southern provinces. You have heard of the unworthy treatment of the Swiss regiment of Ernst. The canton of Berne has bravely recalled them, with a stout letter to the King of France, which must be inserted in all the papers. I now come to the most unpleasant article, our home politics. Bosset and La Motte are condemned to fine and twenty years' imprisonment in the fortress of Arbourg. We have not yet received their official sentence, nor is it believed that the proofs and proceedings against them will be published; an awkward circumstance, which it does not seem easy to justify. Some (though none of note) are taken up, several are fled, many more are suspected and suspicious. All are silent, but it is the silence of fear and discontent; and the secret hatred which rankled against government begins to point against the few who are known to be well-affected. I never knew any place so much changed as Lausanne, even since last year; and though you will not be much obliged to me for the motive, I begin very seriously to think of visiting Sheffield-Place by the month of September next. Yet here again I am frightened, by the dangers of a French, and the difficulties of a German, route. You must send me an account of the passage from Dieppe to Brighton, with an itinerary of the Rhine, distances, expences, &c. As usual, I just save the post, nor have I time to read my letter, which, after wasting the morning in deliberation, has been struck off in a heat since dinner. No news of the Madeira. Your views of S. P. are just received; they are admired, and shall be framed. Severy has spent the carnival at Turin. Trevor is only the best man in the world.

To the Same.   LAUSANNE, May 30, 1792.

AFTER the receipt of your *penultimate*, eight days ago, I expected, with much impatience, the arrival of your next-promised epistle. It arrived this morning, but has not completely answered my expectations. I wanted, and I hoped for a full and fair picture of the present and probable aspect of your political world, with which, at this distance, I seem every day less satisfied. In the slave question you triumphed last session, in this you have been defeated. What is the cause of this alteration? If it proceeded only from an impulse of humanity, I cannot be displeased, even with an error; since it is very likely that my own vote (had I possessed one) would have been added to the majority. But in this rage against slavery, in the numerous petitions against the slave trade, was there no leaven of new democratical principles? no wild ideas of the rights and natural equality of man? It is these, I fear. Some articles in newspapers, some pamphlets of the year, the Jockey Club, have fallen into my hands. I do not infer much from such publications; yet I have never known them of so black and malignant a cast. I shuddered at Grey's motion; disliked the half-support of Fox, admired the firmness of Pitt's declaration, and excused the usual intemperance of Burke. Surely such men as ∗ ∗ ∗, ∗ ∗ ∗, ∗ ∗ ∗, have talents for mischief. I see a club of reform which contains some respectable names. Inform me of the professions, the principles, the plans, the resources, of these reformers. Will they heat the minds of the people? Does the French democracy gain no ground? Will the bulk of your party stand firm to their own interest, and that of their country? Will you not take some active measures to declare your sound opinions, and separate yourselves from your rotten members? If you allow them to perplex government, if you trifle with this solemn business, if you do not resist the spirit of innovation in the first attempt, if you admit the smallest and most specious change in our parliamentary system, you are lost. You will be driven from one step to another; from principles just in theory, to consequences most pernicious in practice; and your first concessions will be productive of every subsequent mischief, for which you will be answerable to your country and to posterity. Do not suffer yourselves to be lulled into a false security; remember the proud fabric of the French monarchy. Not four years ago it stood founded, as it might seem, on the rock of time, force, and opinion, supported by the triple aristocracy of the church, the nobility, and the parliaments. They are crumbled into dust; they are vanished from the earth. If this tremendous warning has no effect on the men of property in England; if it does not open every eye, and raise every arm, you will deserve your fate. If I am too precipitate, enlighten; if I am too desponding, encourage me.

My pen has run into this argument; for, as much as a foreigner as you think me, on this momentous subject, I feel myself an Englishman.

The pleasure of residing at Sheffield-Place is, after all, the first and the ultimate object of my visit to my native country. But when or how will that visit be effected? Clouds and whirlwinds, Austrian Croats and Gallic cannibals, seem on every side to impede my passage. You seem to apprehend the perils or difficulties of the German road, and French peace is more sanguinary than civilized war. I must pass through, perhaps, a thousand republics or municipalities, which neither obey, nor are obeyed. The strictness of passports, and the popular ferment, are much increased since last summer: aristocrat is in every mouth, lanterns hang in every street, and an hasty word, or a casual resemblance, may be fatal. Yet, on the other hand, it is probable that many English, men, women, and children, will traverse the country without any accident before next September; and I am sensible that many things appear more formidable at a distance than on a nearer approach. Without any absolute determination, we must see what the events of the next three or four months will produce. In the meanwhile, I shall expect with impatience your next letter: let it be speedy; my answer shall be prompt.

You will be glad, or sorry, to learn that my gloomy apprehensions are much abated, and that my departure, whenever it takes place, will be an act of choice, rather than of necessity. I do not pretend to affirm, that secret discontent, dark suspicion, private animosity, are very materially assuaged ; but we have not experience, nor do we now apprehend, any dangerous acts of violence, which may compel me to seek a refuge among the friendly Bears (Berne), and to abandon my library to the mercy of the democrats. The firmness and vigour of government have crushed, at least for a time, the spirit of innovation ; and I do not believe that the body of the people, especially the peasants, are disposed for a revolution. From France, praised be the demon of anarchy ! the insurgents of the Pays de Vaud could not at present have much to hope ; and should the *gardes nationales*, of which there is little appearance, attempt an incursion, the country is armed and prepared, and they would be resisted with equal numbers and superior discipline. The Gallic wolves that prowled round Geneva are drawn away, some to the south and some to the north, and the late events in Flanders seem to have diffused a general contempt, as well as abhorrence, for the lawless savages, who fly before the enemy, hang their prisoners, and murder their officers. The brave and patient regiment of Ernest is expected home every day, and as Berne will take them into present pay, that veteran and regular corps will add to the security of our frontier.

I rejoice that we have so little to say on the subject of worldly affairs. * * * This summer we are threatened with an inundation, beside many nameless English and Irish ; but I am anxious for the Duchess of Devonshire and the Lady Elizabeth Foster, who are on their march. Lord Malmsbury, the *audacieux* Harris, will inform you that he has seen me : *him* I would have consented to keep.

One word more before we part ; call upon Mr. John Nicholls, bookseller and Printer, at Cicero's Head, Red-Lion-Passage, Fleet-Street, and ask him whether he did not, about the beginning of March, receive a very polite letter from Mr. Gibbon of Lausanne ? To which, either as a man of business or a civil gentleman, he should have returned an answer. My application related to a domestic article in the Gentleman's Magazine of August, 1788, (p. 698,) which had lately fallen into my hands, and concerning which I requested some farther lights. Mrs. Moss delivered the letters* into my hands, but I doubt whether they will be of much service to me ; the work appears far more difficult in the execution than in the idea, and as I am now taking my leave for some time of the library, I shall not make much progress in the memoirs of P. P. till I am on English ground. But is it indeed true, that I shall eat any Sussex pheasants this autumn ? The event is in the book of Fate, and I cannot unroll the leaves of September and October. Should I reach Sheffield-Place, I hope to find the whole family in a perfect state of existence, except a certain Maria Holroyd, my fair and *generous* correspondent, whose annihilation on proper terms I most fervently desire. I must receive a copious answer before the end of next month, June, and again call upon you for a map of your political world. The chancellor roars ; does he break his chain ? *Vale.*

---

* His letters to me for a certain period, which he desired me to send, to assist him in writing his Memoirs. S.

To the Same.   LAUSANNE, Aug. 23, 1792.

WHEN I inform you, that the design of my English expedition is at last postponed till another year, you will not be much surprised. The public obstacles, the danger of one road, and the difficulties of another, would alone be sufficient to arrest so unwieldy and inactive a being; and these obstacles, on the side of France, are growing every day more insuperable. On the other hand, the terrors which might have driven me from hence have, in a great measure, subsided; our state-prisoners are forgotten: the country begins to recover its old good humour and unsuspecting confidence, and the last revolution of Paris appears to have convinced almost everybody of the fatal consequences of democratical principles, which lead by a path of flowers into the abyss of hell. I may therefore wait with patience and tranquillity till the Duke of Brunswick shall have opened the French road. But if I am not driven from Lausanne, you will ask, I hope with some indignation, whether I am not drawn to England, and more especially to Sheffield-Place? The desire of embracing you and yours is now the strongest, and must gradually become the sole, inducement that can force me from my library and garden, over seas and mountains. The English world will forget and be forgotten, and every year will deprive me of some acquaintance, who by courtesy are styled friends: Lord Guildford and Sir Joshua Reynolds! two of the men, and two of the houses in London, on whom I the most relied for the comforts of society.

Sept. 12, 1792.

THUS far had I written in the full confidence of finishing and sending my letter the next post; but six post-days have unaccountably slipped away, and were you not accustomed to my silence, you would almost begin to think me on the road. How dreadfully, since my last date, has the French road been polluted with blood! and what horrid scenes may be acting at this moment, and may still be aggravated, till the Duke of Brunswick is master of Paris! On every rational principle of calculation he must succeed; yet sometimes, when my spirits are low, I dread the blind efforts of mad and desperate multitudes fighting on their own ground. A few days or weeks must decide the military operations of this year, and perhaps for ever; but on the fairest supposition, I cannot look forwards to any firm settlement, either of a legal or an absolute government. I cannot pretend to give you any Paris news. Should I inform you, as we believe, that *Lally is still among the cannibals,* you would possibly answer, that he is now sitting in the library at Sheffield. Madame de Stael, after miraculously escaping through pikes and poignards, has reached the castle of Copet, where I shall see her before the end of the week. If anything can provoke the King of Sardinia and the Swiss, it must be the foul destruction of *his* cousin Madame de Lamballe, and of *their* regiment of guards. An extraordinary council is summoned at Berne, *but resentment may be checked by prudence.* In spite of Maria's laughter, I applaud your moderation, and sigh for a hearty union of all the sense and property of the country. The times require it; but your last political letter was a cordial to my spirits. The Duchess of D. rather dislikes a coalition; amiable creature! The Eliza (we call her Bess) is furious against you for not writing. We shall lose them in a few days; but the motions of Bess and the Duchess for Italy or England are doubtful. Ladies Spencer and Duncannon certainly pass the Alps. I live with them. Adieu. Since I do not appear in person, I feel the absolute propriety of writing to my lady and Maria; but there is far from the knowledge to the performance of a duty. Ever your's.

To the Same.   LAUSANNE, Oct. 5, 1792.

As our English newspapers must have informed you of the invasion of Savoy by the French, and as it is possible that you may have some trifling apprehensions of my *being killed and eaten by those cannibals,* it has appeared to me that a short extraordinary dispatch might not be unacceptable on this occasion. It is indeed true, that about ten days ago the French army of the South, under the command of M. de Montesquieu, (if any French army can be said to be under any command,) has entered Savoy, and possessed themselves of Chamberry, Montmelian, and several other places. It has always been the practice of the King of Sardinia to abandon his transalpine dominions; but on this occasion the court of Turin appears to have been surprised by the strange eccentric motions of a democracy, which always acts from the passion of the moment, and their inferior troops have retreated, with some loss and disgrace, into the passes of the Alps. Mount Cenis is now impervious, and our English travellers who are bound for Italy, the Duchess of Devonshire, Ancaster, &c. will be forced to explore a long circuitous road through the Tyrol. But the Chablais is yet intact, nor can our telescopes discover the tricolor banners on the other side of the lake. Our accounts of the French numbers seem to vary from fifteen to thirty thousand men; the regulars are few, but they are followed by a rabble-rout, which must soon, however, melt away, as they will find no plunder, and scanty subsistence, in the poverty and barrenness of Savoy. *N.B.*—I have just seen a letter from M. de Montesquieu, who boasts that at his first entrance into Savoy he had only twelve battalions. Our intelligence is far from correct.

The magistrates of Geneva were alarmed by this dangerous neighbourhood, and more especially by the well-known animosity of an exiled citizen, Claviere, who is one of the six ministers of the French republic. It was carried by a small majority in the General Council, to call in the succour of three thousand Swiss, which is stipulated by ancient treaty. The strongest reason or pretence of the minority, was founded on the danger of provoking the French, and they seem to have been justified by the event; since the complaint of the French resident amounts to a declaration of war. The fortifications of Geneva are not contemptible, especially on the side of Savoy; and it is much doubted whether M. de Montesquieu is prepared for a regular siege; but the malcontents are numerous within the walls, and I question whether the spirit of the citizens will hold out against a bombardment. In the mean while the diet has declared that the first cannon fired against Geneva will be considered as an act of hostility against the whole Helvetic body. Berne, as the nearest and most powerful canton, has taken the lead with great vigour and vigilance; the road is filled with the perpetual succession of troops and artillery; and, if some disaffection lurks in the towns, the peasants, especially the Germans, are inflamed with a strong desire of encountering the murderers of their countrymen. M. de Watteville, with whom you dined at my house last year, refused to accept the command of the Swiss succour of Geneva, till it was made his first instruction that he should never, in any case, surrender himself prisoner of war.

In this situation, you may suppose that we have some fears. I have great dependence, however, on the many chances in our favour, the valour of the Swiss, the return of the Piedmontese with their Austrian allies, eight or ten thousand men from the Milanese, a diversion from Spain, the great events (how slowly they proceed) on the side of Paris, the inconstancy and want of discipline of the French, and the near approach of the winter season. I am not nervous, but I will not be rash. It will be painful to abandon my house and library; but, if the danger should approach, I will retreat before it, first to Berne, and gradually to the North. Should I even be forced to take refuge in England (a violent measure so late in the year), you would perhaps receive me as kindly as you do the French priests—a noble act of hospitality! Could I have foreseen this storm, I would have been there six weeks ago; but who can foresee the wild measures of the savages of Gaul? We thought ourselves perfectly out of the hurricane latitudes. Adieu. I am going to bed, and must rise early to visit the Neckers at Rolle, whither they have retired, from the frontier situation of Copet. Severy is on horseback, with his dragoons : his poor father is dangerously ill. It will be shocking if it should be found necessary to remove him. While we are in this very awkward crisis, I will write at least every week. Ever yours. Write instantly, and remember all my commissions.

To the Same.

I WILL keep my promise of sending you a weekly journal of our troubles, that, when the piping times of peace are restored, I may sleep in long and irreproachable silence : but I shall use a smaller paper, as our military exploits will seldom be sufficient to fill the ample size of our English quarto.

Oct. 13, 1792.

Since my last of the 6th, our attack is not more eminent, and our defence is most assuredly stronger, two very important circumstances, at a time when every day is leading us, though not so fast as our impatience could wish, towards the unwarlike month of November; and we observe with pleasure that the troops of M. de Montesquieu, which are chiefly from the Southern Provinces, will not cheerfully entertain the rigor of an Alpine winter. The 7th instant, M. de Chateauneuf, the French resident, took his leave with an haughty mandate, commanding the Genevois, as they valued their safety and the friendship of the republic, to dismiss their Swiss allies, and to punish the magistrates who had traitorously proposed the calling in these foreign troops. It is precisely the fable of the wolves, who offered to make peace with the sheep, provided they would send away their dogs. You know what became of the sheep. This demand appears to have kindled a just and general indignation, since it announced an edict of proscription; and must lead to a democratical revolution, which would probably renew the horrid scenes of Paris and Avignon. A general assembly of the citizens was convened, the message was read, speeches were made, oaths were taken, and it was resolved (with only three dissentient voices) to live and die in the defence of their country. The Genevois muster about three thousand well-armed citizens; and the Swiss, who may easily be increased (in a few hours) to an equal number, add spirit to the timorous, and confidence to the well-affected: their arsenals are filled with arms, their magazines with ammunition. and their granaries with corn. But their fortifications are extensive and imperfect, they are commanded from two adjacent hills; a French faction lurks in the city, the character of the Genevois is rather commercial than military, and their behaviour, lofty promise, and base surrender, in the year 1782, is fresh in our memories. In the mean while, 4000 French at the most are arrived in the neighbouring camp, nor is there yet any appearance of mortars or heavy artillery. Perhaps an haughty menace may be repelled by a firm countenance. If it were worth while talking of justice, what a shameful attack of a feeble, unoffending state! On the news of their danger, all Switzerland, from Schaffouse to the Pays de Vaud, has risen in arms; and a French resident, who has passed through the country, in his way from Ratisbon, declares his intention of informing and admonishing the National Convention. About eleven thousand Bernois are already posted in the neighbourhood of Copet and Nyon; and new reinforcements of men, artillery, &c. arrive every day. Another army is drawn together to oppose M. de Ferrieres, on the side of Bienne and the bishopric of Basle; and the Austrians in Swabia would be easily persuaded to cross the Rhine in our defence. But we are yet ignorant whether our sovereigns mean to wage an offensive or defensive war. If the latter, which is more likely, will the French begin the attack? Should Genoa yield to fear or force, this country is open to an invasion; and though our men are brave, we want generals; and I despise the French much less than I did two months ago. It should seem that our hopes from the King of Sardinia and the Austrians of Milan are faint and distant; Spain sleeps; and the Duke of Brunswick (amazement!) seems to have failed in his great project. For my part, till Geneva falls, I do not think of a retreat; but at all events, I am provided with two strong horses, and an hundred Louis in gold. Zurich would be probably my winter quarters, and the society of the Neckers would make any place agreeable. Their situation is worse than mine: I have no daughter ready to lie in; nor do I fear the French aristocrats on the road. Adieu. Keep my letters. Excuse contradictions and repetitions. The Duchess of Devonshire leaves us next week. Lady Elizabeth abhors you. Ever yours.

To the Same.   Oct. 20, 1792.

SINCE my last, our affairs take a more pacific turn; but I will not venture to affirm that our peace will be either safe or honourable. M. de Montesquieu and three commissioners of the Convention, who are at Carrouge, have had frequent conferences with the magistrates of Geneva; several expresses have been dispatched to and from Paris, and every step of the negotiation is communicated to the deputies of Berne and Zurich. The French troops observe a very tolerable degree of order and discipline; and no act of hostility has yet been committed on the territory of Geneva.

Oct. 27.

My usual temper very readily admitted the excuse, that it would be better to wait another week, till the final settlement of our affairs. The treaty is signed between France and Geneva; and the ratification of the Convention is looked upon as assured, if any thing can be assured in that wild democracy. On condition that the Swiss garrison, with the approbation of Berne and Zurich, be recalled before the first of December, it is stipulated that the independence of Geneva shall be preserved inviolate; that M. de Montesquieu shall immediately send away his heavy artillery; and that no French troops shall approach within ten leagues of the city. As the Swiss have acted only as auxiliaries, they have no occasion for a direct treaty; but they cannot prudently disarm, till they are satisfied of the pacific intentions of France; and no such satisfaction can be given till they have acknowledged the new republic, which they will probably do in a few days, with a deep groan of indignation and sorrow; it has been cemented with the blood of their countrymen! But when the Emperor, the King of Prussia, the first general, and the first army in Europe have failed, less powerful states may acquiesce, without dishonour, in the determination of fortune. Do you understand this most unexpected failure? I will allow an ample share to the badness of the roads and the weather, to famine and disease, to the skill of Dumourier, a heaven-born general! and to the enthusiastic ardour of the new Romans; but still, still there must be some secret and shameful cause at the bottom of this strange retreat. We are now delivered from the impending terrors of siege and invasion. The Geneva *emigrés*, particularly the Neckers, are hastening to their homes; and I shall not be reduced to the hard necessity of seeking a winter asylum at Zurich or Constance: but I am not pleased with our future prospects. It is much to be feared that the present government of Geneva will be soon modelled after the French fashion; the new republic of Savoy is forming on the opposite bank of the Lake; the Jacobin missionaries are powerful and zealous; and the malcontents of this country, who begin again to rear their heads, will be surrounded with temptations, and examples, and allies. I know not whether the Pays de Vaud will long adhere to the dominion of Berne; or whether I shall be permitted to end my days in this little paradise, which I have so happily suited to my taste and circumstances.

Last Monday only I received your letter, which had strangely loitered on the road since its date of the 29th of September. There must surely be some disorder in the posts, since the Eliza departed indignant at never having heard from you.

The case of my wine I think peculiarly hard: to lose my Madeira, and to be scolded for losing it. I am much indebted to Mr. Nichols for his genealogical communications, which I am impatient to receive; but I do not understand why so civil a gentleman could not favour me in six months, with an answer by the post : since he entrusts me with these valuable papers, you have not, I presume, informed him of my negligence and awkwardness in regard to manuscripts. Your reproach rather surprises me, as I suppose I am much the same as I have been for these last twenty years. Should you hold your resolution of writing only such things as may be published at Charing-Cross, our future correspondence would not be very interesting. But I expect and require, at this important crisis, a full and confidential account of your views concerning England, Ireland, and France. You have a strong and clear eye ; and your pen is, perhaps, the most useful quill that ever has been plucked from a goose. Your protection of the French refugees is highly applauded. Rosset and La Motte have escaped from Arbourg, perhaps with connivance to avoid disagreeable demands from the republic. Adieu. Ever yours.

To the Same. Nov. 10, 1792.

RECEIVED this day, November 9th, a most amiable dispatch from the too humble secretary (Miss Holroyd), of the family of Espee (meaning Sheffield-Place), dated October 24th, which I answer the same day. It will be acknowledged, that I have fulfilled my engagements with as much accuracy as our uncertain state and the fragility of human nature would allow. I resume my narrative. At the time when we imagined that all was settled, by an equal treaty between two such unequal powers, as the Geneva Flea and the Leviathan France, we were thunderstruck with the intelligence that the ministers of the republic refused to ratify the conditions ; and they were indignant, with some colour of reason, at the hard obligation of withdrawing their troops to the distance of ten leagues, and of consequently leaving the Pays de Gez naked, and exposed to the Swiss, who had assembled 15,000 men on the frontier, and with whom they had not made any agreement. The messenger who was sent last Sunday from Geneva is not yet returned ; and many persons are afraid of some design and danger in this delay. Montesquieu has acted with politeness, moderation, and apparent sincerity ; but he may resign, he may be superseded, his place may be occupied by an *enragé*, by Servan, or Prince Charles of Hesse, who would aspire to imitate the predatory fame of Custine in Germany. In the mean while, the General holds a wolf by the ears ; an officer who has seen his troops, about 18,000 men (with a tremendous train of artillery), represents them as a black, daring, desperate crew of buccaneers, rather shocking than contemptible ; the officers (scarcely a gentleman among them), without servants, or horses, or baggage, lying *higgledy piggledy* on the ground with the common men, yet maintaining a rough kind of discipline over them. They already begin to accuse and even to suspect their general, and call aloud for blood and plunder : could they have an opportunity of squeezing some of the rich citizens, Geneva would cut up as fat as most towns in Europe. During this suspension of hostilities they are permitted to visit the city without arms, sometimes three or four hundred at a time ; and the magistrates, as well as the Swiss commander, are by no means pleased with this dangerous intercourse, which they dare not prohibit. Such are our fears : yet it should seem on the other side, that the French affect a kind of magnanimous justice towards their little neighbour, and that they are not ambitious of an unprofitable contest with the poor and hardy Swiss. The Swiss are not equal to a long and expensive war ; and as most of our militia have families and trades, the country already sighs for their return. Whatever can be yielded, without absolute danger or disgrace, will doubtless be granted ; and the business will probably end in our owning the sovereignty, and trusting to the good faith of the republic of France : how that word would have sounded four years ago ! The measure is humiliating ; but after the retreat of the Duke of Brunswick, and the failure of the Austrians, the smaller powers may acquiesce without dishonour. Every dog has his day ; and these Gallic dogs have their day, at least, of most insolent prosperity. After forcing or tempting the Prussians to evacuate their country, they conquer Savoy, pillage Germany, threaten Spain : the Low Countries are ere now invaded ; Rome and Italy tremble ; they scour the Mediterranean, and talk of sending a squadron into the South Sea. The whole horizon is so black, that I begin to feel some anxiety for England, the last refuge of liberty and law ; and the more so, as I perceive from Lord Sheffield's last epistle that his firm nerves are a little shaken : but of this more in my next, for I want to unburthen my conscience. If England, with the experience of our happiness and French calamities, should now be seduced to eat the apple of false freedom, we should indeed deserve to be driven from the paradise which we enjoy. I turn aside from the horrid and improbable (yet not impossible) supposition, that, in three or four years' time, myself and my best friends may be reduced to the deplorable state of the French emigrants : they thought it as impossible three or four years ago. Never did a revolution affect, to such a degree, the private existence of such numbers of the first people of a great country: your examples of misery I could easily match with similar examples in this country and the neighbourhood ; and our sympathy is the deeper, as we do not possess, like you, the means of alleviating, in some degree, the misfortunes of the fugitives. But I must have, from the very excellent pen of the Maria, the tragedy of the Archbishop of Arles ; and the longer the better. Madame de Biron has probably been tempted by some faint and (I fear) fallacious promises of clemency to the women, and which have likewise engaged Madame d'Aguesseau and her two daughters to revisit France. Madame de Bouillon stands her ground, and her situation as a foreign princess is less exposed. As Lord S. has assumed the glorious character of protector of the distressed, his name is pronounced with gratitude and respect. The D. of Richmond is praised, on Madame de Biron's account. To the Princess d'Henin, and Lally, I wish to be remembered. The Neckers cannot venture into Geneva, and Madame de Stael will probably lie in at Rolle. He is printing a defence of the King, &c. against their republican Judges ; but the name of Necker is unpopular to all parties, and I much fear that the guillotine will be more speedy than the press. It will, however, be an eloquent performance ; and, if I find an opportunity, I am to send you one, to you Lord S. by his particular desire : he wishes likewise to convey some copies with speed to our principal people, Pitt, Fox, Lord Stormont, &c.

But such is the rapid succession of events, that it will appear like the *Pouvoir Executif,* his best work, after the whole scene has been totally changed. Ever yours.

P.S. The revolution of France, and my triple dispatch by the same post to Sheffield-Place, are, in my opinion, the two most singular events in the eighteenth century. I found the task so easy and pleasant, that I had some thoughts of adding a letter to the gentle Louisa. I am this moment informed, that our troops on the frontier are beginning to move, on their return home; yet we hear nothing of the treaty's being concluded.

EDWARD GIBBON *Esq. to the Hon. Miss* HOLROYD.

LAUSANNE, Nov. 10, 1792.

IN dispatching the weekly political journal to Lord. S. my conscience (for I have some remains of conscience) most powerfully urges me to salute, with some lines of friendship and gratitude, the amiable secretary, who might save herself the trouble of a modest apology. I have not yet forgotten our different behaviour after the much lamented *separation* of October the 4th, 1791, your meritorious punctuality, and my unworthy silence. I have still before me that entertaining narrative, which would have interested me, not only in the progress of the *carissima familia,* but in the motions of a Tartar camp, or the march of a caravan of Arabs; the mixture of just observation and lively imagery, the strong sense of a man, expressed with the easy elegance of a female. I still recollect with pleasure the happy comparison of the Rhine, who had heard so much of liberty on both his banks, that he wandered with mischievous licentiousness over all the adjacent meadows.* The inundation, alas! has now spread much wider; and it is sadly to be feared that the Elbe, the Po, and the Danube, may imitate the vile example of the Rhine: I shall be content, however, if our own Thames still preserves his fair character, of

Strong without rage, without o'erflowing full.

These agreeable epistles of Maria produced only some dumb intentions, and some barren remorse; nor have I designed, except by a brief missive from my chancellor, to express how much I loved the author, and how much I was pleased with the composition. That amiable author I have known and loved from the first dawning of her life and *coquetry,* to the present maturity of her talents; and as long as I remain on this planet, I shall pursue, with the same tender and even anxious concern, the future steps of her establishment and life. That establishment must be splendid; that life must be happy. She is endowed with every gift of nature and fortune; but the advantage which she will derive from them, depends almost entirely on herself. You must not, you shall not, think yourself unworthy to write to any man: there is none whom your correspondence would not amuse and satisfy. I will not undertake a task, which my taste would adopt, and my indolence would too soon relinquish; but I am really curious, from the best motives, to have a particular account of your own studies and

* Mr. Gibbon alludes to letters written by him to Miss Holroyd, when she was returning from Switzerland along the Rhine, to England.   S.

daily occupation. What books do you read ? and how do you employ your time and your pen ? Except some professed scholars, I have often observed that women in general read much more than men; but, for want of a plan, a method, a fixed object, their reading is of little benefit to themselves, or others. If you will inform me of the species of reading to which you have the most propensity, I shall be happy to contribute my share of advice or assistance. I lament that you have not left me some monument of your pencil. Lady Elizabeth Foster has executed a very pretty drawing, taken from the door of the greenhouse where we dined last summer, and including the poor Acacia (now recovered from the cruel shears of the gardener), the end of the terrace, the front of the Pavilion, and a distant view of the country, lake, and mountains. I am almost reconciled to d'Apples' house, which is nearly finished. Instead of the monsters which Lord Hercules Sheffield extirpated, the terrace is already shaded with the new acacias and plantanes ; and although the uncertainty of possession restrains me from building, I myself have planted a bosquet at the bottom of the garden, with such admirable skill that it affords shade without intercepting prospect. The society of the aforesaid Eliza, commonly called Bess, of the Duchess of D. &c. has been very interesting ; but they are now flown beyond the Alps, and pass the winter at Pisa. The Legards, who have long since left this place, should be at present in Italy; but I believe Mrs. Grimstone and her daughter returned to England. The Levades are highly flattered by your remembrance. Since you still retain some attachment to this delightful country, and it is indeed delightful, why should you despair of seeing it once more ? The happy peer or commoner, whose name you may assume, is still concealed in the book of fate : but, whosoever he may be, he will cheerfully obey your commands, of leading you from ——— Castle to Lausanne, and from Lausanne to Rome and Naples. Before that event takes place, I may possibly see you in Sussex ; and, whether as a visitor or a fugitive, I hope to be welcomed with a friendly embrace. The delay of this year was truly painful, but it was inevitable ; and individuals must submit to those storms which have overturned the thrones of the earth. The tragic story of the Archbishop of Arles I have now somewhat a better right to require at your hands. I wish to have it in all its horrid details*; and as you are now so much mingled

---

* The Answer to Mr. Gibbon's Letter is annexed, as giving the best account I have seen of the barbarous transaction alluded to. S.

SHEFFIELD-PLACE, November 1791.

"YOUR three letters received yesterday caused the most sincere pleasure to each individual of this family; to none more than myself. Praise, (I fear, beyond my deserts,) from one whose opinion I so highly value, and whose esteem I so much wish to preserve, is more pleasing than I can describe. I had not neglected to make the collection of facts which you recommend, and which the great variety of unfortunate persons whom we see, or with whom we correspond, enables me to make.

"As to that part of your letter which respects *my studies*, I can only say, the slightest hint on that subject is always received with the greatest gratitude, and attended to with the utmost punctuality; but I must decline that topic for the present, to obey your commands, which require from me the horrid account of the *massacre aux Carmes*.—Eight respectable ecclesiastics landed, about the beginning of October, from an open boat at Seaford, wet as the waves. The natives of the coast were endeavouring to get from them what they had not, (viz.) money, when a gentleman of the neighbourhood came to their protection; and, finding they had nothing, shewed his good sense, by dispatching them to Milord Sheffield : they had been pillaged, and with great difficulty had escaped from Paris. The reception they met with at this house, seemed to make the greatest impression on them ; they were in extacy on finding

with the French exiles, I am of opinion, that were you to keep a journal of all the authentic facts which they relate, it would be an agreeable exercise at present, and a future source of entertainment and instruction.

I should be obliged to you, if you would make, or find, some excuse for my not answering a letter from your aunt, which was presented to me by Mr. Fowler. I shewed him some civilities, but he is now a poor invalid, confined to his room. By her channel and yours I should be glad to have some information of the health, spirits, and situation of Mrs. Gibbon of Bath, whose alarms (if she has any) you may dispel. She is in my debt. Adieu ; most truly yours.

M. de Lally living : they gradually became cheerful, and enjoyed their dinner : they were greatly affected as they recollected themselves, and found us attending on them. Having dined, and drank a glass of wine, they began to discover the beauties of the dining-room, and of the chateau : as they walked about, they were overheard to express their admiration at the treatment they met, and *from Protestants.* We then assembled in the library, formed half a circle round the fire, M. de Lally and Milord occupying the hearth *à l'Angloise,* and questioning the priests concerning their escape. Thus we discovered, that two of these unfortunate men were in the Carmelite Convent at the time of the massacre of the one hundred and twenty priests, and had most miraculously escaped, by climbing trees in the garden, and from thence over the tops of the buildings. One of them, a man of superior appearance, described, in the most pathetic manner, the death of the Archbishop of Arles, (and with such simplicity and feeling, as to leave no doubt of the truth of all that he said,) to the following purport.—On the second of September, about five o'clock in the evening, at the time they were permitted to walk in the garden, expecting every hour to be released, they expressed their surprise at seeing several large pits, which had been digging for two days past : they said, the day is almost spent ; and yet Manuel told a person who interceded for us last Thursday, that on the Sunday following not one should remain in captivity : we are still prisoners : soon after, they heard shouts, and some musquet-shots. An ensign of the national guard, some commissaries of the sections, and some Marseillois rushed in : the miserable victims, who were dispersed in the garden, assembled under the walls of the church, not daring to go in, lest it should be polluted with blood. One man, who was behind the rest, was shot. '*Point de coup de fusils,*' cried one of the chiefs of the assassins, thinking that kind of death too easy. These well-trained fusileers went to the rear ; les piques, les haches, les poignards came forward. They demanded the Archbishop of Arles ; he was immediately surrounded by all the priests. The worthy prelate said to his friends, ' Let me pass ; if my blood will appease them, what signifies it, if I die? Is it not my duty to preserve your lives at the expence of my own?' He asked the eldest of the priests to give him absolution : he knelt to receive it ; and when he arose, forced himself from them, advanced slowly, and with his arms crossed upon his breast, and his eyes raised to heaven, said to the assassins, ' *Je suis celui que vous cherchez.*' His appearance was so dignified and noble, that, during ten minutes, not one of these wretches had courage to lift his hand against him : they upbraided each other with cowardice, and advanced ; one look from this venerable man struck them with awe, and they retired. At last, one of the miscreants struck off the cap of the Archbishop with a pike ; respect once violated, their fury returned, and another from behind cut him through the skull with a sabre. He raised his right hand to his eyes : with another stroke they cut off his hand. The Archbishop said, *O ! mon Dieu !* and raised the other : a third stroke across the face left him sitting ; the fourth extended him lifeless on the ground ; and then all pressed forward, and buried their pikes and poignards in the body. The priests all agreed, that he had been one of the most amiable men in France ; and that his only *crime* was, having, since the revolution, expended his private fortune, to support the necessitous clergy of his diocese. The second victim was the General des Benedictins. Then the national guards obliged the priests to go into the church, telling them, they should appear, one after another, before the Commissaires du section. They had hardly entered, before the people impatiently called for them ; upon which, all kneeling before the altar, the Bishop of Beauvais gave them absolution : they were then obliged to go out, two by two : they passed before a commissaire, who did not question, but only counted, his victims ; they had in their sight the heaps of dead, to which they were going to add. Among the one hundred and twenty priests thus sacrificed, were the Bishops of Zaintes and Beauvais (both of the Rochefoucauld family). I should not omit to remark, that one of the priests observed they were assassinated, because they would not swear to a constitution which their murderers had destroyed. We had (to comfort us for this melancholy story) the most grateful expressions of gratitude towards the English nation, from whom they did not do us the justice to expect such a reception.

"There can be no doubt that the whole business of the massacres was concerted at a meeting at the Duke of Orlean's house. I shall make you as dismal as myself by this narration. I must change the style." * * *

EDWARD GIBBON *Esq. to the Right Hon. Lady* SHEFFIELD.

LAUSANNE, November 10, 1792.

I COULD never forgive myself, were I capable of writing by the same post, a political epistle to the father, and a friendly letter to the daughter, without sending any token of remembrance to the respectable matron, my dearest my Lady, whom I have now loved as a sister for something better or worse than twenty years. No, indeed, the historian may be careless, he may be indolent, he may always intend and never execute, but he is neither a monster nor a statue ; he has a memory, a conscience, a heart, and that heart is sincerely devoted to Lady S——————.

He must even acknowledge the fallacy of a sophism which he has sometimes used, and she has always and most truly denied ; that where the persons of a family are strictly united, the writing to one is in fact writing to all ; and that consequently all his numerous letters to the husband, may be considered as equally addressed to his wife. He feels, on the contrary, that separate minds have their distinct ideas and sentiments, and that each character, either in speaking or writing, has its peculiar tone of conversation. He agrees with the maxim of Rousseau, that three friends who wish to disclose a common secret, will impart it only *deux a deux;* and he is satisfied that, on the present memorable occasion, each of the persons of the Sheffield family will claim a peculiar share in this triple missive, which will communicate, however, a triple satisfaction. The experience of what may be effected by vigorous resolution, encourages the historian to hope that he shall cast the skin of the old serpent, and hereafter show himself a new creature.

I lament, on all our accounts, that the last year's expedition to Lausanne did not take place in a golden period, of health and spirits. But we must reflect, that human felicity is seldom without alloy ; and if we cannot indulge the hope of your making a second visit to Lausanne, we must look forwards to my residence next summer at Sheffield-Place, where I must find you in the full bloom of health, spirits, and beauty. I can perceive, by all public and private intelligence, that your house has been the open hospitable asylum of French fugitives ; and it is a sufficient proof of the firmness of your nerves, that you have not been overwhelmed or agitated by such a concourse of strangers. Curiosity and compassion may, in some degree, have supported you. Every day has presented to your view, some new scene of that strange tragical romance, which occupies all Europe so infinitely beyond any event that has happened in our time, and you have the satisfaction of not being a mere spectator of the distress of so many victims of false liberty. The benevolent fame of Lord S. is widely diffused.

From Angletine's last letter to Maria, you have already some idea of the melancholy state of her poor father. As long as M. de Severy allowed our hopes and fears to fluctuate with the changes of his disorder, I was unwilling to say anything on so painful a subject ; and it is with the deepest concern that I now confess our absolute despair of his recovery. All his particular complaints are now lost in a general dissolution of the whole frame ; every principle of life is exhausted, and as often as I am admitted to his bedside, though he still looks and smiles with the patience of an angel, I have the heart-felt grief of seeing him each day drawing nearer to the term of his existence. A few weeks, possibly a few days, will deprive me of a most excellent friend, and break for ever the most perfect system of domestic happiness, in which I had so large and intimate a share. Wilhelm (who has obtained leave of absence from his military duty) and his sister behave and feel like tender and dutiful children ; but they have a long gay prospect of life; and new connections, new families will make them forget, in due time, the common lot of mortality. But it is Madame de Severy whom I truly pity ; I dread the effects of the first shock, and I dread still more the deep perpetual consuming affliction for a loss which can never be retrieved. You will not wonder that such reflections sadden my own mind, nor can I forget how much my situation is altered since I retired, nine years ago, to the banks of the Leman Lake. The death of poor Deyverdun first deprived me of a domestic companion, who can never be supplied ; and your visit has only served to remind me that man, however amused and occupied in his closet, was not made to live alone. Severy will soon be no more ; his widow for a long time, perhaps for ever, will be lost to herself and her friends, the son will travel, and I shall be left a stranger in the insipid circle of mere common acquaintance. The revolution of France, which first embittered and divided the society of Lausanne, has opposed a barrier to my Sussex visit, and may finally expel me from the paradise which I inhabit. Even that paradise, the expensive and delightful establishment of my house, library, and garden, almost becomes an incumbrance, by rendering it more difficult for me to relinquish my hold, or to form a new system of life in my native country, for which my income, though improved and improving, would be probably insufficient. But every complaint should be silenced by the contemplation of the French ; compared with whose cruel fate, all misery is relative happiness. I perfectly concur in your partiality for Lally ; though Nature might forget some meaner ingredients, of prudence, œconomy, &c. she never formed a purer heart, or a brighter imagination. If he be with you, I beg my kindest salutations to him. I am every day more closely united with the Neckers. Should France break, and this country be over-run, they would be reduced, in very humble circumstances, to seek a refuge ; and where but in England? Adieu, dear Madam, there is, indeed, much pleasure in discharging one's heart to a real friend. Ever yours.

EDWARD GIBBON, *Esq. to the Right Hon. Lord* SHEFFIELD.
[Send me a List of these Letters, with their respective dates.]
LAUSANNE, Nov. 25, 1792.

AFTER the triple labour of my last dispatch, your experience of the creature might tempt you to suspect that it would again relapse into a long slumber. But, partly from the spirit of contradiction, (though I am not a lady,) and partly from the ease and pleasure which I now find in the task, you see me again alive, awake, and almost faithful to my hebdomadal promise. The last week has not, however, afforded any events deserving the notice of an historian. Our affairs are still floating on the waves of the convention, and the ratification of a corrected treaty, which had been fixed for the twentieth, is not yet arrived ; but the

report of the diplomatic committee has been favourable, and it is generally understood that the leaders of the French republic do not wish
to quarrel with the Swiss. We are gradually withdrawing and disbanding our militia. Geneva will be left to sink or swim, according to the
humour of the people ; and our last hope appears to be, that by submission and good behaviour we shall avert for some time the impending
storm. A few days ago an odd accident happened in the French
army ; the desertion of the general. As the Neckers were sitting,
about eight o'clock in the evening, in their drawing-room at Rolle,*
the door flew open, and they were astounded by their servant's announcing *Monsieur le General de Montesquieu ?* On the receipt of some
secret intelligence of a *decret d'accusation,* and an order to arrest him,
he had only time to get on horseback, to gallop through Geneva, to
take boat for Copet, and to escape from his pursuers, who were ordered
to seize him alive or dead. He left the Neckers after supper, passed
through Lausanne in the night, and proceeded to Berne and Basle,
whence he intended to wind his way through Germany, amidst enemies
of every description, and to seek a refuge in England, America, or the
moon. He told Necker, that the sole remnant of his fortune consisted
in a wretched sum of twenty thousand livres ; but the public report, or
suspicion, bespeaks him in much better circumstances. Besides the
reproach of acting with too much tameness and delay, he is accused of
making very foul and exorbitant contracts ; and it is certain that new
Sparta is infected with this vice, beyond the example of the most corrupt monarchy. Kellerman is arrived, to take the command ; and it
is apprehended that on the first of December, after the departure of
the Swiss, the French may *request* the permission of using Geneva, a
friendly city, for their winter quarters. In that case, the democratical
revolution, which we all foresee, will be very speedily effected.

I would ask you, whether you apprehend there was any treason in
the Duke of Brunswick's retreat, and whether you have totally withdrawn your confidence and esteem from that once-famed general?
Will it be possible for England to preserve her neutrality with any
honour or safety? We are bound, as I understand, by treaty, to
guarantee the dominions of the King of Sardinia and the Austrian
provinces of the Netherlands. These countries are now invaded and
over-run by the French. Can we refuse to fulfil our engagements,
without exposing ourselves to all Europe as a perfidious or pusillanimous nation? Yet, on the other hand, can we assist those allies, without plunging headlong into an abyss, whose bottom no man can
discover? But my chief anxiety is for our domestic tranquillity ; for
I must find a retreat in England, should I be driven from Lausanne.
The idea of firm and honourable union of parties pleases me much ;
but you must frankly unfold what are the great difficulties that may
impede so salutary a measure : you write to a man discreet in speech,
and now careful of papers. Yet what can such a coalition avail?
Where is the champion of the constitution? Alas, Lord Guildford !
I am much pleased with the Manchester Ass. The asses or wolves
who sacrified him have cast off the mask too soon ; and such a nonsensical act must open the eyes of many simple patriots, who might

* A considerable town between Lausanne and Geneva.

have been led astray by the specious name of reform. It should be made as notorious as possible. Next winter may be the crisis of our fate, and if you begin to improve the constitution, you may be driven step by step from the disfranchisement of old Sarum to the King in Newgate, the Lords voted useless, the Bishops abolished, and a House of Commons without articles (*sans culottes*). Necker has ordered you a copy of his royal defence, which has met with, and deserved, universal success. The pathetic and argumentative parts are, in my opinion, equally good, and his mild eloquence may persuade without irritating. I have applied to this gentler tone some verses of Ovid, (Metamorph. l. iii. 302, &c.*) which you may read. Madame de Stael has produced a second son. She talks wildly enough of visiting England this winter. She is a pleasant little woman. Poor Severy's condition is hopeless. Should he drag through the winter, Madame de S. would scarcely survive him. She kills herself with grief and fatigue. What a difference in Lausanne? I hope triple answers are on the road. I must write soon; the *times* will not allow me to read or think. Ever yours.

To the same.   LAUSANNE, Dec. 14, 1792.

OUR little storm has now completely subsided, and we are again spectators, though anxious spectators, of the general tempest that invades or threatens almost every country of Europe. Our troops are every day disbanding and returning home, and the greatest part of the French have evacuated the neighbourhood of Geneva. Monsieur Barthelemy, whom you have seen secretary in London, is most courteously entertained, as ambassador, by the Helvetic body. He is now at Berne, where a diet will speedily be convened: the language on both sides is now pacific, and even friendly, and some hopes are given of a provision for the officers of the Swiss guards who have survived the massacres of Paris.

                                            January 1, 1793.

WITH the return of peace I have relapsed into my former indolence; but now awakening, after a fortnight's slumber, I have little or nothing to add, with regard to the internal state of this country, only the revolution of Geneva has already taken place, as I announced, but sooner than I expected. The Swiss troops had no sooner evacuated the place, than the *Egaliseurs*, as they are called, assembled in arms; and as no resistance was made, no blood was shed on the occasion. They seized the gates, disarmed the garrison, imprisoned the magistrates, imparted the rights of citizens to all the rabble of the town and country, and proclaimed a *National* Convention, which has not yet met. They are all for a pure and absolute democracy; but some wish to remain a small independent state, whilst others aspire to become a part of the republic of France; and as the latter, though less

---

* Quà tamen usque potest, vires sibi demere tentat,
Nec, quo centimanum dejecerat igne Typhœa,
Nunc armatur eo : nimiûm feritatis in illo.
Est aliud levius fulmen ; cui dextra Cyclopum
Sævitiæ, flammæque minus, minus addidit iræ ;
Tela secunda vocant Superi.

numerous, are more violent and absurd than their adversaries, it is highly probable that they will succeed. The citizens of the best families and fortunes have retired from Geneva into the Pays de Vaud; but the French methods of recalling or proscribing emigrants, will soon be adopted. You must have observed, that Savoy is now become *le department du Mont Blanc.* I cannot satisfy myself, whether the mass of the people is pleased or displeased with the change; but my noble scenery is clouded by the democratical aspect of twelve leagues of the opposite coast, which every morning obtrude themselves on my view. I here conclude the first part of the history of our Alpine troubles, and now consider myself as disengaged from all promises of periodical writing. Upon the whole, I kept it beyond our expectations; nor do I think that you have been sufficiently astonished by the wonderful effort of the triple dispatch.

You must now succeed to my task, and I shall expect, during the winter, a regular political journal of the events of your greater world. You are on the theatre, and may often be behind the scenes. You can always see, and may sometimes forsee. My own choice has indeed transported me into a foreign land; but I am truly attached, from interest and inclination, to my native country; and even as a citizen of the world, I wish the stability of England, the sole great refuge of mankind, against the opposite mischiefs of despotism and democracy. I was indeed alarmed, and the more so, as I saw that you were not without apprehension; but I now glory in the triumph of reason and genuine patriotism, which seems to pervade the country; nor do I dislike some mixture of popular enthusiasm, which may be requisite to encounter our mad or wicked enemies with equal arms. The behaviour of Fox does not surprise me. You may remember what I told you last year at Lausanne, when you attempted his defence, that * * * You have now crushed the daring subverters of the constitution; but I now fear the moderate well-meaners, reformers. Do not, I beseech you, tamper with parliamentary representation. The present House of Commons forms, in *practice,* a body of gentlemen, who must always sympathise with the interests and opinions of the people; and the slightest innovation launches you, without rudder or compass, on a dark and dangerous ocean of theoretical experiment. On this subject I am indeed serious.

Upon the whole, I like the beginning of ninety-three better than the end of ninety-two. The illusion seems to break away throughout Europe. I think England and Switzerland are safe. Brabant adheres to its old constitution. The Germans are disgusted with the rapine and insolence of their deliverers. The Pope is resolved to head his armies, and the Lazzaroni of Naples have presented St. Januarius with a gold fuzee, to fire on the Brigands François. So much for politics, which till now never had such possession of my mind. Next post I will write about myself and my own designs. Alas, your poor eyes! make the Maria write; I will speedily answer her. My Lady is still dumb. The German posts are now slow and irregular. You had better write by the way of France, under cover. Direct to *Le Citoien Rebours a Pontalier, France.* Adieu; ever yours.

To the Same.   LAUSANNE, Jan. 6, 1793.

THERE was formerly a time when our correspondence was a painful discussion of my private affairs ; a vexatious repetition of losses, of disappointments, of sales, &c. These affairs are decently arranged : but public cares have now succeeded to private anxiety, and our whole attention is lately turned from Lenborough and Beriton, to the political state of France and of Europe. From these politics, however, one letter shall be free, while I talk of myself and of my own plans ; a subject most interesting to a friend, and only to a friend.

I know not whether I am sorry or glad that my expedition has been postponed to the present year. It is true, that I now wish myself in England, and almost repent that I did not grasp the opportunity when the obstacles were comparatively smaller than they are now likely to prove. Yet had I reached you last summer before the month of August, a considerable portion of my time would be now elapsed, and I should already begin to think of my departure. If the gout should spare me this winter, (and as yet I have not felt any symptom,) and if the spring should make a soft and early appearance, it is my intention to be with you in Downing-street before the end of April, and thus to enjoy six weeks or two months of the most agreeable season of London and the neighbourhood, after the hurry of parliament is subsided, and before the great rural dispersion. As the Banks of the Rhine and the Belgic provinces are completely overspread with anarchy and war, I have made up my mind to pass through the territories of the French republic. From the best and most recent information, I am satisfied that there is little or no real danger in the journey; and I must arm myself with patience to support the vexatious insolence of democratical tyranny. I have even a sort of curiosity to spend some days at Paris, to assist at the debates of the Pandæmonium, to seek an introduction to the principal devils, and to contemplate a new form of public and private life, which never existed before, and which I devoutly hope will not long continue to exist. Should the obstacles of health or weather confine me at Lausanne till the month of May, I shall scarcely be able to resist the temptation of passing some part at least of the summer in my own little paradise. But all these schemes must ultimately depend on the great question of peace and war, which will indeed be speedily determined. Should France become impervious to an English traveller, what must I do ? I shall not easily resolve to explore my way through the unknown language and abominable roads of the interior parts of Germany, to embark in Holland, or perhaps at Hamburgh, and to be finally intercepted by a French privateer. My stay in England appears not less doubtful than the means of transporting myself. Should I arrive in the spring, it is possible, and barely possible, that I should return here in the autumn : it is much more probable that I shall pass the winter, and there may be even a chance of my giving my own country a longer trial. In my letter to my Lady I fairly exposed the decline of Lausanne ; but such an establishment as mine must not be lightly abandoned ; nor can I discover what adequate mode of life my private circumstances, easy as they now are, could afford me in England. London and Bath have doubtless their respective merits, and I could wish to reside within a day's journey of Sheffield-Place. But a state of perfect happiness is not to be found here below; and in the possession of my library, house, and garden, with the relics of our society, and a frequent intercourse with the Neckers, I may still be tolerably content. Among the disastrous changes of Lausanne, I must principally reckon the approaching dissolution of poor Severy and his family. He is still alive, but in such a hopeless and painful decay, that we no longer conceal our wishes for his speedy release. I never loved nor esteemed him so much as in this last mortal disease, which he supports with a degree of energy, patience, and even cheerfulness, beyond all belief. His wife, whose whole time and soul are devoted to him, is almost sinking under her long anxiety. The children are most amiably assiduous to both their parents, and, at all events, his filial duties and worldly cares must detain the son some time at home.

And now approach, and let me drop into your most private ear a literary secret. Of the Memoirs little has been done, and with that little I am not satisfied. They must be postponed till a mature season; and I much doubt whether the book and the Author can ever see the light at the same time. But I have long revolved in my mind another scheme of biographical writing : the Lives, or rather the Characters, of the most eminent Persons in Arts and Arms, in Church and State, who have flourished in Britain from the reign of Henry the Eighth to the present age. This work, extensive as it may be, would be an amusement, rather than a toil: the materials are accessible in our own language, and, for the most part, ready to my hands : but the subject, which would afford a rich display of human nature and domestic history, would adress itself to the feelings of every Englishman. The taste or fashion of the times seems to delight in picturesque decorations; and this series of British portraits might aptly be accompanied by the respective heads, taken from originals, and engraved by the best masters. Alderman Boydell, and his son-in-law, Mr. George Nicol, bookseller in Pall-mall, are the great undertakers in this line. On my arrival in England I shall be free to consider, whether it may suit me to proceed in a mere literary work without any other decorations than those which it may derive from the pen of the Author. It is a serious truth, that I am no longer ambitious of fame or money; that my habits of industry are much impaired, and that I have reduced my studies, to be the loose amusement of my morning hours, the repetition of which will insensibly lead me to the last term of existence. And for this very reason I shall not be sorry to bind myself by a liberal engagement, from which I may not with honour recede.

Before I conclude, we must say a word or two of parliamentary and pecuniary concerns. 1. We all admire the generous spirit with which you damned the assassins * *. I hope that * * The opinion of parliament in favour of Louis was declared in a manner worthy of the representatives of a great and wise nation. It will certainly have a powerful effect; and if the poor King be not already murdered, I am satisfied that his life is in safety : but is such a life worth his care? Our debates will now become every day more interesting; and as I expect from you only opinions and anecdotes, I most earnestly conjure you to send me Woodfall's Register as often (and that must be very often) as the occasion deserves it. I now spare no expence for news.

I want some account of Mrs. G.'s health. Will my Lady never write? How can people be so indolent! I suppose this will find you at Sheffield-Place during the recess, and that the heavy baggage will not move till after the birth-day. Shall I be with you by the first of May? The Gods only know. I almost wish that I had accompanied Madame de Stael. Ever yours.

To the Same.   Begun Feb. 9,—ended Feb. 18, 1793.

THE struggle is at length over, and poor de Severy is no more! He expired about ten days ago, after every vital principle had been exhausted by a complication of disorders, which had lasted above five months: and a mortification in one of his legs, that gradually rose to the more noble parts, was the immediate cause of his death. His patience and even cheerfulness supported him to the fatal moment; and he enjoyed every comfort that could alleviate his situation, the skill of his physicians, the assiduous tenderness of his family, and the kind sympathy not only of his particular friends, but even of common acquaintance, and generally of the whole town. The stroke has been severely felt: yet I have the satisfaction to perceive that Madame de Severy's health is not affected; and we may hope that in time she will recover a tolerable share of composure and happiness. Her firmness has checked the violent sallies of grief; her gentleness has preserved her from the worst of symptoms, a dry, silent despair. She loves to talk of her irreparable loss, she descants with pleasure on his virtues; her words are interrupted with tears, but those tears are her best relief; and her tender feelings will insensibly subside into an affectionate remembrance. Wilhelm is much more deeply wounded than I could imagine, or than he expected himself: nor have I ever seen the affliction of a son more lively and sincere. Severy was indeed a very valuable man: without any shining qualifications, he was endowed in a high degree with good sense, honour, and benevolence; and few men have filled with more propriety their circle in private life. For myself, I have had the misfortune of knowing him too late, and of losing him too soon.—But enough of this melancholy subject.

The affairs of this theatre, which must always be minute, are now grown so tame and tranquil, that they no longer deserve the historian's pen. The new constitution of Geneva is slowly forming, without much noise or any bloodshed; and the patriots, who have staid in hopes of guiding and restraining the multitude, flatter themselves that they shall be able at least to prevent their mad countrymen from giving themselves to the French, the only mischief that would be absolutely irretrievable. The revolution of Geneva is of less consequence to us, however, than that of Savoy; but our fate will depend on the general event, rather than on these particular causes. In the mean while we hope to be quiet spectators of the struggle of this year; and we seem to have assurances that both the Emperor and the French will compound for the neutrality of the Swiss. The Helvetic body does not acknowledge the republic of France: but Barthelemy, their ambassador, resides at Baden, and steals, like Chauvelin, into a kind of extra-official negotiation. All spirit of opposition is quelled in the Canton of Berne, and the perpetual banishment of the * * * family has scarcely excited a murmur. It will probably be followed by that of * * *, * * * : the crime alleged in their sentence is the having assisted at the federation-dinner at Rolle two years ago; and as they are absent, I could almost wish that they had been summoned to appear, and heard in their own defence. To the general supineness of the inhabitants of Lausanne I must ascribe, that the death of Louis the Sixteenth has been received with less horror and indignation than I could have wished. I was much tempted to go into mourning, and probably should, had the Duchess been still here ; but, as the only Englishman of any mark, I was afraid of being singular ; more especially as our French emigrants, either from prudence or poverty, do not wear black, nor do even the Neckers. Have you read his discourse for the King ? It might indeed supersede the necessity of mourning. I should judge from your last letter, and from the Diary, that the French declaration of war must have rather surprised you. I wish, although I know not how it could have been avoided, that we might still have continued to enjoy our safe and prosperous neutrality. You will not doubt my best wishes for the destruction of the miscreants ; but I love England still more than I hate France. All reasonable chances are in favour of a confederacy, such as was never opposed to the ambition of Louis the Fourteenth ; but, after the experience of last year, I distrust reason, and confess myself fearful for the event. The French are strong in numbers, activity, enthusiasm ; they are rich in rapine ; and, although their strength may be only that of a phrenzy fever, they may do infinite mischief to their neighbours before they can be reduced to a straight waistcoat. I dread the effects that may be produced on the minds of the people by the increase of debt and taxes, probable losses, and possible mismanagement. Our trade must suffer; and though projects of invasion have been always abortive, I cannot forget that the fleets and armies of Europe have failed before the towns in America, which have been taken and plundered by a handful of Buccaneers. I know nothing of Pitt as a war minister ; but it affords me much satisfaction that the intrepid wisdom of the new chancellor, Lord Loughborough, is introduced into the cabinet. I wish, not merely on your own account, that you were placed in an active, useful station in government. I should not dislike you secretary at war.

I have little more to say of myself, or of my journey to England : you know my intentions, and the great events of Europe must determine whether they can be carried into execution this summer. If * * * has warmly adopted *your* idea, I shall speedily hear from him ; but in truth, I know not what will be my answer : I see difficulties which at first did not occur : I doubt my own perseverance, and my fancy begins to wander into new paths. The amusement of reading and thinking may perhaps satisfy a man who has paid his debt to the public ; and there is more pleasure in building castles in the air than on the ground. I shall contrive some small assistance for your correspondent, though I cannot learn any thing that distinguishes him from many of his countrymen ; we have had our full share of poor emigrants : but if you wish that any thing extraordinary should be done for this

man, you must send me a measure. Adieu. I embrace my Lady and
Maria, as also Louisa, if with you. Perhaps I may soon write, without
expecting an answer. Ever yours.

Death of Lady Sheffield.

To THE SAME.   LAUSANNE, April 27, 1793.

MY dearest Friend, for such you most truly are, nor does there exist
a person who obtains, or shall ever obtain, a superior place in my
esteem and affection.

After too long a silence I was sitting down to write, when, only
yesterday morning (such is now the irregular slowness of the English
post), I was suddenly struck, indeed struck to the heart, by the fatal
intelligence, *the death of Lady Sheffield*, from Sir Henry Clinton and
Mr. de Lally. Alas! what is life, and what are our hopes and projects!
When I embraced her at your departure from Lausanne, could I imagine
that it was for the last time? when I postponed to another summer my
journey to England, could I apprehend that I never, never should see
her again? I always hoped that she would spin her feeble thread to a
long duration, and that her delicate frame would survive (as is often
the case) many constitutions of a stouter appearance. In four days!
in your absence, in that of her children! But she is now at rest; and
if there be a future life, her mild virtues have surely entitled her to the
reward of pure and perfect felicity. It is for you that I feel, and I can
judge of your sentiments by comparing them with my own. I have
lost, it is true, an amiable and affectionate friend, whom I had known
and loved above three-and-twenty years, and whom I often styled by
the endearing name of sister. But you are deprived of the companion
of your life, the wife of your choice, and the mother of your children;
poor children! the liveliness of Maria, and the softness of Louisa,
render them almost equally the objects of my tenderest compassion. I
do not wish to aggravate your grief; but, in the sincerity of friendship,
I cannot hold a different language. I know the impotence of reason,
and I much fear that the strength of your character will serve to make
a sharper and more lasting impression.

The only consolation in these melancholy trials to which human
life is exposed, the only one at least in which I have any confidence, is
the presence of a real friend; and of that, as far as it depends on
myself, you shall not be destitute. I regret the few days that must be
lost in some necessary preparations; but I trust that to-morrow se'n-
night (May the fifth) I shall be able to set forwards on my journey to
England: and when this letter reaches you, I shall be considerably
advanced on my way. As it is yet prudent to keep at a respectful
distance from the banks of the French Rhine, I shall incline a little to
the right, and proceed by Schaffouse and Stutgard to Frankfort and
Cologne: the Austrian Netherlands are now open and safe, and I am
sure of being able at least to pass from Ostend to Dover: whence,
without passing through London, I shall pursue the direct road to
Sheffield-Place. Unless I should meet with some unforeseen accident,
and delays, I hope, before the end of the month to share your solitude,
and sympathize with your grief. All the difficulties of the journeys
which my indolence had probably magnified, have now disappeared

M

before a stronger passion; and you will not be sorry to hear, that, as far as Frankfort to Cologne, I shall enjoy the advantage of the society, the conversation, the German language, and the active assistance of Severy. His attachment to me is the sole motive which prompts him to undertake this troublesome journey; and as soon as he has seen me over the roughest ground, he will immediately return to Lausanne. The poor young man loved Lady S. as a mother, and the whole family is deeply affected by an event which reminds them too painfully of their own misfortune. Adieu. I could write volumes, and shall therefore break off abruptly. I shall write on the road, and hope to find a few lines *à poste restante* at Frankfort and Brussels. Adieu; ever yours.

To the Same.

MY DEAR FRIEND,   LAUSANNE, May 8, 1793.
I MUST write a few lines before my departure, though indeed I scarcely know what to say. Nearly a fortnight has now elapsed since the first melancholy tidings, without my having received the slightest subsequent accounts of your health and situation. Your own silence announces too forcibly how much you are involved in your feelings; and I can but too easily conceive that a letter to me would be more painful than to an indifferent person. But that amiable man Count Lally might surely have written a second time; but your sister, who is probably with you; but Maria,—alas! poor Maria! I am left in a state of darkness to the workings of my own fancy, which imagines everything that is sad and shocking. What can I think of for your relief and comfort? I will not expatiate on those common-place topics, which have never dried a single tear; but let me advise, let me urge you to force yourself into business, as I would try to force myself into study. The mind must not be idle; if it be not exercised on external objects, it will prey on its own vitals. A thousand little arrangements, which must precede a long journey, have postponed my departure three or four days beyond the term which I had first appointed; but all is now in order, and I set off to-morrow, the ninth instant, with my *valet de chambre*, a courier on horseback, and Severy, with his servant, as far as Frankfort. I calculate my arrival at Sheffield-Place (how I dread and desire to see that mansion!) for the first week in June, soon after this letter; but I will try to send you some later intelligence. I never found myself stronger, or in better health. The German road is now cleared, both of enemies and allies, and though I must expect fatigue, I have not any apprehensions of danger. It is scarcely possible that you should meet me at Frankfort, but I shall be much disappointed at not finding a line at Brussels or Ostend. Adieu. If there be any invisible guardians, may they watch over you and yours! Adieu.

To the Same.   FRANKFORT, May 19, 1793.
AND here I am in good health and spirits, after one of the easiest, safest, and pleasantest journies which I ever performed in my whole life; not the appearance of an enemy, and hardly the appearance of a war. Yet I hear, as I am writing, the cannon of the siege of Mayence, at the distance of twenty miles; and long, very long, will it be heard.

It is confessed on all sides, that the French fight with a courage worthy of a better cause. The town of Mayence is strong, their artillery admirable; they are already reduced to horse-flesh, but they have still the resource of eating the inhabitants, and at last of eating one another; and, if that repast could be extended to Paris and the whole country, it might essentially contribute to the relief of mankind. Our operations are carried on with more than German slowness, and when the besieged are quiet, the besiegers are perfectly satisfied with their progress. A spirit of division undoubtedly prevails; and the character of the Prussians for courage and discipline is sunk lower than you can possibly imagine. Their glory has expired with Frederick. I am sorry to have missed Lord Elgin, who is beyond the Rhine with the King of Prussia. As I am impatient, I propose setting forwards to-morrow afternoon, and shall reach Ostend in less than eight days. The passage must depend on winds and packets; and I hope to find at Brussels or Dover a letter which will direct me to Sheffield-Place or Downing-Street. Severy goes back from hence. Adieu: I embrace the dear girls. Ever yours.

From the Same.   BRUSSELS, May 27, 1793.
THIS day, between two and three o'clock in the afternoon, I am arrived at this place in excellent preservation. My expedition, which is now drawing to a close, has been a journey of perseverance rather than speed, of some labour since Frankfort, but without the smallest degree of difficulty or danger. As I have every morning been seated in the chaise soon after sun-rise, I propose indulging to-morrow till eleven o'clock, and going that day no farther than Ghent. On Wednesday the 29th instant I shall reach Ostend in good time, just eight days, according to my former reckoning, from Frankfort. Beyond that I can say nothing positive; but should the winds be propitious, it is possible that I may appear next Saturday, June first, in Downing-Street. After that earliest date, you will expect me day by day till I arrive. Adieu. I embrace the dear girls, and salute Mrs. Holroyd. I rejoice that you have anticipated my advice by plunging into business; but I should now be sorry if that business, however important, detained us long in town. I do not wish to make a public exhibition, and only sigh to enjoy you and the precious remnant in the solitude of Sheffield-Place. Ever yours.

If I am successful I may outstrip or accompany this letter. Your's and Maria's waited for me here, and over-paid the journey.

THE preceding Letters intimate that, in return for my visit to Lausanne in 1791, Mr. Gibbon engaged to pass a year with me in England: that the war having rendered travelling exceedingly inconvenient, especially to a person who, from his bodily infirmities, required every accommodation, prevented his undertaking so formidable a journey at the time he proposed.

The call of friendship, however, was sufficient to make him overlook every personal consideration, when he thought his presence might prove a consolation. I must ever regard it as the most endearing proof of his sensibility, and of his possessing the true spirit of friendship, that after having relinquished the thought of his intended visit, he hastened to England, in spite of encreasing impediments, to soothe me by the most generous sympathy, and to alleviate my domestic affliction; neither his great corpulency, nor his extraordinary bodily infirmities, nor any other consideration, could prevent him a moment from resolving on an undertaking that might have deterred the most active young man. He, almost immediately, with alertness by no means natural to him, undertook a great circuitous journey, along the frontiers of an enemy, worse than savage, within the sound of their cannon, within the range of the light troops of the different armies, and through roads ruined by the enormous machinery of war.

The readiness with which he engaged in this kind office of friendship, at a time when a selfish spirit might have pleaded a thousand reasons for declining so hazardous a journey, conspired, with the peculiar charms of his society to render his arrival a cordial to my mind. I had the satisfaction of finding that his own delicate and precarious health had not suffered in the service of his friend, a service in which he disregarded his own personal infirmities. He arrived in the beginning of June at my house in Downing-Street, safe and in good health; and after we had passed about a month together in London, we settled at Sheffield-Place for the summer; where his wit, learning, and cheerful politeness delighted a great variety of characters.

Although he was inclined to represent his health as better than it really was, his habitual dislike to motion appeared to increase; his inaptness to exercise confined him to the library and dining-room, and there he joined my friend Mr. Frederick North, in pleasant arguments against exercise in general. He ridiculed the unsettled and restless disposition that summer, the most uncomfortable, as he said, of all seasons, generally gives to those who have the free use of their limbs. Such arguments were little required to keep society within doors, when his company was only there to be enjoyed; for neither the fineness of the season, nor the most promising parties of pleasure, could tempt the company of either sex to desert him.

Those who have enjoyed the society of Mr. Gibbon will agree with me, that his conversation was still more captivating than his writings. Perhaps no man ever divided time more fairly between literary labour and social enjoyment; and hence, probably, he derived his peculiar excellence of making his very extensive knowledge contribute, in the highest degree, to the use or pleasure of those with whom he conversed. He united, in the happiest manner imaginable, two characters which are not often found in the same person, the profound scholar and the fascinating companion.

It would be superfluous to attempt a very minute delineation of a character which is so distinctly marked in the Memoirs and Letters. He has described himself without reserve, and with perfect sincerity. The Letters, and especially the extracts from the Journal, which could not have been written with any purpose of being seen, will make the reader perfectly acquainted with the man.

Excepting a visit to Lord Egremont and Mr. Hayley, whom he very particularly esteemed, Mr. Gibbon was not absent from Sheffield-Place till the beginning of October, when we were reluctantly obliged to part with him, that he might perform his engagement to Mrs. Gibbon at Bath, the widow of his father, who had early deserved, and invariably retained, his affection. From Bath he proceeded to Lord Spencer's at Althorp, a family which he always met with uncommon satisfaction. He continued in good health during the whole summer, and in excellent spirits (I never knew him enjoy better); and when he went from Sheffield-Place, little did I imagine it would be the last time I should have the inexpressible pleasure of seeing him there in full possession of health.

The few following short letters, though not important in themselves, will fill up this part of the narrative better, and more agreeably, than any thing I can substitute in their place.

E. GIBBON *to Lord* SHEFFIELD.

Oct. 2, 1793.

THE Cork-Street hotel has answered its recommendation; it is clean, convenient, and quiet. My first evening was passed at home in a very agreeable *tête-à-tête* with my friend Elmsley. Yesterday I. dined at Cranfurd's with an excellent set, in which were Pelham and Lord Egremont. I dine to-day with my Portuguese friend, Madame de Sylva, at Grenier's; most probably with Lady Webster, whom I met last night at Devonshire-House; a constant, though late, resort of society. The Duchess is as good, and Lady Elizabeth as seducing, as ever. No news whatsoever. You will see in the papers Lord Harvey's memorial. I love vigour, but it is surely a strong measure to tell a gentleman you have *resolved* to pass the winter in his house. London is not disagreeable; yet I shall probably leave it Saturday. If any thing should occur, I will write. Adieu; ever yours.

To the same.

SUNDAY afternoon I left London and lay at Reading, and Monday in very good time I reached this place, after a very pleasant airing; and am always so much delighted and improved, with this union of ease and motion, that, were not the expence enormous, I would travel every year some hundred miles, more especially in England. I passed the day with Mrs. G. yesterday. In mind and conversation she is just the same as twenty years ago. She has spirits, appetite, legs, and eyes, and talks (she was then in her eightieth year. S.) of living till ninety. I can say from my heart, Amen. We dine at two, and remain together till nine; but, although we have much to say, I am not sorry that she talks of introducing a third or fourth actor. Lord Spenser expects me about the 20th; but if I can do it without offence, I shall steal away two or three days sooner, and you shall have advice of my motions. The troubles of Bristol have been serious and bloody. I know not who was in fault; but I do not like appeasing the mob by the extinction of the toll, and the removal of the Hereford militia, who had done their duty. Adieu. The girls must dance at Tunbridge. What would dear little aunt say if I was to answer her letter? Ever yours, &c.

YORK-HOUSE, BATH, Oct. 9, 1793.

I still follow the old style, though the Convention has abolished the Christian æra, with months, weeks, days, &c.

To the same.   YORK-HOUSE, BATH, Oct. 13, 1793.

I AM as ignorant of Bath in general as if I were still at Sheffield. My impatience to get away makes me think it better to devote my whole time to Mrs. G.; and dear little aunt, whom I tenderly salute, will excuse me to her two friends, Mrs. Hartley and Preston, if I make little or no use of her kind introduction. A *tête-à-tête* of eight or nine hours every day is rather difficult to support; yet I do assure you, that our conversation flows with more ease and spirit when we are alone, than when any auxiliaries are summoned to our aid. She is indeed a wonderful woman, and I think all her faculties of the mind stronger, and more active, than I have ever known them. I have settled, that ten full days may be sufficient for all the purposes of our interview. I should therefore depart next Friday, the eighteenth instant, and am indeed expected at Althorpe on the twentieth; but I may possibly reckon without my host, as I have not yet apprised Mrs. G. of the term of my visit; and will certainly not quarrel with her for a short delay. Adieu. I must have some political speculations. The campaign, at least on our side, seems to be at an end. Ever yours.

To the same.   ALTHORP LIBRARY, Tues., 4 o'c.

WE have so completely exhausted this morning among the first editions of Cicero, that I can mention only my departure hence tomorrow the sixth instant. I shall lie quietly at Woburn, and reach London in good time Thursday. By the following post I will write somewhat more largely. My stay in London will depend, partly on my amusement, and your being fixed at Sheffield-Place; unless you think I can be comfortably arranged for a week or two with you at Brighton. The military remarks seem good; but now to what purpose? Adieu. I embrace and much rejoice in Louisa's improvement. Lord Ossory was from home at Farning-Woods.

To the same.   LONDON, Frid., Nov. 8, 4 o'c.

WALPOLE has just delivered yours, and I hasten the direction, that you may not be at a loss. I will write to-morrow, but I am now fatigued, and rather unwell. Adieu. I have not seen a soul except Elmsley.

To the same.   ST. JAMES'S-ST., Nov. 9, 1793.

As I dropt yesterday the word *unwell*, I flatter myself that the family would have been a little alarmed by my silence to-day. I am still awkward, though without any suspicions of gout, and have some idea of having recourse to medical advice. Yet I creep out to-day in a chair, to dine with Lord Lucan. But as it will be literally my first going down stairs, and as scarcely any one is apprised of my arrival,

I know nothing, I have heard nothing, I have nothing to say. My present lodging, a house of Elmsley's, is cheerful, convenient, somewhat dear, but not so much as a hotel, a species of habitation for which I have not conceived any great affection. Had you been stationary at Sheffield, you would have seen me before the twentieth; for I am tired of rambling, and pant for my home; that is to say, for your house. But whether I shall have courage to brave * * * and a bleak down, time only can discover. Adieu. I wish you back to Sheffield-Place. The health of dear Louisa is doubtless the first object; but I did not expect Brighton after Tunbridge. Whenever dear little aunt is separate from you, I shall certainly write to her; but at present how is it possible? Ever yours.

To the same at Brighton.   ST. JAMES'S ST., Nov. 11, 1793.

I MUST at length withdraw the veil before my state of health, though the naked truth may alarm you more than a fit of the gout. Have you never observed, through my inexpressibles, a large prominency *circa genitalia*, which, as it was not at all painful, and very little troublesome, I had strangely neglected for many years? But since my departure from Sheffield-Place it has increased (most stupendously,) is increasing, and ought to be diminished. Yesterday I sent for Farquhar, who is allowed to be a very skillful surgeon. After viewing and palping, he very seriously desired to call in assistance, and has examined it again to-day with Mr. Cline, a surgeon, as he says, of the first eminence. They both pronounce it a *hydrocele*, (a collection of water,) which must be let out by the operation of tapping; but, from its magnitude and long neglect, they think it a most extraordinary case, and wish to have another surgeon, Dr. Bayley, present. If the business should go off smoothly, I shall be delivered from my burthen, (it is almost as big as a small child,) and walk about in four or five days with a truss. But the medical gentlemen, who never speak quite plain, insinuate to me the possibility of an inflammation, of fever, &c. I am not appalled at the thoughts of the operation, which is fixed for Wednesday next, twelve o'clock; but it has occurred to me, that you might wish to be present, before and afterwards, till the crisis was past; and to give you that opportunity, I shall solicit a delay till Thursday, or even Friday. In the mean while, I crawl about with some labour, and much indecency, to Devonshire-House (where I left all the fine Ladies making flannel waistcoats); Lady Lucan's, &c. Adieu. Varnish the business for the Ladies: yet I am afraid it will be public;—the advantage of being notorious. Ever yours.

IMMEDIATELY on receiving the last letter, I went the same day from Brighthelmstone to London, and was agreeably surprised to find that Mr. Gibbon had dined at Lord Lucan's, and did not return to his lodgings, where I waited for him till eleven o'clock at night. Those who have seen him within the last eight or ten years, must be surprised to hear, that he could doubt, whether his disorder was apparent. When he returned to England in 1787, I was greatly alarmed by a prodigious increase, which I always conceived to proceed from a rupture. I did not understand why he, who had talked with me on every other subject relative to himself and his affairs without reserve, should never in any shape hint at a malady so troublesome ; but on speaking to his valet de chambre, he told me, Mr. Gibbon could not bear the least allusion to that subject, and never would suffer him to notice it. I consulted some medical persons, who with me supposing it to be a rupture, were of opinion that nothing could be done, and said that he surely must have had advice, and of course had taken all necessary precautions. He now talked freely with me about his disorder ; which, he said, began in the year 1761 ; that he then consulted Mr. Hawkins, the surgeon, who did not decide whether it was the beginning of a rupture, or an hydrocele ; but he desired to see Mr. Gibbon again when he came to town. Mr. Gibbon not feeling any pain, nor suffering any inconvenience, as he said, never returned to Mr. Hawkins ; and although the disorder continued to increase gradually, and of late years very much indeed, he never mentioned it to any person, however incredible it may appear, from 1761 to November 1793. I told him, that I had always supposed there was no doubt of its being a rupture ; his answer was, that he never thought so, and that he, and the surgeons who attended him, were of opinion that it was an hydrocele. It is now certain that it was originally a rupture, and that an hydrocele had lately taken place in the same part ; and it is remarkable that his legs, which had been swelled about the ancle, particularly one of them, since he had the erisipelas in 1790, recovered their former shape, as soon as the water appeared in another part, which did not happen till between the time he left Sheffield-Place, in the beginning of October, and his arrival at Althorpe, towards the latter end of that month. On the Thursday following the date of his last letter, Mr. Gibbon was tapped for the first time ; four quarts of a transparent watery fluid were discharged by that operation. Neither inflammation nor fever ensued ; the tumour was diminished to nearly half its size ; the remaining part was a soft irregular mass. I had been with him two days before, and I continued with him above a week after the first tapping, during which time he enjoyed his usual spirits ; and the three medical gentlemen who attended him will recollect his pleasantry, even during the operation. He was abroad again in a few days, but the water evidently collecting very fast, it was agreed that a second puncture should be made a fortnight after the first. Knowing that I should be wanted at a meeting in the country, he pressed me to attend it, and promised that soon after the second operation was performed he would follow me to Sheffield-Place ; but before he arrived I received the two following Letters :

Mr. GIBBON *to Lord* SHEFFIELD, *at* Brighton.

ST. JAMES'S STREET, Nov. 25, 1793.

THOUGH Farquhar has promised to write you a line, I conceive you may not be sorry to hear directly from me. The operation of yesterday was much longer, more searching, and more painful than the former ; but it has eased and lightened me to a much greater degree.* No inflammation, no fever, a delicious night, leave to go abroad to-morrow, and to go out of town when I please, *en attendant* the

* Three quarts of the same fluid as before were discharged.

future measures of a radical cure. If you hold your intention of returning next Saturday to Sheffield-Place, I shall probably join you about the Tuesday following, after having passed two nights at Eden-Farm, Beckenham. The Devons are going to Bath, and the hospitable Craufurd follows them. I passed a delightful day with Burke; an odd one with Monsignore Erskine, the Pope's Nuncio. Of public news, you and the papers know more than I do. We seem to have strong sea and land hopes; nor do I dislike the Royalists having beaten the Sans Culottes, and taken Dol. How many minutes will it take to guillotine the seventy-three new members of the convention, who are now arrested? Adieu; ever yours.

To the same. ST. JAMES'S-ST., Nov. 30, 1793.

IT will not be in my power to reach Sheffield-Place quite so soon as I wished and expected. Lord Auckland informs me that he shall be at Lambeth next week, Tuesday, Wednesday, and Thursday. I have therefore agreed to dine at Beckenham on Friday. Saturday will be spent there, and unless some extraordinary temptation should detain me another day, you will see me by four o'clock Sunday the ninth of December. I dine to-morrow with the Chancellor at Hampstead, and, what I do not like at this time of the year, without a proposal to stay all night. Yet I would not refuse, more especially as I had denied him on a former day. My health is good; but I shall have a final interview with Farquhar before I leave town. We are still in darkness about Lord Howe and the French ships, but hope seems to preponderate. Adieu. Nothing that relates to Louisa can be forgotten. Ever yours.

Mr. Gibbon generally took the opportunity of passing a night or two with his friend Lord Auckland, at Eden-Farm, (ten miles from London,) on his passage to Sheffield-Place; and notwithstanding his indisposition, he had lately made an excursion thither from London; when he was much pleased by meeting the Archbishop of Canterbury, of whom he expressed an high opinion. He returned to London, to dine with Lord Loughborough, to meet Mr. Burke, Mr. Windham, and particularly Mr. Pitt, with whom he was not acquainted; and in his last journey to Sussex, he re-visited Eden-Farm, and was much gratified by the opportunity of again seeing, during a whole day, Mr. Pitt, who passed the night there. From Lord Auckland's, Mr. Gibbon proceeded to Sheffield-Place; and his discourse was never more brilliant, nor more entertaining, than on his arrival. The parallels he drew, and the comparisons he made, between the leading men of this country, were sketched in his best manner, and were infinitely interesting. However, this last visit to Sheffield-Place became far different from any he had ever made before. That ready, cheerful, various, and illuminating conversation, which we had before admired in him, was not now always to be found in the library or the dining-room. He moved with difficulty, and retired from company sooner than he had been used to do. On the twenty-third of December, his appetite began to fail him. He observed to me, that it was a very bad sign *with him* when he could not eat his breakfast, which he had done at all times very heartily; and this seems to have been the strongest expression of apprehension that he was ever observed to utter. A considerable degree of fever now made its appearance. Inflammation arose, from the weight and the bulk of the tumour. Water again collected very fast, and when the fever went off, he never entirely recovered his appetite even for breakfast. I became very uneasy indeed at his situation towards the end of the month, and thought it necessary to advise him to set out for London. He had before settled his plan to arrive there about the middle of January. I had company in the house, and we expected one of his particular friends; but he was obliged to sacrifice all social pleasure to the immediate attention which his health required. He went to London on the seventh of January, and the next day I received the following billet; *the last he ever wrote:*

EDWARD GIBBON *Esq. to Lord* SHEFFIELD.

ST. JAMES'S STREET, four o'clock, Tuesday.
" THIS date says every thing. I was almost killed between Sheffield-Place and East-Grinsted, by hard, frozen, long, and cross ruts, that would disgrace the approach of an Indian wig-wam. The rest was something less painful; and I reached this place half dead, but not seriously feverish, or ill. I found a dinner invitation from Lord Lucan; but what are dinners to me? I wish they did not know of my departure. I catch the flying post. What an effort! Adieu, till Thursday or Friday.

By his own desire, I did not follow him till Thursday the ninth. I then found him far from well. The tumour more distended than before, inflamed, and ulcerated in several places. Remedies were applied to abate the inflammation; but it was not thought proper to puncture the tumour for the third time, till Monday the 13th of January, when no less than six quarts of fluid were discharged. He seemed much relieved by the evacuation. His spirits continued good. He talked, as usual, of passing his time at houses which he had often frequented with great pleasure, the Duke of Devonshire's, Mr. Craufurd's, Lord Spenser's, Lord Lucan's, Sir Ralph Payne's, and Mr. Batt's; and when I told him that I should not return to the country, as I had intended, he pressed me to go; knowing I had an engagement there on public business, he said, " you may be back on Saturday, and I intend to go on Thursday to Devonshire-House." I had not any apprehension that his life was in danger, although I began to fear that he might not be restored to a comfortable state, and that motion would be very troublesome to him; but he talked of a radical cure. He said, that it was fortunate the disorder had shewn itself while he was in England, where he might procure the best assistance; and if a radical cure could not be obtained before his return to Lausanne, there was an able surgeon at Geneva, who could come to tap him when it should be necessary.
On Tuesday the fourteenth, when the risk of inflammation and

fever from the last operations was supposed to be over, as the medical gentlemen who attended him expressed no fears for his life, I went that afternoon part of the way to Sussex, and the following day reached Sheffield-place. The next morning, the sixteenth, I received by the post a good account of Mr. Gibbon, which mentioned also that he hourly gained strength. In the evening came a letter by express, dated noon that day, which acquainted me that Mr. Gibbon had had a violent attack the preceding night, and that it was not probable he should live till I could come to him. I reached his lodgings in St. James's-street about midnight, and learned that my friend had expired a quarter before one o'clock that day, the sixteenth of January 1794.

After I left him on Tuesday afternoon the fourteenth, he saw some company, Lady Lucan and Lady Spenser, and thought himself well enough at night to omit the opium draught, which he had been used to take for some time. He slept very indifferently; before nine the next morning he rose, but could not eat his breakfast. However, he appeared tolerably well, yet complained at times of a pain in his stomach. At one o'clock he received a visit of an hour from Madame de Sylva, and at three, his friend, Mr. Craufurd, of Auchinames, (whom he always mentioned with particular regard,) called, and stayed with him till past five o'clock. They talked, as usual, on various subjects; and twenty hours before his death, Mr. Gibbon happened to fall into a conversation, not uncommon with him, on the probable duration of his life. He said, that he thought himself a good life for ten, twelve, or perhaps twenty years. About six, he ate the wing of a chicken, and drank three glasses of Madeira. After dinner he became very uneasy and impatient; complained a good deal, and appeared so weak, that his servant was alarmed. Mr. Gibbon had sent to his friend and relation, Mr. Robert Darell, whose house was not far distant, desiring to see him, and adding, that he had something particular to say. But, unfortunately, this desired interview never took place.

During the evening he complained much of his stomach, and of a disposition to vomit. Soon after nine, he took his opium draught, and went to bed. About ten, he complained of much pain, and desired that warm napkins might be applied to his stomach. He almost incessantly expressed a sense of pain till about four o'clock in the morning, when he said he found his stomach much easier. About seven the servant asked, whether he should send for Mr. Farquhar? he answered, no; that he was as well as he had been the day before. At about half past eight, he got out of bed, and said he was "*plus adroit*" than he had been for three months past, and got into bed again, without assistance, better than usual. About nine, he said that he would rise. The servant, however, persuaded him to remain in bed till Mr. Farquhar, who was expected at eleven, should come. Till about that hour he spoke with great facility. Mr. Farquhar came at the time appointed, and he was then visibly dying. When the *valet de chambre* returned, after attending Mr. Farquhar out of the room, Mr. Gibbon said, "*Pourquoi est ce que vous me quittez?*" This was about half-past eleven. At twelve, he drank some brandy and water from a tea-pot, and desired his favourite servant to stay with him. These were the last words he pronounced articulately. To the last he preserved his senses : and when he could no longer speak, his servant having asked a question, he made a sign, to show that he understood him. He was quite tranquil, and did not stir ; his eyes half-shut. About a quarter before one, he ceased to breathe.

The *valet de chambre* observed, that Mr. Gibbon did not, at any time, shew the least sign of alarm, or apprehension of death ; and it does not appear that he ever thought himself in danger, unless his desire to speak to Mr. Darell may be considered in that light.

Perhaps I dwell too long on these minute and melancholy circumstances. Yet the close of such a life can hardly fail to interest every reader ; and I know that the public has received a different and erroneous account of my friend's last hours.

I can never cease to feel regret that I was not by his side at this awful period : a regret so strong, that I can express it only by borrowing (as the eloquent Mr. Mason has done on a similar occasion) the forcible language of Tacitus : *Mihi præter acerbitatem amici erepti, auget mæstitiam quod assidere valetudini, fovere deficientem, satiari vultu, complexu non contigit.* It is some consolation to me, that I have not, like Tacitus, by a long absence, anticipated the loss of my friend several years before his decease. Although I had not the mournful gratification of being near him on the day he expired, yet during his illness I had not failed to attend him with that assiduity which his genius, his virtues, and, above all, our long, uninterrupted, and happy friendship demanded.

POSTSCRIPT.

MR. Gibbon's Will is dated the 1st of October 1791, just before I left Lausanne ; he distinguishes me, as usual, in the most flattering manner :

"I constitute and appoint the Right Honourable John Lord Sheffield, Edward Darell Esquire, and John Thomas Batt Esquire, to be the Executors of this my last Will and Testament ; and as the execution of this trust will not be attended with much difficulty or trouble, I shall indulge these gentlemen, in the pleasure of this last disinterested service, without wronging my feelings, or oppressing my heir, by too light or too weighty a testimony of my gratitude. My obligations to the long and active friendship of Lord Sheffield, I could never sufficiently repay."

He then observes, that the Right Hon. Lady Eliot, of Port-Eliot, is his nearest relation on the father's side ; but that her three sons are in such prosperous circumstances, that he may well be excused for making the two children of his late uncle, Sir Stanier Porten, his heirs ; they being in a very different situation. He bequeaths annuities to two old servants, three thousand pounds, and his furniture, plate, &c., at Lausanne, to Mr. Wilhelme de Severy ; one hundred guineas to the poor of Lausanne, and fifty guineas each to the following persons : Lady Sheffield and daughters, Maria and Louisa, Madame and Mademoiselle de Severy, the Count de Schomberg, Mademoiselle la Chanoinesse de Polier, and M. le Ministre Le Vade, for the purchase of some token which may remind them of a sincere friend.

EPITAPH OF EDWARD GIBBON.

The Remains of Mr. Gibbon were deposited in Lord Sheffield's Family Burial-Place, in Fletching, Sussex; whereon is inscribed the following Epitaph, written at his Lordship's request by a distinguished scholar, the Rev. Dr. Parr:—

EDVARDUS GIBBON
CRITICUS ACRI INGENIO ET MULTIPLICI DOCTRINA ORNATUS
IDEMQUE HISTORICORUM QUI FORTUNAM
IMPERII ROMANI
VEL LABENTIS ET INCLINATI VEL EVERSI ET FUNDITUS DELETI
LITTERIS MANDAVERINT
OMNIUM FACILE PRINCEPS
CUJUS IN MORIBUS ERAT MODERATIO ANIMI
CUM LIBERALI QUADAM SPECIE CONJUNCTA
IN SERMONE
MULTA GRAVITATI COMITAS SUAVITER ADSPERSA
IN SCRIPTIS
COPIOSUM SPLENDIDUM
CONCINNUM ORBE VERBORUM
ET SUMMO ARTIFICIO DISTINCTUM
ORATIONIS GENUS
RECONDITÆ EXQUISITÆQUE SENTENTIÆ
ET IN MONUMENTIS RERUM POLITICARUM OBSERVANDIS
ACUTA ET PERSPICAX PRUDENTIA
VIXIT ANNOS LVI MENS. VII DIES XXVIII
DECESSIT XVII CAL. FEB. ANNO SACRO
MDCCLXXXXIV
ET IN HOC MAUSOLEO SEPULTUS EST
EX VOLUNTATE JOHANNIS DOMINI SHEFFIELD
QUI AMICO BENE MERENTI ET CONVICTORI HUMANISSIMO
H. TAB. P. C.

CORRESPONDENCE.

THE Letters of Mr. Gibbon, from the time of his return to Switzerland in 1788, are annexed to his Memoirs, as the best continuation of them. Among his Letters of an earlier date, I find several which he has alluded to, and others which will illustrate the account he has given of himself. These, I flatter myself, will please the generality of readers; since, when he touches on matters of private business, even subjects of the driest nature become interesting, from his mode of treating them. Many Letters from distinguished persons to him will be introduced, and some that he received at a very early period of life. Although we have not all his own Letters to which these were answers, yet we have enough to testify his ambition, even in youth, to be distinguished as a scholar.

It has been sometimes thought necessary to offer to the Public an apology for the publication of private Letters. I have no scruple to say, that I publish these, because I think they place my friend in an advantageous point of view. He might not, perhaps, have expected that all his Letters should be printed; but I have no reason to believe that he would have been averse to the publication of any. If I had, they never would have been made public, however highly I might have conceived of their excellence.

M. ALLAMAND *to* E. GIBBON.

SIR,   BEX, 12th September 1756.

AFTER escaping from the tumult of public functions, in which the ministers of this church are employed during the holydays, I sit down with much pleasure to converse with you a few minutes on paper; without intending to make any very violent exertion in answering the questions concerning innate ideas, which you propose for my consideration. I am not willing to risk the being obliged to say, with one of Terence's characters, *Magno conatu magnas nugas;* besides, it is long since I looked into Locke, the modern oracle on that subject; and too much time and paper would be requisite completely to canvass so intricate a subject. You will have the goodness, therefore, to be contented with the first reflections that occur to me on some passages of his first book.

In chapter i. § 5, that able writer undertakes to prove that the axioms, "Whatever is, is;" and "It is impossible for the same thing to be and not to be at the same time;" are not innate; because children are totally ignorant of them, as appears from their never taking notice of them; and many persons die without ever perceiving the truth of these axioms; "but it is impossible," Mr. Locke observes, "for an idea to be in the mind, which the mind never takes notice of." It is plain that the whole weight of his reasoning rests on this last assertion; which assertion itself seems to be manifestly contradicted by experience.

Do you perceive, Sir, at this moment all the ideas that are in your mind? Are there not some of them which you may not, perhaps, take notice of for many years? In the efforts which we make to recall things to the memory, are we not sensible that some ideas may be so deeply hidden in its recesses, that instead of continually perceiving them, we have no small trouble in bringing them back to our remembrance? I know that Mr. Locke, c. iii. § 20, endeavours to obviate these objections; but the length and perplexity of that article shews that he was not at ease in writing it. How indeed could he be so? since, as far as I am able to judge, the following is the result of his argument: " I confess that we have ideas in the mind, of which we are not conscious; but then these ideas are in the memory; as appears from this, that we never recall them without remembering that they formerly were objects of our perception. But this is not supposed to hold with regard to what are called innate ideas. When these are perceived for the first time, it is not with reminiscence, which would certainly be the case if they had been in the mind before this first perception of them," &c.

Be pleased to tell me, Sir, whether you think that Mr. Locke himself well understood the distinction which he makes between *being in the mind*, and *being in the memory?* And of what importance is it, that we remember to have formerly had the recalled ideas, provided it be allowed that we had them long, without taking any notice of them, which is the point in question? Besides, Mr. Locke ought to have known that innate ideas are not recalled with reminiscence, because those ideas come originally into the mind in a way that neither excites nor requires our attention; for whatever Mr. Locke may say, every one may be sensible from his own experience, that many even of his acquired ideas could not have come into his mind independently of the presence of certain objects of which he had never taken any notice; or, in general, independently of certain unknown causes, which enriched him, without his being sensible of it, with ideas that he did not believe himself possessed of, till they actually presented themselves to his understanding.

As to the main question, Mr. Locke seems to me perpetually to confound two things extremely different; the idea itself, which is a perception of the mind, and a principle of reasoning; and the expression of that idea in the form of a proposition or definition. It is possible, nay, very probable, that many persons have never formed, or thought of the proposition, "It is impossible for the same thing to be and not to be at the same time." See Locke, b. i. c 1. § 12. But does it follow from this, that they are ignorant of the truth expressed by these words? By no means. Every man who affirms, denies, or speaks; a child who asks, refuses, or complains, must know the truth of this proposition. Does it not appear to you, Sir, that the doctrine of innate ideas may be defended on the same principle by which Mr. Locke attacks it; namely, that many persons have never thought of the propositions or descriptions by which they are expressed? For if without ever having thought of those propositions, they make use of them in their reasonings, and employ them in judging of the justness or absurdity of every discourse which they hear, how could they be so familiar with principles which they never distinctly took notice of, unless they had a natural knowledge or innate perception of them?

In paragraphs 17 and 18, Mr. Locke denies that our consenting to certain propositions at first hearing them, is a proof that the ideas expressed by them are innate; since many propositions, thus assented to, evidently express ideas that had been acquired; for example, *two and two make four*, &c. But does it not appear to you, that he here confounds the definition of words with self-evident truths? at least, all the examples which he gives are mere definitions. The idea expressed by *two and two* is precisely the same with the idea of *four*. Nobody says that our knowledge of the definitions of words is innate, because that would imply language to be so. But the knowledge of this truth, that the whole is greater than its part, does not imply that supposition; since an infant shews itself acquainted with this principle, when, dissatisfied with the half of an apple, it indicates its desire to possess the whole.

Take the trouble, Sir, to examine § 23; in which Mr. Locke endeavours to disprove the assertion, that there are some principles so truly innate, that those who hear them expressed in words for the first time, immediately comprehend them without learning anything new. "First of all," he observes, "it is clear they must have learned the terms of the expression, and the meaning of those terms." But here Mr. Locke manifestly departs from the question. Nobody says that words, which are merely arbitrary signs of our ideas, are innate. He adds, "that the ideas denoted by these expressions are no more born with us than the expressions themselves, and that we acquire the ideas after first learning the terms by which they are expressed." But, 1. Is not this to take for granted the thing to be proved? There are no innate ideas, for all ideas are acquired. Mr. Locke would laugh at his adversaries, were they to make use of such an argument. 2. If words are learned before ideas, at least if that is always the case, as Mr. Locke understands it to be, I would be glad to know how the first language could have been formed, or how it could be possible to communicate to any one the meaning of a word altogether new to him? A person who had no idea of order, for example, would be no more capable of understanding the word order, than a man born blind could understand the word colour.

In paragraph 27, Mr. Locke denies innate ideas, because they are not found in children and idiots, in whom we ought most to expect meeting with them. I answer, 1. Those who admit innate ideas, do not believe them more natural to the mind than its faculties; and as the state and constitution of the body disturbs the faculties of idiots, the same cause may hinder them from showing any signs of innate ideas. 2. The fact is not strictly true. Even idiots and infants have the idea of their existence, individuality, identity, &c.

In the remainder of that paragraph, Mr. Locke diverts himself with the absurdity of those who believe the expressions of abstract maxims to be innate; but the most determined scholastic never maintained any such opinion; and he combats a chimera which is the work of his own fancy.

I know not how it has happened that, instead of a few general reflections which I had intended, I have sent you a long and tiresome criticism on some passages of a single chapter. The remains of lassitude, probably, made it easier for me to follow and dispute with Mr. Locke, than to think and reason alone. Have patience, and pardon me. There are many remarks to make on the second chapter, where he treats of innate practical principles. But I will not tire you with that subject, unless you desire it.

Our newspapers say, that the King of Prussia has beat the Austrians, and killed twenty thousand of their men; with the loss of fifteen thousand of his own. This was the object he had in view when he passed through Leipsic. If the news be true, the war must become general; and, according to appearances, it will be terrible. But I much fear lest his Prussian Majesty meet with the fate of Charles XII. What are his resources for defence against the united strength of France and Austria, and perhaps of Russia?

I have the honour to be, with the most perfect consideration, yours, &c. ALLAMAND.

M. ALLAMAND *to Mr.* GIBBON.

SIR, BEX, October 12, 1756.

I am delighted with your last letter, equally distinguished by accuracy and penetration; and with you, Sir, I believe that the question approaches to its decision.

You are right in saying, that the self-evident propositions, which I mentioned, are not merely ideas, but judgments: yet you will have the goodness to observe, that Mr. Locke having given them as examples of ideas which pass for being innate, but which he does not regard as such, the mistake is chargeable on him, and not on me, who had nothing farther to do than to refute his manner of reasoning. Besides, you will be pleased to remark, that the real question is, whether not only certain ideas, but also certain common and self-evident propositions be innate. The only examples produced of innate ideas are those of God, unity, and existence; the other examples are of innate propositions, which you call judgments.

You ask, whether it be possible that our judgments should be innate, judgment being nothing else but the act of our intellectual faculties in comparing our ideas, and our judgment concerning self-evident truths being merely the perception of those truths by a simple glance of the mind? I grant all that, but would ask, what else is an idea but a glance of the mind? Those who define it otherwise, widely depart from the original sense of the word; and talk unintelligibly, when they say that ideas are species; that is, appearances of things impressed on the mind, as the images of corporeal objects are impressed on the eye. All metaphysicians have committed this mistake; and Mr. Locke, though sensible of it, has chosen in his anger to direct his batteries against the weathercocks, rather than against the building itself. According to the meaning of these metaphysicians, there are surely no innate ideas, because in their sense of the word there are no ideas whatever. An idea is merely an act or perception of the mind: and the question concerning innate ideas is merely to determine, whether certain truths be not so common and so evident, that every mind, not absolutely stupid, must recognize them at a single glance,

N

without the assistance of any teacher, and without the intervention of
any discussion or reasoning ; and often without being sensible that
this glance is cast on them ?   The affirmative appears to me incontro-
vertible ; and the question thereby is solved.

You will please to remark, that this way of explaining the matter is
as favourable to innate ideas, and therefore as opposite to Mr. Locke's
doctrine, as the unintelligible hypothesis above mentioned.   For what
reason do we contend in favour of innate ideas ?   To oppose evidence
and certainty to universal scepticism ; whose cause is ruined by proving certain truths to be so necessary and so natural to man, that they
are universally recognized by a single glance.   This may be proved
according to my meaning of the word idea, as well as according to the
sense in which this word is vulgarly taken ; and the proof would not
have been very pleasing to Mr. Locke, who, without professing himself
a sceptic, yet shows a leaning to the sceptical side ; and whose works
have contributed much to the diffusion of scepticism in the present
age.   His too eager desire of fixing the limits of human knowledge, a
thing highly necessary, has made him leave nothing but limits.

After these general observations on the main question, it is not very
necessary to descend to the particulars in which you think me mistaken.   Yet you will permit me to answer your objections. 1. It is
true, that Mr. Locke, § 5, c. 1, joins the two expressions, " being in the
mind, without being actually perceived by the mind," and " being in
the mind, without having ever been perceived by the mind ;" but at
the conclusion of the paragraph he lays himself open to my criticism,
by expressing himself as follows : " so that to be in the understanding
and not to be understood, to be in the mind and never to be perceived, is
all one as to say, any thing is and is not in the mind or understanding."
It is clear, Sir, that this great philosopher erred in writing this passage ;
maintaining what I took the liberty to contradict, that nothing could
be in the understanding without being perceived to be there.   I doubt
not that he would have corrected this mistake had it been pointed out
to him ; but he certainly falls into it, and employs it as a principle of
reasoning against his adversaries.

2. You think that we ought to admit his distinction between " ideas
in the mind," and " ideas in the memory."   I admit the distinction
with all my heart, provided you take the word idea in the same accep-
tation as I do.   In that sense an idea is in the mind, when the mind
actually considers the proposition which is the object of its idea, that
is, of its glance or perception ; and an idea is in the memory when the
mind, having formerly cast that glance on it, finds thereby a greater
facility in recalling it, remembering at the same time that it formerly
was the object of its perception.   But if you understand by ideas these
chimerical species, the mere fictions of metaphysicians, and, as it seems
to me, not sufficiently disproved by Mr. Locke, I return to my assertion, and maintain that the distinction is unintelligible between " being
in the mind," and " being in the memory."

A violent headache, which I brought with me from our venerable
class, hinders me from continuing this letter, or rendering what I have
already written shorter and more perspicuous.   I intreat you to excuse
its imperfections.   Your penetration will perhaps discern how all diffi-

culties may be solved concerning innate practical principles. Mr. Locke treats this subject better than he does the others ; but in several parts he is somewhat puzzled.

I rejoiced at the hopes of seeing you for a moment at Vevay, and was surprised at being *disappointed.* If I rightly understand this word of your language, it cannot be well translated into ours. I met with Mr. Pavillard only in the assembly.

M. ALLAMAND.

Mr. GIBBON to M. GESNER.

SIR,

THE multitude of your employments affords at once the proof of your own merit, of the justice done to it by the public, of my presumption, and of your goodness. How enviable is the lot of that small number of superior minds whose talents are equally adapted to promote the purposes either of pleasure or utility ? The discernment surely of those princes is worthy of much applause, who, having ventured to dissipate the clouds of envy, calumny, and frivolity, that usually surround thrones, render to the truly great men among their subjects a justice which had been long done to them by the impartial public, and reward their talents, by affording them new opportunities to display them. These are but a small part of the reflections occasioned by your letter, and which, were I to consult my inclination only, would extend to a great length ; but my reason tells me, that I must be contented with assuring you, that you have filled with gratitude a man who will always be proud of being called your scholar. I go shortly to England ; where, perhaps, I may find an opportunity of proving to you the sincerity of my sentiments, at least of rendering my correspondence less tiresome. My residence in London will give me a sort of local merit. I will send you early intelligence of the labours and discoveries of our learned men, whose example I am unable to imitate ; and will expect to learn, in return, what is so proper an object of curiosity, the occupations and studies of your colleagues and disciples at Gottingen. At my return to London I propose to myself a new pleasure in collecting all your works, which I will make it my first business to procure ; and for assisting me in this matter, must request that you will give me the titles of all the curious pieces with which you have enriched the republic of letters. My ignorance of many of them causes both joy and shame. It can only be excused in consideration of my youth, and the place from which this letter is dated.

If I venture to propose some new doubts, it is because you know better than any one, that absolute submission, is due only to reason, either real or apparent. You will believe that my only motive for discussing your lessons is to render myself worthy of them :

" Non ita certandi cupidus, quam propter amorem."*

After this apology, I must confess that I have still some remaining doubts concerning the Piso to whom Horace addresses his Art of Poetry. You think that the manner in which that poet speaks of Virgil does not prove the latter to be still alive ; because Horace does

* Lucret. de Rer. Natur. L. iii. ver. 5, *et seq.*

not oppose the dead to the living, but the ancients to the moderns. I examined the passage again, and that new perusal excited reflections which confirmed me more strongly in my former opinion. Horace thought the Latin tongue too poor and barren, and deficient in words expressive of abstract ideas, which were unknown to Romulus' companions, consisting of shepherds and robbers. This imperfection had been remarked by others. Horace, wishing to remedy it, proposes to the Virgils and Variuses, to co-operate with him in this design, by borrowing from the Greek many energetic terms and phrases which were wanting in Latin. He does not justify a thing already done, but proposes a new enterprise. The futurity which he looks to can only have a reference to authors still alive. The Art of Poetry was therefore written before the year of Rome seven hundred and thirty-five. This explanation agrees so well with the poet's thought, that his opposition between the dead and living poets, concludes with one of the justest and liveliest images that I ever remember to have met with :

> "———— licuit semperque licebit
> Signatum præsente notâ producere nomen."[*]

The *licuit* has a reference to the Terences and the Ceciliuses, who were long dead ; the *licebit*, in the future, to the Variuses and Virgils, who were still alive, and might avail themselves of the maxim.[†]

You say that Piso's eldest son might be ten years old when the Art of Poetry was published ; an age at which Grotius wrote verses. Grotius did so ; but how few boys of that age have not only the fire to write, but the judgment to criticise poetry ? It is not likely that Piso the father should have children at the age of twenty. You well know the paucity of marriages under Augustus, which rendered the conjugal felicity of Germanicus an example so much admired, *Suet. L. II. c.* 34 ; pride, poverty, *Tacit. Annal. ii. c.* 37, and debauchery, deterred the Roman nobles from marriage, especially amidst the civil wars, which, during Piso's youth, desolated the earth. Augustus' laws on that subject only prove the greatness of the evil[‡] ; and Piso was thirty years old, before the first of those laws was enacted §. If an ordinary generation is computed at thirty-three years ||, the generations under the first emperors ought rather to be extended to forty, than reduced to twenty years. These I acknowledge, are but probabilities, but in the science of criticism probabilities destroy possibilities, and are themselves destroyed by proofs. This principle is not to be controverted. The authority of Porphyrio is of too little weight among the learned to be the foundation of an argument ; it might at best help to prop an argument, otherwise well supported. The ancients do not assign to him the first rank among Horace's commentators ¶ ; and the moderns, particularly Mr. Dacier, find in him many errors. I do not see any ground for your first hypothesis. If Piso had a son when he was thirty years old, this son might be sixteen when Horace wrote his

---

* Horat. de Art, Poet. ver. 59.
+ This explanation is the more probable, because Virgil appears in his works to value himself rather on reviving old words, than on borrowing new ones from the Greek. I doubt whether a single passage can be pointed out, in which he followed Horace's advice.
‡ Dion. Hist. Rom. L. lvi. p. 570.   § Horat. Carm. Secular. v 17, &c.   Torrent de Lege Juliâ ad Calc. Horat. p. 75, &c. || Herodot. L. ii.   Newton Chronol. Emendat. p. 41.
¶ Vid. Vitam Horat fine nomine Autoris.

Art of Poetry; an age which you think agrees with every quality required in him. Did you not forget, in writing this sentence, that Horace died in seven hundred and forty-five, when Piso himself was only forty years old?

2. I think it certain that Horace, in the third ode of his third book, meant to show the Romans, that if their prince aspired to divine honours, *V. amque affectat Olympo*, he well merited them by his exploits, which rivalled those of the greatest heroes, Bacchus, Hercules, and Romulus, who, after trampling on their human enemies, and appeasing the jealousy of the gods, had opened for themselves a road to the palace of the immortals. But did the poet also intend, by this ode, to resist and destroy the clamours of the people concerning the infamous supper of the twelve gods? I think he did not. 1. This design does not agree with chronology. Suetonius does not tell us the date of this supper; but since Mark Antony mentioned it, in his letters to Augustus, *Suet. L. ii. c.* 70; it must have happened before the last quarrel of the triumvirs. According to Bentley, *Bentley in Præfat. ad Horat;* whose opinion you adopt, Horace wrote the third book of his odes in the forty-second and forty-third years of his age; that is, in the seven hundred and twenty-eighth and seven hundred and twenty-ninth years of Rome. An apology for Augustus' debaucheries, written seven years after they happened, could have only served to revive the memory of enormities, which the policy of that prince and the gratitude of the Romans had long consigned to oblivion. 2. Augustus supped with eleven men and women, who, as well as himself, were adorned with the emblems of divinities. The poet feated Augustus at the table of the gods, *purpureo bibit ore nectar;* but can we reasonably suppose that he meant to place there the companions of his feast? This would have been to render the honour too common; and his panegyric would have degenerated into a satire. I agree with you, that it is rather desirable than necessary to discover the plan of an ode; the writers of Lyric poetry having always enjoyed the privilege of soaring to heights, which, if admired by fancy, must not be criticised by reason. This fault, if it be one, is compensated by great beauties. The two first stanzas prove the wonderful efficacy of poetry when combined with philosophy. The *justum & tenacem propositi virum* is the sage of the Stoics, their king.* and only happy man; all whose designs are just, and inflexibly persued.† Such a being, exempt from passions and prejudices, never casts his eyes on the tumults of human life, without exclaiming,

"O! curas hominum! O! quantum in rebus inane!"

To the disgrace of mankind, such a character never existed; but it is not a small honour for the species, that such perfect virtue has been described and relished. The climax is beautiful. The sage would resist the clamorous fury of a mad multitude; but this popular rage is often appeased as easily as it is kindled. He would despise the threats of a furious tyrant; but the hearts of tyrants sometimes relent with compassion. He would hear without terror the raging tempest, which over-powers the cries of the wretched; but fortune has often rescued victims

---

* Horat. Serm. L. i. Serm. iii. ver. 124.   † Cicero pro Murenæ, c. 29.   De la Mothe le Vayer, tom. i. p. 606, &c. de la Vertu des Payens.

from the boisterous waves. He would not dread the thunder of Jupiter : here the trembling imagination pauses, fearing lest the poet should either sink into meanness, or swell into bombast ; because it seems impossible to conceive a bolder image than the enraged master of gods and men. But our fear is converted into admiration, when we read " he would sustain unterrified the crashing shock of the universe, by which the elements, men, and gods are involved in one common ruin," *Plin. L. vi. Epist.* 20, I stop here, lest my reflections should tire you ; which if they do, it must be my fault. I shall have attained, however, my purpose, which was to show the point of view under which I consider the most profound erudition. Regarded as a mean or instrument, it merits our highest admiration ; but considered as an ultimate end, it is entitled to nothing but contempt.

3. You remember, Sir, that famous passage of Velleius Paterculus, *Vell. Paterc. L. ii. c.* 125, which has given so much trouble to the learned. It is as follows : * * * * It seems unsusceptible of any meaning, and must be supposed either defective or corrupt. All the critics, therefore, who have examined it, endeavour to restore the text. Burerius, Acidalius, Gruter, Boeclerus, Heinsius, Burman, have, all of them, given conjectures more or less probable, which I shall not here discuss. I shall rather submit an emendation of my own to your judgment. Instead of the common reading, I would substitute *Prisca antiquâque feveritate,* FUSUS *ancipitia sibi tam re quam exemplo perniciosa.* We see at once that this small alteration produces a clear and distinct sense ; and the correction may be proved to be equally conformable to the analogy of the Latin tongue, and agreeable to the truth of history. The best grammarians acknowledge that the Latin, not having a middle voice, admits of a passive participle in an active signification.* Thus, *juratus, punitus,* sometimes denote *qui juravit, qui punivit.* We find *peragratus* used in this meaning by Velleius himself.† *Fusus* may therefore, without impropriety, denote the action of Drusus. History also favours this correction. According to Tacitus, when Drusus arrived in the camp of the rebels, his orders were disobeyed, his offers suspected, the soldiers made him prisoner, they insulted his friends, and waited only for a pretence to begin the slaughter. Such were the dangers that threatened his person ! *Sibi ancipitia tam re.* The severity of the Roman discipline is well known. The generals were the gods of the soldiers, and their orders received as oracles. But ancient maxims were now overturned ; and the sedition of the Pannonian legions created an example most pernicious to posterity. Superstition, which does so much evil, here did good ; an eclipse of the moon frightened the soldiers, and saved the life of the general.

I read with much pleasure your solution of the difficulty in Justin ; and admire your skill in extracting a regular narrative, by bringing the scattered lights in authors to one focus. If any uncertainty still remains, it must be ascribed to the darkness of antiquity and Justin's brevity.

Your suffrage removes all fear about the solidity of my conjecture

* V. Burman ad Vell. Paterc. L. ii. c. 97. Perizon. ad Sanct. Minerv. L. i. c. 15. n. 4.
† Vell. Paterc. L. ii. c. 97.   ‡ Tacit. Annal. i. c. 24, &c.

concerning the death of Catullus. I formerly thought it probable, but begin now to regard it as certain. I have the honour to remain, with the highest consideration and most perfect esteem, yours, &c.

EDWARD GIBBON.

[THIS LETTER, in the early hand-writing of Mr. GIBBON, (probably about the time of his first leaving Lausanne,) seems to be under the assumed character of a Swedish traveller, writing to a Swiss friend, delineating the defects he discovered in the government of Berne. In pointing out those defects he seems to have had the intention of suggesting remedies; but, as he is entering on this topic, the manuscript ends abruptly. The excellence of this curious paper will apologize for its great length.—S.]

No; my dear friend, I will not be a citizen of the world; I reject with scorn that proud title, under which our philosophers conceal an equal indifference for the whole human race. I will love my country; and to love it above all others, there must be reasons for my preference : but, if I am not mistaken, my heart is susceptible of affection for more countries than one. Did I sacrifice all to Sweden, I should only pay my debt of gratitude to the land in which I was born, and to which I owe my life and fortune. Yet life and fortune would have been but melancholy burthens, if, after my banishment from home in early youth, your country had not formed my taste and reason, and taught me more refined morals than our own. I should prove myself unworthy of this goodness, did it not inspire me with the liveliest gratitude : and now that Sweden, enjoying tranquillity under the protection of laws, requires nothing from its subjects but a just sense of their happiness, I may direct my attention, without offence, to the Pays de Vaud, my second country; rejoicing with you in its advantages, or commiserating its misfortunes.

You enjoy a fine climate, a fertile soil, and have conveniences for internal commerce, from which great benefit might be derived. But I consider the people rather than their territory. Philosophy flourishes in London; Paris is the centre of those attracted by the allurements of polished society. Your country, though inferior to those capitals, yet unites in some measure their respective advantages : since it is the only country whose inhabitants, while they think freely and boldly, live politely and elegantly. What then is wanting? Liberty; and deprived of it, you have lost your all.

This truth surprises and offends you. The right of complaining, you answer, that we are not free, is a proof of our liberty. If I wrote at Lausanne, the argument would have weight; yet even there, it would not be convincing; for your masters are not ignorant of Cardinal Mazarine's maxim, and are willing to allow you to talk, provided you allow them to act; so that the process is not yet determined.

If I wrote for the people I would speak to their passions, and hold a language repeated in all ages, that under republics, those who are free are more free, and those who are enslaved, more enslaved, than under any other form of government. But with a friend like you I would seek only the maxims of truth, and employ only the arguments of reason. When I compare your condition with that of surrounding nations, I can sincerely congratulate you on your happiness. Whenever we quit the neighbourhood of your lake and mountains, we find men who, though worthy of a better fate, are plunged in the most abject superstition ; whose property and industry are the spoils of a licentious soldiery; and whose lives are ready every moment to be sacrificed to the caprice of one man, who, when he bears that twenty thousand of his fellow-creatures have fallen sacrifices to his ambition, is contented with saying coldly, " they have done their duty."

You, on the contrary, enjoy a Christianity brought back to the purity of its original principles, taught publicly by worthy ministers, who are loved and respected, but who have it not in their power to become the objects of fear. Your connection with the Swiss cantons has preserved to you the blessings of peace two centuries ; a thing unexampled in history. Your taxes are moderate ; and the public administration is gentle. You have not to complain of those arbitrary sentences, which, without any form of legal procedure, without an accuser, and without a crime, have been known to tear citizens from the bosoms of their families. The sovereign is never seen ; the weight of his authority is rarely felt : yet if liberty consists in being subject to laws, which impartially consult the interests of all the members of the community, you do not enjoy that blessing.

When the injustice of some, and the weakness of others, showed the necessity for civil society, individuals were obliged to renounce their beloved, but pernicious, independence. All particular wills were melted down into the general will of the public ; by which, under the sanction of definite punishments, men became bound to regulate their conduct. But it is a matter of the utmost delicacy to determine with whom that general will ought to be deposited. Shall it reside in the breast of a prince, who thereby becomes absolute ? I know that the true interests of a prince can never be separated from those of his people, and that in exerting himself for their benefit, he labours for his own. This is the language of philosophy, but it is seldom spoken by the preceptors of princes ; and if the latter sometimes read it in their own hearts, the impression is speedily effaced by contrary passions, in themselves, their confessors, their ministers, or mistresses. The groans of the people are not soon heard ; and their master learns only by a fatal experience, that it is the interest of a shepherd to preserve his flock. The legislative power, therefore, cannot safely be entrusted to a single person. A council, whose members mutually instruct, and mutually check each other, appears to be its proper depository. But in this council one condition is essentially requisite. It must consist of deputies from every order in the state, interested by their own safety in opposing every regulation inconsistent with the happiness of that order to which they belong. Such a council will rarely be guilty of gross errors ; and should this sometimes happen, it will soon blush for, and repair them. Is this the picture of your legislature ? When I survey your country, I behold two nations, distinctly characterised by their rights, employments, and manners : the one, consisting of three hundred families, born to command ; the other, consisting of an hundred thousand, doomed to submission. The former are invested, as a body, with all the prerogatives of hereditary monarchs, which are the more humiliating to you their subjects, because they belong to men apparently your equals. The comparison between yourselves and them is made every moment ; no circumstance tends to conceal it from your fancy.

A council of three hundred persons is the sovereign umpire of your dearest interests, which will always be sacrificed when they clash with their own. This council is invested with the executive, as well as the legislative, power ; two branches of authority which can never be united, without rendering each of them too formidable to the subject. When they belong to different persons, or assemblies, the legislature will not venture to form violent resolutions, because these would be of no avail, unless they were carried into execution by another power, always its rival, and often its antogonist. The sword of authority is not only sharpened by this union, but is thereby confined to a smaller number of hands. In the last century the great council of Berne began to elect its own members ; which was a great step towards oligarchy, since it excluded from elections the citizens at large, and thereby narrowed the basis of the government. But this arrangement was liable to other inconveniences. Intrigue, venality, and debauchery signalised the admission of citizens into the sovereign council ; and ambitious men squandered their wealth, that they might purchase a right to indulge their rapacity. A committee of six counsellors, established in the infancy of the republic, to watch the execution of the laws, and whose offices were held at pleasure, became entrusted with the power of naming the members of the grand council, by which this committee itself was appointed. Its number was augmented by sixteen senators, chosen in the manner most favourable to the designs of faction. They exercised their power at first collectively, but by degrees they came to understand that their particular interests would be better promoted by each naming his son, son-in-law, or kinsman. The powerful families which then commanded the senate, still rule in it at present. Thirty places are filled by the Wattevilles and Steiguers. This selfish traffic, by which the members of the little council are elected by the great council, consisting of their own relations, that they may name other relations to seats in the great council, has reduced the number of families, which have a right to sit in the latter, to nearly fourscore. These princely families look down with equal contempt on those who are their fellow-citizens by the law of nature, and those who were rendered such by the constitution of their country. The former class is deprived of a resource which the most absolute princes have seldom ventured to wrest from their subjects ; I mean those courts of justice acknowledged by the prince, and revered by the people, as the organs of public opinion, and the depositories of the laws. The commands of the sovereign are obeyed with cheerfulness only when their propriety is confirmed by the approbation of those tribunals, whose members it has been found difficult either to deceive, to seduce, or to intimidate. Their resistance to oppression is respectful, but firm ; and in exerting it, they display that warmth of eloquence with which reason and liberty inspire good citizens. In the members of those peaceful tribunals, such qualities appear in their greatest lustre. Destitute of arms, their whole strength lies in their talents and their probity. What noble lessons to kings have been given by the Parliament of Paris? What excellent examples to subjects are set by the Mandarines of China? Monarchs *must* hear the groans of their people, when such respectable bodies of men are their organs. The people too learn that they have a country, which they will begin to love, to study its laws, and to form themselves to public virtues. These virtues ripen silently; they are exerted when an opportunity offers; and sometimes they will make an opportunity for their own exhibition. In the Pays de Vaud, which was equally respectable under the kings of Burgundy and the dukes of Savoy, the states formed such a tribunal. They were composed of the nobility, clergy, and deputies from the principal cities, which annually assembled at Moudon, and formed the perpetual council of the prince, without whose consent he could neither enact new laws, nor impose new taxes. Were I on the spot, I could prove the existence of those rights by your most authentic records. At a distance I can only appeal to their testimony, and employ an analogical proof, which will be sufficiently convincing to men of letters. The Barbarians, who overflowed Europe in the fifth century, every where laid the foundation of that form of government which Charlemagne established in the Low Countries, France, Italy, Switzerland, and Germany. The different modes of tenure which were at different times introduced, the various degrees of dependance which one fief came to have on another, the acquisition of lordships by the clergy, and the purchase of franchises by cities; all these circumstances occasioned but slight differences in the ground-work of the constitution, which remained unalterably founded on a firm basis of liberty. The states, their members, and their rights, were invariably maintained; remaining uniformly the same at all times, and in all places.

I think that I hear you, my friend, interrupting me. Hitherto, you say, I have listened to you with patience; but what is your conclusion from this picture of our government? Whatever defects there may be in its principles, we have experienced its salutary consequences; and the states and assemblies which you so much commend, will not easily make us abolish our ancient magistracies, in order to try innovations.

It is time, Sir, to pause; I spoke to you as became a freeman, and you answer me in the language of slavery. Let us admit for a moment your prosperity; to whom do you owe it? You will not answer, to the constitution. It is due then to your rulers. The Romans owed a prosperity yet greater to Titus; but still remained the basest of slaves. Brutus would have taught you that a despot may sometimes choose to promote the public happiness; but that the magistrates of a free people can have no other wish. The advantages actually enjoyed by a citizen and a slave may be the same; but those of the latter are precarious, having no other foundation than the changeable passions of men; whereas those of the former are secure, being solidly supported on those laws which curb guilty passions in the prince as well as in the peasant.

But unfortunately too many faults may be found in your public administration. I shall give you the black list of omissions and oppressions which, notwithstanding that you will exclaim against my malignity, your own memory will augment by an hundred articles, which I may be either ignorant of, or forget to mention. It is the duty of a sovereign to procure for his people all the happiness of which their condition is susceptible. His public spirited exertions may be suspended by the exigencies of defensive war; but as soon as peace is restored, he will be continually and usefully occupied with the interests of religion, laws, morals, sciences, police, commerce, and agriculture. Let us try the merits of the senate of Berne by these maxims. The members of this senate have been masters of the Pays de Vaud since the year one thousand five hundred and thirty-six. When we consider the deplorable condition in those days of France, England, Holland, and Germany, we can scarcely imagine that they were the same countries with those respectively known at present by the same names. Their barbarism has been civilized, their ignorance enlightened, their poverty enriched; their deserts have become cities, and their forests now wave with yellow harvests. These wonders have been effected by their princes and ministers: a Henry the Fourth, a Sully, a Colbert, an Elizabeth, a de Witt, and a Frederick William. The comparative condition of the Pays de Vaud at those two remote æras, does not present so pleasing a picture. There the arts still languish, for want of those encouragements which princes only can bestow: the country is still destitute of commerce and manufactures: we hear not of any projects for promoting the public prosperity: we see nothing but the marks of an universal lethargy. Yet the princes above mentioned had but moments for executing their great designs; the senators of Berne have had ages. What benefits might not those patriotic kings have conferred on their subjects, if, instead of having their thrones continually shaken by war and sedition, they had enjoyed during two centuries the advantage of having loyal subjects and pacific neighbours? I appeal to yourself; point out a single useful establishment which the Pays de Vaud owes to the sovereignty of Berne: but do not tell me of the academy of Lausanne, founded on motives of religion during the zeal of reformation, but since totally neglected, though a worthy magistrate of that city proposed the laudable design of erecting it into an university.

Your masters err not through ignorance. They are not deficient, I know, in political abilities. But while a prince treats with impartial bounty all his subjects, the citizens of an aristocratical capital are apt to behold with jealousy the improvement of the provinces. Their elevation, they think, must pave the way for their own downfal; and if they become their equals in point of knowledge and riches, they will soon be tempted, they imagine, to aspire at an equality with themselves in power. Recal to memory the year 1685; when the wretched policy of Louis the Fourteenth drove from their country the most industrious portion of his subjects, many of whom sought refuge in the Pays de Vaud; a neighbouring district, and speaking their own language. They requested only an asylum, the benefit of which they would richly have repaid by the wealth which they carried with them, and their skill in manufactures, still more valuable. But the narrow policy of Berne took the alarm. " If we make these men citizens of Berne, their interests will coincide with our own. But is it fit that mortals should be raised to the rank of gods ! If they are mixed with the mass of our subjects, our subjects will be enriched by their industry." They concluded therefore, with the ambassadors of Porsenna— "that it was more desirable for a prince to govern a poor but submissive people, than to contend with the unruly passions of men pampered by prosperity."

The emigrants, disgusted at being repeatedly refused what they ought to have been requested to accept, travelled to Holland, Prussia, and England, whose rulers had the good sense to avail themselves of an emergency as favourable as it was singular. A part of them indeed remained in the Pays de Vaud, but the poorest and the idlest, who had neither money nor spirit to travel farther.

These unhappy fugitives had no sooner begun to forget their past sufferings, than they learned by fatal experience that, in order to avoid persecution, it was necessary to fly from the society of men. The sovereigns of the country in which they had settled had imbibed the severe system of Calvin, a stern theologian, who loved liberty too well, to endure that Christians should wear any other chains than those imposed by himself. His near conformity in opinion with a celebrated German philosopher, interested the honour of the German name in supporting his doctrines. But in the Pays de Vaud the asperity of religious opinions had softened with the improvement of society. It became necessary, therefore, to send thither formulas and inquisitors, designed to make as many hypocrites as possible, not indeed by fire and sword, but by threats and deposition from office.

In supporting the rights of man, I would not carry too far the maxims of toleration. It is just that public rewards should be bestowed only on those who teach the religion of the public ; and those bold innovators, who would impart a dangerous light to the people, may very properly be restrained by the arm of the magistrate. But it surely is absurd, that the sovereign should interfere in theological minutiæ, and take part warmly in questions which are incapable of being decided. It is particularly unjust, that he should impose confessions of faith on old ministers, who wish to avoid disputation ; leaving them the miserable alternative of falsehood or beggary. But this persecution has now ceased. What put an end to it ? It was not shame, nor the tears of the people, but the boldness of Davel, that meritorious enthusiast. Even to the present day, a secret inquisition still reigns at Lausanne ; where the names of Arminian and Socinian are often mentioned in the letters written by very honest people to their patrons of Berne ; and offices are often given or withheld according to the reports made of the religious tenets of the candidates.

Having made these strictures on your legislature, which by no means exhaust the subject, I proceed to consider the defects of your executive power ; which is the public force, as the legislature ought to be the public will. But a single council, or a single man, may deliberate and resolve for a whole nation ; the executive power, on the contrary, requires the exertions of many : as it is composed of a great variety of branches, many officers, subordinate one to the other, must actuate the different parts of the machine, to which the chief magistrate can only communicate the first general movement. The honours and emoluments legally attached to such offices, ought to be open to all those citizens who are properly qualified for discharging them. Each individual, as he bears a share of the public burdens, is entitled also to a share of the public rewards. This just arrangement is easily maintained in monarchies; where, with the exception of a few courtiers, who, by being continually about the prince's person, have an opportunity of substituting flattery instead of real services, all the inhabitants of the kingdom are treated with comparative equity. In France, provided a man has court-favour or merit, the question is never asked whether he comes from Provence or Normandy. D'Epernon was born in Gascony; Richelieu, in Champagne; Mazarine, in Rome. But in aristocratical republics, the citizens of one town are not contented with being sovereigns collectively, unless they individually appropriate all offices of honour or emolument. In the canton of Berne talents and information are not of the smallest use to any one who is not born in the capital; and in another sense they are useless to those born there; because they *must* make their way without them. Their subjects in the Pays de Vaud are condemned, by the circumstances of their birth, to a condition of shameful obscurity. They naturally become, therefore, a prey to despair; and neglecting to cultivate talents which they can never enjoy an opportunity to display, those who had capacities for becoming great men are contented with making themselves agreeable companions. Should I propose that the subjects obtained a right to hold the lucrative employments of *Baillis*, or governors of districts, the aristocratical families of Berne would think me guilty of a crime little less than sacrilege. "The emoluments of these offices form the patrimony of the state; and we are the state." It is true, that you in the Pays de Vaud may be deputies to the Baillis; but the advantages belonging to that subordinate magistracy are obtained on certain conditions, which, unless the holder of the office lives a certain number of years, renders his bargain a very bad one for his family.

What encouragement is then left for the gentlemen of the Pays de Vaud? That of foreign service. But to them, even this road to preferment is extremely difficult, and to attain the higher ranks is impossible. I speak not of the brilliant service of France : in that country, expence is unavoidable; the ensign is ruined, the captain can scarcely live, and the colonel cannot save money. You are therefore obliged to the paternal care of the magistrates of Berne, whose treaties for supplying troops to France do not lead you into temptation. Let us only consider the service of Holland, a service more profitable than showy, where officers have nothing to do but to grow rich. By the treaty of 1712, the Canton of Berne granted the use of twenty-four companies to their High Mightinesses, and promised that they should always be allowed to recruit them in their territories. But the command of sixteen of those companies was appropriated by the citizens of Berne, and the remaining eight were left common between them and their subjects in the Pays de Vaud. On the supposition, then, that the interest of both classes of candidates for those companies is equal, the sovereign people will obtain four out of the eight, and twenty out of the whole twenty-four. This proportion appears the more unreasonable, when it is considered that in the canton there are above an 100,000 men fit to bear arms, of whom scarcely 800 are citizens of Berne. Besides, the poorer classes of citizens, proud merely of this title, prefer living in idleness at Berne to honourable exertions abroad, by which they might better their condition. I doubt, therefore, whether fifty citizens of Berne, who are not officers, will be found in the whole of the Swiss Dutch troops.

These inconveniencies, you will tell me, are only felt by men of family; that is to say, by the most respectable, but least numerous, portion of the community; and they disappear amidst the general equity and impartiality of the public administration. But does the tyranny of the *bailiffs* disappear also? The people, a name so dear to humanity, feel the full weight of their oppression. I will not have recourse to particular examples; because you might call in question the authenticity of facts, or object with reason, that general conclusions are not to be drawn from particular principles. I shall be contented with pointing out the extent of their power, and leave to your own knowledge of human nature to infer the abuses with which it must be accompanied. In his own district every bailiff is at the head of religion, of the law, the army, and the finances. As judge, he decides without appeal, all causes to the amount of an hundred franks; a sum of little importance to a gentleman, but which often makes the whole fortune of a peasant; and he decides alone, for the voice of his assessors has not any weight in the scale. He confers, or rather he sells, all the employments in his district. When the injured party wishes to appeal from his sentence, as there is no court of justice at Moudon, he is obliged to remove the cause to Berne; and how few peasants can bear this expence. But if his eagerness to punish his tyrant carries him thither, it is not without many difficulties on his part that the Avoyer or chief magistrate, grants him admission into the council; where, after all his trouble and expence, he is finally allowed to plead his cause before a tribunal, the members of which are connected with his oppressor by the ties of blood, and still more by a conformity of interests and crimes.

Your taxes, moderate as they are, exhaust the country. This observation requires to be explained. While the great kingdoms of Europe, loaded with expences and debts, are driven to expedients which would alarm the wildest prodigal, Berne is the only state which has amassed a large treasure. The secret has been so well kept, that it is not easy to ascertain its amount. Stanyan, the British envoy at Berne, a man inquisitive and possessed of good means of information, estimated forty years ago the money belonging to that republic, in the English funds, at 300,000l., or seven millions of Swiss livres; and the sums remaining in the treasury of Berne, or dispersed through the other funds or banks of Europe, at 1,800,000l., or forty-three millions Swiss. These treasures have not probably diminished since the year 1722. The Canton enriches itself by the simple means of receiving much and expending little. But what is the amount of its receipts? I know not, but I will try to discover it. The twelve bailiwics, or districts, of the Pays de Vaud pay, one with another, during the six years that they are governed by the same magistrate, five hundred thousand Swiss livres. The contributions, therefore, of all the twelve amount to a million of livres annually. I have always been told that the bailiffs or governors, retain ten *per cent.* on the revenues raised within their respective jurisdictions. The million of revenue, diminished by an hundred thousand livres consumed in the appointments of the *bailiffs*, is reduced to three hundred thousand crowns ; of which one hundred thousand may be allowed for the expences of the state, a sum not chosen at random ; and the other two hundred thousand crowns, which in other countries would be employed in the maintenance of a court and army, whose incomes would circulate through the general mass of the people on whom they had been raised, are here buried in the coffers of the sovereignty, or dispersed through the precarious banks of Europe, to become one day a prey to the knavery of a clerk, or the ambition of a conqueror. This continual absorption of specie extinguishes industry, deadens every enterprise that requires the aid of money, and gradually impoverishes the country.

These, Sir, are your hardships. But I think you will say to me, " Have you thus probed our wounds merely to make us feel their smart ? What advice do you give us ?" None, unless you have already anticipated it. I would indeed advise you to remonstrate. But there are evils so deeply rooted in governments, that Plato himself would despair of curing them. What could you expect to obtain from those masters by remonstrances, who have remained during two centuries insensible to the merit of your faithful service? There is another remedy, more prompt, more perfect, and more glorious. William Tell would have prescribed it ; I do not. I know that the spirit of a good citizen is, like that of charity, long-suffering, and hoping all things. The citizen is in the right ; since he knows the evils resulting from his submission, but knows not the greater evils which might be produced by his resistance. You know me too well to be ignorant how much I respect those principles, so friendly to the interests of peace and of human kind. I will never, in the language of a seditious tribune, persuade the people to shake off the yoke of authority, that they may proceed from murmur to sedition, from sedition to anarchy, and from anarchy perhaps to despotism.

Yet, with the freedom which has hitherto guided my pen, I will endeavour to destroy some giants of romance, which might otherwise inspire you with vain terror. Whether you prefer the road of bold enterprise or cautious repose, I wish that reason, not prejudice, should dictate your choice.

The magistrates of Berne have a right to expect your obedience : you fear to do them wrong in withholding it. * * * * *

Mr. GIBBON *to Mrs.* PORTEN.

DEAR MADAM,   LAUSANNE, 1756.

FEAR no reproaches for your negligence, however great ; for your silence, however long. I love you too well to make you any. Nothing, in my opinion, is so ridiculous as some kind of friends, wives, and lovers, who look on no crime as so heinous as the letting slip a post without writing. The charm of friendship is liberty ; and he that would destroy the one, destroys, without designing it, the better half of the other. I compare friendship to charity, and letters to alms; the last signifies nothing without the first, and very often the first is very strong, although it does not shew itself by the other. It is not good-will which is wanting, it is only opportunities or means. However, one month—two months—three months—four months—I began not to be angry, but to be uneasy, for fear some accident had happened to you. I was often on the point of writing, but was always stopped by the hopes of hearing from you by the next post. Besides, not to flatter you, your excuse is a very bad one. *You cannot entertain me by your letters.* I think I ought to know that better than you; and I assure you that one of *your plain sincere letters* entertains me more than the most polished one of Pliny or Cicero. 'Tis your heart speaks, and I look on your heart as much better in its way than either of their heads.

Out of pure politeness I ought to talk of * * * before myself. I was some hours with him in this place, that is to say, almost all the time he was here. I find him always * * *, always good-natured, always amusing, and always trifling. I asked him some questions about Italy; he told me, he hurried out of it as soon as he could, because there was no French comedy, and he did not love the Italian opera. I let slip some words of the pleasure he should have of seeing his native country again, on account of the services he could render her in parliament. "Yes (says he), I want vastly to be at London; there are three years since I have seen Garrick." He spoke to me of you, and indeed not only with consideration, but with affection. Were there nothing else valuable in his character, I should love him, because he loves you. He told me he intended to see you as soon as he should be in England; I am glad he has kept his word. I was so taken up with my old friend, that I could not speak a word to * * *. He appeared, however, a good, sensible, modest young man. Poor Minorca indeed thus lost! but poor Englishmen who have lost it! I think the second exclamation still stronger than the first. Poor Lord Torrington! I can't help pitying him. What a shameful uncle he has! I shall lose all my opinion of my countrymen, if the whole nation, Whigs, Tories, Courtiers, Jacobites, &c. &c. are not unanimous in detesting that man. Pray, is there any truth in a story we had here, of a brother of Admiral Byng's having killed himself out of rage and shame? I did not think he had any brothers alive. It is thought here that Byng will be acquitted. I hope not. Though I do not love rash judgments, I cannot help thinking him guilty.

You ask me, when I shall come into England? How should I know it? The 14th of June I wrote to my father, and saying nothing of my return, which I knew would have been to no purpose, I desired him to give me a fixed allowance of 200l. a year, or, least, to allow me a servant. No answer. About a fortnight ago I renewed my request; and I cannot yet know what will be my success. I design to make a virtue of necessity, to keep quiet during this winter, and to put in use all my machines next spring, in order to come over.* I shall write the strongest, and at the same time the most dutiful letter I can imagine to my father. If all that produces no effect, I don't know what I can do.

* This letter is a curious specimen of the degree in which Mr. Gibbon had lost the English language in a short time. S.

You talk to me of my cousin Ellison's wedding; but you don't say a word of who she is married to. Is it Eliot? Though you have not seen my father yet, I suppose you have heard of him. How was he in town? His wife, was she with him? Has marriage produced any changement in his way of living? Is he to be always at Beriton, or will he come up to London in winter? Pray have you ever seen my mother-in-law, or heard anything more of her character? Compliments to everybody that makes me compliments : to the Gilberts, to the Comarques, to Lord Newnham, &c. When you see the Comarques again, ask them if they did not know, at Putney, Monsieur la Vabre, and his daughters; perhaps you know them yourself. I saw them lately in this country; one of them very well married.

The Englishman who lodges in our house, is little sociable at least for a reasonable person. My health always good, my studies pretty good. I understand Greek pretty well. I have even some kind of correspondence with several learned men, with M. Crevier of Paris, with M. Breitinger of Zurich, and with M. Allamand, a clergyman of this country, the most reasonable divine I ever knew. Do you never read now? I am a little piqued that you say nothing of Sir Charles Grandison; if you have not read it yet, read it for my sake. Perhaps Clarissa does not encourage you; but, in my opinion, it is much superior to Clarissa. When you have read it, read the letters of Madame de Sevigné to her daughter; I don't doubt of their being translated into English. They are properly what I called in the beginning of my letter, letters of the heart; the natural expressions of a mother's fondness; regret at their being at a great distance from one another, and continual schemes to get together again. All that, won't it please you? There is scarce anything else in six whole volumes ; and notwithstanding that, few people read them without finding them too short. Adieu : my paper is at an end. I don't dare to tell you to write soon. Do it, however, if you can. Yours affectionately,

E. GIBBON.

Rev. Dr. WALDGRAVE* *to* EDWARD GIBBON, *Esq. jun.*

DEAR SIR, WASHINGTON, near STORRINGTON, Dec. 7, 1758.
I HAVE read nothing for some time (and I keep reading on still) that has given me so much pleasure as your letter, which I received by the last post. I rejoice at your return to your country, to your father, and to the good principles of truth and reason. Had I in the least suspected your design of leaving us, I should immediately have put you upon reading Mr. Chillingworth's Religion of Protestants; any one page of which is worth a library of Swiss divinity. It will give me great pleasure to see you at Washington; where I am, I thank God, very well and very happy. I desire my respects to Mr. Gibbon; and am, with very great regard, dear Sir,
Your most affectionate humble servant,
THO. WALDGRAVE.

* Tutor to Mr. Gibbon when he first went to Magdalen College, Oxford. S.

O

Mr. GIBBON *to his* FATHER.

DEAR SIR,   1760.

AN address in writing, from a person who has the pleasure of being
with you every day, may appear singular. However, I have preferred
this method, as upon paper I can speak without a blush, and be heard
without interruption. If my letter displeases you, impute it, dear Sir,
only to yourself. You have treated me, not like a son, but like a friend.
Can you be surprised that I should communicate to a friend, all my
thoughts, and all my desires? Unless the friend approve them, let the
father never know them ; or at least, let him know at the same time,
that however reasonable, however eligible, my scheme may appear to
me, I would rather forget it for ever, than cause him the slightest uneasiness.

When I first returned to England, attentive to my future interest,
you were so good as to give me hopes of a seat in parliament. This
seat, it was supposed would be an expence of fifteen hundred pounds.
This design flattered my vanity, as it might enable me to shine in so
august an assembly. It flattered a nobler passion ; I promised myself
that by the means of this seat I might be one day the instrument of
some good to my country. But I soon perceived how little a mere
virtuous inclination, unassisted by talents, could contribute towards
that great end ; and a very short examination discovered to me, that
those talents had not fallen to my lot. Do not, dear Sir, impute this
declaration to a false modesty, the meanest species of pride. Whatever else I may be ignorant of, I think I know myself, and shall always
endeavour to mention my good qualities without vanity, and my defects
without repugnance. I shall say nothing of the most intimate acquaintance with his country and language, so absolutely necessary to every
senator. Since they may be acquired, to alledge my deficiency in
them, would seem only the plea of laziness. But I shall say with great
truth, that I never possessed that gift of speech, the first requisite of an
orator, which use and labour may improve, but which nature alone can
bestow. That my temper, quiet, retired, somewhat reserved, could
neither acquire popularity, bear up against opposition, nor mix with
ease in the crowds of public life. That even my genius (if you will
allow me any) is better qualified for the deliberate compositions of the
closet, than for the extemporary discourses of the parliament. An unexpected objection would disconcert me; and as I am incapable of explaining to others, what I do not thoroughly understand myself, I should
be meditating, while I ought to be answering. I even want necessary
prejudices of party, and of nation. In popular assemblies, it is often
necessary to inspire them ; and never orator inspired well a passion,
which he did not feel himself. Suppose me even mistaken in my own
character ; to set out with the repugnance such an opinion must produce, offers but an indifferent prospect. But I hear you say, it is not
necessary that every man should enter into parliament with such
exalted hopes. It is to acquire a title the most glorious of any in a free
country, and to employ the weight and consideration it gives, in the
service of one's friends. Such motives, though not glorious, yet are
not dishonourable ; and if we had a borough in our command, if you
could bring me in without any great expence, or if our fortune enabled

us to despise that expence, then indeed I should think them of the greatest strength. But with our private fortune, is it worth while to purchase at so high a rate, a title, honourable in itself, but which I must share with every fellow that can lay out fifteen hundred pounds ? Besides, dear Sir, a merchandise is of little value to the owner, when he is resolved not to sell it.

I should affront your penetration, did I not suppose you now see the drift of this letter. It is to appropriate to another use the sum with which you destined to bring me into parliament ; to employ it, not in making me great, but in rendering me happy. I have often heard you say yourself, that the allowance you had been so indulgent as to grant me, though very liberal in regard to your estate, was yet but small, when compared with the almost necessary extravagancies of the age. I have indeed found it so, notwithstanding a good deal of economy, and an exemption from many of the common expences of youth. This, dear Sir, would be a way of supplying these deficiencies, without any additional expence to you.—But I forebear.—If you think my proposals reasonable, you want no entreaties to engage you to comply with them ; if otherwise, all will be without effect.

All that I am afraid of, dear Sir, is, that I should seem not so much asking a favour, as this really is, as exacting a debt. After all I can say, you will still remain the best judge of my good, and your own circumstances. Perhaps, like most landed gentlemen, an addition to my annuity would suit you better, than a sum of money given at once ; perhaps the sum itself may be too considerable. Whatever you shall think proper to bestow upon me, or in whatever manner, will be received with equal gratitude.

I intended to stop here ; but as I abhor the least appearance of art, I think it will be better to lay open my whole scheme at once. The unhappy war which now desolates Europe, will oblige me to defer seeing France till a peace. But that reason can have no influence upon Italy, a country which every scholar must long to see ; should you grant my request, and not disapprove of my manner of employing your bounty, I would leave England this Autumn, and pass the Winter at Lausanne, with M. de Voltaire and my old friends. The armies no longer obstruct my passage, and it must be indifferent to you, whether I am at Lausanne or at London during the Winter, since I shall not be at Beriton. In the spring I would cross the Alps, and after some stay in Italy, as the war must then be terminated, return home through France ; to live happily with you and my dear mother. I am now two-and-twenty ; a tour must take up a considerable time, and though I believe you have no thoughts of settling me soon, (and I am sure I have not,) yet so many things may intervene, that the man who does not travel early, runs a great risk of not travelling at all. But this part of my scheme, as well as the whole, I submit entirely to you.

Permit me, dear Sir, to add, that I do not know whether the complete compliance with my wishes could increase my love and gratitude ; but that I am very sure, no refusal could diminish those sentiments with which I shall always remain, dear Sir,

Your most dutiful and obedient son and servant,

E. GIBBON, junior.

Mr. MALLET *to* Mr. GIBBON.

DEAR SIR, 1761.

I COULD not procure you a ticket for the coronation, without putting you to the expence of ten guineas. But I now send you something much more valuable, which will cost you only a groat. When will your father or you be in town? Desire Becket to send me one of your books, well bound, for myself : all the other copies I gave away, as Duke Desenany drunk out ten dozen of Lord Bolingbroke's Champagne in his absence—to your honour and glory. I need not tell you that I am,

most affectionately, &c.

Turn over, read, and be delighted. D. MALLET.
Let your father too read.

I READ with as much eagerness as pleasure the excellent and agreeable work with which the author presented me. I speak as if Mr. Gibbon had not praised me, and that too warmly. His work is that of a real man of letters, who loves them for their own sake, without exception or prejudice ; and who unites with much talent the more precious gift of good sense, and an impartiality that displays his candour and justice, in spite of the bias that he must have received from the innumerable authors whom he has read and studied. I have therefore perused with the greatest avidity, this little work ; and wish that it was more extensive, and read universally.

I would also express my thanks to Lady Hervey, for making me acquainted with an author who proves in every page that learning is hostile only to ignorance and prejudice ; who deserves to have a Maty for his friend, and who adds honour and strength to our language by the use which he so ably makes of it. Were I more learned I should dwell on the merit of the discussions, and the justness of the observations.

CAYLUS.

GEO. L. SCOTT, *Esq. to* E. GIBBON, *jun.*

SUPPOSING you settled in quarters, dear Sir, I obey your commands, and send you my thoughts, relating to the pursuit of your mathematical studies. You told me, you had read Clairaut's Algebra, and the three first books of l'Hopital's Conic Sections. You did not mention the Elements of Geometry you had perused. Whatever they were, whether Euclid's, or by some other, you will do well, if you have not applied yourself that way for some time past, to go over them again, and render the conclusions familiar to your memory. You may defer, however, a very critical inquiry into the principles and reasoning of geometers, till Dr. Simpson's new edition of Euclid (now in the press) appears. I would have you study that book well ; in the mean time recapitulate Clairaut and l'Hopital, so far as you have gone, and then go through the remainder of the marquis's books with care. The fifth book will be an Introduction to the "*Analyse des Infiniment petits;*"

to which I would advise you to proceed, after finishing the Conic Sections. The *Infiniment petits* may want a comment; Crousaz has written one, but it is a wretched performance : he did not understand the first principles of the science he undertook to illustrate ; and his geometry shews, that he did not understand the first principles of geometry. There is a posthumous work of M. Varignon's, called *Éclaircissemens sur l'Analyse des Infiniment petits.* Paris, 1725, 4to. This will be often of use to you. However, it must be owned, that the notion of the *Infiniment petits,* or *Infinitesimals,* as we call them, is too bold an assumption, and too remote from the principles of the ancients, our masters in geometry : and has given a handle to an ingenious author (Berkeley, late bishop of Cloyne) to atttack the logic of modern mathematicians. He has been answered by many, but by none so clearly as by Mr. Maclaurin, in his Fluxions, (2 vols. 4to,) where you will meet with a collection of the most valuable discoveries in the mathematical and physico-mathematical sciences. I recommend this author to you ; but whether you ought to read him immemediately after M. de l'Hopital, may be a question. I think you may be satisfied at first with reading his introduction, and chap. 1. book I. of the grounds of the Method of Fluxions, and then proceed to chap. 12. of the same book, § 495 to § 505 inclusive, where he treats of the Method of Infinitesimals, and of the Limits of Ratios. You may then read chap. 1. book II. § 697 to § 714 inclusive ; and this you may do immediately after reading the first section of the *Analyse des Infiniment petits :* or if you please, you may postpone a critical inquiry into the principles of Infinitesimals and Fluxions, till you have seen the use and application of this doctrine in the drawing of Tangents, and in finding the Maxima and Minima of Geometrical Magnitudes. *Annal. des Infin. pet.* § 2 *and* 3.

When you have read the beginning of l'Hopital's 4th sect. to sect. 65 inclusive, you may read Maclaurin's chap. 2, 3, and 4 ; where he fully explains the nature of these higher orders of Fluxions, and applies the notion to geometrical figures. Your principles being then firmly established, you may finish M. de l'Hopital.

Your next step must be to the inverse method of Fluxions, called by the French *calcul integral.* M. de Bougainville has given us a treatise upon this subject, Paris, 1754, 4to. under the title *Traité du calcul integral pour servir de suite a l'Analyse des Infiniment petits.* You should have it ; but though he explains the methods hitherto found out for the determination of Fluents from given Fluxions, or in the French style, *pour trouver les integrales des differences données ;* yet as he has not shewn the use and application of this doctrine, as de l'Hopital did, with respect to that part which he treats of, M. de Bougainville's book is, for that reason, not so well suited to beginners as could be wished. You may therefore take Carré's book in 4to, printed at Paris, 1700, and entitled, *Methode peur la Mesure des Surfaces,* &c. *par l'Application du Calcul integral.* Only I must caution you against depending upon him in his fourth section, where he treats of the centre of oscillation and percussion ; he having made several mistakes there, as M. de Mairan has shewn, p. 196. *Mem. de l'Acad. Royale des Sciences,* edit. Paris, 1735. After Carré, you may read Bougainville.

I have recommended French authors to you, because you are a thorough master of that language, and because, by their studying style and clearness of expression, they seem to me best adapted to beginners. Our authors are often profound and acute, but their laconisms, and neglect of expression, often perplex beginners. I except Mr. Maclaurin, who is very clear ; but then he has such a vast variety of matter, that a great part of his book is, on that account, too difficult for a beginner. I might recommend other authors to you, as a course of elements ; for instance, you might read Simpson's Geometry, Algebra, Trigonometry, and Fluxions ; all which contain a great variety of good things. In his Geometry he departs from Euclid without a sufficient reason. However, you may read him after Dr. R. Simson's Euclid, or together with it, and take notice of what is new in Simpson. His Algebra you may join with Clairaut ; and the rather that Clairaut has been sparing of particular problems, and has, besides, omitted several useful applications of Algebra. Simpson's Fluxions may go hand in hand with l'Hopital, Maclaurin, Carré, and Bougainville. If you come to have a competent knowledge of these authors, you will be far advanced, and you may proceed to the works of Newton, Cotes, the Bernoulli's, Dr. Moivre, &c. as your inclination and time will permit. Sir Isaac Newton's treatise of the Quadrature of Curves has been well commented by Mr. Stewart, and is of itself a good institution of Fluxions. Sir Isaac's Algebra is commented in several places by Clairaut, and in more in Maclaurin's Algebra ; and Newton's famous Principia are explained by the *Minims Jacquirs et le Seur*, Geneva, 4 vols. 4to. Cotes is explained by Don Walmesley, in his *Analyse des Mesures*, &c. Paris, 4to. You see you may find work enough. But my paper bids me subscribe myself, dear Sir,

Your most obedient servant,

LEICESTER-SQUARE, May 7, 1762.   GEO. LEWIS SCOTT.

P. S. But I recollect, a little late, that the books I have mentioned, excepting Newton's Principia, and the occasional problems in the rest, treat only of the abstract parts of the Mathematics ; and you are, no doubt, willing to look into the concrete parts, or what is called Mixed Mathematics, and the Physico-mathematical Sciences. Of these the principal are, mechanics, optics, and astronomy. As to the principles of mechanics, M. d'Alembert has recommended M. Trabaud's *Principes du Mouvement et de l'Equilibre*, to beginners ; and you cannot do better than to study this book. In optics we have Dr. Smith's Complete System, 2 vols. 4to. I wish though, we had a good institution, short and clear ; the Doctor's book entering into too great details for beginners. However, you may consider his first book, or popular Treatise, as an Institution, and you will from thence acquire a good deal of knowledge. In astronomy I recommend M. le Monnier's *Institutions Astronomiques*, in 4to. Paris, 1746. It is a translation from Keil's Astronomical Lectures, but with considerable additions. You should also have Cassini's *Elemens d'Astronomie*, 2 vols. 4to. As to the physical causes of the celestial motions, after having read Maclaurin's account of Sir Isaac Newton's philosophical Discoveries, and Dr. Pemberton's View of Sir Isaac's Philosophy, you may read the great author himself, with the comment. But if you read Maclaurin's Fluxions throughout, you will find many points of Sir Isaac's philosophy well explained there. The theory of light and colours should be studied in Sir Isaac himself; in the English edition of his Optics, 8vo. there is a branch of the optical sciences which I have not mentioned, that is,— Perspective. Dr. Brook Taylor's is the best system, but his style and expression is embarrassed and obscure. L'Abbé de la Caille has also given a good treatise of Perspective, at the end of his *Optique :* these are of use to painters ; but the theory of mathematical projection in general is more extensive, and has been well treated of by old writers, Clavius, Aguillonius, Tacquet, and De Chules : and lately M. de la Caille has given a memoir among those of the *Acad. Roy. des Sciences* of Paris, *anno* 1741, *sur le calcul des projections en general.* This subject is necessary for the understanding of the theory of maps and planispheres. Mathematicians have also applied their art to the theory of sounds and music. Dr. Smith's Harmonics is the principal book of the kind.

Thus have I given you some account of the principal elementary authors in the different branches of mathematical knowledge, and it were much to be wished that we had a complete institution, or course, of all these things of a moderate size, which might serve as an introduction to all the good original authors. Wolsius attempted this ; his intention was laudable, but his book is so full of errors of the press, besides some of his own, that I cannot recommend him to a beginner. He might be used occasionally for the signification of terms, and for many historical facts relating to mathematics ; and, besides, may be considered as a collector of problems, which is useful.

Besides the books I have mentioned, it might be of use to you to have M. Montucla's *Historie des Mathematiques,* in 4to. 2 vols. You will there find a history of the progress of the mathematical sciences, and some account of the principal authors relating to this subject.

I mentioned to you in conversation, the superior elegance of the antient method of demonstration. If you incline to examine this point, after being well versed in Euclid, you may proceed to Dr. Simson's Conic Sections ; and to form an idea of the antient analysis or method of investigating the solution of geometrical problems, read Euclid's Data, which Dr. Simson will publish, together with his new edition of Euclid ; and then read his *Loci Plani,* in 4to. The elegance of the method of the ancients is confessed ; but it seems to require the remembrance of a great multitude of propositions, and in complicated problems it does not seem probable that it can be extended so far as the algebraic method.

EDWARD GIBBON, *Esq. to Mrs.* GIBBON, Beriton.

DEAR MADAM,   Paris, Feb. 12, 1763.

YOU remember our agreement,—short and frequent letters. The first part of the treaty you have no doubt of my observing. I think I ought not to leave you any of the second. *A propos* of treaty : our definitive one was signed here yesterday, and this morning the Duke of Bridgewater and Mr. Neville went for London with the news of it. The plenipotentiaries sat up till ten o'clock in the morning at the ambassador of Spain's ball, and then went to sign this treaty, which regulates the fate of Europe.

Paris, in most respects, has fully answered my expectations. I have a number of very good acquaintance, which increase every day ; for nothing is so easy as the making them here. Instead of complaining of the want of them, I begin already to think of making a choice. Next Sunday, for instance, I have only three invitations to dinner. Either in the houses you are already acquainted, you meet with people who ask you to come and see them, or some of your friends offer themselves to introduce you. When I speak of these connections, I mean chiefly for dinner and the evening. Suppers, as yet, I am pretty much a stranger to, and I fancy shall continue so ; for Paris is divided into two species, who have but little communication with each other. The one, who are chiefly connected with the men of letters, dine very much at home, are glad to see their friends, and pass the evenings till about nine, in agreeable and rational conversation. The others are the most fashionable, sup in numerous parties, and always play, or rather game, both before and after supper. You may easily guess which sort suits me best. Indeed, Madam, we may say what we please of the frivolity of the French, but I do assure you, that in a fortnight passed at Paris, I have heard more conversation worth remembering, and seen more men of letters among the people of fashion, than I had done in two or three winters in London.

Amongst my acquaintance I cannot help mentioning M. Helvetius, the author of the famous book *de l'Esprit.* I met him at dinner at Madame Geoffrin's, where he took great notice of me, made me a visit next day, has ever since treated me, not in a polite but a friendly manner. Besides being a sensible man, an agreeable companion, and the worthiest creature in the world, he has a very pretty wife, an hundred thousand livres a year, and one of the best tables in Paris. The only thing I dislike in him is his great attachment to, and admiration for, * * * whose character is indeed at Paris beyond any thing you can conceive. To the great civility of this foreigner, who was not obliged to take the least notice of me, I must just contrast the behaviour of * * *

EDWARD GIBBON *to his* FATHER.

DEAR SIR,   PARIS, Feb., 24, 1763.
I RECEIVED your letter about twelve days after its date, owing, as I apprehend, to Mr. Foley's negligence. My direction is, *à Monsieur* Gibbon, *Gentilhomme Anglois à l'Hotel de Londres, rue de Columbier, Fauxbourg, St. Germains, à Paris.* You see I am still in that part of the town ; and indeed from all the intelligence I could collect, I saw no reason to change, either on account of cheapness or pleasantness. Madame Bontems, Mrs. Mallet's friend, and a Marquis de Mirabeau, (I got acquainted with at her house,) have acted a very friendly part ; though

all their endeavours have only served to convince me that Paris is unavoidably a very dear place. I.am sorry to find my English cloaths look very foreign. The French are now excessively long-waisted. At present we are in mourning for the Bishop of Liege, the king's uncle ; and expect soon another of a singular nature, for the old Pretender, who is very ill. They mourn for him, not as a crowned head, but as a relation of the king's. I am doubtful how the English here will behave ; indeed we can have no difficulties, since we need only follow the example of the Duke of Bedford.

I have now passed nearly a month in this place, and I can say with truth, that it has answered my most sanguine expectations. The buildings of every kind, the libraries, the public diversions, take up a great part of my time ; and I have already found several houses, where it is both very easy and very agreeable to be acquainted. Lady Harvey's recommendation to Madame Geoffrin was a most excellent one. Her house is a very good one ; regular dinners there every Wednesday, and the best company of Paris, in men of letters and people of fashion. It was at her house I connected myself with M. Helvetius, who, from his heart, his head, and his fortune, is a most valuable man.

At his house I was introduced to the Baron d'Olbach, who is a man of parts and fortune, and has two dinners every week. The other houses I am known in, are the Duchess d'Aiguillon's, Madame la Comtesse de Froulay's, Madame du Bocage, Madame Boyer, M. le Marquis de Mirabeau, and M. de Foucemagn. All these people have their different merit ; in some I meet with good dinners ; in others, societies for the evening ; and in all, good sense, entertainment, and civility ; which, as I have no favours to ask, or business to transact with them, is sufficient for me. Their men of letters are as affable and communicative as I expected. My letters to them did me no harm, but were very little necessary. My book had been of great service to me, and the compliments I have received upon it would make me insufferably vain, if I laid any stress on them. When I take notice of the civilities I have received, I must take notice too of what I have seen of a contrary behaviour. You know how much I always built upon the Count de Caylus : he has not been of the least use to me. With great difficulty I have seen him, and that is all. I do not, however, attribute his behaviour to pride, or dislike to me, but solely to the man's general character, which seems to be a very odd one. De la Motte, Mrs. Mallet's friend, has behaved very drily to me, though I have dined with him twice. But I can forgive him a great deal, in consideration of his having introduced me to M. d'Augny (Mrs. Mallet's son). Her men are generally angels or devils ; but here I really think, without being very prone to admiration, that she has said very little too much of him. As far as I can judge, he has certainly an uncommon degree of understanding and knowledge, and, I believe, a great fund of honour and probity. We are very much together, and I think our intimacy seems to be growing into a friendship. Next Sunday we go to Versailles ; the king's guard. is done by a detachment from Paris, which is relieved every four days ; and as he goes upon this command, it is a very good occasion for me to see the palace. I shall not neglect, at the same time, the opportunity of informing myself of the French discipline.

The great news at present is the arrival of a very extraordinary person from the Isle of France in the East Indies. An obscure Frenchman, who was lately come into the island, being very ill, and given over, said, that before he died he must discharge his conscience of a great burden he had upon it, and declared to several people, he was the accomplice of Damien, and the very person who held the horses. Unluckily for him, the man recovered after this declaration, was immediately sent prisoner to Paris, and is just landed at Port l'Orient, from whence he is daily expected here, to unravel the whole mystery of that dark affair. This story (which at first was laughed at) has now gained entire credit, and I apprehend must be founded on real fact.

A lady of Miss Caryll's acquaintance has desired me to convey the inclosed letter to her. You will be so good as to send it over to Ladyholt. I hope I need say nothing of my sentiments towards our friends at Beriton, nor of my readiness to execute any of their commands here.

I am, dear Sir, most affectionately yours,

E. GIBBON.

Mr. GIBBON *to Mr.* HOLROYD *at* Lausanne.

DEAR HOLROYD,   BOROMEAN ISLANDS, May 16, 1764.

HURRY of running about, time taken up with seeing places, &c. &c., are excellent excuses ; but I fancy you will guess that my laziness and aversion to writing to my best friend are the real motives, and I am afraid you will have guessed right.

We are at this minute in a most magnificent palace, in the middle of a vast lake ; ranging about suites of rooms without a soul to interrupt us, and secluded from the rest of the universe. We shall sit down in a moment to supper, attended by all the Count's household. This is the fine side of the medal : turn to the reverse. We are got here wet to the skin ; we have crawled about fine gardens which rain and fogs prevented our seeing ; and if to-morrow does not hold up a little better, we shall be in some doubt whether we can say we have seen these famous islands. Guise says yes, and I say no. The Count is not here : we have our supper from a paultry hedge alehouse, (excuse the bull,) and the servants have offered us beds in the palace, pursuant to their master's directions.

I hardly think you will like Turin ; the court is old and dull ; and in that country every one follows the example of the court. The principal amusement seems to be, driving about in your coach in the evening, and bowing to the people you meet. If you go while the Royal Family is there, you have the additional pleasure of stopping to salute them every time they pass. I had that advantage fifteen times one afternoon. We were presented to a lady who keeps a public assembly, and a very mournful one it is ; the few women that go to it are each taken up by their cicisbeo ; and a poor Englishman, who can neither talk Piedmontois nor play at Faro, stands by himself without one of their haughty nobility doing him the honour of speaking to him. You must not attribute this account to our not not having staid long enough to form connections. It is a general complaint of our countrymen, except of Lord * * *, who has been engaged for about two years in the service of a lady, whose long nose is her most distinguishing fine feature. The most sociable women I have met with are the king's daughters. I chatted for about a quarter of an hour with them, talked about Lausanne, and grew so very free and easy, that I drew my snuff-box, rapped it, took snuff twice (a crime never known before in the presence chamber), and continued my discourse in my usual attitude of my body bent forwards, and my fore finger stretched out.* As it might however have been difficult to keep up this acquaintance, I chiefly employ my time in seeing places, which fully repaid me in pleasure the trouble of my journey. What entertained me the most, was the museum and the citadel. The first is under the care of a M. Bartoli, who received us, without any introduction, in the politest manner in the world, and was of the greatest service to us, as I dare say he will be to you. The citadel is a stupendous work ; and when you have seen the subterraneous part of it, you will scarcely think it possible such a place can ever be taken. As it is however a regular one, it does not pique my curiosity so much as those irregular fortifications hewn out of the Alps, as Exiles, Fenestrelles, and the Brunette would have done, could we have spared the time necessary. Our next stage from Turin has been Milan, where we were mere spectators, as it was not worth while to endeavour at forming connections for so very few days. I think you will be surprised at the great church, but infinitely more so at the regiment of Baden, which is in the citadel. Such steadiness, such alertness in the men, and such exactness in the officers, as exceeded all my expectations. Next Friday I shall see the regiment reviewed by General Serbelloni. Perhaps I may write a particular letter about it. From Milan we proceed to Genoa, and thence to Florence. You stare—But really we find it so inconvenient to travel like mutes, and to lose a number of curious things for want of being able to assist our eyes with our tongues, that we have resumed our original plan, and leave Venice for next year. I think I should advise you to do the same.

MILAN, May 18, 1764.
THE next morning was not fair, but however we were able to take a view of the islands, which, by the help of some imagination, we conclude to be a very delightful, though not an enchanted place. I would certainly advise you to go there from Milan, which you may very well perform in a day and half. Upon our return, we found Lord Tilney and some other English in their way to Venice. We heard a melancholy piece of news from them : Byng died at Bologna a few days ago of a fever. I am sure you will be all very sorry to hear it.
We expect a volume of news from you in relation to Lausanne, and in particular to the alliance of the Duchess with the Frog. Is it already concluded ? How does the bride look after her great revolution ?

* This attitude continued to be characteristic of Mr. Gibbon. S.

Pray embrace her and the adorable, if you can, in both our names; and assure them, as well as all the *Spring*,* that we talk of them very often, but particularly of a Sunday; and that we are so disconsolate, that we have neither of us commenced cicisbeos as yet, whatever we may do at Florence. We have drank the Duchess's health, not forgetting the little woman on the top of Mount Cenis, in the middle of the Lago Maggiore, &c. &c. I expect some account of the said little woman. Who is my successor? I think * * * had began to supplant me before I went. I expect your answer at Florence, and your person at Rome; which the Lord grant. Amen.

Mr. GIBBON *to Mr.* HOLROYD *at* Berlin.

DEAR HOLROYD,   BERITON, Oct. 31, 1765.
   WHY did I not leave a letter for you at Marseilles? For a very plain reason : because I did not go to Marseilles. But, as you have most judiciously added, why did not I send one? Humph. I own that nonplusses me a little. However, hearken to my history. After revolving a variety of plans, and suiting them as well as possible to time and finances, Guise and I at last agreed to pass from Venice to Lyons, swim down the Rhone, wheel round the south of France, and embark at Bourdeaux. Alas! At Lyons I received letters which convinced me that I ought no longer to deprive my country of one of her greatest ornaments. Unwillingly I obeyed, left Guise to execute alone the remainder of our plan, passed about ten delicious days at Paris, and arrived in England about the end of June. Guise followed me about two months afterwards, as I was informed by an epistle from him, which, to his great astonishment, I immediately answered. You perceive there is still some virtue amongst men. *Exempli gratiâ*, your letter is dated Vienna, Oct. 12, 1765 ; it made its appearance at Beriton, Wednesday evening, Oct. 29. I am at this present writing, sitting in my library, on Thursday morning, between the hours of twelve and one. I have ventured to suppose you still at Berlin ; if not, I presume you take care that your letters should follow you. This ideal march to Berlin is the only one I can make at present. I am under command ; and were I to talk of a third sally as yet, I know some certain people who would think it just as ridiculous as the third sally of the renowned Don Quixote. All I ever hoped for was, to be able to take the field once more, after lying quiet a couple of years. I must own that your executing your tour in so complete a manner gives me a little selfish * * *. If I make a summer's escape to Berlin, I cannot hope for the companion I flattered myself with. I am sorry however I have said so much ; but as it is difficult, to encrease your Honour's proper notions of your own perfections, I will e'en let it stand. Indeed I owed you something for your account of the favourable reception my book has met with. I see there are people of taste at Vienna, and no longer wonder at your liking it. Since the court is so agreeable, a thorough reformation must have taken place. The stiffness of the Austrian etiquette, and the haughty magnificence of the Hungarian princes, must

* The society of young ladies mentioned in the Memoirs. S.

have given way to more civilized notions. You have (no doubt) informed yourself of the forces and revenues of the empress. I think (however unfashionably) we always esteemed her. Have you lost or improved that opinion. Princes, like pictures to be admired, must be seen in their proper point of view, which is often a pretty distant one. I am afraid you will find it peculiarly so at Berlin.

I need not desire you to pay a most minute attention to the Austrian and Prussian discipline. You have been bit by a mad serjeant as well as myself; and when we meet, we shall run over every particular which we can approve, blame, or imitate. Since my arrival, I have assumed the august character of Major, received returns, issued orders, &c. &c. I do not intend you shall have the honour of reviewing my troops next summer. Three fourths of the men will be recruits; and during my pilgrimage, discipline seems to have been relaxed. But I summon you to fulfil another engagement. Make me a visit next summer. You will find here a bad house, a pleasant country in summer, some books, and very little *strange* company. Such a plan of life for two or three months must, I should imagine, suit a man who has been for as many years struck from one end of Europe to the other like a tennis-ball. At least I judge of you by myself. I always loved a quiet, studious, indolent life; but never enjoyed the charms of it so truly, as since my return from an agreeable but fatiguing course of motion and hurry. However I shall hear of your arrival, which can scarcely be so soon as January 1766, and shall probably have the misfortune of meeting you in town soon after. We may then settle any plans for the ensuing campaign.

En attendant, (admire me, this is the only scrap of foreign lingo I have imported into this epistle—if you had seen that of Guise to me!) let me tell you a piece of Lausanne news. Nanette Grand is married to Lieutenant-colonel Prevot. Grand wrote to me; and by the next post I congratulated both father and daughter. There is exactness for you. The Curchod (Madame Necker) I saw at Paris. She was very fond of me, and the husband particularly civil. Could they insult me more cruelly? Ask me every evening to supper; go to bed, and leave me alone with his wife—what an impertinent security! it is making an old lover of mighty little consequence. She is as handsome as ever, and much genteeler; seems pleased with her fortune rather than proud of it. I was (perhaps indiscreetly enough) exalting Nanette d'Illens's good luck and the fortune. What fortune? (said she, with an air of contempt)—not above twenty thousand livres a-year. I smiled, and she caught herself immediately.—"What airs I give myself in despising twenty thousand livres a-year, who a year ago looked upon eight hundred as the summit of my wishes."

I must end this tedious scrawl. Let me hear from you: I think I deserve it. Believe me, Dear Holroyd, I share in all your pleasures, and feel all your misfortunes. Poor Bolton! I saw it in the newspaper. Is Ridley with you? I suspect not: but if he is, assure him I do not forget him though he does me. Adieu; and believe me, most affectionately yours,

E. GIBBON Junior.

EDWARD GIBBON *Esq. to* J. HOLROYD *Esq.*

DEAR HOLROYD,   BERITON, April 29, 1767.
I HAPPENED to-night to stumble upon a very odd piece of intelligence in the St. James's Chronicle; it related to the marriage of a certain Monsieur Olroy,* formerly Captain of Hussars. I do not know how it came into my head that this Captain of Hussars was not unknown to me, and that he might possibly be an acquaintance of yours. If I am not mistaken in my conjecture, pray give my compliments to him, and tell him from me, that I am at least as well pleased that he is married as if I were so myself. Assure him, however, that though as a philosopher I may prefer celibacy, yet as a politician I think it highly proper that the species should be propagated by the usual method; assure him even that I am convinced, that if celibacy is exposed to fewer miseries, marriage can alone promise real happiness, since domestic enjoyments are the source of every other good. May such happiness, which is bestowed on few, be given to him; the transient blessings of beauty, and the more durable ones of fortune, good sense, and an amiable disposition.

I can easily conceive, and as easily excuse you, if you have thought mighty little this winter of your poor rusticated friend. I have been confined ever since Christmas, and confined by a succession of very melancholy occupations. 1 had scarcely arrived at Beriton, where I proposed staying only about a fortnight, when a brother of Mrs. Gibbon's died unexpectedly, though after a very long and painful illness. We were scarcely recovered from the confusion which such an event must produce in a family, when my father was taken dangerously ill, and with some intervals has continued so ever since. I can assure you, my dear Holroyd, that the same event appears in a very different light when the danger is serious and immediate; or when, in the gaiety of a tavern dinner, we affect an insensibility that would do us no great honour were it real. My father is now much better; but I have since been assailed by a severe stroke—the loss of a friend. You remember, perhaps, an officer of our militia, whom I sometimes used to compare to yourself. Indeed, the comparison would have done honour to any one. His feelings were tender and noble, and he was always guided by them: his principles were just and generous, and he acted up to them. I shall say no more, and you will excuse my having said so much, of a man with whom you were unacquainted; but my mind is just now so very full of him, that I cannot easily talk, or even think, of any thing else. If I know you right, you will not be offended at my *weakness.*

What rather adds to my uneasiness, is the necessity I am under of joining our militia the day after to-morrow. Though the lively hurry of such a scene might contribute to divert my ideas, yet every circumstance of it, and the place itself, (which was that of his residence,) will give me many a painful moment. I know nothing would better raise my spirits than a visit from you; the request may appear unseasonable, but I think I have heard you speak of *an uncle* you had near Southampton. At all events, I hope you will snatch a moment to write to

* The name was so spelt in the newspapers. S.

me, and give me some account of your present situation and future designs. As you are now fettered, I should expect you will not be such a *hic et ubique,** as you have been since your arrival in England. I stay at Southampton from the first to the twenty-eighth of May, and then propose making a short visit to town : if you are any where in the neighbourhood of it, you may depend upon seeing me. I shall then concert measures for seeing a little more of you next winter, than I have lately done, as I hope to take a pretty long spell in town. I suppose Guise has often fallen in your way : he has never once written to me, nor I to him : in the country we want materials, and in London we want time. I ought to recollect, that you even want time to read my unmeaning scrawl. Believe, however, my dear Holroyd, that it is the sincere expression of a heart entirely yours.

EDWARD GIBBON, *Esq. to* J. B. HOLROYD, *Esq.*
DEAR HOLROYD, BERITON, October 16, 1769.
I RECEIVED your agreeable missive about two days ago ; and am glad to find that, after all your *errors,* you are at last a settled man. I do most sincerely regret that it is not in my power to obey your immediate summons. Some very particular business will not at present permit me to be long absent from Beriton. The same business will carry me to town, about the sixth of next month, for some days. On my return, I do really hope and intend to storm your castle before Christmas, as I presume you will hardly remove sooner. I should be glad to meet Cambridge ; but the plain dish of friendship will satisfy me, without the seasoning of Attic wit. Do you know any thing of Guise ? Have you no inclination to look at the Russians ? We have a bed at your service. *Vale.*
Present my sincere respects to those who are dear to you ; believe me, they are so to me.

The Same to the Same.
DEAR HOLROYD, PALL MALL, Dec. 25, 1769.
SOME dæmon, the enemy of friendship, seems to have determined that we shall not meet at Sheffield-Place. I was fully resolved to make amends for my lazy scruples, and to dine with you to-morrow ; when I received a letter this day from my father, which irresistibly draws me to Beriton for about ten days. The above-mentioned dæmon, though he may defer my projects, shall not however disappoint them. Since you intend to pass the winter in retirement, it will be a far greater compliment to quit active, gay, political London, than the drowsy desert London of the holidays. But I retract. What is both pleasing and sincere, is above that prostituted word *compliment.* Believe me,
Most sincerely yours.
A propos, I forgot the compliments of the season, &c. &c.

The motto of the regiment called Royal Foresters, in which Mr. Holroyd had been Captain.

The Same to the Same.

DEAR HOLROYD,   October 6, 1771.

I SIT down to answer your epistle, after taking a very pleasant ride.
—A ride! and upon what?—Upon a horse.—*You lie!*—I don't.—I
have got a droll little poney, and intend to renew the long-forgotten
practice of equitation, as it was known in the world before the second
of June of the year of our Lord one thousand seven huñdred and sixty-
three. As I used to reason against riding, so I can now argue for it;
and indeed the principal use I know in human reason is, when called
upon, to furnish arguments for what we have an inclination to do.

What do you mean by presuming to affirm, that I am of no use here?
Farmer Gibbon of no use? *Last week* I sold all my hops, and I
believe well, at nine guineas a hundred, to a very responsible man.
Some people think I might have got more at Weyhill Fair, but that
would have been an additional expence, and a great uncertainty. Our
quantity has disappointed us very much; but I think, that besides
hops for the family, there will not be less than 500l.;—no contemptible
sum off thirteen small acres, and two of them planted last year only.
This week I let a little farm in Petersfield by auction, and propose
raising it from 25l. to 35l. *per annum:* and Farmer Gibbon of no use?

To be serious; I have but one reason for resisting your invitation,
and my own wishes; that is, Mrs. Gibbon I left nearly alone all last
winter, and shall do the same this. She submits very cheerfully to
that state of solitude; but, on sounding her, I am convinced that she
would think it unkind were I to leave her at present. I know you so
well, that I am sure you will acquiesce in this reason; and let me
make my next visit to Sheffield-Place from town, which I think may
be a little before Christmas. I should like to hear something of the
precise time, duration, and extent of your intended tour into Bucks.
Adieu.

EDWARD GIBBON *Esq. to* J. B. HOLROYD *Esq.*

MOST RESPECTABLE SOUTH SAXON,   BERITON, Nov. 18, 1771.

IT would ill become me to reproach a dilatory correspondent;

  Quis tulerit Gracchos de seditione querentes?

especially when that correspondent had given me hopes of undertaking a
very troublesome expedition for my sole advantage. Yet thus much I may
say, that I am obliged very soon to go to town upon other business,
which, in that hope, I have hitherto deferred. If by next Sunday I
have no answer, or if I hear that your journey to Denham is put off
sine die, or to a long day, I shall on Monday set off for London, and
wait your future will with *faith, hope, and charity.* Adieu.

EDWARD GIBBON *Esq. to* JOHN BAKER HOLROYD *Esq.*
Sheffield-Place.

DEAR HOLROYD,   LONDON, 1772.

THE sudden change from the sobriety of Sheffield-Place to the irregularities of this town, and to the wicked company of Wilbraham, Clarke,
Damer, &c. having deranged me a good deal, I am forced to employ

one of my secretaries to acquaint you with a piece of news I know nothing about myself. It is certain, some extraordinary intelligence is arrived this morning from Denmark, and as certain that the levee was suddenly prevented by it. The particulars of that intelligence are variously and obscurely told. It is said, that the king had raised a little physician to the rank of minister and Ganymede ; such a mad administration had so disgusted all the nobility, that the fleet and army had rose, and shut up the king in his palace. *La Reine se trouve mêlée la dedans ;* and it is reported that she is confined, but whether in consequence of the insurrection, or some other cause, is not agreed. Such is the rough draft of an affair that nobody yet understands. *Embrassez de ma part Madame, et le reste de la chere famille.*   GIBBON.
                        Et plus bas—WILBRAHAM, Sec.

EDWARD GIBBON *Esq. to* J. B. HOLROYD *Esq.*
                  BOODLE'S, 10 o'clock, Monday night, Feb. 3, 1772.
I LOVE, honour, and respect, every member of Sheffield-Place ; even my great enemy * Datch, to whom you will please to convey my sincere wishes, that no *simpleton* may wait on him at dinner, that his wise papa may not shew him any pictures, and that his much wiser mamma may chain him hand and foot, in direct contradiction to Magna Charta and the bill of rights.

It is difficult to write news, because there is none. Parliament is perfectly quiet ; and I think that Barré, who is just now playing at whist in the room, will not have exercise of the lungs, except, perhaps, on a message much talked of, and soon expected, to recommend it to the wisdom of the House of Commons to provide a proper future remedy against the improper marriages of the younger branches of the Royal Family. The noise of * * * is subsided, but there was some foundation for it. * * *'s expences in his bold enterprise were yet unpaid by government. The hero threatened, assumed the patriot, received a sop, and again sunk into the courtier. As to Denmark, it seems now that the king, who was totally unfit for government, has only passed from the hands of his queen wife, to those of his queen mother-in-law. * * * is said to have indulged a very *vague* taste in her amours. She would not be admitted into the Pantheon, whence the *gentlemen proprietors* exclude all beauty, unless unspotted and immaculate (tautology by the bye). *The gentlemen proprietors,* on the other hand, are friends and patrons of the leopard beauties. Advertising challenges have passed between the two great factions, and a bloody battle is expected Wednesday night. *A propos,* the Pantheon, in point of ennui and magnificence, is the wonder of the eighteenth century and of the British empire. Adieu.

The Same to the Same.   BOODLE'S, Saturday night, Feb. 8, 1772.
    THOUGH it is very late, and the bell tells me that I have not above ten minutes left, I employ them with pleasure in congratulating you on the late victory of our dear mamma the Church of England. She had

* The name by which the child called himself. S.

P

last Thursday seventy-one rebellious sons, who pretended to set aside
her will on account of insanity : but two hundred and seventeen worthy
champions, headed by Lord North, Burke, Hans, Stanley, Charles Fox,
Godfrey Clarke, &c. though they allowed the thirty-nine clauses of her
testament were absurd and unreasonable, supported the validity of it
with infinite humour. By the bye, * * * prepared himself for that
holy war, by passing twenty-two hours in the pious exercise of hazard ;
his devotions cost him only about 500 l. *per* hour—in all 11,000 l. * * *
lost 5000 l. This is from the best authority. I hear too, but will not
warrant it, that * * *, by way of paying his court to * * *, has lost
this winter 12,000 l. How I long to be ruined !

There are two county contests, Sir Thomas Egerton and Colonel
Townley in Lancashire, after the county had for some time gone
a-begging. In Salop, Sir Watkin, supported by Lord Gower, happened
by a punctilio to disoblige Lord Craven, who told us last night, that he
had not quite 9000 l. a-year in that county, and who has set up Pigot
against him. You may suppose we all wish for God Almighty against
that black devil.

I am sorry your journey is deferred. Compliments to Datch. As he
is now in durance, great minds forgive their enemies, and I hope he
may be released by this time.—Coming, Sir. Adieu.

You see the Princess of W. is gone. Hans Stanley says, it is
believed the Empress Queen has taken the same journey.

DEAR HOLROYD,   LONDON, Feb. 13, 1772.

THE papers and plans arrived safe in town last night, and will be in
your hands in their intact virgin state in a day or two. Consider them
at leisure, if that word is known in the rural life. Unite, divide, but
(above all) *raise.* Bring them to London with you : I wait your
orders ; nor shall I, for fear of tumbling, take a single step till your
arrival, which, on many accounts, I hope will not be long deferred.

Clouds still hover over the horizon of Denmark. The public circumstances of the revolution are related, and I understand, very exactly,
in the foreign papers. The secret springs of it still remain unknown.
The town indeed seems at present quite tired of the subject. The
Princess's death, her character, and what she left, engross the conversation. She died without a will ; and as her savings were generally
disposed of in charity, the small remains of her personal fortune will
make a trifling object when divided among her children. Her favourite
the Princess of B. very properly insisted on the king's immediately
sealing up all the papers, to secure her from the idle reports which
would be so readily swallowed by the great English monster. The
business of Lord and Lady * * * is finally compromised, by the arbitration of the Chancellor and Lord * * *. He gives her 1200 l. a-year
separate maintenance, and 1500 l. to set out with : but as her Ladyship
is now a new face, her husband, who has already bestowed on the
public seventy young beauties, has conceived a violent but hopeless
passion for his chaste moiety. * * * Lord Chesterfield is dying.
County oppositions subside. Adieu.

Entirely yours.

DEAR HOLROYD, Feb. 21, 1772.
HOWEVER, notwithstanding my indignation, I will employ five minutes in telling you two or three recent pieces of news.

1. Charles Fox is commenced patriot, and is already attempting to pronounce the words *country, liberty, corruption,* &c. ; with what success, time will discover. Yesterday he resigned the Admiralty. The story is, that he could not prevail on ministry to join with him in his intended repeal of the marriage act, (a favourite measure of his father, who opposed it from its origin,) and that Charles very judiciously thought Lord Holland's friendship imported him more than Lord North's.

2. Yesterday the marriage message came to both Houses of Parliament. You will see the words of it in the papers : and thanks to the submissive piety of this session, it is hoped that * * *.

3. To-day the House of Commons was employed in a very odd way. Tommy Townshend moved, that the sermon of Dr. Knowell, who preached before the house on the 30th of January, (*id est,* before the Speaker and four members,) should be burnt by the common hangman, as containing arbitrary, tory, high-flown doctrines. The House was nearly agreeing to the motion, till they recollected that they had already thanked the Preacher for his excellent discourse, and ordered it to be printed. Knowell's bookseller is much obliged to the Right Honourable Tommy Townshend.

When do you come to town ? I want money, and am tired of sticking to the earth by so many roots. *Embrassez de ma part,* &c. Adieu.

Ever yours.

EDWARD GIBBON *Esq. to Mrs.* GIBBON, Beriton.
DEAR MADAM, LONDON, March 21, 1772
I HAVE advanced with some care and some success in gaining an idea of the Lenborough estate. The tenants are at will, and from a comparison of my rents with the neighbouring ones, particularly Lord * * *, there is great probability that my estate is very much under-let. My friend Holroyd, who is a most invaluable counsellor, is strongly of that opinion. Sir * * * * * * is just come home. I am sorry to see many alterations, and little improvement. From an honest wild English buck he is grown a *philosopher.* Lord * * * displeases everybody by the affectation of consequence : the young baronet disgusts no less by the affectation of wisdom. He speaks in short sentences, quotes Montaigne, seldom smiles, never laughs, drinks only water, professes to command his passions, and intends to marry in five months. The two lords, his uncles, as well as * * *, attempt to shew him, that such behaviour, even were it reasonable, does not suit this country He remains incorrigible, and is every day losing ground in the good opinion of the public, which at his first arrival ran strongly in his favour. Deyverdun is probably on his journey towards England, but is not yet come.

I am, dear Madam, &c. &c.

EDWARD GIBBON *Esq. to* J. B. HOLROYD *Esq.*

DEAR HOLROYD,   PALL MALL, May 26, 1772.
    I WISH you lived nearer, or even that you could pass a week at
Beriton. When shall you be at Richmond, or would there be any *use*
in my going down to Sheffield for a day or two? In you alone I put
my trust, and without you I should be perplexed, discouraged, and
frightened ; for not a single fish has yet bit at the Lenborough bait.
    I dined the other day with Mr. Way at Boodle's. He told me, that
he was just going down to Sheffield Place. As he has probably
unladen all the politics, and Mrs. Way all the scandal of the town, I
shall for *the present only* satisfy myself with the needful ; among which
I shall always reckon my sincere compliments to Madame, and my
profound respects for Mr. Datch.
                            I am, dear H.
                                            Truly yours.
    It is confidently asserted that the Emperor and King of Prussia are
to run for very deep stakes over the Polish course. If the news be
true, I back Austria against the aged horse, provided little Laudohn
rides the match. *N.B.* Crossing and jostling allowed.

EDWARD GIBBON, *Esq. to Mrs.* HOLROYD, *Senior.*

                    BERITON, near PETERSFIELD, HAMPSHIRE,
MADAM,   July 17, 1772.
    THERE is not any event which could have affected me with greater
surprise and deeper concern, than the news in last night's paper, of
the death of our poor little amiable friend Master Holroyd, whom
I loved, not only for his parents' sake, but for his own. Should the
news be true, (for even yet I indulge some faint hopes,) what must
be the distress of our friends at Sheffield ! I so truly sympathise with
them, that I know not how to write to Holroyd ; but must beg to
be informed of the state of the family by a line from you. I have
some company and business here, but would gladly quit them, if I
had the least reason to think that my presence at Sheffield would
afford comfort or satisfaction to the man in the world whom I
love and esteem most. I am, Madam, your most obedient humble
Servant, &c.

EDWARD GIBBON, *Esq. to* J. B. HOLROYD, *Esq.*

MY DEAR HOLROYD,   BERITON, July 30, 1772.
    IT was my intention to set out for Sheffield as soon as I received
your affecting letter, and I hoped to have been with you as to-day ;
but walking very carelessly yesterday morning, I fell down, and put
out a small bone in my ancle. I am now under the surgeon's hands,
but think, and most earnestly hope, that this little accident will not
delay my journey longer than the middle of next week. I share, and
wish I could alleviate your feelings. I beg to be remembered to Mrs.
Holroyd. I am, my dear Holroyd, most truly yours.

EDWARD GIBBON, *Esq. to Mrs.* GIBBON, Beriton.

DEAR MADAM,   SHEFFIELD-PLACE, August 7, 1772.

I SET out at six yesterday morning from Uppark, and got to Brighton about two; a very thin season, everybody gone to Spa. In the evening I reached this place. My friend appears, as he ever will, in a light truly respectable; concealing the most exquisite sufferings under the show of composure, and even cheerfulness, and attempting, though with little success, to confirm the weaker mind of his partner. I find, my friend expresses so much uneasiness at the idea of my leaving him again soon, that I cannot refuse to pass the month here. If Mr. Scott, as I suppose, is at Beriton, he has himself too high a sense of friendship not to excuse my neglecting him. I had some hopes of engaging Mr. and Mrs. Holroyd to make an excursion to Portsmouth, Isle of Wight, Southampton, &c. in which case they would spend a few days at Beriton. A sudden resolution was taken last night in favour of the tour. We set out, Mr. and Mrs. Holroyd, Mr. Fauquier, and myself, next Thursday, and shall dine at Beriton the following day, and stay there, most probably, three or four days. A farm-house, without either cook or housekeeper, will afford but indifferent entertainment; but we must *exert,* and they must *excuse.* Our tour will last about a fortnight; after which my friend presses me to return with him, and in his present situation I shall be at a loss how to refuse him.

I am, dear Madam, &c. &c.

Dr. HURD (*now Bishop of* Worcester) *to Mr.* GIBBON.

SIR,   THURCASTON, August 29, 1772.

YOUR very elegant letter on the antiquity and authenticity of the Book of Daniel, (just now received,) finds me here, if not without leisure, yet without books, and therefore in no condition to enter far into the depths of this controversy; which indeed is the less necessary, as everything that relates to the subject will come of course to be considered by my learned successors in the new lecture. For as the prophecies of Daniel make an important link in *that chain, which,* as you say, *has been let down from heaven to earth,* (but not by the author of the late sermons, who brought into view only what he had not invented,) the grounds on which their authority rests will, without doubt, be carefully examined, and, as I suppose, firmly established.

But in the mean time, and to make at least some small return for the civility of your address to me, I beg leave to trouble you with two or three short remarks, such as occur to me on reading your letter.

Your main difficulties are these two : 1. That the author of the book of Daniel is too clear for a prophet; as appears from his prediction of the Persian and Macedonian affairs: and, 2. too fabulous for a contemporary historian; as is evident, you suppose, from his mistakes, particularly in the sixth chapter.

I. The first of these difficulties is an extraordinary one. For why may not prophecy, if the inspirer think fit, be as clear as history?

Scriptural prophecy, whence your idea of its obscurity is taken, *occasionally* thus clear, I mean after the event ; and Daniel's prophecy of the revolutions in the Grecian empire, would have been obscure enough to Porphyry himself before it.

But your opinion, after all, when you come to explain yourself, really is, as one should expect, that, as a prophet, Daniel is not clear enough; for you enforce the old objection of Porphyry, by observing, that where a pretended prophecy is clear to a certain point of time, and afterwards obscure and shadowy, there common sense leads one to conclude that the author of it was an impostor.

This reasoning is plausible, but not conclusive, unless it be taken for granted, that a prophecy must, in all its parts, be equally clear and precise : whereas, on the supposition of real inspiration, it may be fit, I mean it may suit with the views of the inspirer, to predict some things with more perspicuity, and in terms more obviously and directly applicable to the events in which they were fulfilled, than others. But further, this reasoning, whatever force it may have, has no place here ; at least you evidently beg the question when you urge it ; because the persons you dispute against maintain, that the subsequent prophecies of Daniel are equally distinct with those preceding ones concerning the Persian and Macedonian empires, at least so much of them as they take to have been fulfilled ; and that to judge of the rest, we must wait for the conclusion of them.

However, you admit that the suspicion arising from the clearest prophecy may be removed by direct positive evidence that it was composed before the event. But then you carry your notions of that evidence very far, when you require, "that the existence of such a prophecy, prior to its accomplishment, should be proved by the knowledge of its being generally diffused amongst an enlightened nation previous to that period, and its public existence attested by an unbroken chain of authentic writers."

What you here claim as a matter of *right*, is, without question, very desirable, but should, I think, be accepted, if it be given at all, as a matter of *favour*. For what you describe is the utmost evidence that the case admits : but what right have we in this, or any other subject whatever of natural or revealed religion, to the utmost evidence? Is it not enough that the evidence be sufficient to induce a reasonable assent ? and is not that assent reasonable, which is given to real evidence though of an inferior kind, when uncontrolled by any greater? And such evidence we clearly have for the authenticity of the book of Daniel, in the reception of it by the Jewish nation down to the time of Jesus whose appeal to it supposes and implies that reception to have been constant and general : not to observe, that the testimony of Jesus is further supported by all the considerations that are alleged for his own divine character. To this evidence, which is positive so far as it goes, you have nothing to oppose but surmise and conjectures; that is, nothing that deserves to be called evidence. But I doubt, Sir, you take for granted that the claim of inspiration is never to be allowed, so long as there is a possibility of supposing that it was not given.

II. In the second division of your letter, which is longer, and more elaborate, than the first, you endeavour to shew that the *historical* part of the book of Daniel, chiefly that of the sixth chapter, is false and fabulous, and as such, confutes and overthrows the *prophetical.* What you advance on this head, is contained under *five* articles :

1. You think it strange that Daniel, or any other man, should be promoted to a secret office of state, *for his skill in divination.*

But here, first, you forget that Joseph was thus promoted for the same reason. Or, if you object to this instance, what should hinder the promotion either of Joseph or Daniel, (when their skill in divination had once brought them to the notice and favour of their sovereign,) for what you call *mere human accomplishments ?* For such assuredly both these great men possessed, if we may believe the plain part of their story, which asserts of Joseph, and indeed proves, that he was in no common degree *discreet and wise;* and of Daniel, that *an excellent spirit was found in him;* nay, that *he had knowledge and skill in all learning and wisdom,* over and above his *understanding in all visions and dreams.* In short, Sir, though princes of old might not make it a rule to chuse their ministers out of their soothsayers, yet neither would their being soothsayers, if they were otherwise well accomplished, prevent them from being ministers. Just as in modern times, though churchmen have not often, I will suppose, been made officers of state, even by bigoted princes, because they were churchmen ; yet neither have they been always excluded from serving in those stations when they have been found eminently qualified for them.

2. Your next exception is, that a combination could scarce have been formed in the court of Babylon against the favourite minister, (though such factions are common in other courts,) because the courtiers of Darius *must have apprehended that the piety of Daniel could be asserted by a miraculous interposition;* of which they had seen a recent instance. And here, Sir, you expatiate with a little too much complacency on the strange indifference which the ancient world shewed to the gift of miracles. You do not, I dare say, expect a serious answer to this charge ; or if you do, it may be enough to observe, what I am sure your own reading and experience must have rendered very familiar to you, that the strongest belief, or conviction of the mind, perpetually gives way to the inflamed selfish passions ; and that, when men have any scheme of interest or revenge much at heart, they are not restrained from pursuing it, though the scaffold and the axe stand before them in full view, and have perhaps been streaming but the day before with the blood of other state-criminals. I ask not, whether miracles have ever *actually* existed, but whether you do not think that multitudes have been firmly *persuaded* of their existence ; and yet their indifference about them, is a fact which I readily concede to you.

3. Your third criticism is directed against what is said of *the law of the Medes and Persians, that it altereth not;* where I find nothing to admire, but the extreme rigour of Asiatic despotism. For I consider this irrevocability of the law, when once promulgated by the sovereign, not as contrived to be a check on his will, but rather to shew the irresistible and fatal course of it. And this idea was so much cherished by the despots of Persia, that, rather than revoke the iniquitous law, obtained by surprise, for exterminating the Jews, Ahasuerus took the part, as we read in the book of Esther, (and as Baron Montesquieu, I

remember, observes,) to permit the Jews to defend themselves against the execution of it ; whence we see how consistent this law is with the determination of the judges, quoted by you from Herodotus, "that it was lawful for the king to do whatever he *pleased :*" for we understand that he did *not* please that this law, when once declared by him, should be altered.

You add under this head, " May 1 not assert that the Greek writers, who have so copiously treated of the affairs of Persia, have not left us the smallest vestige of a restraint, equally injurious to the monarch and prejudicial to the people." 1 have not the Greek writers by me to consult, but a common book I chance to have at hand refers me to one such vestige, in a very eminent Greek historian, Diodorus Siculus. *Lowth's Comment. in loc.*

4. A fourth objection to the historic truth of the book of Daniel is taken, with more plausibility, from the matter of this law, which, as you truly observe, was very strange for the king's counsellor to advise, and for any despot whatever to enact.

But, 1. I a little question whether prayer was so constant and considerable a part of Pagan worship as is supposed ; and if it was not, the prejudices of the people would not be so much shocked by this interdict as we are ready to think. Daniel indeed prayed three times a day; but the idolaters might content themselves with praying now and then at a stated solemnity. It is clear, that when you speak of *depriving men of the comforts, and priests of the profits, of religion,* you have Christian, and even modern principles and manners in your eye : perhaps in the *comforts,* you represented to yourself a company of poor inflamed Huguenots under persecution ; and in the *profits,* the lucrative trade of popish masses. But be this as it may, it should be considered, 2. That this law could not, in the nature of the thing, suppress all prayer, if the people had any great propensity to it. It could not suppress *mental* prayer ; it could not even suppress *bodily* worship, if performed, as it easily might be, in the night, or in secret. Daniel, it was well known, was used to pray in open daylight, and in a place exposed to inspection, from his usual manner of praying ; which manner, it was easily concluded, so zealous a votary as he was, would not change or discontinue, on account of the edict.   Lastly, though the edict passed for thirty days, to make sure work, yet there was no doubt but the end proposed would be soon accomplished, and then it was not likely that much care would be taken about the observance of it.

All this put together, I can very well conceive that extreme envy and malice in the courtiers might suggest the idea of such a law, and that an impotent despot might be flattered by it. Certainly, if what we read in the third chapter be admitted, that *one* of these despots required all people, nations, and languages, to worship his image on pain of death, there is no great wonder that *another* of them should demand the exclusive worship of himself for a month ; nay, perhaps, he might think himself civil, and even bounteous to his gods, when he left them a share of the other eleven. For as to the presumption,

" Nihil est quod credere de se
Non possit, cum laudatur diis æqua potestas.—

5. A fifth, and what you seem to think the strongest, objection to the credit of the book of Daniel is, that "no such person as Darius the Mede is to be found in the succession of the Babylonish princes," (you mean as given in Ptolemy's canon and the Greek writers,) "between the time of Nebuchadnezzar and that of Cyrus." In saying this, you do not forget or disown what our ablest chronologers have said on the subject; but then you object that Xenophon's Cyaxares (to serve a turn) has been made to personate Darius the Mede; and yet that Xenophon's book, whether it be a romance or a true history, overturns the use which they have made of this hypothesis.

I permit myself perhaps to be too much flattered by your civility in referring me to my own taste, rather than to the authority of Cicero : but the truth is, I am much disposed to agree with you, that, "if we unravel with any care the fine texture of the Cyropœdia, we shall discover in every thread the Spartan discipline and the philosophy of Socrates." But then, as the judicious author chose to make so recent a story as that of Cyrus, and one so well known, the vehicle of his political and moral instructions, he would be sure to keep up to the truth of the story as far as might be; especially in the leading facts, and in the principal persons, as we may say, of the drama. This obvious rule of decorum such a writer as Xenophon could not fail to observe ; and therefore, on the supposition that his Cyropœdia is a romance, I should conclude certainly that the outline of it was genuine history. But, 2. If it be so, you conclude that there is no ground for thinking that Darius the Mede ever reigned at Babylon, because Cyaxares himself never reigned there.

Now, on the idea of Xenophon's book being a romance, there might be good reason for the author's taking no notice of the short reign of Cyaxares, which would break the unity of his work, and divert the reader's attention too much from the hero of it : while yet the omission could hardly seem to violate historic truth, since the lustre of his hero's fame, and the real power, which, out of question, he reserved to himself, would make us forget or overlook Cyaxares. But, as to the fact, it seems no way incredible that Cyrus should concede to his royal ally, his uncle, and his father-in-law, (for he was all these,) the *nominal* possession of the sovereignty ; or that he should *share* the sovereignty with him ; or, at least, that he should leave the *administration,* as we say, in his hands at Babylon, while he himself was prosecuting his other conquests at a distance. Any of these things is supposable enough ; and I would rather admit any of them than reject the express, the repeated, the circumstantial testimony of a not confessedly fabulous historian.

After all, Sir, I should forfeit I know, your good opinion, if I did not acknowledge that some, at least of these circumstances are such as one should not, perhaps, expect at first sight. But then such is the condition of things here ; and what is true in human life, is not always, I had almost said, not often, that which was previously to be expected ; whence an ordinary romance is, they say, more *probable* than the best history.

But should any or all of these circumstances convince you perfectly, that some degree of error or fiction is to be found in the book of Daniel, it would be too precipitate to conclude that therefore the whole book was of no authority: for, at most, you could but infer, that the historical part, in which those circumstances are observed, namely, the 6th chapter, is not genuine; just as you know has been judged of some other historical tracts which had formerly been inserted in the book of Daniel. For it is not with these collections, which go under the names of the Prophets, as with some regularly connected system, where a charge of falsehood, if made good against one part, shakes the credit of the whole. Fictitious histories may have been joined to true prophecies, when all that bore the name of the same person, or any way related to him, came to be put together in the same volume: but the detection of such misalliance could not affect the prophecies; certainly not those of Daniel, which respect *the latter times;* for these have an intrinsic evidence in themselves, and assert their own authenticity, in proportion as we see, or have reason to admit the accomplishment of them.

And now, Sir, I have only to commit these hasty reflections to your candour; a virtue which cannot be separated from the love of truth, and of which I observe many traces in your agreeable letter; and if you should indulge this quality still further, so as to conceive the possibility of that being *true and reasonable*, in matters of religion, which may seem strange, or, to so lively a fancy as yours, even ridiculous, you would not hurt the credit of your excellent understanding, and would thus remove one, perhaps a principal, occasion of those mists which, as you complain, *hang over these nice and difficult subjects.*

I am with true respect, SIR, yours, &c.

(Signed)   R. H.

[The following Fragment was found with the foregoing Letter, in Mr. GIBBON'S handwriting. S.]

YOUR answers to my five objections against the 6th chapter of Daniel come next to be considered.

1. With regard to Daniel's promotion, I consent to withdraw my opposition, and to allow the cases of Ximenes, Wolsey, and Richlieu as parallel instances; though there is surely some difference between a young foreign soothsayer being *suddenly* rewarded, for the interpretation of a dream, with the government of Babylon, and a priest of the established church, rising gradually to the great offices of state.

2. You apprehend, Sir, that my second objection scarcely deserves a serious answer; and that it is quite sufficient to appeal to my own reading and experience, whether *the strongest conviction of the mind does not perpetually give way to the inflamed and selfish passions.* Since you appeal to me, I shall fairly lay before you the result of my observations on that subject. 1. It must be confessed that the drunkard often sinks into the grave, and the prodigal into a gaol, without a possibility of deceiving or of checking themselves. But they sink by slow degrees; and, whilst they indulge the ruling passion, attend only to the trifling moment of each guinea, or of each bottle, without calculating their accumulated weight, till they feel themselves irretrievably crushed under it. 2. In most of the hazardous interprizes of life there

is a mixture of chance and good fortune; what is called good fortune, is often the effect of skill : and as our vanity flatters us into an opinion of our superior merit, we are neither surprised nor dismayed by the miscarriage of our rash predecessors. *The conspirator turns his eyes from the axe and scaffold, perhaps still streaming with blood,* to the successful boldness of Sylla, of Cæsar, and of Cromwell ; and convinces himself that on such a golden pursuit it is even *prudent* to stake a precarious and insipid life. We may add, that the most daring flights of ambition are as often the effects of necessity as of choice. The princes of Hindostan must either reign or perish ; and when Cæsar passed the Rubicon, it was scarcely possible for him to return to a private station. 3. You think, Sir, we may learn from our own experience, that an indifference concerning miracles is very compatible with a full conviction of their truth ; and so it undoubtedly is with such a conviction as we have an opportunity of observing.

E. GIBBON *Esq. to* J. B. HOLROYD *Esq.*
DEAR HOLROYD, BERITON, Oct. 13, 1772.
I AM just arrived, as well as yourself, at my *dii penates,* but with very different intention. You will ever remain a bigot to those rustic deities ; I propose to abjure them soon, and to reconcile myself to the catholic church of London.

I am so happy, so exquisitely happy, at feeling so many mountains taken off my shoulders, that I can brave your indignation, and even the three-forked lightning of Jupiter himself. My reasons for taking so unwarrantable a step (approved of by Hugonin) were no unmanly despondency, (though it daily became more apparent how much the farm would suffer, both in reality and in reputation, by another year's management). * * * *. I see pleasure but not use in a congress, therefore decline it. I know nothing as yet of a purchaser, and can only give you full and unlimited powers. If you think it necessary, let me know when you sell ; but, however, do as you please.

I am sincerely glad to hear Mrs. H. is better. Still think Bath would suit her. She, and you too, I fear, rather want the physic of the mind, than of the body. Tell me something about yourself. If, among a crowd of acquaintances, one friend can afford you any comfort, I am quite at your service. Once more, adieu.

EDWARD GIBBON *Esq. to* J. HOLROYD *Esq.*
DEAR HOLROYD, PALL-MALL, 11th Dec. 1772.
BY this time, I suppose you returned to the Elysian fields of Sheffield. The country (I do not mean any particular reflections on Sussex) must be vastly pleasant at this time of the year ! For my own part, the punishment of my sins has at length overtaken me. On Thursday the third of December, in the present year of our Lord one thousand seven hundred and seventy-two, between the hours of one and two in the afternoon, as I was crossing St. James's church-yard, I stumbled, and *again sprained my foot;* but, alas ! after two days pain and con-

finement, a horrid monster, *ycleped the gout*, made me a short visit; and though he has now taken his leave, I am full of apprehensions that he may have liked my company well enough to call again.

The parliament, after a few soft murmurs, is gone to sleep, to awake again after Christmas, safely folded in Lord North's arms. The town is gone into the country, and I propose *visiting Sheffield* about Sunday se'nnight, if by that time I can get my household preparations (1 have as good as taken Lady Rous's lease in Bentinck-street) in any forwardness. Shall I *angle for Batt?* No news stirring, except the Duchess of G.'s pregnancy certainly declared. * * * called on me the other day, and has taken my plan with him to consider it; he still wishes to defer till spring; talks of bad roads, &c. and is very absolute. I remonstrated, *but want to know whether I am to submit.* Adieu. *Godfrey Clarke*, who is writing near me, begs to be remembered. The savage is going to hunt foxes in Northamptonshire, Oxfordshire, Gloucestershire, &c.   Yours sincerely.

BOODLE'S, Ten o'Clock, Thursday Evening, Dec. 1772.
DEAR HOLROYD,
   MY schemes with regard to you have been entirely disappointed. The business that called me to town was not ready before the 20th of last month, and the same business has kept me here till now. I have however a very strong inclination to eat a Christmas mince pie with you; and let me tell you that inclination is no small compliment. What are the trees and waters of Sheffield-Place, compared with the comfortable smoke, lazy dinners, and inflammatory Junius's, which we can every day enjoy in town? You have seen the last Junius? He calls on the distant legions to march to the Capitol, and free us from the tyranny of the Prætorian guards. I cannot answer for the ghost of the *hic et ubique*, but the Hampshire militia are determined to keep the peace for fear of a broken head. After all, do I mean to make you a visit next week? Upon my soul, I cannot tell. I tell every body that I shall: I know that I cannot pass the week with any man in the world with whom the pleasure of seeing each other will be more sincere or more reciprocal. Yet, *entre nous*, I do not believe that I shall be able to get out of this town before you come into it. At all events I look forwards, with great impatience, to Bruton-street* and the Romans.†
   Believe me most truly yours.

EDWARD GIBBON *Esq. to* J. HOLROYD *Esq.*
DEAR HOLROYD,   January 12, 1773.
   LENBOROUGH is no more! * * * acted like a Jew, and I dare say now repents it. In his room * * * found me a better man, a rich, brutish, honest horse-dealer, who has got a great fortune by serving the cavalry. On Thursday he saw Lenborough, on Friday came to town with * * *, and this morning at nine o'clock we struck at 20,000l. after a very hard battle. As times go, I am not dissatisfied. * * * and the

---
* Where Mr. Holroyd's family passed a winter.   † The Roman Club.

new Lord of Lenborough (by name * * *) dined with me ; and though we did not speak the same language, yet by the help of signs, such as that of putting about the bottle, the natives seemed well satisfied.

The whole world is going down to Portsmouth, where they will enjoy the pleasures of smoke, noise, heat, bad lodgings, and expensive reckonings. For my own part, I have firmly resisted importunity, declined parties, and mean to pass the busy week in the soft retirement of my *bocage* de Bentinck-street. Yesterday the East India Company positively refused the loan : a noble resolution, could they get money any where else. They are violent ; and it was moved, and the motion heard with some degree of approbation, that they should instantly abandon India to Lord North, Sujah Dowlah, or the Devil, if he chose to take it. Adieu.

The Same to the Same.

DEAR HOLROYD,   BOODLE'S, May 11, 1773.

I AM full of worldly cares, anxious about the great twenty-fourth, plagued with the Public Advertiser, distressed by the most dismal dispatches from Hugonin. Mrs. Lee claims a million of repairs, which will cost a million of money.

The House of Commons sat late last night. Burgoyne made some spirited motions—"that the territorial acquisitions in India belonged to the state (that was the word) ; that grants to the servants of the company (such as jaghires) were illegal ; and that there would be no true repentance without restitution." Wedderburne defended the nabobs with great eloquence, but little argument. The motions were carried without a division ; and the hounds go out again next Friday. They are in high spirits ; but the more sagacious ones have no idea they shall kill. Lord North spoke for the inquiry, but faintly and reluctantly. Lady * * * is said to be in town at her mother's, and a separation is unavoidable ; but there is nothing certain.

Adieu.

Sincerely yours.

EDWARD GIBBON, *Esq. to* J. HOLROYD, *Esq. at* Edinburgh.

DEAR HOLROYD,   BENTINCK-STREET, Aug. 7, 1773.

I BEG ten thousand pardons for not being dead, as I certainly ought to be. But such is my abject nature, that I had rather live in Bentinckstreet, attainted and convicted of the sin of laziness, than enjoy your applause either at old Nick's or even in the Elysian Fields. After all, could you expect that I should honour with my correspondence a wild barbarian of the Bogs of Erin ? Had the natives intercepted my letter, the terrors occasioned by such unknown magic characters might have been fatal to you. But now you have escaped the fury of their hospitality, and are arrived among a *cee-vi-leezed* nation, I may venture to renew my intercourse.

You tell me of a long list of dukes, lords, and chieftains of renown to whom you are introduced ; were I with you, I should prefer one *David* to them all. When you are at Edinburgh, I hope you will not fail to visit the sty of that fattest of Epicurus's hogs, and inform your-self whether there remains no hope of its recovering the use of its right paw. There is another animal of *great*, though not perhaps of *equal* and certainly not of *similar* merit, one Robertson ; has he almost created the new world? Many other men you have undoubtedly seen, in the country where you are at present, who must have commanded your esteem : but when you return, if you are not very honest, you will possess great advantages over me in any dispute concerning Caledonian merit.

Boodle's and Atwood's are now no more. The last stragglers, and Godfrey Clarke in the rear of all, are moved away to their several castles ; and I now enjoy, in the midst of London, a delicious solitude. My library, Kensington Gardens, and a few parties with new acquaintance who are chained to London, (among whom I reckon Goldsmith and Sir Joshua Reynolds,) fill up my time, and the monster *ennui* preserves a very respectful distance. By the bye, your friends, Batt, Sir John Russell, and Lascelles, dined with me one day before they set off; for I sometimes give the prettiest little dinner in the world. But all this composure draws near its conclusion. About the sixteenth of this month, Mr. Eliot carries me away, and after picking up Mrs. Gibbon at Bath, sets me down at Port Eliot : there I shall certainly remain six weeks, or, in other words, to the end of September. My future motions, whether to London, Derbyshire, or a longer stay in Cornwall, (pray is not "motion to stay" rather in the Hibernian style ?) will depend on the life of Port Eliot, the time of the meeting of parliament, and perhaps the impatience of Mr. * * *, Lord of Lenborough. One of my pleasures in town I forgot to mention, the unexpected visit of Deyverdun, who accompanies his young lord (very young indeed !) on a two months' tour to England. He took the opportunity of the Earl's going down to the Duke of * * *, to spend a fortnight (nor do I recollect a more pleasant one) in Bentinck-street. They are now gone together into Yorkshire, and I think it doubtful whether I shall see him again before his return to Leipsic. It is a melancholy reflection, that while one is plagued with acquaintance at the corner of every street, real friends should be separated from each other by unsurmountable bars, and obliged to catch at a few transient moments of interview. I desire that you and my Lady (whom I most respectfully greet) would take your share of that very new and acute observation, not so large a share indeed as my Swiss friend, since nature and fortune give *us* more frequent opportunities of being together. You cannot expect news from a desert, and such is London at present. The papers give you the full harvest of public intelligence ; and I imagine that the eloquent nymphs of Twickenham (Miss Cambridges), communicate all the transactions of the polite, the amorous, and the marrying world. The great pantomime of Portsmouth was universally admired ; and I am angry at my own laziness in neglecting an excellent opportunity of seeing it. Foote has given us the Bankrupt, a serious and sentimental piece, with very severe strictures on the licence of scandal in attacking private characters. Adieu. Forgive and epistolize me. I shall not believe you sincere in the former, unless you make Bentinck-street your inn. I fear I shall be gone ; but Mrs. Ford (his housekeeper) and the parrot will be proud to receive you and my Lady after your long peregrination, from which I expect great improvements. Has she got the brogue upon the tip of her tongue ?*

EDWARD GIBBON, *Esq. to* J. HOLROYD, *Esq.*

DEAR HOLROYD,   PORT ELIOT, Sept. 10, 1773.

BY this time you have surely finished your tour, touched at Edinburgh, where you found a letter, which you have not answered, and are now contemplating the beauties of the Weald of Sussex. I shall demand a long and particular account of your peregrinations, but will excuse it till we meet ; and for the present expect only a short memorandum of your health and situation, together with that of my much-honoured friend Mrs. Abigail Holroyd. A word too, if you please, concerning father and sister ; to the latter I enclose a receipt from Mrs. G. who is now with me at Port Eliot.

Blind as you accuse me of being to the beauties of nature, I am wonderfully pleased with this country. Of her three dull notes, *ground*, *plants*, and *water*, Cornwall possesses the first and last in very high perfection. Think of a hundred solitary streams peacefully gliding between amazing cliffs on one side, and rich meadows on the other, gradually swelling by the aid of the tide into noble rivers, successively losing themselves in each other, and all at length terminating in the harbour of Plymouth, whose broad expanse is irregularly *dotted* with two-and-forty line of battle ships. In plants indeed we are deficient ; and though all the gentlemen now attend to posterity, the country will for a long time be very naked. We have spent several days agreeably enough in little parties ; but in general our time rolls away in complete uniformity. Our landlord possesses neither a pack of hounds, nor a stable of running horses, nor a large farm, nor a good library. The last only could interest me ; but it is singular that a man of fortune, who chooses to pass nine months of the year in the country, should have none of them.

According to our present design, Mrs. G. and myself return to Bath about the beginning of next month. I shall probably make but a short stay with her, and defer my Derbyshire journey till another year. Sufficient for the summer is the evil thereof, *viz.* one distant country excursion. Natural inclination, the prosecution of my great work, and the conclusion of my Lenborough business, plead strongly in favour of London. However I desire, and one always finds time for what one really desires, to visit Sheffield-Place before the end of October, should it only be for a few days. I know several houses where I am invited to think myself at home, but I know no other where I seem inclined to accept of the invitation. I forgot to tell you, that I have declined the publication of Lord Chesterfield's Letters. The public will see them, and upon the whole, I think, with pleasure ; but the family were strongly bent against it ; and especially on Deyverdun's account, I deemed it more prudent to avoid making them my personal enemies.

* Mr. and Mrs. Holroyd made a tour to Ireland and Scotland this summer.

EDWARD GIBBON *Esq. to* J. HOLROYD *Esq.*

January 1774.
I HAVE a letter from Hugonin, a *dreadful* one I believe, but it has
lain four days unperused in my drawer. Let me turn it over to you.
Foster is playing at what he calls whist ; his partner swearing in-
wardly. He would write to you to-night, but he thinks he had rather
write *next* post ; he will think so a good while. Every thing public,
still as death. Our Committee of the Catch Club has done more
business this morning than all those of the House of Commons since
their meeting. Roberts does not petition. This from the best
authority, and yet perhaps totally false. Hare married to Sir Abraham
Hume's daughter. You see how hard pressed I am for news. Besides,
at any time, I had rather talk an hour, than write a page. Therefore
adieu. I am glad to hear of your speedy removal. Remember
Bentinck-street.

The Same to the Same.   January 29, 1774.
I AM now getting acquainted with authors, managers, &c. good company to know, but not to live with. Yesterday I dined at the British
Coffee-house, with Garrick, Coleman, Goldsmith, Macpherson, John
Hume, &c. I am this moment come from Coleman's Man of Business.
We dined at the Shakespeare, and went in a body to support it. Between friends, though we got a verdict for our client, his cause was but
a bad one. It is a very confused miscellany of several plays and tales ;
sets out brilliantly enough, but as we advance the plot grows thicker,
the wit thinner, till the lucky fall of the curtain preserves us from total
chaos.
Bentinck-street has visited Welbeck-street. Sappho is very happy
that she is there yet : on Sheffield-place she squints with regret and
gratitude. Mamma consulted me about buying coals ; we cannot get
any round ones. Quintus is gone to head the civil war. Of Mrs. * * *
I have nothing to say. I have got my intelligence for insuring, and
will immediately get the preservative against fire. Foster has sent me
eight-and-twenty pairs of Paris silk stockings, with an intimation that
my lady wished for half-a-dozen. They are much at her service ; but
if she will look into David Hume's Essay on National Characters, she
will see that I durst not offer them to a Queen of Spain. *Sachez
qu'une reine d'Espagne n'a point de jambes.* Adieu.

EDWARD GIBBON *Esq. to* J. HOLROYD, *Esq.*

1774.
WE have conquered ; * * * was amazed at the tempest just ready to
break over his head. He does not desire to go to law, wishes to live
in peace, has no complaints to make, hopes for a little indulgence.
Hugonin is now in the attitude of St. Michael trampling upon Satan ;
he holds him down, till Andrews has prepared *a little chain of adamant*
to bind the foul fiend. In return, receive my congratulation on your
Irish victory. Batt told me yesterday, as from good authority, that
administration designed a second attempt this session ; but to-day I

have it from much better, that they always discouraged it, and that it was *totally an Hibernian scheme.* You remark that I saw Batt. He passed two hours with me ; a pleasant man ! He and Sir John Russell dine with me *next week :* you will *have both their portraits; the originals are engaged.*

The Same to the Same. February, 1774.

DID you get down safe and early? Is my lady in good spirits and humour? You do not deserve that she should, for hurrying her away. Does Maria coquet with Divedown?'[Dr. Downes.] Adieu. Bentinck-street looks very dismal. You may suppose that nothing very important can have occurred since you left town : but I will send you some account of America after Monday, though indeed my anxiety about an old manor takes away much of my attention from a new continent. The mildness of Godfrey Clarke is roused into military fury; but he is an old Tory, and you only suppose yourself an old Whig. I alone am a true Englishman, Philosopher, and Whig.

The Same to the Same. BOODLES, Wed. Even. March 16, 1774.

I WAS this morning with * * *. He was positive that the attempt to settle the preliminaries of arbitration by letters would lead us on to the middle of the summer, and that a meeting was the only practicable measure. I acquiesced, and we blended his epistle and yours into one, which goes by this post. If you can contrive to suit to it your Oxford journey, your presence at the meeting would be received as the descent of a guardian angel.

Very little that is satisfactory has transpired of America. On Monday Lord North moved for leave to bring in a bill to remove the customs and courts of justice from Boston to New Salem ; a step so detrimental to the former town, as must soon reduce it to your own terms; and yet of so mild an appearance, that it was agreed to without a division, and almost without a debate. Something more is, however, intended, and a committee is appointed to inquire into the general state of America. But the administration keep their secret as well as that of free masonry, and, as Coxe profanely suggests, for the same reason.

Don't you remember that in our pantheon walks we admired the *modest beauty* of Mrs. * * *? *Eh bien,* alas ! she is * * *. You ask me with whom? With * * *, of the guards ; both the * * *'s ; * * *, a steward of * * *'s, her first love, and half the town besides. A meeting of * * *'s friends assembled about a week ago, to consult of the best method of acquainting him with his frontal honours. Edmund Burke was named as the orator, and communicated the transaction in a most eloquent speech.

E. GIBBON *Esq. to* J. HOLROYD *Esq.* March 29, 1774.

AMERICA. Had I written Saturday night, as I once intended, fire and sword, oaths of allegiance and high treason tried in England, in consequence of the refusal, would have formed my letter. Lord North, however, opened a most lenient prescription last night ; and the utmost attempt towards a new settlement seemed to be no more than investing the governors with a greater share of executive power, nomination

Q

of civil officers, (judges, however, for life,) and some regulations of juries. The Boston port bill passed the Lords last night ; some lively conversation, but no division.

Bentinck-street. Rose Fuller was against the Boston port bill, and against his niece's going to Boodle's masquerade. He was laughed at in the first instance, but succeeded in the second. Sappho and Fanny very indifferent (as mamma says) about going. They seem of a different opinion. Adieu.

DEAR HOLROYD,   April 20, 1774.

YOU owe me a letter ; so this extra goes only to acquaint you with a misfortune that has just happened to poor Clarke, and which he really considers as such, the loss of a very excellent father. The blow was sudden ; a thin little man, as abstemious as a hermit, was destroyed by a stroke of apoplexy in his coach as he was going to dinner. He appeared perfectly well, and only two days before had very good-naturedly dined with us at a tavern, a thing he had not done for many years before. I am the only person Clarke wishes to see, except his own family ; and I pass a great part of the day with him. A line from you would be kindly received.

Great news, you see, from India. Tanjour four hundred thousand pounds to the company. Suja Dowla six hundred thousand. Adieu.

The Same to the Same.   April 13, 1774.

AT length I am a little more at liberty. Godfrey Clarke went out of town this morning. Instead of going directly into Derbyshire, where he would have been overwhelmed with visits, &c. he has taken his sister, brother, and aunts to a villa near Farnham, in which he has the happiness of having no neighbourhood. If my esteem and friendship for Godfrey had been capable of any addition, it would have been very much increased by the manner in which he felt and lamented his father's death. He is now in very different circumstances than before ; instead of an easy and ample allowance, he has taken possession of a great estate, with low rents and high incumbrances. I hope the one may make amends for the other : under your conduct I am sure they would, and I have freely offered him your assistance, in case he should wish to apply for it.

In the mean time I must not forget my own affairs, which seem to be covered with inextricable perplexity. * * *, as I mentioned about a century ago, promised to see * * * and his attorney, and to oil the wheels of the arbitration. As yet I have not heard from him. I have some thoughts of writing *myself* to the jockey, stating the various steps of the affair, and offering him, with polite firmness, the *immediate* choice of Chancery or arbitration.

For the time, however, I forgot all these difficulties, in the present enjoyment of Deyverdun's company ; and I glory in thinking, that although my house is small, it is just of a sufficient size to hold my real friends, male and *female ;* among the latter my Lady holds the very first place.

We are all quiet.—American business is suspended and almost forgot. The other day we had a brisk report of a Spanish war. It was said they had taken one of our Leward Islands. It since turns out, that we are the invaders, but the invasion is trifling.

Bien obligé non (at present) for your invitation. I wish my Lady and you would come up to our masquerade the third of May. The finest thing ever seen. We sup in a transparent temple that costs four hundred and fifty pounds.

EDWARD GIBBON, *Esq. to* J. HOLROYD *Esq.*

DEAR HOLROYD,   April 21, 1774.

I BEGIN to flag, and though you already reproach me as a bad correspondent, I much fear that I shall every week become a more hardened sinner. Besides the occasional obstructions of Clarke and Deyverdun, I must intreat you to consider, with your usual candour, 1. The aversion to epistolary conversation, which it has pleased the dæmon to implant in my nature. 2. That I am a very fine gentleman, a subscriber to the masquerade, where you and my Lady ought to come, and am now writing at Boodle's, in a fine velvet coat, with ruffles of my lady's choosing, &c. 3. That the aforesaid fine gentleman is likewise an historian; and in truth, when I am writing a page, I do not only think it a sufficient reason for delay, but even consider myself as writing for you, and that, much more to the purpose than if I were sending you the little tattle of the town, of which indeed there is none stirring. With regard to America, the Minister seems moderate, and the House obedient.

* * *'s last letter, by some unaccountable accident, had never reached me; so that yours, in every instance, amazed me. I immediately dispatched to him groans and approbation. * * *, however, gives me very little uneasiness. I see that he is a bully, and that I have a stick. But the cursed business of Lenborough, in the midst of study, dissipation, and friendship, at times almost distracts me. I am surely in a worse situation than before I sold the estate, and what distresses me is, that

His ego nec metas rerum, nec tempora pono.——

Both Deyverdun and Clarke wish to be remembered to you. The former, who has more taste for the country than * * *, could wish to visit you, but he sets out in a few days for the continent with Lord Midleton. Adieu.

EDWARD GIBBON *Esq. to* J. HOLROYD *Esq.*

DEAR HOLROYD,   May 4, 1774.

LAST night was the triumph of Boodle's. Our masquerade cost two thousand guineas; a sum that might have fertilised a province, (I speak in your own style,) vanished in a few hours, but not without leaving behind it the fame of the most splendid and elegant *fête* that was perhaps ever given in a seat of the arts and opulence. It would be as difficult to describe the magnificence of the scene, as it would be easy to record the humour of the night. The one was above, the other below, all relation. I left the Pantheon about five this morning, rose at ten, took a good walk, and returned home to a more rational entertainment of Batt, Sir John Russell, and Lascelles, who dined with me. They have left me this moment; and were I to enumerate the things said of Sheffield, it would form a much longer letter than I have any inclination to write. Let it suffice, that Sir John means to pass in Sussex the interval of the two terms. Everything, in a word, goes on very pleasantly, except the terrestrial business of Lenborough. Last Saturday se'nnight I wrote to * * *, to press him to see * * *, and urge the arbitration. He has not *condescended* to answer me. All is a dead calm, sometimes more fatal than a storm. For God's sake send me advice. Adieu.

EDWARD GIBBON *Esq. to Mrs.* GIBBON, Bath.

DEAR MADAM,   BOODLE'S, May 24, 1774.
Do you remember that there exists in the world one Edward Gibbon, a housekeeper in Bentinck-street? If the standard of writing and of affection were the same, I am sure he would ill-deserve it. I do not wish to discover, how many days (I am afraid I ought to use another word) have elapsed since the date of my last, or even of your last letter, and yet such is the sluggish nature of the beast, that I am afraid nothing but the arrival of Mrs. Bonfoy, and the expectation of Mr. Eliot, could have roused me from my lethargy. The Lady gave me great satisfaction, by her general account of your health and spirits, but communicated some uneasiness, by the mention of a little encounter, in the style of one of Don Quixote's, but which proved, I hope, as trifling as you at first imagined it. For my own part, I am well in mind and body, busy with my books, (which may perhaps produce something next year, either to tire or amuse the world,) and every day more satisfied with my present mode of life, which I always believed was calculated to make me happy. My only remaining uneasiness is Lenborough, which is not terminated. By Holroyd's advice, I rather try what may be obtained by a little more patience, than rush at once into the horrors of Chancery. But let us talk of something else. Mrs. Porten grows younger every day. You remember, I think, in New-man-street, an agreeable woman, Miss W * * *. The Under-secretary is seriously in love with her, and seriously uneasy that his precarious situation precludes him from happiness. We shall soon see which will get the better, love or reason. I bet three to two on love.

Guess my surprise, when Mrs. Gibbon of Northamptonshire suddenly communicated her arrival. I immediately went to Surrey-street, where she lodged, but though it was no more than half an hour after nine, the Saint had finished her evening devotions, and was already retired to rest. Yesterday morning (by appointment) I breakfasted with her at eight o'clock, dined with her to-day at two in Newman-street, and am just returned from setting her down. She is, in truth, a very great curiosity : her dress and figure exceed anything we had at · the masquerade : her language and ideas belong to the last century. However, in point of religion she was rational; that is to say, silent. I do not believe that she asked a single question, or said the least thing concerning it. To me she behaved with great cordiality, and *in her way* expressed a great regard.

Mrs. Porten tells me, that she has just written to you. She ought to go to a masquerade once a year. Did you think her such a girl? I am, dear Madam, most truly yours.

EDWARD GIBBON Esq. to J. HOLROYD Esq.

BOODLE'S, May 24, 1774.

I WROTE three folio pages to you this morning, and yet you complain. Have reason, and have mercy; consider all the excellent reasons for silence which I gave you in one of my last, and expect my arrival in Sussex, when I shall talk more in a quarter of an hour than I could write in a day. *A propos* of that arrival; never pretend to allure me, by painting in odious colours the dust of London. I love the dust, and whenever I move into the Weald, it is to visit you and my Lady, and not your trees. About this-day-month I mean to give you a *visitation*. I leave it to Guise, Clarke, and the other light horse, to prance down for a day or two. They all talk of mounting, but will not fix the day. Sir John Russell, whom I salute, has brought you, I suppose, all the news of Versailles. Let me only add, that the Mesdames, by attending their father, have both got the small-pox. I can make nothing of * * *, or his lawyer. You will swear at the shortness of this letter.—Swear.

The Same to the Same.

Sat. Even. Aug. 27, 1774.

BY your submission to the voice of reason, you eased me of a heavy load of anxiety. I did not like your enterprise. * * *. As to papers, I will shew you that I can keep them safe till we meet. What think you of the Turks and Russians? Romanzow is a great man. He wrote an account of his amazing success to Mouskin Pouskin here, and declared his intention of retiring as soon as he had conducted the army home; desiring that Pouskin would send him the best plan he could procure of an English gentleman's farm. In his answer, Pouskin promised to get it; but added, that at the same time he should send the Empress *a plan of Blenheim.* A handsome compliment, I think. My Lady and Maria, as usual.

EDWARD GIBBON *Esq. to* J. HOLROYD *Esq.*

BENTINCK-STREET, Sept. 10, 1774.

SINCE Heberden is returned, I think the road lies plain before you, I mean the turnpike road; the only party which in good sense can be embraced is, without delay, to bring my Lady to Bentinck-street, where you may inhabit two or three nights, and have any advice (Turton, Heberden, &c.) which the town may afford, in a case that most assuredly ought not to be trifled with. Do this as you value our good opinion. The Cantabs are strongly in the same sentiments. There can be no apprehensions of late hours, &c. as none of Mrs. H.'s raking acquaintance are in town. * * *. You give me no account of the works. When do you inhabit the library? *Turn over—great things await you.*

It is surely infinite condescension for a senator to bestow his attention on the affairs of a juryman. A senator? Yes, Sir, at last

———*Quod* . . . . *Divûm promittere nemo*
Auderet, volvenda dies, en attulit ultro.———

Yesterday morning, about half an hour after seven, as I was destroy-
ing an army of Barbarians, I heard a double rap at the door, and my
friend * * * was soon introduced. After some idle conversation he
told me, that if I was desirous of being in parliament, he had an
independent seat very much at my service. * * *. This is a fine
prospect opening upon me, and if next spring I should take my seat,
and publish my book, it will be a very memorable æra in my life. I am
ignorant whether my borough will be * * *. You despise boroughs,
and fly at nobler game. Adieu.

The Same to the Same.   Dec. 2, 1774.

I SEND you inclosed a dismal letter from Hugonin. Return it without delay, with observations. A manifesto has been sent to * * *,
which must, I think, produce immediate peace or war. Adieu. We
shall have a warm day on the address next Monday. A number of
young members! Whitshed, *a dry man,* assured me, that he heard
one of them ask, whether the king always sat in that chair, pointing to
the Speaker's. Adieu.

The Same to the Same.   BOODLE'S, Jan. 31, 1775.

SOMETIMES people do not write because they are too idle, and sometimes because they are too busy. The former was usually my case,
but at present it is the latter. The fate of Europe and America seems
fully sufficient to take up the time of one man ; and especially of a
man who gives up a great deal of time for the purpose of public and
private information. I think I have sucked Mauduit and Hutcheson
very dry ; and if my confidence was equal to my eloquence, and my
eloquence to my knowledge, perhaps I might make no very intolerable
speaker. At all events, I fancy I shall try to expose myself.

Semper ego auditor tantum ? nunquamne reponam ?

For my own part, I am more and more convinced that we have both
the right and the power on our side, and that, though the effort may be
accompanied with some melancholy circumstances, we are now arrived
at the decisive moment of preserving, or of losing for ever, both our
trade and empire. We expect next Thursday or Friday to be a very great
day. Hitherto we have been chiefly employed in reading papers, and
rejecting petitions. Petitions were brought from London, Bristol, Nor-
wich, &c. framed by party, and designed to delay. By the aid of some
parliamentary quirks, they have been all referred to a separate inactive
committee, which Burke calls a committee of oblivion, and are now
considered as dead in law. I could write you fifty little House of
Commons stories, but from their number and nature they suit better a
conference than a letter. Our general divisions are about two hundred
and fifty to eighty or ninety. Adieu.

EDWARD GIBBON, *Esq. to Mrs.* GIBBON, Bath.

DEAR MADAM,   LONDON, Jan. 31, 1775.

AN idle man has no time, and a busy man very little. As yet the House of Commons turns out very well to me, and though it should never prove of any real benefit to me, I find it at least a very agreeable coffee-house. We are plunging every day deeper and deeper into the great business of America ; and I have hitherto been a zealous, though silent, friend to the cause of government, which, *in this instance*, I think the cause of England. I passed about ten days, as I designed, at Uppark. I found Lord * * * and fourscore foxhounds.

The troubles of Beriton are perfectly composed, and the insurgents reduced to a state, though not a temper of submission. You may suppose I heard a great dead of Petersfield. L * * * means to convict your friend of bribery, to transport him for using a second time old stamps, and to prove that Petersfield is still a part of the manor of Beriton. I remain an impartial spectator. I am, dear Madam, most truly yours.

EDWARD GIBBON, *Esq. to* J. B. HOLROYD, *Esq.*

February 8, 1775.

I AM not d——d according to your charitable wishes, because I have not acted ; there was such an inundation of speakers, young speakers in every sense of the word, both on Thursday in the grand committee, and Monday on the report to the House, that neither Lord George Germaine nor myself could find room for a single word. The principal men both days were Fox and Wedderburne, on the opposite sides ; the latter displayed his usual talents ; the former, taking the vast compass of the question before us, discovered powers for regular debate, which neither his friends hoped, nor his enemies dreaded. We voted an address, (three hundred and four to one hundred and five,) of lives and fortunes, declaring Massachussets Bay in a state of rebellion. More troops, but I fear not enough, go to America, to make an army of ten thousand men at Boston ; three generals, Howe, Burgoyne, and Clinton. In a few days we stop the ports of New England. I cannot write volumes ; but I am more and more convinced, that with firmness all may go well ; yet I sometimes doubt. I am now writing with ladies, (Sir S. Porten and his bride,) and two card-tables, in the library. As to my silence, judge of my situation by last Monday. I am on the Grenvillian committee of Downton. We always sit from ten to three and a half ; after which, that day, I went into the House, and sat till three in the morning. Adieu.

The Same to the Same.   Feb. 25, 1775.

WE go on with regard to America, if we can be said to go on ; for on last Monday a conciliatory motion of allowing the Colonies to tax themselves, was introduced by Lord North, in the midst of lives and fortunes, war and famine. We went into the House in confusion, every moment expecting that the Bedfords would fly into rebellion against those measures. Lord North rose six times to appease the storm, but all in vain; till at length Sir Gilbert declared for administration, and the troops all rallied under their proper standard. On Wednesday we had the Middlesex election. I was a patriot; sat by the Lord Mayor, who spoke well, and with temper, but before the end of the debate fell fast asleep. I am still a mute; it is more tremendous than I imagined; the great speakers fill me with despair, the bad ones with terror.

When do you move? My lady answered like a woman of sense, spirit, and good nature. Neither she nor I could bear it. She was right, and the Duchess of Braganza would have made the same answer.

Adieu.

EDWARD GIBBON *Esq. to Mrs.* GIBBON.

DEAR MADAM, March 30, 1775.

I HARDLY know how to take up the pen. I talked in my last of two or three posts, and I am almost ashamed to calculate how many have elapsed. I will endeavour for the future to be less scandalous. Only believe that my heart is innocent of the laziness of my hand. I do not mean to have recourse to the stale and absurd excuse of business, though I have really had a very considerable hurry of new parliamentary business : one day, for instance, of seventeen hours, from ten in the morning till between three and four the next morning. It is, upon the whole, an agreeable improvement in my life, and forms just the mixture of business, of study, and of society, which I always imagined I should, and now find I do like. Whether the House of Commons may ever prove of benefit to myself or country, is another question. As yet I have been mute. In the course of our American affairs, I have sometimes had a wish to speak, but though I felt tolerably prepared as to the matter, I dreaded exposing myself in the manner, and remained in my seat safe, but inglorious. Upon the whole, (though I still believe I shall try,) I doubt whether Nature, not that in some instances I am ungrateful, has given me the talents of an orator, and I feel that I came into parliament much too late to exert them. Do you hear of Port Eliot coming to Bath? and, above all, do you hear of Charles-street* coming to Bentinck-street, in its way to Essex, &c.

Adieu. Dear Madam,
I am most truly yours.

EDWARD GIBBON *Esq. to Mrs.* GIBBON.

DEAR MADAM, HOUSE OF COMMONS, May 2, 1775

I ACCEPT of the Pomeranian Lady with gratitude and pleasure, and shall be impatient to form an acquaintance with her. My presentations at St. James's passed graciously. My dinner at Twickenham was attended with less ceremony and more amusement. If they turned out Lord North to-morrow, they would still leave him one of the best companions in the kingdom. By this time I suppose the Eliots are with you. I am sure you will say every thing kind and proper on the

* Mrs. Gibbon's residence at Bath.

occasion. I am glad to hear of the approbation of my constituents for my vote on the Middlesex election. On the subject of America, I have been something more of a courtier. You know, I suppose, that Holroyd is just stepped over to Ireland for a fortnight. He passed three days with me on his way. Deyverdun had left me just before your letter arrived, which I shall soon have an opportunity of conveying to him. Though, I flatter myself, he broke from me with some degree of uneasiness, the engagement could not be declined. At the end of four years he has an annuity of one hundred pounds for life, and may for the remainder of his days enjoy a decent independence in that country, which a philosopher would perhaps prefer to the rest of Europe. For my own part, after the hurry of the town and of parliament, I am now retired to my villa in Bentinck-street, which I begin to find a very pleasing solitude, at least as well as if it were two hundred miles from London ; because when I am tired of the Roman Empire, I can laugh away the evening at Foote's theatre, which I could not do in Hampshire or Cornwall. I am, dear Madam, most truly yours.

EDWARD GIBBON, *Esq. to* J. B. HOLROYD, *Esq.*

BENTINCK-STREET, August 1, 1775.
YOUR apprehensions of a precipitate work, &c. are perfectly groundless. I should be much more addicted to a contrary extreme. The *head* is now printing : true, but it was written last year and the year before. The first chapter has been composed *de nouveau three times ;* the second *twice,* and all the others have undergone reviews, corrections, &c. As to the tail, it is perfectly formed and digested, (and were I so much given to self-content and haste,) it is almost all written. The ecclesiastical part, for instance, is written out in fourteen sheets, which I mean to *refondre* from beginning to end. As to the friendly critic, it is very difficult to find one who has leisure, candour, freedom, and knowledge sufficient. However, Batt and Deyverdun have read and observed. After all, the public is the best critic. I print no more than five hundred copies of the first edition ; and the second (as it happens frequently to my betters) may receive many improvements. So much for Rome. We have nothing new from America. But I can venture to assure you, that administration is now as unanimous and decided as the occasion requires. Something will be done this year ; but in the Spring the force of the country will be exerted to the utmost. Scotch Highlanders, Irish Papists, Hanoverians, Canadians, Indians, &c. will all in various shapes be employed. Parliament meets the first week in November. I think his Catholic Majesty may be satisfied with his Summer's amusement. The Spaniards fought with great bravery, and made a fine retreat ; but our Algerine friends surpassed them as much in conduct as in number. Adieu.
The Duchess has stopped Foote's piece. She sent for him to Kingston-house, and threatened, bribed, argued, and wept for about two hours. He assured her, that if the Chamberlain was obstinate, he should publish it, with a dedication to her Grace.

EDWARD GIBBON, *Esq. to Mrs.* GIBBON, Bath.

DEAR MADAM, LONDON, August, 1775.

WILL you accept my present literary business as an excuse for my not writing? I think you will be in the wrong if you do, since I was just as idle before. At all events, however, it is better to say three words, than to be totally a dumb dog. *A propos* of dog, but not of dumb: your Pomeranian is the comfort of my life ; pretty, impertinent, fantastical, all that a young lady of fashion ought to be. I flatter myself that our passion is reciprocal. I am just at present engaged in a great historical work ; no less than a History of the Decline and Fall of the Roman Empire ; with the first volume of which I may very possibly oppress the public next winter. It would require some pages to give a more particular idea of it ; but I shall only say in general, that the subject is curious, and never yet treated as it deserves ; and that during some years it has been in my thoughts, and even under my pen. Should the attempt fail, it must be by the fault of the execution.

Adieu. Dear Madam, believe me most truly yours.

EDWARD GIBBON, *Esq. to* J. B. HOLROYD, *Esq.*

BENTINCK-STREET, October 14, 1775.

I SEND you two pieces of intelligence from the best authority, and which, unless you hear them from some other quarter, I do not wish you should talk much about. 1st, When the Russians arrive, (if they refresh themselves in England or Ireland,) will you go and see their camp? We have great hopes of getting a body of these Barbarians. In consequence of some very plain advances, King George, with his own hand, wrote a very polite epistle to sister Kitty, requesting her friendly assistance. Full powers and instructions were sent at the same time to Gunning, to agree for any force between five, and twenty thousand men, *carte blanche* for the terms ; on condition, however, that they should serve, not as auxiliaries, but as mercenaries, and that the Russian general should be absolutely under the command of the British. They daily and hourly expect a messenger, and hope to hear that the business is concluded. The worst of it is, that the Baltic will soon be frozen up, and that it must be late next year before they can get to America. 2. In the mean time we are not quite easy about Canada ; and even if it should be safe from an attack, we cannot flatter ourselves with the expectation of bringing down that martial people on the Back Settlements. The priests are ours ; the gentlemen very prudently wait the event, and are disposed to join the stronger party ; but the same lawless spirit and impatience of government which have infected our Colonies, are gone forth among the Canadian peasants, over whom, since the conquest, the noblesse have lost much of their ancient influence. Another thing which will please and surprise, is the assurance which I received from a man who might tell me a lie, but who could not be mistaken, that no arts, no management whatsoever, have been used to procure the addresses which fill the Gazette, and that Lord North was as much surprised at the first that came up, as we could be at Sheffield. We shall have, I suppose, some brisk skirmishing in parliament, but the business will soon be decided by our superior weight of fire. *A pròpos,* I believe there has been some vague but serious conversation about *calling out the militia.* The new levies go on very slowly in Ireland. The Dissenters, both there and here, are violent and active. Adieu. I embrace my Lady and Maria.

GEORGE LEWIS SCOTT, *Esq. to* EDWARD GIBBON, *Esq.*

DEAR SIR,   December 29, 1775.

1 AM obliged to you for the liberty of perusing part of your work. What I have read has given me a great deal of pleasure. I have found but few slips of the press, or the pen.

The style of the work is clear, and every way agreeable ; and I dare say you will be thought to have written with all due moderation and decency with respect to received (at least once received) opinions. The notes and quotations will add not a little to the value of the work. The authority of French writers, so familiar to you, has not infected you, however, with the fault of superficial and careless quotations. I find, since I saw you, that 1 must be in the chair at the Excise Office to-morrow ; which service will confine me too much for a week, to permit me to wait upon you so soon as I could wish.

I am very truly, dear Sir,
            Your most obedient and most humble Servant.

EDWARD GIBBON, *Esq. to* J. B. HOLROYD, *Esq.*

LONDON, January 18, 1776.

How do you do ? Are you alive ? Are you buried under mountains of snow ? I write merely to triumph in the superiority of my own situation, and to rejoice in my own prudence, in not going down to Sheffield-place, as I seriously, but foolishly, intended to do last week. We proceed triumphantly with the Roman Empire, and shall certainly make our appearance before the end of next month. I have nothing public. You know we have got eighteen thousand Germans from Hesse, Brunswick, and Hesse Darmstadt. I think our meeting will be lively ; a spirited minority, and a desponding majority. The higher people are placed, the more gloomy are their countenances, the more melancholy their language. You may call this cowardice, but I fear it arises from their knowledge (a late knowledge) of the difficulty and magnitude of the business. Quebec is not *yet* taken. I hear that Carleton is determined never to capitulate with rebels. A glorious resolution, if it were supported with fifty thousand men ! Adieu. I embrace my Lady and Maria. Make my excuses to the latter, for having neglected her birthday.

EDWARD GIBBON, *Esq. to* J. B. HOLROYD, *Esq.*

January 29, 1776.

HARES, &c. arrived safe ; were received with thanks, and devoured with appetite. Send more *(id est)* of hares. I believe, in my last I forgot saying anything of the son of Fergus ; his letters reached him. What think you of the season ? Siberia, is it not ? A pleasant campaign in America. I read and pondered your last, and think that, in the place of Lord G. G. you might perhaps succeed ; but I much fear that our Leaders have not a genius which can act at the distance of three thousand miles. You know that a large draught of guards are just going to America; poor dear creatures ! We are met ; but no business. Next week may be busy; Scotch militia, &c. Roman Empire (first part) will be finished in a week, or fortnight. At last, I have heard Texier ; wonderful ! Embrace my Lady. The weather too cold to turn over the page. Adieu.

Since this, I received your last, and honour your care of the old women ; a respectable name, which, in spite of my Lady, may suit Judges, Bishops, Generals, &c. I am rejoiced to hear of Maria's inoculation. I know not when you have done so wise a thing. You may depend upon getting an excellent house. Adieu.

EDWARD GIBBON, *Esq. to* J. B. HOLROYD, *Esq.*

BENTINCK-STREET, Feb. 9, 1776.
YOU are mistaken about your dates. It is to-morrow *seven-night,* the seventeenth, that my book will decline into the world.

I am glad to find, that by degrees you begin to understand the advantage of a civilized city. Adieu. No public business ; parliament has sat every day, but we have not had a single debate. I think you will have *the book* on Monday. The parent is not forgot, though I had not a single one to spare.

Extract of a Letter from DR. ROBERTSON *to Mr.* STRAHAN, *dated*
Edinburgh College, March 15, 1776.

* * * SINCE my last I have read Mr. Gibbon's History with much attention, and great pleasure. It is a work of very high merit indeed. He possesses that industry of research, without which no man deserves the name of an Historian. His narrative is perspicuous and interesting ; his style is elegant and forcible, though in some passages I think rather too laboured, and in others too quaint. But these defects are amply compensated by the beauty of the general flow of language, and a very peculiar happiness in many of his expressions. I have traced him in many of his quotations, (for experience has taught me to suspect the accuracy of my brother pen-men,) and I find he refers to no passage but what he has seen with his own eyes. I hope the book will be as successful as it deserves to be. I have not yet read the two last chapters, but am sorry, from what I have heard of them, that he has taken such a tone in them as will give great offence, and hurt the sale of the book.

Mr. FERGUSON *to Mr.* GIBBON.

DEAR SIR, EDINBURGH, March 19, 1776.
I RECEIVED, about eight days ago, after I had been reading your History, the copy which you have been so good as to send me, and for

which I now trouble you with my thanks. But even if I had not been thus called upon to offer you my respects, I could not have refrained from congratulating you on the merit, and undoubted success, of this valuable performance. The persons of this place whose judgment you will value most, agree in opinion, that you have made a great addition to the classical literature of England, and given us what Thucydides proposed leaving with his own countrymen, a *possession in perpetuity*. Men of a certain modesty and merit always exceed the expectations of their friends ; and it is with very great pleasure I tell you, that although you must have observed in me every mark of consideration and regard, that this is, nevertheless, the case, I receive your instruction and study your model with great deference, and join with every one else in applauding the extent of your plan, in hands so well able to execute it. Some of your readers, I find, were impatient to get at the fifteenth chapter, and began at that place. I have not heard much of their criticism, but am told that many doubt of your orthodoxy. I wish to be always of the charitable side, while I own you have proved that the clearest stream may become foul when it comes to run over the muddy bottom of human nature. I have not stayed to make any particular remarks. If any should occur on the second reading, I shall not fail to lay in my claim to a more needed, and more useful admonition from you, in case I ever produce anything that merits your attention. And am, with the greatest respect, dear Sir,

Your most obliged, and most humble Servant,
ADAM FERGUSON.

Extract of a Letter from Mr. DAVID HUME *to Mr.* STRAHAN, *dated*
Edinburgh, April 8, 1776.

* * * I AM very much taken with Mr. Gibbon's Roman History, which came from your press, and am glad to hear of its success. There will no books of reputation now be printed in London but through your hands and Mr. Cadell's. The Author tells me that he is already preparing a second edition. I resolved to have given him my advice with regard to the manner of printing it ; but as I am now writing to you, it is the same thing. He ought certainly to print the number of the chapter at the head of the margin ; and it would be better if something of the contents could also be added. One is also plagued with his notes, according to the present method of printing the book : when a note is announced, you turn to the end of the volume ; and there you often find nothing but a reference to an authority. All these authorities ought only to be printed at the margin, or the bottom of the page. I desire a copy of my new edition should be sent to Mr. Gibbon ; as wishing that gentleman, whom I so highly value, should peruse me in a form the least imperfect to which I can bring my work.

* * * Dr. Smith's performance is another excellent work that has come from your press this winter ; but I have ventured to tell him, that it requires too much thought to be as popular as Mr. Gibbon's.

Mr. FERGUSON *to Mr.* GIBBON.

DEAR SIR,   EDINBURGH, April 18, 1776.

I SHOULD make some apology for not writing you sooner an answer to your obliging letter : but if you should honour me frequently with such requests, you will find, that, with very good intentions, I am a very dilatory and irregular correspondent. I am sorry to tell you, that our respectable friend (Mr. Hume) is still declining in his health : he is greatly emaciated, and loses strength. He talks familiarly of his near prospect of dying. His mother, it seems, died under the same symptoms ; and it appears so little necessary, or proper, to flatter him, that no one attempts it. I never observed his understanding more clear, or his humour more pleasant and lively. He has a great aversion to leave the tranquillity of his own house, to go in search of health among inns and hostlers. And his friends here gave way to him for some time ; but now think it necessary that he should make an effort to try what change of place and air, or anything else Sir John Pringle may advise, can do for him. I left him this morning in the mind to comply in this article, and I hope that he will be prevailed on to set out in a few days. He is just now sixty-five.

I am very glad that the pleasure you give us recoils a little on yourself, through our feeble testimony. I have, as you suppose, been employed at any intervals of leisure or rest I have had for some years, in taking notes, or collecting materials for a History of the distractions that broke down the Roman Republic, and ended in the establishment of Augustus and his immediate successors. The compliment you are pleased to pay, I cannot accept of, even to my subject. Your subject now appears with advantages it was not supposed to have had ; and I suspect that the magnificence of the mouldering ruin will appear more striking, than the same building, when the view is perplexed with scaffolding, workmen, and disorderly lodgers, and the ear is stunned with the noise of destructions and repairs, and the alarms of fire. The night which you begin to describe is solemn, and there are gleams of light superior to what is to be found in any other time. I comfort myself, that as my trade is the study of human nature, I could not fix on a more interesting corner of it, than the end of the Roman Republic. Whether my compilations should ever deserve the attention of any one besides myself, must remain to be determined after they are farther advanced. I take the liberty to trouble you with the enclosed for Mr. Smith, whose uncertain stay in London makes me at a loss how to direct for him. You have both such reason to be pleased with the world just now, that I hope you are pleased with each other.

I am, with the greatest respect, Sir,

ADAM FERGUSON.

EDWARD GIBBON, *Esq. to* J. B. HOLROYD, *Esq.*

LONDON, May 20, 1776.

I AM angry that you should impede my noble designs of visiting foreign parts, more especially as I have an advantage which Sir Wilful had not, that of understanding your foreign lingos. With regard to

Mrs. Gibbon, her intended visit, to which I was not totally a stranger, will do me honour ; and, though it should delay my emigration till the end of July, there will still remain the months of August, September, and October. Above all, abstain from giving the least hint to any Bath correspondent, and perhaps, if I am not provoked by opposition, the thing may not be absolutely certain. At all events, you may depend on a previous visit. At present, I am very busy with the Neckers.· I live with her, just as I used to do twenty years ago, laugh at her Paris varnish, and oblige her to become a simple reasonable Suissesse. The man who might read English husbands' lessons of proper and dutiful behaviour, is a sensible good-natured creature. In about a fortnight I launch again into the world in the shape of a quarto volume. Cadell assures me, that he never remembered so eager and impatient a demand for a second edition. The town is beginning to break up ; the day after to-morrow we have our last day in the House of Commons, to inquire into the instructions of the commissioners. I like the man, and the motion appears plain. Adieu. I dined with Lord Palmerstone to-day; great dinner of catches. I embrace my Lady and the Maria.

EDWARD GIBBON, *Esq. to* J. B. HOLROYD, *Esq.*

To tell you anything of the change, or rather changes, of governors, I must have known something of them myself; but all is darkness, confusion, and uncertainty to such a degree, that people do not even know what lies to invent. The news from America have indeed diverted the public attention into another, and far greater, channel. All that you see in the papers, of the repulse at Quebec, as well as the capture of Lee, rests on the authority (a very unexceptionable one) of the provincial papers, as they have been transmitted by Governor Tryon from New York. Howe is well, and eats plentifully ; and the weather seems to clear up so fast, that, according to the English custom, we have passed from the lowest despondency to a full assurance of success. My new birth happened last Monday ; seven hundred of the fifteen hundred were gone yesterday. I now understand, from pretty good authority, that Dr. * * *, the friend and chaplain of * * *, is actually sharpening his goose quill against the two last chapters. Adieu.

June 6, 1776, from Almack's, where I was chosen last week.

The Same to the Same. Almack's, June 24, 1776.

YES, yes, I am alive, and well ; but what shall I say ? Town grows empty, and this house, where I have passed very agreeable hours, is the only place which still unites the flower of the English youth. The style of living, though *somewhat* expensive, is exceedingly pleasant, and, notwithstanding the rage of play, I have found more entertaining, and even rational society here, than in any other club to which I belong. Mrs. Gibbon still hangs in suspense, and seems to consider a town expedition with horror. I think,·however, that she will be soon in motion ; and when I have her in Bentinck-street, we shall perhaps talk of a Sheffield excursion. I am now deeply engaged in the reign of Constantine, and, from the specimens which I have already seen, I can venture to promise, that the second volume will not be less interesting than the first. The fifteen hundred copies are moving off with decent speed, and the obliging Cadell begins to mutter something of a third edition for next year. No news of Deyverdun, or his French translation. What a lazy dog! Madame Necker has been gone a great while. I gave her, *en partant*, the most solemn assurances of following her *paws* in less than two months ; but the voice of indolence begins to whisper a thousand difficulties, and unless your absurd policy should thoroughly provoke me, the Parisian journey may possibly be deferred. I rejoice in the progress of * * * towards light. We are in expectation of American news. Carleton is made a Knight of the Bath. The old report of Washington's resignation, and quarrel with the Congress, seems to revive. Adieu.

Extract of a Letter from Dr. GEORGE CAMPBELL, *Professor at* Aberdeen, *to Mr.* STRAHAN, *dated* Aberdeen, June 25, 1776.

I HAVE lately read over one of your last winter's publications with very great pleasure, and I hope some instruction. My expectations were indeed high when I began it ; but, I assure you, the entertainment I received greatly exceeded them. What made me fall to it with the greater avidity was, that it had in part a pretty close connection with a subject I had occasion to treat sometimes in my Theological Lectures ; to wit, the Rise and Progress of the Hierarchy ; and you will believe that I was not the less pleased to discover, in an historian of so much learning and penetration, so great a coincidence with my own sentiments, in relation to some obscure points in the Christian antiquities. I suppose I need not now inform you, that the book I mean is Gibbon's History of the Fall of the Roman Empire ; which, in respect of the style and manner, as well as the matter, is a most masterly performance.

EDWARD GIBBON, *Esq. to* J. B. HOLROYD, *Esq.*

Saturday, August, 1776.

WE expect you at five o'clock Tuesday, without a sore throat. You have ere this heard of the shocking accident which takes up the attention of the town. Our old acquaintance * * *. By his own indolence, rather than extravagance, his circumstances were embarrassed, and he had frequently declared himself tired of life. No public news, nor any material expected, till the end of this, or the beginning of next month, when Howe will probably have collected his whole force. A tough business indeed. You see by their declaration, that they have now passed the Rubicon, and rendered the work of a treaty infinitely more difficult. You will perhaps say, so much the better ; but I do assure you, that the *thinking* friends of Government are by no means sanguine. I take the opportunity of eating turtle with Garrick at Hampton. Adieu.

EDWARD GIBBON *Esq. to* J. B. HOLROYD *Esq.*

Saturday, ¼ past Eleven. 1776.

FOR the present I am so deeply engaged, that you must renounce the hasty apparition at Sheffield-place ; but if you should be very impatient, I will try (after the meeting) to run down, between the Friday and Monday, and bring you the last editions of things. At present *nought* but expectation. The attack on me is begun ; an anonymous eighteen-penny pamphlet, which will get the author more glory in the next world than in this. The heavy troops, Watson and another, are on their march. Adieu.

Extract of a Letter from Mr. WALLACE *to Mr.* STRAHAN, *dated* Edinburgh, August 30, 1776.

ALAS, for David Hume ! * His friends have sustained a great loss in his death. He was interred yesterday, at a place he lately pur-chased in the burying-ground on the Calton.

> " For who, to dumb forgetfulness a prey,
> This pleasing anxious being e'er resign'd,
> Left the warm precincts of the cheerful day,
> Nor cast one longing, lingering look behind ? "

A monument on that airy elevated cemetery, which, on account of a magnificent terrace, now carried round the hill, is greatly frequented, will be extremely conspicuous, and must often call his name to remem-brance. It has been remarked, that the same day on which Lucretius died, gave birth to Virgil ; and amidst their late severe loss, philosophy and literature will probably find themselves not wholly disconsolate, on reflecting that the same year in which they were deprived of Hume, Gibbon arose ; his superior in some respects. This Gentleman's His-tory of the Decline of the Roman Empire, appears to me, in point of composition, incomparably the finest production in English, without any exception. I hardly thought the language capable of arriving at his correctness, perspicuity, and strength.

EDWARD GIBBON *Esq. to* J. B. HOLROYD *Esq.*

1776.

I HOPE you bark and growl at my silence ; growl and bark. This is not a time for correspondence. Parliament, visits, dinners, suppers, and an hour or two stolen with difficulty for the Decline, leave but very little leisure. I send you the Gazette, and have scarcely any thing to add, except that about five hundred of them have deserted to us, and that the New York incendiaries were immediately, and very justifiably, destined to the cord. Lord G. G. with whom I had a long conversa-tion last night, was in high spirits, and hopes to reconquer Germany in America. On the side of Canada, he only fears Carleton's *slowness*, but entertains great expectations that the light troops and Indians, under Sir William Johnson, who are sent from Oswego down the

* Mr. Hume died at Edinburgh, August 25, 1776.

Mohawk River to Albany, will oblige the Provincials to give up the defence of the Lakes, for fear of being cut off. The report of a foreign war subsides. House of Commons dull, and opposition talk of suspending hostilities from despair.

An anonymous pamphlet and Dr. Watson out against me; (in my opinion,) the former feeble, and very illiberal ; the latter uncommonly genteel. At last I have had a letter from Deyverdun; wretched excuses ; nothing done ; vexatious enough. To-morrow I write to Suard, a very skilful translator of Paris, who was here in the spring with the Neckers, to get him (if not too late) to undertake it. Adieu.

Mr. GIBBON *to the Rev. Dr.* WATSON (*now Bishop of* Llandaff).

BENTINCK-STREET, November 2, 1776.

MR. Gibbon takes the earliest opportunity of presenting his compliments and thanks to Dr. Watson, and of expressing his sense of the liberal treatment which he has received from so candid an adversary. Mr. Gibbon entirely coincides in opinion with Dr. Watson, that as their different sentiments, on a very important period of history, are now submitted to the Public, they both may employ their time in a manner much more useful, as well as agreeable, than they could possibly do by exhibiting a single combat in the amphitheatre of controversy. Mr. Gibbon is therefore determined to resist the temptation of justifying, in a professed reply, any passages of his History, which might perhaps be easily cleared from censure and misapprehension ; but he still reserves to himself the privilege of inserting in a future edition some occasional remarks and explanations of his meaning. If any calls of pleasure or business should bring Dr. Watson to town, Mr. Gibbon would think himself happy in being permitted to solicit the honour of his acquaintance.

Dr. WATSON *to Mr.* GIBBON.

CAMBRIDGE, November 4, 1776.

DR. Watson accepts with pleasure Mr. Gibbon's polite invitation to a personal acquaintance. If he comes to town this winter, will certainly do himself the honour to wait upon him. Begs, at the same time, to assure Mr. Gibbon, that he will be very happy to have an opportunity of shewing him every civility, if curiosity, or other motives, should bring him to Cambridge. Dr. Watson can have some faint idea of Mr. Gibbon's difficulty in resisting the temptation he speaks of, from having been of late in a situation somewhat similar himself. It would be very extraordinary, if Mr. Gibbon did not feel a parent's partiality for an offspring which has justly excited the admiration of all who have seen it ; and Dr. Watson would be the last person in the world to wish him to suppress any explanation which might tend to exalt its merits.

EDWARD GIBBON *Esq. to* J. B. HOLROYD *Esq.*
ALMACK'S, November 7, 1776.

LETTERS from Burgoyne. They embarked on the Lakes the thirtieth September, with eight hundred British sailors, six thousand regulars, and a naval force superior to any possible opposition : but the season was so far advanced, that they expected only to occupy and strengthen Ticonderoga, and afterwards to return and take up their winter quarters in Canada. Yesterday we had a surprize in the House, from a proclamation of the Howes, which made its first appearance in the Morning Post, and which nobody seems to understand. By this time, my Lady may see that 1 have not much reason to fear my antagonists. Adieu, till next Thursday.

EDWARD GIBBON *Esq. to* J. B. HOLROYD *Esq.*
Friday Evening, November 22.

NEWS from the Lakes. A naval combat, in which the Provincials were repulsed with considerable loss. They burnt and abandoned Crown Point. Carleton is besieging Ticonderoga. Carleton, I say ; for he is there, and it is apprehended that Burgoyne is coming home. We dismissed the Nabobs without a division. Burke and the Attorney General spoke very well. Adieu.

The Same to the Same. BENTINCK-STREET, January 18, 1777.

As I presume, my Lady does not make a practice of tumbling down stairs every day after dinner, by this time the colours must have faded, and the high places (1 mean the temples) are reduced to a proper level. But what, in the name of the great prince, is the meaning of her declining the Urban expedition ? Is it the spontaneous result of her own proud spirit ? or does it proceed from the secret machinations of her domestic tyrant ? At all events, 1 expect you will both remember your engagement of next Saturday in Bentinck-street, with Donna Catherina, the Mountaineer *, &c. Things go on very prosperously in America. Howe is himself in the Jerseys, and will push at least as far as the Delaware River. The continental (perhaps *now* the rebel) army is in a great measure dispersed, and Washington, who wishes to cover Philadelphia, has not more than six or seven thousand men with him. Clinton designs to conquer Rhode Island in his way home. But, what *I* think of much greater consequence, a province made its submission, and desired to be reinstated in the peace of the King. It is indeed only poor little Georgia ; and the application was made to Governor Tonyn of Florida. Some disgust at a violent step of the Congress, who removed the President of their Provincial Assembly, a leading and popular man, co-operated with the fear of the Indians, who began to amuse themselves with the exercise of scalping on their Back Settlements. Town fills, and we are mighty agreeable. Last year, on the Queen's birth-day, Sir G. Warren had his diamond star cut off his coat ;

* The Honourable General Simon Fraser.

this day the same accident happened to him again, with another star worth seven hundred pounds. He had better compound by the year. Adieu.

EDWARD GIBBON, *Esq. to* J. B. HOLROYD, *Esq.*

ALMACK'S, Wednesday Evening.

IN due obedience to thy dread commands I write. But what shall I say? My life, though more lively than yours, is almost as uniform. A very little reading and writing in the morning, bones or guts * from two to four, pleasant dinners from five to eight, and afterwards clubs, with an occasional assembly, or supper. America affords nothing very satisfactory; though we have many flying reports, you may be assured that we are ignorant of the consequences of Trenton, &c. Charles Fox is now at my elbow, declaiming on the impossibility of keeping America, since a victorious army has been unable to maintain any extent of posts in the single province of Jersey. Lord North is out of danger (we trembled for his important existence). I now expect that my Lady and you should fix the time for the promised visitation to Bentinck-street. March and April are open, chuse. Adieu.

The Same to the Same.   1777.

YOU deserve, and we exult in your weather and disappointments. Why would you bury yourself? I dined in Downing-street Thursday last; and I think Wedderburne was at least as agreeable a companion as your timber-surveyor could be. Lee is certainly taken, but Lord North does not apprehend he is coming home. We are not clear whether he behaved with courage or pusillanimity when he surrendered himself; but Colonel Keene told me to-day, that he had seen a letter from Lee since his confinement. " He imputes his being taken, to the alertness of Harcourt, and cowardice of his own guard; hopes he shall meet his fate with fortitude; but laments that freedom is not likely to find a resting-place in any part of the globe." It is said, he was to succeed Washington. We know nothing certain of the Hessians; but there *has* been a blow. Adieu.

The Same to the Same.   Saturday Night, April 12, 1777.

YOUR dispatch is gone to * * *, and I flatter myself that by your assistance I shall be enabled to lose a thousand a year upon Lenborough before I return from Paris. The day of my departure is not absolutely fixed; Sunday seven-night, the twenty-seventh instant, is talked of: But if any India business should come on after the Civil List, it will occasion some delay, otherwise things are in great forward-ness. Mrs. Gibbon is an enemy to the whole plan; and I must

* Mr. Gibbon at this time attended Dr. Hunter's Anatomical Lectures.

answer, in a long letter, two very ingenious objections which she has started. 1st, That I shall be confined, or put to death by the priests; and, 2dly, That I shall sully my *moral* character, by making love to Necker's wife. Before I go, I will consult Newton, about a power of attorney for you. By the bye, I wish you would remember a sort of promise, and give me one day before I go. We talk chiefly of the Marquis de la Fayette, who was here a few weeks ago. He is about twenty, with an hundred and thirty thousand livres a year; the nephew of Noailles, who is ambassador here. He has bought the Duke of Kingston's yacht, and is gone to join the Americans. The Court *appear* to be angry with him. Adieu.

EDWARD GIBBON, *Esq. to* J. B. HOLROYD, *Esq.*
ATWOOD'S, Saturday Night, April 19, 1777.

IT is not possible as yet to fix the day of my departure. That circumstance depends on the state of India, and will not be determined till the General Court of next Wednesday. I know from the *first* authority, if the violence of the Proprietors about the Pigot, can be checked in the India-house by the influence of a Government majority, the Minister does not wish to exert the omnipotence of Parliament; and I shall be dismissed from hence time enough to set forwards on Thursday the first of May. On the contrary, should we be involved in those perplexing affairs, they may easily detain me till the middle of next month. But as all this is very uncertain, I direct you and my Lady to appear in town to-morrow seven-night. I have many things to say. We have been animated this week, and, notwithstanding the strict œconomy recommended by Charles Fox and John Wilkes, we have paid the Royal debts. Adieu.

The Same to the Same. Monday Night, April 21, 1777.

BAD news from Hampshire.———Support Hugonin, comfort me; correct or expel * * * sell Lenborough, and remove my temporal cares. When do you arrive?

The Same to the Same. Wednesday Night, April 23, 1777.

IT is uncertain whether India comes to Westminster this year, and it is certain that Gibbon goes to Paris next Saturday seven-night. Therefore Holroyd must appear in town the beginning of next week. Gibbon wants the cordial of his presence before the journey. My Lady *must* come.

The Same to the Same. DOVER, Tues. Even, May 6, 1777.

MY expedition does not begin very auspiciously. The wind, which for some days had been fair, paid me the compliment of changing on my arrival; and, though I immediately secured a vessel, it has been impossible to make the least use of it during the whole of this tedious day. It seems doubtful, whether I shall get out to-morrow morning; and the Captain assures me, that the passage will have the double advantage of being both cold and rough. Last night a small privateer, fitted out at Dunkirk, with a commission from Dr. Franklin, attacked, took, and has carried into Dunkirk Road, the Harwich Packet. The King's messenger had just time to throw his dispatches over-board. He passed through this town about four o'clock this afternoon, in his return to London. As the alarm is now given, our American friend will probably remain quiet, or will be soon caught ; so that I have not *much* apprehension for my personal safety; but if so daring an outrage is not followed by punishment and restitution, it may become a very serious business, and may possibly shorten my stay at Paris.

Adieu. I shall write by the first opportunity, either from Calais or Philadelphia.

Mr. Gibbon *to Mr.* Holroyd.

CALAIS, Wednesday, May 7, 1777.

Post nubila Phœbus. A pleasant passage, an excellent house, a good dinner, with Lord * * *, whom I found here. Easy Custom-house officers, fine weather, &c. I am detained to-night by the temptation of a French comedy, in a theatre at the end of Dessein's garden ; but shall be in motion to-morrow early, and hope to dine at Paris Saturday. Adieu. I think I am a punctual correspondent ; but this beginning is too good to last.

Dr. William Robertson *to Mr.* Gibbon.

SIR, COLLEGE of EDINBURGH, June 5, 1777.

I have desired Mr. Strahan to take the liberty of sending you, in my name, a copy of the History of America, which I hope you will do me the honour of accepting, as a testimony, not only of my respect, but of my gratitude, for the instruction which I have received from your writings, as well as the credit you have done me, by the most obliging manner in which you have mentioned my name. I wish the present work may not diminish sentiments so flattering to me. I have taken much pains to obtain the approbation of those whose good opinion one ought to be solicitous to secure, and I trust that my industry at least will be applauded.

An unlucky indisposition prevented me from executing a scheme which I had formed, of passing two months of last spring in London. The honour of being made known to you, was one of the pleasures with which I had flattered myself. But I hope to be more fortunate next year ; and beg that you will believe that I am, with great respect, Sir, your most obedient, and most humble servant.

Mr. GIBBON *to Dr.* ROBERTSON.

SIR, PARIS, 1777.

WHEN I ventured to assume the character of Historian, the first, the most natural, but at the same time the most ambitious, wish which I entertained, was to obtain the approbation of Dr. Robertson and of Mr. Hume; two names which friendship united, and which posterity will never separate. I shall not therefore attempt to dissemble, though I cannot easily express, the pleasure which I received from your obliging letter, as well as from the intelligence of your most valuable present. The satisfaction which I should otherwise have enjoyed, in common with the public, will now be heightened by a sentiment of a more personal and flattering nature; and I shall frequently whisper to myself, that I have in some measure deserved the esteem of the writer whom I admire.

A short excursion which I have made to this place, during the summer months, has occasioned some delay in my receiving your letter, and will prevent my possessing, till my return, the copy of your History, which you so politely desired Mr. Strahan to send me. But I have already gratified the eagerness of my impatience; and although I was obliged to return the book much sooner than I could have wished, I have seen enough to convince me, that the present publication will support, and if possible, will extend the fame of the Author; that the materials are collected with diligence, and arranged with skill; that the first book contains a learned and satisfactory account of the progress of discovery; that the achievements, the dangers, and the crimes, of the Spanish adventurers are related with a temperate spirit; and that the most original, perhaps the most curious, portion of the history of human manners is at length rescued from the hands of sophists and declaimers. Lord Stormont, and the few in this Capital, who have had an opportunity of perusing the History of America, unanimously concur in the same sentiments. Your work is already become a favourite topic of public conversation; and Mr. Suard is repeatedly pressed, in my hearing, to fix the time when his translation will appear.

I flatter myself you will not abandon your design of visiting London next winter; as I already anticipate, in my own mind, the advantages which I shall derive from so pleasing and so honourable a connection. In the mean while, I should esteem myself happy, if you could think of any literary commission, in the execution of which I might be useful to you at Paris, where I propose to stay till very near the meeting of Parliament. Let me, for instance, suggest an enquiry, which cannot be indifferent to you, and which might perhaps be within my reach. A few days ago I dined with Bagniousky, the famous adventurer, who escaped from his exile at Kamschatska, and returned into Europe by Japan and China. His narrative was amusing, though I know not how far his veracity, in point of circumstances, may safely be trusted. It was his original design to penetrate through the North East Passage; and he actually followed the coast of Asia as high as the latitude of $67^\circ 35'$, till his progress was stopped by the ice, in a Straight between the two Continents, which was only seven leagues broad. Thence he descended along the coast of America, as low as Cape Mendocin; but was repulsed by contrary winds, in his attempts to reach the port of Acapulco. The Journal of his Voyage, with his original Charts, is now at Versailles, in the *Depôt des Affaires Etrangers;* and if you conceived that it would be of any use to you for a second edition, I would try what might be obtained ; though I am not ignorant of that mean jealousy which you yourself have experienced, and so deservedly stigmatised. I am, &c.

Dr. ROBERTSON *to Mr.* GIBBON.

SIR,

I HAD the honour of your obliging Letter, and I should be a very proud man indeed, if I were not vain of the approbation which you are pleased to bestow upon me. As you will now have had an opportunity to peruse the book, which you had only seen when you wrote to me, I indulge myself in the hopes, that the favourable opinion you had formed of it, is not diminished. I am much pleased with your mentioning my friendship with Mr. Hume ; I have always considered that as one of the most fortunate and honourable circumstances of my life. It is a felicity of the age and country in which we live, that men of letters can enter the same walk of science, and go on successfully, without feeling one sentiment of envy or rivalship. In the intercourse betwᵃᵃn Mr. Hume and me, we always found *something to blame,* as well as *something to commend.* I have received frequently very valuable criticisms on my performances from him ; and I have sometimes ventured to offer him my strictures on his works. Permit me to hope for the same indulgence from you. If in reading the History of America, any thing, either in the matter or style, has occurred to you as reprehensible, I will deem it a most obliging favour if you will communicate it freely to me. I am certain of profiting by such a communication.

I return you thanks for your frank offer of executing any literary commission for me. I accept of it without ceremony, and am flattered with the idea of receiving such aid from your hands. I know nothing of Bagniouski's Adventures, but what was published in some Newspaper. If one can rely on his veracity, what he relates must be very interesting to me. If you had heen writing the History of America, the question concerning the mode of peopling it, might not perhaps have occupied your attention very much. But it was proper for me to consider it more fully. Bagniouski (if he may be credited) has seen what it may be useful for me to know. I can see no reason why the Court of France should be shy about communicating his Journal, and the Charts which illustrate it ; possibly my name may operate somewhat towards obtaining a copy of both ; your interposition, I am confident, will do a great deal. It will be very illiberal indeed, if such a communication were refused. My Lord Stormont (by whose attention I have been much honoured) would not decline to give his aid, were that necessary. But if your Court resembles that of Spain, I am afraid every proposal from an ambassador is received with some degree of jealousy. Your own private application will, I apprehend, be more effectual. As it is probable that a second edition may go to press early in the winter, it will add to the favour, if you can soon inform me concerning the success of your negociation. As this is something in the style of the *Corps Diplomatique*, allow me to recommend one of its members to you. Mr. Fullarton, the new secretary of the embassy, is a particular friend of mine. He is a young man of such qualities both of head and heart, that I am sure you will esteem and love him. Please remember me to him. I have the houour to be, with great respect,

Your obliged humble servant,
WILLIAM ROBERTSON.

EDWARD GIBBON, *Esq. to* J. B. HOLROYD, *Esq.*

PARIS, June 16, 1777.

I TOLD you what would infallibly happen, and you know enough of the nature of the beast not to be surprised at it. I have now been at Paris exactly five weeks ; during which time I have not written to any person whatsoever within the British dominions, except two lines of notification to Mrs. Gibbon. The dæmon of procrastination has at length yielded to the genius of friendship, assisted indeed by the powers of fear and shame. But when I have seated myself before a table, and begin to revolve all that I have seen and tasted during this busy period, I feel myself oppressed and confounded ; and I am very near throwing away the pen, and resigning myself to indolent despair. A complete history would require a volume, at least, as corpulent as the Decline and Fall ; and if I attempt to select and abridge, besides the difficulty of the choice, there occur so many things which cannot properly be entrusted to paper, and so many others of too slight a tex- ture to support the journey, that I am almost tempted to reserve for our future conversations the detail of my pleasures and occupations. But as I am sensible that you are *rigid* and impatient, I will try to convey, in a few words, a general idea of my situation as a man of the world, and as a man of letters. You remember that the Neckers were my principal dependance ; and the reception which I have met with from them very far surpassed my most sanguine expectations. I do not indeed lodge in their house, (as it might incite the jealousy of the husband, and procure me a lettre de cachet,) but I live very much with them, and dine and sup whenever they have company, which is almost every day, and whenever I like it, for they are not in the least *exigeans*. Mr. Walpole gave me an introduction to Madame du Deffand, an agreeable young lady of eighty-two years of age, who has constant suppers, and the best company in Paris. When you see the Duke of Richmond, he will give you an account of that house, where I meet him almost every evening. Ask him about Madame de Cambis. I have met the Duke of Choiseul at his particular request, dined by *accident* with Franklin, conversed with the Emperor, been presented at court, and gradually, or rather rapidly, I find my acquaintance spread- ing over the most valuable parts of Paris. They pretend to like me, and whatever you may think of French professions, I am convinced that some at least are sincere. On the other hand, I feel myself easy and happy in their company, and only regret that I did not come over two or three months sooner. Though Paris throughout the summer promises me a very agreeable society, yet I am hurt every day by the departure of men and women whom I begin to know with some familiarity, the departure of officers for their governments and garrisons, of bishops for their dioceses, and even of country gentlemen for their estates, as a rural taste gains ground in this country. So much for the general idea of my acquaintance ; details would be endless, yet unsatisfactory. You may add, to the pleasures of society, those of the spectacles and promenades, and you will find that I lead a very agreeable life ; let me just condescend to observe, that it is not extravagant. After decking myself out with silks and silver, the ordinary establishment of coach, lodging, servants, eating, and pocket expences, does not exceed sixty pounds *per* month. Yet I have two footmen in handsome liveries behind my coach, and my apartment is hung with damask. Adieu for the present : I have more to say, but were I to attempt any further progress, you must wait another post ; and you have already waited long enough, of all conscience.

Let me just in two words give you an idea of my day. I am now going (nine o'clock) to the King's library, where I shall stay till twelve ; as soon as I am dressed, I set out to dine with the Duke de Nivernois ; shall go from thence to the French comedy, into the Princess de Beaveau's loge grillée, and cannot quite determine whether I shall sup at Madame du Deffand's, Madame Necker's, or the Sardinian Ambassadress's. Once more adieu.

I embrace my Lady and *Bambini*. I shall with cheerfulness execute any of her commissions.

EDWARD GIBBON *Esq. to* J. B. HOLROYD *Esq.*

Paris, August 13, 1777.

WELL, and who is the culprit now ?—Thus far had I written in the pride of my heart, and fully determined to inflict an epistle upon you, even before I received any answer to my former ; I was very near a bull. But this forward half line lay ten days barren and inactive, till its generative powers were excited by the missive which I received yesterday. What a wretched piece of work do we seem to be making of it in America ? The greatest force which any European power ever ventured to transport into that continent, is not strong enough even to attack the enemy ; the naval strength of Great Britain is not sufficient to prevent the Americans (they have almost lost the appellation of Rebels) from receiving every assistance that they wanted ; and in the mean time you are obliged to call out the militia to defend your own coasts against their privateers. You possibly may expect from me some account of the designs and policy of the French court, but I choose to decline that task for two reasons : 1st. Because you may find them laid open in every newspaper ; and 2dly, Because I live too much with their courtiers and ministers to know anything about them. I. shall only say, that I am not under any immediate apprehensions of a war with France. It is much more pleasant as well as profitable to view in safety the raging of the tempest, occasionally to pick up some pieces of the wreck, and to improve their trade, their agriculture, and their finances, while the two countries are *lento collisa duello.* Far from taking any step to put a speedy end to this astonishing dispute, I should not be surprised if next summer they were to lend their cordial assistance to England, as to the weaker party. As to my personal engagement with the D. of R. I recollect a few slight skirmishes, but nothing that deserves the name of a general engagement. The extravagance of some diputants, both French and English, who have espoused the cause of America, sometimes inspires me with an extraordinary vigour. Upon the whole, I find it much easier to defend the justice than the policy of our measures; but there are certain cases, where whatever is repugnant to sound policy ceases to be just.

The more I see of Paris, the more I like it. The regular course of the society in which I live is easy, polite, and entertaining; and almost every day is marked by the acquisition of some new acquaintance, who is worth cultivating, or who, at least, is worth remembering. To the great admiration of the French, I regularly dine and regularly sup, drink a dish of strong coffee after each meal, and find my stomach a citizen of the world. The spectacles, (particularly the Italian, and above all the French Comedies,) which are open the whole summer, afford me an agreeable relaxation from company; and to shew you that I frequent them from taste, and not from idleness, I have not yet seen the Colisee, the Vauxhall, the Boulevards, or any of those places of entertainment which constitute Paris to most of our countrymen. Occasional trips to dine or sup in some of the thousand country-houses which are scattered round the environs of Paris, serve to vary the scene. In the mean while the summer insensibly glides away, and the fatal month of October approaches, when I must change the house of Madame Necker for the House of Commons. I regret that I could not choose the winter, instead of the summer, for this excursion : I should have found many valuable persons, and should have preserved others whom I have lost as I began to know them. The Duke de Choiseul, who deserves attention both for himself, and for keeping the best house in Paris, passes seven months of the year in Touraine; and though l have been tempted, I consider with horror a journey of sixty leagues into the country. The Princess of Beauveau, who is a most superior woman, has been absent above six weeks, and does not return till the 24th of this month. A large body of recruits will be assembled by the Fontainbleau journey; but in order to have a thorough knowledge of this splendid conntry, I ought to stay till the month of January; and if I could be sure that Opposition would be as tranquil as they were last year— I think your life has been as animated, or, at least, as tumultuous, and I envy you Lady Payne, &c. much more than either the Primate, or the Chief-justice. Let not the generous breast of my Lady be torn by the black serpents of envy. She still possesses the first place in the sentiments of her slave : but the adventure of the fan was a mere accident, owing to Lord Carmarthen. Adieu. I think you may be satisfied. I say nothing of my terrestrial affairs.

EDWARD GIBBON *Esq. to* J. B. HOLROYD *Esq.*

BENTINCK-STREET, Saturday, November, 1777.
HAD you four horns as well as four eyes and four hands, I should still maintain that you are the most unreasonable monster in the creation. My pain is lively, my weakness excessive, the season cold, and only twelve days remain to the meeting. Far from thinking of trips into the country, I shall be well satisfied if I am on my legs the 20th, in the medical sense of the word. At present I am a corpse, carried about by four arms which do not belong to me. Yet I try to smile : I salute the hen and chickens. Adieu. Writing is really painful.

The Same to the Same.   Friday, November 14, 1777.
I DO not like this disorder on your eyes : and when I consider your temperance and activity, I cannot understand why any spring of the machine should ever be deranged. With regard to myself, the gout has behaved in a very honourable manner ; after a complete conquest, and after making me feel his power for some days, the generous enemy has disdained to abuse his victory, or to torment any longer an unre-sisting victim. He has already ceased to torture the lower extremities of your humble servant ; the swelling is so amazingly diminished, that they are no longer above twice their ordinary size. Yesterday I moved about the room with the laborious majesty of crutches ; to-day I have exchanged them for a stick ; and by the beginning of next week, I hope, with due precaution, to take the air, and to inure myself for the interesting representation of Thursday. How cursedly unlucky ; I wanted to see you both : a thousand things to say and to hear, and every thing of that kind broken to pieces. If you are not able to come to Bentinck-street, I must contrive to steal three or four vacant days during the session, and run down to Sheffield. The town fills, and I begin to have numerous levees, and couchees ; more properly the latter. We are still in expectation, but in the mean while we believe (I mean ministers) that the news of Howe's victory and the taking of Philadelphia are true. Adieu.

The Same to the Same.   December 2, 1777.
BY the inclosed you will see that America is not *yet* conquered. Opposition are very lively ; and, though in the House we keep our numbers, there seems to be an universal desire of peace, even on the most humble conditions. Are you still fierce?

The Same to the Same.   Monday Night, December, 1777.
I CONGRATULATE your noble firmness, as I suppose it must arise from the knowledge of some hidden resources, which will enable us to open the next campaign with new armies of fifty or sixty thousand men. But I believe you will find yourself obliged to carry on this glorious war almost alone. It would be idle to dispute any more about politics, as we shall so soon have an opportunity of a personal combat. Your journey gives me some hopes that you have not entirely lost your reason. Your bed shall be ready.

EDWARD GIBBON *Esq. to* J. B. HOLROYD *Esq.*

HOUSE OF COMMONS, Thursday, Dec. 4, 1777.

DREADFUL news indeed! You will see them partly in the papers, and we have not yet any particulars. An English army of nearly ten thousand men laid down their arms, and surrendered prisoners of war, on condition of being sent to England, and of never serving against America. They had fought bravely, and were three days without eating. Bourgoyne is said to have received three wounds. General Fraser, with two thousand men, killed. Colonel Ackland likewise killed. A general cry for peace. Adieu. We have constant late days.

The Same to the Same. February 28, 1778.

* * * As to politics, we should easily fill pages, and therefore had better be silent. You are mistaken in supposing that the bills are opposed ; some particular objections have been stated, and in the *only* division I voted with government.

The Same to the Same. February 23, 1778.

YOU do not readily believe in præternatural miscarriages of letters ; nor I neither. Listen, however, to a plain and honest narrative. This morning after breakfast, as I was ruminating on *your* silence, Thomas, my new footman, with confusion in his looks and stammering on his tongue, produced a letter reasonably soiled, which he was to have brought me the day of his arrival, and which had lain forgotten from that time in his pocket. To shorten as much as possible the continuance, 1 immediately enquired, whether any method of conveyance could be devised more expeditious than the post, and was fortunately informed of your coachman's intentions. You probably know the heads of the plan : an Act of Parliament to declare, that we never *had* any intention of taxing America : another Act, to empower the Crown to name Commissioners, authorised to suspend hostilities by sea and land, as well as all obnoxious Acts ; and, in short, to grant every thing, except independence. Opposition, after expressing their doubts whether the lance of Achilles could cure the wound which it had inflicted, could not refuse their assent to the principles of conduct which they themselves had always recommended. Yet you must acknowledge, that in a business of this magnitude there may arise several important questions, which, without a spirit of faction, will deserve to be debated : whether Parliament ought not to name the Commissioners? whether it would not be better to repeal the obnoxious Acts ourselves? I do not find that the world ; that is, a few people whom I happen to converse with ; are much inclined to praise Lord N.'s ductility of temper. In the service of next Friday you will, however, take notice of the injunction given by the Liturgy : "And all the People shall say after the *Minister*, Turn us again, O Lord, and so shall we be turned." While we consider whether we shall negociate, I fear the French have been more diligent. It is positively asserted, both in private and in Parliament, and not contradicted by the

Ministers, that on the fifth of this month a Treaty of Commerce (which naturally leads to a war) was signed at Paris with the independent States of America. Yet there still remains a hope that England may obtain the preference. The two greatest countries in Europe are fairly running a race for the favour of America. Adieu.

EDWARD GIBBON *Esq. to* J. B. HOLROYD *Esq.*

ALMACK'S, Saturday Night, March 21, 1778.

As business thickens, and you may expect me to write sometimes, I shall lay down one rule; totally to avoid political argument, conjecture, lamentation, declamation, &c. which would fill pages, not to say volumes; and to confine myself to short, authentic pieces of intelligence, for which I may be able to afford moments and lines. Hear then—The French Ambassador went off yesterday morning, not without some slight expressions of ill-humour from John Bull. Lord Stormont is probably arrived to-day. No *immediate* declaration, except on our side. A report (but vague) of an action in the Bay, between La Motte Piquet and Digby; the former has five ships and three frigates, with three large store-ships under convoy; the latter has eleven ships of the line. If the Frenchman should sail to the mouth of the Delaware, he may possibly be followed and shut up. When Franklin was received at Versailles, Deane went in the same character to Vienna, and Arthur Lee to Madrid. Notwithstanding the reports of an action in Silesia, they subside; and I have seen a letter from Eliot at Berlin of the tenth instant, without any mention of actual hostilities, and even speaking of the impending war as not absolutely inevitable. Last Tuesday the first payment of the loan of six hundred thousand pounds was certainly made; and as it would otherwise be forfeited, it is a security for the remainder. I have not yet got the intelligence you want about former prices of stock in critical times. There are surely such. *Dixi. Vale.* Send me some good news from Bucks; in spite of the war, I must sell. We want you in town. Simon Fraser is impatient: but if you come without my Lady, every door will be shut.

The Same to the Same.   ALMACK'S, Friday, June 12, 1778.

*   *   *'s Letter gave me that sort of satisfaction which one may receive from a good physician, who, after a careful examination, pronounces your case incurable. But no more of that. I take up the pen, as I suppose by this time you begin to swear at my silence. Yet literally (a bull) I have not a word to say. Since D'Estaing's fleet has passed through the Gut (I leave you to guess where it must have got out) it has been totally forgotten, and the most wonderful lethargy and oblivion, of war and peace, of Europe and of America, seems to prevail. Lord Chatham's funeral was meanly attended, and Government ingeniously contrived to secure the double odium of suffering the thing to be done, and of doing it with an ill grace. Their chief con-

versation at Almack's is about tents, drill-serjeants, subdivisons, firings, &c. and I am revered as a veteran. Adieu. When do you return? If it suits your evolutions, aunt Kitty and myself meditate a Sussex journey next week. I embrace my Lady.

EDWARD GIBBON *Esq. to* J. B. HOLROYD *Esq.*
Wednesday Evening, July 1, 1778.

YOUR plan of operations is clear and distinct; yet, notwithstanding your zeal, and the ideas of ducal discipline, I think you will be more and longer at Sheffield-Place than you imagine. However, I am disposed to advance my journey as much as possible. I want to see you; my martial ardour makes me look to Coxheath, necessity obliges me to think of Beriton, and I feel something of a very new inclination to taste the sweets of the country. Aunt Kitty shares the same sentiments; but various obstacles will not allow us to be with you before Saturday, or perhaps Sunday evening; I say *evening*, as we mean to take the cool part of the day, and shall probably arrive after supper. Keppel's return has occasioned infinite and inexpressible consternation, which gradually changes into discontent against him. He is ordered out again with three or four large ships; two of ninety, two of seventy-four, and the fiftieth regiment, as marines. In the mean time the French, with a superior fleet, are masters of the sea; and our outward-bound East and West India trade is in the most imminent danger. Adieu.

The Same to the Same.　　　　BENTINCK-STREET, July 7, 1778.

EXPECT me —— when you see me; and do not regulate your active motions by my uncertainty. Saturday is impossible. The most probable days are, Tuesday or Friday. I live not unpleasantly, in a round of ministerial dinners; but I am rather impatient to see my white house at Brighton. I cannot find that Sheffield has the same attractions for you *. Lord North, as a mark of his gratitude, observed the other day, that your regiment would make a very good figure in North Carolina. Adieu. I wrote two lines to Mitchel, lest he should think me dead.

The Same to the Same.　　　　Saturday Night, Sept. 25, 1778.

NO news from the fleets; we are so tired of waiting, that our impatience seems gradually to subside into a careless and supine indifference. We sometimes yawn, and ask, just by way of conversation, Whether Spain will join? I believe you may depend on the truth, not the sincerity, of an answer from their Court, that they will not support or acknowledge the independence of the Americans. But, on the other hand, magazines are forming, troops marching, in a stile which mani-

* Mr. Holroyd was then in quarters at Brighthelmstone.

festly threatens Gibraltar. Gib is, however, a hard morsel ; five thousand effectives, and every article of defence in the most complete state.
We are certainly courting Russia. So much for the Republic. Adieu.

EDWARD GIBBON *Esq. to* J. B. HOLROYD *Esq.*

Tuesday Night, Nov. 1778.

YOU sometimes complain that I do not send you early news ; but
you will now be satisfied with receiving a full and true account of all
the parliamentary transactions of *next* Thursday. In town we think it
an excellent piece of humour* (the author is Tickell). Burke and
C. Fox are pleased with their own speeches, but serious patriots groan
that such things should be turned to farce. We seem to have a chance
of an additional Dutch war : you may depend upon its being a very
important business, from which we cannot extricate ourselves without
either loss or shame. *Vale.*

The Same to the Same.   ALMACK'S, Wednesday Evening, 1778.

I DELAYED writing, not so much through indolence, as because I
expected every post to hear from you. The state of Beriton is uncertain, incomprehensible, tremendous. It would be endless to send you
the folios of Hugonin, but I have inclosed you one of his most picturesque epistles, on which you may meditate. Few offers ; one,
promising enough, came from a gentleman at Camberwell. I detected
him, with masterly skill and diligence, to be only an attorney's Clerk,
without money, credit, or experience. I have written as yet in vain to
Sir John Shelley, about Hearsay ; perhaps you might get intelligence.
I much fear that the Beriton expedition is necessary ; but it has occurred
to me, that if I *met*, instead of *accompanying* you, it would save me a
journey of above one hundred miles. That reflection led to another of
a very impudent nature ; *viz.* that if I did not accompany you, I
certainly could be of no use to you or myself on the spot ; that I had
much rather, while you examined the premises, pass the time in a
horse-pond ; and that I had still rather pass it in my library with the
Decline and Fall. But that would be an effort of friendship worthy of
Theseus or Perithous ; modern times would hardly credit, much less
imitate, such exalted virtue. No news from America ; yet there are
people, large ones too, who talk of conquering it next summer with the
help of twenty thousand Russians. I fancy you are better satisfied
with private than public war. The Lisbon packet in coming home
met above forty of our privateers. Adieu. I hardly know whether I
direct right to you, but I think Sheffield-Place the surest.

Dr. WATSON (*now Bishop of* Llandaff) *to Mr.* GIBBON.

SIR,   CAMBRIDGE, January 14, 1779.

IT will give me the greatest pleasure to have an opportunity of

_____
* The Title of the Pamphlet—*Anticipation.*

becoming better acquainted with Mr. Gibbon. I beg he would accept my sincere thanks for the too favourable manner in which he has spoken of a performance, which derives its chief merit from the elegance and importance of the work it attempts to oppose. I have no hope of a future existence, except that which is grounded on the truth of Christianity. I wish not to be deprived of this hope ; but I should be an apostate from the mild principle of the religion I profess, if I could be actuated with the least animosity against those who do not think with me upon this, of all others, the most important subject. I beg your pardon for this declaration of my belief ; but my temper is naturally open, and it ought assuredly to be without disguise to a man whom I wish no longer to look upon as an antagonist, but as a friend. I have the honour to be, with every sentiment of respect, your obliged servant,

RD. WATSON.

EDWARD GIBBON *Esq. to* J. B. HOLROYD *Esq.*

February 6, 1779.

YOU are quiet and peaceable, and do not bark, as usual, at my silence. To reward you, I would send you some news ; but we are asleep ; no foreign intelligence, except the capture of a frigate ; no certain account from the West Indies, and a dissolution of Parliament, which seems to have taken place since Christmas. In the papers you will see negociations, changes of departments, &c. and I have *some* reason to believe that those reports are not entirely without foundation. Portsmouth is no longer an object of speculation ; the whole stream of all men, and all parties, runs one way. Sir Hugh is disgraced, ruined, &c. &c.; and as an old wound has broken out again, they say he must have his leg cut off as soon as he has time. In a night or two we shall be in a blaze of illumination, from the zeal of naval heroes, land patriots, and tallow-chandlers ; the last are not the least sincere. I want to hear some details of your military and familiar proceedings. By your silence I suppose you admire Davis, and dislike my pamphlet ; yet such is the public folly, that we have a second edition in the press : the fashionable style of the clergy, is to say they have not read it. If Maria does not take care, I shall write a much sharper invective against her, for *not* answering my diabolical book. My Lady carried it down, with a solemn promise that I should receive an *unassisted* French letter. Yet I embrace the little animal, as well as my Lady, and the *Spes altera Romæ.* Adieu.

There is a buz about a peace, and Spanish mediation.

Dr. WILLIAM ROBERTSON *to Mr.* GIBBON.

DEAR SIR,   COLLEGE of EDINBURGH, March 10, 1779.

I SHOULD have long since returned you thanks for the pamphlet you took the trouble of sending to me. I hope you are not one of those who estimate kindness by punctuality in correspondence. I read your little performance with much eagerness, and some solicitude. The

S

latter soon ceased. The tone you take with your adversary in this *impar congressus* appears to me perfectly proper; and, though I watched you with some attention, I have not observed any expression which I should, on your own account, wish to be altered. Davis's book never reached us here. Our distance from the Capital operates somewhat like time. Nothing but what has intrinsic value comes down to us. We hear sometimes of the worthless and vile things that float for a day on the stream, but we seldom see them. I am satisfied, however, that it was necessary for you to animadvert on a man who had brought accusations against you, which no gentleman can allow to be made without notice. I am persuaded, that the persons who instigated the man to such an illiberal attack, will now be ashamed of him. At the same time I applaud your resolution, of not degrading yourself, by a second conflict, with such antagonists.

I am ashamed to tell you, how little I have done since I had the pleasure of seeing you. I have been prevented, partly by ill health, partly by causes which I shall explain when we meet : I hope that may be next spring. Believe me to be with great truth,

Your affectionate and faithful humble servant,

WILLIAM ROBERTSON.

EDWARD GIBBON, *Esq. to* J. B. HOLROYD, *Esq.*

May 7, 1779.

BY some of the strangest accidents, (Lord G. G.'s indiscretion, Rigby's boldness, &c.) which it would require ten pages to explain, our wise resolution of last Thursday is changed, and Lord Cornwallis will be examined ; Sir Henry Howe's enquiry will proceed, and we shall be oppressed by the load of information. You have heard of the Jersey invasion ; everybody praises Arbuthnot's decided spirit. Conway went last night to throw himself into the island.

The Same to the Same.

May, 1779.

ALAS ! alas ! fourteen ships of the line : you understand by this, that you have not got a single long-boat. Ministry are more crest-fallen, than I ever knew them, with the last intelligence ; and I am sorry to say, that I see a smile of triumph on some opposition faces. Though the business of the West Indies may still produce something, I am much afraid that we shall have a campaign of immense expence, and little or no action. The most busy scene is at present in the House of Commons ; and we shall be involved, during a great part of next month, in tedious, fruitless, but, in my opinion, proper inquiries. You see how difficult it would be for me to visit Brighton ; and I fancy I must content myself with receiving you on your passage to Ireland. Indeed, I much want to have a *very serious* conversation with you. Another reason, which must in a great measure pin me to Bentinck-street, is the Decline and Fall. I have resolved to bring out the *suite* in the course of next year ; and though I have been tolerably diligent, so much remains to be done, that I can hardly spare a single day from he shop. I can guess but one reason which should prevent you from supposing that the picture in Leicester Fields was intended for the Sheffield library ; viz. my having told you some time ago that I was under a formal engagement to Mr. Walpole.* Probably I should not have been in any great hurry to execute my promise, if Mr. Cadell had not strenuously urged the curiosity of the Public, who may be willing to repay the exorbitant price of *fifty* guineas. It is now finished, and my friends say, that, in every sense of the word, it is a good head. Next week it will be given to Hall the engraver, and I promise you a first impression. Adieu. I embrace my Lady, and infants.

EDWARD GIBBON Esq. to J. B. HOLROYD Esq.

1779.

WHEN do you come to town ? You gave me hopes of a visit, and I want to talk over things in general with you, before you march to the extremities of the West, where the sun goes to sleep in the sea. Mrs. Trevor told me your destination was Exeter ;† and I suppose nothing but truth can proceed from a pretty mouth.—I have been, and am still very diligent ; and, though it is a huge beast, (the Roman Empire,) yet, if I am not mistaken, I see it move a little.—You seem surprised that I was able to get off Bath : very easily, the extreme shortness of our holidays was a fair excuse ; her recovery of health, spirits, &c. made it less necessary, and she accepted my apology, which was however accompanied with an offer, if she chose it, in the prettiest manner possible. A load of business in this House, I write from it will be the amusement of the spring ; motions, enquiries, taxes, &c. &c We are now engaged in Lord Pigott's affair, brought on by a motion from the Admiral, that the Attorney General should prosecute Mr. Stratton and Council ; all the Masters Charles, Burke, Wedderburne, are of the same side, for it ; Lord North seems to make a feeble stand, for the pleasure of being in a minority. The day is hot and dull ; will be long : some curious evidence ; one man who refused three lacks of rupees, (thirty-seven thousand five hundred pounds,) merely not to go to council ; our mouths watered at such royal corruption ; how pitiful is our insular bribery ! A letter from aunt Hester. Adieu.

The Same to the Same.

July 2, 1779.

THE inclosed will inform you of an event,‡ not the most disagreeable of those which I have lately experienced. I have only to add, that it was effected by the firm and sincere friendship of the Attorney General. So many incidents have happened, that I hardly know how to talk of news. You will learn that the Lords have strangely castrated the new Militia Bill. The Ferrol squadron, eight or nine ships, have joined the French. The numbers stand on our side thirty-two, on theirs thirty-seven ; but our force is at least equal, and the general consternation much dispelled. If you do not Hibernize, you might at least Bentinckize. I embrace, &c. Parliament will be prorogued to-morrow.

* The portrait, one of the best of Sir Joshua's, is in the library at Sheffield Place.
† With the Sussex Militia, of which Mr. Holroyd was Major.
‡ His appointment as Lord of Trade.

EDWARD GIBBON *Esq. to Mrs.* GIBBON, Bath.

DEAR MADAM,　　　　　　BENTINCK-STREET, September 17, 1779.
I AM well and happy; two words which you will accept as the substance of a very long letter; and even as a sufficient excuse for a very
long silence. Yet I really do intend to behave better; and to prevent
the abominable consequence of hours and days and posts stealing
away, till the sum total amounts to a formidable account, I have a
great mind to enter into an agreement, of sending you regularly every
month, a *miniature* picture of my actual state and condition on the first
day of the aforesaid month.

I am glad to hear of the very beneficial effects you have derived from
your recent friendship with the goats at Abergavenny; and as I cannot discover in what respect this poor country is more prosperous or
secure than it was last year, I must consider your present confidence
as a proof that you view the prospect through a purer medium, and a
glass of a more cheerful colour. I find myself so much more susceptible of private friendship than of public spirit, that I am very well
satisfied with that conclusion. My summer has been passed in the
town and neighbourhood, which I still maintain to be the best society
and the best retirement; the latter, however, has been sometimes interrupted by the Colonel of Dragoons * with a train of serjeants, trumpets,
recruits, &c. &c. My own time is much and agreeably employed in
the prosecution of my business. After doing much more than I
expected to have done within the time, I find myself much less
advanced than I expected : yet I begin to reckon, and as well as I can
calculate, I believe, that in twelve or fourteen months I shall be
brought to-bed, perhaps of twins : may they live, and prove as healthy
as their eldest brother. With regard to the little foundling which so
many friends or enemies chose to lay at my door, I am perfectly innocent, even of the knowledge of that production; and all the faults or
merits of the History of Opposition must, as I am informed, be
imputed to Macpherson, the author or translator of Fingal. Dear
Madam, most truly yours.

EDWARD GIBBON *Esq. to Colonel* HOLROYD *at* Coventry.

LONDON, Monday, February 7, 1780.
WHEN the Attorney General informed me of the express he had just
sent down to Coventry, I had not the least doubt of your embracing
the bolder resolution. You are indeed obliged to him for his real
friendship, which he feels and expresses warmly; on this occasion I
hope it will be successful, and that in a few days you will find yourself
among us at St. Stephen's in the heat of the battle. But you know
that I am a dastardly, pusillanimous spirit, more inclined to fear than
to hope, and not very eager in the pursuit of *expensive* vanity. On this
vacancy the celerity of your motions may probably prevent opposition;
but at the general election your enemy the corporation will not be
asleep, and I wish, if it be not too late, to warn you against any promises or engagements which may terminate in a defeat, or at least a

* Colonel Holroyd at that time was raising a regiment of Light Dragoons.

contest of ten thousand pounds. Adieu. I could believe (without seeing it under her paw) that my Lady wishes to leave Coventry. No news! foreign or domestic. I did not forget to mention the *companies*, but find people, as I expected, torpid. Burke makes his motion Friday; but I think the rumours of a civil war subside every day : petitions are thought less formidable ; and I hear your Sussex protest gathers signatures in the country.

EDWARD GIBBON *Esq. to Mrs.* GIBBON, Bath.

DEAR MADAM, BENTINCK-STREET, March 10, 1780.

WHEN you awakened me with your pen, it was my intention to have shown some signs of life by the next post. But so uncertain are all human affairs, that I found myself arrested by a mighty unrelenting tyrant, called the gout ; and though my feet were the part on which he chose to exercise his cruelty, he left me neither strength nor spirits to use my hand in relating the melancholy tale. At present, I have the pleasure of informing you, that the fever and inflammation have subsided : but the absolute weakness and monstrous swelling of my two feet confine me to my chair and flannels ; and this confinement most unluckily happens at a very *nice* and important moment of parliamentary affairs. Col. H. pursues those affairs with eager and persevering zeal ; and has the pleasure of undertaking more business than any three men could possibly execute. He is much obliged to you for your kind congratulation. Mrs. Eliot is in town ; but 1 am quite ignorant (not more so than they are themselves) of their intentions. I will write again very soon. 1 am, dear Madam, most truly yours.

The Same to the Same.

DEAR MADAM, June 6, 1780.

As the old story of religion has raised most *formidable* tumults in this town, and as they will of course seem much more formidable at the distance of an hundred miles, you may not be sorry to hear that I am perfectly safe and well : my known attachment to the Protestant religion has most probably saved me. Measures, and effectual measures, are taken to suppress those disorders, and every street is filled with horse and foot. Mrs. Holroyd went out of town yesterday morning ; the Colonel remains, and shows his usual spirit. I am sincerely yours.

EDWARD GIBBON *Esq. to Mrs.* GIBBON, Bath.

DEAR MADAM, LONDON, June 8, 1780.

As a Member of Parliament, I cannot be exposed to any danger, since the House of Commons has adjourned to Monday se'nnight ; as an individual, I do not conceive myself to be obnoxious. I am not apt, without duty or necessity, to thrust myself into a mob : and our part of the town is as quiet as a country village. So much for personal safety; but I cannot give the same assurances of public tranquility: forty thousand Puritans, such as they might be in the time of Cromwell, have started out of their graves; the tumult has been dreadful: and even the remedy of military force and martial law is unpleasant. But Government, with fifteen thousand regulars in town, and every gentleman (but one) on their side, must extinguish the flame. The execution of last night was severe; perhaps it must be repeated tonight: yet, upon the whole, the tumult subsides. Colonel Holroyd was all last night in Holborn among the flames, with the Northumberland Militia, and performed very bold and able service. I will write again in a post or two.

I am, dear Madam, ever yours.

EDWARD GIBBON *Esq. to Mrs.* GIBBON, Bath.

DEAR MADAM,   June 10, 1780.

I SHOULD write with great pleasure, to say that this audacious tumult is perfectly quelled; that Lord George Gordon is sent to the Tower; and that, instead of safety or danger, we are now at leisure to think of justice: but I am now alarmed on your account, as we have just got a report, that a similar disorder has broken out at Bath. I shall be impatient to hear from you; but I flatter myself that your pretty town does not contain much of that scum which has boiled up to the surface in this huge cauldron. I am, dear Madam, most sincerely yours.

The Same to the Same.

DEAR MADAM,   BENTINCK-STREET, June 27, 1780.

I BELIEVE we may now rejoice in our common security. All tumult has perfectly subsided, and we only think of the justice which must be properly and severely inflicted on such flagitious criminals. The measures of Government have been seasonable and vigorous; and even opposition has been forced to confess, that the military power was applied and regulated with the utmost propriety. Our danger is at an end, but our disgrace will be lasting, and the month of June 1780, will ever be marked by a dark and diabolical fanaticism, which I had supposed to be extinct, but which actually subsists in Great Britain, perhaps beyond any other country in Europe. Our parliamentary work draws to a conclusion; and I am much more pleasingly, though laboriously, engaged in revising and correcting for the press, the continuation of my History, two volumes of which will certainly appear next winter. This business fixes me to Bentinck-street more closely than any other part of my literary labour; as it is absolutely necessary that I should be in the midst of all the books which I have at any time used during the composition. But I feel a strong desire (irritated, like all other passions, by repeated obstacles) to escape to Bath.

Dear Madam,
Most truly yours.

EDWARD GIBBON *Esq. to Colonel* HOLROYD.

July 25, 1780.

As your motions are spontaneous, and the stations of the Lord Chief (Lord Mansfield) unalterably fixed, I cannot perceive the necessity of your sending or receiving intelligence. However, your commands are obeyed. You wish I would write, as a sign of life. I am alive; but, as I am immersed in the Decline and Fall, I shall only make the sign. It is made. You may suppose that we are not pleased with the junction of the fleets; nor can an ounce of West India loss be compensated by a pound of East India success: but the circuit will roll down all the news and politics of London. I rejoice to hear that the Sussex regiment of Dragoons (commanded by Colonel Holroyd) are such well-disciplined cannibals; but I want to know when the chief cannibal will return to his den. It would suit me better that it should happen soon. Adieu.

The Same to the Same.   BROOKS'S, November 28, 1780.

PERHAPS the Sheriffs (the Sheriffs of Coventry), the tools of your enemies, may venture to make a false and hostile return, on the presumption that they shall have a whole year of impunity; and that the merits of your petition cannot be heard this session. Some of your most respectable friends in the House of Commons are resolved, (if the return should be such,) to state it forcibly as a special and extraordinary case; and to exert all proper strength for bringing on the trial of your Petition without delay. The knowledge of such a resolution may awe the Sheriffs; and it may be prudent to admonish them of the *impending* danger, in the way that you judge most adviseable. Adieu. God send you a good deliverance.

Mr. GIBBON *to Mrs.* GIBBON, Belvedere, Bath.

DEAR MADAM,   BENTINCK-STREET, December 21, 1780.

THE constant attendance on the Board of Trade almost every day this week, has obliged me to defer till next Monday a visit of inclination and propriety to Lord Loughborough (at Mitcham, in Surrey). I shall not return till Wednesday or Thursday; and, instead of my Christmas, I shall eat my New-year's dinner, at the Belvedere, Bath. May that New Year prove fortunate to you, to me, and to this weary country, which is this day involved in a new war! I shall write again about the middle of next week, with a precise account of my motions. I think the gallant Colonel, who is now Lord Sheffield, will succeed at Coventry; *perhaps* on the return, *certainly* on the petition. I am, dear Madam, ever yours.

EDWARD GIBBON *Esq. to Mrs.* GIBBON, Bath.

DEAR MADAM,　　　　　　BENTINCK-STREET, February 24, 1781.
As you have probably received my last letter of thirteen hundred
pages *, I shall be very concise ; read, judge, pronounce ; and believe
that I sincerely agree with my friend Julian, in esteeming the praise of
those only who will freely censure my defects. Next Thursday I shall
be delivered to the world, for whose inconstant and malicious levity I
am coolly but firmly prepared. Excuse me to Sarah. I see more
clearly than ever, the absolute necessity of confining my presents to
my own family : *that*, and that only, is a determined line, and Lord S.
- is the first to approve his exclusion. He has a strong assurance of
success, and some hopes of a speedy decision. How suddenly your
friend General Pierson disappeared ! You thought him happy. What
is happiness ! My dear Madam, ever yours.

Dr. WILLIAM ROBERTSON *to Mr.* GIBBON.

DEAR SIR,　　　　　　COLLEGE OF EDINBURGH, May 12, 1781.
I AM ashamed of having deferred so long to thank you for the agreeable presents of your two new volumes ; but just as I had finished the
first reading of them, I was taken ill, and continued, for two or three
weeks, nervous, deaf, and languid. I have now recovered as much
spirit as to tell you, with what perfect satisfaction I have not only
perused, but studied, this part of your work. I knew enough of your
talents and industry to expect a great deal, but you have gone far
beyond my expectations. I can recollect no historical work from
which I ever received so much instruction ; and when I consider in
what a barren field you had to glean and pick up materials, I am truly
astonished at the connected and interesting story you have formed.
I like the style of these volumes better than that of the first ; there is
the same beauty, richness, and perspicuity of language, with less of
that quaintness, into which your admiration of Tacitus sometimes
seduced you. I am highly pleased with the reign of Julian. I was a
little afraid that *you* might lean with some partiality towards him ; but
even bigots, I should think, must allow, that you have delineated his
most singular character with a more masterly hand than ever touched
it before. You set me a reading his works, with which I was very
slenderly acquainted ; and I am much struck with the felicity where-
with you have described that odd infusion of Heathen fanaticism and
philosophical coxcombry, which mingled with the great qualities of a
hero and a genius. Your chapter concerning the pastoral nations is
admirable ; and, though I hold myself to be a tolerably good general
historian, a great part of it was new to me. As soon as I have leisure,
I purpose to trace you to your sources of information ; and I have no
doubt of finding you as exact there, as I have found you in other passages where I have made a scrutiny. It was always my idea that an
historian should feel himself a witness giving evidence upon oath. I
am glad to perceive by your minute scrupulosity, that your notions are

* Second and third volumes of the Decline and Fall.

the same. The last chapter in your work is the only one with which I am not entirely satisfied. I imagine you rather anticipate, in describing the jurisprudence and institutions of the Franks; and should think that the account of private war, ordeals, chivalry, &c. would have come in more in its place about the age of Charlemagne, or later : but with respect to this, and some other petty criticisms, I will have an opportunity of talking fully to you soon, as I propose setting out for London on Monday. I have, indeed, many things to say to you ; and as my stay in London is to be very short, I shall hope to find your door (at which I will be very often) always open to me. I cannot conclude without approving of the caution with which the new volumes are written ; I hope it will exempt you from the illiberal abuse the first volume drew upon you. I ever am, yours, faithfully and affectionately,

WILLIAM ROBERTSON.

EDWARD GIBBON *Esq. to Lady* SHEFFIELD, *at* Sheffield-Place.

BENTINCK-STREET, Friday Evening, 10 o'clock, 1781.

OH, oh ! I have given you the slip ; saved thirty miles, by proceeding this day directly from Eartham to town, and am now *comfortably* seated in my library, in *my own* easy chair, and before *my* own fire ; a style which you understand, though it is unintelligible to your Lord. The town is empty ; but I am surrounded with a thousand old acquaintance of all ages and characters, who are ready to answer a thousand questions which I am impatient to ask. I shall not easily be tired of their company ; yet I still remember, and will honorably execute, my promise of visiting you at Brighton about the middle of next month. I have seen nobody, nor learned any thing, in four hours of a town life ; but I can inform you that Lady * * * is now the declared Mistress of Prince Henry of Prussia, whom she encountered at Spa ; and that the Emperor has invited the amiable couple to pass the winter at Vienna : fine encouragement for married women, who behave themselves properly. I spent a very pleasant day in the little paradise of Eartham, and the hermit expressed a desire (no vulgar compliment) to see and to know Lord S. Adieu. I cordially embrace, &c.

Sir WILLIAM JONES *to Mr.* GIBBON.

DEAR SIR, LAMB'S-BUILDINGS, June 30, 1784.

I HAVE more than once sought, without having been so fortunate as to obtain, a proper opportunity of thanking you very sincerely for the elegant compliment which you pay me, in a work abounding in elegance of all kinds.

My *Seven Arabian Poets* will see the light before next winter, and be proud to wait upon you in their English dress. Their wild productions will, I flatter myself, be thought interesting, and not venerable merely on account of their antiquity.

In the mean while, let me request you to honour me with accepting a copy of a Law Tract, which is not yet published : the subject is so generally important, that I make no apology for sending you a professional work.

You must pardon my inveterate hatred of C. Octavianus, basely surnamed Augustus. I feel myself unable to forgive the death of Cicero, which, if he did not promote, he might have prevented. Besides, even Mecænas knew the cruelty of his disposition, and ventured to reproach him with it. In short, I have not *Christian* charity for him.

With regard to Asiatic letters, a necessary attention to my profession will compel me wholly and eternally to abandon them, *unless* Lord North (to whom I am already under no small obligation) should think me worthy to concur in the *improved* administration of justice in Bengal, and should appoint me to supply the vacancy on the India Bench. Were that appointment to take place this year, I should probably travel, for speed, through part of Egypt and Arabia, and should be able, in my way, to procure many Eastern tracts of literature and jurisprudence. I might become a good *Mahomedan* lawyer before I reached Calcutta, and, in my vacations, should find leisure to explain, in my native language, whatever the Arabs, Persians, and Turks, have written on science, history, and the fine arts.

My happiness by no means depends on obtaining this appointment, as I am in easy circumstances without my profession, and have flattering prospects in it; but if the present summer and the ensuing autumn elapse without my receiving any answer, favourable or unfavourable, I shall be forced to consider that silence as a polite refusal, and, having given sincere thanks for past favours, shall entirely drop all thoughts of *Asia,* and "deep as ever plummet sounded, shall drown my *Persian* books." If my politics have given offence, it would be manly in Ministers to tell me so. I shall never be *personally* hostile to them, nor enlist under party banners of any colour; but I will never resign my opinions for *interest,* though I would cheerfully abandon them on *conviction.* My reason, such as it is, can only be controlled by better reason, to which I am ever open. As to my freedom of thought, speech, and action, I shall ever say what Charles XII. wrote under the map of Riga, "*Dieu me l'a donnee; le diable ne me l'otera pas.*" But the fair answer to this objection is, that my system is purely speculative, and has no relation to my seat on the bench in India, where I should hardly think of instructing the Gentoos in the maxims of the Athenians. I believe I should not have troubled you with this letter, if I did not fear that your attendance in Parliament might deprive me of the pleasure of meeting you at the Club next Tuesday; and I shall go to Oxford a few days after. At all times, and in all places, I shall ever be, with undissembled regard, dear Sir, your much obliged and faithful servant,   W. JONES.

Lord HARDWICKE *to Mr.* GIBBON.

SIR,   WIMPLE, September 20, 1781.

As I have perused your History of the Decline, &c. with the greatest pleasure and instruction, I cannot help wishing that, as health and leisure permit, you would gratify your numerous readers and admirers, bv continuing it, at least till the irruption of the Arabs after Mahomet. From that period the History of the East is not very interesting, and often disgusting. I particularly wish to see the reigns of Justin, Justinian, and I think Justin the Second, written by so masterly a hand. There are striking facts and remarkable characters in all those reigns, which have not yet met with an able and sagacious *Historian.* You seemed (as well as I recollect) to think the anecdotes of Procopius spurious; there are strange anecdotes in them, and of a very different cast from his History. Can it be traced up when they first came to light?

Excuse this short interruption from much better employments or amusements; and believe me, Sir, with the greatest regard, your most obedient humble servant,

HARDWICKE.

P.S. It has occurred to me, that a map of the progress and native seat of the northern hives would greatly elucidate and explain that part of your History. It may be done in a second edition.

Dr. ROBERTSON to Mr. GIBBON.

DEAR SIR,   COLLEGE OF EDINBURGH, November 6, 1781.

SOON after my return I had a long conversation with our friend Mr. Smith, in which I stated to him every particular you mentioned to me, with respect to the propriety of going on with your great work. I was happy to find, that his opinion coincided perfectly with that which I had ventured to give you. His decisions, you know, are both prompt and vigorous; and he would not allow that you ought to hesitate a moment in your choice. He promised to write his sentiments to you very fully. But as he may have neglected to do this, for it is not willingly that he puts pen to paper, I thought it might be agreeable to you to know his opinion, though I imagine you could hardly entertain any doubt concerning it. I hope you have brought such a stock of health and spirits from Brighton, that you are set seriously at your desk, and that in two winters or so, you will display the crescent of Mahomet on the dome of St. Sophia. I met t'other day, in a work addressed to yourself, a sensible passage from F. Paul, which perfectly removes one of your chief difficulties, as to the barrenness of some parts of your period. Hayley's Essay on History, p. 133. By the bye, who is this Mr. Hayley? His poetry has more merit than that of most of his contemporaries; but his whiggism is so bigotted, and his Christianity so fierce, that he almost disgusts one with two very good things.

I have got quite well long ago, and am perfectly free from deafness; but I cannot yet place myself in any class but that of the *multa et præclara minantes.* Be so kind as to remember me to Lord Loughborough and Mr. Craufurd, and believe me to be, with most sincere respect and attachment, yours very faithfully,

WILLIAM ROBERTSON.

EDWARD GIBBON *Esq. to Mrs.* GIBBON, Bath.

DEAR MADAM, BRIGHTHELMSTONE, Nov. 2, 1781.

I RETURNED to this place with Lord and Lady Sheffield, with the design of passing two or three weeks in a situation which had so highly delighted me. But how vain are all sublunary hopes! I had forgot that there is some difference between the sunshine of August and the cold fogs (though we have uncommon good weather) of November. Instead of my beautiful sea-shore, I am confined to a dark lodging in the middle of the town; for the place is still full, and our time is now spent in the dull imitation of a London life. To complete my misfortunes, Lord Sheffield was hastily ordered to Canterbury and Deal, to suppress some disturbances, and I was left almost alone with my Lady, in the servile state of a married man. But he returns to-day, and I hope to be seated in my own library by the middle of next week. However, you will not be sorry to hear that I have refreshed myself by a very *idle* summer, and indeed a much idler and more pleasant winter than the House of Commons will ever allow me to enjoy again. ' I had almost forgot Mr. Hayley; ungratefully enough, since I really passed a very simple, but entertaining day with him. His place, though small, is elegant as his mind, which I value much more highly. Mrs. * * * wrote a melancholy story of an American mother, a friend of her friend, who in a short time had lost three sons; one killed by the savages, one run mad from the fright at that accident, and the third taken at sea, now in England, a prisoner in Forton hospital. For *him* something might perhaps be done. Your humanity will prompt you to obtain from Mrs. * * * a more accurate account of names, dates, and circumstances; but you will prudently suppress my request, lest I should raise hopes which it may not be in my power to gratify. Lady S. begs to send her kindest compliments to you. I am, dear Madam, ever yours.

EDWARD GIBBON *Esq. to Mrs.* GIBBON, Bath.

DEAR MADAM, July 3, 1782.

I HOPE you have not had a moment's uneasiness about the delay of my Midsummer letter. Whatever may happen, you may rest fully secure, that the materials of it shall always be *found.* But on this occasion I have missed four or five posts; postponing, as usual, from morning to the evening bell, which now rings, till it has occurred to me, that it might not be amiss to enclose the two essential lines, if I only added that the influenza has been known to me only by the report of others. Lord Rockingham is at last dead; a good man, whatever he might be a minister: his successor is not yet named, and divisions in the Cabinet are suspected. If Lord Shelburne should be the man, as I think he will, the friends of his predecessor will quarrel with him before Christmas. At all events, I foresee much tumult and strong opposition, from which I should be very glad to extricate myself, by quitting the House of Commons with honour. Whatever you may hear, I believe there is not the least intention of dissolving Parliament, which would indeed be a rash and dangerous measure. I hope you like Mr. Hayley's poem; he rises with his subject, and since Pope's death, 1 am satisfied that England has not seen so happy a mixture of strong sense and flowing numbers. Are you not delighted with his address to his mother? I understand that she was in plain prose every thing that he speaks her in verse. This summer I shall stay in town, and work at my trade, till I make some holidays for my Bath excursion. Lady Sheffield is at Brighton, and he is under tents, like the wild Arabs; so that m.y country house is shut up. I am, dear Madam, ever yours.

EDWARD GIBBON *Esq. to the Right Honourable Lord* SHEFFIELD, *Camp*, Coxheath.

BENTINCK-STREET, 1782.
I SYMPATHISE with your fatigues; yet Alexander, Hannibal, &c. have suffered hardships almost equal to yours. At such a moment it is disagreeable (besides laziness) to write, because every hour teems with a new life. As yet, however, only Charles has formally resigned; but Lord John Cavendish, Burke, Keppel, Lord Althorpe, &c. certainly follow; your Lord Lieutenant stays. In short, three months of prosperity has dissolved a phalanx, which had stood ten years' adversity. Next Tuesday, Fox will give his reasons, and possibly be encountered by Pitt, the new Secretary, or Chancellor of the Exchequer, at three-and-twenty. The day will be rare and curious, and, if I were a light dragoon, I would take a gallop on purpose to Westminster. Adieu. I hear the bell. How could I write before I knew where you dwelt?

EDWARD GIBBON *Esq. to the Right Honourable Lord* SHEFFIELD, Coxheath *Camp*.

September 29, 1782.
I SHOULD like to hear sometimes, whether you survive the scenes of action and danger in which a dragoon is continually involved. What a difference between the life of a dragoon and that of a philosopher! and 1 will freely own that I (the philosopher) am much better satisfied with my own independent and tranquil situation, in which I have always something to do, without ever being obliged to do anything. The Hampton Court villa has answered my expectation, and proved no small addition to my comforts; so that I am resolved next summer to hire, borrow, or steal, either the same, or something of the same kind. Every morning I walk a mile or more before breakfast, read and write *quantum sufficit*, mount my chaise and visit in the neighbourhood, accept some invitations, and escape others, use the Lucans as my daily bread, dine pleasantly at home, or sociably abroad, reserve for study an hour or two in the evening, lie in town regularly once a week, &c. &c. I have announced to Mrs. G. my new arrangements; the certainty that October will be fine, and my increasing doubts whether I shall be able to reach Bath before Christmas. Do you intend (but how can you intend anything?) **to pass the winter under**

canvas. Perhaps under the veil of Hampton Court I may lurk ten days or a fortnight at Sheffield, if the enraged Lady does not shut the doors against me. The Warden (Lord North) passed through in his way to Dover. He is not so fat, and more cheerful than ever. I had not any private conversation with him ; but he clearly holds the balance, unless he lets it drop out of his hand. The Pandæmonium (as I understand) does not meet till the twenty-sixth of November. Town is more a desert than I ever knew it. I arrived yesterday, dined at Sir Joshua Reynolds' with a tolerable party ; the chaise is now at the door ; I dine at Richmond, lie at Hampton, &c. Adieu.

EDWARD GIBBON, *Esq. to Lord* SHEFFIELD, *at* Coxheath *Camp.*

BENTINCK-STREET, October 14, 1782.

ON the approach of winter, my paper house at Hampton becomes less comfortable ; my visits to Bentinck-street grow longer and more frequent, and the end of next week will restore me to the town, with a lively wish, however, to repeat the same, or a similar experiment, next summer. I admire the assurance with which you propose a month's residence at Sheffield, when you are not sure of being allowed three days. Here it is currently reported, that camps will not separate till Lord Howe's *return* from Gibraltar, and as yet we have no news of his arrival. Perhaps indeed you may have more intimate correspondence with your old friend Lord Shelburne, and already know the hour of your deliverance. I should like to be informed. As Lady S. has entirely forgotten me, I shall have the pleasure of forming a new acquaintance. I have often thought of writing, but it is now too late to repent.

I am at a loss what to say or think about our parliamentary state. A certain late Secretary of Ireland reckons the House of Commons thus: Minister one hundred and forty, Reynard ninety, Boreas one hundred and twenty, the rest unknown, or uncertain. The last of the three, by self or agents, talks too much of absence, neutrality, moderation. I still think he will discard the game.

I am not in such a fury with the letter of American independence ; but I think it seems ill-timed and useless ; and I am much entertained with the metaphysical disputes between Government and Secession about the meaning of it. Lord Loughborough will be in town Sunday seven-night. I long to see him and Co. I think he will take a very decided part. If he could throw aside his gown, be would make a noble leader. The East India news are excellent. The French gone to Mauritius, Heyder desirous of peace, the Nizam and Mahrattas our friends, and seventy lacks of rupees in the Bengal treasury, while we were voting the recal of Hastings. Adieu. Write soon.

EDWARD GIBBON *Esq. to Lord* SHEFFIELD.

1782.

I HAVE designed writing every post. The air of London is admirable ; my complaints have vanished, and the gout still respects me. Lord

Loughborough, with whom I passed an entire day, is very well satisfied with his Irish expedition, and found the barbarous people very kind to him. The castle is strong, but the volunteers are formidable. London is dead, and all intelligence so totally extinct, that the loss of an army would be a favourable incident. We have not even the advantage of shipwrecks, which must soon, with the society of you and Gerard Hamilton, become the only pleasures of Brighton. My Lady is precious, and deserves to shine in London, when she regains her palace. The workmen are slow, but I hear that the Minister talks of hiring another house after Christmas.* Adieu, till Monday seven-night.

The Same to the Same.

January 17, 1783.

As I arrived about seven o'clock on Wednesday last, we were some time in town in mutual ignorance. Unlucky enough ; yet our loss will be speedily repaired. Your reason for not writing is worthy of an Irish Baron : you thought Sarah might be at Bath, because you directed letters to her at Clifton near Bristol ; where indeed I saw her in a delightful situation, swept by the winter winds, and scorched by the summer sun. A nobler reason for your silence would be the care of the public papers, to record your steps, words, and actions. I was pleased with your Coventry oration : a panegyric on * * * is a subject entirely new, and which no orator before yourself would have dared to undertake. You have acted with prudence and dignity in casting away the military yoke. This next summer you will sit down (if you can sit) in the long lost character of a country gentleman.

For my own part, my late journey has only confirmed me in the opinion, that Number Seven in Bentinck-street is the best house in the world. I find that peace and war alternately, and daily, take their turns of conversation, and this (Friday) is the pacific day. Next week we shall probably hear some questions on that head very strongly asked, and very foolishly answered, &c. Give me a line by return of post, and probably I may visit Downing-street on Monday evening ; late, however, as I am engaged to dinner and cards. Adieu.

[Although Dr. Priestley may not be justified for publishing the following Letters, yet as he thought fit to print them with a volume of sermons soon after Mr. Gibbon's death, it will not be improper to insert them in this collection.]

Mr. GIBBON *to Dr.* PRIESTLEY.

SIR, January 23, 1783.

As a mark of your esteem, I should have accepted with pleasure your History of the Corruptions of Christianity. You have been careful to inform me, that it is intended, not as a gift, but as a challenge, and such a challenge you must permit me to decline. At the

* Lord North, while his house was repairing, inhabited Lord Sheffield's in Downing-street.

same time you glory in outstripping the zeal of the Mufti and the Lama, it may be proper to declare that I should equally refuse the defiance of those venerable divines. Once, and once only, the just defence of my own veracity provoked me to descend into the amphitheatre; but as long as you attack opinions which I have never maintained, or maintain principles which I have never denied, you may safely exult in my silence and your own victory. The difference between us, (on the credibility of miracles,) which you chuse to suppose, and wish to argue, is a trite and antient topic of controversy, and, from the opinion which you entertain of yourself and of me, it does not appear probable that our dispute would either edify or enlighten the Public.

That Public will decide to whom the *invidious* name of Unbeliever more justly belongs; to the Historian, who, without interposing his own sentiments, has delivered a simple narrative of authentic facts, or to the disputant who proudly rejects all natural proofs of the immortality of the soul, overthrows (by circumscribing) the inspiration of the evangelists and apostles, and condemns the religion of every Christian nation, as a fable less innocent, but not less absurd, than Mahomet's journey to the third Heaven.

And now, Sir, since you assume a right to determine the objects of my past and future studies, give me leave to convey to your ear the almost unanimous, and not offensive wish, of the philosophic world :— that you would confine your talents and industry to those sciences in which real and useful improvements *can* be made. Remember the end of your predecessor Servetus, not of his life, (the Calvins of our days are restrained from the use of the same fiery arguments,) but, I mean, the end of his reputation. His theological writings are lost in oblivion; and if his book on the Trinity be still preserved, it is only because it contains the first rudiments of the discovery of the circulation of the blood.

I am, Sir, your obedient humble servant.

Dr. PRIESTLEY *to Mr.* GIBBON.

SIR,   BIRMINGHAM, 3 February, 1783.

It would have been impertinent in me, especially considering the object of my *History*, to have sent you a copy of it as a mark of my *esteem* or *friendship*. What I meant was to act the part of a fair and open *adversary*, and I am truly sorry that you decline the discussion I proposed : for though you are of a different opinion, I do not think that either of us could be better employed ; and, should the Mufti and the Lama, whose challenge, you say, you would also decline, become parties in the business, I should rejoice the more. I do not well know what you can mean by intimating, that I am a greater Unbeliever than yourself ; that I attack opinions which you never maintained, and maintain principles which you never denied. If you mean to assert, that you are a believer in Christianity, and meant to recommend it, I must say, that your mode of writing has been very ill adapted to gain your purpose. If there be any certain method of discovering a man's real object, yours has been to discredit Christianity in fact, while in words you represent yourself as a friend to it : a conduct which I scruple not to call highly unworthy and mean ; an insult on the common sense of the Christian world ; as a method of screening you from the notice of the law, (which is as hostile to me as it is to you,) you must know that it could avail you nothing : and, though that mode of writing might be deemed ingenious and witty in the first inventor of it, it has been too often repeated to deserve that appellation now.

According to your own rule of conduct, this charge ought to provoke you to descend into the amphitheatre once more, as much as the accusation of Mr. Davis : for it is a call upon you to defend, not your *principles* only, but also your *honour.* For what can reflect greater dishonour on a man, than to say one thing and mean another? You have certainly been very far from confining yourself, as you pretend, to a simple narrative of authentic facts, without interposing your own sentiments. I hold no opinions, obnoxious as they are, that I am not ready both to *avow* in the most explicit manner, and also to defend with any person of competent judgment and ability. Had I not considered you in this light, and also as fairly open, by the strain of your writings, to such a challenge, I should not have called upon you as I have done. The Public will form its own judgment both of that and of your silence on the occasion ; and finally decide between you, the *humble historian,* and me, the *proud disputant.*

As to my *reputation,* for which you are so very obligingly concerned, give me leave to observe, that, as far as it is an object with any person, and a thing to be enjoyed by himself, it must depend upon his particular notions and feelings.—Now, odd as it will appear to you, the esteem of a very few rational Christian friends (though I know that it will ensure me the detestation of the greater part of the present nominally Christian world that happened to hear me) gives me more real satisfaction, than the applause of what you call the philosophic world. I admire Servetus, by whose example you wish me to take warning, more for his courage in dying for the cause of important truth, than I should have done if, besides the certain discovery of the circulation of the blood, he had made any other the most celebrated discovery in philosophy.

However, I do not see what my philosophical friends (of whom I have many, and whom I think I value as I ought,) have to do with my metaphysical or theological writings. They may, if they please, consider them as my particular whims or amusements, and accordingly neglect them. They have, in fact, interfered very little with my application to philosophy, since I have had the means of doing it. I was never more busy, or more successfully so, in my philosophical pursuits, than during the time that I have been employed about the History of the Corruptions of Christianity. I am at this very time, *totus in illis,* as my friends know ; and as the Public will know in due time ; which with me is never long, and if you had thought proper to enter into the discussion I proposed, it would not have made me neglect my laboratory, or omit a single experiment that I should otherwise have made.

I am, Sir,
Your very humble servant,
J. PRIESTLEY.

T

Mr. GIBBON *to Dr.* PRIESTLEY.

SIR,   BENTINCK-STREET, February 6, 1783.

AS I do not pretend to judge of the sentiments or intentions of another, I shall not enquire how far you are inclined to suffer, or inflict, martyrdom. It only becomes me to say, that the style and temper of your last letter have satisfied me of the propriety of declining all farther correspondence, whether public or private, with such an adversary. I am, Sir, your humble servant.

Dr. PRIESTLEY *to Mr.* GIBBON.

SIR,   BIRMINGHAM, 10 February, 1783.

I NEITHER requested nor wished to have any *private correspondence* with you. All that my MS. card required, was a simple acknowledgment of the receipt of the copy of my work. You chose, however, to give me a specimen of your temper and feelings; and also, what I thought to be an opening to a further call upon you for a justification of yourself *in public.* Of this I was willing to take advantage; and, at the same time, to satisfy you, that my philosophical pursuits, for which, whether in earnest or not, you were pleased to express some concern, would not be interrupted in consequence of it.

As this correspondence, from the origin and nature of it, cannot be deemed *confidential,* I may, especially if I resume my observations on your conduct as an Historian, give the Public an opportunity of judging of the propriety of my answer to your first extraordinary letter, and also to this last truly *enigmatical* one ; to interpret which requires much more sagacity than to discover your real intentions with respect to Christianity, though you might think you had carefully concealed them from all human inspection.

Wishing to hear from you just as little as you please in private, and just as much as you please in public, I am, Sir, your humble servant.

Mr. GIBBON *to Dr.* PRIESTLEY.

February 22, 1783.

IF Dr. Priestley consults his friends, he will probably learn, that a single copy of a paper, addressed under a seal to a single person, and not relative to any public or official business, must always be considered as *private* correspondence ; which a man of honour is not at liberty to print without the consent of the writer. That consent in the present instance, Mr. Gibbon thinks proper to withhold ; and, as he desires to escape all further altercation, he shall not trouble Dr. Priestley or himself with explaining the motives of his refusal.

Dr. PRIESTLEY *to Mr.* GIBBON.

BIRMINGHAM, February 25, 1783.

DR. PRIESTLEY is as unwilling to be guilty of any real impropriety as Mr. Gibbon can wish him to be : but, as the correspondence between them relates not to any *private*, but only to a *public matter*, he apprehends that it may, according to Mr. Gibbon's own distinction, at the pleasure of either of the parties be laid before the Public ; who, in fact, are interested to know, at least, the result of it. Dr. Priestley's conduct will always be open to animadversion, that of Mr. Gibbon, or of any other person. His appeal is to men of honour, and even men of the world ; and he desires no favour.

Dr. Priestley has sent a single copy of the correspondence to a friend in London, with leave to shew it to any other common friends, but with a prohibition to take any other copy : but between this and *printing* there is no difference, except in *mode* and *extent.* In the eye of the law and of reason both are equally publications ; and has Mr. Gibbon never thought himself at liberty to shew a copy of a letter to a third person ?

Mr. Gibbon may easily escape all further altercation by discontinuing this mutually disagreeable correspondence, by leaving Dr. Priestley to act as his own discretion or indiscretion may dictate ; and for this, himself only, and not Mr. Gibbon, is responsible.

M. GIBBON *à Mons.* DEYVERDUN, à Lausanne.

A LONDRES, ce 20 Mai 1783.

QUE j'aime la douce et parfaite confiance de nos sentimens réciproques ! Nous nous aimons dans l'éloignement et le silence, et il nous suffit à l'un et à l'autre, de savoir de tems en tems, des nouvelles de la santé et du bonheur de son ami. Aujourd'hui j'ai besoin de vous écrire ; je commence sans excuses et sans reproches, comme si nous allions reprendre la conversation familière du jour précédent. Si je proposois de faire un *compte rendu* de mes études, de mes occupations, de mes plaisirs, de mes nouvelles liaisons, de ma politique toujours muette, mais un peu plus rapprochée des grands évenemens, je multiplierois mes *in quarto*, et je ne sais pas encore votre avis sur ceux que je vous ai déjà envoyés. Dans cette histoire moderne, il seroit toujours question de la décadence des empires ; et autant que j'en puis juger sur mes réminiscences et sur le rapport de l'ami Bugnon, vous aimez aussi peu la puissance de l'Angleterre que celle des Romains. Notre chute, cependant, a été plus douce. Apres une guerre sans succès, et une paix assez peu glorieuse, il nous reste de quoi vivre contens et heureux ; et lorsque je me suis dépouillé du rôle de Membre du Parlement, pour redevenir homme, philosophe, et historien, nous pourrions bien nous trouver d'accord sur la plus part des scènes étonnantes qui viennent de se passer devant nos yeux, et qui fourniront une riche matière aux plus habiles de mes successeurs.

Bornons nous à cette heure à un objet moins illustre sans doute, mais plus intéressant pour tous les deux, et c'est beaucoup que le même objet puisse intéresser deux mortels qui ne se sont pas vûs, qui a peine se sont écrit depuis—oui ma foi—depuis huit ans. Ma plume, très paresseuse au commencement, ou plutôt avant le commencement, marche assez vite, lorsqu'elle s'est une fois mise en train ; mais une raison qui m'empêcheroit de lui donner carrière, c'est l'espérance de

pouvoir bientôt me servir avec vous d'un instrument encore plus commode, la langue.   Que l'homme, l'homme Anglois, l'homme Gibbon,
est un sot animal !   Je l'espere, je le desire, je le puis, mais je ne sais
pas si je le veux, encore moins si j'exécuterai cette volonté.   Voici mon
histoire, autant qu'elle pourra vous éclairer, qu'elle pourra m'éclairer
moi-même, sur mes véritables intentions, qui me paroîssent tres
obscures, et tres équivoques ; et vous aurez la bonté de m'apprendre
qu'elle sera ma conduite future.   Il vous souvient, Seigneur, que mon
grand pere a fait sa fortune, que mon pere l'a mangée avec un peu trop
d'appétit, et que je jouis actuellement du fruit, ou plutôt du reste de
leurs travaux.   Vous n'avez pas oublié que je suis entré au Parlement
sans patriotisme, sans ambition, et que toutes mes vues se bornoient à
la place commode et honnête d'un *Lord of Trade.*   Cette place, je l'ai
obtenue enfin ; je l'ai possédée trois ans, depuis 1779 jusqu'à 1782, et
le produit net, qui se montoit à sept cens cinquante livres sterling,
augmentoit mon revenu, au niveau de mes besoins, et de mes desirs.
Mais au printems de l'année précédente, l'orage a grondé sur nos têtes :
Milord North a été renversé, votre serviteur chassé, et le *Board*
même, dont j'étois membre, aboli et cassé pour toujours, par la réfor-
mation de M. Burke, avec beaucoup d'autres places de l'Etat, et de la
maison du Roi.   Pour mon malheur, je suis toujours resté Membre de
la Chambre basse : à la fin du dernier Parlement (en 1780) M. Eliot
à retiré sa nomination ; mais la faveur de Milord North a facilité ma
rentrée, et la reconnoisance m'imposoit le devoir de faire valoir, pour
son service, les droits que je tenois en partie de lui.   Cet hyver nous
avons combatu sous le étendards réunis (vous savez notre histoire) de
Milord North, et de M. Fox ; nous avons triomphé de Milord Shelburne et de la paix, et mon ami (je n'aime pas à profaner ce nom) a
remonté sur sa bête en qualité de Secretaire d'Etat.   C'est à présent
qu'il peut bien me dire : " C'étoit beaucoup pour moi ; ce n'étoit rien
pour vous ;" et malgré les assurances les plus fortes, j'ai trop de raison,
pour avoir de la foi.   Avec beaucoup d'esprit, et des qualités très
respectables, il n'a plus ni le titre, ni le crédit de premier ministre ; des
collegues plus actifs lui enlevent les morceaux les plus friands, qui
sont aussitôt devorés par la voracité de leurs créatures ; nos malheurs
et nos réformes ont diminué le nombre des graces ; par orgueil ou par
paresse, je sollicite aussi mal, et si je parviens enfin, ce sera peut être
à la veille d'une nouvelle révolution, qui me fera perdre dans un
instant, ce qui m'aura coûté tant de soins et de recherches.   Si je ne
consultois que mon cœur et ma raison, je romprois sur le champ cette
indigne chaine de la dépendance ; je quitterois le Parlement, Londres,
l'Angleterre ; je chercherois sous un ciel plus doux, dans un pays plus
tranquille, le repos, la liberté, l'aisance, et une société éclairée et
aimable.   Je coulerois quelques années de ma vie sans espérance, et
sans crainte, j'acheverois mon histoire, et je ne rentrerois dans ma
patrie qu'en homme libre, riche, et respectable par sa position, aussi
bien que par son caractère.   Mes amis, et surtout Milord Sheffield, ne
veulent pas me permettre d'être heureux suivant mon goût et mes
lumières.   Leur prudence exige que je fasse tous mes efforts, pour
obtenir un emploi très sur à la vérité, qui me donneroit mille guinées
de rente, mais qui m'enleveroit cinq jours par semaine.   Je me prête

à leur zele, et je leur ai promis de ne partir qu'en automne, après avoir consacré l'été à cette dernière tentative. Le succès, cependant, est très incertain, et je ne sais si je le desire de bonne foi. Si je parviens à me voir exilé, mon choix ne sera pas douteux. Lansanne a eu mes prémices ; elle me sera toujours chere par le doux souvenir de ma jeunesse. Au bout de trente ans, je me rappelle les polissons qui sont aujourd'hui juges, les petites filles de la société du printems, qui sont devenues grand-meres. Votre pays est charmant, et, malgré le dégoût de Jean Jacques, les mœurs, et l'esprit de ses habitans, me paroissent très assortis aux bords du lac Léman. Mais un trésor que je ne trouverois qu'à Lausanne ; c'est un ami que me convient également par les sentimens, et les idées, avec qui je n'ai jamais connu un instant d'ennui, de sécheresse, ou de réserve. Autrefois dans nos libres épanchemens, nous avons cent fois fait le projet de vivre ensemble, et cent fois nous avons épluché tous les détails du Roman, avec une chaleur qui nous étonnoit nous memes. A présent il demeure, ou plutôt vous demeurez, (car je me lasse de ce ton étudié,) dans une maison charmante et commode ; je vois d'ici mon appartement, nos salles communes, notre table, et nos promenades ; mais ce mariage ne vaut rien, s'il ne convient pas également aux deux époux, et je sens combien des circonstances locales, des goûts nouveaux, de nouvelles liaisons, peuvent s'opposer aux desseins, qui nous ont paru les plus agréables dans le lointain. Pour fixer mes idées, et pour nous épargner des regrets, il faut me dévoiler avec la franchise dont je vous ai donné l'exemple, le tableau extérieur et intérieur de George Deyverdun. Mon amour est trop délicat, pour supporter l'indifférence et les égards, et je rougirois d'un bonheur dont je serois redevable, non à l'inclination, mais à la fidélité de mon ami. Pour m'armer contre les malheurs possibles, helas ! peut être trop vraisemblables, j'ai essayé de me détacher de la pensée de ce projet favori, et de me représenter à Lausanne votre bon voisin, sans être précisement votre commensal. Si j'y étois réduit, je ne voudrois pas tenir maison, autant par raison d'économie, que pour éviter l'ennui de manger seul. D'un autre côté, une pension ouverte, fut elle montée sur l'ancien pied de celle de Mesery, ne conviendroit plus à mon age, ni à mon caractère ? Passerois je ma vie au milieu d'une foule de jeunes Anglois échappés du college, moi qui aimerois Lausanne cent fois davantage, si j'y pouvois être le seul de ma nation ? Il me faudroit donc une maison commode et riante, un état au dessus de la bourgeoisie, un mari instruit, une femme qui ne resembleroit pas à Madame Pavilliard, et l'assurance d'y être reçu comme le filles unique, ou plutôt comme le frere de la famille. Pour nous arranger sans gêne, je meublerait très volontier un joli appartement sous le même toit, ou dans le voisinage, et puisque le ménage le plus foible, laisse encore de l'étoffe pour une forte pension, je ne serois pas obligé de chicaner sur les conditions pecuniaires. Si je me vois déchu de cette dernière espérance, je renoncerois en soupirant à ma seconde patrie, pour chercher un nouvel asyle, non pas à Geneve, triste séjour du travail et de la discorde, mais aux bords du lac de Neufchatel, parmi les bons Savoyards de Chamberry, ou sous le beau climat des Provinces Méridionales de la France. Jes finis brusquement, parceque j'ai mille choses à vous dire. Je pense que nous nous ressemblons pour la correspondance.   Pour le bavardage savant, ou même amical, je suis de tous les hommes le plus paresseux, mais dès qu'il s'agit d'un objet réel, d'un service essentiel, le premier Courier emporte toujours ma réponse.   A la fin d'un mois, je commencerai à compter les semaines, les jours, les heures.   Ne me les faites pas compter trop long tems. Vale.

M. Deyverdun à M. Gibbon.

STRASBOURG, le 10 Juin, 1783.

Je ne saurais vous exprimer, Monsieur et cher ami, la variété et la vivacité des sensations que m'a fait éprouver votre lettre.   Tout cela a fini par un fond de plaisir et d'espérance qui resteront dans mon cœur, jusqu'à ce que vous les en chassiez.

Un rapport singulier de circonstances contribue à me faire espérer que nous sommes destinés à vivre quelque tems agréablement ensemble. Je ne suis pas dégoûté d'une ambition que je ne connus jamais ; mais par d'autres circonstances, je me trouve dans la même situation d'embarras et d'incertitude où vous êtes aussi à cette époque.   Il y a un an que votre lettre, mon cher ami, m'auroit fait plaisir sans doute, mais en ce moment, elle m'en fait bien davantage : elle vient en quelque façon à mon secours.

Depuis mon retour d'Italie, ne pouvant me determiner à vendre ma maison, m'ennuyant d'y être seul (car je suis comme vous, Monsieur, et je déteste de manger sans compagnie) ne voulant pas louer à des étrangers, j'ai pris le parti de m'arranger assez joliment au premier étage, et de donner le second à une famille de mes amis, qui me nourrit, et que je loge.   Cet arrangement a paru pendant long tems contribuer au bonheur des deux parties.   Mais tout est transitoire sur cette terre. Ma maison sera vuide, selon tout apparence, sur la fin de l'été, et je me vois d'avance tout aussi embarassé et incertain, que je l'étais, il y a quelques années, ne sachant quelle nouvelle société choisir, et assez disposé à vendre enfin cette possession qui m'a causé bien des plaisirs, et bien des peines.   Ma maison est donc à votre disposition pour cet automne, et vous y arriveriez comme un Dieu dans une machine qui finit l'embroglio.   Voilà quant à moi ; parlons de vous maintenant avec la même sincérité.

Un mot de préambule.   Quelque intéressé que je sois à votre résolution, convaincu qu'il faut aimer ses amis pour eux mêmes, sentant d'ailleurs combien il seroit affreux pour moi de vous voir des regrets, je vous donne ici ma parole d'honneur, que mon intérêt n'influe en rien sur ce que je vais écrire, et que je ne dirai pas un mot que je ne vous disse, si l'hermite de la grotte etoit un autre que moi.   Vos amis Anglais vous aiment pour eux mêmes : je ne veux moi que votre bonheur. Rappellez vous, mon cher ami, que je vis avec peine votre entrée dans le Parlement, et je crois n'avoir été que trop bon prophete ; je suis sur que cette carrière vous a fait éprouver plus de privations de jouissances, beaucoup plus de peines que de plaisirs ; j'ai cru toujours, depuis que je vous ai connu, que vous étiez destiné à vivre heureux par les plaisirs du cabinet et de la société, que tout autre marche était un écart de la route du bonheur, et que ce n'etait que les qualités réunies d'homme de lettres, et d'homme aimable de société, qui pouvoient vous procurer gloire, honneur, plaisirs, et un suite continuelle de jouissances. Au bout de quelques tours dans votre salle, vous sentirez parfaitement que j'avois bien vu, et que l'évenement a justifié mes idées. Lorsque j'ai appris que vous étiez *Lord of Trade,* j'en ai été faché ; quand j'ai su que vous aviez perdu cette place, je m'en suis réjouis pour vous ; quand on m'a anoncé que Milord North étoit remonté sur sa bête, j'ai cru vous voir très mal à votre aise, en croupe derrière lui, et je m'en suis affligé pour vous. Je suis donc charmé, mon cher ami, de vous savoir à pied, et je vous conseille très sincèrement de rester dans cette position, et bien loin de solliciter la place en question, de la refuser, si elle vous était offerte. Mille guinées vous dédommageront elles de cinq jours pris de la semaine ? Je suppose, ce que cependant j'ai peine à croire, que vous me disiez que oui : et la variété et l'inconstance continuelle de votre ministère, vous promettent elles d'en jouir long tems constamment, et n'est il pas plus désagréable, mon cher Monsieur, de n'avoir plus 1000 livres sterl. de .rente, qu'il n'a été agréable d'en jouir ? D'ailleurs ne pourrez vous par toujours rentrer dans la carrière, si l'ambition ou l'envie de servir la patrie, vous reprennent ; ne rentrerez vous pas avec plus d'honneur, lorsque vos rentes étant augmentées naturellement, vous serez libre et indépendant ?

En faisant cette retraite en Suisse, outre la beauté du pays, et les agrémens de la société, vous acquererez deux biens que vous avez perdus, la liberté et la richesse. Vous ne serez d'ailleurs point inutile ; vos ouvrages continueront à nous éclairer, et independamment de vos talens, l'honnête homme, le galant homme, n'est jamais inutile.

Il me reste à vous présenter le tableau que vous trouveriez. Vous aimiez ma maison et mon jardin, c'est bien autre chose à présent. Au premier étage qui donne sur la descente d'Ouchy, je me suis arrangé un appartement qui me suffit, j'ai une chambre de domestique, deux sallons, et deux cabinets. J'ai au plein pied de la terrasse, deux autres sallons dont l'un sert en été de salle à manger, et l'autre de sallon de compagnie. J'ai fait un nouvel appartement de trois pièces dans le vuide entre la maison et la remise, en forte que j'ai à vous offrir tout le grand appartement, qui consiste actuellement en onze pièces, tant grandes que petites, tournées au Levant et au Midi, meublées sans magnificence déplacée, mais avec une sorte d'élégance dont j'espère que vous seriez satisfait. La terrasse a peu changé ; mais elle est terminée par un grand cabinet mieux proportionné que le précédent, garnie tout du long, de caisses d'orangers, &c. La treille, que ne vous est pas indifférente, a embelli, prospéré, et regne presqu'entièrement. jusqu'au bout ; parvenu à ce bout, vous trouverez un petit chemin qui vous conduira à une chaumière placée dans un coin ; et de ce coin, en suivant le long d'une autre route à l'Anglaise, le mur d'un manége. Vous trouverez au bout, un chalet avec écurie, vacherie, petite porte, petit cabinet, petite bibliothèque, et une galerie de bois doré, d'où l'on voit tout ce qui sort et entre en ville par la porte du Chêne, et tout ce qui se passe dans ce Faubourg. J'ai acquis la vigne au-dessous du jardin ; j'en ai arraché tout ce qui étoit devant la maison ; j'en ai fait un tapis vert, arrosé par l'eau du jet d'eau ; et j'ai fait tout autour de ce petit parc, une promenade très variée par les différens points de vue

et les objets même intérieurs, tantot jardin potager, tantot parterre,
tantot vigne, tantot prés, puis chalet, chaumiere, petite montagne;
bref, les étrangers viennent le voir et l'admirent, et malgré la description
pompeuse que je vous en fais, vous en serez content.
N.B. J'ai planté une quantité d'excellens arbres fruitiers.

Venons à moi; vous comprenez bien que j'ai vieilli, excepté pour la
sensibilité; je suis à la mode, mes nerfs sont attaqués; je suis plus
mélancolique, mais je n'ai pas plus d'humeur; vous ne souffrirez de
mes maux que tout au plus négativement. Ensemble, et séparés par
nos logemens, nous jouirons vis-à-vis l'un de l'autre, de la plus grande
liberté. Nous prendrons une gouvernante douce et entendue, plutôt
par commodité que par nécessité; car je me chargerois sans crainte de
la surintendance. J'ai fait un ménage de quatre, pendant quelque
tems; j'ai fait le mien, et j'ai remarqué que cela marchoit tout seul,
quand c'étoit une fois en train. Les petites gens qui n'ont que ce
mérite, font grand bruit pour rien. Mon jardin nous fournira avec
abondance de bons fruits et d'excellens légumes. Pour le reste de la
table et de la dépense domestique, je ne demanderais pas mieux que
de vous reçevoir chez moi, comme vous m'avez reçu chez vous; mais
nos situations sont différentes à cet egard; cependant si vous etiez plus
ruiné, je vous l'offrirois sans doute, et je devrois le faire; mais avec les
rentes que vous aviez, quand j'étois chez vous, en les supposant même
diminuées, vous vivrez très agréablement à Lausanne. Enfin à cet
égard nous nous arrangerons comme il vous sera le plus agréable, et
en proportion de nos revenus. Toujours serez vous ainsi, à ce qui
j'espère, plus décemment et plus comfortablement, que vous ne seriez
par tout ailleurs au même prix.

Quant à la société, quoique infiniment agréable, je commence ce
chapitre par vous dire que j'éviterois de vous y inviter, si vous étiez
entièrement désœuvré; les jours sont longs alors, èt laissent bien du
vuide; mais homme de lettres, comme vous êtes, je ne connois point
de société qui vous convienne mieux. Nous aurons autour de nous un
cercle, comme il seroit impossible d'en trouver ailleurs dans un aussi
petit espace. Madame de Corcelles, Mademoiselle Sulens, et M. de
Montolieu (Madame est morte), Messrs. Polier et leurs femmes,
Madame de Severy, et M. et Madame de Nassau, Mademoiselle de
Chandieu, Madame de St. Cierge, et M. avec leurs deux silles jolies et
aimables, Madames de Crousaz, Polier, de Charrieres, &c. font un fonds
de bonne compagnie dont on ne se lasse point, et dont M. de Servan est
si content qu'il regrette toujours d'être obligé de retourner dans ses terres,
et ne respire que pours'établir tout à fait à Lausanne. Il passa tout l'hyver
de 1782 avec nous, et il fut, on ne peut plus, agréable. Vous trouverez
les mœurs changées en bien, et plus conformes à nos ages, et à nos
caractères; peu de grandes assemblées, de grands repas, mais beaucoup de petits soupers, de petites assemblées, où l'on fait ce qu'on veut,
où l'on cause, lit, &c. et dont on écarte avec soin les facheux de toute
espece. Il y a le Dimanche une société, où tout ce qu'il y a d'un peu
distingué en étrangères et étrangers, est invité. Cela fait des assemblées de 40 à 50 personnes, où l'on voit ce qu'on ne voit gueres le reste
de la semaine, et ces especes de *rout* font quelquefois plaisir. Nous
sommes fort dégoutés des étrangers, surtout des jeunes gens, et nous

les écartons avec soin de nos petits comités, à moins qu'ils n'ayent du mérite, ou quelques talens. À cet égard un de nos petits travers, c'est l'engouement ; mais vous en profiterez, mon cher Monsieur, comme Edward Gibbon, et comme mon ami ; vous serez d'abord l'homme à la mode, et je vois d'ici que vous soutiendrez fort bien ce rôle, sans vous en fâcher, dût on un peu vous surfaire. *Je sens que tu me flattes, mais tu me fais plaisir,* est peut être le meilleur vers de Destouches. Voilà donc l'hyver ; l'étude le matin, quelques conversations, quand vous serez fatigué, avec quelque homme de lettres, ou amateur, ou du moins qui aura vu quelque chose ; à l'heure qu'il vous plaira un diner, point de fermier général, mais l'honnête épicurien, avec un ou deux amis quand vous voudrez ; puis quelques visites, une soirée, souvent un souper. Quant à l'été, vu votre manière d'aimer la campagne, on diroit que ma remise à été faite pour vous ; pendant que vous vous y promenerez en sénateur, je serai souvent en bon paysan Suisse, devant mon chalet, ou dans ma chaumière ; puis nous nous rencontrerons tout à coup, et tâcherons de nous remettre au niveau l'un de l'autre. Nous fermerons nos portes à l'ordinaire, excepté aux étrangers qui passent leur chemin ; mais quand nous voudrons, nous y aurons toux ceux que nous aimerons à y voir : car on ne demande pas mieux que d'y venir se rejouir. J'ai eu, un beau jour d'Avril ce printems, un déjeûner, qui m'a coûté quelques Louis, ou il y avait plus de 40 personnes, je ne sais combien de petites tables, une bonne musique au milieu du verger, et une quantité de jeunes et jolies personnes dansant des branles, et formant des chifres en cadence ; j'ai vu bien des fêtes, j'en ai peu vu de plus jolies. Quand mon parc vous ennuyera, nous aurons, ou nous louerons ensemble (et ce sera ainsi un plaisir peu cher) un cabriolet léger, avec deux chevaux gentils, et nous irons visiter nos amis dispersés dans les campagnes, qui nous recevront à bras ouverts. Vous en serez content ou des campagnes ; toujours en proportion vous comprenez, et vous trouverez en général un heureux changement pour les agrémens de la société, et une sorte de recherche simple, mais élégante. Les bergères du *printems,* excepté Madame de Vanberg, ne sont sans doute plus présentables, mais il y en a d'autres assez gentilles, et quoiqu'elles ne soyent pas en bien grand nombre, il y en aura toujours assez pour vous, mon cher Monsieur. Peu à peu mon imagination m'a emporté, et mon style s'égaye, comme cela nous arrivait quelquefois dans nos chateaux en Espagne. Il est bien tems de finir cet article, résumons nous plus sérieusement.

Si vous exécutez le plan que vous avez imaginé, j'aimerois même à dire que voue embrassez, surtout d'après ce que vous marquez vous même, *Si je ne consultais que mon cœur et ma raison, je romprois sur le champ cette indigne chaine,* &c. Eh ! que voulez vous consulter, si ce n'est votre cœur et votre raison ? Si, dis-je, vous exécutez ce plan, vous retrouverez une liberté et une indépendance, que vous n'auriez jamais du perdre, et dont vous méritez de jouir, une aisance qui ne vous coûtera qu'un voyage de quelques jours, une tranquillité que vous ne pouvez avoir à Londres, et enfin un ami qui n'a peut être pas été un jour sans penser à vous, et qui malgré ses défauts, ses foiblesses et son infériorité, est encore un des compagnons qui vous convient le mieux.

Il me reste à vous apprendre pourquoi je vous réponds si tard : vous savez déjà actuellement que ce n'est pas manque d'amitié et de zele pour la chose ; mais votre lettre m'a été renvoyée de Lausanne ici, à Strasbourg, et je n'ai passé qu'une poste sans y répondre, ce qui n'est pas trop, vous l'avouerez, pour un pareil bavardage. Je suis parti de Lausanne la veille de Pâques pour venir voir un M. Bourcard de Basle, fort de mes amis ; il est ici auprès du Comte de Cagliostro, pour profiter de ses remédes. Vous aurez entendu parler peut être de cet homme extraordinaire à tous égards. Comme j'ai été assez malade tout l'hyver, je profite aussi de ses remèdes ; mais comme le tems du séjour du Comte ici n'est rien moins que sur, le mieux sera que vous m'écriviez à *M. D. chez M. Bourcard du Kirshgarten, à Basle.*

Vous comprenez combien à tous égards, il est nécessaire m'écrire sans perte de tems, dèsque vous aurez pris une résolution. Adieu, mon cher ami.

M. GIBBON à *M.* DEYVERDUN.

JE reçois votre lettre du 10 Juin, le 21 de ce mois. Aujourd'hui Mardi 24th, je mets la main à la plume (comme dit M. Fréron) pour y répondre, quoique ma missive ne puisse partir par arrangement des postes, que Vendredi prochain, 27 du courant. O merveille, de la grace efficace ! Elle n'agit pas moins puissamment sur vous, et moyennant le secours toujours prêt, et toujours prompt de nos couriers, un mois nous suffit pour la demande et la réponse. Je remercie mille fois le génie de l'amitié, qui m'a poussé, après mille efforts inutiles, à vous écrire enfin au moment le plus critique et le plus favorable. Jamais démarche n'a répondu si parfaitement à tous mes vœux et à toutes mes espérances. Je comptois sans doute sur la durée et la vérité de vos sentimens ; mais j'ignorois (telle est la foiblesse humaine) jusqu'à quel point ils avoient pu être attiédis par le tems et l'éloignement ; et je savois encore moins l'état actuel de votre santé, de votre fortune et de vos liaisons, qui auroient pu opposer tant d'obstacles à notre réunion. Vous m'écrivez, vous m'aimez toujours ; vous désirez avec zele, avec ardeur, de réaliser nos anciens projets ; vous le pouvez, vous le voulez ; vous m'offrez dès l'automne votre maison, et quelle maison ! votre terrasse, et quelle terrasse ! votre société, et quelle société ! L'arrangement nous convient à tous les deux ; je retrouve à la fois le compagnon de ma jeunesse, un sage conseiller, et un peintre qui sait représenter et exagérer même les objets les plus rians. Ces exagérations me font pour le moins autant de plaisir, que la simple vérité. Si votre portrait étoit tout à fait ressemblant, ces agrémens n'existeroient que hors de nous mêmes, et j'aime encore mieux les trouver dans la vivacité de votre cœur et de votre imagination. Ce n'est pas que je ne reconnoisse un grand fond de vérité dans le tableau de Lausanne ; je connois le lieu de la scène, je me transporte en idée sur notre terrasse, je vois ces côteaux, ce lac, ces montagnes, ouvrages favoris de la nature, et je conçois sans peine les embellissemens que votre goût s'est plus y ajouter. Je me rappelle depuis vingt ou trente ans les mœurs, l'esprit, l'aisance de la société, et je comprends que ce véritable ton de la bonne compagnie se perpétue, et s'épure de pere en fils, ou plutôt de mere en fille ; car il m'a toujours paru qu'à Lausanne, aussi bien qu'en France, les femmes sont très supérieures aux hommes. Dans un pareil séjour, je craindrois la dissipation bien plus que l'ennui, et le tourbillon de Lausanne étonneroit un philosophe accoutumé, depuis tant d'années à la tranquillité de Londres. Vous êtes trop instruit pour regarder ce propos, comme une mauvaise plaisanterie ; c'est dans les détroits qu'on est entrainé par la rapidité des courans : il n'y en a point en pleine mer. Dèsqu'on ne recherche plus les plaisirs bruyans, et qu'on s'affranchit volontiers des devoirs pénibles, la liberté d'un simple particulier se fortifie par l'immensité de la ville. Quant à moi, l'application à mon grand ouvrage, l'habitude, et la récompense du travail, m'ont rendu plus studieux, plus séndentaire, plus ami de la retraite. La chambre des communes et les grands dîners exigent beaucoup de tems ; et la tempérance d'un repas Anglois, vous permet de goûter de cinq ou six vins différens, et vous ordonne de boire une bouteille de claret après le désert. Mais enfin je ne soupe jamais, je me couche de bonne heure, je reçois peu de visites, les matinées sont longues, les étés sont libres, et dèsque je ferme ma porte ; je suis oublié du Monde entier. Dans une société plus bornée et plus amicale, les démarches sont publiques, les droits sont réciproques, l'on dine de bonne heure, on se goûte trop pour ne pas passer l'après-midi ensemble ; on soupe, on veille, et les plaisirs de la soirée ne laissent pas de déranger le repos de la nuit, et le travail du lendemain. Quel est cependant le résultat de ces plaintes ? c'est seulement que la mariée est trop belle, et que j'ose me servir de l'excuse honnête de la santé et du privilege d'un homme de lettres ; il ne tiendra qu'à moi de modêrer un peu l'excès de mes jouissances. Pour cet engouement que vous m'annoncez, et qui a toujours été le défaut des peuples les plus spirituels, je l'ai déjà éprouvé sur un plus grand théâtre. Il y a six ans que l'ami de Madame Necker fut reçu à Paris, comme celui de George Deyverdun pourroit l'être à Lausanne. Je ne connois rien de plus flatteur que cet accueil favorable d'un public poli et éclairé. Mais cette faveur, si douce pour l'étranger, n'est-elle pas un peu dangereuse pour l'habitant exposé à voir flétrir ses lauriers, par sa faute ou par l'inconstance des ses juges? Non ; on se soutient toujours, peut être pas précisement, au même point d'élévation. A l'abri de trois gros volumes in quarto en langue étrangère, encore ce qui n'est pas un petit avantage, je conserverai toujours la réputation littéraire, et cette réputation donnera du relief aux qualités sociales, si l'on trouve l'historien sans travers, sans affectation et sans prétensions. Je serai donc charmé et content de votre société, et j'aurois pu dire en deux mots, ce qui j'ai bavardé en deux pages ; mais il y a tant de plaisir à bavarder avec un ami ! car enfin je possède à Lausanne un véritable ami ; et les simples connoissances remplaceront sans beaucoup de peine, tout ce qui s'appelle liaison, et même amitié, dans, ce vaste désert de Londres. Mais au moment ou j'écris, je vois de tous côtés une foule d'objets dont la perte sera bien plus difficile à réparer. Vous. connoissiez ma bibliothèque ; mais je suis en état de vous rendre le propos de votre maison *c'est bien autre chose à cette heure;* formée peu à peu, mais avec beaucoup de soin et de dépense, elle peut se nommer aujourd'hui un beau cabinet de particulier. Non content de remplir à rangs redoublés la meilleure piece qui lui étoit destinée, elle s'est débordée dans la chambre sur la rue, dans votre ancienne chambre à coucher, dans la mienne, dans tous les recoins de la maison de *Bentinck-street*, et jusques dans une chaumière que je me suis donnée à *Hampton Court*.

J'ai mille courtisans rangés autour de moi :
Ma retraite est mon Louvre, et j'y commande en roi.

Le fonds est de la meilleure compagnie Grecque, Latine, Italienne, Françoise, et Angloise, et les auteurs les moins chers à l'homme de goût, des ecclésiastiques, des Byzantins, des Orientaux, sont les plus nécessaires à l'historien de la décadence et de la chute, &c. Vous ne sentez que trop bien le désagrément de laisser, et l'impossibilité de transporter cinq ou six milles volumes, d'autant plus que le ciel n'a pas voulu faire de la Suisse, un pays maritime. Cependant mon zele pour la réussite de nos projets communs, me fait imaginer que ces obstacles pourront s'applanir, et que je puis adoucir ou supporter ces privations douloureuses. Les bons auteurs classiques, la bibliotheque des nations, se retrouvent dans tous les pays. Lausanne n'est pas dépourvu de livres, ni de politesse, et j'ai dans l'esprit qu'on pourroit acquérir pour un certain tems, quelque bibliotheque d'un vieillard ou d'un mineur, dont la famille ne voudroit pas se défaire entièrement. Quant aux outils de mon travail, nous commencerons par examiner l'état de nos richesses ; apres quoi il faudroit faire un petit calcul du prix, du poids et de la rareté de chaque ouvrage, pour juger de ce qu'il seroit nécessaire de transporter de Londres, et de ce qu'on acheteroit plus commodément en Suisse ; à l'égard de ces frais, on devroit les envisager comme les avances d'une manufacture transplantée en pays étranger, et dont on espere retirer dans la suite un profit raisonnable. Malheureusement votre bibliotheque publique, en y ajoutant même celle de M. de Bochat, est assez piteuse ; mais celles de Berne et de Basle sont très nombreuses, et je compterois assez sur la bonhommie Helvétique, pour espérer que, moyennant des recommandations et des cautions, il me seroit permis d'en tirer les livres dont j'aurois essentiellement besoin. Vois êtes très bien placé pour prendre les informations, et pour fixer les démarches convenables ; mais vous voyez du moins combien je me retourne de tous les côtés, pour esquiver la difficulté la plus formidable.

Venons à present à des objets moins relevés, mais très importans à l'existence et au bien être de l'animal, le logement, les domestiques, et la table. Pour mon appartement particulier, une chambre à coucher, avec un grand cabinet et une antichambre, auroient suffi à tous mes besoins ; mais si vous pouvez vous en passer, je me promenerai avec plaisir dans l'immensité de vos onze pieces, qui s'accommoderont sans doute aux heures et aux saisons différentes. L'article des domestiques renferme une assez forte difficulté, sur la quelle je dois vous consulter. Vous connoissez, et vous estimez Caplin mon valet de chambre, maître d'hotel, &c. qui a été nourri dans notre maison, et qui comptoit y finir ses jours. Depuis votre départ, ses talens et ses vertus se sont développés de plus en plus, et je le considere bien moins sur le pied d'un domestique, que sur celui d'un ami. Malheureusement il ne sait que l'Anglois, et jamais il n'apprendra de langue étrangère. Il m'accompagna, il y a six ans, dans mon voyage à Paris, mais il rapporta fidelement à Londres toute l'ignorance, et tous les préjugés d'un bon patriote. A Lausanne il me coûteroit beaucoup, et à l'exception du service personel, il ne nous seroit que d'une très petite utilité. Cependant je supporterois volontiers cette dépense, mais je suis très persuadé que, si son attachement le portoit à me suivre, il s'ennuyeroit à mourir dans un pays où tout lui seroit étranger et désagréable. Il faudroit donc me détacher d'un homme dont je connois le zele, la fidélité, rompre tout d'un coup de petites habitudes qui sont liées avec le bien être journalier et momentané, et se resoudre à lui substituer un visage nouveau, peut être un mauvais sujet, toujours quelque avanturier Suisse pris sur le pavé de Londres. Vous rappellez vous un certain Georges Suisse qui a fait autrefois avec moi, le voyage de France et d'Italie ? Je le crois marié et établi à Lausanne ; s'il vit encore, si vous pouvez l'engager à se rendre ici, pour me ramener en Suisse, la compagnie d'un bon et ancien serviteur ne laisseroit pas d'adoucir la chute, et il resteroit peut être aupres de moi, jusqu'à ce que nous eussions choisi un jeune homme du pays, adroit, modeste et bien élevé, à qui je ferois un parti avantageux. Les autres domestiques, gouvernantes, laquais, cuisinière, &c. se prennent et se renvoyent sans difficulté. Un article bien plus important, c'est notre table, car enfin nous ne sommes pas assez hermites, pour nous contenter des légumes et des fruits de votre jardin, tout excellens qu'ils sont ; mais je n'ai presque rien à ajouter à l'honnêteté de vos propos, qui me donnent beaucoup plus de plaisir que de surprise. Si je me trouvois sans fortune, au lieu de rougir des bienfaits de l'amitié, j'accepterois vos offres aussi simplement que vous les faites. Mais nous ne sommes pas réduits à ce point, et vous comprenez assez qu'une déconfiture Angloise laisse encore une fortune fort décente au Pays de Vaud, et pour vous dire quelque chose de plus précis, je dépenserois sans peine et sans inconvenient cinq ou six cens Louis. Vous connoissez le résultat aussi bien que les détails d'un ménage ; en supposant une petite table de deux philosophes Epicuriens, quatre, cinq, ou six domestiques, des amis assez souvent, des repas assez rarement, beaucoup de sensualité, et peu de luxe, à combien estimez vous en gros le dépense d'un mois et d'une année ? Le partage que vous avez dejà fait, me paroît des plus raisonnables ; vous me logez, et je vous nourris. A votre calcul, j'ajouterois mon entretien personnel, habits, plaisirs, gages de domestiques, &c. et je verrois d'une manière assez nette, l'ensemble de mon petit établissement.

Apres avoir essuyé tant de détails minutieux, le cher lecteur s'imagine sans doute que la résolution de me fixer pendant quelque tems aux bords du Lac Léman, est parfaitement décidée. Helas ! rien n'est moins vrai ; mais je me suis livré au charme délicieux de compter, de sonder, de palper ce bonheur, dont je sens tout le prix, qui est à ma portée, et auquel j'aurai peut être la bêtise de renoncer. Vous avez raison de croire, mais vous ignorez jusqu'à quel point vous l'avez, que ma carrière politique a été plus semée d'épines que de roses. Eh ! quel objet, quel mortel, pourroit me consoler de l'ennui des affaires, et de la honte de la dépendance ? *La gloire ?* Comme homme de letres, j'en jouis, comme orateur je ne l'aurai jamais, et le nom des simples soldats est oublié dans les victoires aussi bien que dans les défaites. *Le devoir.*

Dans ces combats à l'aveugle, où les chefs ne cherchent que leur avantage particulier, il y a toujours à parier que les subalternes feront plus de mal que de bien. *L'attachement personnel?* Les ministres sont rarement dignes de l'inspirer ; jusqu'à present Lord North m'a pas eu à se plaindre de moi, et si je me retire du Parlement, il lui sera très aisé d'y substituer un autre muet, tout aussi affidé que son ancien serviteur. Je suis intimement convaincu, et par la raison, et par le sentiment, qu'il n'y a point de parti, que me convienne aussi bien que de vivre avec vous, et auprès de vous à Lausanne ; et si je parviens à la place (*Commissioner of the Excise or Customs*) où je vise, il y aura toutes les semaines cinq longues matinées, qui m'avertiront de la folie de mon choix. Vous vous trompez à la vérité à l'égard de l'instabilité de ces emplois ; ils sont presques les seuls qui ne se ressentent jamais des révolutions du ministère. Cependant si cette place s'offroit bientôt, je n'aurois pas le bon sens et le courage de la refuser. Quels autres conseillers veux je prendre, si non mon cœur et ma raison ? Il en est de puissans et toujours écoutés : les égards, la mauvaise honte, tous mes amis, ou soi disant tels, s'écrieront que je suis un homme perdu, ruiné, un fou qui se dérobe à ses protecteurs, un misanthrope qui s'exile au bout du monde, et puis les exagérations sur tout ce qui seroit fait en ma faveur, si surement, si promptement, si libéralement. Milord Sheffield opinera à me faire interdire et enfermer ; mes deux tantes et ma belle mere se plaindront que je les quitte pour jamais, &c. Et l'embarras de prendre mon bonnet de nuit, comme disoit le sage Fontenelle, lorsqu'il n'etoit question que de se coucher, combien de bonnets de nuit ne me faudra-t-il pas prendre, et les prendre tout seul, car tout le monde, amis, parens, domestiques, s'opposera à ma fuite. Voila à la vérité des obstacles assez peu redoutables, et en les décrivant, je sens qu'ils s'affoiblissent dans mon esprit. Grace à ce long bavardage vous connoissez mon intérieur, comme moi même, c'est à dire, assez mal ; mais cette incertitude, très amicale pour moi, seroit tres facheuse pour vous. Votre réponse me parviendra vers la fin de Juillet, et huit jours après, je vous promets une replique nette et décisive : *je pars* ou *je reste.* Si je pars, ce sera au milieu de Septembre ; je mangerai les raisons de votre treille, les premiers jours d'Octobre, et vous aurez encore le tems de me charger de vos commissions. Ne me dites plus : *Monsieur, et tres cher ami ;* le premier est froid, le second est superflu.

M. Deyverdun *à M.* Gibbon.

Me voilà un peu embarrassé actuellement ; je ne dois vous appeller ni Monsieur, ni ami. Eh bien ! vous saurez qu'étant parti Samedi de Strasbourg, pendant que je venois ici, votre seconde lettre alloit là, et qu'ainsi je reçus votre troisième, Dimanche, et votre seconde, hier. La mention que vous y faisiez du Suisse George, dont je n'ai pu rien trouver dans la première, m'a fait comprendre qu'il y en avoit une seconde, et j'ai cru devoir attendre un courier, la troisième n'exigeant pas de réponse.

Pour votre parole, permettez que je vous en dispense encore, et même jusqu'au dernier jour, je sens bien qu'un procédé contraire, vous conviendroit ; mais certes il ne me convient pas du tout. Ceci, comme vous le dites, est une espèce de mariage, et pensez vous que malgré les engagemens les plus solemnels, je n'eusse pas reconduit chez elle, du pied des autels, la femme la plus aimable qui m'eut temoigné des regrets. Jamais je ne me consolerois, si je vous voyois mécontent dans la suite, et dans le cas de me faire des reproches. C'est à vous à faire, si vous croyez nécessaire, des demarches de votre côté, qui fortifient votre résolution ; pour moi, je n'en ferai point d'essentielles, jusqu'à ce que j'aye reçu encore une lettre de vous. Après ce petit préambule, parlons toujours comme si l'affaire étoit décidée, et repassons votre lettre. Tout ce que vous dites des grandes et petites villes est très vrai, et votre comparaison des détroits et de la pleine mer est on ne peut pas plus juste et agréable ; mais enfin, *comme on fait son lit, on se couche,* disoit Sancho Pancha d'agréable mémoire, et qui peut mieux faire son lit à sa guise qu'un étranger, qui, n'ayant ni devoirs d'état ni de sang à remplir, peut vivre entièrement isolé, sans que personne y puisse trouver à redire ? Moi même, bourgeois et citoyen de la ville, je suis presqu'entièrement libre. L'été, par exemple, je déteste de m'enfermer le soir dans des chambres chaudes, pour faire une partie. Eh bien ! on m'a persécuté un peu la première année ; à present on me laisse en repos. Il y aura sans doute quelque changement dans votre manière de vivre ; mais il me semble qu'on se fait aisement à cela. Les diners, surtout en femmes, sont très rares ; les soupers peu grands ; on reste plutôt pour être ensemble, que pour manger, et plusieurs personnes ne s'asseyent point. Je crois, tout compté et rabattu, que vous aurez encore plus de tems pour le cabinet qu'à Londres ; on sort peu le matin, et quand nos amis communs viendront chez mois, et vous demanderont, je leur dirai ; " ce n'est pas un oisif comme vous autres, il travaille dans son cabinet," et ils se tairont respectueusement.

Pour les bibliotheques publiques, votre idée ne pourroit, je pense, se réaliser pour un lecteur ou même un écrivain ordinaire, mais un homme qui joue un rôle dans la république des lettres, un homme aimé et considéré, trouvera, je m'imagine, bien des facilités ; d'ailleurs, j'ai de bons amis à Berne, et je prendrai ici des informations.

Passons à la table. Si j'étois à Lausanne, cet article seroit plus sur, je pourrois revoir mes papiers, consulter ; j'ai une chienne de mémoire. A vue de pays cela pourra aller de 20 à 30 Louis par mois, plus ou moins, vous sentez, suivant la friandise, et le plus ou moins de convives. Marquez moi dans votre première combien vous coûte le votre.

Je sens fort bien tous les bonnets de nuit : point de grands changemens sans embarras, même sans regrets ; vous en aurez quelquefois sans doute : par exemple, si votre salle à manger, votre salle de compagnie, sont plus riantes, vous perdrez pour le vase de la bibliotheque. Pour ce qui est des représentations, des discours au moins inutiles, il me semble que le mieux seroit de masquer vos grandes opérations, de ne parler que d'une course, d'une visite chez moi, de six mois ou plus ou moins. Vous feriez bien, je pense, d'aller chez mon ami Louis Teissier ; c'est un brave et honnête homme, qui m'est attaché, qui aime notre pays ; il vous donnera tout plein de bons conseils avec zele, et vous gardera le secret.

Vous aurez quelquefois à votre table un poëte ;—oui, Monsieur, un poëte :—nous en avons un enfin. Procurez vous un volume 8vo. *Poësies Helvetiennes, imprimés l'année passée chez Mouser, à Lausanne.* Vous trouverez cntr'autres dans l'épitre au jardinier de la grotte, votre ami et votre parc. Toute la prose est de votre très humble serviteur, qui désire qu'elle trouve grace devant vous.

Le Comte de Cagliostro a fait un séjour à Londres. On ne sait qui il est, d'où il est, d'où il tire son argent ; il exerce *gratis* ses talens pour la médecine ; il a fait des cures admirables ; mais c'est d'ailleurs le composé le plus étrange. J'ai cessé de prendre ses rémedes qui m'échauffoient—l'homme d'ailleurs me gâtoit le médecin. Je suis revenu à Basle avec mon ami. Adieu ; récrivez moi le plutôt possible.

M. GIBBON *à M.* DEYVERDUN.

HAMPTON COURT, ce 1 Julliet, 1783.

APRES avoir pris ma resolution, l'honneur, et ce qui vaut encore mieux l'amitié, me défendent de vous laisser un moment dans l'incerti-tude. JE PARS. Je vous en donne ma parole, et comme je suis bien aise de me fortifier d'un nouveau lien, je vous prie très sérieusement de ne pas m'en dispenser. Ma possession, sans doute, ne vaut pas celle de Julie ; mais vous serez plus inéxorable que St. Preux. Je ne sens plus qu'une vive impatience pour notre réunion. Mais le mois d'Octobre est encore loin ; 92 jours, et nous aurons tout le tems de prendre, et de nous donner des éclaircissemens dont nous avons besoin. Après un mûr examcn, je renonce au voyage de George Suisse, qui me paroît incertain, cher et difficile. Après tout mon valet de chambre et ma bibliotheque, sont les deux articles les plus embarrassans. Si je ne retenois pas ma plume, je remplirois sans peine la feuille ; mais il ne faut pas passer du silence, à un babil intarissable. Seulement si je connois le Comte de Cagliostro, cet homme extraordinaire, &c. Savez vous le Latin ? oui, sans doute ; mais faites, comme si je ne le savois point. Quand retournez vous à Lausanne vous même ? Je pense que vous y trouverez une petite bête bien aimable, mais tant soit peu méchante, qui se nomme Milady Elizabeth Foster ; parlez lui de moi, mais parlcz en avec discrétion ; elle a des correspondances partout. Vale.

EDWARD GIBBON *Esq. to the Right Hon. Lord* SHEFFIELD.

July 10, 1783.

YOU will read the following lines with more patience and attention than you would probably give to an hasty conference, perpetually inter-rupted by the opening of the door, and perhaps by the quickness of our own tempers. I neither expect nor desire an answer on a subject of extreme importance to myself, but which friendship alone can render interesting to you. We shall soon meet at Sheffield.

It is needless to repeat the reflections which we have sometimes debated together, and which I have often seriously weighed in my silent solitary walks. Notwithstanding your active and ardent spirit, you must allow that there is some perplexity in my present situation, and that my future prospects are distant and cloudy. I have lived too long in the world to entertain a very sanguine idea of the friendship or zeal of ministerial patrons ; and we are all sensible how much the powers of patronage are reduced. * * *. At the end of the Parliament, or rather long before that time, (for their lives are not worth a year's purchase,) our Ministers are kicked downstairs, and I am left their disinterested friend, to fight through another opposition, and to expect the fruits of another revolution. But I will take a more favourable supposition, and conceive myself in six months firmly seated at the board of customs ; before the end of the next six months I should infallibly hang myself. Instead of regretting my disappointment, I rejoice in my escape ; as I am satisfied that no salary could pay me for the irksomeness of attendance, and the drudgery of business so repugnant to my taste, (and I will dare to say,) so unworthy of my character. Without looking forwards to the possibility, still more remote, of exchanging that laborious office for a smaller annuity, there is surely another plan, more reasonable, more simple, and more pleasant ; a temporary retreat to a quiet and less expensive scene. In a four years' residence at Lausanne, I should live within my income, save, and even accumulate, my ready money ; finish my History, an object of profit, as well as fame, expect the contingencies of elderly lives, and return to England at the age of fifty, to form a lasting independent establishment, without courting the smiles of a Minister, or apprehending the downfall of a party. Such have been my serious sober reflections. Yet I much question, whether I should have found courage to follow my reason and my inclination, if a friend had not stretched his hand to draw me out of the dirt. The twentieth of last May I wrote to my friend Deyverdun, after a long interval of silence, to expose my situation, and to consult in what manner I might best arrange myself at Lausanne. From his answer, which I received about a fortnight ago, I have the pleasure to learn that his heart and his house are both open for my reception ; that a family which he had lodged for some years is about to leave him, and that at no other time my company could have been so acceptable and convenient. I shall step, at my arrival, into an excellent apartment and a delightful situation ; the fair division of our expences will render them very moderate, and I shall pass my time with the companion of my youth, whose temper and studies have always been congenial to my own. I have given him my word of honour to be at Lausanne in the beginning of October, and no power or persuasion can divert me from this IRREVOCABLE resolution, which I am every day proceeding to execute.

I wish, but I scarcely hope, to convince you of the propriety of my scheme ; but at least you will allow, that when we are not able to prevent the *follies* of our friends, we should strive to render them as easy and harmless as possible. The arrangement of my house, furniture, and books will be left to meaner hands, but it is to your zeal and judgment alone that I can trust the more important disposal of Lenborough

and * * *.   On these subjects we may go into a committee at Sheffield-Place, but you know it is the rule of a committee, not to hear
any arguments against the *principle* of the bill.   At present I shall
only observe, that neither of these negotiations ought to detain me
here ; the former may be dispatched as well, the latter much better,
in my absence.   *Vale.*

M. GIBBON *à M.* DEYVERDUN.

SHEFFIELD-PLACE, le 31 Juillet, 1783.

VOTRE papier s'est furieusement rappetisé ; vous avez si bien re-
tranché le superflu, que vous oubliez l'essentiel, et ce n'est que pas des
conjectures fines et savantes que je devine la date du tems et du lieu.
Quant à moi je suis actuellement au château de Milord Sheffield, à
quarante milles de Londres, ce qui ajoute deux jours pour l'arrivée et
le départ du courier.   Je reçois votre lettre (je ne sais du quantième)
le 30 Juillet de l'an de grace 1783, je réponds du 31 du dit mois et de
la dite année.   Le zele ne se rallentit point pour la consummation du
grand œuvre.   Je sens votre procédé délicat et généreux, et quoique je
n'eusse pas été faché de trouver dans votre fermeté, un appui à la
mienne, mon inclination est si bien affermie sur la base inébranlable
de l'inclination et de la raison, que je ne crains plus les obstacles ex-
térieurs ni intérieurs.   Dèsque j'ai osé fixer mon départ, les nuages qui
le couvroient, se sont évanouis ; les montagnes s'aplanissoient devant
moi, et les dragons qui s'étoient présentés sur ma route, se sont appri-
voisés.   La semaine passée, je frappai le grand coup par la cassation
du bail de ma maison de *Bentinck-street ;* et après le mois de Septembre, si je ne couche pas à Lausanne, je coucherai dans la rue.   Mes
différens bonnets de nuit s'arrangent tous les jours, avec beaucoup
d'ordre et de facilité.   Lord Sheffield lui même, ce terrible St. George,
vrai champion de l'Angleterre, s'est rendu à mes raisons, ou plutôt aux
votres.   Il est charmé du tableau de votre première lettre, et malgré
l'activité de son ame, au lieu de me condamner, il me porte envie ; et
nous disputons (un peu en l'air) sur le projet d'une visite que lui, son
amiable compagne et sa fille ainée, se proposent de nous faire dans
deux ans aux bords du Lac Léman.   Bien loin de combattre mon
dessein, il me conseille, il me seconde dans l'exécution, et je n'aurai
pas besoin de recourir aux lumières de votre ami Louis Teyssier,
d'autant plus que pour les menus détails de la correspondence étrangère,
je trouve dans le libraire Elmsly un conseiller sage, instruit et discret.
* * *   Votre calcul de la dépense de la maison surpasse, non pas
absolument mes moyens, mais un peu mes espérances et mes conjectures.   La consummation en Suisse n'est point chargée d'impots ; le
vin y coule comme l'eau de fontaine ; votre jardin produit des fruits et
des légumes.   Se peut il que vingt ou trente Louis se dépensent tous
les mois pour le pain, la viande, le bois, la chandelle, quelque peu de
vin étranger, les domestiques de la cuisine, &c. ?   Je me flatte que
dans l'incertitude, vous avez cavé au plus fort ; mais enfin tout ce
détail se réglera suivant nos goûts et nos facultés ; et un mois d'ex-
périence sera plus instructif que cent pages de raisonnemens.   La

comparaison que vous me demandez de mon ménage de Londres, ne meneroit à rien. A la rigueur je ne tiens pas maison ; je ne donne presque jamais à manger : en hyver je dine assez rarement chez moi ; je ne soupe jamais ; et une partie assez considérable de la dépense (celle des clubs et des *tavernes*) n'entre point dans le compte de la maison. Ma nourriture domestique n'excede pas toutefois votre calcul Lausannois ; mais je sens la différence entre le petit couvert triste et mesquin d'un garçon, et la table honnête et hospitalière de deux amis, qui auront d'autres amis, &c.

Votre idée de masquer mes grands opérations est de la plus profonde politique ; mais les déclarations, et même les démarches qui seront nécessaires pour me retirer de la Chambre des Communes, déclareront un peu trop tot l'étendue de mes projets. Cependant on peut tirer quelque parti de cette honnête dissimulation, pour calmer un peu les scrupules, et les regrets des dames agées que vous connoissez, et que vous ne connoissez pas. Mais le moyen le plus efficace pour arrêter, ou pour ne pas écouter les mauvais discours, c'est de s'y dérober par une prompte fuite, et depuis que ma résolution a été prise, je compte les jours et les momens. Le 10 du mois prochain je retournerai à Londres, où je travaillerai vivement à préparer ce grand changement d'état. J'attends tous les jours la réponse de Madame Gibbon, à qui j'ai tâché de persuader qu'une entrevue de trois ou quatre jours à Bath, seroit moins douce qu'amère à tous les deux. Si elle se rend, ou fait semblant de se rendre à mes raisons, je compte que tout sera fini la première, ou du moins la seconde semaine de Septembre, et comme je couperai droit par la Champagne, et la Franche-Comté, je pourrois fort bien me trouver à Lausanne vers le 20 ou le 25 de ce mois là, supposé toujours que cette promptitude vous convienne, que votre maison sera libre, et que vous y serez rendu vous même. J'avois quelque idée de me détourner par Strasbourg, de vous prendre à Basle, et de passer avec vous par Berne, &c. mais, tout bien considéré, j'aime mieux abréger le grand voyage et réserver cette promenade (si nous avions envie de la faire) pour une saison plus tranquille. J'attends votre réponse dans une trentaine de jours ; mais sans l'attendre je vous écrirai de Londres, pour continuer le fil de l'histoire, et peut être pour vous charger de quelques achats de livres, qui se feront plus commodément à Basle qu'à Lausanne. Vous ne me donnez point de commissions. Cependant ce pays n'est pas sans industrie. Milord et Milady Sheffield vous embrassent très amicalement. Ce sera pour mois la perte la plus sensible.

EDWARD GIBBON *Esq. to the Right Hon. Lord* SHEFFIELD.

Monday, August 18, 1783.

IN the preparation of my journey I have not felt any circumstance more deeply than the kind concern of Lady Sheffield and the silent grief of Mrs. Porten. Yet the age of my friends makes a very essential difference. I can scarcely hope ever to see my aunt again ; but I flatter myself, that in less than two years, my *sister* will make me a visit, and that in less than four, I shall return it with a cheerful heart at Sheffield-Place. Business advances; this morning my books were shipped for Rouen, and will reach Lausanne almost as soon as myself. On Thursday morning the bulk of the library moves from Bentinck-street to Downing-street. I shall escape from the noise to Hampton Court, and spend three or four days in taking leave. I want to know your precise motions, what day you arrive in town, whether you visit Lord * * * before the races, &c. I am now impatient to be gone, and shall only wait for a last interview with you. Your medley of judges, advocates, politicians, &c. is rather *useful* than pleasant. Town is a vast solitude. Adieu.

The Same to the Same.   BENTINCK-STREET, Aug. 20, 1783.

I AM now concluding one of the most unpleasant days of my life. Will the day of our meeting again be accompanied with proportionable satisfaction? The business of preparation will serve to agitate and divert *my* thoughts; but I do not like your brooding over melancholy ideas in your solitude, and I heartily wish that both you and my dear Lady S. would immediately go over and pass a week at Brighton. Such is our imperfect nature, that dissipation is a far more efficacious remedy than reflection. At all events, let me hear from you soon. I have passed the evening at home, without gaining any intelligence.

M. DEYVERDUN *à M.* GIBBON.

DE NEUCHATEL, le 20 Aout, 1783.

IL y long tems que je n'ai été aussi mécontent de moi que je le suis dans ce moment; j'ai fait par l'événement une grande étourderie; j'ai manqué à ceux qui me quittent, et à celui qui vient me joindre; enfin je me suis très mal conduit. M. * * *, qui loge chez moi, me paraîssoit si disposé à quitter ma maison, quand je partis au printems, que ne doutant pas qu'il ne trouvât à s'arranger pendant tout l'été, je la regardois dejà d'avance comme vacante. Le plaisir extrême que j'avois à vous l'offrir, n'a pas peu contribué à soutenir cette illusion; enfin n'entendant parler cependant de rien, je lui ai écrit, après avoir reçu il y a six jours votre dernière, et il vient de me répondre qu'il n'a rien trouvé encore, mais qu'il n'épargnera ni soins ni dépenses, pour déloger, je ne lui ai au reste point marqué de quoi il étoit question; mais je l'ai prié de me dire à quelle époque il croyoit que ma maison pourroit être vacante. Je lui récrirai demain, car il me paraît qu'il est piqué, et tel que je le connois, malgré ce que je pourrai lui marquer, il sera fort empressé à décamper; mais malgré cela, il ne faut plus compter sur la maison entière pour votre arrivée.

Je vous demande mille pardons, mon cher ami, je me mets à votre merci; et en vérité si vous me voyiez en ce moment, vous auriez pitié de moi. Que nous reste-t-il à faire? car enfin il ne faut pas perdre la tête. J'ai un appartement de deux chambres sans lit, et deux petits cabinets, où vous pourriez être passablement, en attendant que la maison fût tout à fait libre; le tout est à plein pied de la terrasse, je me procurerois un logement au bout de mon jardin, et nous pourrions nous faire apporter à manger, chose pratiquée par nombre de Grands Seigneurs, entr'autres par Monseigneur le Margrave d'Anspach. 2. Ou bien louer un appartement garni que nous occuperons ensemble. Ou enfin 3, passer l'hyver dans quelle autre ville du Continent qu'il vous plaira choisir, ou j'irai vous joindre et vous porter mes excuses. Une réflexion que je fais dans ce moment ci, et qui me console un peu, c'est que dans votre première lettre, votre résolution ne tenoit point à ma maison, ni même à l'idée de loger et vivre avec moi. Ce second article aura toujours lieu, s'il vous convient, et le premier ne sera que différé ; ainsi appaisez vous, mon cher ami, pardonnez moi, et écrivez moi tout de suite lequel de ces partis vous convient le mieux, pour que je m'y conforme ; ou si vous en imaginez un nouveau, annoncez le moi. Une reflexion qui contribute encore à me consoler, c'est que pendant le tems que nous camperons ainsi en quelque manière, nous aurons le tems de bien voir autour de nous, et de nous arranger à notre aise, d'une manière stable et commode pour notre établissement. Encore une fois cependant, mon cher ami, mille pardons.

Milord Sheffield s'est montré plus raisonnable que je ne l'aurais cru ; diantre ! n'allez pas dire cela à sa seigneurie ; mais dites-lui, je vous prie, combien me plait l'espoir d'avoir l'honneur de le connoitre ; je vois encore d'ici son beau parc et le charmant ruisseau. Son suffrage dans des circonstances qui doivent sans doute le prévenir contre moi, me fait le plus grand plaisir, parceque je le regarde comme une bien forte preuve que vous prenez un parti convenable à votre bonheur. Des commissions, je ne saurais trop que vous dire dans ce moment ; comme vous avez une maison montée, voyez s'il n'y auroit pas des choses Anglaises auxquelles vous êtes accoutumé, et qui vous feroient plaisir, on en pourroit remplir une caisse. Un service de cette porcelaine de Bath, par exemple, nous conviendroit, ce me semble, assez.

Une de mes craintes maintenant, c'est que cette lettre ne vous parvienne peut être point avant votre départ ; cela serait très facheux. Toujours aurai-je soin de me trouver à Lausanne, au moins vers le milieu de mois prochain. Des couriers, comme celui que vous amenez, sont ordinairement de vrais domestiques de Grands Seigneurs, chers et importans ; mais vous les connoitrez en route. Ne soyez pas trop faché contre moi, du contretems que je vous annonce, et pensez qu'il y a enfin un appartement honnête de garçon, ma terrasse, mon jardin et votre ami, qui ne peuvent vous manquer——

Tout à vous,

D.

EDWARD GIBBON *Esq. to the Right Hon. Lord* SHEFFIELD.

Friday, August 22, 1783.

I AM astonished with your apparition and flight, and am at a loss to conjecture the mighty and sudden business of * * *, which could not be delayed till next week. Timeo * * *, their selfish cunning, and your sanguine unsuspecting spirit. Not dreaming of your arrival, I thought it unnecessary to apprise you, that I delayed leaving Hampton to this day; on Monday I shall return, and will expect you Tuesday evening, either in Bentinck or Downing street, as you like best. You have seen the piles of learning accumulated in your parlour; the transportation will be achieved to-day, and Bentinck-street is already reduced to a light, ignorant habitation, which I shall inhabit till about the first of September; four days must be allowed for clearing and packing; these I shall spend in Downing-street, and after seeing you a moment on your return, I shall start about Saturday the sixth. London is a desert, and life, without books, business, or society, will be somewhat tedious. From this state, you will judge that your plan coincides very well, only I think you should give me the whole of Wednesday in Bentinck-street. With regard to Bushy, perhaps as a compliment to Lord L. you had better defer it till your return. I admire Gregory Way, and should envy him, if I did not possess a disposition somewhat similar to his own. My Lady will be reposed and restored at Brighton; the torrent of Lords, Judges, &c. a proper remedy for you, was a medicine ill-suited to her constitution. I *tenderly* embrace her.

EDWARD GIBBON *Esq. to the Right Hon. Lady* SHEFFIELD.

MY DEAR FRIEND, BENTINCK-STREET, August 30, 1783.

FOR the names of Sheffelina, &c. are too playful for the serious temper of my mind. In the whole period of my life I do not recollect a day in which I felt more unpleasant sensations, than that on which I took my leave of Sheffield-Place. I forgot my friend Deyverdun, and the fair prospect of quiet and happiness which awaits me at Lausanne. I lost sight of our almost certain meeting at the end of a term, which, at our age, cannot appear very distant; nor could I amuse my uneasiness with the hopes, the more doubtful prospect, of your visit to Switzerland. The agitation of preparing everything for my departure has, in some degree, diverted these melancholy thoughts; yet I still look forwards to the decisive day (to-morrow se'nnight) with an anxiety of which yourself and Lord S. have the principal share.

Surely never anything was so unlucky as the unseasonable death of Sir John Russel on his passage to his friend at Sheffield-Place, which so strongly reminded us of the instability of human life and human expectations. The inundation of the assizes must have distressed and overpowered you; but I hope and I wish to hear from yourself, that the air of your favourite Brighton, the bathing, and the quiet society of two or three friends have composed and revived your spirits. Present my love to Sarah, and compliments to Miss Carter, &c. Give me a speedy and satisfactory line. I am most truly yours.

EDWARD GIBBON *Esq. to the Right Hon. Lord* SHEFFIELD.

DOWNING-STREET, September 8, 1783.

AS we are not unconscious of each other's feelings, I shall only say, that I am glad you did not go alone into Sussex; an American rebel to dispute with gives a diversion to uneasy spirits, and I heartily wished for such a friend or adversary during the remainder of the day. No letter from Deyverdun ; the post is arrived, but two Flanders' mails are due. Æolus does not seem to approve of my designs, and there is little merit in waiting till Friday. I should wait with more reluctance, did I think there was much chance of success. I dine with Craufurd, and if anything is decided, will send an extraordinary Gazette. You have obliged me beyond expression, by your kindness to aunt Kitty ; she will drink her afternoon tea at Sheffield next Friday. For my sake Lady S. will be kind to the old lady, who will not be troublesome, and will vanish at the first idea of Brighton. Has not that salubrious air already produced some effects ? Peace will be proclaimed to-morrow ; odd ! as war was never declared. The buyers of stock seem as indifferent as yourself about the definitive treaty. Tell Maria, that though you had forgotten the *Annales de la Vertu,* I have directed them to be sent, but know nothing of their plan or merit. Adieu. When you see my Lady, say everything tender and friendly to her. I did not know how much I loved her. She may depend upon my keeping a separate, though not perhaps a very frequent account with her. *A propos,* I think aunt Kitty has a secret wish to sleep in my room ; if it is not occupied, she might be indulged. Once more, adieu.

M. GIBBON *à M.* DEYVERDUN.

DOWNING-STREET, à LONDRES, le 9 Septembre 1783.

SELON ma diligence ordinaire je répondis le 31 Juillet à votre lettre sans date, reçue le jour auparavant. Je voyois couler le mois d'Août, fortement persuadé qu'il ne s'acheveroit point, sans m'apporter votre *ultimatum.* Nous voici au 9 Septembre, quarante jours depuis ma missive, et je n'ai point encore de vos nouvelles ! Il est vrai que des vents contraires nous retiennent deux malles de Flandres, et vos dépêches peuvent et doivent s'y trouver. Mais si elles ne m'apportent rien de votre part, je serai très étonné, et pas moins embarrassé. Se peut-il que vos lettres, ou les miennes se soient égarées en chemin ? êtes vous mort ? êtes vous malade ? avez vous changé d'avis ? est-il survenu des difficultés ? Je vous ai écrit de nouveau le 19 Août ; mais l'incertitude de mes craintes me sait encore hazarder ce billet. Après des travaux inouis, j'ai enfin brisé tous mes liens, et depuis ma résolution, je n'ai pas eu un instant de regrets ; ma vive impatience se fortifie tous les jours, et depuis que j'ai abandonné ma maison et ma bibliotheque, l'ennui a prêté des ailes à l'espérance et à l'amitié. Enfin j'avois fixé mon départ au commencement de la semaine ; à cette heure il est renvoyé a Vendredi prochain, 12 de ce mois, dans la supposition toujours d'une lettre de votre part, car je ne saurois entreprendre ma course, sans être assuré de la réception qui m'attend au bout. Je me ferai toujours précéder par un mot de billet ; mais la saison est tellement orageuse, qu'il me sera impossible d'arrêter le jour de mon arrivée à Lausanne, jusqu'à ce que je me voye en sureté audela de la mer. Adieu. Vous devez être de retour à Lausanne. Annoncez moi aux enfans des mes anciennes connoissances.

EDWARD GIBBON *Esq. to the Right Hon. Lord* SHEFFIELD.

Thursday, September 11, 1783.

THE scheme (which you may impart to my Lady) is completely
vanished, and I support the disappointment with heroic patience.
* * * goes down to Chatsworth to-morrow, and * * * does not recommend my waiting for the event ; yet the appointment is not yet declared,
and I am ignorant of the name and merits of my successful competitor. Is it not wonderful that I am still in suspence, without a
letter from Deyverdun ? No, it is not wonderful, since no Flanders
mail is arrived : to morrow three will be due. I am therefore in a
miserable state of doubt and anxiety ; in a much better house indeed
than my own, but without books, or business, or society. I send or
call two or three times each day to Elmsly's, and can only say that I
shall fly the next day, Saturday, Sunday, &c. after I have got my
quietus. Aunt Kitty was delighted with my Lady's letter ; at her age,
and in her situation, every kind attention is pleasant. I took my leave
this morning ; and as I did not wish to repeat the scene, and thought
she would be better at Sheffield, I suffer her to go to-morrow. Your
discretion will communicate or withhold any tidings of my departure
or delay as you just most expedient. Christie writes to you this post ;
he talks, in his rhetorical way, of many purchasers. Do you approve
of his fixing a day for the auction ? To us he talked of an indefinite
advertisement. No news, except that we keep Negapatnam. The
other day the French Ambassador mentioned that the Empress of
Russia, a precious ——, had proposed to ratify the principles of the
armed neutrality, by a definitive treaty ; but that the French, obliging
creatures ! had declared, that they would neither propose nor accept
an article so disagreeable to England. Grey Elliot was pleased with
your attention, and says you are a perfect master of the subject
(American commerce). Adieu. If I could be sure that no mail would
arrive to-morrow, I would run down with my aunt. My heart is not
light. I embrace my Lady with true affection, but I need not repeat it.

EDWARD GIBBON *Esq. to the Right Hon. Lord* SHEFFIELD.

DOWNING-STREET, Friday, September 12, 1783.

SINCE my departure is near, and inevitable, you and Lady S. will be
rather sorry than glad to hear that I am detained, day after day, by
the caprice of the winds. *Three* Flanders Mails are now due. I
know not how to move without the final letter from Deyverdun, which
I expected a fortnight ago, and my fancy (perfectly unreasonable)
begins to create strange phantoms. A state of suspence is painful,
but it will be alleviated by the short notes which I mean to write, and
hope to receive, every post. A separation has some advantages,
though they are purchased with bitter pangs ; among them is the
pleasure of knowing how dear we are to our friends, and how dear
they are to us. It will be a kind office to sooth aunt Kitty's sorrows,
and " to rock the cradle of declining age." She will be vexed to hear
that I am not yet gone ; but she is reasonable and cheerful. Adieu.
Most truly yours.

EDWARD GIBBON, *Esq. to the Right Hon. Lord* SHEFFIELD.

DOWNING-ST., Sat., Sept. 13, 1783.

Enfin la bombe a crevé.—The three Flanders mails are arrived this day, but without any letters from Deyverdun. Most incomprehensible! After many adverse reflections, I have finally resolved to begin my journey on Monday; a heavy journey, with much apprehension, and much regret. Yet I consider, first, That if he is alive and well, (an unpleasant *if,*) scarcely any event can have happened to disappoint our mutual wishes; and, 2ndly, That, supposing the very worst, even that worst would not overthrow my general plan of living abroad, though it would derange my hopes of a quiet and delightful establishment with my friend. Upon the whole, without giving way to melancholy fears, my reason conjectures that his indolence thought it superfluous to write any more, that it was my business to act and move, and his duty to sit still and receive me with open arms. At least he is well informed of my operations, as I wrote to him (since his last) July thirty-first, from Sheffield-Place; August nineteenth; and this week, September ninth. The two first have already reached him.

As I shall not arrive at, or depart from, Dover till Tuesday night, (alas! I may be confined there a week,) you will have an opportunity, by dispatching a parcel *per* post to Elmsly's, to catch the Monday's post. Let us improve these last short moments: I want to hear how poor Kitty behaves. I am really impatient to be gone. It is provoking to be so near, yet so far from, certain persons. London is a desert. I dine to-morrow with the Paynes, who pass through. Lord Lough-borough was not returned from Buxton yesterday. Sir Henry Clinton found me out this morning: he talks with rapture of visits to be made at Sheffield, and returned at Brighton. I envy him those visits more than the red ribbon. Adieu.

The Same to the Same.   DOVER, Wed., Sept. 17, 1783.

THE best laws are useless without proper guardians. Your letter *per* Sunday's post is not arrived, (its fate is uncertain and irrevocable, you must repeat any material article,) but that *per* Monday's post reached me last night. Oliver is more insolent than his great-grandfather; but you will cope with one, and would not have been much afraid of the other. Last night the wind was so high, that the vessel could not stir from the harbour; this day it is brisk and fair. We are flattered with the hope of making Calais harbour by the same tide, in three hours and a half; but any delay will leave the disagreeable option of a tottering boat or a tossing night. What a cursed thing to live in an island, this step is more awkward than the whole journey! The triumvirate of this memorable embarkation will consist of the grand Gibbon, Henry Laurence Esquire, President of Congress, and Mr. Secretary, Colonel, Admiral, Philosopher, Thompson, attended by three horses, who are not the most agreeable fellow-passengers. If we survive, l will finish and seal my letter at Calais. Our salvation shall be ascribed to the prayers of my Lady and Aunt; for I do believe they both pray.

BOULOGNE, Thursday Morning, Ten o'clock.
Instead of Calais, the wind has driven us to Boulogne, where we landed in the evening, without much noise and difficulty. The night is passed, the custom-house is despatched, the post-horses are ordered, and I shall start about eleven o'clock. I had not the least symptom of sea-sickness, while my companions were spewing round me. Laurence has read the pamphlet,* and thinks it has done much mischief. A good sign! Adieu. The Captain is impatient. I shall reach Lausanne by the end of next week, but may probably write on the road.

EDWARD GIBBON, *Esq. to the Right Hon. Lord* SHEFFIELD.

LANGRES, Sept. 23, 1783.
LET the geographical Maria place before you the map of France, and trace my progress as far as this place, through the following towns: Boulogne, (where I was forced to land,) St. Omer, (where I recovered my road,) Aire, Bethune, Douay, Cambray, St. Quintin, La Fere, Laon, Rheims, Chalons, St. Dizier, and Langres, where I have just finished my supper. The Inns, in general, more agreeable to the palate, than to the sight or smell. But, with some short exceptions of time and place, I have enjoyed good weather and good roads, and at the end of the ninth day, I feel so little fatigued, that the journey appears no more than a pleasant airing. I have generally conversed with Homer and Lord Clarendon, often with Caplin and Muff (his dog); sometimes with the French postillions, of the above mentioned animals the least rational. To-morrow I lie at Besançon, and, according to the arrangement of post or hired horses, shall either sup at Lausanne on Friday, or dine there Saturday. I feel some suspense and uneasiness with regard to Deyverdun; but in the scale both of reason and constitution, my hopes preponderate very much above my fears. From Lausanne I will immediately write. I embrace my Lady. If aunt Kitty's gratitude and good-breeding have not driven her away upon the first whisper of Brighton, she will share this intelligence; if she is gone, a line from you would be humane and attentive. *Monsieur les Chevaux seront prets a cinq heurs.* Adieu. I am going into an excellent bed, about six feet high from the ground.

EDWARD GIBBON, *Esq. to the Right Hon. Lord* SHEFFIELD.

LAUSANNE, Sept. 30, 1783.
I ARRIVED safe in harbour last Saturday, the 27th instant, about ten o'clock in the morning; but as the post only goes out twice a week, it was not in my power to write before this day. Except one day, between Langres and Besançon, which was laborious enough, I finished my easy and gentle airing without any fatigue, either of mind or body. I found Deyverdun well and happy, but much more happy at the sight of a friend, and the accomplishment of a scheme which he had so long and impatiently desired. His garden, terrace, and *park*, have even

* Lord Sheffield's Observations on the Commerce of the American States.

exceeded the most sanguine of my expectations and remembrances; and you yourself cannot have forgotten the charming prospect of the lake, the mountains, and the declivity of the Pays de Vaud. But as human life is perpetually chequered with good and evil, 1 have found some disappointments on my arrival. The easy nature of Deyverdun, his indolence, and his impatience, had prompted him to reckon too positively that his house would be vacant at Michaelmas; some unforeseen difficulties have arisen, or have been discovered when it was already too late, and the consummation of our hopes is (I am much afraid) postponed to next spring. At first, I was knocked down by the unexpected thunderbolt, but I have gradually been reconciled to my fate, and have granted a free and gracious pardon to my friend. As his own apartment, which afforded me a temporary shelter, is much too narrow for a settled residence, we hired for the winter a convenient ready furnished apartment in the nearest part of the Rue de Bourg, whose back door leads in three steps to the terrace and garden, as often as a tolerable day shall tempt us to enjoy their beauties; and this arrangement has even its advantage, of giving us time to deliberate and provide, before we enter on a larger and more regular establishment. But this is not the sum of my misfortunes; hear and pity! The day after my arrival (Sunday) we had just finished a very temperate dinner, and intended to begin a round of visits on foot, *chapeau sous le bras*, when, most unfortunately, Deyverdun proposed to shew me something in the court; we boldly and successfully ascended a flight of stone steps, but in the descent I missed my footing, and strained, or sprained, my ancle in a painful manner. My old latent enemy, (I do not mean the Devil,) who is always on the watch, has made an ungenerous use of his advantage, and I much fear that my arrival at Lausanne will be marked with a fit of the gout, though it is quite unnecessary that the intelligence or suspicion should find its way to Bath. Yesterday afternoon I lay, or at least sat, in state to receive visits, and at the same moment my room was filled with four different nations. The loudest of these nations was the single voice of the Abbé Raynal, who, like your friend, has chosen this place for the asylum of freedom and history. His conversation, which might be very agreeable, is intolerably loud, peremptory, and insolent; and you would imagine that he alone was the monarch and legislator of the world. Adieu. I embrace my Lady and the infants. With regard to the important transactions for which you are constituted plenipotentiary, I expect with some impatience, but with perfect confidence, the result of your labours. You may remember what I mentioned of my conversation with * * * about the place of Minister at Berne; I have talked it over with Deyverdun, who does not dislike the idea, provided this place was allowed to be my villa during at least two-thirds of the year; but for my part, I am sure that * * * are worth more than ministerial friendship and gratitude; so I am inclined to think, that they are preferable to an office which would be procured with difficulty, enjoyed with constraint and expence, and lost, perhaps, next April, in the annual revolutions of our domestic Government. Again adieu.

EDWARD GIBBON, *Esq. to the Right. Hon. Lady* SHEFFIELD.

LAUSANNE, October 28, 1783.

THE progress of my gout is in general so regular, and there is so much uniformity in the History of its Decline and Fall, that I have hitherto indulged my laziness, without much shame or remorse, without supposing that you would be very anxious for my safety, which has been sufficiently provided for by the triple care of my friend Deyverdun, my humbler friend Caplin, and a very conversable physician, (not the famous Tissot,) whose ordinary fee is ten batz, or rather fifteen pence English. After the usual increase and decrease of the member (for it has been confined to the injured part) the gout has retired in good order, and the remains of weakness, which obliged me to move on the rugged pavement of Lausanne with a stick, or rather small crutch, are to be ascribed to the sprain, which might have been a much more serious business. As I have now spent a month at Lausanne, you will enquire with much curiosity, more kindness, and some mixture of spite and malignity, how far the place has answered my expectations, and whether I do not repent of a resolution which has appeared so rash and ridiculous to my ambitious friends? To this question, however natural and reasonable, I shall not return an immediate answer, for two reasons : 1. *I have not yet made a fair trial.* The disappointment and delay with regard to Deyverdun's house, will confine us this winter to lodgings, rather convenient than spacious or pleasant. I am only beginning to recover my strength and liberty, and to look about on persons and things ; the greatest part of those persons are in the country taken up with their vintage ; my books are not yet arrived, and, in short, I cannot look upon myself as settled in that comfortable way which you and I understand and relish. Yet the weather has been heavenly, and till this time, the end of October, we enjoy the brightness of the sun, and somewhat gently complain of its immoderate heat. 2. If I should be too sanguine in explaining my satisfaction in what I have done, you would ascribe that satisfaction to the novelty of the scene, and the inconstancy of man ; and I deem it far more safe and prudent to postpone any positive declaration, till I am placed by experience beyond the danger of repentance and recantation. Yet of one thing I am sure, that I possess in this country, as well as in England, the best cordial of life, a sincere, tender, and sensible friend, adorned with the most valuable and pleasant qualities both of the heart and head. The inferior enjoyments of leisure and society are likewise in my power ; and in the short excursions which I have hitherto made, I have commenced or renewed my acquaintance with a certain number of persons, more especially women, (who, at least in France and this country, are undoubtedly superior to our prouder sex,) of rational minds and elegant manners. I breakfast alone, and have declared that I receive no visits in a morning, which you will easily suppose is devoted to study. I find it impossible, without inconvenience, to defer my dinner beyond two o'clock. We have got a very good woman cook. Deyverdun, who is somewhat of an Epicurean philosopher, understands the management of a table, and we frequently invite a guest or two to share our luxurious, but not extravagant repasts. The afternoons are (and will be much more so hereafter) devoted to society, and I shall find it necessary to play at cards much oftener than in London : but I do not dislike that way of passing a couple of hours, and I shall not be ruined at shilling whist. As yet I have not supped, but in the course of the winter I must sometimes sacrifice an evening abroad, and in exchange I hope sometimes to steal a day at home, without going into company * * *. I have all this time been talking to Lord Sheffield ; I hope that he has dispatched my affairs, and it would give me pleasure to hear that I am no longer member for Lymington, nor Lord of *Lenborough*. Adieu. I feel every day that the distance serves only to make me think with more tenderness of the persons whom I love.

EDWARD GIBBON, *Esq. to the Right Hon. Lord* SHEFFIELD.

LAUSANNE, Nov. 14, 1783.

LAST Tuesday, November eleventh, after plaguing and vexing yourself all the morning, about some business of your fertile creation, you went to the House of Commons, and passed the afternoon, the evening, and perhaps the night, without sleep or food, stifled in a close room by the heated respiration of six hundred politicians, inflamed by party and passion, and tired of the repetition of dull nonsense, which, in that illustrious assembly, so far outweighs the proportion of reason and eloquence. On the same day, after a studious morning, a friendly dinner, and a cheerful assembly of both sexes, I retired to rest at eleven o'clock, satisfied with the past day, and certain that the next would afford me the return of the same quiet and rational enjoyments. *Which has the better bargain ?* Seriously, I am every hour more greatful to my own judgment and resolution, and only regret that I so long delayed the execution of a favourite plan, which I am convinced is the best adapted to my character and inclinations. Your conjecture of the revolutions of my face, when I heard that the house was for this winter inaccessible, is probable, but false. I bore my disappointment with the temper of a sage, and only use it to render the prospect of next year still more pleasing to my imagination. You are likewise mistaken in imputing my fall to the awkwardness of my limbs. The same accident might have happened to Slingsby himself, or to any *hero* of the age, the most distinguished for his *bodily activity.* I have now resumed my entire strength, and walk with caution, yet with speed and safety, through the streets of this mountainous city. After a month of the finest autumn I ever saw, the *bise* (the N.E. wind) made me feel my old acquaintance ; the weather is now milder, and this present day is dark and rainy, not much better than what you probably enjoy in England. The town is comparatively empty, but the Noblesse are returning every day from their chateaux, and I already perceive that I shall have more reason to complain of dissipation than of dulness. As I told Lady S. I am afraid of being too rash and hasty in expressing my satisfaction ; but I must again repeat, that appearances are extremely favourable. I am sensible that general praise conveys no distinct ideas, but it is very difficult to enter into particulars where the individuals are unknown, or indifferent to our correspondent. You have forgotten the *old* gencration, and in twenty years a new one is grown up. Death has swept many from the world, and chance or choice has brought many to this place. If you enquire after your old acquaintance Catherine, you must be told, that she is solitary, ugly, blind, and universally forgotten. Your later flame, and our common goddess, the Eliza, passed a month at the inn. She came to consult Tissot, and was acquainted with Cerjat. And now to business. * * * With regard to meaner cases, these are two, which you can and will undertake. 1. As I have not renounced my country, I should be glad to hear of your parliamentary squabbles, which may be done with small trouble and expence. After an interesting debate, my Lady in due time may cut the speeches from Woodfall. You will write or dictate any curious anecdote, and the whole, inclosed in a letter, may be dispatched to Lausanne. 2. A set of Wedgewood china, which we talked of in London, and which would be most acceptable here. As you have a *sort* of a taste, I leave to your own choice the colour and the pattern ; but as I have the inclination and means to live very handsomely *here*, I desire that the size and number of things may be adequate to a plentiful table. If you see Lord North, assure him of my gratitude ; had he been a more successful friend, I should now be drudging at the Board of Customs, or vexed with business in the amiable society of———. To Lord Loughborough present an affectionate sentiment ; I am satisfied of his intention to serve me, if I had not been in such a fidget. I am sure you will not fail, while you are in town, to visit and comfort poor aunt Kitty. I wrote to her on my first arrival, and she may be assured that I will not neglect her. To my Lady I say nothing; we have now our private correspondence, into which the eye of an husband should not be permitted to intrude. I am really satisfied with the success of the pamphlet ;* not only because I have a sneaking kindness for the author, but as it shews me that plain sense, full information, and warm spirit, are still acceptable in the world. You talk of Lausanne as a place of retirement, yet, from the situation and freedom of the Pays de Vaud, all nations, and all extraordinary characters, are astonished to meet each other. The Abbé Raynal, the grand Gibbon, and Mercier, author of the *Tableau de Paris*, have been in the same room. The other day the Prince and Princess de Ligne, the Duke and Duchess d'Ursel, &c. came from Brussels on purpose (literally true) to act a comedy at * * * in the country. He was dying, and could not appear ; but we had comedy, ball, and supper. The event seems to have revived him ; for that great man is fallen from his ancient glory, and his nearest relations refuse to see him. I told you of poor Catherine's deplorable state ; but Madame de Mesery, at the age of sixty-nine, is still handsome. Adieu.

EDWARD GIBBON, *Esq. to the Right Hon. Lord* SHEFFIELD.

LAUSANNE, Dec. 20, 1783.

I HAVE received both your epistles ; and as any excuse will serve a man who is at the same time very busy and very idle, I patiently expected the second, before I entertained any thoughts of answering the first. * * * * I therefore conclude, that on every principle of

* Observations on the Commerce with the American States.

common sense, before this moment your active zeal has already expelled me from the house, to which, without regret, I bid an everlasting farewell. The agreeable hour of five o'clock in the morning, at which you commonly retire, does not tend to revive my attachment; but if you add the soft hours of your morning Committee,* in the discussion of taxes, customs, frauds, smugglers, &c. I think I should beg to be released and quietly sent to the gallies, as a place of leisure and freedom. Yet I do not depart from my general principles of toleration. Some animals are made to live in the water, others on the earth, many in the air, and some, as it is now believed, even in fire. Your present hurry of Parliament I perfectly understand; when opposition make the attack,

——— *Horæ*
Momento cita mors venit, aut victoria læta.

But when the Minister brings forward any strong and decisive measure, he at length prevails; but his progress is retarded at every step, and in every stage of the bill, by a pertinacious, though unsuccessful, minority. I am not sorry to hear of the splendour of Fox; I am proud, in a foreign country, of his fame and abilities, and our little animosities are extinguished by my retreat from the English stage. With regard to the substance of the business, I scarcely know what to think : the vices of the Company (East India Company), both in their persons and their constitution, were manifold and manifest ; the danger was imminent, and such an empire, with thirty millions of subjects, was not to be lost for trifles. Yet, on the other hand, the faith of charters, the rights of property ! I hesitate and tremble. Such an innovation would at least require that the remedy should be as certain as the evil, and the proprietors may perhaps insinuate, that *they* were as competent guardians of their own affairs, as either * * * or * * *. Their acting without a salary, seems childish, and their not being removable by the Crown, is a strange and dangerous precedent. But enough of politics, which I now begin to view through a thin, cold, distant cloud, yet not without a reasonable degree of curiosity and patriotism. From the papers (especially when you add an occasional slice of the Chronicle) I shall be amply informed of facts and debates. From you I expect the causes, rather than the events, the true springs of action, and those interesting anecdotes which seldom ascend the garret of a Fleet-street editor. You say that many friends (alias acquaintance) have expressed curiosity and concern ; I should not wish to be immediately forgotten. That others (you once mentioned Gerard Hamilton) condemn Government, for suffering the departure of a man who might have done them some credit and some service, perhaps as much as * * * himself. To you, in the confidence of friendship, and without either pride or resentment, I will fairly own that I am somewhat of Gerard's opinion ; and if I did not compare it with the rest of his character, I should be astonished that * * * suffered me to depart, without even a civil answer to my letter. Were I capable of hating a man, whom it is not easy to hate, I should find myself amply revenged by * * *. But the happy souls in Paradise are susceptible only of love and pity, and though

* A select Committee for inquiring into frauds committed in respect to the revenue.

Lausanne is not a Paradise, more especially in winter, I do assure you, in sober prose, that it has hitherto fulfilled, and even surpassed, my warmest expectation. Yet I often cast a look toward Sheffield-Place, where you now repose, if you can repose, during the Christmas recess. Embrace my Lady, the young Baroness, and the gentle Louisa, and insinuate to your silent Consort, that separate letters require separate answers. Had I an air balloon, the great topic of modern conversation, I would call upon you till the meeting of Parliament. *Vale.*

EDWARD GIBBON, Esq. to Mrs. PORTEN.

DEAR MADAM,   LAUSANNE, Dec. 27, 1783.

THE unfortunate are loud and loquacious in their complaints, but real happiness is content with its own silent enjoyment ; and if that happiness is of a quiet uniform kind, we suffer days and weeks to elapse without communicating our sensations to a distant friend. By you, therefore, whose temper and understanding have extracted from human life on every occasion the best and most comfortable ingredients, my silence will always be interpreted as an evidence of content, and you would only be alarmed (the danger is not at hand) by the too frequent repetition of my letters. Perhaps I should have continued to slumber, I don't know how long, had I not been awakened by the anxiety which you express in your last letter. * * *

From this base subject I ascend to one which more seriously and strongly engages your thoughts, the consideration of my health and happiness. And you will give me credit when I assure you with sincerity, that I have not repented a single moment of the step which I have taken, and that I only regret the not having executed the same design two, or five, or even ten years ago. By this time I might have returned independent and rich to my native country ; I should have escaped many disagreeable events that have happened in the meanwhile, and I should have avoided the parliamentary life, which experience has proved to be neither suitable to my temper, nor conducive to my fortune. In speaking of the happiness which I enjoy, you will agree with me, in giving the preference to a sincere and sensible friend ; and though you cannot discern the full extent of his merit, you will easily believe that Deyverdun is the man. Perhaps two persons so perfectly fitted to live together, were never formed by Nature and education. We have both read and seen a great variety of objects ; the lights and shades of our different characters are happily blended, and a friendship of thirty years has taught us to enjoy our mutual advantages, and to support our unavoidable imperfections. In love and marriage, some harsh sounds will sometimes interrupt the harmony, and in the course of time, like our neighbours, we must expect some disagreeable moments ; but confidence and freedom are the two pillars of our union, and I am much mistaken, if the building be not solid and comfortable. One disappointment I have indeed experienced, and patiently supported. The family who were settled in Deyverdun's house started some unexpected difficulties, and will not leave it till the spring ; so that you must not yet expect any poetical, or even historical, description of the beauties of my habitation. During the dull months of winter we are satisfied with a very comfortable apartment in the middle of the town, and even derive some advantage from this delay; as it gives us time to arrange some plans of alteration and furniture, which will embellish our future and more elegant dwelling. In this season I rise (not at four in the morning) but a little before eight; at nine, I am called from my study to breakfast, which I always perform alone, in the English style, and, with the aid of Caplin, I perceive no difference between Lausanne and Bentinck-street. Our mornings are usually passed in separate studies; we never approach each other's door without a previous message, or thrice knocking, and my apartment is already sacred and formidable to strangers. I dress at half past one, and at two (an early hour, to which I am not perfectly reconciled,) we sit down to dinner. We have hired a female cook, well-skilled in her profession, and accustomed to the taste of every nation; as for instance, we had excellent mince-pies yesterday. After dinner, and the departure of our company, one, two, or three friends, we read together some amusing book, or play at chess, or retire to our rooms, or make visits, or go to the coffee-house. Between six and seven the assemblies begin, and I am oppressed only with their number and variety. Whist, at shillings or half-crowns, is the game I generally play, and I play three rubbers with pleasure. Between nine and ten we withdraw to our bread and cheese, and friendly converse, which sends us to bed at eleven; but these sober hours are too often interrupted by private or numerous suppers, which I have not the courage to resist, though I practise a laudable abstinence at the best furnished tables. Such is the skeleton of my life; it is impossible to communicate a perfect idea of the vital and substantial parts, the characters of the men and women with whom I have very easily connected myself in looser and closer bonds, according to their inclination and my own. If I do not deceive myself and if Deyverdun does not flatter me, I am already a general favourite; and as our likings and dislikes are commonly mutual, I am equally satisfied with the freedom and elegance of manners, and (after proper allowances and exceptions) with the worthy and amiable qualities of many individuals. The autumn has been beautiful, and the winter hitherto mild, but in January we must expect some severe frost. Instead of rolling in a coach, I walk the streets, wrapped up in a fur cloak; but this exercise is wholesome, and except an accidental fit of the gout of a few days, I never enjoyed better health. I am no longer in Pavillard's house, where I was almost starved with cold and hunger, and you may be assured that I now enjoy every benefit of comfort, plenty, and even decent luxury. You wish me happy; acknowledge that such a life is more conducive to happiness, than five nights in the week passed in the House of Commons, or five mornings spent at the Custom-house. Send me, in return, a fair account of your own situation in mind and body. I am satisfied your own good sense would have reconciled you to inevitable separation; but there never was a more suitable diversion than your visit to Sheffield-Place. Among the innumerable proofs of friendship which I have received from that family, there are none which affect me more sensibly than their kind civilities to you, though I am persuaded that they are

x

at least as much on your account as on mine. At length Madame de
* * * is delivered by her tyrant's death ; her daughter, a valuable
woman of this place, has made some enquiries, and though her own
circumstances are narrow, she will not suffer her father's widow to be
left totally destitute. I am glad you derived so much melancholy
pleasure from the letters, yet had I known it, I should have withheld
* * *.

EDWARD GIBBON, *Esq. to the Right Hon. Lord* SHEFFIELD.

LAUSANNE, Jan. 24, 1784.

WITHIN two or three days after your last *gracious* epistle, your complaints were silenced, and your enquiries were satisfied, by an ample
dispatch of four pages, which overflowed the inside of the cover, and
in which I exposed my opinions of things in general, public as well as
private, as they existed in my mind, in my state of ignorance and error,
about the eighteenth or twentieth of last month. Within a week after
that date I epistolised, in the same rich and copious strain, the two
venerable females of Newman-street and Bath, whose murmurings
must now be changed into songs of gratitude and applause. My correspondence with the holy matron of Northamptonshire has been less
lively and loquacious. You have not forgotten the author's vindication
of himself from the foul calumnies of pretended Christians. Within a
fortnight after his arrival at Lausanne, he communicated the joyful
event to Mrs. Esther Gibbon. She answered, *per* return of post, both
letters at the same time, and in very dutiful language, almost excusing
her advice, which was intended for my spiritual as well as temporal
good, and assuring me, that *nobody should be able to injure me with
her.* Unless the saint is an hypocrite, such an expression must convey
a favourable and important meaning. At all events, it is worth giving
ourselves some trouble about her, without indulging any sanguine
expectations of inheritance. So much for my females ; with regard to
my male correspondents, you are the only one to whom I have given
any signs of my existence, though I have formed many a generous
resolution. Yet I am not insensible of the kind and friendly manner
in which Lord Loughborough has distinguished me. He could have
no inducements of interest, and now that I view the distant picture
with impartial eyes, I am convinced that (for a statesman) he was sincere in his wishes to serve me. When you see *him*, the Paynes, Eden,
Crauford, &c. tell them that I am well, happy, and ashamed. On
your side, the zeal and diligence of your pen has surprised and delighted
me, and your letters, at this interesting moment, are exactly such as I
wished them to be—authentic anecdotes, and rational speculations,
worthy of a man who acts a part in the great theatre, and who fills a
seat, not only in the general Pandæmonium, but in the private council
of the Princes of the infernal regions. With regard to the detail of
parliamentary operations, I must repeat my request to you, or rather
to my Lady, who will now be on the spot, that she will write, not with
her pen, but with her scissors, and that after every debate which
deserves to pass the sea and the mountains, she will dissect the faithful

narrative of Woodfall, and send it off by the next post, as an agreeable supplement to the meagre accounts of our weekly papers. The wonderful revolutions of last month have sounded to my ear more like the shifting scenes of a comedy, or comic opera, than like the sober events of real and modern history ; and the irregularity of our winter posts, which sometimes retarded, and sometimes hastened, the arrival of the dispatches, has increased the confusion of our ideas. Surely the Lord has blinded the eyes of Pharaoh and of his servants ; the obstinacy of last spring was nothing compared to the headstrong and headlong madness of this winter. I expect with much impatience the first days of your meeting ; the purity and integrity of the coalition will suffer a fiery trial ; but if they are true to themselves and to each other, a majority of the House of Commons must prevail ; the rebellion of the young gentlemen will be crushed, and the masters will resume the government of the school. After the address and answer, I have no conception that Parliament can be dissolved during the session ; but if the present Ministry can outlive the storm, I think the death-warrant will infallibly be signed in the summer. *Here* I blush for my country, without confessing her shame. Fox acted like a man of honour, yet surely his union with Pitt affords the only hope of salvation. How miserably are we wasting the season of peace !

I have written three pages before I come to my own business and feelings. In the first place, I most sincerely rejoice that I left the ship, and swam ashore on a plank : the daily and hourly agitation in which I must have lived would have made me truly miserable ; and if I had obtained a place during pleasure, * * *, for instance ? On the first news of the dissolution, I considered my seat as so totally and irrecoverably gone, that I have been less afflicted with * * *'s obstinacy. * * *. On this occasion remember you are acting for a *poor* friend ; dismiss a little of the spirit of faction and patriotism, and stoop to a prudential line of conduct, which in your own case you might possibly disdain. * * * Perhaps you will abuse my prudence and patriotism, when I inform you, that I have already vested a part (thirty thousand livres, about one thousand three hundred pounds) in the new loan of the King of France. I get eight *per cent.* on the joint lives of Deyverdun and myself, besides thirty tickets in a very advantageous lottery, of which the highest prize is an annuity of forty thousand livres (one thousand seven hundred pounds) a year. At this moment, the beginning of a peace, and probably a long peace, I think (and the world seems to think) the French funds at least as solid as our own, I have empowered my agent, M. de Lessart, a capital banker at Paris, to draw upon Gosling for the money two months hence ; and to avoid all accidents that may result from untoward delays, and mercantile churlishness, I expect that you will support my credit in Fleet-street with your own more respectable name. * * * What say you now ? Am I not a wise man ? My letter is enormous, and the post on the wing. In a few days I will write to my Lady herself, and enter something more into the details of domestic life. Suffice it to say, that the scene becomes each day more pleasant and comfortable, and that I complain only of the dissipation of Lausanne. In the course of March or April we shall take possession of Deyverdun's house. My books, which, by some strange neglect, did not leave Paris till the third of this month, will arrive in a few weeks; and I shall resume the continuation of my History, which I shall prosecute with the more vigour, as the completion affords me a distant prospect of a visit to England. Adieu. Ever yours.

EDWARD GIBBON, *Esq. to the Right Hon. Lord* SHEFFIELD.

BARON!   LAUSANNE, Feb. 20, 1784.

AFTER my last enormous dispatch, nothing can remain, except some small gleanings, or occasional hints; and thus in order: I am not conscious that any of your valuable MSS. have miscarried, or that I have omitted to answer any essential particulars. They stand in my bureau carefully arranged, and docketed under the following dates; September twenty-three, October twenty-three, November eighteen, December two, December fifteen, December nineteen, December twenty-three, December twenty-nine, January sixteen, which last I have received this day, February 2nd. For greater perspicuity, it will not be amiss (on either side) to number our future epistles, by a conspicuous Roman character inscribed in the front, to which we may at any time refer. But instead of writing by Ostend, the shorter and surer way, especially on all occasions that deserve celerity, will be to inclose them to my banker, M. de Lessart at Paris, who will forward them to me. Through Germany the passage by sea is more uncertain, the roads worse, and the distance greater: we often complain of delay and irregularity at this interesting moment. By your last I find that you have boldly and generously opened a treaty with the enemy, which I proposed with fear and hesitation. I impatiently expect the result; and again repeat, that *whatever* you can obtain for * * *, I shall consider it as so much saved out of the fire, &c. &c. Do you remember Dunning's motion (in the year 1780) to address the Crown against a dissolution of Parliament; a simple address we rejected, as an infringement on the prerogative? yet how far short of these strong democratical measures, for which you have probably voted, as I should probably have done: such is the contagion of party. Fox drives most furiously, yet I should not be surprised if Pitt's moderation and character should insensibly win the nation, and even the House, to espouse his cause. * * * Unless when I look back on England with a selfish or a tender regard, my hours roll away very pleasantly, and I can again repeat with truth, that I have not regretted one single moment the step which I have taken. We are now at the height of the winter dissipation, and I am peculiarly happy when I can steal away from great assemblies, and suppers of twenty or thirty people, to a more private party of some of those persons whom I begin to call my friends. Till we are settled in our house little can be expected on our side; yet I have already given two or three handsome dinners; and though everything is grown dearer, I am not alarmed at the general view of my expence. Deyverdun salutes you; and we are agreed that few married couples are better entitled to the flitch of bacon than we shall be at the end of the year. When I had written about half this epistle my books arrived: at our first meeting all was rapture and confusion, and two or three posts, from the second to this day, the fourteenth, have been suffered to depart unnoticed. Your letter of the twenty-seventh of January, which was not received till yesterday, has again awakened me, and I thought the surest way would be to send off this single sheet without any farther delay.

I sincerely rejoice in the stability of Parliament ;* and the first faint dawn of reconciliation, which must however be effected by the equal balance of parties, rather than by the wisdom of the country gentlemen (at the St. Alban's Tavern).

My Lady!—But it would be highly incongruous to begin my letter at the bottom of the page. Adieu, therefore, till next post.

EDWARD GIBBON, *Esq. to the Right Hon. Lord* SHEFFIELD.

LAUSANNE, May 11, 1784.

ALAS! alas! alas! We may now exchange our mutual condolence. Last Christmas, on the change of administration, I was struck with the thunderbolt of the unexpected event, and in the approaching dissolution I foresaw the loss of * * *. The long continuance and various changes of the tempest rendered me by degrees callous and insensible ; when the art of the mariners was exhausted I felt that we were sinking, I expected the ship to founder, and when the fatal moment arrived, I was even pleased to be delivered from hope and fear, to the calmness of despair. I now turn my eyes, not on the past, but on the present and the future ; what is lost I try to consider as if it never had existed ; and every day I congratulate my own good fortune, let me say my prudence and resolution, in migrating from your noisy stage to a scene of repose and content. But even in this separate state, I was still anxious for my friend upon English earth, and at first was much delighted with your hint, that you were setting off for Coventry, without any prospect of an opposition. Every post, Wednesdays and Saturdays, I eagerly looked for the intelligence of your victory ; and in spite of my misbehaviour, which I do not deny, I must abuse *my Lady*, rather than you, for leaving me in so painful a situation. Each day raised and increased my apprehension ; the *Courier de l'Europe* first announced the contest, the English papers proclaimed your defeat, and your last letter, which I received four days ago, shewed me that you exerted first the spirit, and at last the temper of an hero. I am not much surprised that you should have been swept away in the general unpopularity, since even in this quiet place, your friends are considered as a factious crew, acting in direct opposition both to the King and people. For yourself I am at a loss what to say. If this repulse should teach you to renounce all connection with Kings and Ministers, and Patriots and Parties, and Parliaments ; for all of which you are by many degrees too honest ; I should exclaim, with Teague of respectable memory, " By my shoul, dear joy, you have *gained* a loss." Private life, whether contemplative or active, has surely more solid and independent charms ; you have *some* domestic comforts ; Sheffield-Place is still susceptible of useful and ornamental

* This supposition was founded on Mr. Banks's declaration in the name of Mr. Pitt.

improvements, (alas ! how much better might even the last * * * have been laid out !) and if these cares are not sufficient to occupy your leisure, I can trust your restless and enterprising spirit to find new methods to preserve you from the insipidity of repose. But I much fear your discontent and regret at being excluded from that Pandæmonium which we have so often cursed, as long as you were obliged to attend it. The leaders of the party will flatter you with the opinion of their friendship and your own importance ; the warmth of your temper makes you credulous and unsuspicious ; and, like the rest of our species, male and female, you are not absolutely deaf to the voice of praise. Some other place will be suggested, easy, honourable, certain, where nothing is wanted but a man of character and spirit to head a superior interest ; the opposition, if any, is contemptible, and the expence cannot be large. You will go down, find almost every circumstance falsely stated, repent that you had engaged yourself, but you cannot desert those friends who are firmly attached to your cause ; besides, the money you have already spent would have been thrown away ; another thousand will complete the business : deeper and deeper will you plunge, and the last evil will be worse than the first. You see I am a free-spoken counsellor ; may I not be a true prophet ! Did I consult my own wishes, I should observe to you, that as you are no longer a slave, you might soon be transported, as you seem to desire, to one of the Alpine hills. The purity and calmness of the air is the best calculated to allay the heat of a political fever ; the education of the two Princesses might be successfully conducted under your eye and that of my Lady ; and if you had resolution to determine on a residence, not a visit, at Lausanne, your worldly affairs might repose themselves after their late fatigues. But you know that *I* am a friend to toleration, and am always disposed to make the largest allowance for the different natures of animals ; a lion and a lamb, an eagle and a worm. I am afraid we are too quiet for you ; here it would not be easy for you to create any business ; you have for some time neglected books, and I doubt whether you would not think our suppers and assemblies somewhat trifling and insipid. You are far more difficult than I am ; you are in search of knowledge, and you are not content with your company, unless you can derive from them information or extraordinary amusement. For my part, I like to draw information from books, and I am satisfied with polite attention and easy manners. Finally, 1 am happy to tell, and you will be happy to hear, that this place has in every respect exceeded my best and most sanguine hopes. How often have you said, as often as I expressed any ill-humour against the hurry, the expence, and the precarious condition of my London life, " Ay, that is a nonsensical scheme of retiring to Lausanne that you have got into your head, a pretty fancy ; you remember how much you liked it in your youth, but you have now seen more of the world, and if you were to try it again, you would find yourself woefully disappointed ? " 1 had it in my head, in my heart, I have tried it, I have not been disappointed, and my knowledge of the world has served only to convince me, that a capital and a crowd may contain much less real society than the small circle of this gentle retirement. The winter has been longer, but, as far as I can learn, less rigorous than in the rest of Europe. The spring is now bursting upon us, and in our own garden it is displayed in all its glory. I already occupy a temporary apartment, and we live in the lower part of the house; before you receive this we shall be in full possession. We have much to enjoy and something to do, which I take to be the happiest condition of human life. Now for business, the kind of subject which I always undertake with the most reluctance, and leave with the most pleasure. * * * Adieu.

And now, my Lady,

LET me approach your gentle, not grimalkin, presence, with deep remorse. You have indirectly been informed of my state of mind and body; (the whole winter I have not had the slightest return of the gout, or any other complaint whatsoever;) you have been apprised, and are now apprised, of my motions, or rather of my perfect and agreeable repose; yet I must confess (and I *feel*) that something of a direct and personal exchange of sentiment has been neglected on my side, though I still *persuade* myself that when I am settled in my new house I shall have more subject, as well as leisure, to write. Such tricks of laziness your active spirit is a stranger to, though Mrs. * * * complains that she has never had an answer to her last letters. Poor Lady Pembroke! *you* will feel for her; after a cruel alternative of hope and fear, her only daughter, Lady Charlotte, died at *Aix en Provence;* they have persuaded her to come to this place, where she is intimately connected with the Cerjat family. She has taken an agreeable house, about three miles from the town, and lives retired. I have seen her; her behaviour is calm, but her affliction ——. I accept with gratitude your friendly proposal of Wedgewood's ware, and should be glad to have it bought and packed, and sent without delay through Germany; and I shall only say, that I wish to have a very complete service for two courses and a dessert, and that our suppers are numerous, frequently fifteen or twenty persons. Adieu. I do not mean this as your letter. You are very good to poor Kitty. With you I do not condole about Coventry.

EDWARD GIBBON, *Esq. to Mrs.* GIBBON, Bath.

DEAR MADAM,   LAUSANNE, May 28, 1784.

I BEGIN without preface or apology, as if I had received your letter by the last post. In my own defence I know not what to say; but if I were disposed to recriminate, I might observe that you yourself are not perfectly free from the sin of laziness and procrastination. I have often wondered why we are not fonder of letter-writing. We all delight to talk of ourselves, and it is only in letters, in writing to a friend, that we can enjoy that conversation, not only without reproach or interruption, but with the highest propriety and mutual satisfaction; sure that the person whom we address feels an equal, or at least a strong and lively interest in the consideration of the pleasing subject. On the subject therefore of *self* I will entertain a friend, to whom none of my thoughts or actions, none of my pains or pleasures, can ever be indifferent. When I first cherished the design of retiring to Lausanne, I was much more apprehensive of wounding your tender attachment, than of offending Lord Sheffield's manly and vehement friendship. In the abolition of the Board of Trade the motives for my retreat became more urgent and forcible ; I wished to break loose, yet I delayed above a year before I could take my final resolution ; and the letter in which I disclosed it to you cost me one of the most painful struggles of my life. As soon as I had conquered that difficulty, all meaner obstacles fell before me, and in a few weeks I found myself at Lausanne, aston-ished at my firmness and my success. Perhaps you still blame or still lament the step which I have taken. If on your own account, I can only sympathize with your feelings, the recollection of which often costs me a sigh : if on mine, let me fairly state what I have escaped in Eng-land, and what I have found at Lausanne. Recollect the tempests of this winter, how many anxious days 1 should have passed, how many noisy, turbulent, hot, unwholesome nights, while my political existence, and that of my friends, was at stake ; yet these feeble efforts would have been unavailing ; I should have lost my seat in parliament, and after the extraordinary expence of another year, I must still have pursued the road of Switzerland, unless I had been tempted by some selfish patron, or by Lord S.'s aspiring spirit, to incur a most incon-venient expence for a new seat ; and once more, at the beginning of an opposition, to engage in new scenes of business. As to the immediate prospect of anything like a quiet and profitable retreat, I should not know where to look ; my friends are no longer in power. With * * * and his party I have no connection ; and were he disposed to favour a man of letters, it is difficult to say what he could give, or what I would accept ; the reign of pensions and sinecures is at an end, and a com-mission in the Excise or Customs, the summit of my hopes, would give me income at the expence of leisure and liberty. When I revolve these circumstances in my mind, my only regret, I repeat it again and again, is, that 1 did not embrace this salutary measure three, five, ten years ago. Thus much I thought it necessary to say, and shall now dismiss this unpleasing part of the subject. For my situation here, health is the first consideration ; and on that head your tenderness had conceived some degree of anxiety. I know not whether it has reached you that I had a fit of the gout the day after my arrival. The deed is true, but the cause was accidental ; carelessly stepping down a flight of stairs, 1 sprained my ancle ; and my ungenerous enemy instantly took advantage of my weakness. But since my breaking that double chain, I have enjoyed a winter of the most perfect health that 1 have perhaps ever known, without any mixture of the little flying incommodi-ties which in my best days have sometimes disturbed the tranquillity of my English life. You are not ignorant of Dr. Tissot's reputation, and his merit is even above his reputation. He assures me, that in his opinion, the moisture of England and Holland is most pernicious ; the dry pure air of Switzerland most favourable to a gouty constitution : that experience justifies the theory ; and that there are fewer martyrs of that disorder in this, than in any other country in Europe. This winter has everywhere been most uncommonly severe : and you seem in England to have had your full share of the general hardship : but in this corner, surrounded by the Alps, it has rather been long than rigorous; and its duration stole away our spring, and left us no interval between furs and silks. We now enjoy the genial influence of the climate and the season; and no station was ever more calculated to enjoy them than Deyverdun's house and garden, which are now become my own. You will not expect that the pen should describe, what the pencil would imperfectly delineate. A few circumstances may, however, be mentioned. My library is about the same size with that in Bentinck-street, with this difference, however, that instead of looking on a paved court, twelve feet square, I command a boundless prospect of vale, mountain, and water, from my three windows. My apartment is completed by a spacious light closet, or store-room, with a bed-chamber and dressing-room. Deyverdun's habitation is pleasant and convenient, though less extensive : for our common use we have a very handsome winter apartment of four rooms ; and on the ground-floor, two cool saloons for the summer, with a sufficiency, or rather super-fluity, of offices, &c. A terrace, one hundred yards long, extends beyond the front of the house, and leads to a close impenetrable shrub-bery ; and from thence the circuit of a long and various walk carries me round a meadow and vineyard. The intervals afford abundant supply of fruit, and every sort of vegetables ; and if you add, that this villa (which has been much ornamented by my friend) touches the best and most sociable part of the town, you will agree with me, that few persons, either princes or philosophers, enjoy a more desirable residence. Deyverdun, who is proud of his own works, often walks me round, pointing out, with acknowledgment and enthusiasm, the beau-ties that change with every step and with every variation of light. I share, or at least, I sympathize with his pleasure. He appears con-tented with my progress, and has already told several people, that he does not despair of making me a gardener. Be that as it may, you will be glad to hear that I am, by my own choice, infinitely more in motion, and in the open air, than I ever have been formerly ; yet my perfect liberty and leisure leave me many studious hours ; and as the circle of our acquaintance retire into the country, I shall be much less engaged in company and diversion. I have seriously resumed the prosecution of my History ; each day and each month adds something to the completion of the great work. The progress is slow, the labour continual, and the end remote and uncertain ; yet every day brings its amusement, as well as labour ; and though I dare not fix a term, even in my own fancy, I advance, with the pleasing reflection, that the business of publication (should I be detained here so long) must enforce my return to England, and restore me to the best of mothers and friends. In the mean while, with health and competence, a full independence of mind and action, a delightful habitation, a true friend, and many pleasant acquaintance ; you will allow that I am rather an object of envy than of pity ; and if you were more conversant with the use of the French language, I would seriously propose to you to repose yourself with us in this fine country. My indirect intelligence (on which I sometimes depend with more implicit faith than on the kind dissimulation of your friendship) gives me reason to hope that the last winter has been more favourable to your health than the preceding one. Assure me of it yourself honestly and truly, and you will afford me one of the most lively pleasures.

EDWARD GIBBON *Esq. to the Right Hon. Lord* SHEFFIELD.

LAUSANNE, June 19, 1784.

* * * IN this glorious season I frequently give tea and supper to a dozen men and women with ease and reputation, and heartily wish you and my Lady were among them. In this corner of Europe we enjoy, or shall speedily enjoy, (besides threescore English, with Lady Pembroke, and forty French, with the Duchess de Sivrac at their head,) M. and Madame Necker, the Abbé Raynal, the Hereditary Prince of Brunswick, Prince Henry of Prussia, perhaps the Duke of Cumberland; yet I am still more content with the humble natives, than with *most* of these illustrious *names.* Adieu. The post is on the wing, and you owe me a long epistle. I am, as usual, in the firm intention of writing next week to my Lady.

The Same to the Same.   LAUSANNE, Oct. 18, 1784.

SINCE my retreat to Lausanne our correspondence has never received so long an interruption; and as I have been equally taciturn with the rest of the English world, it may now be a problem among that sceptical nation, whether the Historian of the Decline and Fall be a living substance or an empty name. So tremendous is the sleepy power of laziness and habit, that the silence of each post operated still more strongly to benumb the hand, and to freeze the *epistolary* ink. How or when I should have naturally awakened, I cannot tell; but the pressure of my affairs and the arrival of your last letter, compel me to remember that you are entrusted with the final amputation of the best limb of my property. The subject is in itself so painful, that I have postponed it, like a child's physic, from day to day; and losing whole mornings, as I walked about my library, in useless regret and impotent resolution, you will be amazed to hear that (after peeping to see if you are all well, and returned from Ireland) I have not yet had the courage to peruse your letter, for fear of meeting with some gloomy intelligence; and I will now finish what I have to say of pecuniary matters, before I know whether its contents will fortify or overthrow my unbiassed sentiments. * * * To what purpose (will you say) are these tardy and useless repinings? To arraign your manager? No, I am satisfied with the skill and firmness of the pilot, and complain only of the untoward violence of the tempest. To repent of your retreat into Switzerland? No, surely, every subsequent event has tended to make it as necessary as it has proved agreeable. Why then these lamentations? Hear and attend—It is to interest (if possible more strongly) your zeal and friendship, to justify a sort of avarice, a love of money, very foreign to my character, but with which I cling to these last fragments of my fortune. * * * As far as I can judge from the experience of a year, though I find Lausanne much more expensive than I imagined, yet my style of living (and a very handsome style it is) will be brought *nearly* within my ordinary revenues. I wish our poor country could say as much! But it was always my favourite and rational wish, that at the winding up of my affairs I might possess a sum, from one to two thousand pounds, neither buried in land, nor locked up in the funds, but free, light, and ready to obey any call of interest, or pleasure, or virtue; to defray any extraordinary expence, support any delay, or remove any obstacle. For the attainment of this object, I trust in your assistance. * * * Thus much for this money transaction; to you I need add no other stimulative, than to say that my ease and comfort very much depend on the success of this plan.

As I thought every man of sense and fortune in Ireland must be satisfied, I did not conceive the cloud so dark as you represent it. I will seriously peruse the 8vo. and in due time the 4to. edition;* it would become a classic book, if you could find leisure (will you ever find it?) to introduce order and ornament. You must negociate *directly* with Deyverdun; but the state will not hear of parting (alluding to his portrait) with their only Reynolds. I embrace my Lady; let her be angry, provided she be well. Adieu. Yours.

P. S. The care of Ireland may have amused you in the summer; but how do you mean to employ the winter? Do you not cast a longing, lingering look at St. Stephen's chapel? With your fiery spirit, and firm judgment, I almost wish you there; not for your benefit, but for the public. If you resolve to recover your seat, do not listen to any fallacious and infinite projects of interest, contest, return petition, &c. but limit your expence.

EDWARD GIBBON *Esq. to the Right Hon. Lady* SHEFFIELD.

LAUSANNE, Oct. 22, 1784.

A FEW weeks ago, as I was walking on our terrace with M. Tissot, the celebrated physician; M. Mercier, the author of the *Tableau de Paris;* the Abbé Raynal; Monsieur, Madame, and Mademoiselle Necker; the Abbé de Bourbon, a natural son of Lewis the Fifteenth, the Hereditary Prince of Brunswick, Prince Henry of Prussia, and a dozen Counts, Barons, and extraordinary persons, among whom was a natural son of the Empress of Russia——Are you satisfied with this list? which I could enlarge and embellish, without departing from truth; and was not the Baron of Sheffield (profound as he is on the subject of the American trade) doubly mistaken with regard to Gibbon and Lausanne? Whenever I used to hint my design of retiring, that illustrious Baron, after a proper effusion of d——d fools, condescended to observe, that such an obscure nook in Switzerland might please me in the ignorance of youth, but that after tasting for so many years the various society of Paris and London, I should soon be tired with the dull and uniform round of a provincial town. In the winter, Lausanne is indeed reduced to its native powers; but during the summer, it is possibly, after Spa, one of the most favourite places of general resort. The tour of Switzerland, the Alps, and the Glaciers, is become a

* Of Observations on the Commerce with the American States.

fashion. Tissot attracts the invalids, especially from France ; and a colony of English have taken up the habit of spending their winters at Nice, and their summers in the Pays de Vaud. Such are the splendour and variety of our summer visitors ; and *you* will agree with me more readily than the Baron, when I say that this variety, instead of being a merit, is, in my opinion one of the very few objections to the residence of Lausanne. After the dissipation of the winter I expected to have enjoyed, with more freedom and solitude, myself, my friend, my books, and this delicious paradise ; but my position and character make me here a sort of a public character, and oblige me to see and be seen. However, it is my firm resolution for next summer to assume the independence of a philosopher, and to be visible only to the persons whom I like. On that principle I should not, most assuredly, have avoided the Neckers and Prince Henry. The former have purchased the barony of Copet near Geneva ; and as the buildings were very much out of repair, they passed this summer at a country-house at the gates of Lausanne. They afford a new example, that persons who have tasted of greatness can seldom return with pleasure to a private station. In the moments when we were alone he conversed with me freely, and I believe truly, on the subject of his administration and fall ; and has opened several passages of modern history, which would make a very good figure in *the* American book.* If they spent the summers at the castle of Copet, about nine leagues from hence, a fortnight or three weeks visit would be a pleasant and healthful excursion ; but, alas ! I fear there is little appearance of its being executed. *Her* health is impaired by the agitation of her mind : instead of returning to Paris, she is ordered to pass the winter in the southern provinces of France, and our last parting was solemn ; as I very much doubt whether I shall ever see her again. They have now a very troublesome charge, which you will experience in a few years, the disposal of a Baroness ; Mademoiselle (now Madame de Stael) Necker, one of the greatest heiresses in Europe is now about eighteen, wild, vain, but good-natured, and with a much larger provision of wit than of beauty : what increases their difficulties is their religious obstinacy of marrying her only to a protestant. It would be an excellent opportunity for a young Englishman of a great name and a fair reputation. Prince Henry must be a man of sense ; for he took more notice, and expressed more esteem for me, than any body else. He is certainly (without touching his military character) a very lively and entertaining companion. He talked with freedom, and generally with contempt, of most of the princes of Europe ; with respect of the Empress of Russia, but never mentioned the name of his brother, except once, when he hinted that it was *he himself* that won the battle of Rosbach. His nephew, and our nephew, the hereditary Prince of Brunswick is here for his education. Of the English, who live very much as a national colony, you will like to hear of Mrs. Fraser and *one* more. Donna Catherina (the Hon. Mrs. Fraser) pleases every body, by the perfect simplicity of her state of nature. You know she has had the resolution to return from England (where she told me she saw you) to Lausanne, for the sake of Miss Bristow, who is in bad health, and in a few days they set

* Observations on the Commerce with the American States.

off for Nice. *The other* is the Eliza; she passed through Lausanne, in her road from Italy to England; poorly in health, but still adorable, (nay, do not frown!) and I enjoyed some delightful hours by her bed-side. She wrote me a line from Paris, but has not executed her promise of visiting Lausanne in the month of October. My pen has run much faster, and much farther, than I intended on the subject of others; yet, in describing them, I have thrown some light over myself and my situation. A year, a very short one, has now elapsed since my arrival at Lausanne; and after a cool review of my sentiments, I can sincerely declare, that I have never, during a single moment, repented of having executed my *absurd* project of retiring to Lausanne. It is needless to dwell on the fatigue, the hurry, the vexation which I must have felt in the narrow and dirty circle of English politics. My present life wants no foil, and shines by its own native light. The chosen part of my library is now arrived, and arranged in a room full as good as that in Bentinck-street, with this difference indeed, that instead of looking on a stone court, twelve feet square, I command, from three windows of plate-glass, an unbounded prospect of many a league of vineyard, of fields, of wood, of lake, and of mountains; a scene which Lord Shef-field will tell you is superior to all you can imagine. The climate, though severe in winter, has perfectly agreed with my constitution, and the year is accomplished without any return of the gout. An excellent house, a good table, a pleasant garden, are no contemptible ingredients in human happiness. The general style of society hits my fancy; I have cultivated a large and agreeable circle of acquaintance, and I am much deceived if I have not laid the foundations of two or three more intimate and valuable connections; but their names would be indif-ferent, and it would require pages, or rather volumes, to describe their persons and characters. With regard to my standing dish, my domestic friend, I could not be much disappointed, after an intimacy of eight-and-twenty years. His heart and his head are excellent; he has the warmest attachment for me, he is satisfied that I have the same for him: some slight imperfections must be mutually supported; two batchelors, who have lived so long alone and independent, have their peculiar fancies and humours, and when the mask of form and cere-mony is laid aside, every moment in a family-life has not the sweetness of the honey-moon, even between the husbands and wives who have the truest and most tender regard for each other. Should you be very much surprised to hear of my being married? Amazing as it may seem, I do assure you that the event is less improbable than it would have appeared to myself a twelvemonth ago. Deyverdun and I have often agreed, in jest and in earnest, that a house like ours would be regulated, and graced, and enlivened, by an agreeable female com-panion; but each of us seems desirous that his friend should sacrifice himself for the public good. Since my residence here I have lived much in women's company; and, to your credit be it spoken, I like you the better the more I see of you. Not that I am in love with any particular person. I have discovered about half-a-dozen *wives* who would please me in different ways, and by various merits: one as a mistress (a widow, vastly like *the* Eliza; if she returns I am to bring them together); a second, a lively entertaining acquaintance; a third, a sincere good-natured friend; a fourth, who would represent with grace and dignity at the head of my table and family; a fifth, an excellent œconomist and housekeeper; and a sixth, a very useful nurse. Could I find all these qualities united in a single person, I should dare to make my addresses, and should deserve to be refused. You hint in some of your letters, or rather postscripts, that you consider me as having renounced England, and having fixed myself for the rest of my life in Switzerland, and that you suspect the sincerity of my vague or insidious schemes of purchase or return. To remove, as far as I can, your doubts and suspicions, I will tell you, on that interesting subject, fairly and simply as much as I know of my own intentions. There is little appearance that I shall be suddenly recalled by the offer of a place or pension. I have no claim to the friendship of your young minister, and should he propose a Commissioner of the Customs, or Secretary at Paris, the supposed objects of my low ambition, Adam in Paradise would refuse them with contempt. *Here* therefore I shall certainly live till I have finished the remainder of my History; an arduous work, which does not proceed so fast as I expected, amidst the avocations of society, and miscellaneous study. As soon as it is completed, most probably in three or *four* years, I shall infallibly return to England, about the month of May or June; and the necessary labour of printing with care two or three quarto volumes, will detain me till their publication, in the ensuing spring. Lord Sheffield and yourself will be the loadstone that most forcibly attracts me; and as I shall be a vagabond on the face of the earth, I shall be the better qualified to domesticate myself with you, both in town and country. Here then, at no very extravagant distance, we have the certainty (if we live) of spending a year together, in the peace and freedom of a friendly intercourse; and a year is no very contemptible portion of this mortal existence. Beyond that period all is dark, but not gloomy. Whether, after the final completion of my History, I shall return to Lausanne, or settle in England, must depend on a thousand events which lie beyond the reach of human foresight, the state of public and private affairs, my own health, the health and life of Deyverdun, the various changes which may have rendered Lausanne more dear, or less agreeable, to me than at present. But without losing ourselves in this distant futurity, which perhaps we may never see, and without giving any positive answer to Maria's parting question, whether I shall be buried in England or Switzerland, let me seriously and earnestly ask you, whether you do not mean to visit me next summer? The defeat at Coventry would, I should think, facilitate the project; since the Baron is no longer detained the whole winter from his domestic affairs, nor is there any attendance on the House that keeps him till Midsummer in dust and dispute. I can send you a pleasant route, through Normandy, Paris, and Lyons, a visit to the Glaciers, and your return down the Rhine, which would be commodiously executed in three or four months, at no very extravagant expence, and would be productive of health and spirits to you, of entertainment to you both, and of instruction to *the* Maria. Without the smallest inconvenience to myself, I am able to lodge yourselves and family, by arranging you in the winter apartment, which in the summer season is not of any use to us. I think you will be satisfied with your habitation, and already see you in your dressing-room; a small pleasant room, with a delightful prospect to the west and south. If poor aunt Kitty (you oblige me beyond expression by your tender care of that excellent woman) if she were only ten years younger, I would desire you to take her with you, but I much fear we shall never meet again. You will not complain of the brevity of this epistle; I expect, in return, a full and fair account of yourself, your thoughts and actions, soul and body, present and future, in the safe, though unreserved, confidence of friendship. The Baron in two words hinted but an indifferent account of your health; you are a fine machine; but as he was absent in Ireland, I hope I understand the cause and the remedy. Next to yourself, I want to hear of the two Baronesses. You must give me a faithful picture (and though a mother you can give it) of their present external and internal forms; for a year has now elapsed, and in *their* lives a year is an age. Adieu. Ever yours.

EDWARD GIBBON *Esq. to the Right Hon. Lord* SHEFFIELD.

LAUSANNE, March 13, 1785.
MY long silence (and it has been long) must not, on this occasion, be imputed to laziness, though that little devil may likewise have been busy. But you cannot forget how many weeks I remained in suspense, expecting every post the final sentence, and not knowing what to say in that passive uncertainty. It is now something more than a fortnight since your last letter, and that of Gosling informed me of the event. I have intended every day to write, and every day I have started back with reluctance and disgust, from the consideration of the wretched subject. Lenborough irrecoverably gone, for three-fourths of its real, at least of its ancient, value; my seat in parliament sunk in the abyss of your cursed politics, and a balance neatly cyphered and summed by Gosling, which shews me a very shallow purse, in which others have a clearer right to dip than myself.

March 21.
ANOTHER week is now elapsed, and though nothing is changed in this too faithful state of my affairs, I feel myself able to encounter them with more spirit and resolution; to look on the future, rather than the past, on the fair, rather than on the foul side of the prospect. I shall speak in the confidence of friendship, and while you listen to the more doleful tale of my wants and wishes, you will have the satisfaction of hearing some circumstances in my present situation of a less unpleasing nature. 1. In the first place, I most heartily rejoice in the sale, however unfavourable, of the Bucks estate. Considering the dullness of the times, and the high interest of money, it is not a little to obtain even a tolerable price, and I am sensible how much your patience and industry have been exercised to extort the payment. 2. Your resistance to my Swiss expedition was more friendly than wise. Had I yielded, after eighteen months of suspense and anxiety, I should now, a still poorer man, be driven to embrace the same resource, which has

succeeded according to, or even beyond, my most sanguine expectations. I do not pretend to have discovered the terrestrial paradise,
which has not been known in this world since the fall of Adam ; but I
can truly declare, (now the charms of novelty are long since faded,)
that I have found the plan of life the best adapted to my temper and
my situation. I am now writing to you in a room as good as that in
Bentinck-street, which commands the country, the lake, and the mountains, and the opening prospect of the spring. The aforesaid room
is furnished without magnificence, but with every conveniency for
warmth, ease, and study, and the walls are already covered with more
than two thousand volumes, the choice of a chosen library. I have
health, friends, an amusing society, and perfect freedom. A Commissioner of the Excise ! the idea makes me sick. If you ask me what
I have saved by my retreat to Lausanne? I will fairly tell you (in the
two great articles of a carriage and a house in town, both which were
indispensable, and are now annihilated, with the difference of clubs,
public places, servants' wages, &c.) about four hundred pounds, or
guineas, a year ; no inconsiderable sum, when it must be annually
found as addition to an expense which is somewhat larger than my
present revenue. 3. *What is then, you will ask, my present establishment ?* *This* is not by any means a cheap country ; and, except in the
article of wine, I could give a dinner, or make a coat, perhaps for the
same price in London as at Lausanne. My chief advantage arises
from the things which I do not want ; and in some respects my style
of living is enlarged by the increase of my relative importance, an
obscure batchelor in England, the master of a considerable house at
Lausanne. Here I am expected to return entertainments, to receive
ladies, &c. and to perform many duties of society, which, though agreeable enough in themselves, contribute to inflame the housekeeper's
bills. From the disbursements of the first year I cannot form any just
estimate ; the extraordinary expenses of the journey, carriage of heavy
goods from England, the acquisition of many books, which it was not
expedient to transport, the purchase of furniture, wine, fitting up my
library, and the irregularity of a new menage, have consumed a pretty
large sum. But in a quiet, prudent, regular course of life, I think I
can support myself with comfort and honour for six or seven hundred
pounds a year, instead of a thousand or eleven hundred in England.
Besides these uncertainties, (uncertain at least as to the time,) I have
a sure and honourable supply from my own pen. I continue my History
with pleasure and assiduity ; the way is long and laborious, yet I see
the end, and I can almost promise to land in England next September
twelvemonth, with a manuscript of the current value of about four
thousand pounds, which will afford either a small income or a large
capital. 5. It is in the meanwhile that my situation is somewhat
difficult. * * * Such are the services and revenues of the year ; proceed we now, in the style of the budget, to the ways and means of
extraordinary supplies. * * * I will not affront your friendship, by
observing that you will incur little or no risk on this occasion. Read,
consider, act, and write.

It is the privilege of friendship to make our friend a patient hearer,
and active associate in our own affairs ; and I have now written five

pages on my private affairs, without saying a word either of the public, or of yourself. Of the public I have little to say ; I never was a very warm patriot, and I grow every day a citizen of the world. The scramble for power or profit at Westminster or St. James's, and the names of Pitt and Fox, become less interesting to me than those of Cæsar and Pompey. You are not a friend of the young Minister, but he is a great favourite on the continent, as he appears to be still ; and you must own that the fairness of his character, his eloquence, his application to business, and even his youth, must prepossess at least the ignorant in his favour. Of the merit or defects of his administration I cannot pretend to speak ; but I find, from the complaints of some interested persons, that his restraints on the smuggling of tea have already ruined the East India Companies of Antwerp and Sweden, and that even the Dutch will scarcely find it worth their while to send any ships to China. Your Irish friends appear to be more quiet, at least the volunteers and national congress seem to subside. How far that tranquillity must be purchased on our side, by any pernicious sacrifices, you will best decide ; and from some hint in your last letters, I am inclined to think that you are less affected than might be supposed with national or local prejudice. Your introduction I have attentively read ; the matter, though most important in itself, is out of the line of my studies and habits, and the subordinate beauties of style you disclaim. Yet I can say with truth, that I never met with more curious and diligent investigation, more strong sense, more liberal spirit, and more cool and impartial temper in the same number of pages. By this time you have probably read Necker's book on the finances. Perhaps for you there is too much French enthusiasm and paint ; but in many respects you must have gained a knowledge of his country ; and on the whole, you must have been pleased with the picture of a great and benevolent mind. In your attack on Deyverdun for my picture I cannot promise you much success ; he seems resolved to maintain his right of possession, and your only chance would be a personal assault. The next summer (how time slips away !) was fixed for your visit to Lausanne. We are prepared at all points to receive *you*, my Lady, and a princess or two, with their train ; and if you have a proper contempt for St. Stephen's chapel, you are perfectly free, and at leisure (can you ever be at leisure ?) for the summer season. As you are now in a great measure disengaged from any affairs, you may find time to inform me of your proceedings and your projects. At present I do not even know whether you pass the winter at Sheffield-Place or in Downing-street. My Lady revenges herself of my long silence ; yet I embrace her and the infants. Adieu. You have deranged the Decline and Fall this morning. I have finished my epistle since dinner, and am now going to a pleasant party and good supper.

EDWARD GIBBON *Esq. to the Right Hon. Lord* SHEFFIELD.

LAUSANNE, September 5, 1785.

EXTRACT from a weekly English Paper, September 5, 1785. "It is reported, but we hope without foundation, that the celebrated Mr

Gibbon, who had retired to Lausanne in Switzerland to finish his valuable History, lately died in that city."

The hope of the Newspaper-writer is very handsome and obliging to the Historian; yet there are several weighty reasons which would incline me to believe that the intelligence may be true. *Prima,* It must one day be true; and therefore may very probably be so at present. *Secundo,* We may always depend on the impartiality, accuracy, and veracity of an English Newspaper. *Tertio,* which is indeed the strongest argument, We are credibly informed that for a long time past the said celebrated Historian has not written to any of his friends in England; and as that respectable personage had always the reputation of a most exact and regular correspondent, it may be fairly concluded from his silence, that he either is, or ought to be dead. The only objection that I can foresee, is the assurance that Mr. G—— himself read the article as he was eating his breakfast, and laughed very heartily at the mistake of his brother Historian; but as he might be desirous of concealing that unpleasant event, we shall not insist on his apparent health and spirits, which might be affected by that subtle politician. He affirms, however, not only that he is alive, and was so on the fifth of September, but that his head, his heart, his stomach, are in the most perfect state, and that the climate of Lausanne has been congenial both to his mind and body. He confesses indeed, that after the last severe winter, the gout, his old enemy, from whom he hoped to have escaped, pursued him to his retreat among the mountains of Helvetia, and that the siege was long, though more languid than in his precedent attacks; after some exercise of patience he began to creep, and gradually to walk; and though he can neither run, nor fly, nor dance, he supports himself with firmness on his two legs, and would willingly kick the impertinent Gazetteer; impertinent enough, though more easily to be forgiven than the insolent *Courier du Bas Rhin,* who about three years ago amused himself and his readers with a fictitious epistle from Mr. Gibbon to Dr. Robertson.

Perhaps now you think, Baron, that I shall apologize in humble style for my silence and neglect. But, on the contrary, I do assure you that I am truly provoked at your Lordship's not condescending to be in a passion. I might really have been dead, I might have been sick; if I were neither dead nor sick, I deserved a volley of curses and reproaches for my infernal laziness, and you have defrauded me of my just dues. Had I been silent till Christmas, till doomsday, you would never have thought it worth your while to abuse me. Why then (let me ask in your name) did you not write before? That is indeed a very curious question of natural and moral philosophy. Certainly I am not lazy: elaborate quartos have proved, and will abundantly prove my diligence. I *can* write; spare my modesty on that subject. I like to converse with my friends by pen or tongue, and as soon as I can set myself a-going, I know no moments that run off more pleasantly. I am so well convinced of that truth, and so much ashamed of forcing people that I love to forget me, that I have now resolved to set apart the first hour of each day for the discharge of my obligations; beginning, *comme de raison,* with yourself, and regularly proceeding to Lord Loughborough and the rest. May heaven give me strength and grace to accomplish this laudable intention! Amen. Certainly (yet I do not know whether it be so certain) I should write much oftener to you if we were not linked in business, and if my business had not always been of the un‧ pleasant and mortifying kind. Even now I shove the ugly monster to the end of this epistle, and will confine him to a page by himself, that he may not infect the purer air of our correspondence. Of my situation here I have little new to say, except a very comfortable and singular truth, that my passion for my wife or mistress (Fanny Lausanne) is not palled by satiety and possession of two years. I have seen her in all seasons, and in all humours, and though she is not without faults, they are infinitely overbalanced by her good qualities. Her face is not handsome, but her person, and everything about her, has admirable grace and beauty : she is of a very cheerful sociable temper ; without much learning, she is endowed with taste and good sense ; and though not rich, the simplicity of her education makes her a very good œcono‐ mist ; she is forbid by her parents to wear any expensive finery ; and though her limbs are not much calculated for walking, she has not yet asked me to keep her a coach. Last spring (not to wear the metaphor to rags) I saw Lausanne in a new light, during my long fit of the gout, and must boldly declare, that either in health or sickness I find it far more comfortable than your huge metropolis. In London my confine- ment was sad and solitary ; the many forgot my existence when they saw me no longer at Brookes's ; and the few, who sometimes cast a thought or an eye on their friend, were detained by business or pleasure, the distance of the way, or the hours of the House of Commons, and I was proud and happy if I could prevail on Elmsly to enliven the dul- ness of the evening. Here the objects are nearer, and much more dis- tinct, and I myself am an object of much larger magnitude. People are not kinder, but they are more idle, and it must be confessed that, of all nations on the globe, the English are the least attentive to the old and infirm ; I do not mean in acts of charity, but in the offices of civil life. During three months I have had round my chair a succession of agree- able men and women, who came with a smile, and vanished at a nod ; and as soon as it was agreeable I had a constant party at cards, which was sometimes dismissed to their respective homes, and sometimes detained by Deyverdun to supper, without the least trouble or incon- venience to myself. In a word, my plan has most completely answered ; and I solemnly protest, after two years' trial, that I have never, in a single moment repented of my transmigration. The only disagreeable circumstance is the increase of a race of animals with which this coun- try has been long infested, and who are said to come from an island in the Northern Ocean. I am told, but it seems incredible, that upwards of forty thousand English, masters and servants, are now absent on the continent ; and I am sure we have our full proportion, both in town and country, from the month of June to that of October. The occupa- tions of the closet, indifferent health, want of horses, in some measure plead my excuse ; yet I do too much to please myself, and probably too little to satisfy my countrymen. What is still more unlucky is, that a part of the colony of this present year are really good company, people one knows, &c. ; the Astons, Hales, Hampdens, Trevors, Lady Clarges, and Miss Carter, Lord Northington, &c. I have seen Trevor several times, who talks of you, and seems to be a more exact correspondent than myself. *His wife* is much improved by her diplomatic life, and shines in every company, as a woman of fashion and elegance. But those who have repaid me for the rest, were Lord and Lady Spencer. I saw them almost every day, at my house or their own, during their stay of a month ; for they were hastening to Italy, that they might return to London next February. He is a valuable man, and where he is familiar, a pleasant companion ; she a charming woman, who, with sense and spirit, has the simplicity and playfulness of a child. You are not ignorant of her talents, of which she has left me an agreeable specimen, a drawing of the Historic Muse, sitting in a thoughtful posture to compose. So much of self and Co. let us now talk a little of your house and your two countries. Does my Lady ever join in the abuse which I have merited from you ? Is she satisfied with her own behaviour, her unpardonable silence, to one of the prettiest, most obliging, most entertaining, most, &c. epistles that ever was penned since the epistles of * * *. Will she not *mew* one word of reply ? I want some account of her spirits, health, amusements, of the elegant accomplishments of Maria, and the opening graces of Louisa : of yourself I wish to have some of those details which she is most likely to transmit. Are you patient in your exclusion from the House ? Are you satisfied with legislating with your pen ? Do you pass the whole winter in town? Have you resumed the pursuits of farming, &c. ? What new connections, public or private, have you formed ? A tour to the continent would be the best medicine for the shattered nerves of a soldier and politician. By this expression you will perceive that your letter to Deyverdun is received ; it landed last post, after I had already written the two first pages of this composition. On the whole my friend was pleased and flattered ; but instead of surrendering, or capitulating, he seems to be making preparations for an obstinate defence. He already talks of the right of possession,* of the duties of a good citizen, of a *writ ne exeat regnum*, and of a vote of the two hundred, that whomsoever shall, directly or indirectly, &c. is an enemy to his country. Between you be the strife, while I sit with my scales in my hand, like Jupiter n Mount Ida. I begin to view with the same indifference the combat of Achilles, Pitt, and Hector Fox ; for such, as it should now seem, must be the comparison of the two warriors. * * *.

At this distance I am much less angry with bills, taxes, and propositions, than I am pleased with Pitt for making a friend and a deserving man happy, for releasing Batt from the shackles of the law, and for enhancing the gift of a secure and honourable competency, by the handsome manner in which it was conferred. This I understand to be the case, from the unsuspicious evidence of Lord Northington and Chief Baron Skinner ; and if I can find time, (*resolution*,) I will send him a hearty congratulation ; if I fail, you may at least communicate my intentions. Of Ireland I know nothing, and while I am writing the Decline of a great Empire, I have not leisure to attend to the affairs of a remote and petty province. I see that your friend Foster has been hooted by the mob, and unanimously chosen Speaker of the House of Commons. How could Pitt expose himself to the

* His portrait, painted by Sir Joshua Reynolds.

disgrace of withdrawing his propositions after a public attempt ? Have Ministers no way of computing beforehand the sense or nonsense of an Irish Parliament ? I am quite in the dark ; your pamphlet, or book, would probably have opened my eyes ; but, whatever may have been the reason, I give you *my word of honour,* that I have never seen nor heard of it. Here we are much more engaged with continental politics. In general we hate the Emperor, as the enemy of peace, without daring to make war. The old lion of Prussia acts a much more glorious part, as the champion of public tranquillity, and the independence of the German states.

And now for the bitter and nauseous pill of pecuniary business, upon which I shall be as concise as possible in the two articles of my discourse, land and money. * * * It is impossible to hate more than I do this odious necessity of owing, borrowing, anticipating, and I look forwards with impatience to the happy period when the supplies will always be raised within the year, with a decent and useful surplus in the treasury. I now trust to the conclusion of my History, and it will hasten and secure the principal comforts of my life. You will believe I am not lazy; yet I fear the term is somewhat more distant than I thought. My long gout lost me three months in the spring ; in every great work unforeseen dangers, and difficulties, and delays will arise ; and I should be rather sorry than surprised if next autumn was postponed to the ensuing spring. If my Lady (a good creature) should write to Mrs. Porten, she may convey news of my life and health, without saying anything of this *possible* delay. Adieu. I embrace, &c.

LAUSANNE, October 1, 1785.

EDWARD GIBBON *Esq. to the Right Hon. Lord* SHEFFIELD.

LAUSANNE, January 17, 1786.

HEAR, all ye nations ! An epistle from Sheffield-Place, received the seventeenth of January, is answered the same day ; and to say the truth, this method, which is the best, is at the same time the most easy and pleasant. Yet I do not allow that on the last past silence and delay you have any more reason to swear than myself. Our letters crossed each other, our claims were equal, and if both had been stiffly maintained, our mutual silence must have continued till the day of judgment. The balance was doubtless in my favour, if you recollect the length, the fulness, the variety of pleasant and instructive matter of my last dispatch. Even at present, of myself, my occupations, my designs, I have little or nothing to add ; and can only speak dryly and briefly to very dry and disagreeable business. * * * But we shall both agree, that the true criminal is my Lady ; and though I do suppose that a letter is on the road, which will make some amends, her obstinate, contumacious, dilatory silence, so many months or years since my valuable letter, is worthy a royal tigress. * * * Notwithstanding your gloomy politicians, I do love the funds ; and were the next war to reduce them to half, the remainder would be a better and pleasanter property, than a similar value in your dirty acres. We are now in the height of our winter amusements; balls, great suppers, comedies, &c. and, except St. Stephen's, I certainly lead a more gay and dissipated life here, among the Alps, (by the bye, a most extraordinary mild winter,) than in the midst of London. Yet my mornings, and sometimes an afternoon, are diligently employed. My work advances, but much remains, indeed much more than I imagined ; but a great book, like a great house, was never yet finished at the given time. When I talk of the spring of eighty-seven, I suppose all my time well bestowed ; and what do you think of a fit of the gout, that may disqualify me for two or three months ? You may growl, but if you calmly reflect on my pecuniary and sentimental state, you will believe that I most earnestly desire to complete my labour, and *visit* England. Adieu.

EDWARD GIBBON *Esq. to the Right Hon. Lord* SHEFFIELD.

May 10, 1786.

BY the difference, I suppose, of the posts of France and Germany, Sir Stanier's letter, though first written, is still on the road, and yours, which I received yesterday morning, brought me the first account of poor Mrs. Porten's departure. There are few events that could afflict me more deeply, and I have been ever since in a state of mind more deserving of your pity than of your reproaches. I certainly am not ignorant that we have nothing better to wish for ourselves than the fate of that best humoured woman, as you very justly style her; a good understanding and an excellent heart, with health, spirits, and a competency, to live in the midst of her friends till the age of fourscore, and then to shut her eyes without pain or remorse. Death can have deprived her only of some years of weakness, perhaps of misery ; and for myself, it is surely less painful to lose her at present, than to find her in my visit to England next year sinking under the weight of age and infirmities, and perhaps forgetful of herself and of the persons once the dearest to her. All this is perfectly true : but all these reflections will not dispel a thousand sad and tender remembrances that rush upon my mind. To her care I am indebted in earliest infancy for the preservation of my life and health. I was a puny child, neglected by my mother, starved by my nurse, and of whose being very little care or expectation was entertained ; without her maternal vigilance I should either have been in my grave, or imperfectly lived a crooked ricketty monster, a burden to myself and others. To her instructions I owe the first rudiments of knowledge, the first exercise of reason, and a taste for books, which is still the pleasure and glory of my life ; and though she taught me neither language nor science, she was certainly the most useful preceptor I ever had. As I grew up, an intercourse of thirty years endeared her to me, as the faithful friend and the agreeable companion. You have seen with what freedom and confidence we lived together, and have often admired her character and conversation, which could alike please the young and the old. All this is now lost, finally, irrecoverably lost ! I will agree with my Lady, that the immortality of the soul is at some times a very comfortable doctrine. A thousand thanks to her for her constant kind attention to that poor woman who is no more. I wish I had as much to applaud, and as little to reproach, in my own behaviour towards Mrs. Porten since I left England ; and when I reflect that my letters would have soothed and comforted her decline, I feel more deeply than I can express, the real neglect, and seeming indifference, of my silence. To delay a letter from the Wednesday to the Saturday, and then from the Saturday to the Wednesday, appears a very slight offence ; yet in the repetition of such delay, weeks, months, and years will elapse, till the omission may become irretrievable, and the consequence mischievous or fatal. After a long lethargy, I had roused myself last week, and wrote to the three old Ladies ; my letter for Mrs. Porten went away last post, Saturday night, and yours did not arrive till Monday morning. Sir Stanier will probably open it, and read the true picture of my senti-ments for a friend who, when I wrote, was already extinct. There is something sad and awful in the thought, yet, on the whole, I am not sorry that even this tardy epistle preceded my knowledge of her death : but it did not precede (you will observe) the information of her dan-gerous and declining state, which I conveyed in my last letter, and her anxious concern that she should never see or *hear* from me again. This idea, and the hard thoughts which you must entertain of me, press so much on my mind, that I must frankly acknowledge a strange inexcusable supineness, on which I desire you would make no comment, and which in some measure may account for my delays in corresponding with you. The unpleasant nature of business, and the apprehension of finding something disagreeable, tempted me to post-pone from day to day, not only the answering, but even the opening, your penultimate epistle ; and when I received your last, yesterday morning, the seal of the former was still unbroken. Oblige me so far as to make no reflections ; my own may be of service to me hereafter. Thus far (except the last sentence) I have run on with a sort of melan-choly pleasure, and find my heart much relieved by unfolding it to a friend. And the subject so strongly holds me, so much disqualifies me for other discourse, either serious or pleasant, that here I would willingly stop, and reserve all miscellaneous matter for a second volunteer epistle. But we both know how frail are promises, how dangerous are delays, and there are some pecuniary objects on which I think it necessary to give you an immediate, though now tardy, explanation.

I do not return you any formal thanks for * * * I have really a hundred things to say of myself, of you and Co. of your works, of mine, of my books in Downing-street, of Lausanne, of politics, &c. &c. After this, some epistolary debts must and SHALL be paid ; and to proceed with order, I have fixed this day fortnight (May twenty-fifth) for the date and dispatch of your second epistle. Give me credit once more. Pray does my Lady think herself absolved from all obligation of writing to me ? To her at least I am not in arrear. Adieu.

EDWARD GIBBON *Esq. to Sir* STANIER PORTEN, Kensington-Palace.
MY DEAR SIR,   LAUSANNE, May 12, 1786.
    THE melancholy event which you have communicated, in your last obliging letter of the twenty-fourth of April, might indeed be too

naturally feared and expected. If we consult our reason, we can wish nothing better for ourselves than the lot of that dear and valuable friend whom we have now lost.* A warm heart, a strong and clear understanding, a most invaluable happiness of temper, which showed her the agreeable or comfortable side of every object, and every situation ; an easy competency, the reward of her own attention ; private friendship, general esteem, a mature age, and a placid decline. But these rational motives of consolation are insufficient to check a thousand soft and sad remembrances that rush into my mind ; the intimacy of a whole life : of mine, at least, from the earliest dawn of my infancy ; the maternal and assiduous care of my health, and afterwards of my mind ; the freedom and frequency of our conversations ; the regret which I felt in our last separation, and the hope, however faint and precarious, of seeing her again. Time alone can reconcile us to this irreparable loss, and to his healing power I must recommend your grief as well as my own. I sincerely applaud her very proper and natural disposal of her effects, and am proud of the pre-eminence which she has allowed me in a list of dear and worthy relations.

I am too full of a single idea to expatiate, as I should otherwise do, on indifferent matters ; yet not totally indifferent to my friends, since they relate to my present situation. My health is in general perfectly good, and the only drawbacks some occasional visits of the gout, which abate, however, in strength, and are grown, I think, less frequent and lasting. The life which I lead is temperate and tranquil, and the distemper itself is not common in the purity and dryness of the climate. After a long trial, I can now approve my own choice of retiring to Switzerland. My delightful habitation, at once in town and country ; my library, and the society of agreeable men and women, compose a very eligible plan of life, which is shaded with very few, and very slight exceptions. I prosecute with ease, and regular diligence, the conclusion of my History ; and, as far as I can judge, I may hope to deliver it to the press in the course of next year. That important business will recall me to England, and detain me there some months ; and I shall rejoice in the opportunity of revisiting my country and my friends ; among them those of Kensington-Palace hold a high and distinguished place.

I truly sympathize, my dear Sir, in your paternal feelings, in the health and progress of your very promising children. May that, and every other blessing, attend both yourself and Lady Porten. My friend M. Deyverdun desires to assure you of his respect and good wishes. I am, dear Sir, most affectionately yours.

EDWARD GIBBON *Esq. to the Right Hon. Lord* SHEFFIELD.

LAUSANNE, July 22, 1786.

* * * Since I have another page, and some leisure moments, we may as well employ it in friendly converse ; the more so, as the greater letter to which I alluded is wonderfully precarious and uncertain : the more so likewise, as our correspondence for some time past has been of an

* His aunt, Mrs. Catherine Porten.

abrupt and disagreeable cast. Let us first talk of Sheffield's works : they are of two sorts : *Primo*, Two nymphs, whom I much desire to see; the sprightly Maria and the gentle Louisa. I perfectly represent them both in the eye of fancy ; each of them accomplished according to her age and character, yet totally different in their external and internal forms. *Secundo*, Three pamphlets ; pamphlets ! I cry you mercy ; three weighty treatises, almost as useful as an inquiry into the state of the primitive church. And here let me justify, if I have not before, my silence on a subject which we authors do not easily forgive. The first, whose first editions had seen the light before I left England, followed me here in a more complete condition ; and that Treatise on the American Trade has been read, judged, approved, and reported. The second, on Ireland, I have seen by accident the copy you sent to Mr. Trevor, who passed last summer (eighty-five) here. The third, and in my present situation the most interesting, on the French Commerce,* I have not yet seen by any means whatsoever, and you who know what orders you have given to Elmsly or others, will best discern on whom should be laid the fault and the blame. By the bye, Mrs. Trevor is now here, without her husband, and I am just going to see her, about a mile out of town : she is judged elegant and amiable. But to return to your books, all that I have seen must do you honour, and might do the public service ; you are above the trifling decorations of style ; but your sense is strong, your views impartial, and your industry laudable. I find that your American Tract is just translated into German. Do you still correspond with * * *? If he could establish a beneficial intercourse between the two first nations in the world, I would excuse him some little political tergiversation. At some distance of time and place, those domestic squabbles lose much of their importance ; and though I should not forgive him any breach of private friendship or confidence, I cannot much blame him if he chose rather to serve his family and his country, than to persevere in a hopeless and, as I suspect, an unpopular opposition. You have never told me clearly and correctly how you support your inactive retreat from the House of Commons ; whether you have resumed your long forgotten taste for rural and domestic pleasures, and whether you have never cast a look towards Coventry, or some other borough equally pure and respectable. In the short space that is left I will only repeat more distinctly, that in the present contemplation of my work, June or July of next year is the earliest term at which I can hope to see England ; and if I have a fit of the gout? I have indeed been free from the monster this last twelvemonth ; but he is most arbitrary and capricious. Of my own situation let me say with truth that it is tranquil, easy, and well adapted to my character. All enthusiasm is now at an end ; I see things in their true light, and I applaud the judgment and choice of my retirement. I am well, happy, and diligent ; but your kind hint of the London house is perfectly superfluous ; as instead of the *spring*, we must already read the *summer* of next year. Do not be childish or passionate ; trust me, I wish to appear in England ; but it must be with my book in my hand ; and a book takes more time in making than a pudding. Adieu. Will my Lady never write ?

* A mistake—Lord Sheffield did not PUBLISH any tract on French Commerce.

You see why I have left a blank in the first page; and when I begun I had no design of going beyond it; and now, unless I have some extraordinary fit of diligence and zeal, shall probably wait till the return of your epistle. A word before we part, about the least unpleasant of my business; my library in Downing-street. Excuse the accidental derangement; I shall send for no more books, and only beg you to give them shelter in your uninhabited parlour till my arrival. Two or three mornings will suffice for personal review, and the subsequent steps of sale or travel will most properly be executed under my own eye. Once more adieu.

EDWARD GIBBON *Esq. to Mr.* CADELL, *Bookseller*, London.

DEAR SIR,   LAUSANNE, December 16, 1786.

I RECEIVED your letter this morning (the 16th instant), and answer it the same day. I am a sad correspondent, but it has been my constant endeavour that my negligence should never affect the interest or happiness of my friends.

The report you so kindly mention is somewhat incorrect. I never could fix a particular day for dining with Lord Sheffield, nor should I think of performing the journey in the winter month of February. The last autumn was the term which I had fixed in my hopes, and long since in my letters to him. It has been changed to next spring, and by the spring I must now understand the middle of the summer, which I can at present ascertain with some confidence, from a nearer prospect of the end of my work, which I shall bring over for the press. It will consist of three more quarto volumes, somewhat thinner, perhaps, than their predecessors; but as that difference cannot be enough to affect the price, it will be so much saved on the author's pains, and the printer's expences. I am happy to understand the public entertain the same opinion of the past, and the same impatience for the remainder; and, unless I am strangely deceived, their expectation will not be disappointed. The three last volumes are laboured at least with equal diligence; they contain a longer period of time, and a far greater variety of events; and the whole will comprise a general series of history, from the reign of Trajan and the Antonines, to the taking of Constantinople by Mahomet the Second; with a review of Mahomet and his successors, the Crusades and the Turks, as far as in their utmost latitude they are connected with the fate of the Eastern or Western Empire. With regard to our pecuniary arrangements, I persuade myself that we shall have no more difficulties now than heretofore; that you will cheerfully assign the same value to the three younger as to the three elder brothers; and that so important a transaction will have been concluded in the first instance by three minutes of conversation, and in the second by three lines of a letter; a memorable example in the annals of authors and booksellers. If you agree with me on this subject, you may provide paper, &c. as soon as you please in the spring, in the full confidence of seeing me with my book in the summer; and I should not be sorry to learn what time (in using the utmost expedition) would be sufficient for printing, and how late you would consent to publish in the ensuing spring. At this moment, when I am straining every nerve to conclude my living labours, I am ill-disposed to lose any time in the dull dead work of correcting a new edition. When I am in England, quiet in the country, there would be room and leisure for a complete revision ; and I should have no objection to place at the end of the sixth volume a string of amendments and improvements, which hereafter might be inserted in their proper places. We shall likewise have occasion for a good and general index to the whole.

I sincerely condole with you in your various losses ; Rose and Strahan were indeed valuable men. For myself, you will rejoice to hear that I am satisfied with my Swiss retirement ; and that, except some mild and transient fits of the gout, I enjoy as much health and happiness as is compatible with the lot of man. I expect with much impatience Dr. Robertson's improved edition. There are three or four books which I should like to have without delay : that work, Pennant's Arctic Zoology, White's Sermons (the Arabic professor), the Annual Registers since the year 1782. With Elmsley's assistance (he is a sad dog, but I will write to him soon) could you not inclose them in a small box, with any other recent publications of merit, and dispatch them instantly by some more costly and expeditious mode of conveyance ? I am, most faithfully yours.

EDWARD GIBBON *Esq. to the Right Hon. Lord* SHEFFIELD.

LAUSANNE, January 20, 1787.

AFTER some sallies of wrath, you seem at length to have subsided in sullen silence, and I must confess not totally without reason. Yet if your mind be still open to truth, you will confess that I am not so black as I appear. 1. Your Lordship has shown much less activity and eloquence than formerly, and your last letter was an answer to mine, which I had expected some time with impatience. Bad examples are dangerous to young people. 2. Formerly I have neglected answering your epistles on essential, though unpleasant, business ; and the *respublica* or *privata* may have suffered by my neglect. Supposing therefore we had no transactions, why should I write so often ? To exchange sentimental compliments or to relate the various and important transactions of the republic of Lausanne. As long as I do not inform you of my death, you have good grounds to believe me alive and well. You have a general, and will soon have a more particular idea of my system and arrangement here. One day glides away after another in tranquil uniformity. Every object must have sides and moments less luminous than others ; but, upon the whole, the life and the place which I have chosen are most happily adapted to my character and circumstances : and I can now repeat, at the end of three years, what I soon and sincerely affirmed, that never, in a single instant, have I repented of my scheme of retirement to Lausanne ; a retirement which was judged by my best and wisest friend a project little short of insanity. The place, the people, the climate, have answered or exceeded my warmest expectations. And though I truly rejoice in my approaching visit to England, Mr. Pitt, were he your friend and mine, would not find it an easy task to prevent my return. 3. And now let me add a third reason, which often diverted me from writing ; namely, my impatience to see you this next summer. I am building a great book, which, besides the three stories already exposed to the public eye, will have three stories more before we reach the roof and battlements. You too have built or altered a great Gothic castle with baronial battlements. Did you finish it within the time you intended? As that time drew near, did you not find a thousand nameless and unexpected works that must be performed ; each of them calling for a portion of time and labour? and had you not despised, nobly despised, the minute diligence of finishing, fitting up, and furnishing the apartments, you would have discovered a new train of indispensable business. Such, at least, has been my case. A long while ago, when I contemplated the distant prospect of my work, I gave you and myself some hopes of landing in England last autumn ; but, alas! when autumn grew near, hills began to rise on hills, Alps on Alps, and I found my journey far more tedious and toilsome than I had imagined. When I look back on the length of the undertaking, and the variety of materials, I cannot accuse, or suffer myself to be accused of idleness ; yet it appeared that unless I doubled my diligence, another year, and perhaps more, would elapse before I could embark with my complete manuscript. Under these circumstances I took, and am still executing, a bold and meritorious resolution. The mornings in winter, and in a country of early dinners, are very concise ; to them, my usual period of study, I now frequently add the evenings, renounce cards and society, refuse the most agreeable evenings, or perhaps make my appearance at a late supper. By this extraordinary industry, which I never practised before, and to which I hope never to be again reduced, I see the last part of my History growing apace under my hands ; all my materials are collected and arranged ; I can exactly compute, by the square foot, or the square page, all that remains to be done ; and after concluding text and notes, after a general review of my time and my ground, I now can decisively ascertain the final period of the Decline and Fall, and can boldly promise that I will dine with you at Sheffield-Place in the month of August, or perhaps of July, in the present year ; within less than a twelvemonth of the term which I had loosely and originally fixed ; and perhaps it would not be easy to find a work of that size and importance in which the workman has so tolerably kept his word with himself and the public. But in this situation, oppressed with this particular object, and stealing every hour from my amusement, to the fatigue of the pen, and the eyes, you will conceive, or you might conceive, how little stomach I have for the epistolary style ; and that instead of idle, though friendly, correspondence I think it far more agreeable to employ my time in the effectual measures that may hasten and exhilarate our personal interview. About a month ago I had a voluntary, and not unpleasing, epistle from Cadell ; he informs me that he is going to print a new octavo edition, the former being exhausted, and that the public expect with impatience the conclusion of that excellent work, whose reputation increases every day, &c. I answered him by the return of the post, to inform him of the period and extent of my labours, and to express a reasonable hope that he would set the same value on the three last as he had done on the three former volumes. Should we conclude in this easy manner a transaction so honourable to the author and bookseller, my way is clear and open before me; in pecuniary matters I think I am assured for the rest of my life of never troubling my friends, or being troubled myself; a state to which I aspire, and which I indeed deserve, if not by my management, at least by moderation.

In your last, you talk more of the French treaty than of yourself and your wife and family; a true English *quid nunc!* For my part, in this remote, inland, neutral country, you will suppose, that after a slight glance on the papers, I have neither had the means nor the inclination to think very deeply about it. As a citizen of the world, a character to which I am every day rising or sinking, I must rejoice in every agreement that diminishes the separation between neighbouring countries, which softens their prejudices, unites their interests and industry, and renders their future hostilities less frequent and less implacable. With regard to the present treaty, I hope both nations are gainers; since otherwise it cannot be lasting; and such double mutual gain is surely possible in fair trade, though it could not easily happen in the mischievous amusements of war and gaming. * * * What a delightful hand have these great statesmen made of it since my departure! without power, and, as far as I can see, without hope. When we meet I shall advise you to digest all your political and commercial knowledge, (England, Ireland, France, America,) and, with some attention to style and order, to make the whole a classic book, which may preserve your name and benefit your country. I know not whether you have seen Sir Henry Clinton since his return: he passed a day with me, and seemed pleased with my reception and place. We talked over you and the American war. I embrace the *silent my Lady* and the two honourable Misses, whom I sigh to behold and admire. Adieu. Ever yours.

Though I can part with land, you find I cannot part with books: the remainder of my library has so long embarrassed your room, that it may now await my presence and final judgment. Has my Lady read a novel intitled Caroline de Litchfield, of our home manufacture; I may say of ours, since Deyverdun and myself were the judges and patrons of the manuscript. The author, who is since married a second time, (Madame de Crousaz, now Montolicu,) is a charming woman. I was in some danger. Once more, bar a long fit of the gout, and the Historian will land at Dover before the end of July. Adieu.

EDWARD GIBBON *Esq. to Mr.* CADELL, London.

DEAR SIR,　　　　　　　　　　　　LAUSANNE, February 24, 1787.

I AM perfectly satisfied with your's and Mr. Strahan's cheerful and liberal assent to my proposal, and am glad to find that your partner has not degenerated from his worthy father, whose loss I sincerely lament. The sole remaining difficulty (of the volumes falling below the guinea price) it is unnecessary for the present to discuss, as I think it unlikely to happen. As I am resolved to finish and revise the work before I leave Lausanne, it will depend on yourself to arrange your preparations of paper, &c. in such a manner that we may lose no time, but go to press the first week after my arrival. But in the mean while I wish you to reflect and inquire; 1st, In how many months the impression of the three volumes may be completed, either with ordinary or extraordinary diligence. And, 2dly, How late in next year you would be desirous or willing to publish. On my revisal I may find more alterations and improvements to make than I at present foresee; I may be disabled by a fit of the gout; and your speedy answer will inform me of the utmost latitude in which I may be indulged, without totally disconcerting our common interest. You probably agree with me in the necessity of a good general index for the six volumes. If you are possessed of an intelligent workman, he might without delay take in hand the first three volumes; but in that case I must desire him to send me as soon as possible a *short* specimen by the post. I have thought on the subject of index-making, and can give him some advice, which will abridge the size, without impairing the use and value of his alphabetical table. By a letter of the thirteenth instant, Elmsley informs me that he is on the point of sending the books; and I hope to have them here before the end of next month. I propose writing to him very soon; but as the events of life are uncertain, it may be safer to answer his question through your channel: "The author of Caroline (Madame de Crousaz) is now become Madame la Baronne de Montolieu by second marriage, and has other cares and pleasures besides those of writing. Her pen is not idle, but her new schemes of romance are not in any degree of forwardness or maturity. Perhaps an handsome proposal from an English bookseller might stimulate her diligence." I am sincerely yours.

In our style of negociation it is almost superfluous to say that I reserve about a score of copies for myself and my friends.

EDWARD GIBBON *Esq. to the Right Hon. Lord* SHEFFIELD.

LAUSANNE, June 2, 1787.

I BEGIN to discover that if I wait till I could achieve a just and satisfactory epistle, equally pleasant and instructive, you would have a poor chance of hearing from me. I will therefore content myself with a simple answer to a question, which (I love to believe) you repeat with some impatience: "When may we expect you in England?" My great building is, as it were, completed, and some slight ornaments, the painting and glazing of the last finished rooms may be dispatched without inconvenience in the autumnal residence of Sheffield-Place. It is therefore my sincere and peremptory intention to depart from Lausanne about the twentieth of July, and to find myself (*me trouver*) in London on or before the glorious first of August. I know of nothing that can prevent it but a fit of the gout, the capricious tyrant, who obeys no laws either of time or place; and so unfortunately are we circumstanced, that such a fit, if it came late and lasted long, would effectually disable me from coming till next spring; since thereby I should lose the season, the monsoon, for the impression of three quarto volumes, which will require nine months (a regular parturition), and cannot advantageously appear after the beginning or middle of May. At the same time do not be apprehensive that I mean to play you a dog's trick. From a thousand motives it is my wish to come over this year : the desire of seeing you, and the *silent sullen* my Lady ; the family arrangements, discharge of servants, which I have already made ; the strong wish of settling my three youngest children in a manner honourable to them and beneficial to their parents. Much miscellaneous matter rises to my pen, but I will not be tempted to turn the leaf. Expect me therefore at Sheffield-Place, with ·strong probability, about the fifteenth of August. Adieu. Yours.

EDWARD GIBBON *Esq. to the Right Hon. Lord* SHEFFIELD.

LAUSANNE, July 21, 1787.

THE twentieth of July is past, and I am still at Lausanne ; but the march of heavy bodies, such as armies and historians, can seldom be foreseen or fixed to a precise day. Some particular reasons have engaged me to allow myself another week ; and the day of my departure is now (*I believe*) determined for Sunday the twenty-ninth instant. You know the road and the distance. I am no rapid English traveller, and my servant is not accustomed to ride post. I was never fond of deeds of darkness, and if the weather be hot, we must repose in the middle of the day. Yet the roads are in general good : between sun and sun the interval is long ; and, barring the accidents of winds and waves, I think it possible to reach London in ten or twelve days ; *viz.* on or before the ninth of August. With your active spirit, you will scarce understand how I can look on this easy journey with some degree of reluctance and apprehension ; but after a tranquil sedentary life of four years, (having lain but a single night out of my own bed,) I see mountains and monsters in the way ; and so happy do I feel myself *at home*, that nothing but the strongest calls of friendship and interest could drag me from hence. You ingeniously propose that I should turn off at Sittingbourne, and seem to wonder what business I can find, or make, for an immediate residence in the capital. Have you totally forgot that I bring over three quarto volumes for the press ? and are you ignorant that not a moment must be lost, if we are desirous of appearing at a proper season ; and that I must set the machine in motion before I can secede to Sheffield-Place with an easy mind, and for a reasonable term ? Of this be assured, that I shall not be less impatient than yourself, and that, of human two-legged animals, yourself and yours are the first whom I shall wish to see in England. For myself, I do not regret the occupancy of Downing-street ; in my first visit to London, a lodging or hotel in the Adelphi will be more convenient ; but I have some anxiety about my books, and must try whether I can approach those holy relics, without offending the delicacy of an amiable Duchess. Our interview is so near, that I have little more to add, except a caution about my own concerns, in which, you will confess, that from ——, and ——, to ——, I have been generally unlucky. If anything remains, present or future, it must be agitated and decided ; but all retrospects are useless and painful, and we have so many pleasant subjects of conversation, that all such odious matters may be buried in oblivion. Adieu. I embrace my Lady and Louisa, but I no longer presume, even on paper, to embrace the blooming Maria. Ever yours.

EDWARD GIBBON *Esq. to the Right-Hon. Lord* SHEFFIELD.

ADELPHI HOTEL, August 8, 1787.
INTELLIGENCE EXTRAORDINARY. This day (August the seventh) the celebrated E. G. arrived with a numerous retinue (one servant). We hear that he has brought over from Lausanne the remainder of his History for immediate publication. The post had left town before my arrival. I am pleased, but indeed astonished, to find myself in London, after a journey of six hundred miles, and hardly yet conceive how I had resolution to undertake it. I find myself not a little fatigued, and have devoted this hot day to privacy and repose, without having seen anybody except Cadell and Elmsley, and my neighbour Batt, whose civility amounts to kindness and real friendship. But you may depend on it, that instead of sauntering in town, or giving way to every temptation, I will dispatch my necessary work, and hasten with impatience to the groves of Sheffield-Place ; a project somewhat more rational than the hasty turbulent visit which your vigour had imagined. If you come up to quicken my diligence we shall meet the sooner ; but I see no appearance of my leaving town before the end of next week. I embrace, &c. Adieu.

The Same to the Same. Monday Afternoon, 1787.
I PRECIPITATE, I inconvenience ! Alas! alas! I am a poor miserable cripple, confined to my chair. Last Wednesday evening I felt some flying symptoms of the gout : for two succeeding days I struggled bravely, and went in a chair to dine with Batt and Lord Loughborough : but on Saturday I yielded to my conqueror. I have now passed three wearisome days without amusement, and three miserable nights without sleep. Yet my acquaintance are charitable ; and as virtue should never be made too difficult, I feel that a man has more friends in Pall-mall than in Bentinck-street. This fit is remarkably painful ; the enemy is possessed of the left foot and knee, and how far he may carry the war God only knows. Of futurity it is impossible to speak ; but it will be fortunate if I am able to leave town by the end, not of this, but of the ensuing week. What may be the future progress, whether slow or rapid, fluctuating or steady, time alone will determine ; and to that master of human knowledge I must leave our Bath journey. Pity me, magnanimous Baron ; pity me, tender females ; pity me, Swiss exile (M. Wilhel. de Severy) ; and believe me, it is far better to be learning English at Uckfield. I write with difficulty, as the least motion or constraint in my attitude is repeated by all the nerves and sinews in

my knee. But you shall find each day a note or bulletin of my health. To-morrow I must give pain to Mrs. G——. Adieu. Ever yours.

EDWARD GIBBON *Esq. to the Right Hon. Lady* SHEFFIELD.

BATH, December 18, 1787.

ALAS! alas! alas! How vain and fallacious are all the designs of man. This is now the eighteenth of December, precisely one month since my departure from Sheffield-Place; and it was firmly my wish, my hope, my resolution, that after dispatching some needful business in London, and accomplishing a pious duty at Bath, I should by this day be restored to the tranquil leisure, and friendly society, of Sheffield-Place. A cruel tyrant has disconcerted all my plans; my business in town has been neglected, my attendance at Bath is just begun, and my return is yet distant. I was not a little edified to hear of some expressions of regret and discontent on my departure; and though I am not able to produce as good evidence, you will perhaps believe that in the solitude of a London lodging I often railed at the gout for maliciously delaying his attack till I was removed from a place where my sufferings would have been alleviated by every kind and comfortable attention. I grew at last so desperately impatient, as to resolve on immediate flight, without waiting till I had totally expelled the foe, and recovered my strength. I performed the journey with tolerable ease, but the motion has agitated the remains of the humour. I am very lame, and a second fit may possibly be the punishment of my rashness.

As yet I have seen nothing of Bath except Mrs. G—— ; and weakness, as well as propriety, will confine me very closely to her. Lord Sheffield, with Mrs. Holroyd and Maria, dined with us yesterday. We begin to throw out hints of the shortness of our stay, and indispensable business; and, unless I should be confined by the gout, it is resolved in our cabinet to leave Bath on Thursday the twenty-sixth, and passing through Lord Loughborough's and town, to settle at Sheffield-Place, most assuredly, before the end of the year. For my own part I can say with truth, that did not the press loudly demand my presence, I could, without a sigh, allow the Duchess to reign in Downing-street the greatest part of the winter, and should be happy in the society of two persons (no common blessing) whom I love, and by whom I am beloved.

Adieu, dear Madam, and believe me, with the affection of a friend and a brother, ever yours.

Dr. WILLIAM ROBERTSON *to Mr.* GIBBON.

MY DEAR SIR,   COLLEGE of EDINBURGH, February 27, 1788.

THOUGH you have now been some time in London, yet as I heard of your welfare by different channels, and as I know from experience how much a man has to do who is printing three quartos, even after he thinks they are altogether ready for the press, I have hitherto forborne to interrupt you by any letter or inquiry of mine. But there is such a

z

general impatience to see your new publication among people of letters here; and, as your friend, I am so frequently interrogated about the length it has advanced, and the time when it will appear, that I begin to be ashamed of knowing nothing more about it than other people. I must request of you then to furnish me with such information as may both preserve my credit, and gratify my own curiosity. My expectations from this part of your work are, indeed, very high. Your materials begin to improve, and are certainly much more copious than during a great part of the period you have gone through. You have three or four events as great, and splendid, and singular, as the heart of an historian could wish to delineate. The contemporary writers will furnish you with all the necessary facts. To adorn them as elegant writers, or to account for them as philosophers, never entered into their heads. This they have left to you.

Since you went to the continent I have not done so much as I wished. My health, until lately, has been more shattered; and as I advance in life, (I am now sixty-six,) though my faculties, I imagine, are still entire, yet I find my mind less active and ardent. I have, however, finished a very careful revise of all my works, and have given them the last polish they will receive from my hand. I have made some additions to each of them, and in the History of Scotland pretty considerable ones. I have desired Mr. Strahan to send to you a copy of them uniformly bound, and hope you will accept of them, as a memorial of my esteem and affection. You will see that I have got in Mr. Whitaker an adversary so bigotted and zealous, that though I have denied no article of faith, and am at least as orthodox as he himself, yet he rails against me with all the asperity of theological hatred. I shall adhere to my fixed maxim of making no reply. May I hope that when you see Lord Loughborough you will remember me to him with kindness and respect. Our friend Mr. Smith, whom we were in great danger of losing, is now almost perfectly re-established. I have the honour to be, with great truth, your most faithful humble servant,

WILLIAM ROBERTSON.

EDWARD GIBBON, *Esq. to the Right Hon. Lord* SHEFFIELD.

DOWNING-STREET, June 21, 1788.

INSTEAD of the Historian you receive a short letter, in your eyes an indispensible tribute. This day, at length, after long delay and frequent expostulation, I have received the writings, which I am now in the act of signing, sealing, and delivering, according to the lawyer's directions. * * * I long to be at Sheffield-Place. You see my departure is not postponed a moment by idleness or pleasure, but the precise day still hangs on contingencies, and we must all be patient, if our wishes should be thwarted. I say our wishes, for I sincerely desire to be with you. I have had many dinners, some splendid and memorable, with Hastings last Thursday, with the Prince of Wales next Tuesday at Craufurd's. But the town empties, Texier is silent, and in an evening, I *desiderate* the resources of a family or a club. Caplin has finished the Herculean labour, and seven majestic boxes

will abdicate on Monday your hall. Severy has likewise dispatched
his affairs, and secured his companion Clarke, who is arrived in town ;
but his schemes are abridged by the inexorable rigour of Lord Howe,
who has assured our great and fair intercessors, that by the King's
order the dockyards are shut against all strangers. We therefore give
up Portsmouth, and content ourselves with two short trips ; one to
Stowe and Oxford, the other to Chatham ; and if we can catch a
launch and review, *encore vit on.* He (Severy, not Lord Howe,) salutes
with me the family. Adieu. Yours.

EDWARD GIBBON, *Esq. to the Right Hon. Lord* SHEFFIELD.

DOWNING-STREET, Saturday.
ACCORDING to your imperious law I write a line to postpone my
arrival till Friday, or perhaps Saturday, but I hope Friday, and I promise you that not a moment shall be wasted. And now let me add a
cool word as to my final departure, which is irrevocably fixed between
the tenth and fifteenth of July. After a full and free enjoyment of each
other's society, let us submit, without a struggle, to reason and fate.
It would be idle to pretend business at Lausanne ; but a complete
year will elapse before my return. Severy and myself are now expected with some impatience. I am thankful for your hospitable
entertainment ; but I wish you to remember Homer's admirable
precept :

"Welcome the coming, *speed* the parting guest."

Spare me, therefore, spare yourself, the trouble of a fruitless contest,
in which, according to a great author, I foresee a certain loss of time,
and a probable loss of temper. I believe we shall have both Craufurd
and Hugonin at Sheffield-Place. Adieu.

The Same to the Same. DOWNING-ST., Sat., June, 1788.
I HAVE but a moment between my return home and my dressing,
and heartily tired I am ; for I am now involved in the horrors of
shopping, packing, &c. yet I must write four lines, to prevent a growl,
which might salute the arrival of an empty-handed post on Sunday.
I hope the whole caravan, Christians and Pagans, arrived in good
health at the castle ; that the turrets begin to rise to the third heaven ;
that each has found a proper occupation ; and that Tuft* enjoys the
freedom and felicity of the lawn. Yesterday the august scene was
closed for this year. Sheridan surpassed himself ; and though I am
far from considering him as a perfect orator, there were many beautiful
passages in his speech, on justice, filial love, &c. ; one of the closest
chains of argument I ever heard, to prove that Hastings was responsible for the acts of Middleton ; and a compliment, much admired, to
a certain Historian of your acquaintance. Sheridan, in the close of
his speech, sunk into Burke's arms ; but I called this morning, he is

* Lady Sheffield's lap-dog.

perfectly well. I fear that I shall not be able to dine at home a single day. To-morrow Severy and myself go to Bushy. I hope to be with you by Sunday the twenty-second instant. The casing of my books is a prodigious operation. Adieu.

Dr. WILLIAM ROBERTSON *to Mr.* GIBBON.

DEAR SIR,   COLLEGE of EDINBURGH, July 30, 1788.
   LONG before this I should have acknowledged the receipt of your most acceptable present ; but for several weeks I have been afflicted with a violent fit of deafness, and that unsocial malady is always accompanied with such a degree of languor, as renders even the writing of a letter an effort. During my solitude the perusal of your book has been my chief amusement and consolation. I have gone through it once with great attention, and am now advanced to the last volume in my second reading. I ventured to predict the superior excellence of the volumes lately published, and I have not been a false prophet. Indeed, when I consider the extent of your undertaking, and the immense labour of historical and philosophic research requisite towards executing every part of it, I am astonished that all this should have been accomplished by one man. I know no example, in any age or nation, of such a vast body of valuable and elegant information communicated by any individual. I feel, however, some degree of mortification mingled with my astonishment. Before you began your historic career, I used to pride myself in being at least the most industrious historian of the age ; but now, alas ! I can pretend no longer even to that praise, and must say, as Pliny did his uncle, *Si comparer illi sum desidiosissimus.* Your style appears to me improved in these new volumes ; by the habit of writing, you write with greater ease. I am sorry to find that our ideas on the effects of the Crusades do not altogether coincide. I considered that point with great care, and cannot help thinking still that my opinion was well founded. I shall consult the authorities to which I refer ; for when my sentiments differ from yours, I have some reason to distrust them, and I may possibly trouble you with a letter on the subject. I am much flattered with the manner in which you have so often mentioned my name. *Lætus sum laudari a te laudato viro.* I feel much satisfaction in having been distinguished by the two historians of my own times, whose favourable opinion I was most ambitious of obtaining.
   I hope this letter may find you still in England. When you return to Lausanne, permit me to recommend to your good offices my youngest son, who is now at Yverdun on account of his health, and lives with M. Herman, a clergyman there. You will find the young man (if you can rely on the partial testimony of a father) sensible, modest, and well-bred, and though no great scholar, he has seen much ; having returned from India, where he served last war, by Bassora, Bagdat, Moussul, and Aleppo. He is now a Captain in the twenty-third regiment. If you have any friend at Yverdun, be so good as to recommend him. It will do him credit to have your countenance. I have

desired him to pay his respects to you at Lausanne. Farewell, my dear Sir. I ever am yours most faithfully,

WILLIAM ROBERTSON.

Dr. ADAM SMITH *to Mr.* GIBBON.

MY DEAR FRIEND, EDINBURGH, December 10, 1788.
I HAVE ten thousand apologies to make, for not having long ago returned you my best thanks for the very agreeable present you made me of the three last volumes of your History. I cannot express to you the pleasure it gives me to find, that by the universal assent of every man of taste and learning, whom I either know or correspond with, it sets you at the very head of the whole literary tribe at present existing in Europe. I ever am, my dear friend, most affectionately yours,

ADAM SMITH.

Mr. GIBBON *to Mr.* CADELL, *Bookseller*, London.

LAUSANNE, February 11, 1789.
I SHOULD be much more ashamed of my silence, were I not satisfied that you have received a recent and favourable account of me from some of our friends who have visited this place since my return. But I should be inexcusable, did I not thank you for your kind and seasonable wishes, which I can return with equal sincerity. I do not propose making any improvements or corrections in the octavo edition which you meditate ; some slight alterations would give me more trouble than pleasure. A thorough revision of the whole work would be the labour of many months ; it may be the amusement of my old age, and will be a valuable legacy, to renew your copyright at the expiration of the last fourteen years. In the mean while, some expedition may be useful to guard your property from the unexpected invasion of *foreign* pirates. Eight volumes in octavo are already printed at Basil, and the remainder is expected every day. I am both glad and sorry to inform you, that the type is neat, the paper tolerable, and the text *wonderfully* correct. I hear of another English edition in Saxony, and of two French translations advancing with speed and emulation at Paris. Of the success of the work at home you are best qualified, and most interested, to judge ; and I am happy to find that you express yourself, with some reserve, satisfied with the sale. From some reports of angry criticisms, and from the use and abuse of my name in the papers, I perceive that I am not forgotten. Before a year has elapsed from the time of publication, my History will have been perused by some thousand readers of various characters and understandings. Each will probably find something to blame, and I hope something to commend ;' and the balance of their private judgments will fix the public estimate of its merit and reputation. Since my return, I have been, as I promise in the preface, very busy and very idle in my library ; several ideal works have been embraced and thrown aside ; but if the warm weather should ripen any project to form and maturity, you may depend on the

earliest intelligence. I have received a very friendly and flattering letter from Dr. Robertson, and have had the pleasure of shewing some civilities to his son during his residence in this place. If you can, send me a good account of Adam Smith; there is no man more sincerely interested in his welfare than myself. I beg you will present my compliments to all our friends, particularly to Mr. Strahan and Dr. Gillies. Tell Elmsley, that I have received with due contrition his *third* letter; unless you are speedy, my answer *will* anticipate your information. I am most faithfully yours.

EDWARD GIBBON *Esq. to Lady* PORTEN, Kensington-palace.

DEAR MADAM,   LAUSANNE, June 27, 1789.

I RECEIVED with more concern than surprize, your kind notification of my poor uncle's departure. My own knowledge of his many valuable qualities teaches me to sympathize in your loss; but his long infirmities and gradual decay must have prepared you for the melancholy event, and your own reason will suggest the best and strongest motives of consolation; among these is your regard for the amiable children whom he has left behind. Your labours for their future happiness will be assisted by all your friends, who are attached to his memory; and for my own part, I beg leave to assure you, that on every occasion I shall consider them as my near and dear relations. When I had last the pleasure of seeing Charlotte at Kensington, I was delighted with her innocent cheerfulness, with her assiduous care of her poor father, and with an appearance of sense and discretion far beyond her years. How happy should I think myself, if I had a daughter of her age and disposition, who in a short time would be qualified to govern my family, and to be my companion and comfort in the decline of life!

You will, I am sure, be pleased to hear that my situation at Lausanne continues, almost in every respect, as agreeable as I could wish. The only circumstance which embitters my happiness, is the declining health of my friend Mons. Deyverdun. I cannot long flatter myself with the hope of possessing him. I am, dear Madam, &c.

Mr. GIBBON *to Mr.* CADELL.

DEAR SIR,   LAUSANNE, November 17, 1790.

I SHOULD indeed be inexcusable for my long neglect of your last obliging letter, had it not reached me in a moment of pain and weakness, in a fit of the gout, the longest and most severe that I have ever known. A letter with me is no trifling enterprize; and before I could find strength, and time, and resolution, the occasion on which you so handsomely consulted me was already past. I suppose that the abridgment of my History is now freely circulated, either with or without your name; nor can I foresee any possible mischief, either for *my* reputation or *your* interest. A translation, an abridgment, or even a criticism, always proves the success, and consequently extends the sale, of any popular work.

As I am inclined to flatter myself that you have no reason to be displeased with your purchase, I now wish to ask you whether you feel yourself disposed to add a seventh, or supplemental volume to my History? The materials of which it will be composed will naturally he classed under the three following heads : 1. A series of fragments, disquisitions, digressions, &c. more or less connected with the principal subject. 2. Several tables of geography, chronology, coins, weights and measures, &c.; nor should I despair of obtaining from a gentleman at Paris some accurate and well-adapted maps. 3. A critical review of all the authors whom I have used and quoted.* 1 am convinced such a supplement might be rendered entertaining, as well as useful ; and that few purchasers would refuse to *complete* their Decline and Fall. But as the writer could not derive either fame or amusement from these obscure labours, he must be encouraged by other motives ; and, in plain English, I should expect the same reward for the seventh, as for any of the preceding volumes. You think and act with too much liberality, to confound such a large original supplement with the occa-sional improvements of a new edition, which are already your property by the terms of our former covenant. But as I am jealous of standing clear, not only in law and equity, but in your esteem and my own, I shall instantly renounce the undertaking, if it appears by your answer that you have the shadow of an objection. Should you tempt me to proceed, this supplement will be only the employment of my leisure hours ; and I foresee that full two years will elapse before I can deliver it into the hands of the printer.

Our friend Elmsley, who possibly thinks me dead and buried, will be, or will not be, surprised when you inform him that I have now a letter of two pages in my bureau addressed to him, dated the twenty-sixth of May, and not yet finished. Hunger, literary hunger, will soon, however, compel me to write ; as I have many questions to ask, and many commissions to give. In the mean while I thirst for Mr. Burke's Reflections on the Revolutions of France. Intreat Elmsley, in my name, to dispatch it to Lausanne with care and speed, by *any* mode of conveyance less expensive than the post. He may add to the parcel the new edition of Adam Smith's Theory of Moral Sentiments. I heard of his death with more concern than surprise. What a loss to letters, philosophy, and mankind !

I beg you would remember me to Mr. Strahan and all our friends. In my happy exile, my public and private affections remind me that I am an Englishman. Pray thank Dr. Moore, in my name, for the pleasure which I have received from Zeluco, the best philosophical romance of the age. If he cultivates his talents by any similar publi-cations, I only wish that he would place the scene at home ; we may describe the characters, but we can never paint the *manners* of foreigners, and the quarrel of the two Scotchmen is doubtless the best chapter in the book. I am, dear Sir, most faithfully yours.

* Mr. Gibbon soon became tired of this plan, and expressed a wish it had not been men-tioned. He said his History was a critical review of the authors he had used. S.

Mr. GIBBON *to* Mr. CADELL.

DEAR SIR,   LAUSANNE, April 27, 1791.
TOO many posts have slipped away since my receipt of your last letter, without my assuring you that every shadow of misapprehension has vanished from my mind, and that 1 am perfectly satisfied with the liberality of your sentiments and conduct. But 1 am every day more inclined to believe that on the present occasion they will not be put to the trial. On a closer inspection, I discover more difficulty and less advantage than I had at first imagined in the plan of a supplement; and I feel the objection, which you so handsomely decline, against increasing the weight and price of so voluminous a work. Perhaps it would have been better if my crude idea had not been so hastily announced to the public; but even this venial indiscretion is a proof of your zeal and regard. The intelligence of any new designs shall be delayed till they are ripe for execution; but you may be assured that I am now awake.

I am very happy to hear that our respectable friend Dr. Robertson is not asleep; and much do I expect from the subject and the pen. 1 had once a design not totally unconnected with his own, but it is now in far abler hands. Boswell's book will be curious, or at least whimsical: his hero, who can so long detain the public curiosity, must be no common animal. I see you now advertise an octavo edition of Dr. Henry's History of England. Is not the author dead? His plan is excellent, and I wish you could engage some diligent and sensible man to undertake the continuation. Alas! if Dr. Campbell were still alive! I have desired Elmsley to ask you for three octavo copies of my own work. Whenever he sends me a box of books, 1 should be glad if you would enrich it with any of your own valuable publications. Your name is a recommendation; but the chastity of that name cannot be too religiously preserved. My health and spirits are now remarkably good, and it will give me great pleasure to receive as favourable an account of yourself. I am most faithfully yours.

EDWARD GIBBON *Esq. to Mrs.* GIBBON, Belvidere, Bath.

DEAR MADAM,   LAUSANNE, May 18, 1791.
As much as I am accustomed to my own sins, I am shocked, really shocked, when I think of my long and most inexcusable silence; nor do I dare to compute how many months I have suffered to elapse without sending a single line (Oh shame! shame!) to the best and dearest of my friends, who indeed has been very seldom out of my thoughts. I have sometimes imagined that if the opportunities of writing occurred less frequently, they would be seized with more diligence; but the unfortunate departure of the post twice every week encourages procrastination, and each short successive delay is indulged without scruple, till the whole has swelled to a tremendous account. I will try, alas! to reform; and, although I am afraid that writing grows painful to you, I have the confidence to solicit a *speedy line*, to say that you love and forgive me. After a long experience of the unfeeling doubts and delays of the law, you will probably soon hear from Lord Sheffield that the

Beriton transaction is at last concluded, and I hope that you will be satisfied with the full and firm security of your annuity. That you may long continue to enjoy it is the first and most sincere wish of my heart.

In the placid course of our lives, at Lausanne and Bath, we have few events to relate, and fewer changes to describe ; but I indulge myself in the pleasing belief that we are both as well and as happy as the common order of nature will allow us to expect. I should be satisfied, had 1 received from time to time some indirect, but agreeable, information of your health. For myself, I have no complaint, except the gout ; and though the visits of my old enemy are somewhat longer, and more enfeebling, they are confined to my feet and knees ; the pain is moderate, and my imprisonment to my chamber, or my chair, is much alleviated by the daily kindness of my friends. I wish it were in my power to give you an adequate idea of the conveniency of my house, and the beauty of my garden ; both of which I have improved at a considerable expence since the death of poor Deyverdun. But the loss of a friend is indeed irreparable. Were I ten years younger, I might possibly think of a female companion ; but the choice is difficult, the success doubtful, the engagement perpetual, and at fifty-four a man should never think of altering the whole system of his life and habits. The disposal of Beriton, and the death of my aunt Hester, who has left me her estate in Sussex, makes me very easy in my worldly affairs : my income is equal to my expence, and my expence is adequate to my wishes. You may possibly have heard of literary projects which are ascribed to me by the public without my knowledge : but it is much more probable that I have closed the account ; and though I shall never lay aside the pleasing occupations of study, you may be assured that I have no serious settled thoughts of a new work. Next year I shall meditate, and I trust shall execute, a visit to England, in which the Belvidere is one of my powerful loadstones. I often reflect with a painful emotion on the imperious circumstances which have thrown us at such a distance from each other.

In the moving picture of the world, you cannot be indifferent to the strange revolution which has humbled all that was high, and exalted all that was low, in France. The irregular and lively spirit of the nation has disgraced their liberty, and instead of building a free constitution, they have only exchanged despotism for anarchy. This town and country are crowded with noble exiles ; and we sometimes count in an assembly a dozen Princesses and Duchesses. Burke, if I remember right, is no favourite of yours ; but there is surely much eloquence and much sense in his book. The prosperity of England forms a proud contrast with the disorders of France ; but I hope we shall avoid the folly of a Russian war. Pitt, in this instance, seems too like his father. Mr. Helrard, a sensible man, and his pupil have left us. They found, as your friends will always find, the weight of your recommendation with me. I am, dearest Madam, ever most affectionately yours.

Dr. WILLIAM ROBERTSON *to Mr.* GIBBON.

DEAR SIR,   LENNEL-HOUSE, August 25, 1791.
SOME time before the publication of my Historical Disquisition concerning India I desired our friend Mr. Cadell to send a copy of it to you in my name. I hope you received it long ago, and will allow it to remain in your library, as a memorial of my respect and friendship. No man had formed a more decided resolution of retreating early from public view, and of spending the eve of life in the tranquillity of professional and domestic occupations ; but, directly in the face of that purpose, I step forth with a new work, when just on the brink of threescore and ten. The preface of the book gives a fair and simple account how this happened. Hitherto I have no cause to repent of a step which I took with hesitation and anxiety. My book has met with a reception beyond what the *spe lentus, pavidusque futuri,* dared to expect. I find, however, like other parents, that I have a partial fondness for this child of my old age ; and cannot set my heart quite at ease, until I know your opinion of it. I need not say with what perfect confidence I rest upon your judgment, and how happy it will make me to find that this production meets with your approbation. Nothing will add so much to that pleasure, as your communicating to me any remarks that occurred to you in perusing it. While I was engaged in composing the Disquisition it often occurred to me, that I was more upon your ground than in any of my former works ; and I often wished that I had been so near to you as to profit by your advice and information. Next to that will be the benefit I may derive from your friendly strictures.` Be so kind then as to mention to me any error or omission you have observed; every criticism of yours will be instructive.

Permit me to request another favour. You allowed me to hope, that as soon as you fixed upon a new subject you would let me know, and give me the satisfaction of indulging the hopes of living until you finished it. I trust that you are not idle still. I may now tell you with authority, that you are yet far from that period of life when you should lay down your pen. I can say from experience, that the busiest season of life is the most happy ; and I have no doubt that you will concur with me in this sentiment. Let me know then, my dear Sir, how you are, what you are doing, and what progress you make. As for my part, I enjoy good health ; and, except some fits of deafness, am little troubled with the infirmities of old age. I write this at my son-in-law's, Mr. Brydone, who, if he had not a wife and family, loves Switzerland so well, and has so many friends in Lausanne, that I believe he would gladly join you there. Believe me to be, with great respect, your most faithful and obedient servant,

WILLIAM ROBERTSON.

EDWARD GIBBON, *Esq. to Mrs.* GIBBON, Bath.

MY DEAREST MADAM,   LAUSANNE, August 1, 1792.
NOTWITHSTANDING all the arts of our great enemy, the dæmon of procrastination, I should not have postponed for so many months a pleasing duty, which may at any time be performed in a single hour,

had I not for some time past entertained a lively and probable hope of visiting you this autumn in person; had I not flattered myself, that the very next post I might be able to fix the day of my departure from Lausanne, and almost of my arrival at the Belvidere. That hope is now vanished, and my journey to England is unavoidably delayed till the spring or summer of next year. The extraordinary state of public affairs in France opposes an insuperable bar to my passage; and every prudent stranger will avoid that inhospitable land, in which a people of slaves is suddenly become a nation of tyrants and cannibals. The German road is indeed safe, but, independent of a great addition of fatigue and expence, the armies of Austria and Prussia now cover that frontier; and though the generals are polite, and the troops well disciplined, I am not desirous of passing through the clouds of hussars and pandours that attend their motions. These public reasons are fortified by some private motives, and to this delay I resign myself, with a sigh for the present, and a hope for the future.

What a strange wild world do we live in! You will allow me to be a tolerable historian, yet, on a fair review of ancient and modern times, I can find none that bear any affinity with the present. My knowledge of your discerning mind, and my recollection of your political principles, assure me, that you are no more a *democrat* than myself. Had the French improved their glorious opportunity to erect a free constitutional monarchy on the ruins of arbitrary power and the Bastille, I should applaud their generous effort; but this total subversion of all rank, order, and government could be productive only of a popular monster, which, after devouring everything else, must finally devour itself. I was once apprehensive that this monster would propagate some imps in our happy island, but they seem to have been crushed in their cradle; and I acknowledge with pleasure and pride the good sense of the English nation, who seem truly conscious of the blessings which they enjoy: and I am happy to find that the most respectable part of Opposition has cordially joined in the support of "things as they are." Even this country has been somewhat tainted with the democratical infection; the vigilance of government has been exerted, the malcontents have been awed, the misguided have been undeceived, the fever in the blood has gradually subsided, and I flatter myself that we have secured the tranquil enjoyment of obscure felicity, which we had been almost tempted to despise.

You have heard, most probably, from Mrs. Holroyd, of the long-expected though transient satisfaction which I received from the visit of Lord Sheffield's family. He appeared highly satisfied with my arrangements here, my house, garden, and situation, at once in town and country, which are indeed singular in their kind, and which have often made me regret the impossibility of shewing them to my dearest friend of the Belvidere. Lord Sheffield is still, and will ever continue, the same active being; always employed for himself, his friends, and the public, and always persuading himself that he wishes for leisure and repose. There are various roads to happiness; but when I compare his situation with mine, I do not, upon the whole, repent that I have given the preference to a life of celibacy and retirement. Although I have been long a spectator of the great world, my unambitious temper has been content with the occupations and rewards of study; and although my library be still my favourite room, I am now no longer stimulated by the prosecution of any literary work. The society of Lausanne is adapted to my taste; my house is open to many agreeable acquaintance, and some real friends; the uniformity of the natives is enlivened by travellers of all nations; and this summer I am happy in a familiar intercourse with Lady Spencer, the Duchess of Devonshire, Lady Elizabeth Foster, and Lady Duncannon, who seems to be gradually recovering from her severe complaints. My health is remarkably good. I have now enjoyed a long interval from the gout; and I endeavour to use with moderation Dr. Cadogan's best remedies, temperance, exercise, and cheerfulness. Adieu, dear Madam; may every blessing that nature can allow be attendant on your latter season. Your age and my habits will not permit a very close correspondence; but I wish to hear, and I _presume_ to ask, a speedy _direct_ account of your own situation. May it be such as I shall hear with pleasure! Once more adieu; I live in hopes of embracing you next summer at the Belvidere, but you may be assured that I bring over nothing for the press.

EDWARD GIBBON, _Esq. to the Right Hon. Lady_ * * * _at_ Florence.

LAUSANNE, November 8, 1792.

I REMEMBER it has been observed of Augustus and Cromwell, that they should never have been born, or never have died; and I am sometimes tempted to apply the same remark to certain beings of a softer nature, who, after a short residence on the banks of the Leman Lake, are now flown far away over the Alps and the Appenines, and have abandoned their votaries to the insipidity of common life. The remark, however, would be unreasonable, and the sentiment ungrateful. The pleasures of the summer, the lighter and the graver moments of the society of _petit Ouchy_,* are indeed past, perhaps never to return; but the remembrance of that delightful period is itself a pleasure, and I enjoy, I cherish the flattering persuasion that it is remembered with some satisfaction in the gallery of Florence, as well as in _the library_ of Lausanne. Long before we were reduced to seek a refuge from the savages of Gaul, I had secretly indulged the thought, or at least the wish, of asking leave to attend _mes bonnes amis_ over Mount Cenis, of basking once more in an Italian sun, and of paying once more my devotions to the Apollo of the Vatican. But my aged and gouty limbs would have failed me in the bold attempt of scaling St. Bernard, and I wanted patience to undertake the tedious circumitineration of the Tirol. Your return to the Pays de Vaud next summer I hold to be extremely doubtful; but my anxiety on that head is somewhat diminished by the sure and certain hope of our all meeting in England the ensuing winter. I flatter myself that the Porter of Devonshire-house will not be inexorable; yet I am afraid of losing you amidst the smoke and tumult of fashionable London, in which the night is devoted to pleasure and the morning to sleep. My ambition may

* A beautiful villa near the lake, about a mile from Lausanne.

perhaps aspire to pass some hours in the palladian Chiswick, or even some days at Chatsworth ; but these princely mansions will not recal the freedom, the ease, the *primitive* solitude of dear little Ouchy. Indeed ! indeed ! your fair friend was made for something better than a Duchess.

Although you most magnanimously abandoned us in the crisis of our fate, yet as you seem to interest yourself in the hopes and fears of this little country, it is my duty to inform you, that we still hang in a state of suspense ; inclining, however, to the side of hope, rather than of despair. The garrison, and even the bourgeoisie, of Geneva shewed a vigorous resolution of defending the city ; and our frontiers have been gradually covered with fifteen thousand intrepid Swiss. But the threats of a bombardment, the weight of expence, and, above all, the victorious ascendant of the French republic, have abated much of the first heroic ardour. Monsieur de Montesquiou displayed a pacific, and even yielding, temper ; and a treaty was signed, dismissing the Swiss garrison from Geneva, and removing the French troops to the distance of ten leagues. But this last condition, which is indeed objectionable, displeased the convention, who refused to ratify the agreement. New conferences were held, new messengers have been dispatched ; but unless they are determined to find or to make a subject of quarrel, it is probable that we shall purchase peace by submission. As Geneva has a very dangerous democratical party within her walls, and as the national guards are already allowed to enter the city, and to tamper with the inhabitants and the garrison, I will not ensure that poor little republic from one week to another. For ourselves, the approaches of danger must be more gradual. I think we are now safe for this winter, and I no longer run to the window to see whether the French are coming. But with so many enemies without, and so many within, the government of Berne, and the tranquillity of this happy country, will be suspended by a very slender twig ; and I begin to fear that Satan will drive me out of the possession of Paradise. My only comfort will be, that I shall have been expelled by the power, and not seduced by the arts, of the blackest dæmon in hell, the dæmon of democracy. Where indeed will this tremendous inundation, this conspiracy of numbers against rank and property, be finally stopped ? Europe seems to be universally tainted, and wherever the French can light a match, they may blow up a mine. Our only hope is now in their devouring one another ; they are furious and hungry monsters, and war is almost declared between the convention and the city of Paris, between the moderate republicans and the absolute levellers. A majority of the convention wishes to spare the royal victims, but they must yield to the rage of the people and the thirst of popularity, and a few hours may produce a trial, a sentence, and a guillotine. Mr. Necker is publishing a pamphlet in defence of the august sufferers ; but his feeble and tardy efforts will rather do credit to himself than service to his clients. You kindly ask after the situation of poor Severy. Alas ! it is now hopeless ; all his complaints are increased, all his resources are exhausted ; where nature cannot work, the effect of art is vain, and his best friends begin to wish him a quiet release. His wife, I had almost said his widow, is truly an object of compassion. The dragoon is returned for a few days ; and if his domestic sorrows gave him leave, he would almost regret the want of an occasion to deserve his feather and cockade. Your note has been communicated to Madame de Montelieu ; but as she is engaged with a dying aunt, I have not yet seen her. Madame Dagaisseau has hastily left us ; the last decrees seemed to give the *emigrés* only the option of starving abroad or hanging at home ; yet she has ventured into France, on some faint glimpse of clemency for the women and children. Madame de Bouillon does not appear to move. Madame de Stael, whom I saw last week at Rolle, is still uncertain where she shall drop her burthen ; but she must soon resolve, for the young lady or gentleman is at the door ;

———— Demanding life, impatient for the skies.

By this time you have joined the Ladies Spencer and Duncannon, whom I beg leave to salute with the proper shades of respect and tenderness. You may, if you please *be, belle comme un ange ;* but I do not like your comparison of the archangel. Those of Milton, with whom I am better acquainted at present than with Guido, are all masculine manly figures, with a great sword by their side, and six wings folding round them. The heathen goddesses would please me as little. Your friend is less severe than Minerva, more decent than Venus, less cold than Diana, and not quite so great a vixen as the ox-eyed Juno. To express that infallible mixture of grace, sweetness, and dignity, a new race of beings must be invented, and I am a mere prose narrator of matter of fact. Bess is much nearer the level of a mortal, but a mortal for whom the wisest man, historic or medical, would throw away two or three worlds, if he had them in his possession. From the aforesaid Bess I have received three marks of kind remembrance, from the foot of St. Bernard, with an exquisite monument of art and friendship, from Turin, and finally, from Milan, with a most valuable insertion from the Duchess. At birds in the air it is difficult to take aim, and I fear or hope that I shall sustain some reproaches on your not finding this long epistle at Florence. I will mark it No. 1. ; and why should I despair of my future   since I can say with truth, that since your departure I have not spent so agreeable a morning. To each of the dear little Caro's pray deliver nine kisses for me, which shall be repaid on demand. My best compliments to Mr. Pelham, if he is with you.

———

EDWARD GIBBON, *Esq. to the Right Hon. Lady * * * at* Florence.

LAUSANNE, April 4, 1793.

HAD I not given previous notice of my own unworthiness, the plea of being an old incorrigible offender would serve only to aggravate my guilt ; it is still sufficiently black, and I can patiently hear every reproach, except the cruel and unjust imputation of having forgotten my fair friends of the Arno and the Tyber. They would indeed have been less present to my thoughts, had I maintained a regular *weekly* correspondence ; since, by the effect of my negligence, not a *day* has elapsed without a serious, though fruitless, resolution of writing by the very next post. What may have somewhat contributed, besides original sin, to this vile procrastination, is the course of events that has filled this abominable winter. As long as the poor King's fate was on suspense, one waited from post to post, between hope and fear, and when the blow was struck, even Shakespeare's language was inadequate to express our grief and indignation. I have never approved the execution of Charles the First ; yet Charles had invaded, in many respects, the ancient constitution of England, and the question had been judged in the field of Naseby before it was tried in West-minster-hall. But Louis had given and suffered everything. The cruelty of the French was aggravated by ingratitude, and a life of innocence was crowned by the death of a saint, or, what is far better, of a virtuous prince, who deserves our pity and esteem. He might have lived and reigned, had he possessed as much active courage as he was endowed with patient fortitude. When I read the accounts from home, of the universal grief and indignation which that fatal event excited, I indeed gloried in the character of an Englishman. Our national fame is now pure and splendid ; we have nobly stood forth in the common cause of mankind ; and although our armaments are somewhat slow, I still persuade myself that we shall give the last deadly wound to the Gallic hydra. The King of Prussia is likewise slow, and your poor friend, the Duke of Brunswick, is now not censured but forgotten. We turn our eyes to the Prince of Cobourg and his Austrians, and it must be confessed, that the deliverance of Holland and Brabant from such a dragon as Dumourier is a very tolerable employment for the month of March. These blossoms of the spring will be followed, it may be fairly hoped, by the fruits of summer ; and in the meanwhile the troubles of Paris, and the revolt of the pro-vinces, may promote, by the increase of anarchy, the restoration of order. I see that restoration through a dark cloud ; but if France be lost, the rest of Europe, I believe and trust, will be saved. But amidst the hurricane, I dare not fix my eyes on the *Temple.* So much for politics, which now engross the waking and sleeping thoughts of every feeling and thinking animal. In this country we are tranquil, and I believe safe, at least for this summer ; though peace has been purchased at some expence of national honour, of the old reputation of Swiss courage, we have crouched before the tiger, and stroked him till he has sheathed his claws, and ceased for a moment to roar. My journey to England this year must depend on the events of the cam-paign ; as I am fully resolved rather to remain quiet another autumn and winter in my sweet habitation, than to encounter the dangers of the sea and land. I envy the pleasures which you and your com-panions have enjoyed at Florence and Rome ; nor can I decide which have tasted the most perfect delight, those to whom such beauties were new, or those to whom they were familiar. A fine eye, correct judgment, and elegant sensibility, are requisite to qualify the studious traveller ; and these gifts have been liberally dispensed among the Ouchy caravan. But when you have been gratified, though not satiated, with the Hesperian prospect, to what fortunate clime will you direct your footsteps ? Have we any hopes of meeting (for my journey, at all events, would be late) in the shades, or rather in the sunshine, of Ouchy? Should Mount Cenis be still imperious, you have trampled on St. Bernard in a more rigorous season ; and whatsoever may be the state of the world, the Pays de Vaud will afford you a secure asylum, or a pleasant station. I rejoice to hear of Lady Besborough's improvement. Will that new title make any difference in the plan ? Is the Duchess very impatient to revisit England ? Except some trifling considerations of children, &c. all countries may be indifferent to her ; as she is sure of being loved and admired in all.

Mr. GIBBON *to Lord* * * *.

MY LORD, ROLLE,* February 23, 1793.

I DO not merely congratulate your Lordship's promotion to an office which your abilities have long deserved. My satisfaction does not arise from an assurance of the wisdom and vigour which administration will derive from the support of so respectable an ally. But as a friend to government in general, I most sincerely rejoice that you are now armed in the common cause against the most dangerous fanatics that have ever invaded the peace of Europe ; against the new barbarians, who labour to confound the order and happiness of society ; and who, in the opinion of thinking men, are not less the enemies of subjects than of kings. The hopes of the wise and good are now fixed on the success of England ; and I am persuaded that my personal attachment to your Lordship will be amply gratified by the important share which your counsels will assume in that success. I could wish that some of your former associates possessed sufficient strength of mind to extricate themselves from the toils of prejudice and party.

Mr. Necker, in whose house I am now residing on a visit of some days, wishes me to express the sentiments of esteem and consideration which he entertains for your Lordship's character. As a friend to the interests of mankind, he is warmly attached to the welfare of Great Britain, which he has long revered as the first, and perhaps as the last asylum of genuine liberty. His late eloquent work *Du pouvoir executif,* which your Lordship has assuredly read, is a valuable testimony of his esteem for our constitution ; and the testimony of an impartial stranger may have taught some of our countrymen to value the political blessings which they have been tempted to despise.

I cherish a lively hope of being in England, and of paying my respects to your Lordship before the end of the summer : but the events of the year are so uncertain, and the sea and land are encompassed with so many difficulties and dangers, that I am doubtful whether it will be practicable for me to execute my purpose.

---

* A town between Lausanne and Geneva, where M. Necker then resided.

[For Index see end of Volume.]

THE HISTORY

OF

THE CRUSADES.

THE CRUSADES.

SINCE the first conquests of the caliphs, the establishment of the Turks in Anatolia or Asia Minor was the most deplorable loss which the church and empire had sustained. By the propagation of the Moslem faith, Soliman the sultan, deserved the name of *Gazi*, a holy champion ; and his new kingdom of the Romans, or of *Roum*, was added to the tables of Oriental geography. It is described as extending from the Euphrates to Constantinople, from the Black Sea to the confines of Syria ; pregnant with mines of silver and iron, of alum and copper, fruitful in corn and wine, and productive of cattle and excellent horses. The wealth of Lydia, the arts of the Greeks, the splendour of the Augustan age, existed only in books and in ruins, which were equally obscure in the eyes of the Scythian conquerors. Yet in the present decay, Anatolia still contains *some* wealthy and populous cities ; and, under the Byzantine empire, they were far more flourishing in numbers, size, and opulence. By the choice of the sultan, Nice, the metropolis of Bithynia, was preferred for his palace and fortress : the seat of the Seljukian dynasty of Roum was planted 100 miles from Constantinople ; and the Divinity of Christ was denied and derided in the same temple in which it had been pronounced by the first general synod of the Catholics. The unity of God, and the mission of Mahomet, were preached from the mosques, the Arabian learning was taught in the schools ; the Cadis judged according to the law of the Koran : the Turkish manners and language prevailed in the cities ; and Turkman camps were scattered over the plains and mountains of Anatolia. On the hard conditions of tribute and servitude, the Greek Christians might enjoy the exercise of their religion ; but their most holy churches were profaned ; their priests and bishops were insulted : they were compelled to suffer the triumph of the *Pagans*, and the apostacy of their brethren ; many thousand children were marked by the knife of circumcision : and many thousand captives were devoted to the service or the pleasures of their masters. After the loss of Asia, Antioch still maintained her primitive allegiance to Christ and Cæsar ;

but the solitary province was separated from all Roman aid, and surrounded on all sides by the Mahometan powers. The despair of Philaretus the governor prepared the sacrifice of his religion and loyalty, had not his guilt been prevented by his son, who hastened to the Nicene palace, and offered to deliver this valuable prize into the hands of Soliman. The ambitious sultan mounted on horseback, and in twelve nights (for he reposed in the day) performed a march of six hundred miles. Antioch was oppressed by the speed and secresy of his enterprise ; and the dependent cities, as far as Laodicea, and the confines of Aleppo, obeyed the example of the metropolis. From Laodicea to the Thracian Bosphorus, or arm of St. George, the conquests and reign of Soliman extended thirty days' journey in length, and in breadth about ten or fifteen, between the rocks of Lycia and the Black Sea. The Turkish ignorance of navigation protected, for a while, the inglorious safety of the emperor ; but no sooner had a fleet of two hundred ships been constructed by the hands of the captive Greeks, than Alexius trembled behind the walls of his capital. His plaintive epistles were dispersed over Europe, to excite the compassion of the Latins, and to paint the danger, the weakness, and the riches, of the city of Constantine.

But the most interesting conquest of the Seljukian Turks, was that of Jerusalem, which soon became the theatre of nations. In their capitulation with Omar, the inhabitants had stipulated the assurance of their religion and property ; but the articles were interpreted by a master against whom it was dangerous to dispute; and in the four hundred years (A.D. 638—1099) of the reign of the caliphs, the political climate of Jerusalem was exposed to the vicissitudes of storms and sunshine. By the increase of proselytes and population, the Mahometans might excuse their usurpation of three-fourths of the city : but a peculiar quarter was reserved for the patriarch with his clergy and people ; a tribute of two pieces of gold was the price of protection; and the sepulchre of Christ, with the church of the Resurrection, was still left in the hands of his votaries. Of these votaries, the most numerous and respectable portion were strangers to Jerusalem : the pilgrimages to the Holy Land had been stimulated, rather than suppressed, by the conquest of the Arabs ; and the enthusiasm which had always prompted these perilous journeys, was nourished by the congenial passions of grief and indignation. A crowd of pilgrims from the East and West continued to visit the holy sepulchre, and the adjacent sanctuaries, more especially at the festival of Easter : and the Greeks and Latins, the Nestorians and Jacobites, the Copts and Abyssinians, the Armenians and Georgians, maintained the chapels, the clergy, and the poor of their respective communions. The harmony of prayer in so many various tongues, the worship of so many nations in the common temple of their religion, might have afforded a spectacle of edification and peace ; but the zeal of the Christian sects was embittered by hatred and revenge ; and in the kingdom of a suffering Messiah, who had pardoned his enemies, they aspired to command and persecute their spiritual brethren. The pre-eminence was asserted by the spirit and number of the Franks ; and the greatness of Charlemagne protected both the Latin pilgrims and the Catholics of the East. The poverty of Carthage, Alexandria, and Jerusalem, was relieved by the alms of that pious emperor ; and many monasteries of Palestine were founded or restored by his liberal devotion. Harun Alrashid, the greatest of the Abassides, esteemed in his Christian brother a similar supremacy of genius and power : their friendship was cemented by a frequent intercourse of gifts and embassies ; and the caliph, without resigning the substantial dominion, presented the emperor with the keys of the holy sepulchre, and perhaps of the city of Jerusalem. In the decline of the Carlovingian monarchy, the republic of Amalphi promoted the interest of trade and religion in the East. Her vessels transported the Latin pilgrims to the coasts of Egypt and Palestine, and deserved, by their useful imports, the favour and alliance of the Fatimite caliphs : an annual fair was instituted on mount Calvary ; and the Italian merchants founded the convent and hospital of St. John of Jerusalem, the cradle of the monastic and military order which has since reigned in the isles of Rhodes and of Malta. Had the Christian pilgrims been content to revere the tomb of a prophet, the disciples of Mahomet, instead of blaming, would have imitated, their piety : but these rigid *Unitarians* were scandalised by a worship which represents the birth, death, and resurrection, of a God ; the Catholic images were branded with the name of idols ; and the Moslems smiled with indignation at the miraculous flame, which was kindled on the eve of Easter in the holy sepulchre. This pious fraud, first devised in the ninth century, was devoutly cherished by the Latin crusaders, and is annually repeated by the clergy of the Greek, Armenian, and Coptic sects, who impose on the credulous spectators for their own benefit, and that of their tyrants. In every age, a principle of toleration has been fortified by a sense of interest ; and the revenue of the prince and his emir was increased each year, by the expence and tribute of so many thousand strangers.

The revolution which transferred the sceptre (A.D. 969—1076) from the Abassides to the Fatimites was a benefit, rather than an injury, to the Holy Land. A sovereign resident in Egypt was more sensible of the importance of Christian trade ; and the emirs of Palestine were less remote from the justice and power of the throne. But the third of these Fatimite caliphs was the famous Hakem, a frantic youth, who was delivered by his impiety and despotism from the fear either of God or man ; and whose reign was a wild mixture of vice and folly. Regardless of the most ancient customs of Egypt, he imposed on the women an absolute confinement : the restraint excited the clamours of both sexes ; their clamours provoked his fury ; a part of Old Cairo was delivered to the flames ; and the guards and citizens were engaged many days in a bloody conflict. At first the caliph declared himself a zealous Mussulman, the founder or benefactor of mosques and colleges : twelve hundred and ninety copies of the Koran were transcribed at his expence in letters of gold ; and his edict extirpated the vineyards of the Upper Egypt. But his vanity was soon flattered by the hope of introducing a new religion ; he aspired above the fame of a prophet and styled himself the visible image of the most high God, who, after nine apparitions on earth, was at length manifest in his royal person. At the name of Hakem, the lord of the living and the dead, every knee was bent in religious adoration : his mysteries were performed on à mountain near Cairo : sixteen thousand converts had signed his profession of faith ; and at the present hour, a free and warlike people, the Druses of Mount Libanus, are persuaded of the life and divinity of a madman and tyrant. In his divine character, Hakem hated the Jews and Christians, as the servants of his rivals : while some remains of prejudice or prudence still pleaded in favour of the law of Mahomet. Both in Egypt and Palestine, his cruel and wanton persecution made some martyrs and many apostates : the common rights and special privileges of the sectaries were equally disregarded ; and a general interdict was laid on the devotion of strangers and natives. The temple of the Christian world, the church of the Resurrection, was (A.D. 1009) demolished to its foundations ; the luminous prodigy of Easter was interrupted, and much profane labour was exhausted to destroy the cave in the rock which properly constitutes the holy sepulchre. At the report of this sacrilege, the nations of Europe were astonished and afflicted : but instead of arming in the defence of the Holy Land, they contented themselves with burning, or banishing, the Jews, as the secret advisers of the impious Barbarian. Yet the calamities of Jerusalem were in some measure alleviated by the inconstancy or repentance of Hakem himself ; and the royal mandate was sealed for the restitution of the churches, when the tyrant was assassinated by the emissaries of his sister. The succeeding caliphs resumed the maxims of religion and policy ; a free toleration was again granted ; with the pious aid of the emperor of Constantinople, the holy sepulchre arose from its ruins ; and, after a short abstinence, the pilgrims returned with an increase of appetite to the spiritual feast. In the sea-voyage of Palestine, the dangers were frequent, and the opportunities rare : but the conversion of Hungary opened a safe communication between Germany and Greece. The charity of St. Stephen, the apostle of his kingdom, relieved and conducted his itinerant brethren : and from Belgrade to Antioch, they traversed 1500 miles of a Christian empire. Among the Franks, the zeal of pilgrimage prevailed (A.D.

1024, &c.) beyond the example of former times : and the roads were covered with multitudes of either sex, and of every rank, who professed their contempt of life, so soon as they should have kissed the tomb of their Redeemer. Princes and prelates abandoned the care of their dominions ; and the numbers of these pious caravans were a prelude to the armies which marched in the ensuing age under the banner of the cross. About thirty years before the first crusade, the archbishop of Mentz, with the bishops of Utrecht, Bamberb, and Ratisbon, undertook this laborious journey from the Rhine to the Jordan ; and the multitude of their followers amounted to 7000 persons. At Constantinople, they were hospitably entertained by the emperor ; but the ostentation of their wealth provoked the assault of the wild Arabs ; they drew their swords with scrupulous reluctance, and sustained a siege in the village of Capernaum, till they were rescued by the venal protection of the Fatimite emir. After visiting the holy places, they embarked for Italy, but only a remnant of 2000 arrived in safety in their native land. Ingulphus, a secretary of William the Conqueror, was a companion of this pilgrimage : he observes that they sallied from Normandy, thirty stout and well-appointed horsemen ; but that they repassed the Alps, twenty miserable palmers, with the staff in their hand, and the wallet at their back.

After the defeat of the Romans, the tranquillity of the Fatimite caliphs was invaded (A.D. 1076—1096) by the Turks. One of the lieutenants of Malek Shah, Atsiz the Carizmian, marched into Syria at the head of a powerful army, and reduced Damascus by famine and the sword. Hems, and the other cities of the province, acknowledged the caliph of Bagdad and the sultan of Persia : and the victorious emir advanced without resistance to the banks of the Nile : the Fatimite was preparing to fly into the heart of Africa ; but the negroes of his guard and the inhabitants of Cairo made a desperate sally, and repulsed the Turk from the confines of Egypt. In his retreat, he indulged the licence of slaughter and rapine : the judge and notaries of Jerusalem were invited to his camp ; and their execution was followed by the massacre of 3000 citizens. The cruelty or the defeat of Atsiz was soon punished by the sultan Toucush, the brother of Malek Shah, who, with a higher title and more formidable powers, asserted the dominion of Syria and Palestine. The house of Seljuk reigned about twenty years in Jerusalem ; but the hereditary command of the holy city and territory was entrusted or abandoned to the emir Ortok, the chief of a tribe of Turkmans, whose children, after their expulsion from Palestine, formed two dynasties on the borders of Armenia and Assyria. The Oriental Christians and the Latin pilgrims deplored a revolution, which, instead of the regular government and old alliance of the caliphs, imposed on their necks the iron yoke of the strangers of the north. In his court and camp the great sultan had adopted in some degree the arts and manners of Persia ; but the body of the Turkish nation, and more especially the pastoral tribes, still breathed the fierceness of the desert. From Nice to Jerusalem, the western countries of Asia were a scene of foreign and domestic hostility : and the shepherds of Palestine, who held a precarious sway on a doubtful frontier, had neither leisure nor capacity to await the slow profits of commercial and religious freedom. The pilgrims who, through innumerable perils, had reached the gates of Jerusalem, were the victims of private rapine or public oppression, and often sunk under the pressure of famine and disease, before they were permitted to salute the holy sepulchre. A spirit of native bar- barism, or recent zeal, prompted the Turkmans to insult the clergy of every sect : the patriarch was dragged by the hair along the pavement, and cast into a dungeon, to extort a ransom from the sympathy of his flock ; and the divine worship in the church of the resurrection was often disturbed by the savage rudeness of its masters. The pathetic tale excited the millions of the West to march under the standard of the cross to the relief of the holy land : and yet how trifling is the sum of these accumulated evils, if compared with the single act of the sacri lege of Hakem, which had been so patiently endured by the Latin Christians ! A slighter provocation inflamed the more irascible tem- per of their descendants : a new spirit had arisen of religious chivalry and papal dominion : a nerve was touched of exquisite feeling; and the sensation vibrated to the heart of Europe.

About twenty years after the conquest of Jerusalem by the Turks (A.D. 1095—1099), the holy sepulchre was visited by an hermit of the name of Peter, a native of Amiens, in the province of Picardy in France. His resentment and sympathy were excited by his own in- juries, and the oppression of the Christian name ; he mingled his tears with those of the patriarch, and earnestly inquired, if no hopes of relief could be entertained from the Greek emperors of the East. The patriarch exposed the vices and weakness of the successors of Con- stantine. " I will rouse," exclaimed the hermit, " the martial nations of Europe in your cause ;" and Europe was obedient to the call of the hermit. The astonished patriarch dismissed him with epistles of credit and complaint, and no sooner did he land at Bari, than Peter hastened to kiss the feet of the Roman pontiff. His stature was small, his appearance contemptible ; but his eye was keen and lively ; and he possessed that vehemence of speech, which seldom fails to impart the persuasion of the soul. He was born of a gentleman's family (for we must now adopt a modern idiom), and his military service was under the neighbouring counts of Boulogne, the heroes of the first crusade. But he soon relinquished the sword and the world ; and if it be true, that his wife, however noble, was aged and ugly, he might withdraw, with the less reluctance, from her bed to a convent, and at length to an hermitage. In this austere solitude, his body was emaciated, his fancy was inflamed : whatever he wished, he believed ; whatever he believed, he *saw* in dreams and revelations. From Jerusalem, the pilgrim returned an accomplished fanatic ; but as he excelled in the popular madness of the times, pope Urban the second received him as a prophet, applauded his glorious design, promised to support it in a general council, and encouraged him to proclaim the deliverance of the Holy Land. Invigorated by the approbation of the pontiff, this zealous missionary traversed, with speed and success, the provinces of Italy and France. His diet was abstemious, his prayers long and fervent, and the alms which he received with one hand, he distributed with the other : his head was bare, his feet naked, his meagre body was wrapt in a coarse garment ; he bore and displayed a weighty crucifix ; and the ass on which he rode, was sanctified in the public eye by the service of the man of God. He preached to innumerable crowds in the churches, the streets, and the highways : the hermit entered with equal confidence the palace and the cottage : and the people, for all were people, were impetuously moved by his call to repentance and arms. When he painted the sufferings of the natives and pilgrims of Palestine, every heart was melted to compassion ; every breast glowed with indignation, when he challenged the warriors of the age to defend their brethren and rescue their Saviour : his ignorance of art and language was compensated by sighs, and tears, and ejaculations ; and Peter supplied the deficiency of reason by loud and frequent appeals to Christ and his Mother, to the saints and angels of paradise, with whom he had personally conversed. The most perfect orator of Athens might have envied the success of his eloquence : the rustic enthusiast inspired the passions which he felt, and Christendom expected with impatience the counsels and decrees of the supreme pontiff.

The magnanimous spirit of Gregory the seventh had already embraced the design of arming Europe against Asia ; the ardour of his zeal and ambition still breathes in his epistles : from either side of the Alps, 50,000 Catholics had enlisted under the banner of St. Peter ; and his successor reveals *his* intention of marching at their head against the impious sectaries of Mahomet. But the glory or reproach of executing, though not in person, this holy enterprise, was reserved for the pope, Urban the second, the most faithful of his disciples. He undertook the conquest of the East, whilst the larger portion of Rome was possessed and fortified by his rival Guibert of Ravenna, who contended with Urban for the name and honours of the pontificate. He attempted to unite the powers of the West, at a time when the princes were separated from the church, and the people from their princes, by the excommunication which himself and his predecessors had thundered against the emperor and the king of France. Philip the first, of France, supported with patience the censures which

he had provoked by his scandalous life and adulterous marriage.
Henry the fourth, of Germany, asserted the right of investitures, the
prerogative of confirming his bishops by the delivery of the ring and
crosier. But the emperor's party was crushed in Italy by the arms of
the Normans and the countess Matilda; and the long quarrel had
been recently envenomed by the revolt of his son Conrad and the
shame of his wife. So popular was the cause of Urban, so weighty was
his influence, that the council which he (A.D. 1095. March) summoned
at Placentia was composed of 200 bishops of Italy, France, Burgundy, Swabia, and Bavaria. Four thousand of the clergy, and 30,000
of the laity, attended this important meeting : and as the most spacious
cathedral would have been inadequate to the multitude, the session of
seven days was held in a plain adjacent to the city. The ambassadors
of the Greek emperor, Alexius Comnenus,. were introduced to plead
the distress of their sovereign and the danger of Constantinople, which
was divided only by a narrow sea from the victorious Turks, the common enemies of the Christian name. In their suppliant address they
flattered the pride of the Latin princes ; and, appealing at once to
their policy and religion, exhorted them to repel the Barbarians on the
confines of Asia, rather than to expect them in the heart of Europe.
At the sad tale of the misery and perils of their Eastern brethren the
assembly burst into tears : the most eager champions declared their
readiness to march ; and the Greek ambassadors were dismissed with
the assurance of a speedy and powerful succour. The relief of Constantinople was included in the larger and most distant project of the
deliverance of Jerusalem ; but the prudent Urban adjourned the final
decision to a second synod, which he proposed to celebrate in some
city of France in the autumn of the same year. The short delay
would propagate the flame of enthusiasm ; and his firmest hope was in
a nation of soldiers still proud of the pre-eminence of their name,
and ambitious to emulate their hero Charlemagne, who, in the popular
romance of Turpin, had achieved the conquest of the Holy Land. A
latent motive of affection or vanity might influence the choice of Urban :
he was himself a native of France, a monk of Clugny, and the first of
his countrymen who ascended the throne of St. Peter. The pope had
illustrated his family and province ; nor is there perhaps a more exquisite gratification than to revisit, in a conspicuous dignity, the humble
and laborious scenes of our youth.

It may occasion some surprise that the Roman pontiff should erect,
in the heart of France, the tribunal from whence he hurled his anathemas against the king. But our surprise will vanish so soon as we
form a just estimate of a king of France of the eleventh century.
Philip the first was the great-grandson of Hugh Capet the founder of
the present race, who, in the decline of Charlemagne's posterity, added
the regal title to his patrimonial estates of Paris and Orleans. In

this narrow compass, he was possessed of wealth and jurisdiction ; but in the rest of France, Hugh and his first descendants were no more than the feudal lords of about sixty dukes and counts, of independent and hereditary power, who disdained the control of laws and legal assemblies, and whose disregard of their sovereign was revenged by the disobedience of their inferior vassals. At Clermont, in the territories of the count of Auvergne, the pope might brave with impunity the resentment of Philip ; and the council which he convened (A.D. 1095. Nov.) in that city was not less numerous or respectable than the synod of Placentia. Besides his court and council of Roman cardinals, he was supported by 13 archbishops and 225 bishops ; the number of mitred prelates was computed at 400 ; and the fathers of the church were blessed by the saints, and enlightened by the doctors of the age. From the adjacent kingdoms, a martial train of lords and knights of power and renown, attended the council in high expectation of its resolves ; and such was the ardour of zeal and curiosity, that the city was filled, and many thousands, in the month of November, erected their tents or huts in the open field. A session of eight days produced some useful or edifying canons for the reformation of manners ; a severe censure was pronounced against the licence of private war ; the truce of God was confirmed, a suspension of hostilities during four days of the week ; women and priests were placed under the safeguard of the church ; and a protection of three years was extended to husbandmen and merchants, the defenceless victims of military rapine. But a law, however venerable be the sanction, cannot suddenly transform the temper of the times ; and the benevolent efforts of Urban deserve the less praise, since he laboured to appease some domestic quarrels that he might spread the flames of war from the Atlantic to the Euphrates. From the synod of Placentia, the rumour of his great design had gone forth among the nations : the clergy on their return had preached in every diocese the merit and glory of the deliverance of the Holy Land ; and when the pope ascended a lofty scaffold in the market-place of Clermont, his eloquence was addressed to a well-prepared and impatient audience. His topics were obvious, his exhortation was vehement, his success inevitable. The orator was interrupted by the shout of thousands, who with one voice, and in their rustic idiom, exclaimed aloud, " God wills it, God wills it." " It is indeed the will of God," replied the pope ; " and let this memorable word, the inspiration surely of the Holy Spirit, be for ever adopted as your cry of battle to animate the devotion and courage of the champions of Christ. His cross is the symbol of your salvation ; wear it, a red, a bloody cross, as an external mark on your breasts or shoulders, as a pledge of your sacred and irrevocable engagement." The proposal was joyfully accepted ; great numbers both of the clergy and laity impressed on their garments the sign of the cross, and solicited the pope to march at their head. This dangerous honour was declined by the more prudent successor of Gregory, who alleged the schism of the church, and the duties of his pastoral office, recommending to the faithful, who were disqualified by sex or profession, by age or infirmity, to aid, with their prayers and alms, the personal service of their robust brethren. The name and powers of his legate he devolved on Adhemar bishop of Puy, the first who had received the cross at his hands. The foremost of the temporal chiefs was Raymond count of Toulouse, whose ambassadors in the council excused the absence, and pledged the honour of their master. After the confession and absolution of their sins, the champions of the cross were dismissed with a superfluous admonition to invite their countrymen and friends ; and their departure for the Holy Land was fixed to the festival of the Assumption, the fifteenth of August, of the ensuing year.

So familiar, and as it were so natural to man, is the practice of violence, that our indulgence allows the slightest provocation, the most disputable right, as a sufficient ground of national hostility. But the name and nature of an *holy war* demands a more rigorous scrutiny ; nor can we hastily believe, that the servants of the Prince of peace would unsheath the sword of destruction, unless the motive were pure, the quarrel legitimate, and the necessity inevitable. The policy of an action may be determined from the tardy lessons of experience ; but, before we act, our conscience should be satisfied of the justice and propriety of our enterprise. In the age of the crusades, the Christians, both of the East and West, were persuaded of their lawfulness and merit ; their arguments are clouded by the perpetual abuse of Scripture and rhetoric ; but they seem to insist on the right of natural and religious defence, their peculiar title to the Holy Land, and the impiety of their Pagan and Mahometan foes. I. The right of a just defence may fairly include our civil and spiritual allies : it depends on the existence of danger ; and that danger must be estimated by the twofold consideration of the malice, and the power, of our enemies. A pernicious tenet has been imputed to the Mahometans, the duty of *extirpating* all other religions by the sword. This charge of ignorance and bigotry is refuted by the Koran, by the history of the Mussulman conquerors, and by their public and legal toleration of the Christian worship. But it cannot be denied, that the Oriental churches are depressed under their iron yoke ; that, in peace and war, they asserted a divine and indefeasible claim of universal empire ; and that, in their orthodox creed, the unbelieving nations are continually threatened with the loss of religion or liberty. In the eleventh century, the victorious arms of the Turks presented a real and urgent apprehension of these losses. They had subdued in less than thirty years the kingdoms of Asia, as far as Jerusalem and the Hellespont ; and the Greek empire tottered on the verge of destruction. Besides an honest sympathy for their brethren, the Latins had a right and interest in the support of Constantinople, the most important barrier of the West; and the privilege of defence must reach to prevent, as well as to repel, an impending assault. But this salutary purpose might have been accomplished by a moderate succour; and our calmer reason might disclaim the innumerable hosts and remote operations, which overwhelmed Asia and depopulated Europe. II. Palestine could add nothing to the strength or safety of the Latins; and fanaticism alone could pretend to justify the conquest of that distant and narrow province. The Christians affirmed that their inalienable title to the promised land had been sealed by the blood of their divine Saviour: it was their right and duty to rescue their inheritance from the unjust possessors, who profaned his sepulchre, and oppressed the pilgrimage of his disciples. Vainly would it be alleged that the pre-eminence of Jerusalem, and the sanctity of Palestine have been abolished with the Mosaic law; that the God of the Christians is not a local deity, and that the recovery of Bethlem or Calvary, his cradle or his tomb, will not atone for the violation of the moral precepts of the gospel. Such arguments glance aside from the leaden shield of superstition; and the religious mind will not easily relinquish its hold on the sacred ground of mystery and miracle. III. But the holy wars which have been waged in every climate of the globe, from Egypt to Livonia, and from Peru to Hindostan, require the support of some more general and flexible tenet. It has been often supposed, and sometimes affirmed, that a difference of religion is a worthy cause of hostility; that obstinate unbelievers may be slain or subdued by the champions of the cross; and that grace is the sole fountain of dominion as well as of mercy. Above four hundred years before the first crusade, the eastern and western provinces of the Roman empire had been acquired about the same time, and in the same manner, by the Barbarians of Germany and Arabia. Time and treaties had legitimated the conquests of the *Christian* Franks; but in the eyes of their subjects and neighbours, the Mahometan princes were still tyrants and usurpers, who, by the arms of war or rebellion, might be lawfully driven from their unlawful possession.

As the manners of the Christians were relaxed, their discipline of penance was enforced; and with the multiplication of sins, the remedies were multiplied. In the primitive church, a voluntary and open confession prepared the work of atonement. In the middle ages, the bishops and priests interrogated the criminal; compelled him to account for his thoughts, words, and actions; and prescribed the terms of his reconciliation with God. But as this discretionary power might alternately be abused by indulgence and tyranny, a rule of discipline was framed, to inform and regulate the spiritual judges. This mode of legislation was invented by the Greeks; their *penitentials* were translated, or imitated, in the Latin church; and, in the time of Charlemagne, the clergy of every diocese were provided with a code, which they prudently concealed from the knowledge of the vulgar. In this dangerous estimate of crimes and punishments, each case was supposed, each difference was remarked, by the experience or penetration of the monks ; some sins are enumerated which innocence could not have suspected, and others which reason cannot believe ; and the more ordinary offences of fornication and adultery, of perjury and sacrilege, of rapine and murder, were expiated by a penance, which, according to the various circumstances, was prolonged from forty days to seven years. During this term of mortification, the patient was healed, the criminal was absolved, by a salutary regimen of fasts and prayers : the disorder of his dress was expressive of grief and remorse ; and he humbly abstained from all the business and pleasure of social life. But the rigid execution of these laws would have depopulated the palace, the camp, and the city : the Barbarians of the West believed and trembled ; but nature often rebelled against principle ; and the magistrate laboured without effect to enforce the jurisdiction of the priest. A literal accomplishment of penance was indeed impracticable ; the guilt of adultery was multiplied ; that of homicide might involve the massacre of a whole people ; each act was separately numbered ; and, in those times of anarchy and vice, a modest sinner might easily incur a debt of 300 years. His insolvency was relieved by a commutation, or *indulgence:* a year of penance was appreciated at 26 *solidi* of silver, about four pounds sterling, for the rich ; at 3 solidi, or nine shillings, for the indigent : and these alms were soon appropriated to the use of the church, which derived, from the redemption of sins, an inexhaustible source of opulence and dominion. A debt of 300 years, or £1200, was enough to impoverish a plentiful fortune : the scarcity of gold and silver was supplied by the alienation of land ; and the princely donations of Pepin and Charlemagne are expressly given for the *remedy* of their soul. It is a maxim of the civil law, that whosoever cannot pay with his purse, must pay with his body ; and the practice of flagellation was adopted by the monks, a cheap, though painful, equivalent. By a fantastic arithmetic, a year of penance was taxed at 3000 lashes ; and such was the skill and patience of a famous hermit, St. Dominic of the Iron Cuirass, that in six days he could discharge an entire century, by a whipping of 300,000 stripes. His example was followed by many penitents of both sexes ; and, as a vicarious sacrifice was accepted, a sturdy disciplinarian might expiate on his own back the sins of his benefactors. These compensations of the purse and the person introduced, in the eleventh century, a more honourable mode of satisfaction. The merit of military service against the Saracens of Africa and Spain, had been allowed by the predecessors of Urban the second. In the council of Clermont, that pope proclaimed a *plenary indulgence* to those who should enlist under the banner of the cross ; the absolution of *all* their sins, and a full receipt for *all* that might be due of canonical penance. The cold philosophy of modern times is incapable of feeling the impression that was made on a sinful and fanatic world. At the voice of their pastor, the robber, the incendiary, the homicide, arose by thousands to redeem their souls, by repeating on the infidels the same deeds which they had exercised against their Christian brethren ; and the terms of atonement were eagerly embraced by offenders of every rank and denomination. None were pure ; none were exempt from the guilt and penalty of sin ; and those who were the least amenable to the justice of God and the church, were the best entitled to the temporal and eternal recompence of their pious courage. If they fell, the spirit of the Latin clergy did not hesitate to adorn their tomb with the crown of martyrdom ; and should they survive, they could expect without impatience the delay and increase of their heavenly reward. They offered their blood to the Son of God, who had laid down his life for their salvation : they took up the cross, and entered with confidence into the way of the Lord. His providence would watch over their safety ; perhaps his visible and miraculous power would smooth the difficulties of their holy enterprise. The cloud and pillar of Jehovah had marched before the Israelites into the promised land. Might not the Christians more reasonably hope that the rivers would open for their passage ; that the walls of the strongest cities would fall at the sound of their trumpets ; and that the sun would be arrested in his mid-career, to allow them time for the destruction of the infidels?

Of the chiefs and soldiers who marched to the holy sepulchre, I will dare to affirm, that *all* were prompted by the spirit of enthusiasm ; the belief of merit, the hope of reward, and the assurance of divine aid. But I am equally persuaded, that in *many* it was not the sole, that in *some* it was not the leading, principle of action. The use and abuse of religion are feeble to stem, they are strong and irresistible to impel the stream of national manners. Against the private wars of the Barbarians, their bloody tournaments, licentious loves, and judicial duels, the popes and synods might ineffectually thunder. It is a more easy task to provoke the metaphysical disputes of the Greeks, to drive into the cloister the victims of anarchy or despotism, to sanctify the patience of slaves and cowards, or to assume the merit of the humanity and benevolence of modern Christians. War and exercise were the reigning passions of the Franks or Latins ; they were enjoined, as a penance, to gratify those passions, to visit distant lands, and to draw their swords against the nations of the East. Their victory, or even their attempt, would immortalize the names of the intrepid heroes of the cross ; and the purest piety could not be insensible to the most splendid prospect of military glory. In the petty quarrels of Europe, they shed the blood of their friends and countrymen, for the acquisition perhaps of a castle or a village. They could march with alacrity against the distant and hostile nations who were devoted to their arms : their fancy already grasped the golden sceptres of Asia ; and the conquest of Apulia and Sicily by the Normans might exalt to royalty the hopes of the most private adventurer. Christendom, in her rudest state, must have yielded to the climate and cultivation of the Mahometan countries ; and their natural and artificial wealth had been magnified by the tales of pilgrims, and the gifts of an imperfect commerce. The vulgar, both the great and small, were taught to believe every wonder, of lands flowing with milk and honey, of mines and treasures, of gold and diamonds, of palaces of marble and jasper, and of odoriferous groves of cinnamon and frankincense. In this earthly paradise, each warrior depended on his sword to carve a plenteous and honourable establishment, which he measured only by the extent of his wishes. Their vassals and soldiers trusted their fortunes to God and their master : the spoils of a Turkish emir might enrich the meanest follower of the camp ; and the flavour of the wines, the beauty of the Grecian women, were temptations more adapted to the nature, than to the profession, of the champions of the cross. The love of freedom was a powerful incitement to the multitudes who were oppressed by feudal or ecclesiastical tyranny. Under this holy sign the peasants and burghers, who were attached to the servitude of the glebe, might escape from an haughty lord, and transplant themselves and their families to a land of liberty. The monk might release himself from the discipline of his convent : the debtor might suspend the accumulation of usury, and the pursuit of his creditors ; and outlaws and malefactors of every cast might continue to brave the laws and elude the punishment of their crimes.

These motives were potent and numerous : when we have singly computed their weight on the mind of each individual, we must add the infinite series, the multiplying powers of example and fashion. The first proselytes became the warmest and most effectual missionaries of the cross : among their friends and countrymen they preached the duty, the merit, and the recompense, of their holy vow ; and the most reluctant hearers were insensibly drawn within the whirlpool of persuasion and authority. The martial youths were fired by the reproach or suspicion of cowardice ; the opportunity of visiting with an army the sepulchre of Christ, was embraced by the old and infirm, by women and children, who consulted rather their zeal than their strength ; and those who in the evening had derided the folly of their companions, were the most eager, the ensuing day, to tread in their footsteps. The ignorance which magnified the hopes, diminished the perils, of the enterprise. Since the Turkish conquest, the paths of pilgrimage were obliterated : the chiefs themselves had an imperfect notion of the length of their way and the state of their enemies; and such was the stupidity of the people, that, at the sight of the first city or castle beyond the limits of their knowledge, they were ready to ask whether that was not the Jerusalem, the term and object of their labours. Yet the more prudent of the crusaders, who were not sure that they should be fed from heaven with a shower of quails or manna, provided themselves with those precious metals, which, in every country, are the representatives of every commodity. To defray, according to their rank, the expences of the road, princes alienated their provinces, nobles their lands and cattle, peasants their castles and the instruments of husbandry. The value of property was depreciated by the eager competition of multitudes; while the price of arms and horses was raised to an exorbitant height by the wants and impatience of the buyers. Those who remained at home, with sense and money, were enriched by the epidemical disease: the sovereigns acquired at a cheap rate the domains of their vassals; and the ecclesiastical purchasers completed the payment by the assurance of their prayers. The cross, which was commonly sewn on the garment, in cloth or silk, was inscribed by some zealots on their skin: an hot iron, or indelible liquor, was applied to perpetuate the mark; and a crafty monk, who showed the miraculous impression on his breast, was repaid with the popular veneration and the richest benefices of Palestine.

The fifteenth of August had been fixed in the council of Clermont for the departure of the pilgrims: but the day was anticipated by the thoughtless and needy crowd of plebeians; and I shall briefly dispatch the calamities which they inflicted and suffered, before I enter on the more serious and successful enterprise of the chiefs. Early in the spring (A.D. 1096, March, May, &c.), from the confines of France and Lorraine, above 60,000 of the populace of both sexes flocked round the first missionary of the crusade, and pressed him with clamorous importunity to lead them to the holy sepulchre. The hermit, assuming the character, without the talents or authority, of a general, impelled or obeyed the forward impulse of his votaries along the banks of the Rhine and Danube. Their wants and numbers soon compelled them to separate, and his lieutenant, Walter the Pennyless, a valiant though needy soldier, conducted a vanguard of pilgrims, whose condition may be determined from the proportion of 8 horsemen to 50,000 foot. The example and footsteps of Peter were closely pursued by another fanatic, the monk Godescal, whose sermons had swept away 15,000 or 20,000 peasants from the villages of Germany. Their rear was again pressed by an herd of 200,000, the most stupid and savage refuse of the people, who mingled with their devotion a brutal licence of rapine and drunkenness. Some counts and gentlemen, at the head of 3000 horse, attended the motions of the multitude to partake in the spoil; but their genuine leaders (may we credit such folly?) were a goose and a goat, who were carried in the front, and to whom these worthy Christians ascribed an infusion of the divine spirit. Of these, and of other bands of enthusiasts, the first and most easy warfare was against the Jews, the murderers of the Son of God. In the trading cities of the Moselle and the Rhine, their colonies were numerous and rich; and they enjoyed, under the protection of the emperor and the bishops, the free exercise of their religion. At Verdun, Treves, Mentz, Spires, Worms, many thousands of that unhappy people were pillaged and massacred: nor had they felt a more bloody stroke since the persecution of Hadrian. A remnant was saved by the firmness of their bishops, who accepted a feigned and transient conversion; but the more obstinate Jews who opposed their fanaticism to the fanaticism of the Christians, barricadoed their houses, and precipitating themselves, their families, and their wealth, into the rivers or the flames, disappointed the malice, or at least the avarice, of their implacable foes.

Between the frontiers of Austria and the seat of the Byzantine monarchy, the crusaders were compelled to traverse an interval of six hundred miles; the wild and desolate countries of Hungary and Bulgaria. The soil is fruitful, and intersected with rivers; but it was then covered with morasses and forests, which spread to a boundless extent whenever man has ceased to exercise his dominion over the earth. Both nations had imbibed the rudiments of Christianity; the Hungarians were ruled by their native princes; the Bulgarians by a lieutenant of the Greek emperor; but, on the slightest provocation, their ferocious nature was rekindled, and ample provocation was afforded by the disorders of the first pilgrims. Agriculture must have been unskilful and languid among a people whose cities were built of reeds and timber, which were deserted in the summer season for the tents of hunters and shepherds. A scanty supply of provisions was rudely demanded, forcibly seized, and greedily consumed; and on the first quarrel, the crusaders gave a loose to indignation and revenge. But their ignorance of the country, of war, and discipline, exposed them to every snare. The Greek præfect of Bulgaria commanded a regular force; at the trumpet of the Hungarian king, the eighth or the tenth of his martial subjects bent their bows and mounted on horseback; their policy was insidious, and their retaliation on these pious robbers was unrelenting and bloody. About a third of the naked fugitives, and the hermit Peter was of the number, escaped to the Thracian mountains; and the emperor, who respected the pilgrimage and succour of the Latins, conducted them by secure and easy journeys to Constantinople, and advised them to await the arrival of their brethren. For a while they remembered their faults and losses; but no sooner were they revived by the hospitable entertainment, than their venom was again inflamed; they stung their benefactor, and neither gardens, nor palaces, nor churches, were safe from their depredations. For his own safety, Alexius allured them to pass over to the Asiatic side of the

Bosphorus; but their blind impetuosity soon urged them to desert the station which he had assigned, and to rush headlong against the Turks, who occupied the road of Jerusalem. The hermit, conscious of his shame, had withdrawn from the camp to Constantinople; and his lieutenant, Walter the Pennyless, who was worthy of a better command, attempted without success to introduce some order and prudence among the herd of savages. They separated in quest of prey, and themselves fell an easy prey to the arts of the sultan. By a rumour that their foremost companions were rioting in the spoils of his capital, Soliman tempted the main body to descend into the plain of Nice; they were overwhelmed by the Turkish arrows; and a pyramid of bones informed their companions of the place of their defeat. Of the first crusaders, 300,000 had already perished, before a single city was rescued from the infidels, before their graver and more noble brethren had completed the preparations of their enterprise.

None of the great sovereigns of Europe embarked their persons in the first crusade. . The emperor Henry the fourth was not disposed to obey the summons of the pope: Philip the first of France was occupied by his pleasures; William Rufus of England by a recent conquest; the kings of Spain were engaged in a domestic war against the Moors; and the northern monarchs of Scotland, Denmark, Sweden, and Poland, were yet strangers to the passions and interests of the South. The religious ardour was more strongly felt by the princes of the second order, who held an important place in the feudal system. Their situation will naturally cast under four distinct heads the review of other names and characters; but I may escape some needless repetition, by observing at once, that courage and the exercise of arms are the common attribute of these Christian adventurers. I. The first rank both in war and council is justly due to Godfrey of Bouillon; and happy would it have been for the crusaders, if they had trusted themselves to the sole conduct of that accomplished hero, a worthy representative of Charlemagne, from whom he was descended in the female line. His father was of the noble race of the counts of Boulogne : Brabant, the lower province of Lorraine, was the inheritance of his mother; and by the emperor's bounty, he was himself invested with that ducal title, which has been improperly transferred to his lordship of Bouillon in the Ardennes. In the service of Henry the fourth, he bore the great standard of the empire, and pierced with his lance the breast of Rodolph, the rebel king : Godfrey was the first who ascended the walls of Rome; and his sickness, his vow, perhaps his remorse for bearing arms against the pope, confirmed an early resolution of visiting the holy sepulchre, not as a pilgrim, but a deliverer. His valour was matured by prudence and moderation; his piety, though blind, was sincere; and, in the tumult of a camp, he practised the real and fictitious virtues of a convent. Superior to the private factions of the chiefs, he reserved his enmity for the enemies of Christ; and though he gained a kingdom by the attempt, his pure and disinterested zeal was acknowledged by his rivals. Godfrey of Bouillon was accompanied by his two brothers, by Eustace the elder, who had succeeded to the county of Boulogne, and by the younger, Baldwin, a character of more ambiguous virtue. The duke of Lorraine was alike celebrated on either side of the Rhine: from his birth and education he was equally conversant with the French and Teutonic languages: the barons of France, Germany, and Lorraine, assembled their vassals; and the confederate force that marched under his banner was composed of 80,000 foot and about 10,000 horse. II. In the parliament that was held at Paris, in the king's presence, about two months after the council of Clermont, Hugh count of Vermandois was the most conspicuous of the princes who assumed the cross. But the appellation of *the great* was applied, not so much to his merit or possessions (though neither were contemptible), as to the royal birth of the brother of the king of France. Robert duke of Normandy was the eldest son of William the Conqueror; but on his father's death he was deprived of the kingdom of England, by his own indolence and the activity of his brother Rufus. The worth of Robert was degraded by an excessive levity and easiness of temper: his cheerfulness seduced him to the indulgence of pleasure; his profuse liberality impoverished the prince and people; his indiscriminate clemency multiplied the number of offenders; and the amiable qualities of a private man became the essential defects of a sovereign. For the trifling sum of 10,000 marks he mortgaged Normandy during his absence to the English usurper; but his engagement and behaviour in the holy war, announced in Robert a reformation of manners, and restored him in some degree to the public esteem. Another Robert was count of Flanders, a royal province, which, in this century, gave three queens to the thrones of France, England, and Denmark: he was surnamed the sword and lance of the Christians; but in the exploits of a soldier, he sometimes forgot the duties of a general. Stephen, count of Chartres, of Blois, and of Troyes, was one of the richest princes of the age; and the number of his castles has been compared to the 365 days of the year. His mind was improved by literature; and in the council of the chiefs, the eloquent Stephen was chosen to discharge the office of their president. These four were the principal leaders of the French, the Normans, and the pilgrims of the British isles: but the list of the barons who were possessed of three or four towns, would exceed, says a contemporary, the catalogue of the Trojan war. III. In the south of France, the command was assumed by Adhemar, bishop of Puy, the pope's legate, and by Raymond, count of St. Giles and Toulouse, who added the prouder titles of duke of Narbonne and marquis of Provence. The former was a respectable prelate, alike qualified for this world and the next. The latter was a veteran warrior, who had fought against the Saracens of Spain, and who consecrated his declining age, not only to the deliverance, but to the perpetual service, of the holy sepulchre. His experience and riches gave him a strong ascendant in the Christian camp, whose distress he was often able, and sometimes willing, to relieve. But it was easier for him to extort the praise of the · Infidels, than to preserve the love of his subjects and associates. His eminent qualities were clouded by a temper, haughty, envious, and obstinate ; and though he resigned an ample patrimony for the cause of God, his piety in the public opinion, was not exempt from avarice and ambition. A mercantile, rather than a martial spirit, prevailed among his *provincials*, a common name, which included the natives of Auvergne and Languedoc, the vassals of the kingdom of Burgundy or Arles. From the adjacent frontier of Spain, he drew a band of hardy adventurers ; as he marched through Lombardy, a crowd of Italians flocked to his standard, and his united force consisted of 100,000 horse and foot. If Raymond was the first to enlist and the last to depart, the delay may be excused by the greatness of his preparation and the promise of an everlasting farewell. IV. The name of Bohemond, the son of Robert Guiscard, was already famous by his double victory over the Greek emperor : but his father's will had reduced him to· the principality of Tarentum, and the remembrance of his Eastern trophies, still he was awakened by the rumour and passage of the French pilgrims. It is in the person of this Norman chief that we may seek for the coolest policy and ambition with a small alloy of religious fanaticism. His conduct may justify a belief that he had secretly directed the design of the pope, which he affected to second with astonishment and zeal : at the siege of Amalphi, his example and discourse inflamed the passions of a confederate army ; he instantly tore his garment to supply crosses for the numerous candidates, and prepared to visit Constantinople and Asia at the head of 10,000 horse and 20,000 foot. Several princes of the Norman race accompanied this veteran general ; and his cousin Tancred was the partner, rather than the servant, of the war. In the accomplished character of Tancred, we discover all the virtues of a perfect knight, the true spirit of chivalry, which inspired the generous sentiments and social offices of man, far better than the base philosophy, or the baser religion of the times.

Between the age of Charlemagne and that of the crusades, a revolution had taken place among the Spaniards, the Normans, and the French, which was gradually extended to the rest of Europe. The service of the infantry was degraded to the plebeians ; the cavalry formed the strength of the armies, and the honourable name of *miles*, or soldier, was confined to the gentlemen who served on horseback, and were invested with the character of knighthood. The dukes and counts, who had usurped the rights of sovereignty, divided the provinces among their faithful barons : the barons distributed among their vassals the fiefs or benefices of their jurisdiction ; and these military tenants, the peers of each other and of their lord, composed the noble or equestrian order, which disdained to conceive the peasant or burgher as of the same species with themselves. The dignity of their birth was preserved by pure and equal alliances ; their sons alone, who could produce four quarters or lines of ancestry, without spot or reproach, might legally pretend to the honour of knighthood ; but a valiant plebeian was sometimes enriched and ennobled by the sword, and became the father of a new race. A single knight could impart, according to his judgment, the character which he received ; and the warlike sovereigns of Europe derived more glory from this personal distinction than from the lustre of their diadem. This ceremony, of which some traces may be found in Tacitus and the woods of Germany, was in its origin simple and profane ; the candidate, after some previous trial, was invested with the sword and spurs ; and his cheek or shoulder was touched with a slight blow, as an emblem of the last affront which it was lawful for him to endure. But superstition mingled in every public and private action of life ; in the holy wars, it sanctified the profession of arms ; and the order of chivalry was assimilated in its rights and privileges to the sacred orders of priesthood. The bath and white garment of the novice, were an indecent copy of the regeneration of baptism ; his sword, which he offered on the altar, was blessed by the ministers of religion ; his solemn reception was preceded by fasts and vigils ; and he was created a knight in the name of God, of St. George, and of St. Michael the archangel. He swore to accomplish the duties of his profession ; and education, example, and the public opinion, were the inviolable guardians of his oath. As the champion of God and the ladies (I blush to unite such discordant names), he devoted himself to speak the truth ; to maintain the right ; to protect the distressed ; to practise *courtesy*, a virtue less familiar to the ancients ; to pursue the infidels ; to despise the allurements of ease and safety; and to vindicate in every perilous adventure the honour of his character. The abuse of the same spirit provoked the illiterate knight to disdain the arts of industry and peace; to esteem himself the sole judge and avenger of his own injuries; and proudly to neglect the laws of civil society and military discipline. Yet the benefits of this institution, to refine the temper of Barbarians, and to infuse some principles of faith, justice, and humanity, were strongly felt, and have been often observed. The asperity of national prejudice was softened; and the community of religion and arms spread a similar colour and generous emulation over the face of Christendom. Abroad in enterprise and pilgrimage, at home in martial exercise, the warriors of every country were perpetually associated;

and impartial taste must prefer a Gothic tournament to the Olympic games of classic antiquity. Instead of the naked spectacles which corrupted the manners of the Greeks; the pompous decoration of the lists was crowned with the presence of high-born beauty, from whose hands the conqueror received the prize of his dexterity and courage. The skill and strength that were exerted in wrestling and boxing, bear a distant and doubtful relation to the merit of a soldier; but the tournaments, as they were invented in France, and eagerly adopted both in the East and West, presented a lively image of the business of the field. The single combats, the general skirmish, the defence of a pass, or castle, were rehearsed as in actual service; and the contest, both in real and mimic war, was decided by the superior management of the horse and lance. The lance was the proper and peculiar weapon of the knight: his horse was of a large and heavy breed; but this charger, till he was roused by the approaching danger, was usually led by an attendant, and he quietly rode a pad or palfrey of a more easy pace. His helmet, and sword, his greaves, and buckler, it would be superfluous to describe; but I may remark, that at the period of the crusades, the armour was less ponderous than in later times; and that, instead of a massy cuirass, his breast was defended by an hauberk or coat of mail. When their long lances were fixed in the rest, the warriors furiously spurred their horses against the foe; and the light cavalry of the Turks and Arabs could seldom stand against the direct and impetuous weight of their charge. Each knight was attended to the field by his faithful squire, a youth of equal birth and similar hopes; he was followed by his archers and men at arms, and four, or five, or six soldiers, were computed as the furniture of a complete *lance.* In the expeditions to the neighbouring kingdoms or the Holy Land, the duties of the feudal tenure no longer subsisted; the voluntary service of the knights and their followers was either prompted by zeal or attachment, or purchased with rewards and promises; and the numbers of each squadron were measured by the power, the wealth, and the fame of each independent chieftain. They were distinguished by his banner, his armorial coat, and his cry of war; and the most ancient families of Europe must seek in these achievements the origin and proof of their nobility. In this portrait of chivalry, I have been urged to anticipate on the story of the crusades, at once an effect and a cause, of this memorable institution.

Such were the troops, and such the leaders, who assumed the cross for the deliverance of the holy sepulchre. As soon as they were relieved (A.D. 1096, Aug. 15—A.D. 1097, May) by the absence of the plebeian multitude, they encouraged each other, by interviews and messages, to accomplish their vow and hasten their departure. Their wives and sisters were desirous of partaking the danger and merit of the pilgrimage; their portable treasures were conveyed in bars of silver and gold ; and the princes and barons were attended by their equipage of hounds and hawks to amuse their leisure and to supply their table. The difficulty of procuring subsistence for so many myriads of men and horses, engaged them to separate their forces; their choice or situation determined the road ; and it was agreed to meet in the neighbourhood of Constantinople, and from thence to begin their operations against the Turks. From the banks of the Meuse and the Moselle, Godfrey of Bouillon followed the direct way of Germany, Hungary, and Bulgaria : and, as long as he exercised the sole command, every step afforded some proof of his prudence and virtue. On the confines of Hungary he was stopped three weeks by a Christian people, to whom the name, or at least the abuse, of the cross was justly odious. The Hungarians still smarted with the wounds which they had received from the first pilgrims : in their turn they had abused the right of defence and retaliation ; and they had reason to apprehend a severe revenge from an hero of the same nation, and who was engaged in the same cause. But, after weighing the motives and the events, the virtuous duke was content to pity the crimes and misfortunes of his worthless brethren ; and his twelve deputies, the messengers of peace, requested in his name a free passage and an equal market. To remove their suspicions, Godfrey trusted himself, and afterwards his brother, to the faith of Carloman king of Hungary, who treated them with a simple but hospitable entertainment : the treaty was sanctified by their common gospel ; and a proclamation, under pain of death, restrained the animosity and licence of the Latin soldiers. From Austria to Belgrade, they traversed the plains of Hungary, without enduring or offering an injury ; and the proximity of Carloman, who hovered on their flanks with his numerous cavalry, was a precaution not less useful for their safety than for his own. They reached the banks of the Save ; and no sooner had they passed the river than the king of Hungary restored the hostages, and saluted their departure with the fairest wishes for the success of their enterprise. With the same conduct and discipline, Godfrey pervaded the woods of Bulgaria and the frontiers of Thrace ; and might congratulate himself, that he had almost reached the first term of his pilgrimage, without drawing his sword against a Christian adversary. After an easy and pleasant journey through Lombardy, from Turin to Aquileia, Raymond and his provincials marched forty days through the savage country of Dalmatia and Sclavonia. The weather was a perpetual fog : the land was mountainous and desolate ; the natives were either fugitive or hostile : loose in their religion and government, they refused to furnish provisions or guides ; murdered the stragglers ; and exercised by night and .day the vigilance of the count, who derived more security from the punishment of some captive robbers than from his interview and treaty with the prince of Scodra. His march between Durazzo and Constantinople was harassed, without being stopped, by the peasants and soldiers of the Greek emperor ; and the same faint and ambiguous hostility was prepared for the remaining chiefs, who passed the Hadriatic from the coast of Italy. Bohemond had arms and vessels, and foresight and discipline ; and his name was not forgotten in the provinces of Epirus and Thessaly. Whatever obstacles he encountered were surmounted by his military conduct and the valour of Tancred ; and if the Norman prince affected to spare the Greeks, he gorged his soldiers with the full plunder of an heretical castle. The nobles of France pressed forward with the vain and thoughtless ardour of which their nation has been sometimes accused. From the Alps to Apulia the march of Hugh the Great, of the two Roberts, and of Stephen of Chartres, through a wealthy country, and amidst the applauding Catholics, was a devout or triumphant progress : they kissed the feet of the Roman pontiff ; and the golden standard of St. Peter was delivered to the brother of the French monarch. But in this visit of piety and pleasure, they neglected to secure the season, and the means, of their embarkation : the winter was insensibly lost ; their troops were scattered and corrupted in the towns of Italy. They separately accomplished their passage, regardless of safety or dignity : and within nine months from the feast of the Assumption, the day appointed by Urban, all the Latin princes had reached Constantinople. But the count of Vermandois was produced as a captive ; his foremost vessels were scattered by a tempest ; and his person, against the law of nations, was detained by the lieutenants of Alexius. Yet the arrival of Hugh had been announced by four-and-twenty knights in golden armour, who commanded the emperor to revere the general of the Latin Christians, the brother of the King of kings.

In some Oriental tale I have read the fable of a shepherd who was ruined by the accomplishment of his own wishes : he had prayed for water ; the Ganges was turned into his grounds, and his flock and cottage were swept away by the inundation. Such was the fortune, or at least the apprehension, of the Greek emperor Alexius Comnenus (A.D. 1096. Dec.—A.D. 1097. May), whose name has already appeared in this history, and whose conduct is so differently represented by his daughter Anne, and by the Latin writers. In the council of Placentia, his ambassadors had solicited a moderate succour, perhaps of 10,000 soldiers : but he was astonished by the approach of so many potent chiefs and fanatic nations. The emperor fluctuated between hope and fear, between timidity and courage ; but in the crooked policy which he mistook for wisdom, I cannot believe, I cannot discern that he maliciously conspired against the life or honour of the French heroes. The promiscuous multitudes of Peter the hermit, were savage beasts, alike destitute of humanity and reason : nor was it possible for Alexius to prevent or deplore their destruction. The troops of Godfrey and his peers were less contemptible, but not less suspicious, to the Greek emperor. Their motives *might* be pure and pious; but he was equally alarmed by his knowledge of the ambitious Bohemond, and his ignorance of the Transalpine chiefs: the courage of the French was blind and headstrong; they might be tempted by the luxury and wealth of Greece, and elated by the view and opinion of their invincible strength; and Jerusalem might be forgotten in the prospect of Constantinople. After a long march and painful abstinence, the troops of Godfrey encamped in the plains of Thrace; they heard with indignation that their brother, the count of Vermandois, was imprisoned by the Greeks; and their reluctant duke was compelled to indulge them in some freedom of retaliation and rapine. They were appeased by the submission of Alexius; he promised to supply their camp; and as they refused, in the midst of winter, to pass the Bosphorus, their quarters were assigned among the gardens and palaces on the shores of that narrow sea. But an incurable jealousy still rankled in the minds of the two nations, who despised each other as slaves and Barbarians. Ignorance is the ground of suspicion, and suspicion was inflamed into daily provocations: prejudice is blind, hunger is deaf; and Alexius is accused of a design to starve or assault the Latins in a dangerous post, on all sides encompassed with the waters. Godfrey sounded his trumpet, burst the net, overspread the plain, and insulted the suburbs; but the gates of Constantinople were strongly fortified; the ramparts were lined with archers; and after a doubtful conflict, both parties listened to the voice of peace and religion. The gifts and promises of the emperor insensibly soothed the fierce spirit of the western strangers; as a Christian warrior, he rekindled their zeal for the prosecution of their holy enterprise, which he engaged to second with his troops and treasures. On the return of spring, Godfrey was persuaded to occupy a pleasant and plentiful camp in Asia; and no sooner had he passed the Bosphorus, than the Greek vessels were suddenly recalled to the opposite shore. The same policy was repeated with the succeeding chiefs, who were swayed by the example, and weakened by the departure, of their foremost companions. By his skill and diligence, Alexius prevented the union of any two of the confederate armies at the same moment under the walls of Constantinople; and before the feast of the Pentecost not a Latin pilgrim was left on the coast of Europe.

The same arms which threatened Europe, might deliver Asia, and repel the Turks from the neighbouring shores of the Bosphorus and Hellespont. The fair provinces from Nice to Antioch were the recent patrimony of the Roman emperor; and his ancient and perpetual claim still embraced the kingdoms of Syria and Egypt. In his enthusiasm Alexius indulged, or affected, the ambitious hope of leading his new allies to subvert the thrones of the East : but the calmer dictates of reason and temper dissuaded him from exposing his royal person to the faith of unknown and lawless Barbarians. His prudence, or his pride, was content with extorting from the French princes an oath of homage and fidelity, and a solemn promise, that they would either restore, or hold, their Asiatic conquests, as the humble and loyal vassals of the Roman empire. Their independent spirit was fired at the mention of this foreign and voluntary servitude ; they successively yielded to the dexterous application of gifts and flattery ; and the first proselytes became the most eloquent and effectual missionaries to multiply the companions of their shame. The pride of Hugh of Vermandois was soothed by the honours of his captivity ; and in the brother of the French king, the example of submission was prevalent and weighty. In the mind of Godfrey of Bouillon every human consideration was subordinate to the glory of God and the success of the crusade. He had firmly resisted the temptations of Bohemond and Raymond, who urged the attack and conquest of Constantinople. Alexius esteemed his virtues, deservedly named him the champion of the empire, and dignified his homage with the filial name and the rites of adoption. The hateful Bohemond was received as a true and ancient ally ; and if the emperor reminded him of former hostilities, it was only to praise the valour that he had displayed, and the glory that he had acquired, in the fields of Durazzo and Larissa. The son of Guiscard was lodged and entertained, and served with imperial pomp : one day, as he passed through the gallery of the palace, a door was carelessly left open to expose a pile of gold and silver, of silk and gems, of curious and costly furniture, that was heaped, in seeming disorder, from the floor to the roof of the chamber. "What conquests," exclaimed the ambitious miser, "might not be achieved by the possession of such a treasure ?" "It is your own," replied a Greek attendant who watched the motions of his soul ; and Bohemond, after some hesitation, condescended to accept this magnificent present. The Norman was flattered by the assurance of an independent principality, and Alexius eluded, rather than denied, his daring demand of the office of great domestic, or general, of the East. The two Roberts, the son of the conqueror of England, and the kinsman of three queens, bowed in their turn before the Byzantine throne. A private letter of Stephen of Chartres attests his admiration of the emperor, the most excellent and liberal of men, who taught him to believe that he was a favourite, and promised to educate and establish his youngest son. In his southern province, the count of St. Giles and Toulouse faintly recognized the supremacy of the king of France, a prince of a foreign nation and language. At the head of 100,000 men, he declared, that he was the soldier and servant of Christ alone, and that the Greek might be satisfied with an equal treaty of alliance and friendship. His obstinate resistance enhanced the value and the price of his submission ; and he shone, says the princess Anna, among the Barbarians, as the sun amidst the stars of heaven.   His disgust of the noise and insolence of the French, his suspicions of the designs of Bohemond, the emperor imparted to his faithful Raymond ; and that aged statesman might clearly discern, that however false in friendship, he was sincere in his enmity.   The spirit of chivalry was last subdued in the person of Tancred; and none could deem themselves dishonoured by the imitation of that gallant knight.   He disdained the gold and flattery of the Greek monarch ; assaulted in his presence an insolent patrician ; escaped to Asia in the habit of a private soldier ; and yielded with a sigh to the authority of Bohemond and the interest of the Christian cause.   The best and most ostensible reason was the impossibility of passing the sea and accomplishing their vow, without the licence and the vessels of Alexius ; but they cherished a secret hope, that as soon as they trod the continent of Asia, their swords would obliterate their shame, and dissolve the engagement, which on his side might not be very faithfully performed.   The ceremony of their homage was grateful to a people who had long since considered pride as the substitute of power.   High on his throne, the emperor sat mute and immovable : his majesty was adored by the Latin princes ; and they submitted to kiss either his feet or his knees, an indignity which their own writers are ashamed to confess and unable to deny.

Private or public interest suppressed the murmurs of the dukes and counts ; but a French baron (he is supposed to be Robert of Paris) presumed to ascend the throne, and to place himself by the side of Alexius.   The sage reproof of Baldwin provoked him to exclaim, in his barbarous idiom, " Who is this rustic, that keeps his seat while so many valiant captains are standing round him ?"   The emperor maintained his silence, dissembled his indignation, and questioned his interpreter concerning the meaning of the words, which he partly suspected from the universal language of gesture and countenance. Before the departure of the pilgrims, he endeavoured to learn the name and condition of the audacious baron.   " I am a Frenchman," replied Robert, " of the purest and most ancient nobility of my country.   All that I know is, that there is a church in my neighbourhood, the resort of those who are desirous of approving their valour in single combat.   Till an enemy appears, they address their prayers to God and his saints.   That church I have frequently visited, but never have I found an antagonist who dared to accept my defiance." Alexius dismissed the challenger with some prudent advice for his conduct in the Turkish warfare ; and history repeats with pleasure this lively example of the manners of his age and country.

The conquest of Asia was undertaken and achieved by Alexander, with 35,000 Macedonians and Greeks ; and his best hope was in the strength and discipline of his phalanx of infantry.   The principal force of the crusaders consisted in their cavalry; and when that force was mustered in the plains of Bithynia (A.D. 1097. May) the knights and their martial attendants on horseback amounted to 100,000 fighting men, completely armed with the helmet and coat of mail. The value of these soldiers deserved a strict and authentic account; and the flower of European chivalry might furnish, in a first effort, this formidable body of heavy horse. A part of the infantry might be enrolled for the service of scouts, pioneers, and archers; but the promiscuous crowd were lost in their own disorder; and we depend not on the eyes or knowledge, but on the belief and fancy, of a chaplain of count Baldwin, in the estimate of 600,000 pilgrims able to bear arms, besides the priests and monks, the women and children, of the Latin camp. The reader starts; but before he is recovered from his surprise, I shall add, on the same testimony, that if all who took the cross had accomplished their vow, above SIX MILLIONS would have migrated from Europe to Asia. Under this oppression of faith, I derive some relief from a more sagacious and thinking writer, who, after the same review of the cavalry, accuses the credulity of the priest of Chartres, and even doubts whether the *Cisalpine* regions (in the geography of a Frenchman) were sufficient to produce and pour forth such incredible multitudes. The coolest scepticism will remember, that these religious volunteers great numbers never beheld Constantinople and Nice. Of enthusiasm the influence is irregular and transient : many were detained at home by reason or cowardice, by poverty or weakness; and many were repulsed by the obstacles of the way, the more insuperable as they were unforeseen to these ignorant fanatics. The savage countries of Hungary and Bulgaria were whitened with their bones : their vanguard was cut in pieces by the Turkish sultan; and the loss of the first adventure by the sword, or climate, or fatigue, has already been stated at 300,000 men. Yet the myriads that survived, that marched, that pressed forwards on the holy pilgrimage, were a subject of astonishment to themselves and to the Greeks. The copious energy of her language sinks under the efforts of the princess Anna : the images of locusts, of leaves and flowers, of the sands of the sea, or the stars of heaven, imperfectly represent what she had seen and heard; and the daughter of Alexius exclaims, that Europe was loosened from its foundations, and hurled against Asia. The ancient hosts of Darius and Xerxes labour under the same doubt of a vague and indefinite magnitude ; but I am inclined to believe, that a larger number has never been contained within the lines of a single camp than at the siege of Nice, the first operation of the Latin princes. Their motives, their characters, and their arms, have been already displayed. Of their troops, the most numerous portion were natives of France : the Low Countries, the banks of the Rhine, and Apulia, sent a powerful reinforcement : some bands of adventurers were drawn from Spain, Lombardy, and England ; and from the distant bogs and mountains of Ireland or Scotland issued some naked and savage fanatics, ferocious at home but unwarlike abroad. Had not super-stition condemned the sacrilegious prudence of depriving the poorest or weakest Christian of the merit of the pilgrimage, the useless crowd, with mouths but without hands, might have been stationed in the Greek empire, till their companions had opened and secured the way of the Lord. A small remnant of the pilgrims, who passed the Bos-phorus, was permitted to visit the holy sepulchre. Their northern constitution was scorched by the rays, and infected by the vapours, of a Syrian sun. They consumed, with heedless prodigality, their stores of water and provision : their numbers exhausted the inland country ; the sea was remote, the Greeks were unfriendly, and the Christians of every sect fled before the voracious and cruel rapine of their brethren. In the dire necessity of famine, they sometimes roasted and devoured the flesh of their infant or adult captives. Among the Turks and Saracens, the idolaters of Europe were rendered more odious by the name and reputation of cannibals : the spies who in-troduced themselves into the kitchen of Bohemond, were shown several human bodies turning on the spit ; and the artful Norman en-couraged a report, which increased at the same time the abhorrence and the terror of the infidels.

I have expatiated with pleasure on the first steps of the crusaders, as they paint the manners and character of Europe : but I shall abridge the tedious and uniform narrative of their blind achievements, which were performed by strength and are described by ignorance. From their first station in the neighbourhood of Nicomedia, they advanced in successive divisions ; passed the contracted limit of the Greek em-pire ; opened a road through the hills, and commenced (A.D. 1097. May 14—June 20), by the siege of his capital, their pious warfare against the Turkish sultan. His kingdom of Roum extended from the Hellespont to the confines of Syria, and barred the pilgrimage of Jerusalem : his name was Kilidge-Arslan, or Soliman, of the race of Seljuk, and son of the first conqueror ; and in the defence of a land which the Turks considered as their own, he deserved the praise of his enemies, by whom alone he is known to posterity. Yielding to the first impulse of the torrent, he deposited his family and treasure in Nice ; retired to the mountains with 50,000 horse ; and twice descend-ed to assault the camps or quarters of the Christian besiegers, which formed an imperfect circle of above six miles. The lofty and solid walls of Nice were covered by a deep ditch, and flanked by 370 towers; and on the verge of Christendom, the Moslems were trained in arms and inflamed by religion. Before this city, the French princes occu-pied their stations, and prosecuted their attacks without correspond-ence or subordination : emulation prompted their valour; but their valour was sullied by cruelty, and their emulation degenerated into envy and civil discord. In the siege of Nice the arts and engines of antiquity were employed by the Latins ; the mine and the battering-ram, the tortoise, and the belfry or movable turret, artificial fire, and the *catapult* and *balist*, the sling, and the cross-bow for the casting of stones and darts. In the space of seven weeks, much labour and blood were expended, and some progress, especially by count Raymond, was made on the side of the besiegers. But the Turks could protract their resistance, and secure their escape, as long as they were masters of the lake Ascanius, which stretches several miles to the westward of the city. The means of conquest were supplied by the prudence and industry of Alexius ; a great number of boats was transported on sledges from the sea to the lake ; they were filled with the most dexterous of his archers ; the flight of the sultana was intercepted ; Nice was invested by land and water ; and a Greek emissary persuaded the inhabitants to accept his master's protection, and to save themselves by a timely surrender, from the rage of the savages of Europe. In the moment of victory, or at least of hope, the crusaders, thirsting for blood and plunder, were awed by the Imperial banner that streamed from the citadel ; and Alexius guarded with jealous vigilance this important conquest. The murmurs of the chiefs were stifled by honour or interest ; and after an halt of nine days, they directed their march towards Phrygia under the guidance of a Greek general, whom they suspected of secret connivance with the sultan. The consort and the principal servants of Soliman had been honourably restored without ransom ; and the emperor's generosity to the *miscreants** was interpreted as treason to the Christian cause.

Soliman was rather provoked than dismayed by the loss of his capital : he admonished his subjects and allies of this strange invasion of the western Barbarians ; the Turkish emirs obeyed the call of loyalty or religion ; the Turkman hordes encamped round his standard ; and his whole force is loosely stated by the Christians at 200,000, or even 360,000 horse. Yet he patiently waited till they had left behind them the sea and the Greek frontier ; and hovering on the flanks, observed their careless and confident progress in two columns beyond the view of each other. Some miles before they could reach Dorylæum in Phrygia, the left, and least numerous division was surprised and attacked (A.D. 1097. July 4), and almost oppressed by the Turkish cavalry. The heat of the weather, the clouds of arrows, and the barbarous onset, overwhelmed the crusaders ; they lost their order and confidence, and the fainting fight was sustained by the personal valour, rather than by the military conduct, of Bohemond, Tancred, and

---

* *Mecreant*, a word invented by the French crusaders, and confined in that language to its primitive sense. It should seem, that the zeal of our ancestors boiled higher, and that they branded every unbeliever as a rascal. A similar prejudice still lurks in the minds of many who think themselves Christians.

Robert of Normandy. They were revived by the welcome banners of duke Godfrey, who flew to their succour with the count of Vermandois, and 60,000 horse; and was followed by Raymond of Toulouse, the bishop of Puy, and the remainder of the sacred army. Without a moment's pause, they formed in new order, and advanced to a second battle. They were received with equal resolution; and, in their common disdain for the unwarlike people of Greece and Asia, it was confessed on both sides, that the Turks and the Franks were the only nations entitled to the appellation of soldiers. Their encounter was varied and balanced by the contrast of arms and discipline; of the direct charge, and wheeling evolutions; of the couched lance, and the brandished javelin; of a weighty broad-sword and a crooked sabre; of cumbrous armour, and thin flowing robes; and of the long Tartar bow, and the *arbalist* or cross-bow, a deadly weapon, yet unknown to the Orientals. As long as the horses were fresh and the quivers full, Soliman maintained the advantage of the day; and 4000 Christians were pierced by the Turkish arrows. In the evening, swiftness yielded to strength; on either side the numbers were equal, or at least as great as any ground could hold, or any generals could manage; but in turning the hills, the last division of Raymond and his *provincials* was led, perhaps without design, on the rear of an exhausted enemy; and the long contest was determined. Besides a nameless and unaccounted multitude, 3000 *Pagan* knights were slain in the battle and pursuit; the camp of Soliman was pillaged; and in the variety of precious spoil, the curiosity of the Latins was amused with foreign arms and apparel, and the new aspect of dromedaries and camels. The importance of the victory was proved by the hasty retreat of the sultan: reserving 10,000 guards of the relics of his army, Soliman evacuated the kingdom of Roum, and hastened to implore the aid and kindle the resentment, of his Eastern brethren. In a march of 500 miles, the crusaders (July—Sept.) traversed the lesser Asia through a wasted land and deserted towns, without either finding a friend or an enemy. The geographer may trace the position of Dorylæum, Antioch, of Pisidia, Iconium, Archelais, and Germanicia, and may compare those classic appellations with the modern names of Eskishehr the old city, Akshehr the white city, Cogni, Erekli, and Marash. As the pilgrims passed over a desert, where a draught of water is exchanged for silver, they were tormented by intolerable thirst; and on the banks of the first rivulet, their haste and intemperance were still more pernicious to the disorderly throng. They climbed with toil and danger the steep and slippery sides of mount Taurus: many of the soldiers cast away their arms to secure their footsteps; and had not terror preceded their van, the long and trembling file might have been driven down the precipice by a handful of resolute enemies. Two of their most respectable chiefs, the duke of Lorraine and the count of Toulouse, were carried in litters : Raymond was raised, as it is said by miracle, from an hopeless malady ; and Godfrey had been torn by a bear, as he pursued that rough and perilous chace in the mountains of Pisidia. To improve the general consternation, the cousin of Bohemond and the brother of Godfrey were detached from the main army with their respective squadrons of five, and of seven hundred knights. They over-ran in a rapid career the hills and sea-coast of Cilicia, from Cogni to the Syrian gates : the Norman standard was first planted on the walls of Tarsus and Malmistra ; but the proud injustice of Baldwin at length provoked the patient and generous Italian ; and they turned their consecrated swords against each other in a private and profane quarrel. Honour was the motive, and fame the reward, of Tancred ; but fortune smiled on the more selfish enterprise of his rival. He was called to the assistance of a Greek or Armenian tyrant, who had been suffered under the Turkish yoke to reign over the Christians of Edessa. Baldwin accepted the character of his son and champion ; but no sooner was he introduced into the city, than he inflamed the people to the massacre of his father, occupied the throne and treasure, extended his conquests over the hills of Armenia and the plain of Mesopotamia, and founded (A.D. 1097—1151) the first principality of the Franks or Latins, which subsisted fifty-four years beyond the Euphrates.

Before the Franks could enter Syria, the summer, and even the autumn, were completely wasted : the siege of Antioch (A.D. 1097, Oct. 21), or the separation and repose of the army during the winter season, was strongly debated in their council : the love of arms and the holy sepulchre urged them to advance ; and reason perhaps was on the side of resolution, since every hour of delay abates the fame and force of the invader, and multiplies the resources of defensive war. The capital of Syria was protected by the river Orontes ; and the *iron bridge*, of nine arches, derives its name from the massy gates of the two towers which are constructed at either end. They were opened (A.D. 1098. June 3) by the sword of the duke of Normandy : his victory gave entrance to 300,000 crusaders, an account which may allow some scope for losses and desertion, but which clearly detects much exaggeration in the review of Nice. In the description of Antioch, it is not easy to define a middle term between her ancient magnificence, under the successors of Alexander and Augustus, and the modern aspect of Turkish desolation. The Tetrapolis, or four cities, if they retained their name and position, must have left a large vacuity in a circumference of twelve miles ; and that measure, as well as the number of four hundred towers, are not perfectly consistent with the five gates, so often mentioned in the history of the siege. Yet Antioch must have still flourished as a great and populous capital. At the head of the Turkish emirs, Baghisian, a veteran chief, commanded in the place : his garrison was composed of six or seven thousand

horse, and fifteen or twenty thousand foot : one hundred thousand
Moslems are said to have fallen by the sword ; and their numbers
were probably inferior to the Greeks, Armenians, and Syrians, who
had been no more than fourteen years the slaves of the house of Seljuk.
From the remains of a solid and stately wall, it appears to have arisen
to the height of three-score feet in the valleys ; and wherever less art
and labour had been applied, the ground was supposed to be defended
by the river, the morass, and the mountains. Notwithstanding these
fortifications, the city had been repeatedly taken by the Persians, the
Arabs, the Greeks, and the Turks ; so large a circuit must have yielded
many pervious points of attack ; and in a siege that was formed about
the middle of October, the vigour of the execution could alone justify
the boldness of the attempt. Whatever strength and valour could
perform in the field was abundantly discharged by the champions of
the cross : in the frequent occasions of sallies, of forage, of the attack
and defence of convoys, they were often victorious, and we can only
complain, that their exploits are sometimes enlarged beyond the scale
of probability and truth. The sword of Godfrey divided a Turk from
the shoulder to the haunch ; and one half of the infidel fell to the
ground, while the other was transported by his horse to the city gate.
As Robert of Normandy rode against his antagonist, " I devote thy
head," he piously exclaimed, " to the dæmons of hell ;" and that
head was instantly cloven to the breast by the resistless stroke of his
descending faulchion. But the reality or report of such gigantic
prowess must have taught the Moslems to keep within their walls ;
and against those walls of earth or stone, the sword and the lance
were unavailing weapons. In the slow and successive labours of a
siege, the crusaders were supine and ignorant, without skill to contrive,
or money to purchase, or industry to use, the artificial engines and
implements of assault. In the conquest of Nice, they had been
powerfully assisted by the wealth and knowledge of the Greek emperor :
his absence was poorly supplied by some Genoese and Pisan vessels,
that were attracted by religion or trade to the coast of Syria : the stores
were scanty, the return precarious, and the communication difficult
and dangerous. Indolence or weakness had prevented the Franks
from investing the entire circuit ; and the perpetual freedom of two
gates relieved the wants and recruited the garrison of the city. At the
end of seven months, after the ruin of their cavalry, and an enormous
loss by famine, desertion, and fatigue, the progress of the crusaders
was imperceptible, and their success remote, if the Latin Ulysses, the
artful and ambitious Bohemond, had not employed the arms of cunning
and deceit. The Christians of Antioch were numerous and discontented : Phirouz, a Syrian renegado, had acquired the favour of the
emir and the command of three towers ; and the merit of his repentance
disguised to the Latins, and perhaps to himself, the foul design of
perfidy and treason. A secret correspondence, for their mutual interest,

was soon established between Phirouz and the prince of Tarento ; and Bohemond declared in the council of the chiefs, that he could deliver the city into their hands. But he claimed the sovereignty of Antioch as the reward of his service ; and the proposal which had been rejected by the envy, was at length extorted by the distress, of his equals. The nocturnal surprise was executed by the French and Norman princes, who ascended in person the scaling-ladders that were thrown from the walls : their new proselyte, after the murder of his too scrupulous brother, embraced and introduced the servants of Christ ; the army rushed through the gates ; and the Moslems soon found, that although mercy was hopeless, resistance was impotent. But the citadel still refused to surrender ; and the victors themselves were speedily encompassed and besieged by the innumerable forces of Kerboga, prince of Mosul, who, with twenty-eight Turkish emirs, advanced to the deliverance of Antioch. Five-and-twenty days the Christians spent on the verge of destruction ; and the proud lieutenant of the caliph and the sultan left them only the choice of servitude or death. In this extremity they collected the relics of their strength, sallied from the town, and in a single memorable day (A.D. 1098. June 28) annihilated or dispersed the host of Turks and Arabians, which they might safely report to have consisted of 600,000 men. Their supernatural allies I shall proceed to consider : the human causes of the victory of Antioch were the fearless despair of the Franks ; and the surprise, the discord, perhaps the errors, of their unskilful and presumptuous adversaries. The battle is described with as much disorder as it was fought ; but we may observe the tent of Kerboga, a movable palace, enriched with the luxury of Asia, and capable of holding above 2000 persons ; we may distinguish his 3000 guards, who were cased, the horses as well as the men, in complete steel.

In the eventful period of the siege and defence of Antioch, the crusaders were alternately exalted by victory or sunk in despair ; either swelled with plenty or emaciated with hunger. A speculative reasoner might suppose, that their faith had a strong and serious influence on their practice ; and that the soldiers of the cross, the deliverers of the holy sepulchre, prepared themselves by a sober and virtuous life for the daily contemplation of martyrdom. Experience blows away this charitable illusion : and seldom does the history of profane war display such scenes of intemperance as were exhibited under the walls of Antioch. The grove of Daphne no longer flourished ; but the Syrian air was still impregnated with the same vices ; the Christians were seduced by every temptation that nature either prompts or reprobates ; the authority of the chiefs was despised ; and sermons and edicts were alike fruitless against those scandalous disorders, not less pernicious to military discipline, than repugnant to evangelic purity. In the first days of the siege and the possession of Antioch, the Franks

consumed with wanton and thoughtless prodigality the frugal subsistence of weeks and months : the desolate country no longer yielded
a supply ; and from that country they were at length excluded by the
arms of the besieging Turks. Disease, the faithful companion of want,
was envenomed by the rains of the winter, the summer heats, unwholesome food, and the close imprisonment of multitudes. The pictures
of famine and pestilence are always the same, and always disgustful ;
and our imagination may suggest the nature of their sufferings and
their resources. The remains of treasure or spoil were eagerly lavished
in the purchase of the vilest nourishment ; and dreadful must have
been the calamities of the poor, since, after paying three marks of silver for a goat, and fifteen for a lean camel, the count of Flanders was
reduced to beg a dinner, and duke Godfrey to borrow a horse. Sixty
thousand horses had been reviewed in the camp : before the end of
the siege they were diminished to 2000, and scarcely 200 fit for service
could be mustered on the day of battle. Weakness of body, and
terror of mind, extinguished the ardent enthusiasm of the pilgrims ;
and every motive of honour and religion was subdued by the desire of
life. Among the chiefs, three heroes may be found without fear or
reproach : Godfrey of Bouillon was supported by his magnanimous
piety ; Bohemond by ambition and interest ; and Tancred declared,
in the true spirit of chivalry, that as long as he was at the head of
forty knights, he would never relinquish the enterprise of Palestine.
But the count of Toulouse and Provence was suspected of a voluntary
indisposition ; the duke of Normandy was recalled from the sea-shore
by the censures of the church ; Hugh the Great, though he led the
vanguard of the battle, embraced an ambiguous opportunity of returning to France ; and Stephen count of Chartres basely deserted the
standard which he bore, and the council in which he presided. The
soldiers were discouraged by the flight of William, viscount of Melun,
surnamed the *Carpenter*, from the weighty strokes of his axe ; and the
saints were scandalized by the fall of Peter the Hermit, who, after arming Europe against Asia, attempted to escape from the penance of a
necessary fast. Of the multitude of recreant warriors, the names (says
an historian) are blotted from the book of life ; and the opprobrious
epithet of the rope-dancers was applied to the deserters who dropt in
the night from the walls of Antioch. The emperor Alexius, who seemed
to advance to the succour of the Latins, was dismayed by the assurance
of their hopeless condition. They expected their fate in silent despair ;
oaths and punishments were tried without effect ; and to rouse the
soldiers to the defence of the walls, it was found necessary to set fire
to their quarters.

For their salvation and victory, they were indebted to the same
fanaticism which had led them to the brink of ruin. In such a cause,
and in such an army, visions, prophecies, and miracles, were frequent

and familiar. In the distress of Antioch, they were repeated with unusual energy and success : St. Ambrose had assured a pious ecclesiastic, that two years of trial must precede the season of deliverance and grace ; the deserters were stopped by the presence and reproaches of Christ himself ; the dead had promised to rise and combat with their brethren ; the Virgin had obtained the pardon of their sins ; and their confidence was relieved by a visible sign, the seasonable and splendid discovery of the HOLY LANCE. The policy of their chiefs has on this occasion been ˜dmired, and might surely be excused ; but a pious fraud is seldom produced by the cool conspiracy of many persons ; and a voluntary impostor might depend on the support of the wise and the credulity of the people. Of the diocese of Marseilles, there was a priest of low cunning and loose manners, and his name was Peter Bartholemy. He presented himself at the door of the council-chamber, to disclose an apparition of St. Andrew, which had been thrice reiterated in his sleep, with a dreadful menace, if he presumed to suppress the commands of heaven. " At Antioch," said the apostle, " in the church of my brother St. Peter, near the high altar, is concealed the steel head of the lance that pierced the˜side of our Redeemer. In three days, that instrument of eternal, and now of temporal salvation, will be manifested to his disciples. Search and ye shall find ; bear it aloft in battle ; and that mystic weapon shall penetrate the souls of the miscreants." The pope's legate, the bishop of Puy, affected to listen with coldness and distrust ; but the revelation was eagerly accepted by count Raymond, whom his faithful subject, in the name of the apostle, had chosen for the guardian of the holy lance. The experiment was resolved ; and on the third day, after a due preparation of prayer and fasting, the priest of Marseilles introduced twelve trusty spectators, among whom were the count and his chaplain ; and the church-doors were barred against the impetuous multitude. The ground was opened in the appointed place ; but the workmen, who relieved each other, dug to the depth of twelve feet without discovering the object of their search. In the evening, when count Raymond had withdrawn to his post, and the weary assistants began to murmur, Bartholemy, in his shirt, and without his shoes, boldly descended into the pit ; the darkness of the hour and of the place enabled him to secrete and deposit the head of a Saracen lance ; and the first sound, the first gleam, of the steel, was saluted with a devout rapture. The holy lance was drawn from its recess, wrapt in a veil of silk and gold, and. exposed to the veneration of the crusaders ; their anxious suspense burst forth in a general shout of joy and hope, and the desponding troops were again inflamed with the enthusiasm of valour. Whatever had been the arts, and whatever might be the sentiments, of the chiefs, they skilfully improved this fortunate revolution by every aid that discipline and devotion could afford. The soldiers were dismissed to their quarters with an injunction to fortify their minds and bodies for the approaching conflict, freely to bestow their last pittance on themselves and their horses, and to expect with the dawn of day the signal of victory. On the festival of St. Peter and St. Paul, the gates of Antioch were thrown open ; a martial psalm, " Let the Lord arise, and let his enemies be scattered !" was chaunted by a procession of priests and monks ; the battle-array was marshalled in twelve divisions, in honour of the twelve apostles ; and the holy lance, in the absence of Raymond, was entrusted to the hands of his chaplain. The influence of this relic or trophy was felt by the servants, and perhaps by the enemies of Christ ; and its potent energy was heightened by an accident, a stratagem, or a rumour, of a miraculous complexion. Three knights, in white garments and resplendent arms, either issued, or seemed to issue, from the hills : the voice of Adhemar, the pope's legate, proclaimed them as the martyrs St. George, St. Theodore, and ' St. Maurice ; the tumult of battle allowed no time for doubt or scrutiny ; and the welcome apparition dazzled the eyes or the imagination of a fanatic army. In the season of danger and triumph, the revelation of Bartholemy of Marseillès was unanimously asserted ; but as soon as the temporary service was accomplished, the personal dignity and liberal alms which the count of Toulouse derived from the custody of the holy lance, provoked the envy, and awakened the reason, of his rivals. A Norman clerk presumed to sift, with a philosophic spirit, the truth of the legend, the circumstances of the discovery, and the character of the prophet ; and the pious Bohemond ascribed their deliverance to the merits and intercession of Christ alone. ' For a while, the Provincials defended their national palladium with clamours and arms ; and new visions condemned to death and hell the profane sceptics, who presumed to scrutinise the truth and merit of the discovery. The prevalence of incredulity compelled the author to submit his life and veracity to the judgment of God. A pile of dry faggots, four feet high, and fourteen long, was erected in the midst of the camp ; the flames burnt fiercely to the elevation of thirty cubits ; and a narrow path of twelve inches was left for the perilous trial. The unfortunate priest of Marseilles traversed the fire with dexterity and speed ; but his thighs and belly were scorched by the intense heat ; he expired the next day ; and the logic of believing minds will pay some regard to his dying protestations of innocence and truth. Some efforts were made by the Provincials to substitute a cross, a ring, or a tabernacle, in the place of the holy lance, which soon vanished in contempt and oblivion. Yet the revelation of Antioch is gravely asserted by succeeding historians ; and such is credulity, that miracles most doubtful on the spot and at the moment, will be received with implicit faith at a convenient distance of time and space.

The prudence or fortune of the Franks had delayed their invasion till the decline of the Turkish empire. Under the manly government of the three first sultans, the kingdoms of Asia were united in peace and justice ; and the innumerable armies which they led in person were equal in courage, and superior in discipline, to the Barbarians of the West. But at the time of the crusade, the inheritance of Malek Shaw was disputed by his four sons ; their private ambition was insensible of the public danger ; and, in the vicissitudes of their fortune, the royal vassals were ignorant, or regardless, of the true object of their allegiance. The twenty-eight emirs, who marched with the standard of Kerboga, were his rivals or enemies ; their hasty levies were drawn from the towns and tents of Mesopotamia and Syria ; and the Turkish veterans were employed or consumed in the civil wars beyond the Tigris. The caliph of Egypt embraced this opportunity of weakness and discord, to recover his ancient possessions ; and his sultan Aphdal besieged Jerusalem and Tyre, expelled the children of Ortok, and restored in Palestine the civil and ecclesiastical authority of the Fatimites. They heard with astonishment of the vast armies of Christians that had passed from Europe to Asia, and rejoiced in the sieges and battles which broke the power of the Turks, the adversaries of their sect and monarchy. But the same Christians were the enemies of the prophet ; and from the overthrow of Nice and Antioch, the motive of their enterprise, which was gradually understood, would urge them forwards to the banks of the Jordan, or perhaps of the Nile. An intercourse of epistles and embassies, which rose and fell with the events of war, was maintained between the throne of Cairo and the camp of the Latins ; and their adverse pride was the result of ignorance and enthusiasm. The ministers of Egypt declared in an haughty, or insinuated in a milder, tone, that their sovereign, the true and lawful commander of the faithful, had rescued Jerusalem from the Turkish yoke ; and that the pilgrims, if they would divide their numbers, and lay aside their arms, should find a safe and hospitable reception at the sepulchre of Jesus. In the belief of their lost condition, the caliph Mostali despised their arms, and imprisoned their deputies : the conquest and victory of Antioch prompted him to solicit those formidable champions with gifts of horses and silk robes, of vases, and purses of gold and silver ; and in his estimate of their merit or power, the first place was assigned to Bohemond, and the second to Godfrey. In either fortune the answer of the crusaders was firm and uniform : they disdained to inquire into the private claims or possessions of the followers of Mahomet : whatsoever was his name or nation, the usurper of Jerusalem was their enemy ; and instead of prescribing the mode and terms of their pilgrimage, it was only by a timely surrender of the city and province, their sacred right, that he could deserve their alliance, or deprecate their impending and irresistible attack.

Yet this attack, when they were within the view and reach of their glorious prize, was suspended (A.D. 1098, July—A.D. 1099, May) above ten months after the defeat of Kerboga. The zeal and courage of the crusaders were chilled in the moment of victory : and, instead of marching to improve the consternation, they hastily dispersed to enjoy the luxury, of Syria. The causes of this strange delay may be found in the want of strength and subordination. In the painful and various service of Antioch, the cavalry was annihilated ; many thousands of every rank had been lost by famine, sickness, and desertion : the same abuse of plenty had been productive of a third famine ; and the alternative of intemperance and distress, had generated a pestilence, which swept away above 50,000 of the pilgrims. Few were able to command, and none were willing to obey : the domestic feuds, which had been stifled by common fear, were again renewed in acts, or at least in sentiments, of hostility ; the fortune of Baldwin and Bohemond excited the envy of their companions ; the bravest knights were enlisted for the defence of their new principalities ; and count Raymond exhausted his troops and treasures in an idle expedition into the heart of Syria. The winter was consumed in discord and disorder ; a sense of honour and religion was rekindled in the spring ; and the private soldiers, less susceptible of ambition and jealousy, awakened with angry clamours the indolence of their chiefs. In the month of May, (A.D. 1099. May 13), the relics of this mighty host proceeded from Antioch to Laodicea ; about 40,000 Latins, of whom no more than 1500 horse, and 20,000 foot, were capable of immediate service. Their easy march was continued between mount Libanus and the sea-shore ; their wants were liberally supplied by the coasting traders of Genoa and Pisa ; and they drew large contributions from the emirs of Tripoli, Tyre, Sidon, Acre, and Cæsarea, who granted a free passage, and promised to follow the example of Jerusalem. From Cæsarea they advanced into the midland country ; their clerks recognized the sacred geography of Lydda, Ramla, Emaus, and Bethlem, and as soon (June 6) as they descried the holy city, the crusaders forgot their toils and claimed their reward.

Jerusalem has derived some reputation from the number and importance of her memorable sieges. It was not till after a long and obstinate contest that Babylon and Rome could prevail against the obstinacy of the people, the craggy ground that might supersede the necessity of fortifications, and the walls and towers that would have fortified the most accessible plain. These obstacles were diminished in the age of the crusades. The bulwarks had been completely destroyed and imperfectly restored : the Jews, their nation and worship, were for ever banished ; but nature is less changeable than man, and the site of Jerusalem, though somewhat softened and somewhat removed, was still strong against the assaults of an enemy. By the experience of a recent siege, and a three years' possession, the Saracens of Egypt had been taught to discern, and in some degree to remedy, the defects of a place, which religion as well as honour forbade them to resign. Aladin or Iftikhar, the caliph's lieutenant, was entrusted with the defence : his policy strove to restrain the native Christians by the dread of their own ruin and that of the holy sepulchre ; to animate the Moslems by the assurance of temporal and eternal rewards. His garrison is said to have consisted of 40,000 Turks and Arabians ; and if he could muster 20,000 of the inhabitants, it must be confessed that the besieged were more numerous than the besieging army. Had the diminished strength and numbers of the Latins allowed them to grasp the whole circumference of 4000 yards (about two English miles and a half), to what useful purpose should they have descended into the valley of Ben Himmon and torrent of Cedron, or approached the precipices of the south and east, from whence they had nothing either to hope or fear ? Their siege (A.D. 1099. June 7—July 15) was more reasonably directed against the northern and western sides of the city. Godfrey of Bouillon erected his standard on the first swell of mount Calvary : to the left, as far as St. Stephen's gate, the line of attack was continued by Tancred and the two Roberts ; and count Raymond established his quarters from the citadel to the foot of mount Sion, which was no longer included within the precincts of the city. On the fifth day, the crusaders made a general assault, in the fanatic hope of battering down the walls without engines, and of scaling them without ladders. By the dint of brutal force, they burst the first barrier, but they were driven back with shame and slaughter to the camp : the influence of vision and prophecy was deadened by the too frequent abuse of those pious stratagems ; and time and labour were found to be the only means of victory. The time of the siege was indeed fulfilled in forty days, but they were forty days of calamity and anguish. A repetition of the old complaint of famine may be imputed in some degree to the voracious or disorderly appetite of the Franks ; but the stony soil of Jerusalem is almost destitute of water ; the scanty springs and hasty torrents were dry in the summer season ; nor was the thirst of the besiegers relieved, as in the city, by the artificial supply of cisterns and aqueducts. The circumjacent country is equally destitute of trees for the uses of shade or building ; but some large beams were discovered in a cave by the crusaders : a wood near Sichem, the enchanted grove of Tasso, was cut down : the necessary timber was transported to the camp by the vigour and dexterity of Tancred ; and the engines were framed by some Genoese artists, who had fortunately landed in the harbour of Jaffa. Two movable turrets were constructed at the expence, and in the stations, of the duke of Lorraine and the count of Toulouse, and rolled forwards with devout labour, not to the most accessible, but to the most neglected, parts of the fortification.

Raymond's tower was reduced to ashes by the fire of the besieged, but his colleague was more vigilant and successful ; the enemies were driven by his archers from the rampart ; the draw-bridge was let down ; and on a Friday at three in the afternoon, the day and hour of the Passion, Godfrey of Bouillon stood victorious on the walls of Jerusalem. His example was followed on every side by the emulation of valour ; and about 460 years after the conquest of Omar, the holy city was rescued from the Mahometan yoke. In the pillage of public and private wealth, the adventurers had agreed to respect the exclusive property of the first occupant ; and the spoils of the great mosque, seventy lamps and massy vases of gold and silver, rewarded the diligence, and displayed the generosity, of Tancred. A bloody sacrifice was offered by his mistaken votaries to the God of the Christians. resistance might provoke, but neither age nor sex could mollify, their implacable rage : they indulged themselves three days in a promiscuous massacre ; and the infection of the dead bodies produced an epidemical disease. After 70,000 Moslems had been put to the sword, and the harmless Jews had been burnt in their synagogue, they could still reserve a multitude of captives, whom interest or lassitude persuaded them to spare. Of these savage heroes of the cross, Tancred alone betrayed some sentiments of compassion ; yet we may praise the more selfish lenity of Raymond, who granted a capitulation and safe-conduct to the garrison of the citadel. The holy sepulchre was now free ; and the bloody victors prepared to accomplish their vow. Bare-headed and barefoot, with contrite hearts, and in an humble posture, they ascended the hill of Calvary, amidst the loud anthems of the clergy ; kissed the stone which had covered the Saviour of the world ; and bedewed with tears of joy and penitence the monument of their redemption. This union of the fiercest and most tender passions has been variously considered by two philosophers ; by the one as easy and natural ; by the other as absurd and incredible. Perhaps it is too rigorously applied to the same persons and the same hour : the example of the virtuous Godfrey awakened the piety of his companions ; while they cleansed their bodies, they purified their minds ; nor shall I believe that the most ardent in slaughter and rapine were the foremost in the procession to the holy sepulchre.

Eight days (A.D. 1099. July 23) after this memorable event, which pope Urban did not live to hear, the Latin chiefs proceeded to the election of a king, to guard and govern their conquests in Palestine. Hugh the Great, and Stephen of Chartres, had retired with some loss of reputation, which they strove to regain by a second crusade and an honourable death. Baldwin was established at Edessa, and Bohemond at Antioch, and two Roberts, the duke of Normandy and the count of Flanders, preferred their fair inheritance in the West, to a doubtful competition or a barren sceptre. The jealousy and ambition of Ray-

mond were condemned by his own followers, and the free, the just, the
unanimous voice of the army, proclaimed Godfrey of Bouillon the first
and most worthy of the champions of Christendom. His magnanimity accepted a trust as full of danger as of glory; but in a city where
his Saviour had been crowned with thorns, the devout pilgrim rejected
the name and ensigns of royalty; and the founder of the kingdom of
Jerusalem contented himself with the modest title of Defender and
Baron of the Holy Sepulchre. His government of a single year (A.D.
1100. July 18), too short for the public happiness, was interrupted in
the first fortnight by a summons to the field by the approach of the
vizier or sultan of Egypt, who had been too slow to prevent, but who ˉ
was impatient to avenge, the loss of Jerusalem. His total overthrow
in the battle of Ascalon (A.D. 1099. Aug. 12) sealed the establishment
of the Latins in Syria, and signalized the valour of the French princes,
who in this action bade a long farewell to the holy wars. Some glory
might be derived from the prodigious inequality of numbers, though I
shall not count the myriads of horse and foot on the side of the Fatimites; but, except 3000 Ethiopians or blacks, who were armed with
flails, or scourges of iron, the Barbarians of the South fled on the first
onset, and afforded a pleasing comparison between the active valour of
the Turks and the sloth and effeminacy of the natives of Egypt. After
suspending before the holy sepulchre the sword and standard of the
sultan, the new king (he deserves the title) embraced his departing
companions, and could retain only with the gallant Tancred 300
knights, and 2000 foot soldiers, for the defence of Palestine. His
sovereignty was soon attacked by a new enemy, the only one against
whom Godfrey was a coward. Adhemer, bishop of Puy, who excelled
both in council and action, had been swept away in the last plague of
Antioch: the remaining ecclesiastics preserved only the pride and
avarice of their character; and their seditious clamours had required
that the choice of a bishop should precede that of a king. The
revenue and jurisdiction of the lawful patriarch were usurped by the
Latin clergy: the exclusion of the Greeks and Syrians was justified by
the reproach of heresy or schism; and, under the iron yoke of their
deliverers, the Oriental Christians regretted the tolerating government
of the Arabian caliphs. Daimbert, archbishop of Pisa, had long been
trained in the secret policy of Rome: he brought a fleet of his countrymen to the succour of the Holy Land, and was installed, without a ⎰
competitor, the spiritual and temporal head of the church. The new
patriarch immediately grasped the sceptre which had been acquired by
the toil and blood of the victorious pilgrims; and both Godfrey and
Bohemond submitted to receive at his hands the investiture of their
feudal possessions. Nor was this sufficient; Daimbert claimed the
immediate property of Jerusalem and Jaffa: instead of a firm and
generous refusal, the hero negociated with the priest; a quarter of

either city was ceded to the church ; and the modest bishop was satisfied with an eventual reversion of the rest, on the death of Godfrey without children, or on the future acquisition of a new seat at Cairo or Damascus.

Without this indulgence, the conqueror would have almost been stripped of his infant kingdom (A.D. 1099—1187) which consisted only of Jerusalem and Jaffa, with about twenty villages and towns of the adjacent country. Within this narrow verge, the Mahometans were still lodged in some impregnable castles ; and the husbandman, the trader, and the pilgrims, were exposed to daily and domestic hostility. By the arms of Godfrey himself, and of the two Baldwins, his brother and cousin, who succeeded to the throne, the Latins breathed with more ease and safety; and at length they equalled, in the extent of their dominions, though not in the millions of their subjects, the ancient princes of Judah and Israel.* After the reduction of the maritime cities of Laodicea, Tripoli, Tyre, and Ascalon, which were powerfully assisted by the fleets of Venice, Genoa, and Pisa, and even of Flanders and Norway, the range of sea-coast from Scanderoon to the borders of Egypt was possessed by the Christian pilgrims. If the prince of Antioch disclaimed his supremacy, the counts of Edessa and Tripoli owned themselves the vassals of the king of Jerusalem : the Latins reigned beyond the Euphrates ; and the four cities of Hems, Hamah, Damascus and Aleppo, were the only relics of the Mahometan conquests in Syriá. The laws and language, the manners and titles, of the French nation and Latin church, were introduced into these transmarine colonies. According to the feudal jurisprudence, the principal states and subordinate baronies descended in the line of male and female succession ; but the children of the first conquerors, a motley and degenerate race, were dissolved by the luxury of the climate ; the arrival of new crusaders from Europe, was a doubtful hope, and a casual event. The service of the feudal tenures was performed by 666 knights, who might expect the aid of 200 more under the banner of the count of Tripoli; and each knight was attended to the field by four squires or archers on horseback. Five thousand and seventy-five *sergeants,* most probably foot soldiers, were supplied by the churches and cities : and the whole legal militia of the kingdom could not exceed 11,000 men, a slender defence against the surrounding myriads of Saracens and Turks. But the firmest bulwark of Jerusalem was founded on the knights of the hospital of St. John, and of the temple of Solomon ; on the strange association of a monastic and military life, which fanaticism might suggest, but which policy must approve. The flower of the nobility of Europe aspired to wear the

---

* An actual muster, not including the tribes of Levi and Benjamin, gave David an army of 1,300,000, or 1,574,000 fighting men ; which, with the addition of women, children, and slaves, may imply a population of 13,000,000, in a country 60 leagues in length, and 30 broad

cross, an i to profess the vows, of these respectable orders ; their spirit and discipline were immortal; and the speedy donation of 28,000 farms or manors, enabled them to support a regular force of cavalry and infantry for the defence of Palestine. The austerity of the convent soon evaporated in the exercise of arms : the world was scandalized by the pride, avarice, and corruption of these Christian soldiers ; their claims of immunity and jurisdiction disturbed the harmony of the church and state; and the public peace was endangered by their jealous emulation. But in their most dissolute period, the knights of the hospital and temple maintained their fearless and fanatic character : they neglected to live, but they were prepared to die, in the service of Christ; and the spirit of chivalry, the parent and offspring of the crusades, was transplanted by this institution from the holy sepulchre to the isle of Malta.

The spirit of freedom, which pervades the feudal institutions, was felt in its strongest energy by the volunteers of the cross, who elected for their chief the most deserving of his peers. Amidst the slaves of Asia, unconscious of the lesson or example, a model of political liberty was introduced : and the laws of the French kingdom are derived from the purest source of equality and justice. Of such laws, the first and indispensable condition is the assent of those, whose obedience they require, and for whose benefit they are designed. No sooner had Godfrey of Bouillon accepted the office of supreme magistrate than he solicited the public and private advice of the Latin pilgrims, who were the best skilled in the statutes and customs of Europe. From these materials, with the council and approbation of the patriarch and barons, of the clergy and laity, Godfrey composed the ASSISE OF JERUSALEM, a precious monument of feudal jurisprudence. The new code, attested by the seals of the king, the patriarch, and the viscount of Jerusalem, was deposited in the holy sepulchre, enriched with the improvements of succeeding times, and respectfully consulted as often as any doubtful question arose in the tribunals of Palestine. With the kingdom and city, all was lost, the fragments of the written law were preserved (A.D. 1099—1369) by jealous tradition and variable practice till the middle of the thirteenth century : the code was restored by the pen of John d'Ibelin, count of Jaffa, one of the principal feudatories; and the final revision was accomplished in the year 1369, for the use of the Latin kingdom of Cyprus.

The justice and freedom of the constitution were maintained by two tribunals of unequal dignity, which were instituted by Godfrey of Bouillon after the conquest of Jerusalem. The king, in person, presiding in the upper court, the court of the barons. Of these, the four most conspicuous were the prince of Galilee, the lord of Sidon and Cæsarea, and the counts of Jaffa and Tripoli, who, perhaps with the constable and marshal, were in a special manner the compeers and

judges of each other. But all the nobles, who held their lands immediately of the crown, were entitled and bound to attend the king's
court; and each baron exercised a similar jurisdiction in the subordinate assemblies of his own feudatories. The connexion of lord
and vassal was honourable and voluntary : reverence was due to the
benefactor, protection to the dependent; but they mutually pledged
their faith to each other ; and the obligation on either side might be >
suspended by neglect or dissolved by injury. The cognizance of marriages and testaments was blended with religion and usurped by the ·
clergy ; but the civil and criminal causes of the nobles, the inheritance
and tenure of their fiefs, formed the proper occupation of the supreme court. Each member was the judge and guardian both of
public and private rights. It was his duty to assert with his tongue
and sword the lawful claims of the lord ; but if an unjust superior
presumed to violate the freedom or property of a vassal, the confederate peers stood forth to maintain his quarrel by word and deed.
They boldly affirmed his innocence and his wrongs ; demanded the
restitution of his liberty or his lands ; suspended, after a fruitless demand, their own service ; rescued their brother from prison ; and employed every weapon in his defence, without offering direct violence to
the person of their lord, which was ever sacred in their eyes. In
their pleadings, replies, and rejoinders, the advocates of the court were
subtile and copious ; but the use of argument and evidence was often
superseded by judicial combat ; and the Assise of Jerusalem admits
in many cases this barbarous institution, which has been slowly abolished by the laws and manners of Europe.

The trial by battle was established in all criminal cases, which
affected the life, or limb, or honour, of any person ; and in all civil
transactions, of or above the value of one mark of silver. It appears,
that in criminal cases the combat was the privilege of the accuser,
who, except in a charge of treason, avenged his personal injury, or the
death of those persons whom he had a right to represent ; but wherever, from the nature of the charge, testimony could be obtained, it
was necessary for him to produce witnesses of the fact. In civil cases,
the combat was not allowed as the means of establishing the claim of
the demandant ; but he was obliged to produce witnesses who had,
or assumed to have, knowledge of the fact. The combat was then
the privilege of the defendant ; because he charged the witness with
an attempt by perjury to take away his right. He came therefore to
be in the same situation as the appellant in criminal cases. It was
not then as a mode of proof that the combat was received, nor as
making negative evidence (according to the supposition of Montesquieu ;) but in every case the right to offer battle was founded on the
right to pursue by arms the redress of an injury ; and the judicial
combat was fought on the same principle, and with the same spirit, as

a private duel. Champions were only allowed to women, and to men maimed or past the age of sixty. The consequence of a defeat was death to the person accused, or to the champion or witness, as well as to the accuser himself; but in civil cases the demandant was punished with infamy and the loss of his suit, while his witness and champion suffered an ignominious death. In many cases it was in the option of the judge to award or to refuse the combat : but two are specified, in which it was the inevitable result of the challenge; if a faithful vassal gave the lie to his compeer, who unjustly claimed any portion of their lord's demesnes; or if an unsuccessful suitor presumed to impeach the judgment and veracity of the court. He might impeach them, but the terms were severe and perilous : in the same day he successively fought *all* the members of the tribunal, even those who had been absent : a single defeat was followed by death and infamy ; and where none could hope for victory, it is highly probable that none would adventure the trial. In the Assise of Jerusalem, the legal subtlety of the count of Jaffa is more laudably employed to elude, than to facilitate, the judicial combat, which he derives from a principle of honour rather than of superstition.

Among the causes which enfranchised the plebeians from the yoke of feudal tyranny, the institution of cities and corporations is one of the most powerful ; and if those of Palestine are coeval with the first crusade, they may be ranked with the most ancient of the Latin world. Many of the pilgrims had escaped from their lords under the banner of the cross ; and it was the policy of the French princes to tempt their stay by the assurance of the rights and privileges of freemen. It is expressly declared in the Assise of Jerusalem, that after instituting, for his knights and barons, the court of peers, in which he presided himself, Godfrey of Bouillon established a second tribunal, in which his person was represented by his viscount. The jurisdiction of this inferior court extended over the burgesses of the kingdom ; and it was composed of a select number of the most discreet and worthy citizens, who were sworn to judge, according to the laws, of the actions and fortunes of their equals. In the conquest and settlement of new cities, the example of Jerusalem was imitated by the kings and their great vassals ; and above thirty similar corporations were founded before the loss of the Holy Land. Another class of subjects, the Syrians, or Oriental Christians, were oppressed by the zeal of the clergy, and protected by the toleration of the state. Godfrey listened to their reasonable prayer, that they might be judged by their own national laws. A third court was instituted for their use, of limited and domestic jurisdiction : the sworn members were Syrians, in blood, language, and religion ; but the office of the president (in Arabic, of the *rais*) was sometimes exercised by the viscount of the city. At an immeasurable distance below the *nobles*, the *burgesses*, and the *strangers*, the Assise of Jerusalem condescends to mention the *villains* and *slaves*, the peasants of the land and the captives of war, who were almost equally considered as the objects of property. The relief or protection of these unhappy men was not esteemed worthy of the care of the legislator; but he diligently provides for the recovery, though not indeed for the punishment, of the fugitives. Like hounds, or hawks, who had strayed from the lawful owner, they might be lost and claimed : the slave and falcon were of the same value; but three slaves, or twelve oxen, were accumulated to equal the price of the war-horse; and a sum of three hundred pieces of gold was fixed, in the age of chivalry, as the equivalent of the more noble animal.

In a style less grave than that of history, I should perhaps compare the emperor Alexius (A.D. 1097—1118) to the jackall, who is said to follow the steps, and to devour the leavings, of the lion. Whatever had been his fears and toils in the passage of the first crusade, they were amply recompensed by the subsequent benefits which he derived from the exploits of the Franks. His dexterity and vigilance secured their first conquest of Nice; and from this threatening station the Turks were compelled to evacuate the neighbourhood of Constantinople. While the crusaders, with blind valour, advanced into the midland counties of Asia, the crafty Greek improved the favourable occasion when the emirs of the sea-coast were recalled to the standard of the sultan. The Turks were driven from the isles of Rhodes and Chios : the cities of Ephesus and Smyrna, of Sardes, Philadelphia, and Laodicea, were restored to the empire, which Alexius enlarged from the Hellespont to the banks of the Mæander, and the rocky shores of Pamphylia. The churches resumed their splendour; the towns were rebuilt and fortified; and the desert country was peopled with colonies of Christians, who were gently removed from the more distant and dangerous frontier. In these paternal cares, we may forgive Alexius, if he forgot the deliverance of the holy sepulchre; but, by the Latins, he was stigmatized with the foul reproach of treason and desertion. They had sworn fidelity and obedience to his throne; but *he* had promised to assist their enterprise in person, or, at least, with his troops and treasures; his base retreat dissolved their obligations; and the sword, which had been the instrument of their victory, was the pledge and title of their just independence. It does not appear that the emperor attempted to revive his obsolete claims over the kingdom of Jerusalem; but the borders of Cilicia and Syria were more recent in his possession, and more accessible to his arms. The great army of the crusaders was annihilated or dispersed; the principality of Antioch was left without a head, by the surprise and captivity of Bohemond : his ransom had oppressed him with a heavy debt; and his Norman followers were insufficient to repel the hostilis of the Greeks and Turks. In this distress, Bohemond embraced a magnanimous resolution, of leaving the defence of Antioch to his kinsman, the faithful Tancred; of arming the West against the Byzantine empire, and of executing the design which he inherited from the lessons and example of his father Guiscard. His embarkation was clandestine: and if we may credit a tale of the princess Anna, he passed the hostile sea, closely secreted in a coffin. But his reception in France was dignified by the public applause, and his marriage with the king's daughter; his return was glorious, since the bravest spirits of the age enlisted under his veteran command; and he repassed the Hadriatic at the head of 5,000 horse and 40,000 foot, assembled from the most remote climates of Europe. The strength of Durazzo, and prudence of Alexius, the progress of famine, and approach of winter, eluded his ambitious hopes; and the venal confederates were seduced from his standard. A treaty of peace suspended the fears of the Greeks; and they were finally delivered by the death of an adversary, whom neither oaths could bind, nor dangers could appal, nor prosperity could satiate. His children succeeded to the principality of Antioch: but the boundaries were strictly defined, the homage was clearly stipulated, and the cities of Tarsus and Malmistra were restored to the Byzantine emperors. Of the coast of Anatolia, they possessed the entire circuit from Trebizond to the Syrian gates. The Seljukian dynasty of Roum was separated on all sides from the sea and their Mussulman brethren; the power of the sultans was shaken by the victories, and even the defeats, of the Franks; and after the loss of Nice, they removed their throne to Cogni or Iconium, an obscure and inland town above 300 miles from Constantinople. Instead of trembling for their capital, the Comnenian princes waged an offensive war against the Turks, and the first crusade prevented the fall of the declining empire.

In the twelfth century, three great emigrations marched by land from the West to the relief of Palestine. The soldiers and pilgrims o' Lombardy, France, and Germany, were excited by the example and success of the first crusade (A.D. 1101). Forty-eight years (A.D. 1147) after the deliverance of the holy sepulchre, the emperor and the French king, Conrad the third and Louis the seventh, undertook the second crusade to support the falling fortunes of the Latins. A grand division of the third crusade was led (A.D. 1189) by the emperor Frederic Barbarossa, who sympathized with his brothers of France and England in the common loss of Jerusalem. These three expeditions may be compared in their resemblance of the greatness of numbers, their passage through the Greek empire, and the nature and event of their Turkish warfare, and a brief parallel may save the repetition of a tedious narrative. However splendid it may seem, a regular story of the crusades would exhibit the perpetual return of the same causes and effects; and the frequent attempts for the defence or recovery o' the Holy Land, would appear so many faint and unsuccessful copies of the original.

I. Of the swarms that so closely trod in the footsteps of the first pilgrims, the chiefs were equal in rank, though unequal in fame and merit, to Godfrey of Bouillon and his fellow-adventurers. At their head were displayed the banners of the dukes of Burgundy, Bavaria, and Aquitain : the first a descendant of Hugh Capet, the second a father of the Brunswick line : the archbishop of Milan, a temporal prince, transported, for the benefit of the Turks, the treasures and ornaments of his church and palace ; and the veteran crusaders, Hugh the Great and Stephen of Chartres, returned to consummate their unfinished vow. The huge and disorderly bodies of their followers moved forwards in two columns ; and if the first consisted of 260,000 persons, the second might possibly amount to 60,000 horse, and 100,000 foot. The armies of the second crusade might have claimed the conquest of Asia : the nobles of France and Germany were animated by the presence of their sovereigns ; and both the rank and personal characters of Conrad and Louis, gave a dignity to their cause, and a discipline to their force, which might be vainly expected from the feudatory chiefs. The cavalry of the emperor, and that of the king, was each composed of 70,000 knights and their immediate attendants in the field ; and if the light-armed troops, the peasant infantry, the women and children, the priests and monks, be rigorously excluded, the full account will scarcely be satisfied with 400,000 souls. The West, from Rome to Britain, was called into action ; the king of Poland and Bohemia obeyed the summons of Conrad ; and it is affirmed by the Greeks and Latins, that in the passage of a strait or river, the Byzantine agents, after a tale of 900,000, desisted from the endless and formidable computation. In the third crusade, as the French and English preferred the navigation of the Mediterranean, the host of Frederic Barbarossa was less numerous. Fifteen thousand knights, and as many squires, were the flower of the German chivalry : 60,000 horse, and 100,000 foot, were mustered by the emperor in the plains of Hungary ; and after such repetitions we shall no longer be startled at the 600,000 pilgrims, which credulity has ascribed to this last emigration. Such extravagant reckonings prove only the astonishment of contemporaries ; but their astonishment most strongly bears testimony to the existence of an enormous though indefinite multitude. The Greeks might applaud their superior knowledge of the arts and stratagems of war, but they confessed the strength and courage of the French cavalry and the infantry of the Germans ; and the strangers are described as an iron race, of gigantic stature, who darted fire from their eyes, and spilt blood like water on the ground. Under the banners of Conrad, a troop of females rode in the attitude and armour of men ; and the chief of these Amazons, from her gilt spurs and buskins, obtained the epithet of the Golden-footed Dame.

II, The numbers and character of the strangers was an object of terror to the effeminate Greeks, and the sentiment of fear is nearly allied to that of hatred. This aversion was suspended or softened by the apprehension of the Turkish power; and the invectives of the Latins will not bias our more candid belief, that the emperor Alexius dissembled their insolence, eluded their hostilities, counselled their rashness, and opened to their ardour the road of pilgrimage and conquest. But when the Turks had been driven from Nice and the sea coast, when the Byzantine princes no longer dreaded the distant sultans of Cogni, they felt with purer indignation the free and frequent passage of the Western Barbarians, who violated the majesty, and endangered the safety, of the empire. The second and third crusades were undertaken under the reign of Manuel Comnenus and Isaac Angelus, Of the former, the passions were always impetuous, and often malevolent; and the natural union of a cowardly and a mischievous temper was exemplified in the latter, who, without merit or mercy, could punish a tyrant, and occupy his throne. It was secretly, and perhaps tacitly, resolved by the prince and people to destroy, or at least to discourage, the pilgrims, by every species of injury and oppression; and their want of prudence and discipline continually afforded the pretence or the opportunity. The Western monarchs had stipulated a safe passage and fair market in the country of their Christian brethren; the treaty had been ratified by oaths and hostages; and the poorest soldier of Frederic's army was furnished with three marks of silver to defray his expences on the road. But every engagement was violated by treachery and injustice; and the complaints of the Latins are attested by the honest confession of a Greek historian, who ha: dared to prefer truth to his country. Instead of an hospitable reception, the gates of the cities, both in Europe and Asia, were closely barred against the crusaders; and the scanty pittance of food was let down in baskets from the walls. Experience or foresight might excuse this timid jealousy; but the common duties of humanity prohibited the mixture of chalk, or other poisonous ingredients, in the bread; and should Manuel be acquitted of any foul connivance, he is guilty of coining base money for the purpose of trading with the pilgrims. In every step of their march they were stopped or misled: the governors had private orders to fortify the passes and break down the bridges against them: the stragglers were pillaged and murdered . the soldiers and horses were pierced in the woods by arrows from an invisible hand; the sick were burnt in their beds: and the dead bodies were hung on gibbets along the highways. These injuries exasperated the champions of the cross, who were not endowed with evangelical patience; and the Byzantine princes, who had provoked the unequal conflict, promoted the embarkation and march of these formidable guests. On the verge of the Turkish frontier Barbarossa spared the guilty Philadelphia, rewarded the hospitable Laodicea, and deplored the hard necessity that had stained his sword with any drops of Chris tian blood. In their intercourse with the monarchs of Germany and France, the pride of the Greeks was exposed to an anxious trial. They might boast that on the first interview the seat of Louis was a low stool, beside the throne of Manuel; but no sooner had the French king transported his army beyond the Bosphorus, than he refused the offer of a second conference, unless his brother would meet him on equal terms, either on the sea or land. With Conrad and Frederic, the ceremonial was still nicer and more difficult: like the successors of Constantine, they styled themselves emperors of the Romans; and firmly maintained the purity of their title and dignity. The first of these representatives of Charlemagne would only converse with Manuel on horseback in the open field; the second, by passing the Helles pont rather than the Bosphorus, declined the view of Constantinople and its sovereign. An emperor, who had been crowned at Rome, was reduced in the Greek epistles to the .humble appellation of *Rex*, or prince of the Alemanni; and the vain and feeble Angelus affected to be ignorant of the name of one of the greatest men and monarchs of the age. While they viewed with hatred and suspicion the Latin pil grims, the Greek emperors maintained a strict, though secret, alliance with the Turks and Saracens. Isaac Angelus complained, that by his friendship for the great Saladin he had incurred the enmity of the Franks; and a mosque was founded at Constantinople for the public exercise of the religion of Mahomet.*

III. The swarms that followed the first crusade, were destroyed in Anatolia by famine, pestilence, and the Turkish arrows: and the princes only escaped with some squadrons of horse to accomplish their lamentable pilgrimage. A just opinion may be formed of their know ledge and humanity; of their knowledge, from the design of subduing Persia and Chorasan in their way to Jerusalem; of their humanity, from the massacre of the Christian people, a friendly city, who came out to meet them with palms and crosses in their hands. The arms of Conrad and Louis were less cruel and imprudent; but the event of the second crusade was still more ruinous to Christendom; and the Greek Manuel is accused by his own subjects of giving seasonable intelligence to the sultan, and treacherous guides to the Latin princes. Instead of crushing the common foe, by a double attack at the same time but on different sides, the Germans were urged by emulation, and the French were retarded by jealousy. Louis had scarcely passed the Bosphorus when he was met by the returning emperor, who had lost the greatest part of his army in glorious, but unsuccessful, actions on the banks of the Mæander. The contrast of the pomp of his rival

* In the Epist. of Innoc. III. (xiii. 184), and the Hist. of Bohadin (p. 129), see the views of a pope and a cadi on this *singular* toleration.

hastened the retreat of Conrad : the desertion of his independent vassals reduced him to his hereditary troops ; and he borrowed some Greek vessels to execute by sea the pilgrimage of Palestine. Without studying the lessons of experience, or the nature of war, the king of France advanced through the same country to a similar fate. The vanguard, which bore the royal banner and the oriflamme of St. Denys,* had doubled their march with rash and inconsiderate speed ; and the rear which the king commanded in person no longer found their companions in the evening camp. In darkness and disorder they were encompassed, assaulted, and overwhelmed by the innumerable host of Turks, who in the art of war were superior to the Christians of the twelfth century. Louis, who climbed a tree in the general discomfiture, was saved by his own valour and the ignorance of his adversaries ; and with the dawn of day he escaped alive, but almost alone, to the camp of the vanguard. But instead of pursuing his expedition by land, he was rejoiced to shelter the relics of his army in the friendly seaport of Satalia. From thence he embarked for Antioch ; but so penurious was the supply of Greek vessels, that they could only afford room for his knights and nobles ; and the plebeian crowd of infantry was left to perish at the foot of the Pamphylian hills. The emperor and the king embraced and wept at Jerusalem ; their martial trains, the remnant of mighty armies, were joined to the Christian powers of Syria, and a fruitless siege of Damascus was the final effort of the second crusade. Conrad and Louis embarked for Europe with the personal fame of piety and courage ; but the Orientals had braved these potent monarchs of the Franks, with whose names and military forces they had been so often threatened. Perhaps they had still more to fear from the veteran genius of Frederic the first, who in his youth had served in Asia, under his uncle Conrad. Forty campaigns in Germany and Italy had taught Barbarossa to command ; and his soldiers, even the princes of the empire, were accustomed under his reign to obey. As soon as he lost sight of Philadelphia and Laodicea, the last cities of the Greek frontier, he plunged into the salt and barren desert, a land (says the historian) of horror and tribulation. During twenty days, every step of his fainting and sickly march was besieged by the innumerable hordes of Turkmans, whose numbers and fury seemed after each defeat to multiply and inflame. The emperor continued to struggle and to suffer ; and such was the measure of his calamities, that when he reached the gates of Iconium, no more than 1000 knights were able to serve on horseback. By a sudden and resolute assault, he defeated the guards, and stormed the capital of the sultan, who humbly sued for pardon and peace. The road was

---

* As counts of Vexin, the kings of France were the vassals and advocates of the monastery of St. Denys. The saint's peculiar banner, which they received from the abbot, was of a square form, and a red or *flaming* colour. The *oriflamme* appeared at the head of the French armies from the xiith to the xvth century.

now open, and Frederic advanced in a career of triumph, till he was unfortunately drowned in a petty torrent of Cilicia. The remainder of his Germans was consumed by sickness and desertion ; and the emperor's son expired with the greatest part of his Swabian vassals at the siege of Acre. Among the Latin heroes, Godfrey of Bouillon and Frederic Barbarossa alone could achieve the passage of the Lesser Asia ; yet even their success was a warning ; and in the last and most experienced age of the crusades, every nation preferred the sea to the toils and perils of an inland expedition.

The enthusiasm of the first crusade is a natural and simple event, while hope was fresh, danger untried, and enterprise congenial to the spirit of the times. But the obstinate perseverance of Europe may indeed excite our pity and admiration ; that no instruction should have been drawn from constant and adverse experience ; that the same confidence should have repeatedly grown from the same failures ; that six succeeding generations should have rushed headlong down the precipice that was open before them ; and that men of every condition should have staked their public and private fortunes, on the desperate adventure of possessing or recovering a tomb-stone 2000 miles from their country. In a period of two centuries after the council of Clermont, each spring and summer produced a new emigration of pilgrim warriors for the defence of the Holy Land ; but the seven great armaments or crusades were excited by some impending or recent calamity : the nations were moved by the authority of their pontiffs, and the example of their kings : their zeal was kindled, and their reason was silenced, by the voice of their holy orators ; and among these, Bernard, the monk, or the saint, may claim (A.D. 1091—1153) the most honourable place. About eight years before the first conquest of Jerusalem, he was born of a noble family, in Burgundy ; at the age of three-and-twenty, he buried himself in the monastery of Citeaux, then in the primitive fervour of the institution ; at the end of two years he led forth her third colony, or daughter, to the valley of Clairvaux in Champagne ; and was content, till the hour of his death, with the humble station of Abbot of his own community. A philosophic age has abolished, with too liberal and indiscriminate disdain, the honours of these spiritual heroes. The meanest among them are distinguished by some energies of the mind ; they were at least superior to their votaries and disciples ; and, in the race of superstition, they attained the prize for which such numbers contended. In speech, in writing, in action, Bernard stood high above his rivals and contemporaries ; his compositions are not devoid of wit and eloquence ; and he seems to have preserved as much reason and humanity as may be reconciled with the character of a saint. In secular life, he would have shared the seventh part of a private inheritance ; by a vow of poverty and penance, by closing his eyes against the visible world, by the refusal of all ecclesiastical dignities, the abbot of Clairvaux became the oracle of Europe, and the founder of one hundred and sixty convents. Princes and pontiffs trembled at the freedom of his apostolical censures; France, England, and Milan, consulted and obeyed his judgment in a schism of the church : the debt was repaid by the gratitude of Innocent the second ; and his successor Eugenius the third was the friend and disciple of the holy Bernard. It was in the proclamation of the second crusade that he shone as the missionary and prophet of God, who called the nations to the defence of his holy sepulchre. At the parliament of Vezelay he spoke before the king ; and Louis the seventh, with his nobles, received their crosses from his hand. The abbot of Clairvaux then marched to the less easy conquest of the emperor Conrad : a phlegmatic people, ignorant of his language, was transported by the pathetic vehemence of his tone and gestures ; and his progress, from Constance to Cologne, was the triumph of eloquence and zeal. Bernard applauds his own success in the depopulation of Europe ; affirms that cities and castles were emptied of their inhabitants ; and computes, that only one man was left behind for the consolation of seven widows. The blind fanatics were desirous of electing him for their general ; but the example of the hermit Peter was before his eyes ; and while he assured the Crusaders of the divine favour, he prudently declined a military command, in which failure and victory would have been almost equally disgraceful to his character. Yet, after the calamitous event, the abbot of Clairvaux was loudly accused as a false prophet, the author of the public and private mourning ; his enemies exulted, his friends blushed, and his apology was slow and unsatisfactory. He justifies his obedience to the commands of the pope ; expatiates on the mysterious ways of providence ; imputes the misfortunes of the pilgrims to their own sins ; and modestly insinuates, that his mission had been approved by signs and wonders. Had the fact been certain, the argument would be decisive ; and his faithful disciples, who enumerate twenty or thirty miracles in a day, appeal to the public assemblies of France and Germany, in which they were performed. At the present hour, such prodigies will not obtain credit beyond the precincts of Clairvaux ; but in the preternatural cures of the blind, the lame, and the sick, who were presented to the man of God, it is impossible for us to ascertain the separate shares of accident, of fancy, of imposture, and of fiction.

Omnipotence itself cannot escape the murmurs of its discordant votaries ; since the same dispensation which was applauded as a deliverance in Europe, was deplored, and perhaps arraigned, as a calamity in Asia. After the loss of Jerusalem, the Syrian fugitives diffused their consternation and sorrow : Bagdad mourned in the dust ; the cadi Zeineddin of Damascus tore his beard in the caliph's presence ; and the whole divan shed tears at his melancholy tale. But the con-

manders of the faithful could only weep ; they were themselves captives in the hands of the Turks ; some temporal power was restored to
the last age of the Abbassides ; but their humble ambition was confined to Bagdad and the adjacent province. Their tyrants, the Seljukian sultans, had followed the common law of the Asiatic dynasties,
the unceasing round of valour, greatness, discord, degeneracy, and
decay : their spirit and power were unequal to the defence of religion ;
and, in his distant realm of Persia, the Christians were strangers to the
name and the arms of Sangier, the last hero of his race. While the
sultans were involved in the silken web of the harem, the pious task
was undertaken by their slaves, the Atabeks ; a Turkish name, which,
like the Byzantine patricians, may be translated by Father of the
Prince. Ascansar, a valiant Turk, had been the favourite of Malek
Shaw, from whom he received the privilege of standing on the right
hand of the throne ; but, in the civil wars that ensued on the monarch's
death, he lost his head and the government of Aleppo. His domestic
emirs persevered in their attachment to his son Zenghi (A.D. 1127—
1145), who proved his first arms against the Franks in the defeat of
Antioch : thirty campaigns in the service of the caliph and sultan
established his military fame ; and he was invested with the command
of Mosul, as the only champion that could avenge the cause of the
prophet. The public hope was not disappointed : after a siege of
twenty-five days, he stormed the city of Edessa, and recovered from
the Franks their conquests beyond the Euphrates : the martial tribes
of Curdistan were subdued by the independent sovereign of Mosul
and Aleppo : his soldiers were taught to behold the camp as their only
country ; they trusted to his liberality for their rewards ; and their absent families were protected by the vigilance of Zenghi. At the head
of these veterans, his son Noureddin gradually (A.D. 1145—1174)
united the Mahometan powers ; added the kingdom of Damascus to
that of Aleppo, and waged a long and successful war against the Christians of Syria ; he spread his ample reign from the Tigris to the Nile,
and the Abbassides rewarded their faithful servant with all the titles
and prerogatives of royalty. The Latins themselves were compelled to
own the wisdom and courage, and even the justice and piety, of this
implacable adversary. In his life and government, the holy warrior
revived the zeal and simplicity of the first caliphs. Gold and silk were
banished from his palace ; the use of wine from his dominions, the
public revenue was scrupulously applied to the public service ; and the
frugal household of Noureddin was maintained from his legitimate
share of the spoil, which he vested in the purchase of a private estate.
His favourite Sultana sighed for some female object of expence.
" Alas," replied the king, " I fear God, and am no more than the
treasurer of the Moslems. Their property I cannot alienate ; but I
still possess three shops in the city of Hems : these you may take ;

and these alone can I bestow." His chamber of justice was the terror of the great and the refuge of the poor. Some years after the Sultan's death, an oppressed subject called aloud in the streets of Damascus, " O Noureddin, Noureddin, where art thou now? Arise, arise, to pity and protect us!" A tumult was apprehended, and a living tyrant trembled at the name of a departed monarch.

By the arms of the Turks and Franks, the Fatimites had been deprived of Syria. In Egypt, the decay of their character and influence was still more essential. Yet they were still revered as the descendants and successors of the prophet ; they maintained their invisible state in the palace of Cairo ; and their person was seldom violated by the profane eyes of subjects or strangers. The Latin ambassadors have described their own introduction through a series of gloomy passages and glittering porticoes : the scene was enlivened by the warbling of birds and the murmur of fountains ; it was enriched by a display of rich furniture, and rare animals : of the Imperial treasures, something was shown, and much was supposed ; and the long order of unfolding doors was guarded by black soldiers and domestic eunuchs. The sanctuary of the presence-chamber was veiled with a curtain ; and the vizir, who conducted the ambassadors, laid aside his scymetar, and prostrated himself three times on the ground ; the veil was then removed ; and they beheld the commander of the faithful, who signified his pleasure to the first slave of the throne. But this slave was his master : the vizirs or sultans had usurped the supreme administration of Egypt ; the claims of the rival candidates were decided by arms ; and the name of the most worthy, of the strongest, was inserted in the royal patent of command. The factions of Dargham and Shawer alternately expelled each other from the capital and country ; and the weaker side implored the dangerous protection of the sultan of Damascus or the king of Jerusalem, the perpetual enemies of the sect and monarchy of the Fatimites. By his arms and religion, the Turk was most formidable ; but the Frank, in an easy direct march, could advance from Gaza to the Nile ; while the intermediate situation of his realm compelled the troops of Noureddin to wheel round the skirts of Arabia, a long and painful circuit, which exposed them to thirst, fatigue, and the burning winds of the desert. The secret zeal and ambition of the Turkish prince aspired to reign in Egypt under the name of the Abbassides ; but the restoration of the suppliant Shawer was the ostensible motive of the first expedition ; and the success was (A.D. 1163) entrusted to the emir Shiracouh, a valiant and veteran commander. Dargham was oppressed and slain ; but the ingratitude, the jealousy, the just apprehensions, of his more fortunate rival, soon provoked him to invite the king of Jerusalem to deliver Egypt from his insolent benefactors. To this union, the forces of Shiracouh were unequal ; he relinquished the premature conquest ;

and the evacuation of Belbeis or Pelusium was the condition of his safe retreat. As the Turks defiled before the enemy, and their general closed the rear, with a vigilant eye, and a battle-axe in his hand, a Frank presumed to ask him if he were not afraid of an attack? "It is doubtless in your power to begin the attack," replied the intrepid emir ; "but rest assured, that not one of my soldiers will go to paradise till he has sent an infidel to hell." His report of the riches of the land, the effeminacy of the natives, and the disorders of the government, revived the hopes of Noureddin ; the caliph of Bagdad applauded the pious design ; and Shiracouh descended into Egypt a second time with 12,000 Turks and 11,000 Arabs. Yet his forces were still inferior to the confederate armies of the Franks and Saracens ; and I can discern an unusual degree of military art, in his passage of the Nile, his retreat into Thebais, his masterly evolutions in the battle of Babain, the surprise of Alexandria, and his marches and counter-marches in the flats and valley of Egypt, from the tropic to the sea. His conduct was seconded by the courage of his troops, and on the eve of action a Mameluke exclaimed, "If we cannot wrest Egypt from the Christian dogs, why do we not renounce the honours and rewards of the sultan, and retire to labour with the peasants, or to spin with the females of the harem ?" Yet, after all his efforts in the field, after the obstinate defence of Alexandria by his nephew Saladin, an honorable capitulation and retreat concluded the second enterprise of Shiracouh ; and Noureddin reserved his abilities for a third and more propitious occasion. It was soon offered by the ambition and avarice of Almaric or Amaury, king of Jerusalem, who had imbibed the pernicious maxim, that no faith should be kept with the enemies of God. A religious warrior, the great master of the hospital, encouraged him to proceed ; the emperor of Constantinople either gave, or promised, a fleet to act with the armies of Syria ; and the perfidious Christian, unsatisfied with spoil and subsidy, aspired to the conquest of Egypt. In this emergency, the Moslems turned their eyes towards the sultan of Damascus ; the vizir, whom danger encompassed on all sides, yielded to their unanimous wishes, and Noureddin seemed to be tempted by the fair offer of one third of the revenue of the kingdom. The Franks were already at the gates of Cairo ; but the suburbs, the old city, were burnt on their approach ; they were deceived by an insidious negociation ; and their vessels were unable to surmount the barriers of the Nile. They prudently declined a contest with the Turks, in the midst of an hostile country ; and Amaury retired into Palestine, with the shame and reproach that always adhere to unsuccessful injustice. After this deliverance, Shiracouh was invested (A.D. 1169) with a robe of honour, which he soon stained with the blood of the unfortunate Shawer. For a while, the Turkish emirs condescended to hold the office of vizir ; but this foreign conquest precipitated the fall of the Fatimites themselves; and the bloodless change was accomplished by a message and a word. The caliphs had been degraded by their own weakness and the tyranny of the vizirs : their subjects blushed, when the descendant and successor of the prophet presented his naked hand to the rude gripe of a Latin ambassador; they wept when he sent the hair of his women, a sad emblem of their grief and terror, to excite the pity of the sultan of Damascus. By the command of Noureddin (A.D. 1171), and the sentence of the doctors, the holy names of Abubeker, Omar, and Othman, were solemnly restored : the caliph Mosthadi, of Bagdad, was acknowledged in the public prayers as the true commander of the faithful ; and the green livery of the sons of Ali was exchanged for the black colour of the Abbassides. The last of his race, the caliph Adhed, who survived only ten days, expired in happy ignorance of his fate : his treasures secured the loyalty of the soldiers and silenced the murmurs of the sectaries; and in all subsequent revolutions, Egypt has never departed from the orthodox tradition of the Moslems.

The hilly country beyond the Tigris is occupied by the pastoral tribes of the Curds : a people hardy, strong, savage, impatient of the yoke, addicted to rapine, and tenacious of the government of their national chiefs. The resemblance of name, situation, and manners, seem to identify them with the Carducians of the Greeks ; and they still defend against the Ottoman Porte the antique freedom which they asserted against the successors of Cyrus. Poverty and ambition prompted them to embrace the profession of mercenary soldiers : the service of his father and uncle prepared the reign of the great Saladin (A.D. 1171—1193) ; and the son of Job or Ayub, a simple Curd, magnanimously smiled at his pedigree, which flattery deduced from the Arabian caliphs. So unconscious was Noureddin of the impending ruin of his house, that he constrained the reluctant youth to follow his uncle Shiracouh into Egypt : his military character was established by the defence of Alexandria ; and if we may believe the Latins, he solicited and obtained from the Christian general the *profane* honours of knighthood. On the death of Shiracouh, the office of grand visir was bestowed on Saladin, as the youngest and least powerful of the emirs ; but with the advice of his father, whom he invited to Cairo, his genius obtained the ascendant over his equals, and attached the army to his person and interest. While Noureddin lived, these ambitious Curds were the most humble of his slaves ; and the indiscreet murmurs of the divan were silenced by the prudent Ayub, who loudly protested that at the command of the sultan he himself would lead his son in chains to the foot of the throne. " Such language," he added in private, " was prudent and proper in an assembly of your rivals ; but we are now above fear and obedience ; and the threats of Noureddin shall not extort the tribute of a sugar-cane."

His seasonable death relieved them from the odious and doubtful conflict : his son, a minor of eleven years of age, was left for a while to the emirs of Damascus ; and the new lord of Egypt was decorated by the caliph with every title that could sanctify his usurpation in the eyes of the people. Nor was Saladin long content with the possession of Egypt : he despoiled the Christians of Jerusalem, and the Atabeks of Damascus, Aleppo, and Diarbekir ; Mecca and Medina acknowledged him for their temporal protector ; his brother subdued the distant regions of Yemen, or the happy Arabia ; and at the hour of his death, his empire was spread from the African Tripoli to the Tigris, and from the Indian ocean to the mountains of Armenia. In the judgment of his character, the reproaches of treason and ingratitude strike forcibly on *our* minds, impressed, as they are, with the principle and experience of law and loyalty. But his ambition may in some measure be excused by the revolutions of Asia, which had erased every notion of legitimate succession ; by the recent example of the Atabeks themselves ; by his reverence to the son of his benefactor, his humane and generous behaviour to the collateral branches ; by *their* incapacity and *his* merit ; by the approbation of the caliph, the sole source of all legitimate power ; and, above all, by the wishes and interests of the people, whose happiness is the first object of government.   In *his* virtues, and in those of his patron, they admired the singular union of the hero and the saint ; for both Noureddin and Saladin are ranked among the Mahometan saints ; and the constant meditation of the holy war appears to have shed a serious and sober colour over their lives and actions.   The youth of the latter was addicted to wine and women : but his aspiring spirit soon renounced the temptations of pleasure, for the graver follies of fame and dominion ; the garment of Saladin was of coarse woollen ; water was his only drink ; and while he emulated the temperance, he surpassed the chastity, of his Arabian prophet. Both in faith and practice he was a rigid Mussulman ; he ever deplored that the defence of religion had not allowed him to accomplish the pilgrimage of Mecca ; but at the stated hours, five times each day, the sultan devoutly prayed with his brethren : the involuntary omission of fasting was scrupulously repaid ; and his perusal of the Koran on horseback between the approaching armies, may be quoted as a proof, however ostentatious, of piety and courage. The superstitious doctrine of the sect of Shafei was the only study that he deigned to encourage : the poets were safe in his contempt ; but all profane science was the object of his aversion ; and a philosopher, who had vented some speculative novelties, was seized and strangled by the command of the royal saint. The justice of his divan was accessible to the meanest suppliants against himself or his ministers ; and it was only for a kingdom that Saladin would deviate from the rule of equity. While the descendants of Seljuk and Zenghi held his stirrup and smoothed his garments, he was affable and patient with the meanest of his servants. So boundless was his liberality, that he distributed 12,000 horses at the siege of Acre; and, at the time of his death, no more than forty-seven drachms of silver, and one piece of gold coin were found in the treasury; yet in a martial reign, the tributes were diminished, and the wealthy citizens enjoyed without fear or danger, the fruits of their industry. Egypt, Syria, and Arabia, were adorned by the royal foundations of hospitals, colleges, and mosques, and Cairo was fortified with a wall and citadel; but his works were consecrated to public use, nor did the sultan indulge himself in a garden or palace of private luxury. In a fanatic age, himself a fanatic, the genuine virtues of Saladin commanded the esteem of the Christians : the emperor of Germany gloried in his friendship; the Greek emperor solicited his alliance; and the conquest of Jerusalem diffused, and perhaps magnified, his fame both in the East and West.

During its short existence, the kingdom of Jerusalem was supported by the discord of the Turks and Saracens; and both the Fatimite caliphs and the sultans of Damascus were tempted to sacrifice the cause of their religion to the meaner considerations of private and present advantage. But the powers of Egypt, Syria, and Arabia, were now united by an hero, whom nature and fortune had armed against the Christians. All without now bore the most threatening aspect; and all was feeble and hollow in the internal state of Jerusalem. After the two first Baldwins, the brother and cousin of Godfrey of Bouillon, the sceptre devolved by female succession to Melisenda, daughter of the second Baldwin, and her husband Fulk, count of Anjou, the father, by a former marriage, of our English Plantagenets. Their two sons, Baldwin the third and Amaury, waged a strenuous, and not unsuccessful, war against the infidels; but the son of Amaury, Baldwin the fourth, was deprived, by the leprosy, a gift of the crusades, of the faculties both of mind and body. His sister, Sybilla, the mother of Baldwin the fifth, was his natural heiress : after the suspicious death of her child, she crowned her second husband, Guy of Lusignan, a prince of handsome person, but of such base renown, that his own brother Jeffrey was heard to exclaim, " Since they have made *him* a king, surely they would have made *me* a god !" The choice was generally blamed; and the most powerful vassal, Raymond count of Tripoli, who had been excluded from the succession and regency, entertained an implacable hatred against the king, and exposed his honour and conscience to the temptations of the sultan. Such were the guardians of the holy city; a leper, a child, a woman, a coward, and a traitor : yet its fate was delayed twelve years by some supplies from Europe, by the valour of the military orders, and by the distant or domestic avocations of their great enemy. At length, on every side the sinking state was encircled and pressed by an hostile line; and the truce was violated by the

Franks, whose existence it protected. A soldier of fortune, Reginald of Chatillon, had seized a fortress on the edge of the desert, from whence he pillaged the caravans, insulted Mahomet, and threatened the cities of Mecca and Medina. Saladin condescended to complain; rejoiced in the denial of justice; and at the head of 80,000 horse and foot, invaded the Holy Land. The choice of Tiberias for his first siege was suggested by the count of Tripoli, to whom it belonged; and the king of Jerusalem was persuaded to drain his garrisons, and to arm his people for the relief of that important place. By the advice of the perfidious Raymond, the Christians were betrayed into a camp destitute of water : he fled on the first onset with the curses of both nations : Lusignan was overthrown (A.D. 1187. July 3) with the loss of 30,000 men ; and the wood of the true cross, a dire misfortune ! was left in the power of the infidels. The royal captive was conducted to the tent of Saladin ; and as he fainted with thirst and terror, the generous victor presented him with a cup of sherbet cooled in snow, without suffering his companion, Reginald of Chatillon, to partake of this pledge of hospitality and pardon. "The person and dignity of a king," said the sultan, "are sacred ; but this impious robber must instantly acknowledge the prophet, whom he has blasphemed, or meet the death which he has so often deserved." On the proud or conscientious refusal of the Christian warrior, Saladin struck him on the head with his scymetar, and Reginald was dispatched by the guards. The trembling Lusignan was sent to Damascus to an honourable prison and speedy ransom; but the victory was stained by the execution of 230 knights of the hospital, the intrepid champions and martyrs of their faith. The kingdom was left without a head ; and of the two grand masters of the military orders, the one was slain and the other was a prisoner. From all the cities, both of the sea-coast and the inland country, the garrisons had been drawn away for this fatal field : Tyre and Tripoli alone could escape the rapid inroad of Saladin ; and three months after the battle of Tiberias he appeared in arms before the gates of Jerusalem.

He might expect, that the siege of a city, so venerable on earth and in heaven, so interesting to Europe and Asia, would rekindle the last sparks of enthusiasm ; and that, of 60,000 Christians, every man would be a soldier, and every soldier a candidate for martyrdom. But queen Sybilla trembled for herself and her captive husband ; and the barons and knights, who had escaped from the sword and chains of the Turks, displayed the same factious and selfish spirit in the public ruin. The most numerous portion of the inhabitants were composed of the Greek and Oriental Christians, whom experience had taught to prefer the Mahometan before the Latin yoke ; and the holy sepulchre attracted a base and needy crowd, without arms or courage, who subsisted only on the charity of the pilgrims. Some feeble and hasty efforts were made for the defence of Jerusalem ; but in the space of fourteen (A.D.

1187. Oct. 2) days, a victorious army drove back the sallies of the besieged, planted their engines, opened the wall to the breadth of fifteen cubits, applied their scaling-ladders, and erected on the breach twelve banners of the prophet and the sultan. It was in vain that a bare-foot procession of the queen, the women, and the monks, implored the Son of God to save his tomb and his inheritance from impious violation. Their sole hope was in the mercy of the conqueror, and to their first suppliant deputation that mercy was sternly denied. " He had sworn to avenge the patience and long-suffering of the Moslems ; the hour of forgiveness was elapsed, and the moment has now arrived to expiate in blood, the innocent blood which had been spilt by Godfrey and the first crusaders." But a desperate and successful struggle of the Franks admonished the sultan that his triumph was not yet secure ; he listened with reverence to a solemn adjuration in the name of the common Father of mankind ; and a sentiment of human sympathy mollified the rigour of fanaticism and conquest. He consented to accept the city, and to spare the inhabitants. The Greek and Oriental Christians were permitted to live under his dominion ; but it was stipulated, that in forty days all the Franks and Latins should evacuate Jerusalem, and be safely conducted to the sea-ports of Syria and Egypt ; that ten pieces of gold should be paid for each man, five for each woman, and one for every child ; and that those who were unable to purchase their freedom should be detained in perpetual slavery. Of some writers it is a favourite and invidious theme to compare the humanity of Saladin with the massacre of the first crusade. The difference would be merely personal ; but we should not forget that the Christians had offered to capitulate, and that the Mahometans of Jerusalem sustained the last extremities of an assault and storm. Justice is indeed due to the fidelity with which the Turkish conqueror fulfilled the conditions of the treaty ; and he may be deservedly praised for the glance of pity which he cast on the misery of the vanquished. Instead of a rigorous exaction of his debt, he accepted a sum of 30,000 byzants, for the ransom of 7000 poor ; 2000 or 3000 more were dismissed by his gratuitous clemency : and the number of slaves was reduced to 11,000 or 14,000 persons. In his interview with the queen, his words, and even his tears, suggested the kindest consolations ; his liberal alms were distributed among those who had been made orphans or widows by the fortune of war ; and while the knights of the hospital were in arms against him, he allowed their more pious brethren to continue during the term of a year, the care and the service of the sick. In these acts of mercy the virtue of Saladin deserves our admiration and love : he was above the necessity of dissimulation, and his stern fanaticism would have prompted him to dissemble, rather than to affect, this profane compassion for the enemies of the Koran. After Jerusalem had been delivered from the presence of the strangers, the sultan made his triumphant entry, his banners waving in the wind and to the harmony of martial music. The great mosque of Omar, which had been converted into a church, was again consecrated to one God and his prophet Mahomet; the walls and pavement were purified with rosewater; and a pulpit, the labour of Noureddin, was erected in the sanctuary. But when the golden cross that glittered on the dome was cast down, and dragged through the streets, the Christians of every sect uttered a lamentable groan, which was answered by the joyful shouts of the Moslems. In four ivory chests the patriarch had collected the crosses, the images, the vases, and the relics of the holy place : they were seized by the conqueror, who was desirous of presenting the caliph with the trophies of Christian idolatry. He was persuaded however to entrust them to the patriarch and prince of Antioch ; and the pious pledge was redeemed by Richard of England, at the expense of 52,000 byzants of gold.

The nations might fear and hope the immediate and final expulsion of the Latins from Syria ; which was yet delayed (A.D. 1188) above a century after the death of Saladin. In the career of victory, he was first checked by the resistance of Tyre ; the troops and garrisons which had capitulated, were imprudently conducted to the same port: their numbers were adequate to the defence of the place ; and the arrival of Conrad of Montferrat inspired the disorderly crowd with confidence and union. His father, a venerable pilgrim, had been made prisoner in the battle of Tiberias ; but that disaster was unknown in Italy and Greece, when the son was urged by ambition and piety to visit the inheritance of his royal nephew, the infant Baldwin. The view of the Turkish banners warned him from the hostile coast of Jaffa ; and Conrad was unanimously hailed as the prince and champion of Tyre, which was already besieged by the conqueror of Jerusalem. The firmness of his zeal, and perhaps his knowledge of a generous foe, enabled him to brave the threats of the sultan, and to declare, that should his aged parent be exposed before the walls, he himself would discharge the first arrow, and glory in his descent from a Christian martyr. The Egyptian fleet was allowed to enter the harbour of Tyre ; but the chain was suddenly drawn, and five galleys were either sunk or taken : 1000 Turks were slain in a sally ; and Saladin, after burning his engines, concluded a glorious campaign by a disgraceful retreat to Damascus. He was soon assailed by a more formidable tempest. The pathetic narratives, and even the pictures, that represented in lively colours the servitude and profanation of Jerusalem, awakened the torpid sensibility of Europe : the emperor Frederic Barbarossa, and the kings of France and England, assumed the cross ; and the tardy magnitude of their armaments was anticipated by the maritime states of the Mediterranean and the Ocean. The skilful and provident Italians first embarked in the ships of Genoa,

Pisa, and Venice. They were speedily followed by the most eager pilgrims of France, Normandy, and the Western Isles. The powerful succour of Flanders, Frise, and Dènmark, filled near a hundred vessels ; and the northern warriors were distinguished in the field by a lofty stature and a ponderous battle-axe. Their increasing multitudes could no longer be confined within the walls of Tyre, or remain obedient to the voice of Conrad. They pitied the misfortunes, and revered the dignity of Lusignan, who was released from prison, perhaps to divide the army of the Franks. He proposed the recovery of Ptolemais, or Acre, thirty miles to the south of Tyre ; and the place was first invested by 2000 horse and 30,000 foot under his nominal command. I shall not expatiate on the story of this memorable siege, which lasted near two years, and consumed (A.D. 1189, July—A.D. 1191. July) in a narrow space, the forces of Europe and Asia. Never did the flame of enthusiasm burn with fiercer and more destructive rage ; nor could the true believers, a common appellation, who consecrated their own martyrs, refuse some applause to the mistaken zeal and courage of their adversaries. At the sound of the holy trumpet, the Moslems of Egypt, Syria, Arabia, and the Oriental provinces, assembled under the servant of the prophet : his camp was pitched and removed within a few miles of Acre : and he laboured, night and day, for the relief of his brethren and the annoyance of the Franks. Nine battles not unworthy of the name, were fought, in the neighbourhood of mount Carmel, with such vicissitude of fortune, that in one attack, the sultan forced his way into the city ; that in one sally the Christians penetrated to the royal tent. By the means of divers and pigeons, a regular correspondence was maintained with the besieged : and, as often as the sea was left open, the exhausted garrison was withdrawn, and a fresh supply was poured into the place. The Latin camp was thinned by famine, the sword, and the climate ; but the tents of the dead were replenished with new pilgrims, who exaggerated the strength and speed of their approaching countrymen. The vulgar was astonished by the report, that the pope himself, with an innumerable crusade, was advanced as far as Constantinople. The march of the emperor filled the East with more serious alarms ; the obstacles which he encountered in Asia, and perhaps in Greece, were raised by the policy of Saladin ; his joy on the death of Barbarossa was measured by his esteem ; and the Christians were rather dismayed than encouraged at the sight of the duke of Swabia and his wayworn remnant of 5000 Germans. At length, in the spring of the second year, the royal fleets of France and England cast anchor in the bay of Acre, and the siege was more vigorously prosecuted by the youthful emulation of the two kings, Philip Augustus, and Richard Plantagenet. After every source had been tried, and every hope was exhausted, the defenders of Acre submitted to their fate ; a capitulation was granted, but their lives and liberties were taxed at the hard conditions of a ransom of 200,000 pieces of gold, the deliverance of 100 nobles and 1500 inferior captives, and the restoration of the wood of the holy cross. Some doubts in the agreement, and some delay in the execution, rekindled the fury of the Franks, and 3000 Moslems, almost in the Sultan's view, were beheaded by the command of the sanguinary Richard. By the conquest of Acre, the Latin powers acquired a strong town and a convenient harbour; but the advantage was most dearly purchased. The minister and historian of Saladin computes from the report of the enemy, that their numbers, at different periods, amounted to 500,000 or 600,000; that more than 100,000 Christians were slain; that a far greater number was lost by disease or shipwreck; and that a small portion of this mighty host could return in safety to their native countries.

Philip Augustus, and Richard the first, are the only kings of France and England, who (A.D. 1191, 1192), have fought under the same banners; but the holy service, in which they were enlisted, was incessantly disturbed by their national jealousy; and the two factions, which they protected in Palestine, were more averse to each other than to the common enemy. In the eyes of the Orientals, the French monarch was superior in dignity and power; and in the emperor's absence, the Latins revered him as their temporal chief. His exploits were not adequate to his fame. Philip was brave, but the statesman predominated in his character; he was soon weary of sacrificing his health and interest on a barren coast; the surrender of Acre became the signal of his departure; nor could he justify this unpopular desertion, by leaving the duke of Burgundy, with 500 knights and 10,000 foot, for the service of the Holy Land. The king of England, though inferior in dignity, surpassed his rival in wealth and military renown; and if heroism be confined to brutal and ferocious valour, Richard Plantagenet will stand high among the heroes of the age. The memory of *Cœur de Lion*, of the lion-hearted prince, was long dear and glorious to his English subjects; and, at the distance of sixty years, it was celebrated in proverbial sayings by the grandsons of the Turks and Saracens, against whom he had fought: his tremendous name was employed by the Syrian mothers to silence their infants; and if an horse suddenly started from the way, his rider was wont to exclaim, "Dost thou think king Richard is in that bush?" His cruelty to the Mahometans was the effect of temper and zeal; but I cannot believe that a soldier, so free and fearless in the use of his lance, would have descended to whet a dagger against his valiant brother Conrad of Montferrat, who was slain at Tyre by some secret assassins. After the surrender of Acre, and the departure of Philip, the king of England led the crusaders to the recovery of the sea-coast; and the cities of Cæsarea and Jaffa were added to the fragments of the kingdom of Lusignan. A march of 100 miles from Acre to Ascalon, was a great and perpetual battle of eleven days. In the disorder of his troops, Saladin remained on the field with seventeen guards, without lowering his standard, or suspending the sound of his brazen kettle-drum : he again rallied and renewed the charge ; and his preachers or heralds called aloud on the *unitarians*, manfully to stand up against the Christian idolaters. But the progress of these idolaters was irresistible : and it was only by demolishing the walls and buildings of Ascalon, that the sultan could prevent them from occupying an important fortress on the confines of Egypt. During a severe winter, the armies slept ; but in the spring, the Franks advanced within a day's march of Jerusalem, under the leading standard of the English king ; and his active spirit intercepted a convoy, or caravan, of 7000 camels. Saladin had fixed his station in the holy city ; but the city was struck with consternation and discord : he fasted ; he prayed ; he preached ; he offered to share the dangers of the siege ; but his Mamalukes, who remembered the fate of their companions at Acre, pressed the sultan with loyal or seditious clamours, to reserve *his* person and *their* courage for the future defence of the religion and empire. The Moslems were delivered by the sudden, or, as they deemed, the miraculous, retreat of the Christians ; and the laurels of Richard were blasted by the prudence, or envy of his companions. The hero, ascending an hill, and veiling his face, exclaimed with an indignant voice, " Those who are unwilling to rescue, are unworthy to view, the sepulchre of Christ !" After his return to Acre, on the news that Jaffa was surprised by the sultan, he sailed with some merchant vessels, and leaped foremost on the beach ; the castle was relieved by his presence ; and 60,000 Turks and Saracens fled before his arms. The discovery of his weakness provoked them to return in the morning ; and they found him carelessly encamped before the gates with only seventeen knights and three hundred archers. Without counting their numbers, he sustained their charge ; and we learn from the evidence of his enemies, that the king of England, grasping his lance, rode furiously along their front, from the right to the left wing, without meeting an adversary who dared to encounter his career. Am I writing the history of Orlando or Amadis ?

During these hostilities, a languid and tedious negociation between the Franks and Moslems was started, and continued, and broken, and again resumed, and again broken. Some acts of royal courtesy, the gift of snow and fruit, the exchange of Norway hawks and Arabian horses, softened the asperity of religious war : from the vicissitude of success, the monarchs might learn to suspect that Heaven was neutral in the quarrel ; nor, after the trial of each other, could either hope for a decisive victory. The health both of Richard and Saladin appeared to be in a declining state ; and they respectively suffered the evils of distant and domestic warfare : Plantagenet was impatient to punish a perfidious rival who had invaded Normandy in his absence ; and the indefatigable sultan was subdued by the cries of the people, who was the victim, and of the soldiers, who were the instruments, of his martial zeal. The first demands of the king of England were the restitution of Jerusalem, Palestine, and the true cross ; and he firmly declared, that himself and his brother pilgrims would end their lives in the pious labour, rather than return to Europe with ignominy and remorse. But the conscience of Saladin refused, without some weighty compensation, to restore the idols, or promote the idolatry, of the Christians : he asserted, with equal firmness, his religious and civil claim to the sovereignty of Palestine ; descanted on the importance and sanctity of Jerusalem ; and rejected all terms of the establishment, or partition, of the Latins. The marriage which Richard proposed, of his sister with the sultan's brother, was defeated by the difference of faith. A personal interview was declined by Saladin, who alleged their mutual ignorance of each other's language; and the negociation was managed with much art and delay by their interpreters and envoys. The final agreement (A.D. 1192. Sept.) was equally disapproved by the zealots of both parties, by the Roman pontiff and the caliph of Bagdad. It was stipulated that Jerusalem and the holy sepulchre should be open, without tribute or vexation, to the pilgrimage of the Latin Christians ; that, after the demolition of Ascalon, they should inclusively possess the sea-coast from Jaffa to Tyre ; that the count of Tripoli and the prince of Antioch should be compromised in the truce ; and that, during three years and three months, all hostilities should cease. The principal chiefs of the two armies swore to the observance of the treaty ; but the monarchs were satisfied with giving their word and their right-hand : and the royal majesty was excused from an oath, which always implies some suspicion of falsehood and dishonour. Richard embarked for Europe to seek a long captivity and a premature grave; and the space of a few months (A.D. 1193. Mar. 4) concluded the life and glories of Saladin. The Orientals describe his edifying death, which happened at Damascus ; but they seem ignorant of the equal distribution of his alms among the three religions, or of the display of a shroud, instead of a standard, to admonish the East of the instability of human greatness. The unity of empire was dissolved by his death ; his sons were oppressed by the stronger arm of their uncle Saphadin ; the hostile interests of the sultans of Egypt, Damascus, and Aleppo, were again revived ; and the Franks or Latins stood, and breathed, and hoped, in their fortresses along the Syrian coast.

The noblest monument of a conqueror's fame, and of the terror which he inspired, is the Saladine tenth, a general tax, which was imposed on the laity, and even the clergy, of the Latin church for the service of the holy war. The practice was too lucrative to expire with the occasion ; and this tribute became the foundation of all the tithes and tenths on ecclesiastical benefices, which have been granted by the Roman pontiffs to Catholic sovereigns, or reserved for the immediate use of the apostolic see. This pecuniary emolument must have tended to increase the interest of the popes in the recovery of Palestine ; after the death of Saladin they preached the crusade, by their epistles, their legates, and their missionaries ; and the accomplishment of the pious work might have been expected from the zeal (A.D. 1198—1216) and talents of Innocent the third. Under that young and ambitious priest, the successors of St. Peter attained the full meridian of their greatness ; and in a reign of eighteen years, he exercised a despotic command over the emperors and kings, whom he raised and deposed ; over the nations, whom an interdict of months or years deprived, for the offence of their rulers, of the exercise of Christian worship. In the council of the Lateran he acted as the ecclesiastical, almost as the temporal, sovereign of the East and West. It was at the feet of his legate that John of England surrendered his crown ; and Innocent may boast of the two most signal triumphs over sense and humanity, the establishment of transubstantiation, and the origin of the inquisition. At his voice, two crusades, the fourth and the fifth, were undertaken ; but except a king of Hungary, the princes of the second order were at the head of the pilgrims ; the forces were inadequate to the design ; nor did the effects correspond with the hopes and wishes of the pope and the people. The fourth crusade (A.D. 1203) was diverted from Syria to Constantinople ; and the conquest of the Greek or Roman empire by the Latins will form the proper and important subject of succeeding pages. In the fifth (A.D. 1218) 200,000 Franks were landed at the eastern mouth of the Nile. They reasonably hoped that Palestine must be subdued in Egypt, the seat and storehouse of the sultan ; and, after a siege of six teen months, the Moslems deplored the loss of Damietta. But the Christian army was ruined by the pride and insolence of the legate Pelagius, who, in the pope's name, assumed the character of general : the sickly Franks were encompassed by the waters of the Nile and the Oriental forces ; and it was by the evacuation of Damietta that they obtained a safe retreat, some concessions for the pilgrims, and the tardy restitution of the doubtful relic of the true cross. The failure may in some measure be ascribed to the abuse and multiplication of the crusades, which were preached at the same time against the Pagans of Livonia, the Moors of Spain, the Albigeois of France, and the kings of Sicily of the Imperial family. In these meritorious services, the volunteers might acquire at home the same spiritual indulgence, and a larger measure of temporal rewards ; and even the popes, in their zeal against a domestic enemy, were sometimes tempted to forget the distress of their Syrian brethren. From the last age of the crusades they derived the occasional command of an army and revenue ; and some deep reasoners have suspected that the whole enterprise, from the first synod of Placentia, was contrived and executed by the policy of Rome. The suspicion is not founded either in nature or in fact. The successors of St. Peter appear to have followed, rather than guided, the impulse of manners and prejudice; without much foresight of the seasons, or cultivation of the soil, they gathered the ripe and spontaneous fruits of the superstition of the times. They gathered these fruits without toil or personal danger : in the council of the Lateran, Innocent the third declared an ambiguous resolution of animating the crusaders by his example ; but the pilot of the sacred vessel could not abandon the helm ; nor was Palestine ever blessed with the presence of a Roman pontiff.

The persons, the families, and estates of the pilgrims, were under the immediate protection of the popes ; and these spiritual patrons soon claimed the prerogative of directing their operations, and enforcing, by commands and censures, the accomplishment of their vow. Frederic the second, the grandson of Barbarossa, was successively the pupil, the enemy, and the victim, of the church. At the age of twenty-one years, and in obedience to his guardian Innocent the third, he assumed (A.D. 1228) the cross ; the same promise was repeated at his royal and imperial coronations ; and his marriage with the heiress of Jerusalem for ever bound him to defend the kingdom of his son Conrad. But as Frederic advanced in age and authority, he repented of the rash engagements of his youth : his liberal sense and knowledge taught him to despise the phantoms of superstition and the crowns of Asia : he no longer entertained the same reverence for the successors of Innocent ; and his ambition was occupied by the restoration of the Italian monarchy from Sicily to the Alps. But the success of this project would have reduced the popes to their primitive simplicity; and, after the delays and excuses of twelve years, they urged the emperor, with entreaties and threats, to fix the time and place of his departure for Palestine. In the harbours of Sicily and Apulia, he prepared a fleet of 100 galleys, and of 100 vessels, that were framed to transport and land 2500 knights, with their horses and attendants : his vassals of Naples and Germany formed a powerful army ; and the number of English crusaders was magnified to 60,000 by the report of fame. But the inevitable, or affected, slowness of these mighty preparations, consumed the strength and provisions of the more indigent pilgrims : the multitude was thinned by sickness and desertion ; and the sultry summer of Calabria anticipated the mischiefs of a Syrian campaign. At length the emperor hoisted sail at Brundusium, with a fleet and army of 40,000 men ; but he kept the sea no more than three days ; and his hasty retreat, which was ascribed by his friends to a grievous indis-

position, was accused by his enemies as a voluntary and obstinate disobedience. For suspending his vow was Frederic excommunicated by
Gregory the ninth; for presuming, the next year, to accomplish his
vow, he was again excommunicated by the same pope. While he
served under the banner of the cross, a crusade was preached against
him in Italy; and after his return he was compelled to ask pardon for
the injuries which he had suffered. The clergy and military orders of
Palestine were previously instructed to renounce his communion and
dispute his commands; and in his own kingdom, the emperor was
forced to consent that the orders of the camp should be issued in the
name of God and of the Christian republic. Frederic entered Jerusalem in triumph : and with his own hands (for no priest would perform the office) he took the crown from the altar of the holy sepulchre.
But the patriarch cast an interdict on the church which his presence
had profaned; and the knights of the hospital and temple informed
the sultan how easily he might be surprised and slain in his unguarded
visit to the river Jordan. In such a state of fanaticism and faction,
victory was hopeless and defence was difficult ; but the conclusion of
an advantageous peace may be imputed to the discord of the Mahometans, and their personal esteem for the character of Frederic.
The enemy of the church is accused of maintaining with the miscreants
an intercourse of hospitality and friendship, unworthy of a Christian ;
of despising the barrenness of the land ; and of indulging a profane
thought, that if Jehovah had seen the kingdom of Naples, he never
would have selected Palestine for the inheritance of his chosen people.
Yet Frederic obtained from the sultan the restitution of Jerusalem, of
Bethlem and Nazareth, of Tyre and Sidon : the Latins were allowed
to inhabit and fortify the city; an equal code of civil and religious
freedom was ratified for the sectaries of Jesus and those of Mahomet :
and, while the former worshipped at the holy sepulchre, the latter
might pray and preach in the mosque of the temple, from whence the
prophet undertook his nocturnal journey to heaven. The clergy deplored this scandalous toleration ; and the weaker Moslems were
gradually expelled : but every rational object of the crusades was accomplished without bloodshed ; the churches were restored, the monasteries
were replenished ; and in the space of fifteen years, the Latins of Jerusalem exceeded the number of six thousand. This peace and prosperity, for which they were ungrateful to their benefactor, was terminated (A.D. 1243) by the irruption of the strange and savage hordes
of Carizmians. Flying from the arms of the Moguls, those shepherds
of the Caspian rolled headlong on Syria ; and the union of the Franks
with the sultans of Aleppo, Hems, and Damascus, was insufficient to
stem the violence of the torrent. Whatever stood against them, was
cut off by the sword, or dragged into captivity ; the military orders
were almost exterminated in a single battle ; and in the pillage of the

city, in the profanation of the holy sepulchre, the Latins confess and regret the modesty and discipline of the Turks and Saracens.

Of the seven crusades, the two last were undertaken by Louis the ninth, king of France (A.D. 1248—1254); who lost his liberty in Egypt, and his life on the coast of Africa. Twenty-eight years after his death, he was canonized at Rome; and sixty-five miracles were readily found, and solemnly attested, to justify the claim of the royal saint. The voice of history renders a more honourable testimony, that he united the virtues of a king, an hero, and a man; and his martial spirit was tempered by the love of private and public justice; and that Louis was the father of his people, the friend of his neighbours, and the terror of the infidels. Superstition alone, in all the extent of her baleful influence, corrupted his understanding and his heart; his devotion stooped to admire and imitate the begging friars of Francis and Dominic; he pursued with blind and cruel zeal the enemies of the faith; and the best of kings twice descended from his throne to seek the adventures of a spiritual knight-errant. A monkish historian would have been content to applaud the most despicable part of his character; but the noble and gallant Joinville, who shared the friendship and captivity of Louis, has traced with the pencil of nature the free portrait of his virtues as well as of his failings. From this intimate knowledge, we may learn to suspect the political views of depressing their great vassals, which are so often imputed to the royal authors of the crusades. Above all the princes of the middle ages, Louis the ninth successfully laboured to restore the prerogatives of the crown; but it was at home, and not in the East, that he acquired for himself and his posterity; his vow was the result of enthusiasm and sickness: and if he were the promoter, he was likewise the victim, of his holy madness. For the invasion of Egypt, France was exhausted of her troops and treasures; he covered the sea of Cyprus with 1800 sails; the most modest enumeration amounts to 50,000 men; and, if we might trust his own confession, as it is reported by Oriental vanity, he disembarked 9500 horse, and 130,000 foot, who performed their pilgrimage under the shadow of his power.

In complete armour, the oriflamme waving before him, Louis leaped foremost on the beach; and the strong city of Damietta, which had cost his predecessors a siege of sixteen months, was (A.D. 1249) abandoned on the first assault by the trembling Moslems. But Damietta was the first and the last of his conquests: and in the fifth and sixth crusades, the same causes, almost on the same ground, were productive of similar calamities. After a ruinous delay, which introduced into the camp the seeds of an epidemical disease, the Franks advanced from the sea-coast towards the capital of Egypt, and strove to surmount the unseasonable inundation of the Nile, which opposed their progress. Under the eye of their intrepid monarch, the barons and knights of

France displayed their invincible contempt of danger and discipline : his brother, the count of Artois, stormed with inconsiderable valour the town of Massoura ; and the carrier pigeons announced to the inhabitants of Cairo, that all was lost. But a soldier, who afterwards usurped the sceptre, rallied the flying troops : the main body of the Christians was far behind their vanguard ; and Artois was overpowered and slain. A shower of Greek fire was incessantly poured on the invaders ; the Nile was commanded by the Egyptian galleys, the open country by the Arabs ; all provisions were intercepted ; each day aggravated the sickness and famine ; and about the same time a retreat was found to be necessary and impracticable. The Oriental writers confess, that Louis might have escaped, if he would have deserted his subjects : he was made prisoner, with the greatest part of his nobles ; all who could not redeem their lives by service or ransom, were inhumanly massacred ; and the walls of Cairo were decorated with a circle of Christian heads. The king of France was (A.D. 1250, April 5—May 6) loaded with chains ; but the generous victor, a great grandson of the brother of Saladin, sent a robe of honour to his royal captive ; and his deliverance, with that of his soldiers, was obtained by the restitution of Damietta and the payment of 400,000 pieces of gold. In a soft and luxurious climate, the degenerate children of the companions of Noureddin and Saladin were incapable of resisting the flower of European chivalry : they triumphed by the arms of their slaves or Mamalukes, the hardy natives of Tartary, who at a tender age had been purchased of the Syrian merchants, and were educated in the camp and palace of the sultan. But Egypt soon afforded a new example of the danger of prætorian bands : and the rage of these ferocious animals, who had been let loose on the strangers, was provoked to devour their benefactor. In the pride of conquest, Touran Shaw, the last of his race, was murdered by his Mamalukes ; and the most daring of the assassins entered the chamber of the captive king, with drawn scymetars, and their hands imbrued in the blood of their sultan. The firmness of Louis commanded their respect ; their avarice prevailed over cruelty and zeal ; the treaty was accomplished ; and the king of France, with the relics of his army, was permitted to embark for Palestine. He wasted four years within the walls of Acre, unable to visit Jerusalem, and unwilling to return to his native country.

The memory of his defeat excited Louis, after sixteen years of wisdom and repose, to undertake the seventh and last of the crusades. His finances were restored, his kingdom was enlarged ; a new generation of warriors had arisen, and he embarked with fresh confidence at the head of 6000 horse and 30,000 foot. The loss of Antioch had provoked the enterprise : a wild hope of baptizing the king of Tunis, tempted him to steer for the African coast ; and the report of an immense treasure reconciled his troops to the delay of their voyage to the Holy Land. Instead of a proselyte, he found a siege ; the French panted and died on the burning sands ; St. Louis expired (A.D. 1270, Aug. 25) in his tent ; and no sooner had he closed his eyes, than his son and successor gave the signal of the retreat. " It is thus," says Voltaire, " that a Christian king died near the ruins of Carthage, waging war against the sectaries of Mahomet, in a land to which Dido had introduced the deities of Syria."

A more unjust and absurd constitution cannot be devised, than that which condemns the natives of a country to perpetual servitude, under the arbitrary dominion of strangers and slaves. Yet such has been the state of Egypt above five hundred years. The most illustrious sultans of the Baharite and Borgite dynasties (A.D. 1250—1517), were themselves promoted from the Tartar and Circassian bands ; and the four-and-twenty beys or military chiefs, have ever been succeeded, not by their sons, but by their servants. They produce the great charter of their liberties, the treaty of Selim the first with the republic ; and the Othman emperor still accepts from Egypt a slight acknowledgment of tribute and subjection. With some breathing intervals of peace and order, the two dynasties are marked as a period of rapine and blood-shed : but their throne, however shaken, reposed on the two pillars of discipline and valour ; their sway extended over Egypt, Nubia, Arabia, and Syria ; their Mamalukes were multiplied from 800 to 25,000 horse ; and their numbers were increased by a provincial militia of 107,000 foot, and the occasional aid of 66,000 Arabs. Princes of such power and spirit could not long endure on their coast an hostile and independent nation ; and if the ruin of the Franks was postponed about forty years, they were indebted to the cares of an unsettled reign, to the invasion of the Moguls, and to the occasional aid of some warlike pilgrims. Among these, the English reader will observe the name of our first Edward, who assumed the cross in the lifetime of his father Henry. At the head of a thousand soldiers, the future conqueror of Wales and Scotland delivered Acre from a siege ; marched as far as Nazareth with an army of 9000 men ; emulated the fame of his uncle Richard ; extorted, by his valour, a ten years' truce ; and escaped, with a dangerous wound, from the dagger of a fanatic *assassin.* Antioch, whose situation had been less exposed to the calamities of the holy war, was (A.D. 1268, June 12) finally occupied and ruined by Bondocdar, or Bibars, sultan of Egypt and Syria ; the Latin principality was extinguished ; and the first seat of the Christian name was dispeopled by the slaughter of 17,000, and the captivity of 100,000 of her inhabitants. The maritime towns of Laodicea, Gabala, Tripoli, Berytus, Sidon, Tyre, and Jaffa, and the stronger castles of the Hospitalers and Templars, successively fell ; and the whole existence of the Franks was confined to the city and colony of St. John of Acre, which is sometimes described by the more classic title of Ptolemais.

After the loss of Jerusalem, Acre, which is distant about 70 miles, became the metropolis of the Latin Christians, and was adorned with strong and stately buildings, with aqueducts, an artificial port, and a double wall. The population was increased by the incessant streams of pilgrims and fugitives; in the pauses of hostility, the trade of the East and West was attracted to this convenient station; and the market could offer the produce of every clime and the interpreters of every tongue. But in this conflux of nations, every vice was propagated and practised: of all the disciples of Jesus and Mahomet, the male and female inhabitants of Acre were esteemed the most corrupt; nor could the abuse of religion be corrected by the discipline of law. The city had many sovereigns, and no government. The kings of Jerusalem and Cyprus, of the house of Lusignan, the princes of Antioch, the counts of Tripoli and Sidon, the great masters of the hospital, the temple, and the Teutonic order, the republics of Venice, Genoa, and Pisa, the pope's legate, the kings of France and England, assumed an independent command: seventeen tribunals exercised the power of life and death; every criminal was protected in the adjacent quarter; and the perpetual jealousy of the nations often burst forth in acts of violence and blood. Some adventurers, who disgraced the ensign of the cross, compensated their want of pay by the plunder of the Mahometan villages: nineteen Syrian merchants, who traded under the public faith, were despoiled and hanged by the Christians; and the denial of satisfaction justified the arms of the sultan Khalil. He marched against Acre at the head of 60,000 horse and 140,000 foot: his train of artillery (if I may use the word) was numerous and weighty; the separate timbers of a single engine were transported in one hundred waggons; and the royal historian Abulfeda, who served with the troops of Hamah, was himself a spectator of the holy war. Whatever might be the vices of the Franks, their courage was rekindled by enthusiasm and despair; but they were torn by the discord of seventeen chiefs, and overwhelmed on all sides by the powers of the sultan. After a siege of thirty-three days, the double wall was (A.D. 1291, May 18) forced by the Moslems; the principal tower yielded to their engines; the Mamalukes made a general assault; the city was stormed; and death or slavery was the lot of 60,000 Christians. The convent, or rather fortress, of the Templars, resisted three days longer; but the great master was pierced with an arrow; and, of 500 knights, only ten were left alive, less happy than the victims of the sword, if they lived to suffer on a scaffold in the unjust and cruel proscription of the whole order. The king of Jerusalem, the patriarch, and the great master of the hospital, effected their retreat to the shore; but the sea was rough; the vessels were insufficient: and great numbers of the fugitives were drowned before they could reach the isle of Cyprus, which might comfort Lusignan for the loss of Palestine. By the command of the sultan, the churches and fortifications of the Latin cities were demolished ; a motive of avarice or fear still opened the holy sepulchre to some devout and defenceless pilgrims ; and a mournful and solitary silence prevailed along the coast which had so long resounded with the WORLD'S DEBATE.

The restoration of the Western empire by Charlemagne, was speedily followed by the separation of the Greek and Latin churches. A religious and national animosity still divides the two largest communions of the Christian world ; and the schism of Constantinople, by alienating her most useful allies, and provoking her most dangerous enemies, has precipitated the decline and fall of the Roman empire in the East.

In the course of the present history, the aversion of the Greeks for the Latins has been often visible and conspicuous. It was originally derived from the disdain of servitude, inflamed, after the time of Constantine, by the pride of equality or dominion ; and finally exasperated by the preference which their rebellious subjects had given to the alliance of the Franks. In every age, the Greeks were proud of their superiority in profane and religious knowledge : they had first received the light of Christianity ; they had pronounced the decrees of the seven general councils : they alone possessed the language of Scripture and philosophy ; nor should the Barbarians, immersed in the darkness of the West, presume to argue on the high and mysterious questions of theological science. Those Barbarians despised in their turn the restless and subtle levity of the Orientals, the authors of every heresy ; and blessed their own simplicity, which was content to hold the tradition of the apostolic church. Yet, in the seventh century, the synods of Spain, and afterwards of France, improved or corrupted the Nicene creed, on the mysterious subject of the third person of the Trinity. In the long controversies of the East, the nature and generation of the Christ had been scrupulously defined ; and the well-known relation of father and son seemed to convey a faint image to the human mind. The idea of birth was less analogous to the Holy Spirit, who, instead of a divine gift or attribute, was considered by the Catholics, as a substance, a person, a god ; he was not begotten, but in the orthodox style, he *proceeded*. Did he proceed from the Father alone, perhaps *by* the Son ? or from the Father and Son ? The first of these opinions was asserted by the Greeks, the second by the Latins ; and the addition to the Nicene creed of the word *filioque*, kindled the flame of discord between the Oriental and the Gallic churches. In the origin of the dispute, the Roman pontiffs affected a character of neutrality and moderation : they condemned the innovation, but they acquiesced in the sentiment, of their Transalpine brethren : they seemed desirous of casting a veil of silence and charity over the superfluous research ; and in the correspondence of Charlemagne and Leo the third, the pope assumes the liberality of a statesman, and the prince descends to the passions and prejudices of a priest. But the orthodoxy of Rome spon-taneously obeyed the impulse of her temporal policy ; and the *filioque* which Leo wished to erase, was transcribed in the symbol and chaunted in the liturgy of the Vatican. The Nicene and Athanasian creeds are held as the Catholic faith, without which none can be saved ; and both Papists and Protestants must now sustain and return the anathemas of the Greeks, who deny the procession of the Holy Ghost from the Son, as well as from the Father. Such articles of faith are not susceptible of treaty ; but the rules of discipline will vary in remote and indepen-dent churches ; and the reason, even of divines, might allow, that the difference is inevitable and harmless. The craft or superstition of Rome has imposed on her priests and deacons the rigid obligation of celibacy ; among the Greeks it is confined to the bishops ; the loss is compensated by dignity or annihilated by age ; and the parochial clergy, the papas, enjoy the conjugal society of the wives whom they have married before their entrance into holy orders. A question concerning the *Azyms* was fiercely debated in the eleventh century, and the essence of the Eucharist was supposed, in the East and West, to depend on the use of leavened or unleavened bread. Shall I mention in a serious history the furious reproaches that were urged against the Latins, who, for a long while, remained on the defensive ? They neglected to ab-stain, according to the apostolic decree, from things strangled, and from blood : they fasted, a Jewish observance ! on the Saturday of each week : during the first week of Lent they permitted the use of milk and cheese ; their infirm monks were indulged in the taste of flesh ; and animal grease was substituted for the want of vegetable oil : the holy chrism or unction in baptism, was reserved to the episcopal order : the bishops, as the bridegrooms of their churches, were decorated with rings ; their priests shaved their faces, and baptized by a single im-mersion. Such were the crimes which provoked the zeal of the patri-archs of Constantinople, and which were justified with equal zeal by the doctors of the Latin church.

Bigotry and national aversion are powerful magnifiers of every ob-ject of dispute ; but the immediate cause of the schism of the Greeks may be traced in the emulation of the leading prelates, who maintained the supremacy of the old metropolis superior to all, and of the reigning capital, inferior to none, in the Christian world. About the middle of the ninth century, Photius, an ambitious layman, the captain of the guard and principal secretary, was promoted (A.D. 857—886) by merit and favour to the more desirable office of patriarch of Constantinople. In science, even ecclesiastical science, he surpassed the clergy of the age ; and the purity of his morals has never been impeached : but his ordination was hasty, his rise was irregular ; and Ignatius, his abdi-cated predecessor, was yet supported by the public compassion and the obstinacy of his adherents.   They appealed to the tribunal of Nicholas the first, one of the proudest and most aspiring of the Roman pontiffs, who embraced the welcome opportunity of judging and condemning his rival of the East.   Their quarrel was embittered by a conflict of jurisdiction over the king and nation of the Bulgarians; nor was their recent conversion to Christianity of much avail to either prelate, unless he could number the proselytes among the subjects of his power.   With the aid of his court the Greek patriarch was victorious; but in the furious contest he deposed in his turn the successor of St. Peter, and involved the Latin church in the reproach of heresy and schism.   Photius sacrificed the peace of the world to a short and precarious reign : he fell with his patron, the Cæsar Bardas; and Basil the Macedonian performed an act of justice in the restoration of Ignatius, whose age and dignity had not been sufficiently respected. From his monastery, or prison, Photius solicited the favour of the emperor by pathetic complaints and artful flattery ; and the eyes of his rival were scarcely closed, when he was again restored to the throne of Constantinople.   After the death of Basil, he experienced the vicissitudes of courts and the ingratitude of a royal pupil : the patriarch was again deposed, and in his last solitary hours he might regret the freedom of a secular and studious life.   In each revolution, the breath, the nod, of the sovereign had been accepted by a submissive clergy ; and a synod of 300 bishops was always prepared to hail the triumph, or to stigmatise the fall, of the holy, or the execrable Photius. By a delusive promise of succour or reward, the popes were tempted to countenance these various proceedings ; and the synods of Constantinople were ratified by their epistles or legates.   But the court and the people, Ignatius and Photius, were equally adverse to their claims; their ministers were insulted or imprisoned ; the procession of the Holy Ghost was forgotten ; Bulgaria was for ever annexed to the Byzantine throne ; and the schism was prolonged by the rigid censure of all the multiplied ordinations of an irregular patriarch. The darkness and corruption of the tenth century suspended the intercourse, without reconciling the minds, of the two nations.   But when the Norman sword restored the churches of Apulia to the jurisdiction of Rome, the departing flock was warned, by a petulant epistle of the Greek patriarch, to avoid and abhor the errors of the Latins. The rising majesty of Rome could no longer brook the insolence of a rebel ; and Michael Cerularius was excommunicated in the heart of Constantinople by the pope's legates.   Shaking the dust from their feet, they (A.D. 1054. July 16) deposited on the altar of St. Sophia a direful anathema, which enumerates the seven mortal heresies of the Greeks, and devotes the guilty teachers, and their unhappy sectaries, to the eternal society of the devil and his angels.   According to the emergencies of the church and state, a friendly correspondence was sometimes resumed ; the language of charity and concord was some-times affected ; but the Greeks have never recanted their errors ; the popes have never repealed their sentence : and from this thunder-bolt we may date the consummation of the schism. It was en-larged by each ambitious step of the Roman pontiffs : the emperors blushed and trembled at the ignominious fate of their royal brethren of Germany ; and the people were scandalized by the temporal power and military life of the Latin clergy.

The aversion of the Greeks and Latins was nourished and mani-fested (A.D. 1100—1200) in the three first expeditions to the Holy Land. Alexius Comnenus contrived the absence at least of the formidable pilgrims : his successors, Manuel and Isaac Angelus, con-spired with the Moslems for the ruin of the greatest princes of the Franks ; and their crooked and malignant policy was seconded by the active and voluntary obedience of every order of their subjects. Of this hostile temper, a large portion may doubtless be ascribed to the difference of language, dress, and manners, which severs and alienates the nations of the globe. The pride, as well as the prudence, of the sovereign was deeply wounded by the intrusion of foreign armies, that claimed a right of traversing his dominions and passing under the walls of his capital : his subjects were insulted and plundered by the rude strangers of the West ; and the hatred of the pusillanimous Greeks was sharpened by secret envy of the bold and pious enter-prises of the Franks. But these profane causes of national enmity were fortified and inflamed by the venom of religious zeal. Instead of a kind embrace, an hospitable reception, from their Christian brethren of the East, every tongue was taught to repeat the names of schismatic and heretic, more odious to an orthodox ear than those of pagan and infidel : instead of being loved for the general conformity of faith and worship, they were abhorred for some rules of discipline, some questions of theology, in which themselves or their teachers might differ from the Oriental church. In the crusade of Louis the seventh, the Greek clergy washed and purified the altars which had been defiled by the sacrifice of a French priest. The companions of Frederic Barbarossa deplore the injuries which they endured, both in word and deed, from the peculiar rancour of the bishops and monks. Their prayers and sermons excited the people against the impious Barbarians ; and the patriarch is accused of declaring, that the faith-ful might obtain the redemption of all their sins by the extirpation of the schismatics. An enthusiast, named Dorotheus, alarmed the fears, and restored the confidence, of the emperor, by a prophetic assurance, that the German heretic, after assaulting the gate of Blachernes, would be made a signal example of the divine vengeance. The passage of these mighty armies were rare and perilous events ; but the crusades introduced a frequent and familiar intercourse between the two nations, which enlarged their knowledge without abating their prejudices. The wealth and luxury of Constantinople demanded the productions of every climate : these imports were balanced by the art and labour of her numerous inhabitants; her situation invites the commerce of the world ; and, in every period of her existence, that commerce has been in the hands of foreigners. After the decline of Amalphi, the Venetians, Pisans, and Genoese, introduced their fac- tories and settlements into the capital of the empire : their services were rewarded with honours and immunities ; they acquired the pos- session of lands and houses; their families were multiplied by mar- riages with the natives; and, after the toleration of a Mahometan mosque, it was impossible to interdict the churches of the Roman rite. The two wives of Manuel Comnenus were of the race of the Franks ; the first, a sister-in-law of the emperor Conrad ; the second, a daughter of the prince of Antioch : he obtained for his son Alexius a daughter of Philip Augustus king of France ; and he bestowed his own daughter on a marquis of Montferrat, who was educated and dig- nified in the palace of Constantinople. The Greek encountered the arms, and aspired to the empire, of the West ; he esteemed the valour, and trusted the fidelity, of the Franks ; their military talents were un- fitly recompensed by the lucrative offices of judges and treasurers; the policy of Manuel had solicited the alliance of the pope ; and the popu- lar voice accused him of a partial bias to the nation and religion of the Latins. During his reign, and that of his successor Alexius, they were exposed at Constantinople to the reproach of foreigners, heretics, and favourites ; and this triple guilt was severely expiated in the tumult, which announced the return and elevation of Andronicus. The people rose (A.D. 1183) in arms ; from the Asiatic shore the tyrant dispatched his troops and galleys to assist the national revenge ; and the hopeless resistance of the strangers served only to justify the rage, and sharpen the daggers, of the assassins. Neither age, nor sex, nor the ties of friendship or kindred, could save the victims of national hatred, and avarice, and religious zeal : the Latins were slaughtered in their houses and in the streets ; their quarter was reduced to ashes; the clergy were burnt in their churches, and the sick in their hospitals; and some estimate may be formed of the slain from the clemency which sold above 4000 Christians in perpetual slavery to the Turks. The priests and monks were the loudest and most active in the de- struction of the schismatics ; and they chaunted a thanksgiving to the Lord, when the head of a Roman cardinal, the pope's legate, was severed from his body, fastened to the tail of a dog, and dragged, with savage mockery, through the city. The more diligent of the strangers had retreated, on the first alarm, to their vessels, and escaped through the Hellespont from the scene of blood. In their flight, they burnt and ravaged 200 miles of the sea-coast ; inflicted a severe revenge on the guiltless subjects of the empire ; marked the priests and monks as their peculiar enemies ; and compensated, by the accumulation of plunder, the loss of their property and friends. On their return, they exposed to Italy and Europe the wealth and weakness, the perfidy and malice, of the Greeks, whose vices were painted as the genuine characters of heresy and schism. The scruples of the first crusaders had neglected the fairest opportunities of securing, by the possession of Constantinople, the way to the Holy Land : a domestic revolution invited, and almost compelled, the French and Venetians to achieve the conquest of the Roman empire of the east.

In the series of the Byzantine princes, I have exhibited the hypocrisy and ambition, the tyranny and fall, of Andronicus, the last male of the Comnenian family who reigned at Constantinople. The revolution, which cast him headlong from the throne, saved and exalted Isaac Angelus (A.D. 1185—1195, Sept. 12), who descended by the females from the same imperial dynasty. The successor of a second Nero might have found it an easy task to deserve the esteem and affection of his subjects : they sometimes had reason to regret the administration of Andronicus. The sound and vigorous mind of the tyrant was capable of discerning the connexion between his own and the public interest ; and while he was feared by all who could inspire him with fear, the unsuspected people, and the remote provinces, might bless the inexorable justice of their master. But his successor was vain and jealous of the supreme power, which he wanted courage and abilities to exercise ; his vices were pernicious, his virtues (if he possessed any virtues) were useless to mankind ; and the Greeks, who imputed their calamities to his negligence, denied him the merit of any transient or accidental benefits of the times. Isaac slept on the throne, and was awakened only by the sound of pleasure : his vacant hours were amused by comedians and buffoons, and even to these buffoons the emperor was an object of contempt ; his feasts and buildings exceeded the examples of royal luxury ; the number of his eunuchs and domestics amounted to 20,000 ; and a daily sum of 4000 pounds of silver would swell to four millions sterling the annual expence of his household and table. His poverty was relieved by oppression ; and the public discontent was inflamed by equal abuses in the collection, and the application, of the revenue. While the Greeks numbered the days of their servitude, a flattering prophet, whom he rewarded with the dignity of patriarch, assured him of a long and victorious reign of thirty-two years ; during which he should extend his sway to mount Libanus, and his conquests beyond the Euphrates. But his only step towards the accomplishment of the prediction, was a splendid and scandalous embassy to Saladin, to demand the restitution of the holy sepulchre, and to propose an offensive and defensive league with the enemy of the Christian name.

F F

In these unworthy hands, of Isaac and his brother, the remains of the Greek empire crumbled into dust. The island of Cyprus, whose name excites the ideas of elegance and pleasure, was usurped by his namesake, a Comnenian prince : and by a strange concatenation of events, the sword of our Richard bestowed that kingdom on the house of Lusignan, a rich compensation for the loss of Jerusalem.

The honour of the monarchy, and the safety of the capital, were deeply wounded by the revolt (A.D. 1186) of the Bulgarians and Wallachians. Since the victory of the second Basil, they had supported, above 170 years, the loose dominion of the Byzantine princes ; but no effectual measures had been adopted to impose the yoke of laws and manners on these savage tribes. By the command of Isaac, their sole means of subsistence, their flocks and herds, were driven away, to contribute towards the pomp of the royal nuptials : and their fierce warriors were exasperated by the denial of equal rank and pay in the military service. Peter and Asan, two powerful chiefs, of the race of the ancient kings, asserted their own rights and the national freedom : their demoniac impostors proclaimed to the crowd that their glorious patron St. Demetrius had for ever deserted the cause of the Greeks ; and the conflagration spread from the banks of the Danube to the hills of Macedonia and Thrace. After some faint efforts, Isaac Angelus and his brother acquiesced in their independence ; and the Imperial troops were soon discouraged by the bones of their fellow-soldiers, that were scattered along the passes of mount Hæmus. By the arms and policy of John or Joannices, the second kingdom of Bulgaria was firmly established. The subtle Barbarian sent an embassy to Innocent the third, to acknowledge himself a genuine son of Rome in descent and religion ; and humbly received from the pope the licence of coining money, the royal title, and a Latin archbishop or patriarch. The Vatican exulted in the spiritual conquest of Bulgaria, the first object of the schism ; and if the Greeks could have preserved the prerogatives of the church, they would gladly have resigned the rights of the monarchy.

The Bulgarians were malicious enough to pray for the long life of Isaac Angelus, the surest pledge of their freedom and prosperity. Yet their chiefs could involve in the same indiscriminate contempt, the family and nation of the emperor. " In all the Greeks," said Asan to his troops, " the same climate, and character, and education, will be productive of the same fruits. Behold my lance," continued the warrior, " and the long streamers that float in the wind. They differ only in colour ; they are formed of the same silk and fashioned by the same workman ; nor has the stripe that is stained in purple any superior price or value above its fellows." Several of these candidates for the purple successively rose and fell under the empire of Isaac : a general who had repelled the fleets of Sicily, was driven to revolt and ruin by the ingratitude of the prince ; and his luxurious repose was disturbed by secret conspiracies and popular insurrections. The emperor was saved by accident, or the merit of his servants : he was at length oppressed by an ambitious brother, who, for the hope of a precarious diadem, forgot the obligations of nature, of loyalty, and of friendship. While Isaac in the Thracian valleys pursued the idle and solitary pleasures of the chase, his brother, Alexius Angelus, was (A.D. 1203, April 8) invested with the purple, by the unanimous suffrage of the camp : the capital and the clergy subscribed to their choice ; and the vanity of the new sovereign rejected the name of his fathers, for the lofty and royal appellation of the Comnenian race. On the despicable character of Isaac I have exhausted the language of contempt ; and can only add, that in a reign of eight years, the baser Alexius was supported by the masculine vices of his wife Euphrosyne. The first intelligence of his fall was conveyed to the late emperor by the hostile aspect and pursuit of the guards, no longer his own : he fled before them above fifty miles as far as Stagyra in Macedonia ; but the fugitive, without an object or a follower, was arrested, brought back to Constantinople, deprived of his eyes, and confined in a lonesome tower, on a scanty allowance of bread and water. At the moment of the revolution, his son Alexius, whom he educated in the hope of empire, was twelve years of age. He was spared by the usurper, and reduced to attend his triumph both in peace and war ; but as the army was encamped on the sea-shore, an Italian vessel facilitated the escape of the royal youth ; and, in the disguise of a common sailor, he eluded the search of his enemies, passed the Hellespont, and found a secure refuge in the isle of Sicily. After saluting the threshold of the apostles, and imploring the protection of Pope Innocent the third, Alexius accepted the kind invitation of his sister Irene, the wife of Philip of Swabia, king of the Romans. But in his passage through Italy he heard that the flower of Western chivalry was assembled at Venice for the deliverance of the Holy Land ; and a ray of hope was kindled in his bosom, that their invincible swords might be employed in his father's restoration.

About ten or twelve years after the loss of Jerusalem, the nobles of France were (A.D. 1198) again summoned to the holy war by the voice of a third prophet, less extravagant, perhaps, than Peter the hermit, but far below St. Bernard in the merit of an orator and a statesman. An illiterate priest of the neighbourhood of Paris, Fulk of Neuilly, forsook his parochial duty, to assume the more flattering character of a popular and itinerant missionary. The fame of his sanctity and miracles was spread over the land ; he declaimed, with severity and vehemence, against the vices of the age ; and his sermons, which he preached in the streets of Paris, converted the robbers, the usurers, the prostitutes, and even the doctors and scholars of the university. No sooner did Innocent the third ascend the chair of St. Peter, than he proclaimed in Italy, Germany and France, the obligation of a new crusade. The eloquent pontiff described the ruin of Jerusalem, the triumph of the Pagans, and the shame of Christendom : his liberality proposed the redemption of sins, a plenary indulgence to all who should serve in Palestine, either a year in person, or two years by a substitute ; and among his legates and orators who blew the sacred trumpet, Fulk of Neuilly was the loudest and most successful. The situation of the principal monarchs was averse to the pious summons. The emperor Frederic the second was a child ; and his kingdom of Germany was disputed by the rival houses of Brunswick and Swabia, the memorable factions of the Guelphs and Ghibelines. Philip Augustus of France had performed, and could not be persuaded to renew, the perilous vow ; but as he was not less ambitious of praise than of power, he cheerfully instituted a perpetual fund for the defence of the Holy Land. Richard of England was satiated with the glory and misfortunes of his first adventure, and he presumed to deride the exhortations of Fulk of Neuilly, who was not abashed in the presence of kings. "You advise me," said Plantagenet, "to dismiss my three daughters, pride, avarice, and incontinence : I bequeath them to the most deserving ; my pride to the knights-templars, my avarice to the monks of Cisteaux, and my incontinence to the prelates." But the preacher was heard and obeyed by the great vassals, the princes of the . second order ; and Theobald, or Thibaut, count of Champagne, was the foremost in the holy race. The valiant youth, at the age of twenty-two years, was encouraged by the domestic examples of his father, who marched in the second crusade, and of his elder brother, who had ended his days in Palestine with the title of king of Jerusalem : two thousand two hundred knights owed service and homage to his peerage : the nobles of Champagne excelled in all the exercises of war ; and by his marriage with the heiress of Navarre, Thibaut could draw a band of hardy Gascons from either side of the Pyrenæan mountains. His companion in arms was Louis, count of Blois and Chartres ; like himself of regal lineage, for both the princes were nephews, at the same time, of the kings of France and England. In a crowd of prelates and barons, who imitated their zeal, I distinguish the birth and merit of Matthew of Montmorency ; the famous Simon of Montfort, the scourge of the Albigeois ; and a valiant noble, Jeffrey of Villehardouin, marshal of Champagne, who has condescended, in the rude idiom of his age and country, to write or dictate an original narrative of the councils and actions, in which he bore a memorable part. At the same time, Baldwin count of Flanders, who had married the sister of Thibaut, assumed the cross at Bruges, with his brother Henry and the principal knights and citizens of that rich and industrious province. The vow which the chiefs had pronounced in churches, they ratified in tournaments . the operations of the war were debated in full and frequent assemblies ; and it was resolved to seek the deliverance of Palestine in Egypt, a country, since Saladin's death, which was almost ruined by famine and civil war. But the fate of so many royal armies displayed the toils and perils of a land expedition ; and, if the Flemings dwelt along the ocean, the French barons were destitute of ships and ignorant of navigation. They embraced the wise resolution of chusing six deputies or representatives, of whom Villehardouin was one, with a discretionary trust to direct the motions, and to pledge the faith, of the whole confederacy. The maritime states of Italy were alone possessed of the means of transporting the holy warriors with their arms and horses ; and the six deputies proceeded to Venice to solicit, on motives of piety or interest, the aid of that powerful republic.

In the invasion of Italy by Attila, I have mentioned the flight (A.D. 697) of the Venetians from the fallen cities of the continent, and their obscure shelter in the chain of islands that line the extremity of the Hadriatic gulf. In the midst of the waters, free, indigent, laborious, and inaccessible, they gradually coalesced into a republic : the first foundations of Venice were laid in the island of Rialto ; and the annual election of the twelve tribunes was superseded by the permanent office of a duke or doge. On the verge of the two empires the Venetians exult in the belief of primitive and perpetual independence. Against the Latins, their antique freedom has been asserted by the sword, and may be justified by the pen. Charlemagne himself resigned all claims of sovereignty to the islands of the Hadriatic gulf ; his son Pepin was repulsed in the attacks of the *lagunas* or canals, too deep for the cavalry, and too shallow for the vessels ; and in every age, under the German Cæsars, the lands of the republic have been clearly distinguished from the kingdom of Italy. But the inhabitants of Venice were considered by themselves, by strangers, and by their sovereigns, as an inalienable portion of the Greek empire ; in the ninth and tenth centuries, the proofs of their subjection are numerous and unquestionable ; and the vain titles, the servile honours, of the Byzantine court, so ambitiously solicited by their dukes, would have degraded the magistrates of a free people. But the bands of this dependence, which was never absolute or rigid, were imperceptibly relaxed by the ambition of Venice and the weakness of Constantinople. Obedience was softened into respect, privilege ripened into prerogative, and the freedom of domestic government was fortified by the independence of foreign dominion. The maritime cities of Istria and Dalmatia bowed to the sovereigns of the Hadriatic ; and when they armed against the Normans in the cause of Alexius, the emperor applied, not to the duty of his subjects, but to the gratitude and generosity of his faithful allies. The sea was their patrimony : the western parts of the

Mediterranean, from Tuscany to Gibraltar, were indeed abandoned to their rivals of Pisa and Genoa ; but the Venetians acquired an early and lucrative share of the commerce of Greece and Egypt. Their riches increased with the increasing demand of Europe : their manufactures of silk and glass, perhaps the institution of their bank, are of high antiquity ; and they enjoyed the fruits of their industry in the magnificence of public and private life. To assert her flag, to avenge her injuries, to protect the freedom of navigation, the republic could launch and man a fleet of an hundred galleys ; and the Greeks, the Saracens, and the Normans, were encountered by her naval arms. The Franks of Syria were assisted by the Venetians in the reduction of the sea-coast ; but their zeal was neither blind nor disinterested ; and in the conquest of Tyre, they shared the sovereignty of a city, the first seat of the commerce of the world. The policy of Venice was marked by the avarice of a trading, and the insolence of a maritime power ; yet her ambition was prudent ; nor did she often forget that if armed galleys were the effect and safeguard, merchant vessels were the cause and supply, of her greatness. In her religion she avoided the schism of the Greeks, without yielding a servile obedience to the Roman pontiff ; and a free intercourse with the infidels of every clime appears to have allayed betimes the fever of superstition. Her primitive government was a loose mixture of democracy and monarchy : the doge was elected by the votes of the general assembly; as long as he was popular and successful, he reigned with the pomp and authority of a prince ; but in the frequent revolutions of the state, he was deposed, or banished, or slain, by the justice or injustice of the multitude. The twelfth century produced the first rudiments of the wise and jealous aristocracy, which has reduced the doge to a pageant and the people to a cipher.

When the six ambassadors of the French pilgrims arrived (A.D. 1201) at Venice, they were hospitably entertained in the palace of St. Mark, by the reigning doge : his name was Henry Dandolo ; and he shone in the last period of human life as one of the most illustrious characters of the times. Under the weight of years, and after the loss of his eyes, Dandolo retained a sound understanding and a manly courage ; the spirit of an hero, ambitious to signalize his reign by some memorable exploits, and the wisdom of a patriot, anxious to build his fame on the glory and advantage of his country. He praised the bold enthusiasm and liberal confidence of the barons and their deputies ; in such a cause, and with such associates, he should aspire, were he a private man, to terminate his life ; but he was the servant of the republic, and some delay was requisite to consult, on this arduous business, the judgment of his colleagues. The proposal of the French was first debated by the six *sages* who had been recently appointed to control the administration of the doge : it was next disclosed to the forty members of the council of state ; and finally communicated to the legislative assembly of four hundred and fifty representatives, who were annually chosen in the six quarters of the city. In peace and war, the doge was still the chief of the republic ; his legal authority was supported by the personal reputation of Dandolo : his arguments of public interest were balanced and approved ; and he was authorized to inform the ambassadors of the following conditions [of the treaty. It was proposed that the crusaders should assemble at Venice, on the feast of St. John of the ensuing year : that flat-bottomed vessels should be prepared for 4500 horses, and 9000 squires, with a number of ships sufficient for the embarkation of 4500 knights, and 20,000 foot ; that during a term of nine months they should be supplied with provisions, and transported to whatsoever coast the service of God and Christendom should require ; and that the republic should join the armament with a squadron of fifty galleys. It was required, that the pilgrims should pay, before their departure, a sum of 85,000 marks of silver; and that all conquests, by sea and land, should be equally divided between the confederates. The terms were hard ; but the emergency was pressing, and the French barons were not less profuse of money than of blood. A general assembly was convened to ratify the treaty ; the stately chapel and place of St. Mark were filled with 10,000 citizens ; and the noble deputies were taught a new lesson of humbling themselves before the majesty of the people. " Illustrious Venetians," said the marshal of Champagne, " we are sent by the greatest and most powerful barons of France, to implore the aid of the masters of the sea for the deliverance of Jerusalem. They have enjoined us to fall prostrate at your feet ; nor will we rise from the ground, till you have promised to avenge with us the injuries of Christ." The eloquence of their [words and tears, their martial aspect, and suppliant attitude, were applauded by an universal shout ; as it were, says Jeffrey, by the sound of an earthquake. The venerable doge ascended the pulpit to urge their request by those motives of honour and virtue, which alone can be offered to a popular assembly ; the treaty was transcribed on parchment ; attested with oaths and seals, mutually accepted by the weeping and joyful representatives of France and Venice ; and despatched to Rome for the approbation of pope Innocent the third. Two thousand marks were borrowed of the merchants for the first expences of the armament. Of the six deputies, two repassed the Alps to announce their success while their four companions made a fruitless trial of the zeal and emulation of the republics of Genoa and Pisa.

The execution of the treaty was still opposed by unforeseen difficulties and delays. The marshal, on his return to Troyes, was embraced and approved by Thibaut count of Champagne, who had been unanimously chosen general of the confederates. But the health of that valiant youth already declined, and soon became hopeless ; and he deplored the untimely fate, which condemned him to expire, not in a field of battle, but on a bed of sickness. To his brave and numerous vassals, the dying prince distributed his treasures : they swore in his presence to accomplish his vow and their own ; but some there were, says the marshal, who accepted his gifts and forfeited their word. The more resolute champions of the cross held a parliament at Soissons for the election of a new general, but such was the incapacity, or jealousy, or reluctance of the princes of France, that none could be found both able and willing to assume the conduct of the enterprise. They acquiesced in the choice of a stranger, of Boniface marquis of Montferrat, descended of a race of heroes, and himself of conspicuous fame in the wars and negociations of the times ; nor could the piety or ambition of the Italian chief decline this honourable invitation. After visiting the French court, where he was received as a friend and kinsman, the marquis, in the church of Soissons, was invested with the cross of a pilgrim and the staff of a general ; and immediately repassed the Alps, to prepare for the distant expedition of the East. About the festival of the Pentecost he displayed his banner, and marched towards Venice at the head of the Italians : he was preceded or followed by the counts of Flanders and Blois, and the most respectable barons of France ; and their numbers were swelled by the pilgrims of Germany, whose object and motives were similar to their own. The Venetians had fulfilled, and even surpassed, their engagements : stables were constructed for the horses, and barracks for the troops ; the magazines were abundantly replenished with forage and provisions ; and the fleet of transports, ships, and galleys was ready to hoist sail, as soon as the republic had received the price of the freight and armament. But that price far exceeded the wealth of the crusaders who were assembled at Venice. The Flemings, whose obedience to their count was voluntary and precarious, had embarked in their vessels for the long navigation of the ocean and Mediterranean ; and many of the French and Italians had preferred a cheaper and more convenient passage from Marseilles and Apulia to the Holy Land. Each pilgrim might complain that after he had furnished his own contribution he was made responsible for the deficiency of his absent brethren : the gold and silver plate of the chiefs, which they freely delivered to the treasury of St. Mark, was a generous but inadequate sacrifice ; and after all their efforts, 34,000 marks were still wanting to complete the stipulated sum. The obstacle was removed by the policy and patriotism of the doge, who proposed (A.D. 1202. October 8) to the barons, that if they would join their arms in reducing some revolted cities of Dalmatia, he would expose his person in the holy war, and obtain from the republic a long indulgence, till some wealthy conquest should afford the means of satisfying the debt. After much scruple and hesitation they chose rather to accept the offer than to relinquish the enterprise ; and the first hostilities of the fleet and army were (Nov. 10) directed against Zara, a strong city of the Sclavonian coast, which had renounced its allegiance to Venice, and implored the protection of the king of Hungary. The crusaders burst the chain or boom of the harbour ; landed their horses, troops, and military engines ; and compelled the inhabitants, after a defence of five days, to surrender at discretion ; their lives were spared, but the revolt was punished by the pillage of their houses and the demolition of their walls. The season was far advanced ; the French and Venetians resolved to pass the winter in a secure harbour and plentiful country ; but their repose was disturbed by national and tumultuous quarrels of the soldiers and mariners. The conquest of Zara had scattered the seeds of discord and scandal : the arms of the allies had been stained in their outset with the blood, not of infidels, but of Christians : the king of Hungary and his new subjects were themselves enlisted under the banner of the cross ; and the scruples of the devout were magnified by the fear or lassitude of the reluctant pilgrims. The pope had excommunicated the false crusaders who had pillaged and massacred their brethren, and only the marquis Boniface and Simon of Montfort escaped these spiritual thunders ; the one by his absence from the siege, the other by his final departure from the camp. Innocent might absolve the simple and submissive penitents of France ; but he was provoked by the stubborn reason of the Venetians, who refused to confess their guilt, to accept their pardon, or to allow, in their temporal concerns, the interposition of a priest.

The assembly of such formidable powers by sea and land, had revived the hopes of young Alexius ; and, both at Venice and Zara, he solicited the arms of the crusaders, for his own restoration and his father's deliverance. The royal youth was recommended by Philip king of Germany : his prayers and presence excited the compassion of the camp ; and his cause was embraced and pleaded by the marquis of Montferrat and the doge of Venice. A double alliance, and the dignity of Cæsar, had connected with the Imperial family the two elder brothers of Boniface : he expected to derive a kingdom from the important service ; and the more generous ambition of Dandolo was eager to secure the inestimable benefits of trade and dominion that might accrue to his country. Their influence procured a favourable audience for the ambassadors of Alexius ; and if the magnitude of his offers excited some suspicion, the motives and rewards which he displayed might justify the delay and diversion of those forces which had been consecrated to the deliverance of Jerusalem. He promised, in his own and his father's name, that as soon as they should be seated on the throne of Constantinople, they would terminate the long schism of the Greeks, and submit themselves and their people to the lawful supremacy of the Roman church. He engaged to recompense the labours and merits of the crusaders, by the immediate payment of 200,000 marks of silver ; to accompany them in person to Egypt; or, if it should be judged more advantageous, to maintain during a year, 10,000 men, and, during his life, 500 knights, for the service of the Holy Land. These tempting conditions were accepted by the republic of Venice ; and the eloquence of the doge and marquis persuaded the counts of Flanders, Blois, and St. Pol, with eight barons of France, to join in the glorious enterprise. A treaty of offensive and defensive alliance was confirmed by their oaths and seals ; and each individual, according to his situation and character, was swayed by the hope of public or private advantage : by the honour of restoring an exiled monarch ; or by the sincere and probable opinion, that their efforts in Palestine would be fruitless and unavailing, and that the acquisition of Constantinople must precede and prepare the recovery of Jerusalem. But they were the chiefs or equals of a valiant band of freemen and volunteers, who thought and acted for themselves : the soldiers and clergy were divided ; and, if a large majority subscribed to the alliance, the numbers and arguments of the dissidents were strong and respectable. The boldest hearts were appalled by the report of the naval power and impregnable strength of Constantinople ; and their apprehensions were disguised to the world, and perhaps to themselves, by the more decent objections of religion and duty. They alleged the sanctity of a vow, which had drawn them from their families and homes to the rescue of the holy sepulchre ; nor should the dark and crooked counsels of human policy divert them from a pursuit, the event of which was in the hands of the Almighty. Their first offence, the attack of Zara, had been severely punished by the reproach of their conscience and the censures of the pope ; nor would they again imbrue their hands in the blood of their fellow-Christians. The apostle of Rome had pronounced ; nor would they usurp the right of avenging with the sword the schism of the Greeks, and the doubtful usurpation of the Byzantine monarch. On these principles or pretences, many pilgrims, the most distinguished for their valour and piety, withdrew from the camp ; and their retreat was less pernicious than the open or secret opposition of a discontented party, that laboured, on every occasion, to separate the army and disappoint the enterprise.

Notwithstanding this defection, the departure of the fleet and army was vigorously pressed by the Venetians ; whose zeal for the service of the royal youth concealed a just resentment to his nation and family. They were mortified (A.D. 1203. April 7—June 24) by the recent preference which had been given to Pisa, the rival of their trade; they had a long arrear of debt and injury to liquidate with the Byzantine court ; and Dandolo might not discourage the popular tale, that he had been deprived of his eyes by the emperor Manuel, who perfidiously violated the sanctity of an ambassador. A similar armament, for ages, had not rode the Hadriatic : it was composed of 120 flat-bottomed vessels or *palanders* for the horses ; 240 transports filled with men and arms ; 70 storeships laden with provisions ; and 50 stout galleys, well prepared for the encounter of an enemy, While the wind was favourable, the sky serene, and the water smooth, every eye was fixed with wonder and delight on the scene of military and naval pomp which overspread the sea. The shields of the knights and squires, at once an ornament and a defence, were arranged on either side of the ships ; the banners of the nations and families were displayed from the stern ; our modern artillery was supplied by 300 engines for casting stones and darts ; the fatigues of the way were cheered with the sound of music ; and the spirits of the adventurers were raised by the mutual assurance, that 40,000 Christian heroes were equal to the conquest of the world. In the navigation from Venice and Zara, the fleet was successfully steered by the skill and experience of the Venetian pilots : at Durazzo, the confederates first landed on the territories of the Greek empire : the isle of Corfu afforded a station and repose ; they doubled without accident the perilous cape of Malea, the southern point of Peloponnesus or the Morea ; made a descent in the islands of Negropont and Andros ; and cast anchor in Abydos on the Asiatic side of the Hellespont. These preludes of conquest were easy and bloodless : the Greeks of the provinces, without patriotism or courage, were crushed by an irresistible force ; the presence of the lawful heir might justify their obedience ; and it was rewarded by the modesty and discipline of the Latins. As they penetrated through the Hellespont, the magnitude of their navy was compressed in a narrow channel ; and the face of the waters was darkened with innumerable sails. They again expanded in the bason of the Propontis, and traversed that placid sea, till they approached the European shore, at the abbey of St. Stephen, three leagues to the west of Constantinople. The prudent doge dissuaded them from dispersing themselves in a populous and hostile land ; and as their stock of provisions was reduced, it was resolved, in the season of harvest, to replenish their storeships in the fertile islands of the Propontis. With this resolution, they directed their course ; but a strong gale, and their own impatience, drove them to the eastward ; and so near did they run to the shore and the city, that some volleys of stones and darts were exchanged between the ships and the rampart. As they passed along, they gazed with admiration on the capital of the East, or, as it should seem, of the earth ; rising from her seven hills, and towering over the continents of Europe and Asia. The swelling domes and lofty spires of 500 palaces and churches were gilded by the sun and reflected in the waters ; the walls were crowded with soldiers and spectators, whose numbers they beheld, of whose temper they were ignorant ; and each heart was chilled by the reflection, that, since the beginning of the world, such an enterprize had never been undertaken by such an handful of warriors. But the momentary apprehension was dispelled by hope and valour; and every man, says the marshal of Champagne, glanced his eye on the sword or lance which he must speedily use in the glorious conflict. The Latins cast anchor before Chalcedon; the mariners only were left in the vessels; the soldiers, horses, and arms, were safely landed; and in the luxury of an Imperial palace, the barons tasted the first fruits of their success. On the third day, the fleet and army moved towards Scutari, the Asiatic suburb of Constantinople; a detachment of 500 Greek horse was surprised and defeated by 80 French knights; and in a halt of nine days, the camp was plentifully supplied with forage and provisions.

In relating the invasion of a great empire, it may seem strange that I have not described the obstacles which should have checked the progress of the strangers. The Greeks, in truth, were an unwarlike people; but they were rich, industrious, and subject to the will of a single man : had that man been capable of fear, when his enemies were at a distance, or of courage when they approached his person. The first rumour of his nephew's alliance with the French and Venetians was despised by the usurper Alexius; his flatterers persuaded him, that in this contempt he was bold and sincere; and each evening, in the close of the banquet, he thrice discomfited the Barbarians of the West. These Barbarians had been justly terrified by the report of his naval power; and the 1600 fishing boats of Constantinople could have manned a fleet, to sink them in the Hadriatic, or stop their entrance in the mouth of the Hellespont. But all force may be annihilated by the negligence of the prince and the venality of his ministers. The great duke, or admiral, made a scandalous, almost a public, auction of the sails, the masts, and the rigging; the royal forests were reserved for the more important purpose of the chase; and the trees, says Nicetas, were guarded by the eunuchs, like the groves of religious worship. From his dream of pride, Alexius was awakened by the siege of Zara and the rapid advances of the Latins; as soon as he saw the danger was real, he thought it inevitable; and his vain presumption was lost in abject despondency and.despair. He suffered these contemptible Barbarians to pitch their camp in the sight of the palace; and his apprehensions were thinly disguised by the pomp and menace of a suppliant embassy. The sovereign of the Romans was astonished (his ambassadors were instructed to say) at the hostile appearance of the strangers. If these pilgrims were sincere in their vow for the deliverance of Jerusalem, his voice must applaud, and his treasures should assist, their pious design : but should they dare to invade the sanctuary of empire, their numbers, were they ten time. more considerable, should not protect them from his just resentment. The answer of the doge and barons was simple and magnanimous.

" In the cause of honour and justice," they said, "we despise the usurper of Greece, his threats, and his offers. *Our* friendship and *his* allegiance are due to the lawful heir, to the young prince who is seated among us, and to his father, the emperor Isaac, who has been deprived of his sceptre, his freedom, and his eyes, by the crime of an ungrateful brother. Let that brother confess his guilt, and implore forgiveness, and we ourselves will intercede, that he may be permitted to live in affluence and security. But let him not insult us by a second message : our reply will be made in arms, in the palace of Constantinople."

On the tenth day (July 6) of their encampment at Scutari, the cru-saders prepared themselves, as soldiers and as Catholics, for the passage of the Bosphorus. Perilous indeed was the adventure ; the stream was broad and rapid : in a calm the current of the Euxine might drive down the liquid and unextinguishable fires of the Greeks ; and the opposite shores of Europe were defended by 70,000 horse and foot in formidable array. On this memorable day, which hap-pened to be bright and pleasant, the Latins were distributed in six battles or divisions ; the first, or vanguard, was led by the count of Flanders, one of the most powerful of the Christian princes in the skill and number of his cross-bows. The four successive battles of the French were commanded by his brother Henry, the counts of St. Pol and Blois, and Matthew of Montmorency, the last of whom was hon-oured by the voluntary service of the marshal and nobles of Champagne. The sixth division, the rear-guard and reserve of the army, was con-ducted by the marquis of Montferrat, at the head of the Germans and Lombards. The chargers, saddled, with their long caparisons dragging on the ground, were embarked in the flat *palanders;* and the knights stood by the side of their horses, in complete armour, their helmets laced, and their lances in their hands. Their numerous train of *serjeants* and archers occupied the transports ; and each trans-port was towed by the strength and swiftness of a galley. The six divisions traversed the Bosphorus, without encountering an enemy or an obstacle ; to land the foremost was the wish, to conquer or die was the resolution, of every division and of every soldier. Jealous of the pre-eminence of danger, the knights in their heavy armour leaped into the sea, when it rose as high as their girdle ; the serjeants and archers were animated by their valour ; and the squires, letting down the draw-bridges of the palanders, led the horses to the shore. Before the squadrons could mount, and form and couch their lances, the 70,000 Greeks had vanished from their sight ; the timid Alexius gave the example to his troops : and it was only by the plunder of his rich pavilions that the Latins were informed that they had fought against an emperor. In the first consternation of a flying enemy, they resolved by a double attack to open the entrance of the harbour.

The tower of Galata, in the suburb of Pera, was attacked and stormed
by the French, while the Venetians assumed the more difficult task
of forcing the boom or chain that was stretched from the tower to the
Byzantine shore. After some fruitless attempts, their intrepid perseverance prevailed : twenty ships of war, the relics of the Grecian navy,
were either sunk or taken : the enormous and massy links of iron were
cut asunder by the shears, or broken by the weight, of the galleys;
and the Venetian fleet, safe and triumphant, rode at anchor in the
port of Constantinople. By these daring achievements, a remnant
of 20,000 Latins solicited the licence of besieging a capital which contained above 400,000 inhabitants, able, though not willing, to bear
arms in defence of their country. Such an account would indeed
suppose a population of near two millions ; but whatever abatement
may be required in the numbers of the Greeks, the *belief* of those numbers will equally exalt the fearless spirit of their assailants.

In the choice of the attack, the French and Venetians were divided
by their habits of life and warfare. The former affirmed with truth,
that Constantinople was most accessible on the side of the sea and the
harbour. The latter might assert with honour, that they had long
enough trusted their lives and fortunes to a frail bark and a precarious
element, and loudly demanded a trial of knighthood, a firm ground,
and a close onset, either on foot or horseback. After a prudent compromise, of employing the two nations by sea and land, in the service
best suited to their character, the fleet covering the army, they both
proceeded from the entrance to the extremity of the harbour : the stone
bridge of the river was hastily repaired ; and the six battles of the
French formed their encampment against the front of the capital, the
basis of the triangle which runs about four miles from the port of the
Propontis. On the edge of a broad ditch, at the foot of a lofty rampart, they had leisure to contemplate the difficulties of their enterprise.
The gates to the right and left of their narrow camp poured forth frequent sallies of cavalry and light-infantry, which cut off their stragglers,
swept the country of provisions, sounded the alarm five or six times in
the course of each day, and compelled them to plant a palisade, and
sink an entrenchment, for their immediate safety. In the supplies and
convoys the Venetians had been too sparing, or the Franks too voracious : the usual complaints of hunger and scarcity were heard, and
perhaps felt : their stock of flour would be exhausted in three weeks ;
and their disgust of salt meat tempted them to taste the flesh of their
horses. The trembling usurper was supported by Theodore Lascaris,
his son-in-law, a valiant youth, who aspired to save and to rule his
country ; the Greeks, regardless of that country, were awakened to the
defence of their religion ; but their firmest hope was in the strength
and spirit of the Varangian guards, of the Danes and English, as they
are named in the writers of the times. After ten days' (July 7—18

incessant labour, the ground was levelled, the ditch filled, the approaches of the besiegers were regularly made, and 250 engines of assault exercised their various powers to clear the rampart, to batter the walls and to sap the foundations. On the first appearance of a breach, the scaling ladders were applied : the numbers that defended the vantage-ground repulsed and oppressed the adventurous Latins ; but they admired the resolution of fifteen knights and serjeants, who had gained the ascent, and maintained their perilous station till they were precipitated or made prisoners by the Imperial guards. On the side of the harbour the naval attack was more successfully conducted by the Venetians ; and that industrious people employed every resource that was known and practised before the invention of gunpowder. A double line, three bow-shots in front, was formed by the galleys and ships ; and the swift motion of the former was supported by the weight and loftiness of the latter, whose decks and poops, and turret, were the platforms of military engines, that discharged their shot over the heads of the first line. The soldiers, who leaped from the galleys on shore, immediately planted and ascended their scaling-ladders, while the large ships, advancing more slowly into the intervals, and lowering a drawbridge, opened a way through the air from their masts to the rampart. In the midst of the conflict, the doge, a venerable and conspicuous form, stood aloft in complete armour on the prow of the galley. The great standard of St. Mark was displayed before him ; his threats, promises, and exhortations, urged the diligence of the rowers ; his vessel was the first that struck ; and Dandolo was the first warrior on the shore. The nations admired the magnanimity of the blind old man, without reflecting that his age and infirmities diminished the price of life, and enhanced the value of immortal glory. On a sudden, by an invisible hand (for the standard-bearer was probably slain), the banner of the republic was fixed on the rampart : twenty-five towers were rapidly occupied ; and, by the cruel expedient of fire, the Greeks were driven from the adjacent quarter. The doge had despatched the intelligence of his success, when he was checked by the danger of his confederates. Nobly declaring that he would rather die with the pilgrims than gain a victory by their destruction, Dandolo relinquished his advantage, recalled his troops, and hastened to the scene of action. He found the six weary diminutive *battles* of the French encompassed by sixty squadrons of the Greek cavalry, the least of which was more numerous than the largest of their divisions. Shame and despair had provoked Alexius to the last effort of a general sally ; but he was awed by the firm order and manly aspect of the Latins : and, after skirmishing at a distance, withdrew his troops in the close of the evening. The silence or tumult of the night exasperated his fears ; and the timid usurper, collecting a treasure of 10,000 pounds of gold, basely deserted his wife, his people, and his fortune ; threw himself into a bark, stole through the Bosphorus, and landed in shameful safety in an obscure harbour of Thrace. As soon as they were apprised of his flight, the Greek nobles sought pardon and peace in the dungeon where the blind Isaac expected each hour the visit of the executioner. Again saved and exalted by the vicissitudes of fortune, the captive in his imperial robes was replaced on the throne, and surrounded with prostrate slaves, whose real terror and affected joy he was incapable of discerning. At the dawn of day hostilities were suspended; and the Latin chiefs were surprised by a message from the lawful and reigning emperor, who was impatient to embrace his son and to reward his generous deliverers.

But these generous deliverers were unwilling to release their hostage, till they had obtained from his father the payment, or at least the promise, of their recompense. They chose four ambassadors, Matthew of Montmorency, our historian the marshal of Champagne, and two Venetians, to congratulate the emperor. The gates (July 19) were thrown open on their approach, the streets on both sides were lined with the battle-axes of the Danish and English guard : the presence-chamber glittered with gold and jewels, the false substitutes of virtue and power; by the side of the blind Isaac, his wife was seated, the sister of the king of Hungary ; and by her appearance, the noble matrons of Greece were drawn from their domestic retirement, and mingled with the circle of senators and soldiers. The Latins, by the mouth of the marshal, spoke like men, conscious of their merits, but who respected, the work of their own hands ; and the emperor clearly understood that his son's engagements with Venice and the pilgrims must be ratified without hesitation or delay. Withdrawing into a private chamber with the empress, a chamberlain, an interpreter, and the four ambassadors, the father of young Alexius inquired with some anxiety into the nature of his stipulations. The submission of the Eastern empire to the pope, the succour of the Holy Land, and a present contribution of 200,000 marks of silver—"These conditions are weighty," was his prudent reply ; "they are hard to accept, and difficult to perform. But no conditions can exceed the measure of your services and deserts." After this satisfactory assurance, the barons mounted on horseback, and introduced the heir of Constantinople to the city and palace : his youth and marvellous adventures engaged every heart in his favour, and Alexius was solemnly crowned with his father in the dome of St. Sophia. In the first days of his reign, the people, already blessed with the restoration of plenty and peace, were delighted by the joyful catastrophe of the tragedy ; and the discontent of the nobles, their regret and their fears, were covered by the polished surface of pleasure and loyalty. The mixture of two discordant nations in the same capital might have been pregnant with mischief and danger ; and the suburb of Galata, or Pera, was assigned for the quarters of the French and Venetians. But the liberty of trade and familiar intercourse was allowed between the friendly nations ; and each day the pilgrims were tempted by devotion or curiosity to visit the churches and palaces of Constantinople. Their rude minds, insensible perhaps of the finer arts, were astonished by the magnificent scenery : and the poverty of their native towns enhanced the populousness and riches of the first metropolis of Christendom. Descending from his state, young Alexius was prompted by interest and gratitude to repeat his frequent and familiar visits to his Latin allies ; and in the freedom of the table, the gay petulance of the French sometimes forgot the emperor of the East. In their more serious conferences, it was agreed, that the re-union of the two churches must be the result of patience and time ; but avarice was less tractable than zeal ; and a large sum was instantly disbursed to appease the wants, and silence the importunity, of the crusaders. Alexius was alarmed by the approaching hour of their departure : their absence might have relieved him from the engagement which he was yet incapable of performing ; but his friends would have left him, naked and alone, to the caprice and prejudice of a perfidious nation. He wished to bribe their stay, the delay of a year, by undertaking to defray their expence, and to satisfy, in their name, the freight of the Venetian vessels. The offer was agitated in the council of the barons ; and, after a repetition of their debates and scruples, a majority of votes again acquiesced in the advice of the doge and the prayer of the young emperor. At the price of 1600 pounds of gold, he prevailed on the marquis of Montferrat to lead him with an army round the provinces of Europe ; to establish his authority, and pursue his uncle, while Constantinople was awed by the presence of Baldwin and his confederates of France and Flanders. The expedition was successful ; the blind emperor exulted in the success of his arms, and listened to the predictions of his flatterers, that the same Providence which had raised him from the dungeon to the throne, would heal his gout, restore his sight, and watch over the long prosperity of his reign. Yet the mind of the suspicious old man was tormented by the rising glories of his son ; nor could his pride conceal from his envoy, that, while his own name was pronounced in faint and reluctant acclamations, the royal youth was the theme of spontaneous and universal praise.

By the recent invasion, the Greeks were awakened from a dream of nine centuries ; from the vain presumption that the capital of the Roman empire was impregnable to foreign arms. The strangers of the West had violated the city, and bestowed the sceptre, of Constantine : their Imperial clients soon became as unpopular as themselves : the well-known vices of Isaac were rendered still more contemptible by his infirmities ; and the young Alexius was hated as an apostate, who had renounced the manners and religion of his country. His secret covenant with the Latins was divulged or suspected; the people, and especially the clergy, were devoutly attached to their faith and superstition; and every convent, and every shop, resounded with the danger of the church and the tyranny of the pope. An empty treasury could ill supply the demands of regal luxury and foreign extortion: the Greeks refused to avert, by a general tax, the impending evils of servitude and pillage; the oppression of the rich excited a more dangerous and personal resentment: and if the emperor melted the plate, and despoiled the images, of the sanctuary, he seemed to justify the complaints of heresy and sacrilege. During the absence of marquis Boniface and his Imperial pupil, Constantinople was visited with a calamity which might be justly imputed to the zeal and indiscretion of the Flemish pilgrims. In one of their visits to the city, they were scandalized by the aspect of a mosque or synagogue, in which one God was worshipped, without a partner or a son. Their effectual mode of controversy was to attack the infidels with the sword, and their habitation with fire: but the infidels, and some Christian neighbours, presumed to defend their lives and properties; and the flames which bigotry had kindled consumed the most orthodox and innocent structures. During eight days and nights, the conflagration spread above a league in front, from the harbour to the Propontis, over the thickest and most populous regions of the city. It is not easy to count the stately churches and palaces that were reduced to a smoking ruin, to value the merchandise that perished in the trading streets, or to number the families that were involved in the common destruction. By this outrage, which the doge and the barons in vain affected to disclaim, the name of the Latins became still more unpopular; and the colony of that nation, above 15,000 persons, consulted their safety in a hasty retreat from the city to the protection of their standard in the suburb of Pera. The emperor returned in triumph; but the firmest and most dexterous policy would have been insufficient to steer him through the tempest, which overwhelmed the person and government of that unhappy youth. His own inclination, and his father's advice, attached him to his benefactors; but Alexius hesitated between gratitude and patriotism, between the fear of his subjects and of his allies. By his feeble and fluctuating conduct he lost the esteem and confidence of both; and, while he invited the marquis of Montferrat to occupy the palace, he suffered the nobles to conspire, and the people to arm, for the deliverance of their country. Regardless of his painful situation, the Latin chiefs repeated their demands, resented his delays, suspected his intentions, and exacted a decisive answer of peace or war. The haughty summons was delivered by three French knights and three Venetian deputies, who girded their swords, mounted their horses, pierced through the angry multitude, and entered with a fearless countenance the palace and presence of the Greek emperor. In a peremptory tone,

they recapitulated their services and his engagements ; and boldly declared, that unless their just claims were fully and immediately satisfied,
they should no longer hold him either as a sovereign or a friend. After
this defiance, the first that had ever wounded an Imperial ear, they departed without betraying any symptoms of fear ; but their escape from
a servile palace and a furious city astonished the ambassadors ; and
their return to the camp was the signal of mutual hostility.

Among the Greeks, all authority and wisdom were overborne by the
impetuous multitude, who (A.D. 1204) mistook their rage for valour,
their numbers for strength, and their fanaticism for the support and
inspiration of Heaven. In the eyes of both nations Alexius was false
and contemptible : the base and spurious race of the Angeli was rejected with clamourous disdain ; and the people of Constantinople encompassed the senate, to demand at their hands a more worthy emperor. To every senator, conspicuous by his birth or dignity, they
successively presented the purple : by each senator the deadly garment
was repulsed : the contest lasted three days ; and we may learn from
the historian Nicetas, one of the members of the assembly, that fear
and weakness were the guardians of their loyalty. A phantom, who
vanished in oblivion, was forcibly proclaimed by the crowd ; but the
author of the tumult, and the leader of the war, was a prince of the
house of Ducas ; and his common appellation of Alexius must be dis-
criminated by the epithet of Mourzoufle, which in the vulgar idiom
expressed the close junction of his black and shaggy eyebrows. At
once a patriot and a courtier, the perfidious Mourzoufle, who was not
destitute of cunning and courage, opposed the Latins both in speech
and action, inflamed the passions and prejudices of the Greeks, and
insinuated himself into the favour and confidence of Alexius, who
trusted him with the office of great chamberlain, and tinged his buskins
with the colours of royalty. At the dead of night he rushed into the
bed-chamber with an affrighted aspect, exclaiming, that the palace was
attacked by the people and betrayed by the guards. Starting from his
couch, the unsuspecting prince threw himself into the arms of his
enemy, who had contrived his escape by a private staircase. But that
staircase terminated in a prison ; Alexius was (Feb. 8) seized, stripped,
and loaded with chains ; and, after tasting some days the bitterness of
death, he was poisoned, or strangled, or beaten with clubs, at the command, and in the presence, of the tyrant. The emperor Isaac Angelus
soon followed his son to the grave, and Mourzoufle, perhaps, might
spare the superfluous crime of hastening the extinction of impotence
and blindness.

The death of the emperors, and the usurpation of Mourzoufle, had
changed the nature of the quarrel. It was no longer the disagree-
ment of allies who over-valued their services, or neglected their
obligations : the French and Venetians forgot their complaints against

Alexius, dropt a tear on the untimely fate of their companion, and swore revenge against the perfidious nation who had crowned his assassin. Yet the prudent doge was still inclined to negociate; he asked as a debt, a subsidy, or a fine, 50,000 pounds of gold, about £2,000,000; nor would the conference have been abruptly broken, if the zeal, or policy, of Mourzoufle had not refused to sacrifice the Greek church to the safety of the state. Amidst the invective of his foreign and domestic enemies, we may discern, that he was not unworthy of the character which he had assumed, of the public champion: the second siege (Jan.—April) of Constantinople was far more laborious than the first; the treasury was replenished, and discipline was restored, by a severe inquisition into the abuses of the former reign; and Mourzoufle, an iron mace in his hand, visiting the posts, and affecting the port and aspect of a warrior, was an object of terror to his soldiers, at least, and to his kinsmen. Before and after the death of Alexius, the Greeks made two vigorous and well-conducted attempts to burn the navy in the harbour; but the skill and courage of the Venetians repulsed the fire-ships; and the vagrant flames wasted themselves without injury in the sea. In a nocturnal sally the Greek emperor was vanquished by Henry, brother of the count of Flanders: the advantages of number and surprise aggravated the shame of his defeat; his buckler was found on the field of battle; and the Imperial standard, a divine image of the Virgin, was presented, as a trophy and a relic, to the Cistercian monks, the disciples of St. Bernard. Near three months, without excepting the holy season of Lent, were consumed in skirmishes and preparations, before the Latins were ready or resolved for a general assault. The land-fortifications had been found impregnable; and the Venetian pilots represented, that, on the shore of the Propontis, the anchorage was unsafe, and the ships must be driven by the current far away to the straits of the Hellespont; a prospect not unpleasing to the reluctant pilgrims, who sought every opportunity of breaking the army. From the harbour, therefore, the assault was determined by the assailants, and expected by the besieged; and the emperor had placed his scarlet pavilions on a neighbouring height, to direct and animate the efforts of his troops. A fearless spectator, whose mind could entertain the ideas of pomp and pleasure, might have admired the long array of two embattled armies, which extended above half a league, the one on the ships and galleys, the other on the walls and towers raised above the ordinary level by several stages of wooden turrets. Their first fury was spent in the discharge of darts, stones, and fire, from the engines; but the water was deep; the French were bold; the Venetians were skilful; they approached the walls; and a desperate conflict of swords, spears, and battle-axes, was fought on the trembling bridges that grappled the floating, to the stable, batteries. In more than an hundred places the assault was urged, and the defence was sustained; till the superiority of ground and numbers finally prevailed, and the Latin trumpets sounded a retreat. On the ensuing days, the attack was renewed with equal vigour, and a similar event; and in the night, the doge and the barons held a council, apprehensive only for the public danger: not a voice pronounced the words of escape or treaty; and each warrior, according to his temper, embraced the hope of victory or the assurance of a glorious death. By the experience of the former siege, the Greeks were instructed, but the Latins were animated; and the knowledge that Constantinople *might* be taken, was of more avail than the local precautions which that knowledge had inspired for its defence. In the third assault, two ships were linked together to double their strength; a strong north wind drove them on the shore; the bishops of Troyes and Soissons led the van; and the auspicious names of the *pilgrim* and the *paradise* resounded along the line. The episcopal banners were displayed on the walls; an hundred marks of silver had been promised to the first adventurers; and if their reward was intercepted by death, their names have been immortalized by fame. Four towers were scaled; three gates were burst open; and the French knights, who might tremble on the waves, felt themselves invincible on horseback on the solid ground. Shall I relate that the thousands who guarded the emperor's person fled on the approach and before the lance of a single warrior? Their ignominious flight is attested by their countryman Nicetas; an army of phantoms marched with the French hero, and he was magnified to a giant in the eyes of the Greeks. While the fugitives deserted their posts and cast away their arms, the Latins entered the city under the banners of their leaders: the streets and gates opened for their passage; and either design or accident kindled a third conflagration, which consumed in a few hours the measure of three of the largest cities of France. In the close of evening, the barons checked their troops and fortified their stations; they were awed by the extent and populousness of the capital, which might yet require the labour of a month, if the churches and palaces were conscious of their internal strength. But in the morning, a suppliant procession, with crosses and images, announced the submission of the Greeks, and deprecated the wrath of the conquerors; the usurper escaped through the golden gate; the palaces of Blachernæ and Boucoleon were occupied by the count of Flanders and the marquis of Montferrat; and the empire which still bore the name of Constantine, and the title of Roman, was subverted by the arms of the Latin pilgrims.

Constantinople had been taken by storm; and no restraints, except those of religion and humanity, were imposed on the conquerors by the laws of war. Boniface marquis of Montferrat still acted as their general: and the Greeks, who revered his name as that of their future sovereign, were heard to exclaim in a lamentable tone, "Holy marquis-king, have mercy upon us !" His prudence or compassion opened the gates of the city to the fugitives ; and he exhorted the soldiers of the cross to spare the lives of their fellow-Christians. The streams of blood that flow down the pages of Nicetas may be reduced to the slaughter of 2000 of his unresisting countrymen ; and the greater part was massacred, not by the strangers, but by the Latins, who had been driven from the city, and who exercised the revenge of a triumphant faction. Yet of these exiles, some were less mindful of injuries than of benefits ; and Nicetas himself was indebted for his safety to the generosity of a Venetian merchant. Pope Innocent the third accuses the pilgrims of respecting neither age nor sex, nor religious profession ; and bitterly laments that the deeds of darkness were perpetrated in open day. It is indeed probable that the licence of victory prompted and covered a multitude of sins ; the marquis of Montferrat was the patron of discipline and decency ; the count of Flanders was the mirror of chastity : they had forbidden, under pain of death, the rape of married women, or virgins, or nuns ; and the proclamation was sometimes invoked by the vanquished, and respected by the victors. Their cruelty and lust were moderated by the authority of the chiefs, and feelings of the soldiers ; for we are no longer describing an irruption of the northern savages ; and however ferocious they might still appear, time, policy, and religion, had civilized the manners of the French, and still more of the Italians. But a free scope was allowed to their avarice, which was glutted, even in the holy week, by the pillage of Constantinople. The right of victory, unshackled by any promise or treaty, had confiscated the public and private wealth of the Greeks ; and every hand, according to its size and strength, might lawfully execute the sentence and seize the forfeiture. A portable and universal standard of exchange was found in the coined and uncoined metals of gold and silver, which each captor at home or abroad might convert into the possessions most suitable to his temper and situation. Of the treasures, which trade and luxury had accumulated, the silks, velvets, furs, the gems, spices, and rich movables, were the most precious, as they could not be procured for money in the ruder countries of Europe. An order of rapine was instituted ; nor was the share of each individual abandoned to industry or chance. Under the tremendous penalties of perjury, excommunication, and death, the Latins were bound to deliver their plunder into the common stock ; three churches were selected for the deposit and distribution of the spoil : a single share was allotted to a foot soldier ; two for a serjeant on horseback ; four to a knight ; and larger proportions according to the rank and merit of the barons and princes. For violating this sacred engagement, a knight belonging to the count of St. Pol was hanged with his shield and coat of arms round his neck : his example might render similar offenders more art-ful and discreet ; but avarice was more powerful than fear ; and it is generally believed, that the secret far exceeded the acknowledged plun-der. Yet the magnitude of the prize surpassed the largest scale of experience or expectation. After the whole had been equally divided between the French and Venetians, 50,000 marks were deducted to satisfy the debts of the former and the demands of the latter. The residue of the French amounted to 400,000 marks of silver, about £800,000 ; nor can I better appreciate the value of that sum in the public and private transactions of the age, than by defining it as seven times the annual revenue of the kingdom of England.

In this great revolution we enjoy the singular felicity of comparing the narratives of Villehardouin and Nicetas, the opposite feelings of the marshal of Champagne and the Byzantine senator. At the first view it should seem that the wealth of Constantinople was only trans-ferred from one nation to another ; and that the loss and sorrow of the Greeks is exactly balanced by the joy and advantage of the Latins. But in the miserable account of war, the gain is never equivalent to the loss, the pleasure to the pain : the smiles of the Latins were tran-sient and fallacious ; the Greeks for ever wept over the ruins of their country ; and their real calamities were aggravated by sacrilege and mockery. What benefits accrued to the conquerors from the three fires which annihilated so vast a portion of the buildings and riches of the city ! What a stock of such things as could neither be used nor transported, was maliciously or wantonly destroyed ! How much treasure was idly wasted in gaming, debauchery, and riot ! And what precious objects were bartered for a vile price by the impatience or ignorance of the soldiers, whose reward was stolen by the base in-dustry of the last of the Greeks ! Those alone, who had nothing to lose, might derive some profit from the revolution ; but the misery of the upper ranks of society is strongly painted in the personal adven-tures of Nicetas himself. His stately palace had been reduced to ashes in the second conflagration ; and the senator, with his family and friends, found an obscure shelter in another house which he possessed near the church of St. Sophia. It was the door of this mean habita-tion that his friend the Venetian merchant guarded in the disguise of a soldier, till Nicetas could save, by a precipitate flight, the relics of his fortune and the chastity of his daughter. In a cold wintry season, these fugitives, nursed in the lap of prosperity, departed on foot ; his wife was with child ; the desertion of their slaves compelled them to carry their baggage on their own shoulders ; and their women, whom they placed in the centre, were exhorted to conceal their beauty with dirt, instead of adorning it with paint and jewels. Every step was exposed to insult and danger ; the threats of the strangers were less painful than the taunts of the plebeians, with whom they were now levelled ;

nor did the exiles breathe in safety till their mournful pilgrimage was concluded at Selymbria, above forty miles from the capital. On their way they overtook the patriarch, without attendance and almost without apparel, riding on an ass, and reduced to a state of apostolical poverty, which, had it been voluntary, might perhaps have been meritorious. In the mean while, his desolate churches were profaned by the licentiousness and party zeal of the Latins. After stripping the gems and pearls, they converted the chalices into drinking-cups; their tables, on which they gamed and feasted, were covered with the pictures of Christ and the saints; and they trampled under foot the most venerable objects of the Christian worship. In the cathedral of St. Sophia, the ample veil of the sanctuary was rent asunder for the sake of the golden fringe; and the altar, a monument of art and riches, was broken in pieces and shared among the captors. Their mules and horses were laden with the wrought silver and gilt carvings, which they tore down from the doors and pulpit; and if the beasts stumbled under the burthen, they were stabbed by their impatient drivers, and the holy pavement streamed with their impure blood. Nor were the repositories of the royal dead secure from violation: in the church of the apostles, the tombs of the emperors were rifled; and it is said, that after six centuries the corpse of Justinian was found without any signs of decay or putrefaction. In the streets, the French and Flemings clothed themselves and their horses in painted robes and flowing head-dresses of linen; and the coarse intemperance of their feasts insulted the splendid sobriety of the East. To expose the arms of a people of scribes, they affected to display a pen, an ink-horn, and a sheet of paper, without discerning that the instruments of science and valour were *alike* feeble and useless in the hands of the modern Greeks.

Their reputation and their language encouraged them, however, to despise the ignorance, and to overlook the progress, of the Latins. In the love of the arts, the national difference was still more obvious and real; the Greeks preserved with reverence the works of their ancestors, which they could not imitate; and, in the destruction of the statues of Constantinople, we are provoked to join in the complaints and invectives of the Byzantine historian. We have seen how the rising city was adorned by the vanity and despotism of the Imperial founder: in the ruins of paganism, some gods and heroes were saved from the axe of superstition; and the forum and hippodrome were dignified with the relics of a better age. Several of these are described by Nicetas in a florid and affected style; and, from his descriptions, I shall select some interesting particulars. 1. The victorious charioteers were cast in bronze, at their own, or the public, charge, and fitly placed aloft in the hippodrome: they stood aloft in their chariots, wheeling round the goal; the spectators could admire their attitude, and judge of the resemblance; and of these figures, the most perfect might have been transported from the Olympic stadium. 2. The sphinx, river-horse, and crocodile, denote the climate and manufacture of Egypt, and the spoils of that ancient province. 3. The she-wolf suckling Romulus and Remus; a subject alike pleasing to the *old* and the *new* Romans; but which could rarely be treated before the decline of the Greek sculpture. 4. An eagle holding and tearing a serpent in his talons; a domestic monument of the Byzantines, which they ascribed not to a human artist, but to the magic power of the philosopher Apollonius, who, by this talisman, delivered the city from such venomous reptiles. 5. An ass and his driver; which were erected by Augustus in his colony of Nicopolis, to commemorate a verbal omen of the victory of Actium. 6. An equestrian statue; which passed, in the vulgar opinion, for Joshua, the Jewish conqueror, stretching out his hand to stop the course of the descending sun. A more classical tradition recognized the figures of Bellerophon and Pegasus; and the free attitude of the steed seemed to mark that he trod on air, rather than on the earth. 7. A square and lofty obelisk of brass; the sides were embossed with a variety of picturesque and rural scenes : birds singing; rustics labouring, or playing on their pipes; sheep bleating; lambs skipping; the sea, and a scene of fish and fishing; little naked cupids laughing, playing, and pelting each other with apples; and, on the summit, a female figure turning with the slightest breath, and thence denominated *the wind's attendant.* 8. The Phrygian shepherd presenting to Venus the prize of beauty, the apple of discord. 9. The incomparable statue of Helen; which is delineated by Nicetas in the words of admiration and love : her well-turned feet, snowy arms, rosy lips, bewitching smiles, swimming eyes, arched eye-brows, the harmony of her shape, the lightness of her drapery, and her flowing locks that waved in the wind : a beauty that might have moved her Barbarian destroyers to pity and remorse. 10. The manly or divine form of Hercules, as he was restored to life by the master-hand of Lysippus; of such magnitude, that his thumb was equal to the waist, his leg to the stature, of a common man; his chest ample, his shoulders broad, his limbs strong and muscular, his hair curled, his aspect commanding. Without his bow, or quiver, or club, his lion's skin carelessly thrown over him, he was seated on an osier basket, his right leg and arm stretched to the utmost, his left knee bent, and supporting his elbow, his head reclining on his left hand, his countenance indignant and pensive. 11. A colossal statue of Juno, which had once adorned her temple of Samos; the enormous head by four yoke of oxen was laboriously drawn to the palace. 12. Another colossus, of Pallas or Minerva, thirty feet in height, and representing with admirable spirit the attributes and character of the martial maid. Before we accuse the Latins, it is just to remark, that this Pallas was destroyed after the first siege, by the fear and superstition of the Greeks themselves. The other statues of brass which I have enumerated, were broken and melted by the unfeeling avarice of the crusaders : the cost and labour were consumed in a moment ; the soul of genius evaporated in smoke ; and the remnant of base metal was coined into money for the payment of the troops. Bronze is not the most durable of monuments : from the marble forms of Phidias and Praxiteles, the Latins might turn aside with stupid contempt ; but unless they were crushed by some accidental injury, those useless stones stood secure on their pedestals. The most enlightened of the strangers, above the gross and sensual pursuits of their countrymen, more piously exercised the right of conquest in the search and seizure of the relics of the saints. Immense was the supply of heads and bones, crosses and images, that were scattered by this revolution over the churches of Europe ; and such was the increase of pilgrimage and oblation, that no branch, perhaps, of more lucrative plunder was imported from the East. Of the writings of antiquity, many that still existed in the twelfth century are now lost. But the pilgrims were not solicitous to save or transport the volumes of an unknown tongue : the perishable substance of paper or parchment can only be preserved by the multiplicity of copies ; the literature of the Greeks had almost centred in the metropolis : and, without computing the extent of our loss, we may drop a tear over the libraries that have perished in the triple fire of Constantinople.

After the death of the lawful princes, the French and Venetians, confident of justice and victory, agreed to divide and regulate their future possessions. It was stipulated by treaty, that twelve electors, six of either nation, should be nominated ; that a majority should chuse the emperor of the East ; and that, if the votes were equal, the decision of chance should ascertain the successful candidate. To him, with all the titles and prerogatives of the Byzantine throne, they assigned the two palaces of Boucoleon and Blachernæ, with a fourth part of the Greek monarchy. It was defined that the three remaining portions should be equally shared between the republic of Venice and the barons of France ; that each feudatory, with an honourable exception for the doge, should acknowledge and perform the duties of homage and military service to the supreme head of the empire : that the nation which gave an emperor, should resign to their brethren the choice of a patriarch ; and that the pilgrims, whatever might be their impatience to visit the Holy Land, should devote another year to the conquest and defence of the Greek provinces. After the conquest of Constantinople by the Latins, the treaty was confirmed and executed, and the first and most important step was the creation of an emperor. The six electors of the French nation were all ecclesiastics, the abbot of Loces, the archbishop elect of Acre in Palestine, and the bishops of Troyes, Soissons, Halberstadt, and Bethlehem, the last of whom exercised in the camp the office of pope's legate : their profession and knowledge were respectable ; and as *they* could not be the objects, they were best qualified to be the authors, of the choice. The six Venetians were the principal servants of the state, and in this list the noble families of Querini and Contarini are still proud to discover their ancestors. The twelve assembled in the chapel of the palace ; and after the solemn invocation of the Holy Ghost, they proceeded to deliberate and vote. A just impulse of respect and gratitude prompted them to crown the virtues of the doge ; his wisdom had inspired their enterprise ; and the most youthful knights might envy and applaud the exploits of blindness and age. But the patriot Dandolo was devoid of all personal ambition, and fully satisfied that he had been judged worthy to reign. His nomination was over-ruled by the Venetians themselves ; his countrymen, and perhaps his friends, represented, with the eloquence of truth, the mischiefs that might arise to national freedom and the common cause, from the union of two incompatible characters, of the first magistrate of a republic and the emperor of the East. The exclusion of the doge left room for the more equal merits of Boniface and Baldwin ; and at their names all meaner candidates respectfully withdrew. The marquis of Montferrat was recommended by his mature age and fair reputation, by the choice of the adventurers and the wishes of the Greeks ; nor can I believe that Venice, the mistress of the sea, could be seriously apprehensive of a petty lord at the foot of the Alps. But the count of Flanders was the chief of a wealthy and warlike people ; he was valiant and pious ; in the prime of life, since he was only thirty-two years of age, a descendant of Charlemagne, a cousin of the king of France, and a compeer of the prelates and barons who had yielded with reluctance to the command of a foreigner. Without the chapel, these barons, with the doge and marquis at their head, expected the decision of the twelve electors. It was (A.D. 1204. May 9—16) announced by the bishop of Soissons, in the name of his colleagues : " Ye have sworn to obey the prince whom we should chuse ; by our unanimous suffrage, Baldwin count of Flanders and Hainault is now your sovereign, and the emperor of the East." He was saluted with loud applause, and the proclamation was re-echoed through the city by the joy of the Latins and the trembling adulation of the Greeks. Boniface was the first to kiss the hand of his rival, and to raise him on the buckler ; and Baldwin was transported to the cathedral, and solemnly invested with the purple buskins. At the end of three weeks he was crowned by the legate, in the vacancy of a patriarch ; but the Venetian clergy soon filled the chapter of St. Sophia, seated Thomas Morosini on the ecclesiastical throne, and employed every art to perpetuate in their own nation the honours and benefices of the Greek church. Without delay, the successor of Constantine instructed Palestine, France, and Rome of this memorable revolution. To Palestine he sent, as a trophy, the gates of Constantinople, and the chain of the harbour ; and adopted, from the Assise of Jerusalem, the laws or customs best adapted to a French colony and conquest in the East. In his epistles, the natives of France are encouraged to swell that colony, and to secure that conquest, to people a magnificent city and a fertile land, which will reward the labours both of the priest and the soldier. He congratulates the Roman pontiff on the restoration of his authority in the East ; invites him to extinguish the Greek schism by his presence in a general council ; and implores his blessing and forgiveness for the disobedient pilgrims. Prudence and dignity are blended in the answer of Innocent. In the subversion of the Byzantine empire, he arraigns the vices of man, and adores the providence of God : the conquerors will be absolved or condemned by their future conduct ; the validity of their treaty depends on the judgment of St. Peter ; but he inculcates their most sacred duty of establishing a just subordination of obedience and tribute, from the Greeks to the Latins, from the magistrate to the clergy, and from the clergy to the pope.

In the division of the Greek provinces, the share of the Venetians was more ample than that of the Latin emperor. No more than one fourth was appropriated to his domain : a clear moiety of the remainder was reserved for Venice ; and the other moiety was distributed among the adventurers of France and Lombardy. The venerable Dandolo was proclaimed despot of Romania, and invested after the Greek fashion with the purple buskins. He ended at Constantinople his long and glorious life ; and if the prerogative was personal, the title was used by his successors till the middle of the fourteenth century, with the singular though true addition of lords of one fourth and a half of the Roman empire. The doge, a slave of state, was seldom permitted to depart from the helm of the republic ; but his place was supplied by the *bail* or regent, who exercised a supreme jurisdiction over the colony of Venetians : they possessed three of the eight quarters of the city ; and his independent tribunal was composed of six judges, four counsellors, two chamberlains, two fiscal advocates, and a constable. Their long experience of the eastern trade enabled them to select their portion with discernment : they had rashly accepted the dominion and defence of Hadrianople ; but it was the more reasonable aim of their policy to form a chain of factories, and cities, and islands, along the maritime coast, from the neighbourhood of Ragusa to the Hellespont and the Bosphorus. The labour and cost of such extensive conquests exhausted their treasury : they abandoned their maxims of government, adopted a feudal system, and contented themselves with the homage of their nobles, for the possessions which these private vassals undertook to reduce and maintain. And thus it was, that the family of Sanut acquired the duchy of Naxos, which involved the greatest part of the Archipelago. For the price of 10,000 marks, the republic purchased of the marquis of Montferrat the fertile island of Crete or Candia with the ruins of an hundred cities : but its improvement was stinted by the proud and narrow spirit of an aristocracy ; and the wisest senators would confess that the sea, not the land, was the treasury of St. Mark. In the moiety of the adventurers, the marquis Boniface might claim the most liberal reward ; and, besides the isle of Crete, his exclusion from the throne was compensated by the royal title and the provinces beyond the Hellespont. But he prudently exchanged that distant and difficult conquest for the kingdom of Thessalonica or Macedonia, twelve days' journey from the capital, where he might be supported by the neighbouring powers of his brother-in-law the king of Hungary. His progress was hailed by the voluntary or reluctant acclamations of the natives ; and Greece, the proper and ancient Greece, again received a Latin conqueror, who trod with indifference that classic ground. He viewed with a careless eye the beauties of the valley of Tempe ; traversed with a cautious step the straits of Thermopylæ ; occupied the unknown cities of Thebes, Athens, and Argos ; and assaulted the fortifications of Corinth and Napoli, which resisted his arms. The lots of the Latin pilgrims were regulated by chance, or choice, or subsequent exchange ; and they abused, with intemperate joy, their triumph over the lives and fortunes of a great people. After a minute survey of the provinces, they weighed in the scales of avarice the revenue of each district, the advantage of the situation, and the ample or scanty supplies for the maintenance of soldiers and horses. Their presumption claimed and divided the long-lost dependencies of the Roman sceptre : the Nile and Euphrates rolled through their imaginary realms ; and happy was the warrior who drew for his prize the palace of the Turkish sultan of Iconium. I shall not descend to the pedigree of families and the rent-roll of estates, but I wish to specify that the counts of Blois and St. Pol were invested with the duchy of Nice and the lordship of Demotica : the principal fiefs were held by the service of constable, chamberlain, cup-bearer, butler, and chief cook ; and our historian, Jeffrey of Villehardouin, obtained a fair establishment on the banks of the Hebrus, and united the double office of marshal of Champagne and Romania. At the head of his knights and archers, each baron mounted on horseback to secure the possession of his share, and their first efforts were generally successful. But the public force was weakened by their dispersion ; and a thousand quarrels must arise under a law, and among men, whose sole umpire was the sword. Within three months after the conquest of Constantinople, the emperor and the king of Thessalonica drew their hostile followers into the field ; they were reconciled by the authority of the doge, the advice of the marshal, and the firm freedom of their peers.

Two fugitives, who had reigned at Constantinople, still asserted the title of emperor; and the subjects of their fallen throne might be moved to pity by the misfortunes of the elder Alexius, or excited to revenge by the spirit of Mourzoufle. A domestic alliance (A.D. 1204, &c.), a common interest, a similar guilt, and the merit of extinguishing his enemies, a brother and a nephew, induced the more recent usurper to unite with the former the relics of his power. Mourzoufle was received with smiles and honours in the camp of his father Alexius; but the wicked can never love, and should rarely trust, their fellow-criminals: he was seized in the bath, deprived of his eyes, stripped of his troops and treasures, and turned out to wander an object of horror and contempt to those who with more propriety could hate, and with more justice could punish, the assassin of the emperor Isaac, and his son. As the tyrant, pursued by fear or remorse, was stealing over to Asia, he was seized by the Latins of Constantinople, and condemned, after an open trial, to an ignominious death. His judges debated the mode of his execution, the axe, the wheel, or the stake; and it was resolved that Mourzoufle should ascend the Theodosian column, a pillar of white marble of one hundred and forty-seven feet in height. From the summit he was cast down headlong, and dashed in pieces on the pavement, in the presence of innumerable spectators, who filled the forum of Taurus, and admired the accomplishment of an old prediction, which was explained by this singular event. The fate of Alexius is less tragical: he was sent by the marquis a captive to Italy, and a gift to the king of the Romans; but he had not much to applaud his fortune, if the sentence of imprisonment and exile were changed from a fortress in the Alps to a monastery in Asia. But his daughter, before the national calamity, had been given in marriage to a young hero who continued the succession, and restored the throne, of the Greek princes. The valour of Theodore Lascaris (A.D. 1204—1222), was signalized in the two sieges of Constantinople. After the flight of Mourzoufle, when the Latins were already in the city, he offered himself as their emperor to the soldiers and people: and his ambition, which might be virtuous, was undoubtedly brave. Could he have infused a soul into the multitude, they might have crushed the strangers under their feet: their abject despair refused his aid, and Theodore retired to breath the air of freedom in Anatolia, beyond the immediate view and pursuit of the conquerors. Under the title, at first of despot, and afterwards of emperor, he drew to his standard the bolder spirits, who were fortified against slavery by the contempt of life; and as every means was lawful for the public safety, implored, without scruple, the alliance of the Turkish sultan. Nice, where Theodore established his residence, Prusa and Philadelphia, Smyrna and Ephesus, opened their gates to their deliverer: he derived strength and reputation from his victories, and even from his defeats, and the successor of Constantine preserved a fragment of the empire from the banks of the Mæander to the suburbs of Nicomedia, and at length of Constantinople. Another portion, distant and obscure, was possessed by the lineal heir of the Comneni, a son of the virtuous Manuel, a grandson of the tyrant Andronicus. His name was Alexius ; and the epithet of great was applied perhaps to his stature, rather than to his exploits. By the indulgence of the Angeli, he was appointed governor, or duke of Trebizond : his birth gave him ambition, the revolution independence ; and without changing his title, he reigned in peace from Sinope to the Phasis, along the coast of the Black Sea. His nameless son and successor is described as the vassal of the sultan, whom he served with two hundred lances ; that Comnenian prince was no more than duke of Trebizond, and the title of Emperor was first assumed by the pride and envy of the grandson of Alexius. In the West a third fragment was saved from the common shipwreck by Michael, a bastard of the house of Angeli, who, before the revolution, had been known as an hostage, a soldier, and a rebel. His flight from the camp of the marquis Boniface secured his freedom ; by his marriage with the governor's daughter, he commanded the important place of Durazzo, assumed the title of despot, and founded a strong and conspicuous principality in Epirus, Ætolia, and Thessaly, which have ever been peopled by a warlike race. The Greeks who had offered their service to their new sovereigns, were excluded by the haughty Latins from all civil and military honours, as a nation born to tremble and obey. Their resentment prompted them to show that they might have been useful friends, since they could be dangerous enemies : their nerves were braced by adversity : whatever was learned or holy, whatever was noble or valiant, rolled away into the independent states of Trebizond, Epirus, and Nice ; and a single patrician is marked by the ambiguous praise of attachment and loyalty to the Franks. The vulgar herd of the cities and the country, would have gladly submitted to a mild and regular servitude ; and the transient disorders of war would have been obliterated by some years of industry and peace. But peace was banished, and industry was crushed, in the disorders of the feudal system. The *Roman* emperors of Constantinople, if they were endowed with abilities, were armed with power for the protection of their subjects : their laws were wise, and their administration was simple. The Latin throne was filled by a titular prince, the chief, and often the servant, of his licentious confederates : the fiefs of the empire, from a kingdom to a castle, were held and ruled by the sword of the barons : and their discord, poverty, and ignorance extended the ramifications of tyranny to the most sequestered villages. The Greeks were oppressed by the double weight of the priest, who was invested with temporal power, and of the soldier, who was inflamed by fanatic hatred : and the insuperable bar of religion and language for ever separated the stranger and the native. As long as the crusaders were united at Constantinople, the memory of their conquest, and the terror of their arms, imposed silence on the captive land : their dispersion betrayed the smallness of their numbers and the defects of their discipline ; and some failures and mischances revealed the secret, that they were not invincible. As the fear of the Greeks abated, their hatred increased. They murmured ; they. conspired ; and before a year of slavery had elapsed, they implored, or accepted, the succour of a Barbarian, whose power they had felt, and whose gratitude they trusted.

The Latin conquerors had been saluted with a solemn and early embassy from John, or Joannice, or Calo-John, the revolted chief ot the Bulgarians and Walachians. He deemed (A.D. 1205) himself their brother, as the votary of the Roman pontiff, from whom he had received the regal title and an holy banner ; and in the subversion of the Greek monarchy, he might aspire to the name of their friend and accomplice. But Calo-John was astonished to find, that the count of Flanders had assumed the pomp and pride of the successors of Constantine ; and his ambassadors were dismissed with an haughty message, that the rebel must deserve a pardon, by touching with his forehead the footstool of the imperial throne. His resentment would have exhaled in acts of violence and blood ; his cooler policy watched the rising discontent of the Greeks ; affected a tender concern for their sufferings ; and promised, that their first struggles for freedom should be supported by his person and kingdom. The conspiracy was propagated by national hatred, the firmest band of association and secrecy : the Greeks were impatient to sheath their daggers in the breasts of the victorious strangers ; but the execution was prudently delayed, till Henry, the emperor's brother, had transported the flower of his troops beyond the Hellespont. Most of the towns and villages of Thrace were true to the moment and the signal : and the Latins, without arms or suspicion, were slaughtered by the vile and merciless revenge of their slaves. From Demotica, the first scene of the massacre, the surviving vassals of the count of St. Pol escaped to Hadrianople ; but the French and Venetians, who occupied that city, were slain or expelled by the furious multitude ; the garrisons that could effect their retreat fell back on each other towards the metropolis ; and the fortresses, that separately stood against the rebels, were ignorant of each other's and of their sovereign's fate. The voice of fame and fear announced the revolt of the Greeks and the rapid approach of their Bulgarian ally ; and Calo-John, not depending wholly on his own kingdom, had drawn from the Scythian wilderness a body of 14,000 Comans, who drank, as it was said, the blood of their captives, and sacrificed the Christians on the altars of their gods.

Alarmed by this sudden and growing danger, the emperor dispatched a swift messenger to recall count Henry and his troops ;

and had Baldwin expected the return of his gallant brother, with a supply of 20,000 Armenians, he might have encountered the invader with equal numbers and a decisive superiority of arms and discipline. But the spirit of chivalry could seldom discriminate caution from cowardice ; and the emperor took (March) the field with an hundred and forty knights, and their train of archers and serjeants. The marshal, who dissuaded and obeyed, led the vanguard in their march to Hadrianople ; the main body was commanded by the count of Blois ; the aged doge of Venice followed with the rear ; and their scanty numbers were increased from all sides by the fugitive Latins. They undertook to besiege the rebels of Hadrianople ; and such was the pious tendency of the crusades, that they employed the holy week in pillaging the country for their subsistence, and in framing engines for the destruction of their fellow-Christians. But the Latins were soon interrupted and alarmed by the light cavalry of the Comans, who boldly skirmished to the edge of their imperfect lines : and a proclamation was issued by the marshal of Romania, that, on the trumpet's sound, the cavalry should mount and form ; but that none, under pain of death, should abandon themselves to a desultory and dangerous pursuit. This wise injunction was first disobeyed by the count of Blois, who involved the emperor in his rashness and ruin. The Comans, of the Parthian or Tartar school, fled before their first charge ; but after a career of two leagues, when the knights and their horses were almost breathless, they suddenly turned, rallied, and encompassed the heavy squadrons of the Franks. The count was slain on the field ; the emperor was (A.D. 1205, April 15) made prisoner ; and if the one disdained to fly, if the other refused to yield, their personal bravery made a poor atonement for their neglect of the duties of a general.

Proud of his victory and his royal prize, the Bulgarian advanced to relieve Hadrianople and achieve the destruction of the Latins. They must inevitably have been destroyed, if the marshal of Romania had not displayed a cool courage and consummate skill ; uncommon in all ages, but most uncommon in those times, when war was a passion, rather than a science. His grief and fears were poured into the firm and faithful bosom of the doge ; but in the camp he diffused an assurance of safety, which could only be realized by the general belief. All day he maintained his perilous station between the city and the Barbarians : Villehardouin decamped in silence, at the dead of night ; and his masterly retreat of three days would have deserved the praise of Xenophon and the ten thousand. In the rear the marshal supported the weight of the pursuit ; in the front he moderated the impatience of the fugitives ; and wherever the Comans approached, they were repelled by a line of impenetrable spears. On the third day, the weary troops beheld the sea, the solitary town of Rodosto, and their friends, who had landed from the Asiatic shore. They embraced, they wept ; but they united their arms and counsels ; and, in his brother's absence, count Henry assumed the regency of the empire, at once in a state of childhood and caducity. If the Comans withdrew from the summer heats, 7000 Latins, in the hour of danger, deserted Constantinople, their brethren, and their vows. Some partial success was overbalanced by the loss of 120 knights in the field of Rusium ; and of the Imperial domain, no more was left, than the capital, with two or three adjacent fortresses on the shores of Europe and Asia. The king of Bulgaria was resistless and inexorable ; and Calo-John respectfully eluded the demands of the pope, who conjured his new proselyte to restore peace and the emperor to the afflicted Latins. The deliverance of Baldwin was no longer, he said, in the power of man : that prince had died in prison ; and the manner of his death is variously related by ignorance and credulity. About twenty years afterwards, in a wood of the Netherlands, an hermit announced himself as the true Baldwin, the emperor of Constantinople, and lawful sovereign of Flanders. He related the wonders of his escape, his adventures, and his penance, among a people prone to believe and to rebel ; and, in the first transport, Flanders acknowledged her long-lost sovereign. A short examination before the French court detected the impostor, who was punished with an ignominious death ; but the Flemings still adhered to the pleasing error ; and the countess Jane is accused by the gravest historians of sacrificing to her ambition the life of an unfortunate father.

In all civilized hostility, a treaty is established for the exchange or ransom of prisoners ; and if their captivity be prolonged, their condition is known, and they are treated according to their rank with humanity or honour. But the savage Bulgarian was a stranger to the laws of war ; his prisons were involved in darkness and silence ; and above a year elapsed before the Latins could be assured of the death of Baldwin, before his brother, the regent Henry (A.D. 1206, Aug. 20— A.D. 1216, June 11), would consent to assume the title of emperor. His moderation was applauded by the Greeks as an act of rare and inimitable virtue. Their light and perfidious ambition was eager to seize or anticipate the moment of a vacancy, while a law of succession, the guardian both of the prince and people, was gradually defined and confirmed in the hereditary monarchies of Europe. In the support of the Eastern empire, Henry was gradually left without an associate, as the heroes of the crusade retired from the world or from the war. The doge of Venice, the venerable Dandolo, in the fulness of years and glory, sunk into the grave. The marquis of Monferrat was slowly recalled from the Peloponnesian war to the revenge of Baldwin and the defence of Thessalonica. Some nice disputes of feudal homage and service, were reconciled in a personal interview between the emperor and the king : they were firmly united by mutual esteem and the common danger : and their alliance was sealed by the nuptials of Henry with the daughter of the Italian prince. He soon deplored the loss of his friend and father. At the persuasion of some faithful Greeks, Boniface made a bold and successful inroad among the hills of Rhodope : the Bulgarians fled on his approach ; they assembled to harass his retreat. On the intelligence that his rear was attacked, without waiting for any defensive armour, he leaped on horseback, couched his lance, and drove the enemies before him ; but in the rash pursuit he was pierced with a mortal wound ; and the head of the king of Thessalonica was presented to Calo-John, who enjoyed the honours, without the merit of victory. It is here, at this melancholy event, that the pen or the voice of Jeffrey of Villehardouin seems to drop or to expire ; and if he still exercised his military office of marshal of Romania, his subsequent exploits are buried in oblivion. The character of Henry was not unequal to his arduous situation : in the siege of Constantinople, and beyond the Hellespont, he had deserved the fame of a valiant knight and a skilful commander ; and his courage was tempered with a degree of prudence and mildness unknown to his impetuous brother. In the double war against the Greeks of Asia and the Bulgarians of Europe, he was ever the foremost on shipboard or on horseback ; and though he cautiously provided for the success of his arms, the drooping Latins were often roused by his example to save and to second their fearless emperor. But such efforts, and some supplies of men and money from France, were of less avail than the errors, the cruelty, and death of their most formidable adversary. When the despair of the Greek subjects invited Calo-John as their deliverer, they hoped that he would protect their liberty and adopt their laws : they were soon taught to compare the degrees of national ferocity, and to execrate the savage conqueror, who no longer dissembled his intention of dispeopling Thrace, of demolishing the cities, and of transplanting the inhabitants beyond the Danube. Many towns and villages of Thrace were already evacuated : an heap of ruins marked the place of Philippopolis, and a similar calamity was expected at Demotica and Hadrianople, by the first authors of the revolt. They raised a cry of grief and repentance to the throne of Henry ; the emperor alone had the magnanimity to forgive and trust them. No more than 400 knights, with their serjeants and archers, could be assembled under his banner ; and with this slender force he fought and repulsed the Bulgarian, who, besides his infantry, was at the head of 40,000 horse. In this expedition, Henry felt the difference between an hostile and a friendly country ; the remaining cities were preserved by his arms ; and the savage, with shame and loss, was compelled to relinquish his prey. The siege of Thessalonica was the last of the evils which Calo-John inflicted or suffered : he was stabbed in the night in his tent ; and the general, perhaps the assassin, who found him weltering in his blood, ascribed the blow with general applause to the lance of St. Demetrius. After several victories, the prudence of Henry concluded an honourable peace with the successor of the tyrant, and with the Greek princes of Nice and Epirus. If he ceded some doubtful limits, an ample kingdom was reserved for himself and his feudatories ; and his reign, which lasted only ten years, afforded a short interval of prosperity and peace. Far above the narrow policy of Baldwin and Boniface, he freely entrusted to the Greeks the most important offices of the state and army : and this liberality of sentiment and practice was the more seasonable, as the princes of Nice and Epirus had already learned to seduce and employ the mercenary valour of the Latins. It was the aim of Henry to unite and reward his deserving subjects of every nation and language ; but he appeared less solicitous to accomplish the impracticable union of the two churches. Pelagius, the pope's legate, who acted as the sovereign of Constantinople, had interdicted the worship of the Greeks, and sternly imposed the payment of tithes, the double procession of the Holy Ghost, and a blind obedience to the Roman pontiff. As the weaker party, they pleaded the duties of conscience, and implored the rights of toleration : " Our bodies," they said, " are Cæsar's, but our souls belong only to God." The persecution was checked by the firmness of the emperor ; and if we can believe that the same prince was poisoned by the Greeks themselves, we must entertain a contemptible idea of the sense and gratitude of mankind. His valour was a vulgar attribute, which he shared with ten thousand knights ; but Henry possessed the superior courage to oppose, in a superstitious age, the pride and avarice of the clergy. In the cathedral of St. Sophia he presumed to place his throne on the right hand of the patriarch ; and this presumption excited the sharpest censure of pope Innocent the third. By a salutary edict, one of the first examples of the laws of mortmain, he prohibited the alienation of fiefs ; many of the Latins, desirous of returning to Europe, resigned their estates to the church for a spiritual or temporal reward ; these holy lands were immediately discharged from military service ; and a colony of soldiers would have been gradually transformed into a college of priests.

The virtuous Henry died at Thessalonica, in the defence of that kingdom, and of an infant, the son of his friend Boniface. In the two first emperors of Constantinople the male line of the counts of Flanders was extinct. But their sister Yolande was the wife of a French prince, the mother of a numerous progeny ; and one of her daughters had married Andrew king of Hungary, a brave and pious champion of the cross. By seating him on the Byzantine throne, the barons of Romania would have acquired the forces of a neighbouring and warlike kingdom ; but the prudent Andrew revered the laws of succession ; and the princess Yolande, with her husband Peter of Courtenay, count

of Auxerre, was invited by the Latins to assume (A.D. 1217. April 9)
the empire of the East. The royal birth of his father, the noble origin
of his mother, recommended to the barons of France the first cousin
of their king. His reputation was fair, his possessions were ample,
and, in the bloody crusade against the Albigeois, the soldiers and the
priests had been abundantly satisfied of his zeal and valour. Vanity
might applaud the elevation of a French emperor of Constantinople;
but prudence must pity, rather than envy, his treacherous and imaginary greatness. To assert and adorn his title, he was reduced to sell
or mortgage the best of his patrimony. By these expedients, the
liberality of his royal kinsman Philip Augustus, and the national spirit
of chivalry, he was enabled to pass the Alps at the head of 140 knights,
and 5500 serjeants and archers. After some hesitation, pope Honorius
the third was persuaded to crown the successor of Constantine; but he
performed the ceremony in a church without the walls, lest he should
seem to imply or to bestow any right of sovereignty over the ancient
capital of the empire. The Venetians had engaged to transport Peter
and his forces beyond the Hadriatic, and the empress, with her four
children, to the Byzantine palace; but they required, as the price of
their service, that he should recover Durazzo from the despot of Epirus.
Michael Angelus, or Comnenus, the first of his dynasty, had bequeathed
the succession of his power and ambition to Theodore, his legitimate
brother, who already threatened and invaded the establishments of
the Latins. After discharging his debt by a fruitless assault, the emperor raised the siege to prosecute a long and perilous journey over
land from Durazzo to Thessalonica. He was soon lost in the mountains of Epirus: the passes were fortified; his provisions exhausted:
he was delayed and deceived by a treacherous negociation; and, after
Peter of Courtenay and the Roman legate had been arrested in a banquet, the French troops, without leaders or hopes, were eager to exchange their arms for the delusive promise of mercy and bread. The
Vatican thundered; and the impious Theodore was threatened with
the vengeance of earth and heaven; but the captive emperor and his
soldiers were forgotten, and the reproaches of the pope are confined to
the imprisonment of his legate. No sooner was he satisfied by the
deliverance of the priest and a promise of spiritual obedience, than he
pardoned and protected the despot of Epirus. His peremptory commands suspended the ardour of the Venetians and the king of Hungary; and it was only by a natural or untimely death that Peter of
Courtenay was released from his hopeless (A.D. 1217—1219) captivity.
   The long ignorance of his fate, and the presence of the lawful sovereign, of Yolande, his wife or widow, delayed the proclamation of a
new emperor. Before her death, and in the midst of her grief, she
was delivered of a son, who was named Baldwin, the last and most
unfortunate of the Latin princes of Constantinople. His birth endeared

him to the barons of Romania ; but his childhood would have prolonged the troubles of a minority, and his claims were superseded by
the elder claims of his brethren. The first of these, Philip of Courtenay, who derived from his mother the inheritance of Namur, had the
wisdom to prefer the substance of a marquisate to the shadow of an
empire ; and on his refusal, Robert, the second of the sons of Peter
and Yolande, was called to the throne (A.D. 1221—1228) of Constantinople. Warned by his father's mischance, he pursued his slow and
secure journey through Germany and along the Danube : a passage
was opened by his sister's marriage with the king of Hungary ; and
the emperor Robert was crowned by the patriarch in the cathedral of
St. Sophia. But his reign was an æra of calamity and disgrace ; and
the colony, as it was styled, of NEW FRANCE yielded on all sides to
the Greeks of Nice and Epirus. After a victory which he owed to
his perfidy rather than his courage, Theodore Angelus entered the
kingdom of Thessalonica, expelled the feeble Demetrius, the son of
the marquis Boniface, erected his standard on the walls of Hadrianople ;
and added, by his vanity, a third or fourth name to the list of rival
emperors. The relics of the Asiatic province were swept away by
John Vataces, the son-in-law and successor of Theodore Lascaris,
and who, in a triumphant reign of thirty-three years, displayed the
virtues both of peace and war. Under his discipline the swords of
the French mercenaries were the most effectual instrument of his conquests, and their desertion from the service of their country was at
once a symptom and a cause of the rising ascendant of the Greeks.
By the construction of a fleet, he obtained the command of the Hellespont, reduced the islands of Lesbos and Rhodes, attacked the Venetians
of Candia, and intercepted the rare and parsimonious succours of the
West. Once, and once only, the Latin emperor sent an army against
Vataces ; and in the defeat of that army, the veteran knights, the last
of the original conquerors, were left on the field of battle. But the
success of a foreign enemy was less painful to the pusillanimous Robert
than the insolence of his Latin subjects, who confounded the weakness
of the emperor and of the empire. His personal misfortunes will prove
the anarchy of the government and the ferociousness of the times.
The amorous youth had neglected his Greek bride, the daughter of
Vataces, to introduce into the palace a beautiful maid, of a private,
though noble, family of Artois ; and her mother had been tempted by
the lustre of the purple to forfeit her engagements with a gentleman of
Burgundy. His love was converted into rage ; he assembled his friends,
forced the palace gates, threw the mother into the sea, and inhumanly
cut off the nose and lips of the wife or concubine of the emperor.
Instead of punishing the offender, the barons avowed and applauded
the savage deed, which, as a prince and as a man, it was impossible
that Robert should forgive. He escaped from the guilty city to im-

plore the justice or compassion of the pope : the emperor was coolly exhorted to return to his station ; before he could obey, he sank under the weight of grief, shame, and impotent resentment.

It was only in the age of chivalry, that valour could ascend from a private station to the thrones of Jerusalem and Constantinople. The titular kingdom of Jerusalem had devolved to Mary, the daughter of Isabel and Conrad of Montferrat, and the grand-daughter of Almeric or Amaury. She was given to John of Brienne (A.D. 1228—1237), of a noble family in Champagne, by the public voice and the judgment of Philip Augustus, who named him as the most worthy champion of the Holy Land. In the fifth crusade, he led 100,000 Latins to the con quest of Egypt ; by him the siege of Damietta was achieved ; and the subsequent failure was justly ascribed to the pride and avarice of the legate. After the marriage of his daughter with Frederic the second, he was provoked by the emperor's ingratitude to accept the command of the army of the church ; and though advanced in life, and despoiled of royalty, the sword and spirit of John of Brienne were still ready for the service of Christendom. In the seven years of his brother's reign, Baldwin of Courtenay had not emerged from a state of childhood, and the barons of Romania felt the strong necessity of placing the sceptre in the hands of a man and an hero. The veteran king of Jerusalem might have disdained the name and office of regent ; they agreed to invest him for his life with the title and prerogatives of emperor, on the sole condition that Baldwin should marry his second daughter, and succeed at a mature age to the throne of Constantinople. The expectation both of the Greeks and Latins, was kindled by the renown, the choice, and the presence of John of Brienne : and they admired his martial aspect, his green and vigorous age of more than fourscore years, and his size and stature, which surpassed the common measure of mankind. But avarice, and the love of ease, appeared to have chilled the ardour of enterprise : his troops were disbanded, and two years rolled away without action or honour, till he was awakened by the dangerous alliance of Vataces emperor of Nice, and of Azan king of Bulgaria. They besieged Constantinople by sea and land, with an army of 100,000 men, and a fleet of 300 ships of war ; while the entire force of the Latin emperor was reduced to 160 knights, and a small addition of serjeants and archers. I tremble to relate, that instead of defending the city, the hero made a sally at the head of his cavalry ; and that of forty-eight squadrons of the enemy, no more than three escaped from the edge of his invincible sword. Fired by his example, the infantry and the citizens boarded the vessels that anchored close to the walls : and twenty-five were dragged in triumph into the harbour of Constantinople. At the summons of the emperor, the vassals and allies armed in her defence ; broke through every obstacle that opposed their passage ; and, in the succeeding year obtained a second victory over the same enemies. By the rude poets of the age, John of Brienne is compared to Hector, Roland, and Judas Machabæus ; but their credit, and his glory, receives some abatement from the silence of the Greeks. The empire was soon deprived of the last of her champions ; and the dying monarch was ambitious to enter paradise in the habit of a Franciscan friar.

In the double victory of John of Brienne, I cannot discover the name or exploits of his pupil Baldwin ; who had attained the age of military service, and who succeeded (A.D. 1237. Mar. 23—A.D. 1261. July 25) to the Imperial dignity on the decease of his adoptive father. The royal youth was employed on a commission more suitable to his temper ; he was sent to visit the Western courts, of the pope more especially, and of the king of France ; to excite their pity by the view of his innocence and distress ; and to obtain some supplies of men or money for the relief of the sinking empire. He thrice repeated these mendicant visits, in which he seemed to prolong his stay and postpone his return : of the five-and-twenty years of his reign, a greater number were spent abroad than at home ; and in no place did the emperor deem himself less free and secure, than in his native country and his capital. On some public occasions, his vanity might be soothed by the title of Augustus, and by the honours of the purple ; and at the general council of Lyons, when Frederic the second was excommunicated and deposed, his Oriental colleague was enthroned on the right-hand of the pope. But how often was the exile, the vagrant, the Imperial beggar, humbled with scorn, insulted with pity, and degraded in his own eyes and those of the nations ! In his first visit to England, he was stopped at Dover, by a severe reprimand, that he should presume, without leave, to enter an independent kingdom. After some delay, Baldwin however was permitted to pursue his journey, was entertained with cold civility, and thankfully departed with a present of seven hundred marks. From the avarice of Rome he could only obtain the proclamation of a crusade and a treasure of indulgences ; a coin, whose currency was depreciated by too frequent and indiscriminate abuse. His birth and misfortunes recommended him to the generosity of his cousin Lewis the ninth ; but the martial zeal of the saint was diverted from Constantinople to Egypt and Palestine ; and the public and private property of Baldwin was alleviated, for a moment, by the alienation of the marquisite of Namur and the lordship of Courtenay, the last remains of his inheritance. By such shameful or ruinous expedients, he once more returned to Romania, with an army of 30,000 soldiers, whose numbers were doubled in the apprehension of the Greeks. His first despatches to France and England announced his victories and his hopes : he had reduced the country round the capital to the distance of three days' journey ; and if he succeeded against an important, though nameless city (most probably Chiorli), the frontier would be safe and the passage accessible.

But these expectations (if Baldwin was sincere) quickly vanished like a dream : the troops and treasures of France melted away in his unskilful hands ; and the throne of the Latin emperor was protected by a dishonourable alliance with the Turks and Comans. To secure the former, he consented to bestow his niece on the unbelieving sultan of Cogni ; to please the latter he complied with their pagan rites ; a dog was sacrificed between the two armies ; and the contracting parties tasted each other's blood, as a pledge of their fidelity. In the palace or prison of Constantinople, the successor of Augustus demolished the vacant houses for winter fuel, and stripped the lead from the churches for the daily expence of his family. Some usurious loans were dealt with a scanty hand by the merchants of Italy ; and Philip, his son and heir, was pawned at Venice as the security for a debt. Thirst, hunger, and nakedness are positive evils ; but wealth is relative ; and a prince, who would be rich in a private station, may be exposed by the increase of his wants to all the anxiety and bitterness of poverty.

But in this abject distress, the emperor and empire were still possessed of an ideal treasure, which drew its fantastic value from the superstition of the Christian world. The merit of the true cross was somewhat impaired by its frequent division ; and a long captivity among the infidels might shed some suspicion on the fragments that were produced in the East and West. But another relic of the Passion was preserved in the Imperial chapel of Constantinople ; and the crown of thorns which had been placed on the head of Christ was equally precious and authentic. It had formerly been the practice of the Egyptian debtors to deposit, as a security, the mummies of their parents ; and both their honour and religion were bound for the redemption of the pledge. In the same manner, and in the absence of the emperor, the barons of Romania borrowed the sum of 13,134 pieces of gold, on the credit of the holy crown : they failed in the performance of their contract ; and a rich Venetian, Nicholas Querini, undertook to satisfy their impatient creditors, on condition that the relic should be lodged at Venice, to become his absolute property, if it were not redeemed within a short and definite term. The barons apprised their sovereign of the hard treaty and impending loss ; and as the empire could not afford a ransom of £7000, Baldwin was anxious to snatch the prize from the Venetians, and to vest it with more honour and emolument in the hands of the most Christian king. Yet the negociation was attended with some delicacy. In the purchase of relics, the saint would have started at the guilt of simony ; but if the mode of expression were changed, he might lawfully repay the debt, accept the gift, and acknowledge the obligation. His ambassadors two Dominicans, were dispatched to Venice, to redeem and receive the holy crown, which had escaped the dangers of the sea and the galleys of Vataces. On opening a wooden box, they recognized the seals of the doge and barons, which were applied on a shrine of silver: and within this shrine, the monument of the Passion was inclosed in a golden vase. The reluctant Venetians yielded to justice and power: the emperor Frederic granted a free and honourable passage; the court of France advanced as far as Troyes in Champagne, to meet with devotion this inestimable relic : it was borne in triumph through Paris by the king himself, barefoot, and in his shirt; and a free gift of 10,000 marks of silver reconciled Baldwin to his loss. The success of this transaction tempted the Latin emperor to offer with the same generosity the remaining furniture of his chapel ; a large and authentic portion of the true cross ; the baby-linen of the Son of God ; the lance, the spunge, and the chain of his Passion ; the rod of Moses, and part of the skull of St. John the Baptist. For the reception of these spiritual treasures, 20,000 marks were expended by St. Louis on a stately foundation, the holy chapel of Paris, on which the muse of Boileau has bestowed a comic immortality. The truth of such remote and ancient relics, which cannot be proved by any human testimony, must be admitted, by those who believe in the miracles which they have performed. About the middle of the last age, an inveterate ulcer was touched and cured by an holy prickle of the holy crown : the prodigy is attested by the most pious and enlightened Christians of France ; nor will the fact be easily disproved, except by those who are armed with a general antidote against religious credulity.

The Latins of Constantinople were on all sides encompassed (A.D. 1237—1261) and pressed : their sole hope, the last delay of their ruin, was in the division of their Greek and Bulgarian enemies ; and of this hope they were deprived by the superior arms and policy of Vataces emperor of Nice. From the Propontis to the rocky coast of Pamphylia, Asia was peaceful and prosperous under his reign : and the events of every campaign extended his influence in Europe. The strong cities of the hills of Macedonia and Thrace, were rescued from the Bulgarians ; and their kingdom was circumscribed by its present and proper limits, along the southern banks of the Danube. The sole emperor of the Romans could no longer brook that a lord of Epirus, a Comnenian prince of the West, should presume to dispute or share the honours of the purple ; and the humble Demetrius changed the colour of his buskins and accepted with gratitude the appellation of despot. His own subjects were exasperated by his baseness and incapacity : they implored the protection of their supreme lord. After some resistance, the kingdom of Thessalonica was united to the empire of Nice ; and Vataces reigned without a competitor from the Turkish borders to the Hadriatic gulf. The princes of Europe revered his merit and power; and had he subscribed an orthodox creed, it should seem that the pope would have abandoned without reluctance the Latin throne of Constantinople. But the death of Vataces, the short and busy reign of Theodore his son, and the helpless infancy of his grandson John, suspended the restoration of the Greeks: The young prince was oppressed by the ambition of his guardian and colleague (A.D. 1259. Dec. 1) Michael Palæologus, who displayed the virtues and vices that belong to the founder of a new dynasty. The emperor Baldwin had flattered himself, that he might recover some provinces or cities by an impotent negociation. His ambassadors were dismissed from Nice with mockery and contempt. At every place which they named, Palæologus alleged some special reason, which rendered it dear and valuable in his eyes : in the one he was born ; in another he had been first promoted to military command ; and in a third he had enjoyed, and hoped long to enjoy, the pleasures of the chace. " And what then do you propose to give us ?" said the astonished deputies. " Nothing," replied the Greek, " not a foot of land. If your master be desirous of peace, let him pay me as an annual tribute, the sum which he receives from the trade and customs of Constantinople. On these terms, I may allow him to reign. If he refuses, it is war. I am not ignorant of the art of war, and I trust the event to God and my sword." An expedition against the despot of Epirus was the first prelude of his arms. If a victory was followed by a defeat ; if the race of Comneni or Angeli survived in those mountains his efforts and his reign ; the captivity of Villehardouin, prince of Achaia, deprived the Latins of the most active and powerful vassal of their expiring monarchy. The republics of Venice and Genoa disputed, in the first of their naval wars, the command of the sea and the commerce of the East. Pride and interest attached the Venetians to the defence of Constantinople : their rivals were tempted to promote the designs of her enemies, and the alliance of the Genoese with the schismatic conqueror provoked the indignation of the Latin Church.

Intent on this great object, the emperor Michael visited in person and strengthened the troops and fortifications of Thrace. The remains of the Latins were driven from their last possessions : he assaulted without success the suburb of Galata ; and corresponded with a perfidious baron, who proved unwilling, or unable, to open the gates of the metropolis. The next spring, his favourite general, Alexius Stratego-pulus, whom he had decorated with the title of Cæsar, passed the Hellespont with eight hundred horse and some infantry, on a secret expedition. His instructions enjoined him to approach, to listen, to watch, but not to risk any doubtful or dangerous enterprise against the city. The adjacent territory between the Propontis and the Black Sea, was cultivated by an hardy race of peasants and outlaws, exercised in arms, uncertain in their allegiance, but inclined by language, religion, and present advantage, to the party of the Greeks. They were styled the *volunteers*, and by their free service, the army of Alexius, with the regulars of Thrace and the Coman auxiliaries, was augmented to the number of 25,000 men. By the ardour of the volunteers, and by his own ambition, the Cæsar was stimulated to disobey the precise orders of his master, in the just confidence that success would plead his pardon and reward. The weakness of Constantinople, and the distress and terror of the Latins, were familiar to the observation of the volunteers : and they represented the present moment as the most propitious to surprise and conquest. A rash youth, the new governor of the Venetian colony, had sailed away with thirty galleys and the best of the French knights, on a wild expedition to Daphnusia, a town on the Black Sea, at the distance of forty leagues ; and the remaining Latins were without strength or suspicion. They were informed that Alexius had passed the Hellespont ; but their apprehensions were lulled by the smallness of his original numbers ; and their imprudence had not watched the subsequent increase of his army. If he left his main body to second and support his operations, he might advance unperceived in the night with a chosen detachment. While some applied (A.D. 1261. July 25) scaling ladders to the lowest part of the walls, they were secure of an old Greek, who could introduce their companions through a subterraneous passage into his house ; they could soon on the inside break an entrance through the golden gate, which had been long obstructed ; and the conqueror would be in the heart of the city, before the Latins were conscious of their danger. After some debate, the Cæsar resigned himself to the faith of the volunteers ; they were trusty, bold, and successful ; and in describing the plan, I have already related the execution and success. But no sooner had Alexius passed the threshold of the golden gate, than he trembled at his own rashness ; he paused, he deliberated ; till the desperate volunteers urged him forwards, by the assurance that in retreat lay the greatest and most inevitable danger. Whilst the Cæsar kept his regulars in firm array, the Comans dispersed themselves on all sides ; an alarm was sounded, and the threats of fire and pillage compelled the citizens to a decisive resolution. The Greeks of Constantinople remembered their native sovereigns ; the Genoese merchants, their recent alliance and Venetian foes ; every quarter was in arms ; and the air resounded with a general acclamation of " Long life and victory to Michael and John, the august emperors of the Romans !" Their rival, Baldwin, was awakened by the sound ; but the most pressing danger could not prompt him to draw his sword in the defence of a city which he deserted, perhaps, with more pleasure than regret ; he fled from the palace to the sea-shore, where he descried the welcome sails of the fleet returning from the vain and fruitless attempt on Daphnusia. Constantinople was irrecoverably lost ; but the Latin Emperor and the principal families embarked on board the Venetian galleys, and steered for the isle of Euboea, and afterwards for Italy, where the royal fugitive was entertained by the pope and Sicilian king with a mixture of contempt and pity. From the loss of Constantinople to his death, he consumed thirteen years, soliciting the Catholic powers to join in his restoration; the lesson had been familiar to his youth; nor was his last exile more indigent or shameful than his three former pilgrimages to the courts of Europe. His son Philip was the heir of an ideal empire; and the pretensions of *his* daughter Catherine were transported by her marriage to Charles of Valois, the brother of Philip the Fair king of France. The house of Courtenay was represented in the female line by successive alliances, till the title of emperor of Constantinople, too bulky and sonorous for a private name, modestly expired in silence and oblivion.

After this narrative of the expeditions of the Latins to Palestine and Constantinople, I cannot dismiss the subject without revolving the general consequences on the countries that were the scene, and on the nations that were the actors of these memorable crusades. As soon as the arms of the Franks were withdrawn, the impression, though not the memory, was erased in the Mahometan realms of Egypt and Syria. The faithful disciples of the prophet were never tempted by a profane desire to study the laws or language of the idolaters; nor did the simplicity of their primitive manners receive the slightest alteration from their intercourse in peace and war with the unknown strangers of the West. The Greeks, who thought themselves proud, but who were only vain, showed a disposition somewhat less inflexible. In the efforts for the recovery of their empire, they emulated the valour, discipline, and tactics, of their antagonists. The modern literature of the West they might justly despise; but its free spirit would instruct them in the rights of man; and some institutions of public and private life were adopted from the French. The correspondence of Constantinople and Italy diffused the knowledge of the Latin tongue; and several of the fathers and classics were at length honoured with a Greek version. But the national and religious prejudices of the Orientals were inflamed by persecution; and the reign of the Latins confirmed the separation of the two churches.

If we compare, at the æra of the crusades, the Latins of Europe with the Greeks and Arabians, their respective degrees of knowledge, industry, and art, our rude ancestors must be content with the third rank in the scale of nations. Their successive improvement and present superiority may be ascribed to a peculiar energy of character, to an active and imitative spirit, unknown to their more polished rivals, who at that time were in a stationary or retrograde state. With such a disposition, the Latins should have derived the most early and essential benefits from a series of events which opened to their eyes the prospect of the world, and introduced them to a long and frequent intercourse with the more cultivated regions of the East. The first and most obvious progress was in trade and manufactures, in the arts which are strongly prompted by the thirst of wealth, the calls of necessity, and the gratification of the sense or vanity. Among the crowd of unthinking fanatics, a captive or a pilgrim might sometimes observe the superior refinements of Cairo and Constantinople : the first importer of wind-mills* was the benefactor of nations ; and if such blessings are enjoyed without any grateful remembrance, history has condescended to notice the more apparent luxuries of silk and sugar, which were transported into Italy from Greece and Egypt. But the intellectual wants of the Latins were more slowly felt and supplied ; the ardour of studious curiosity was awakened in Europe by different causes and more recent events ; and, in the age of the crusades, they viewed with careless indifference the literature of the Greeks and Arabians. Some rudiments of mathematical and medicinal knowledge might be imparted in practice and in figures ; necessity might produce some interpreters for the grosser business of merchants and soldiers ; but the commerce of the Orientals had not diffused the study and knowledge of their languages in the schools of Europe. If a similar principle of religion repulsed the idiom of the Koran, it should have excited their patience and curiosity to understand the original text of the Gospel ; and the same grammar would have unfolded the sense of Plato and the beauties of Homer. Yet in a reign of sixty years the Latins of Constantinople disdained the speech and learning of their subjects ; and the manuscripts were the only treasures which the natives might enjoy without rapine or envy. Aristotle was indeed the oracle of the Western universities ; but it was a barbarous Aristotle ; and, instead of ascending to the fountain-head, his Latin votaries humbly accepted a corrupt and remote version from the Jews and Moors of Andalusia. The principle of the crusades was a savage fanaticism ; and the most important effects were analogous to the cause. Each pilgrim was ambitious to return with his sacred spoils, the relics of Greece and Palestine ; and each relic was preceded and followed by a train of miracles and visions. The belief of the Catholics was corrupted by new legends, their practice by new superstitions ; and the establishment of the inquisition, the mendicant orders of monks and friars, the last abuse of indulgences, and the final progress of idolatry, flowed from the baleful fountain of the holy war. The active spirit of the Latins preyed on the vitals of their reason and religion ; and if the ninth and tenth centuries were the times of darkness, the thirteenth and fourteenth were the age of absurdity and fable.

In the profession of Christianity, in the cultivation of a fertile land, the northern conquerors of the Roman empire insensibly mingled with the provincials, and rekindled the embers of the arts of antiquity. Their settlements about the age of Charlemagne had acquired some

* Windmills, first invented in the dry country of Asia Minor, and used in Normandy in 1105.

degree of order and stability, when they were overwhelmed by new swarms of invaders, the Normans, Saracens, and Hungarians, who replunged the western countries of Europe into their former state of anarchy and barbarism. About the eleventh century, the second tempest had subsided by the expulsion or conversion of the enemies of Christendom : the tide of civilization, which had so long ebbed, began to flow with a steady and accelerated course ; and a fairer prospect was opened to the hopes and efforts of the rising generations.

Great was the increase, and rapid the progress, during the two hundred years of the crusades ; and some philosophers have applauded the propitious influence of these holy wars, which appear to me to have checked rather than forwarded the maturity of Europe. The lives and labours of millions, which were buried in the East, would have been more profitably employed in the improvement of their native country : the accumulated stock of industry and wealth would have overflowed in navigation and trade ; and the Latins would have been enriched and enlightened by a pure and friendly correspondence with the climates of the East. In one respect I can indeed perceive the accidental operation of the crusades, not so much in producing a benefit as in removing an evil. The larger portion of the inhabitants of Europe was chained to the soil, without freedom, or property, or knowledge ; and the two orders of ecclesiastics and nobles, whose numbers were comparatively small, alone deserved the name of citizens and men. This oppressive system was supported by the arts of the clergy and the swords of the barons. The authority of the priests operated in the darker ages as a salutary antidote : they prevented the total extinction of letters, mitigated the fierceness of the times, sheltered the poor and defenceless, and preserved or revived the peace and order of civil society. But the independence, rapine, and discord of the feudal lords were unmixed with any semblance of good ; and every hope of industry and improvement was crushed by the iron weight of the martial aristocracy. Among the causes that undermined that Gothic edifice, a conspicuous place must be allowed to the crusades. The estates of the barons were dissipated, and their race was often extinguished, in these costly and perilous expeditions. Their poverty extorted from their pride those charters of freedom which unlocked the fetters of the slave, secured the farm of the peasant and the shop of the artificer, and gradually restored a substance and a soul to the most numerous and useful part of the community. The conflagration which destroyed the tall and barren trees of the forest, gave air and scope to the vegetation of the smaller and nutritive plants of the soil.

But the best school of moral discipline which the middle ages afforded was the institution of chivalry. There are, if 1 may say so, three powerful spirits which have from time to time moved over the face of the waters, and given a predominant impulse to the moral sentiments and energies of mankind. These are the spirits of liberty, of religion, and of honour. It was the principal business of chivalry to animate and cherish the last of these three. And whatever high magnanimous energy the love of liberty or religious zeal has ever imparted, was equalled by the exquisite sense of honour which this institution preserved.

It appears probable, that the custom of receiving arms at the age of manhood with some solemnity was of immemorial antiquity among the nations that overthrew the Roman empire. This ceremony, however, would perhaps of itself have done little towards forming that intrinsic principle which characterised the genuine chivalry. Certain feudal tenants, and I suppose also allodial proprietors, were bound to serve on horseback, equipped with the coat of mail. These were called Caballarii, from which the word chevaliers is an obvious corruption. But he who fought on horseback, and had been invested with peculiar arms in a solemn manner, wanted nothing more to render him a knight. We may, however, go farther, and observe that these distinctive advantages above ordinary combatants were probably the sources of that remarkable valour and that keen thirst for glory, which became the essential attributes of a knightly character. The soul of chivalry was individual honour, coveted in so entire and absolute a perfection that it must not be shared with an army or a nation. Most of the virtues it inspired were what we may call independent, as opposed to those which are founded upon social relations. The knights-errant of romance perform their best exploits from the love of renown, or from a sort of abstract sense of justice, rather than from any solicitude to promote the happiness of mankind.

In the first state of chivalry, it was closely connected with the military service of fiefs. The Caballarii in the Capitularies, the Milites of the eleventh and twelfth centuries, were landholders who followed their lord or sovereign into the field. A certain value of land was termed in England a knight's fee, or, in Normandy, feudum loricæ, fief de haubert, from the coat of mail which it entitled and required the tenant to wear ; a military tenure was said to be by service in chivalry. A younger brother, leaving the paternal estate, in which he took a slender share, might look to wealth and dignity in the service of a powerful count. Knighthood, which he could not claim as his legal right, became the object of his chief ambition. It raised him in the scale of society, equalling him in dress, in arms, and in title, to the rich landholders. As it was due to his merit, it did much more than equal him to those who had no pretensions but from wealth ; and the territorial knights became by degrees ashamed of assuming the title till they could challenge it by real desert.

This class of noble and gallant cavaliers, serving commonly for pay, but on the most honourable footing, became far more numerous through the crusades ; a great epoch in the history of European society. During the period of the crusades, we find the institution of chivalry acquire its full vigour as an order of personal nobility; and its original connexion with feudal tenure, if not effaced, became in a great measure forgotten in the splendour and dignity of the new form which it wore. The crusades, however, changed in more than one respect the character of chivalry. Before that epoch it appears to have had no particular reference to religion. We can hardly perceive indeed why the assumption of arms to be used in butchering mankind should be treated as a religious ceremony. But the purposes for which men bore arms in a crusade so sanctified their use, that chivalry acquired the character as much of a religious as a military institution. For many centuries, the recovery of the Holy Land was constantly at the heart of a brave and superstitious nobility; and every knight was supposed at his creation to pledge himself, as occasion should arise, to that cause. Meanwhile, the defence of God's law against infidels was his primary and standing duty. A knight, whenever present at mass, held the point of his sword before him while the Gospel was read, to signify his readiness to support it. The candidate passed nights in prayer among priests in a church; he received the sacraments; he entered into a bath, and was clad with a white robe, in allusion to the presumed purification of his life; his sword was solemnly blessed; everything, in short, was contrived to identify his new condition with the defence of religion, or at least with that of the church.

Courtesy had always been the proper attribute of knighthood; protection of the weak its legitimate duty; but these were heightened to a pitch of enthusiasm when woman became their object. There was little jealousy shown in the treatment of that sex, at least in France, the fountain of chivalry; they were present at festivals, at tournaments, and sat promiscuously in the halls of their castles.

Next therefore, or even equal to devotion, stood gallantry among the principles of knighthood. But all comparison between the two was saved by blending them together. The love of God and the ladies was enjoined as a single duty. But neither that emulous valour which chivalry excited, nor the religion and gallantry which were its animating principles, alloyed as the latter were by the corruption of those ages, could have rendered its institution materially conducive to the moral improvement of society. There were, however, excellences of a very high class which it equally encouraged. In the books professedly written to lay down the duties of knighthood they appear to spread over the whole compass of human obligations. A juster estimate of chivalrous manners is to be deduced from romances. From history itself, we may infer the tendency of chivalry to elevate and purify the moral feelings. Three virtues may particularly be noticed as essential, in the estimation of mankind, to the character of a knight,—loyalty, courtesy, and munificence.

The first of these, in its original sense, may be defined fidelity to engagements; whether actual promises, or such tacit obligations as bound a vassal to his lord, and a subject to his prince. Breach of faith, and especially of an express promise, was held a disgrace that no valour could redeem. This is one of the most striking changes produced by chivalry. Treachery, the usual vice of savage as well as corrupt nations, became infamous during the vigour of that discipline. As

I I

personal rather than national feelings actuated its heroes, they never felt that hatred, much less that fear, of their enemies which blind men to the heinousness of ill faith. Though avarice may have been the rimary motive of ransoming prisoners, instead of putting them to death, their permission to return home on the word of honour, in order to procure the stipulated sum—an indulgence never refused—could only be founded on experienced confidence in the principles of chivalry.

A knight was unfit to remain a member of the order if he violated his faith ; he was ill-acquainted with its duties if he proved wanting in courtesy. Besides the grace which this beautiful virtue threw over the habits of social life, it softened down the natural roughness of war, and gradually introduced that indulgent treatment of prisoners which was almost unknown to antiquity. Liberality, and disdain of money, might also be reckoned among the essential virtues of chivalry.

Valour, loyalty, courtesy, munificence, formed collectively the character of an accomplished knight, so far as was displayed in the ordinary tenor of his life, reflecting these virtues as an unsullied mirror. Yet something more was required for the perfect idea of chivalry, and enjoined by its principles ; an active sense of justice, an ardent indignation against wrong, a determination of courage to its best end, the prevention or redress of injury.

The characteristic virtues of chivalry bear so much resemblance to those which Eastern writers of the same period extol, that I am a little disposed to suspect Europe of having derived some improvement from imitation of Asia. Though the crusades began in abhorrence of infidels, this sentiment wore off in some degree before their cessation ; and the regular intercourse of commerce, sometimes of alliance, between the Christians of Palestine and the Saracens, must have removed part of the prejudice, while experience of their enemy's courage and generosity in war would with these gallant knights serve to lighten the remainder. Excepting that romantic gallantry towards women, which their customs would not admit, the Mahomedan chieftains were abundantly qualified to fulfil the duties of European chivalry.

The licence of times so imperfectly civilized could not be expected to yield to institutions which, like those of religion, fell prodigiously short in their practical result of the reformation which they were designed to work. An undue thirst for military renown was a fault that chivalry must have nourished ; and the love of war, sufficiently pernicious in any shape, was more founded on personal feelings of honour, and less on public spirit, than in the citizens of free states. The character of knighthood widened the separation between the classes of society, and confirmed that aristocratical spirit of high birth, by which the large mass of mankind were kept in unjust degradation.

INDEX.

INDEX TO THE AUTOBIOGRAPHY.

PRÉCIS OF LETTERS.

Bentinck-street, Nov. 1777 :—Complains of his friend's unreasonableness and his own ill health, 256.

Nov. 14th, 1777 :—The gout nearly gone—anxious to see him—hopes the American news is true, 256.

Dec. 2nd, 1777 :—America not conquered, 256.

Dec. 1777 :—A letter of badinage, 256.

House of Commons, Dec. 4th, 1777 :—Dreadful news from America—a general cry for peace, 257.

Feb. 28th, 1778 :—Votes with the Government, 257.

Calais, May 7th, 1777 :—A pleasant passage—a French comedy, 250.

Feb. 23rd, 1778 :—A plain narrative—heads of the plan in Parliament—a Treaty of Commerce signed at Paris with America, 257, 258.

Almack's, March 21st, 1778 :—Authentic pieces of intelligence—wants his friend and his wife, 258.

Almack's, June 12th, 1778 :—No news stirring—Lord Chatham's funeral—intends to go to Sussex, 258, 259.

July 1st, 1778 :—Feels inclined to visit the country—Keppel's return—East and West India trade in danger, 259.

Bentinck-street, July 7th, 1778 :—Gossip, 259.

Sept. 25th, 1778 :—No news from the fleets—intentions of Spain—we court Russia, 259, 260.

Nov. 1778 :—Early news, 260.

Almack's, 1778 :—A letter of Hugonin's on the state of Beriton—no news from America, 260.

Feb. 6th, 1779 :—No foreign intelligence—his pamphlet, a second edition—a talk of peace, 261.

May 7th, 1779 :—Political news, 262.

May, 1779 :—Shipping disasters—distress of Ministers—promises an impression of his portrait, 262, 263.

1779 :—Gossip and political news, 263.

July, 2nd, 1779 :—Appointed Lord of Trade—news of the Navy, 263.

London, Feb. 7th, 1780 :—Remarks on his friend's election—no news foreign or domestic, 264, 265.

July 26th, 1780 :—Gossip, 267.

Brooks's, Nov. 28th, 1780 :—Probability that the Sheriffs of Coventry should make a false return—effect in Parliament, 267.

Gibbon to Mrs. Holroyd, senior—*Beriton, July 17th,* 1772 :—Sorrow at the death of Master Holroyd—sympathizes with the family at Sheffield Place, 216.

Gibbon to Miss Holroyd—*Lausanne, Nov. 9th,* 1791 :— Receives great pleasure from her letters—regrets her departure from Lausanne—Rosset and La Motte at the Castle of Chillon—French society an agreeable addition—receives a hogshead of Madeira, 136-138.

Lausanne, Nov. 10th, 1792 :—Acknowledges her punctuality and the reverse on his side—praises her capabilities of mind—wishes an account of her daily occupations—and of the tragic story of the Archbishop of Arles, 153-155.

Gibbon to Mrs. Porten—*Lausanne,* 1756 :—Protests his friendship for her—reports his request for an allowance from his father—no answer—his health good—Madame de Sévigné's letters, 195-197.

Lausanne, Dec. 27th, 1783 :—Describes his habits of life, 308-310.

Gibbon to Lady Porten—*Lausanne, June 27th,* 1789 :—Letter of condolence in reply to one announcing the death of her husband, 344.

Gibbon to Sir Stainer Porten—*Lausanne, May 12th,* 1786 :—Acknowledges receipt of letter informing him of the death of his aunt—probable date of the completion of the History, 331, 332.

Gibbon to Dr. Priestley—*Feb. 22nd,* 1703 :—Defines his ideas of private correspondence—refuses his consent to publish the letters, 278.

Jan. 23rd, 1783 :—Accepts his book—defends his own opinions—disdains his attempts to determine the objects of his studies, 275, 276.

Bentinck-street, Feb. 6th, 1783 :—Declines all further correspondence, 278.

Gibbon to Dr. Robertson—*Paris,* 1777 :—Is gratified with his approbation—admires his work on America—suggests an inquiry, 251, 252.

Gibbon under the assumed character of a Swedish traveller to a Swiss friend :—Delineates the defects he discovers in the government of Berne—intends to suggest remedies—but ends abruptly, 187-195.

Gibbon to Lady Sheffield (see also Mrs. Holroyd)—*Bentinck-street,* 1781 :—Friendly gossip, 269.

Bentinck-street, Aug. 30th, 1783 :—His feelings on taking leave of Sheffield Place—regret at the death of Sir John Russell—allusion to minor matters, 298.

Lausanne, May 11th, 1784 :—Letter of gossip—thanks for a present of Wedgwood china, 315.

Lausanne, Oct 22nd, 1784 :—His companions—opinion of Prince Henry of Prussia—

of Madame de Staël—the Hon. Mrs. Fraser—review of his stay in Lausanne—opinion of its society, on the question of marriage—his intended stay in Lausanne—invitation to Lausanne—inquiries after her health, 319-323.

Bath, Dec. 18*th*, 1787 :—Apologizes for not having yet come to Sheffield Place—the absolute necessity of his returning to town, 341.

Lausanne, Nov. 8*th*, 1792 :—A letter of friendship and gossip—refers to the action of the convention with reference to the Royalists, 351-354.

Lausanne, Nov. 10*th*, 1792 :—His devotion to her—his ideas on writing to several members of a family—M. Severy's health his pity for the family—the misery of the French, 156, 157.

Lausanne, April 4*th*, 1793 :—Another letter of friendship and gossip—again touching on the troubles in France, 354-356.

Gibbon to Lord Sheffield (see also Mr. Holroyd)—*Bentinck-street*, 1782 :—Sympathizes with his fatigues—resignation of various members of the Ministry, 273.

Sept. 29*th*, 1782 :—Wholly gossip, 273, 274.

Bentinck-street, Oct. 14*th*, 1782 :—Meditates remaining in town—speculations of state of Parliament—letter of American Independence, 274.

1782 :—Restored to health—no news, 274, 275.

Jan. 17*th*, 1783 :—Satirical gossip, 275.

July 10*th*, 1783 :—Intimates a visit to Sheffield Place—the reasons for his intentions, and the stay he can make, 292-294.

Aug. 18*th*, 1783 :—The movements of his books—intends a flying visit to Hampton Court—opinion of town, 295, 296.

Bentinck-street, Aug. 20*th*, 1783 :—Expresses a desire that Lord and Lady Sheffield should spend a week at Brighton, 296.

Aug. 22*nd*, 1783 :—Narrates his movements, and expresses himself strongly dissatisfied with London, 297, 298.

Downing-street, Sept. 8*th*, 1783 :—Narrates his movements—expresses thanks for the attention bestowed on his aunt—the indifference of stockbuyers as to the definite treaty with America—desires to be remembered to Lady Sheffield, 298, 299.

Sept. 11*th*, 1783 :—Comments on the absence of letters from Deyverdun—the proposition of the Emperor of Russia as to the armed neutrality—political and social gossip, 300.

Downing-street, Sept. 12*th*, 1783 :—The non-arrival of the Flanders mails, 300.

Downing-street, Sept. 13*th*, 1783 :—Arrival of the Flanders mails, but without letters from Deyverdun—speculations as to the cause of his silence—fashionable intelligence, 301.

Dover, Sept. 17*th*, 1783 :—Defects of the post-office—the wind—passengers on board the Calais packet.

Boulogne, 18*th Sept.* 1783 :—The passage of the Channel, and the landing—probable arrival at Lausanne, 302.

Langres, Sept. 23*rd*, 1871 :—His route from Boulogne to this point—promises to write from Lausanne—his bed, 302.

Lausanne, Sept. 30*th*, 1783 :—His journey from Langres—obliged to go into lodgings —their character—fears of the gout—on the chance of being made a Minister at Berne— the conversation of the Abbé Reynal, 302, 303.

Oct. 28*th*, 1783 :—Staying on at Lausanne—comparison between the comforts afforded here and in England, 304, 305.

Lausanne, Nov. 14*th*, 1783 :—Comparison of their daily occupations—opinion of the society around—messages of thanks to Lords North and Loughborough—opinion on Lord Sheffield's pamphlet—some of the people at Lausanne, 305, 306.

Lausanne, Dec. 20*th*, 1783:—Acknowledges receipt of two letters—banters Lord Sheffield on the burdens of a parliamentary life—opinion of the attitude of the Government towards the East India Company, and the conduct of the Company—on Gerard Hamilton's opinion on the Government allowing his (the writer's) self-exile, 306-308.

Lausanne, Jan. 24*th*, 1784 :—His epistolatory labours—comments on the possible proceedings of Parliament—his investment in the French loan—his probable movements in Lausanne, 310-312.

Lausanne, Feb. 20*th*, 1784 :—A letter of gossip, 312, 313.

Lausanne, May 11*th*, 1784 :—Condoles with his lordship on the defeat of his party in the House of Commons—criticism on Parliamentary intrigues—his life at Lausanne, 312-315.

Lausanne, June 19*th*, 1784 :—A list of his friends and acquaintances, 318.

Lausanne, Oct. 18*th*, 1784 :—On the tardiness of the completion of the History—asks for assistance in the winding up of his estates—inquires how his lordship intends passing the winter, 318, 319.

Lausanne, March 13*th*, 1785 :—Review of his position, 323.

March 21*st*, 1785 :—Approves of the sum obtained for the Bucks estate—shows that wisdom of his retirement to Lausanne—his mode of living—the privileges of friend ship —reminds his lordship of his promised visit to Lausanne, 323-326.

Lausanne, Sept. 5th, 1785 :—On his reported death—his praises of Lausanne—on the people staying there—inquiries as to what his lordship is doing with himself—on Deyverdun's refusal to part with the picture—his pecuniary condition, 325-329.

Lausanne, Jan. 17th, 1786 :—Calls attention to the promptness of his reply—comparison of his habits of life in England and Lausanne—expected attack of the gout, 329, 330.

May 10th, 1786 :—Sentiments arising from the intimation of the death of his aunt—promises another letter, 330, 331.

Lausanne, July 22nd, 1786 :—Letter of gossip, 332, 333.

Lausanne, Jan. 20th, 1787 :—On the course of their correspondence—his daily life—looks forward to his visit to England—review of the progress of the History—advice to his lordship—the probable date of his landing in England, 335-337.

Lausanne, June 2nd, 1787 :—What would be the consequence of a fit of the gout, 338, 339.

Lausanne, July 21st, 1787 :—Apology for remaining at Lausanne longer than he intended, and for his going to London previous to visiting Sheffield Place, 339, 340.

Adelphi Hotel, Aug. 8th, 1787 :—Narrates his arrival in London, 340.

Monday afternoon :—The course of an attack of the gout, 340, 341.

Downing-street, June 21st, 1788 :—Intimates that he is free and will soon be at Sheffield Place, 342, 343.

Downing-street, Saturday:—Postpones his arrival. Indicates the length of his stay, 343.

Downing-street, Saturday, June, 1788 :—A speech of Sheridan's, 343, 344.

Lausanne, July 30th, 1788 :—Arrival at Lausanne—opinion of the journey and of his companion—serious state of Deyverdun, 113.

Lausanne, Oct. 1st, 1788 :—Half apology for not writing sooner, 113.

Lausanne, Oct. 4th, 1788 :—Instance of his procrastination—mention of the Severys—what he proposes to do—sudden and serious illness of Deyverdun—intercourse with Mr. Fox—M. Necker and the States Generales, 114, 115.

Lausanne, Nov. 29th, 1788 :—Acknowledging thankfully the sketch of the state of England, owing to illness of the King, 115.

Lausanne, Dec. 13th, 1788 :—Desirous of increasing the circle of correspondents—Deyverdun's health, 115, 116.

Lausanne, April 23rd, 1789 :—On the sale o f his estate—the Government of Berne, and a pipe of wine—Deyverdun's health—contemplated necessary steps against the arrival of the addressed, 116.

Lausanne, April 25th, 1789 :—Anxiety for news of the estate—satisfied with the mortgage—civility of the Government of Berne—Deyverdun's health—possession for life of house and garden—happy at the King's recovery, and its consequences—anxiety for a letter—Count de Mirabeau's great work, 116.

Lausanne, June 13th, 1789 :—Admiration of his friend, and sorrow at giving him trouble—Mrs. Gibbon's consent required for the sale of the estate—anxiety for her health and comfort, 116, 117.

Lausanne, July 14th, 1789 :—Deyverdun's death—requires advice how to act with regard to purchase of house—gives full statement of facts and wishes, 117-119.

Lausanne, Aug. 1789 :—Seriously distressed at the contents of a letter just received—doubts of selling or mortgaging the estate—health of the Severys at Mex—regret at the loss of Deyverdun—attachment to Lausanne, yet doubtful whether to return to England—death of Sir Stainer Porten—romantic idea of adopting Charlotte Porten—thoughts on the French Revolution, 119, 121.

Lausanne, Sept. 9th, 1789 :—Procrastination in answering letters—decides not to purchase house at Lausanne—will hold it for his life—allows M. de Montagny a mortgage—Paris an independent Republic—requires news of Mr. and Mrs. Douglas, 121, 122.

Lausanne, Sept. 25th, 1789 :—Discovers the obstacle to selling the estate—an amicable lawsuit—satisfied with his decision about the house—reasons why—starting for Rolle—bad health of M. Severy—wants a pipe of Madeira—France in a state of dissolution, 122, 123.

Lausanne, Dec. 15th, 1789 :—Excuses himself for neglect of business—does not know in what to invest his money—affairs of France—exiles at Lausanne—anxiety about his wine, 123-125.

Lausanne, Jan. 27th, 1790 :—Delay of correspondent's letters—agreement about the estate—astonished at Elmsley's silence, 125.

Lausanne, May 15th, 1790 :—Continued grief at the loss of Deyverdun—anxious for domestic society—suffering from gout—receives the portrait—sends his own in return—pleasure at Lord Sheffield retiring from Coventry—wants the African pamphlet—health of the Severys, 125-127.

1790 :—Serious illness—a visit to M. Necker—opinion on Burke's book—pleasure in expecting the Madeira, 127, 128.

Lausanne, Aug. 7th, 1790 :—Congratulations on the election for Bristol—talks of getting married—still wishes to adopt Charlotte Porten—her mother objects—illness and partial recovery—government of Berne overturned—French exiles, 129, 130.

INDEX TO THE CRUSADES.

THE END.

BRADBURY, AGNEW, & CO., PRINTERS, WHITEFRIARS.